Athenæum Press Series

SELECTIONS FROM De QUINCEY

EDITED

WITH AN INTRODUCTION AND NOTES

BY

MILTON HAIGHT TURK, Ph.D.

PROFESSOR OF THE ENGLISH LANGUAGE AND LITERATURE IN
HOBART COLLEGE

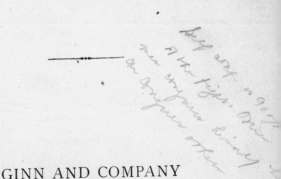

GINN AND COMPANY

BOSTON · NEW YORK · CHICAGO · LONDON
ATLANTA · DALLAS · COLUMBUS · SAN FRANCISCO

𝕿𝖍𝖊 𝕬𝖙𝖍𝖊𝖓𝖆𝖚𝖒 𝕻𝖗𝖊𝖘𝖘
GINN AND COMPANY · PRO-
PRIETORS · BOSTON · U.S.A.

TO A VERY KIND READER

TO WHOSE INDULGENCE I OWE FAR MORE
THAN THE CERTAINTY OF AN AUDIENCE
THIS VOLUME IS INSCRIBED
BY HER SON

PREFACE

THIS volume contains — besides the *Confessions*, several of the *Suspiria*, and other popular pieces — the most important parts of De Quincey's *Autobiographic Sketches* and some of his most interesting *Literary Reminiscences*. It is hoped that the selections will serve to illustrate pretty fully De Quincey's varied literary activity, while at the same time they throw light upon his life and character. A portion of the Introduction is devoted to the study of his personality. The text adopted is, except in the case of the *Confessions*, the latest to which De Quincey gave his approval. For the use of the original *Confessions* in place of the greatly enlarged version of 1856, there appears to be a better excuse than that of brevity. As will be pointed out in the Introduction, it is at least a question whether the earlier form had not the preference of the author himself.

The editor takes pleasure in acknowledging in this place some obligations incurred during the preparation of this volume and not specifically mentioned elsewhere. My debt to the general editors is very considerable. I have to thank for assistance on the Notes Professor F. P. Nash of Hobart College, and Professor J. C. Kirtland, Jr., of The Phillips Academy, Exeter, N.H. Some valuable additions to the Bibliography I owe to the courtesy of Beverly Chew, Esq., of New York, and Professor C. D. Vail, the Librarian of Hobart College. Finally, Professor Edward Dowden of Dublin has come to my aid, in one or two important matters, with a ready kindness that no personal claim of mine could have increased.

M. H. T.

HOBART COLLEGE, GENEVA, N.Y.,
      November 2, 1901.

CONTENTS

		PAGE
PREFACE	. . . .	vii

INTRODUCTION

I. GENERAL REMARKS	. . . . . .	xi
II. DE QUINCEY'S EARLY LIFE	. . . .	xvi
III. DE QUINCEY AS AUTHOR	. . . .	xxvii
IV. DE QUINCEY'S CHARACTER	. . . .	xxxvi
V. CLASSIFICATION OF DE QUINCEY'S WORKS. HIS ESSAYS		xlii
VI. DE QUINCEY'S IMAGINATIVE PROSE	. . .	li
VII. SOME COMMENTS ON DE QUINCEY'S STYLE	.	lxiii
VIII. A BRIEF BIBLIOGRAPHY	. . . . .	lxviii

SELECTIONS

THE AFFLICTION OF CHILDHOOD	. . .	1
INTRODUCTION TO THE WORLD OF STRIFE	. .	21
A MEETING WITH LAMB	. . . . .	93
A MEETING WITH COLERIDGE	. . . .	106
RECOLLECTIONS OF WORDSWORTH	. . .	124
CONFESSIONS OF AN ENGLISH OPIUM-EATER	.	151
FROM THE "SUSPIRIA DE PROFUNDIS"	. .	265
THE ENGLISH MAIL-COACH	. . . .	277
ON MURDER CONSIDERED AS ONE OF THE FINE ARTS.		
SECOND PAPER	. . . . . .	340
JOAN OF ARC	. . . .	356
ON THE KNOCKING AT THE GATE IN "MACBETH"	.	395

| NOTES | . . . . | 401 |

INTRODUCTION

1

In De Quincey's *Letters to a Young Man whose Education has been Neglected* occurs the following significant statement: "I have passed more of my life in absolute and unmitigated solitude, voluntarily, and for intellectual purposes, than any person of my age whom I have ever either met with, heard of, or read of."[1] Thus De Quincey at the age of thirty-seven. Twenty years later Professor Wilson, of whom De Quincey speaks as his "one intimate male friend," gives this account of their relation: "I was very intimate with him, and believe I am now more intimate with him than any other person, and yet I hardly ever see him. . . . I have not seen him above four times in six years (if I remember rightly), and yet his family ask tidings of him from me."[2] The last years of De Quincey's life brought him a little circle of admiring acquaintances who, attracted by the fame of his writings, were attached to him still more closely by the brilliancy of his conversation. But, while these incursions of kindly curiosity must have interrupted his periods of solitude, they did not, it appears, diminish the real isolation of De Quincey's existence.

Having thus lived apart from men, after his death it was his fate to be kept apart from them and to be judged

[1] De Quincey, *Works*, Masson's Ed., Vol. X, p. 14; Riverside Ed., Vol. IX, p. 7.

[2] Mason, *Personal Traits of British Authors: Scott, Hogg, Campbell, Chalmers, Wilson, De Quincey, Jeffrey*, p. 248. (Lord Cranbrook in *National Review*, April, 1884.)

according to other than ordinary human standards. In truth, for a score of years after he died the De Quincey of tradition was hardly a man at all. To the readers of his most popular book it seemed that if he did not drop from the clouds, it was only that he had chosen cloudland as his permanent abode; and this impression was deepened by many anecdotes, eagerly caught up by the public press, concerning the oddities of the Opium-Eater. Thus it came about that so expert a critic as Mr. Leslie Stephen wrote in 1871, and thereafter repeatedly republished, the following generalization on De Quincey's life: "For seventy-three years De Quincey had been carrying on an operation which for want of a better term we must describe as living, but which would be more fitly described by some mode of speech indicating an existence on the borders of dreamland and reality." The growth of this flourishing De Quincey myth was arrested by the appearance in 1877 of Page's [1] (Dr. Japp's) *Life;* and it may be said to have ceased finally since the publication of such works as Findlay's *Recollections*, Woodhouse's *Conversations*, and Japp's *Memorials.* The growth of interest in De Quincey and the academic study of his style have also conduced to a better knowledge and a more judicious estimate of his personality. At this day we can record the final capitulation of the myth-makers in the withdrawal from the last edition of *Hours in a Library* of the sentence just quoted.

The men that have wrought this change, inspired by a deep admiration for their subject, have gathered with the assistance of his family and friends the materials for a fairly adequate account of De Quincey's life; the more comprehensive writings have not failed to discuss

[1] H. A. Page is the pseudonym used in this case by Dr. Alexander H. Japp, whose later publications concerning De Quincey bear his own name.

his personality. In this last respect, however, the reader cannot be blind to an inconclusiveness unusual in the treatment of a man of letters so prominent and one by whom and of whom so much has been said. We know very well what he did; who has told us what he was? If this latter is the more difficult question of the two, it is also no doubt the more important. In De Quincey's case the difficulty of the investigation can hardly be magnified. The inquiring student finds him entrenched in solitude and provisioned with silence. As the biographer of John Wilson says concerning this author of several volumes of autobiography: "He indeed knew how to analyze the human heart, through all its deep windings, but in return he offered no key of access to his own." De Quincey's writings, however, are no more baffling than was his conversation. Every new volume of personal recollections adds another proof that in this respect his friends and his family were not much more fortunate than the wider public.

I have attributed the prevalence of hazy notions of De Quincey's life to his solitude; to his silence we may in part ascribe a perhaps more serious perplexity concerning his personality. Dr. Japp, his chief biographer, has frankly acknowledged what he terms the "critical puzzle of De Quincey's character." His words may serve us now as a point of departure: "that in combination with dreamy abstraction, helplessness and over-sensibility amounting to disease" there should exist "great powers of observation, sympathy, humour, self-possession, dignity and courtesy of manner."[1] The first part of this comparison conveys quite adequately the problem which engages the biographer's attention. The dreamy abstraction, helplessness, and over-sensibility argue a mental deficiency which the great powers of observation and analysis deny. On the one side, as

[1] Page, *Life*, Vol. II, p. 184.

Dr. Japp shows, De Quincey seems marked by powerless-
ness towards the facts of life; on the other he seems equally
distinguished by ability to grasp and control them.

So much for the question of intellect involved. It is at
the words "self-possession, dignity and courtesy of manner"
that we pause. Not, however, to deny that the Opium-
Eater displayed all these characteristics. We have heard
and have been touched by the wonderful tales of his gentleness and his consideration for the feelings of others.
Servants were ladies to him, and ladies goddesses. He
burnt his poor diseased stomach once with a boiling hot
potato rather than keep — not his lady-love — his landlady waiting at his door. Here was a knight, we say, in a
greatcoat and one stocking![1] But surely there is another
side of De Quincey which Dr. Japp — too often his apologist — has not adequately presented to us in his memoir;
surely there are actions recorded of him in which he displays neither self-possession, dignity, nor courtesy of manner. What of his criticisms of Mrs. Wordsworth's brains
and of her husband's legs?[2] What of the remarks upon
Mrs. Coleridge, Bath milliners, and marital unhappiness, for
which Southey prescribed a cudgel?[3] Worse than all these,
by reason of their lack of even the meanest excuse, are the
animadversions — conversational though they be — upon
John Wilson which are recounted for us by Mr. Findlay.[4]

[1] So De Quincey appeared on one occasion. For similar stories, *cf.*
Mrs. Baird Smith in Page, *Life*, Vol. I, p. 361; Burton, *Bookhunter*,
p. 33; Hogg, *De Quincey and his Friends*, p. 129. See also Hogg,
p. 172.

[2] See *Works*, Masson's Ed., Vol. III, p. 202; Riverside Ed., Vol. III,
p. 612; also below, p. 139.

[3] *Works*, Masson's Ed., Vol. II, p. 157; Riverside Ed., Vol. III,
p. 176; and Carlyle, *Reminiscences* (ed. Froude), p. 518.

[4] Findlay, *Personal Recollections*, p. 47; also in Hogg, *De Quincey
and his Friends*, p. 151.

Wilson, we remember, was the "one intimate male friend"; he had been the embarrassed but patient recipient of many a draft signed "T. Q."; he was the author of the judgment of the Opium-Eater in the *Noctes:* "He is a man of a million." But De Quincey tells Findlay of Wilson's "love to be surrounded by parasites"; he ridicules "the sickly, false sentiment of his works and their evidently insincere and vulgar, overwrought religionism"; Wilson's "tales, at least, were a jest among the Wordsworths"; and much more.

Professor Masson, a just though kindly critic, admits freely the "very considerable fund of prejudice, temper, opinionativeness, animosity, pugnacity, on which De Quincey could draw when he liked."[1] This, or much of it, might be said, no doubt, of many another man. What surprises us most in De Quincey is the sort of person or occasion which calls forth these qualities. If Wordsworth or Coleridge had lost all claims to his consideration, as has been suggested, through a failure to prize highly the acquaintance of Mrs. de Quincey, for what did poor Wilson suffer? Unwilling as we may be to follow Miss Martineau in making "malignant gossip" a feature of De Quincey's conversation, we are forced to confess that his behavior on these occasions seems as excessive and as causeless as the knightly performances referred to above. Two such extremes of conduct in the same man form a moral contradiction not less marked, it would seem, than the "critical puzzle" that engages Dr. Japp's attention.

Both these questions — the intellectual and the moral — must be settled before we can know De Quincey as nowadays we insist upon knowing our men of letters; both questions, too, have something of that wider human interest which attaches to all that concerns the Opium-Eater.

---

[1] Masson, *De Quincey* (English Men of Letters), p. 129.

And, in spite of his habitual isolation and persistent silence, his life, when reviewed as a whole, must still yield up something of his real personality to inquiry so near in time as ours. With this end in view I shall, in relating the life of De Quincey, attempt to trace at the same time the growth and development of his intellect and character.

II

"Our family has been in England since the Conquest," said the young De Quincey to George III. Of Norman — ultimately of Norse — origin, the De Quinceys had greatly improved their position after their settlement in England, until a certain De Quincey, Earl of Winchester, was beheaded; whereupon the noble *gens* "exploded and scattered its ruins all over the central provinces of England."[1] The De Quinceys, or Quinceys,[2] as they were now to be called for many centuries, took up commerce, and throve both in England and in America.[3] Our author's father, Thomas Quincey, was very successful in trade with America and the West Indies. He was a man of sterling worth and withal of some taste for letters. His library was very extensive, "comprising the whole general literature of England and Scotland for the preceding generation"; and he was even an author: *A Short Tour in the Midland Counties of England*, which was published in 1775, most of it having first appeared in the *Gentleman's Magazine*,

[1] De Quincey, *Posthumous Works* (ed. Japp), Vol. I, p. 201.

[2] "Not De Quincey himself, but his mother it was that assumed or resumed the 'De,' and then some time after, when she became deeply evangelical in her religious views, was inclined to drop it as a worldly vanity." — JAPP, *De Quincey Memorials*, Vol. I, p. 52. It is amusing to observe that her most severe letters are sure to be signed " E. Quincey " or "E. Q." *Cf. Memorials*, Vol. I, pp. 79, 85, 87, 88, 93, with *ibid.*, p. 97.

[3] Josiah Quincy, of Boston, belonged to this family.

May to September, 1774, was a thoroughly intelligent piece of work. Unhappily, Thomas Quincey was a consumptive; he spent a great deal of time in tropical climates, and the younger Thomas did not know him by sight until he came home in 1793 to die. An influence that might have been potent for good in the wayward life of the son was thus represented by a faint and fading memory ; of De Quincey's mother, who was Elizabeth Penson, we shall hear more.

Thomas, the Opium-Eater, was the fifth child [1] and was born in Manchester on the 15th of August, 1785. He was almost immediately taken to " The Farm," a small suburban dwelling, and in 1791 or 1792 to *Greenhay*,[2] a larger country place. Here he lived until his eleventh year a life of rustic solitude, disturbed only by the experiences of which he has told in his autobiographic writings.[3] In 1796 his mother removed to Bath and placed him in the grammar school there.

De Quincey was of opinion that he inherited a consumptive tendency, which his opium-eating kept in check. Be that as it may, he was certainly from the beginning a small and rather weak child ; apart from the siege of ague that made him an invalid from his second to his fourth year, his recollections of early childhood all point to one of those frail existences that arouse in vigorous humanity more pity than real sympathy. Though De Quincey may have heightened somewhat the contrast between himself and his brother, " the son of eternal racket," the " passion for being despised " to which he confesses is a trait that in a boy indicates a refusal on the part of body and mind

---

[1] See note 1 16.

[2] Both places are now within the city of Manchester, and the latter has given its name, in the form *Greenheys*, to one of the districts of that city.

[3] See below, pp. 1–92, and note 3 4.

to grapple with the world in the struggle which youth is generally but too glad to enter. In very early years, then, De Quincey sank into himself. His autobiography contains pathetic testimony to his refuge in those days. "God speaks to children in dreams," runs, in part, the well-known passage, "and by the oracles that lurk in darkness, but in solitude . . . God holds with little children communion undisturbed."[1] Nourished in this way, the childish sensibility and imaginativeness that are wont to be excessive in frail bodies became in De Quincey extreme.[2]

Herein lie, no doubt, the beginnings of mental infirmity and disease, and here the efforts of discerning parents afford, perhaps, the one hope of relief. De Quincey says that his life was saved by his "introduction to the world of strife" through his brother. But with his mother lay, in these days, his fate. Mrs. de Quincey was a woman of considerable intellectual power.[3] She was also beyond a doubt deeply and unselfishly devoted to her fatherless children; in later years she reduced herself almost to poverty to meet their loose expenditures. But Mrs. de Quincey was decidedly an austere woman; we are told that a servant who was advised to appeal on some point from the housekeeper to the mistress exclaimed in horror, "Speak to mistress! Would I speak to a ghost?" Mrs. de Quincey was moreover a friend of Hannah More and an ardent believer in the tenets of the ultra-evangelical Clapham sect. She took De Quincey out of Bath School, he affirms, because he was too much praised, and in his earlier days, at least, she seems to have been by no means free from the abominable religionist notion that human

[1] See below, pp. 18–19, and note 18 31.

[2] See the second selection in this volume, especially pp. 64 *et seq.*

[3] See, for example, the interesting letter in Japp's *Memorials*, Vol. II, pp. 91–95.

affections deeply enjoyed must lead astray from the path of duty. A love of formality seems to have been another weakness of this good lady. De Quincey tells us with some humor of the daily regulation according to which the brothers and sisters were carried before their mother for morning parade in her dressing-room; "when we were pronounced to be in proper trim," he continues, "we were dismissed, but with two ceremonies that were to us mysterious and allegorical, — first, that our hair and faces were sprinkled with lavender-water and milk of roses; secondly, that we received a kiss on the forehead."

This bearing Mrs. de Quincey consistently maintained; a few years later we find her corresponding with her son about his general welfare in a tone of logical controversy that is really amazing.[1] No one can doubt the sincerity of the earnest protestations of devotion with which she closes these letters; but she seems to have been utterly unable to apply affection, so to speak, to the practical end of removing differences. Her watchword for all men is Duty; the duty of children is to love God and obey their parents: these principles she finds laid down clearly in Holy Writ, especially in the Old Testament, to which her sect continually appealed. Disregard of these principles on the part of children, she knows, incurs divine wrath; failure of parents to insist upon them must therefore be nothing less than a crime. The result of all this is a system of child-rearing as inflexible as a machine. All children are thrown into this moral hopper; if they can get through, they are ground out good boys and girls; if not, they are merely ground to pieces.

Now De Quincey, as we have seen, was by physical weakness, as well as by intellectual superiority, an unusual

[1] These highly interesting letters are given in Japp's *Memorials*, Vol. I, pp. 70–85.

child; he was even from the beginning, by reason of his tendency to self-absorption, in some respects abnormal. The result of his mother's policy was therefore certain to be unfortunate; we should predict with confidence a further mental and moral twist as the outcome of it. Those springs of natural affection that may be said to water the roots of a child's growing moral ideas were in great measure dried up. On the other hand, an almost unparalleled precocity in intellectual pursuits was developed; in those which remove the student farthest from his immediate surroundings, and which on that account are least enjoyed by most boys, De Quincey excelled at an absurdly early age. "That boy," said his master at Bath School, "that boy could harangue an Athenian mob better than you or I could address an English one"; he might have added, "and better than *he* could address an English one, too."

But our frail and precocious schoolboy was soon to be transferred to a sterner discipline; Mrs. de Quincey's system of training was to end in a very commonplace revolt. To return to his days at Bath School. In 1799 an accidental blow on the head kept the young scholar at home ill for a time. Mrs. de Quincey read him such books as Milner's *Church History* and Johnson's *Rambler*, and, as he grew stronger, put him under tutors. On his complete recovery, however, she transferred him from Bath School, which he liked, to Winkfield School in Wiltshire, in which he found nothing to commend but "the religious character of the master." After finishing the scholastic year there, he joined a Bath School friend, young Lord Westport, at Eton for a visit to the latter's home in Ireland. After seeing the last of the Irish Parliament, and having made a strong impression on his friend's father, Lord Altamont, one of the prominent Irish peers, our young scholar made his way to Laxton in Northamptonshire to visit a friend of the

De Quinceys, Lady Carbery, and incidentally to teach her to read her New Testament in Greek. De Quincey was now, at the age of fifteen, ready for Oxford, and he begged to be allowed to go there. His duty was otherwise interpreted for him, and that he might secure ultimately a scholarship at Brasenose, he was sent to Manchester Grammar School to mark time intellectually and be "nosed by cotton-bags" (so writes this scion of the prosperous Manchester merchant) for three years. There followed nineteen months of acquiescence tempered by argument. Lady Carbery relieved the tedium of his surroundings for a little while, and, having now progressed greatly in her Bible studies, repaid his early instruction by teaching him Hebrew; he formed some friendships with thinking men in Manchester and Liverpool; but there was little or nothing for him to learn in school, and to increase the irksomeness of his position, the hours were very long. In a final appeal to his mother he bursts forth thus, and there is a touch of the older and greater De Quincey in his affluence of phrase:

"I ask whether a person can be happy, or even simply easy, who is in a situation which deprives him of *health*, of *society*, of *amusement*, of *liberty*, of *congeniality of pursuits*, and which, to complete the precious picture, admits of no *variety*. I think you will hardly say he can, and yet this description was taken from my own case."

But the guardians, his mother included, were firm; he must either stay where he was, or choose a profession at once. So De Quincey, like many other young rogues and heroes, ran away from school.

His first plan had been to reach Wordsworth, whose *Lyrical Ballads* (1798) had solaced him in fits of melancholy and had awakened in him a deep reverence for the neglected poet. His timidity preventing this, he made his way to Chester, where his mother then lived, in the hope of seeing a sister; was apprehended by the older members of the family; and through the intercession of his uncle, Colonel Penson, received the promise of a guinea a week to carry out his later project of a solitary tramp through Wales. From July to November, 1802, De Quincey then led a wayfarer's life.[1] He soon lost his guinea, however, by ceasing to keep his family informed of his whereabouts, and subsisted for a time with great difficulty. Still apparently fearing pursuit, with a little borrowed money he broke away entirely from his home by exchanging the solitude of Wales for the greater wilderness of London.[2] Failing there to raise money on his expected patrimony, he for some time deliberately clung to a life of degradation and starvation rather than return to his lawful governors. This fact, in giving us De Quincey's opinion of the early conduct of his affairs, offers us also an instructive view of the state of mind to which that policy had brought him.

Discovered by chance by his friends, De Quincey was brought home, — by April 22, 1803, he has been for some time with an old friend of the family, Mrs. Best, in Liverpool, — and after much consultation he was permitted to go to Oxford. As only £100 a year was allowed him for expenses (the income from his own patrimony was £150), he entered Worcester, one of the less expensive colleges. Our reports of his doings at the University, though both meagre and conflicting, leave on the whole no doubt that he was already a deeply marked man. The best opportunities for association with men of equal age and similar intellectual attainments failed to bring him back to the

[1] For all this period see below, pp. 165–171, and, in the notes to these pages, extracts from the revised *Confessions*.

[2] *Cf.* below, p. 66, where De Quincey recommends to the fugitive the "frantic publicities of London" in preference to the "quiet privacies of the country."

world. De Quincey speaks of himself in an autobiograph-
ical paper as having "sought solitude at that early age in
morbid excess." "For the first two years," he says again,
"I compute that I did not utter one hundred words."[1]
"He came to be looked upon as a strange being who associated with no one," records Woodhouse. He made one
important acquaintance at this time, however, — one potent
friend and relentless foe, — opium. Out of this chance meeting[2] sprang, as everybody knows, De Quincey's first and
greatest literary success, and, to no slight extent, the popular notion of his character ; to it also he owed those periods
of utter incapacity and misery that remained in his memory
as the plague-spots of his life. Yet in the discussion of
De Quincey's personality it would seem that opium has
played too large a part. He was twenty-eight years old when
he first really succumbed to the drug ; he had lived for more
than a year a solitary and a stricken man at Oxford before
he knew the *pharmakon nepenthes* at all. What De Quincey
was to be was already determined, and opium entered his life,
except for certain not extended periods, only to strengthen
habits already well established. Even the faculty of magnificent dreaming was his, as he insists, long before.

De Quincey took no degree. He went through part of
the examination, but having been disappointed in the
first place at not being allowed to answer in Greek,[3] and

---

[1] *Cf. The Spectator*, No. 1. "I had not been long at the University
before I distinguished myself by a most profound silence; for, during
the space of eight years, excepting in the public exercises of the college,
I scarce uttered the quantity of an hundred words."

[2] How it happened De Quincey tells below, pp. 198–200. See also
pp. 158, 168; as to the appalling disease of the stomach, see note 158 1.

[3] See Woodhouse's *Conversations* (Garnett, *Confessions of an English
Opium-Eater*, p. 226, or Hogg, *De Quincey and his Friends*, p. 97) for
this story related by De Quincey to Taylor; for another version, see
Masson, *De Quincey*, p. 39.

generally displeased at the methods employed, after one day's experience he vanished. Notwithstanding, he had made good use of his time at Oxford in several ways: he had studied Hebrew and German with his tutors and had fairly ransacked both Greek and Latin literature; more than that, and better in his opinion, he had greatly extended his acquaintance with the best writers in his own tongue. And now also his connection begins with the men who make literature. Unable to summon up the courage to visit Wordsworth, in 1803 he wrote to him, and in time received from him several letters of great dignity and very high moral tone. In 1804, through the kindness of a "literary friend," he met Lamb in London, and in 1807 he found Coleridge at Bridgwater after much seeking. Later in that year an opportunity was afforded him to conduct Mrs. Coleridge and her two children to Southey at Keswick; they stopped at Grasmere, and at the door of Dove Cottage he at last had the happiness of taking Wordsworth's hand. Three days later he made the acquaintance of Southey.

De Quincey remained on the books of his College until 1810, and he includes 1808 in the period of his residence at Oxford; but, although the time when he appeared for his degree is unknown, it would seem that his active connection with the University ends with this visit to the poets. His meeting with them seems to have conduced to their benefit as well as to that of their admirer. Coleridge received in November, 1807, through Cottle, the Bristol bookseller, £300 (it is said to have been 15 per cent of De Quincey's remaining funds) from a "young man of fortune who admired his talents." In the next year De Quincey was much in London; apparently he was already entered as a "student and member of the Honourable Society of the Middle Temple," and was now supposed to be "eating" his terms for the bar; really he saw more of Lamb and Coleridge and extended his acquaintance among men of letters. From November, 1808, till February, 1809, he was with the Wordsworths at Grasmere. Returning to London, he made himself very useful to Wordsworth by seeing his *Convention of Cintra* pamphlet through the press and adding a postscript quite as good as the original. In the meantime Dorothy Wordsworth was fitting up for a new occupant Dove Cottage, which her brother's family had now outgrown, and in November, 1809, De Quincey was able to return to the Lakes as a permanent resident.

De Quincey settled at Grasmere at this time, partly in search of retirement, partly to attach himself to the Wordsworths. As might be expected of him, he succeeded in the former far better than in the latter object. He has ascribed the estrangement that followed to Wordsworth's character, — which certainly was not pliant, — to Mrs. Wordsworth's intellectual deficiencies, to the communicativeness of the servant that Dorothy Wordsworth had hired for him; others have found the difficulty, and the animus of the articles twenty years later, in De Quincey's marriage, which took place in 1816.[1] Margaret Simpson, a

---

[1] The following extremely enlightening remarks formed the close of a letter from De Quincey's mother, dated Sept. 9, 1816 (when·the marriage had already taken place):

"I have wavered often while writing this note, and at last resolve to say a word of the report which we now suppose had no truth in it. It seemed to come from high authority that you were about to marry, and nothing short of an oracular Voice could have made us listen to the tale, considering your want of means to meet the demands of a family. I am, however, so much entitled, and do really feel so affectionate an interest in your happiness, that I cannot help begging you to let me know your designs, and also to consider well before you trust the mere impulse of feeling, if, as I have just now heard, the sober judgment of your Friends cannot approve the step. I can abate much of what the world demands in marriage, but I know there are congruities which are indispensable to *you*, which you may overlook in the delusion of fancy, and be forced

De Quinceyan vision in literature, was in life the daughter of a well-to-do dalesman; she was no doubt in social rank the inferior of Mrs. Wordsworth (who was also a native of Westmoreland), and Mrs. Wordsworth did not see fit to overlook the difference between them. This is much, no doubt; add to this, however, what we know of Wordsworth's strenuous ways; superadd that De Quincey had by this time gone through those first terrible battles royal with opium described in the *Confessions;* and we may agree with him that his separation from the Wordsworths was from the beginning sure to take place.[1] Opium still held its power over our author, and the recovery, before his marriage, from his terrible lapse of 1813 was followed, soon after that event, by the second fall in 1817, and that by yet another in 1823. In his respites from the drug he read German literature and metaphysics and political economy.

His marriage worked, in one way, an important change in De Quincey's life,—his patrimony was soon quite exhausted. Necessity addressed the husband and father in no uncertain terms; and, after several appeals to his mother and uncle, De Quincey became an editor. The *Westmoreland Gazette* had been started at Kendal in the Tory interest. De Quincey gravely set about to transform this dalesman's sheet into a national journal of philosophy, more particularly into an organ of modern transcendental metaphysics. He assured his readers that his friends could float the *Gazette*, backed by his knowledge of German philosophy

to see every moment of your life after to be wanting to your comfort, when you come to yourself. I am, my dear Thomas, your sincerely affectionate Mother, E. QUINCEY."

The identity of the "oracular Voice" can hardly be mistaken; perhaps we have here the true explanation of De Quincey's estrangement from Wordsworth.

[1] See De Quincey's account of the matter, *Works*, Masson's Ed., Vol. III, p. 197; Riverside Ed., Vol. III, p. 607.

and literature, into every section and division of the three great Universities. "I so managed it as to preserve my independence," said the Opium-Eater to Woodhouse: it is a pity that no one has recorded a colloquy of two West-moreland farmers on these plans of the new editor. Next to metaphysics, murder trials seem to have been the staple of this journal in the days of De Quincey.[1] The whole episode might deserve to be a national jest, were it not so pathetic a testimony to the hopeless failure of our author in all practical affairs.

III

In 1821, this journalistic employment having been aban-doned, De Quincey went to London. "Certain pecuniary embarrassments," he writes in his far-away fashion, "had rendered it necessary that I should extricate myself by literary toils." Introduced by Lamb and Talfourd to Taylor and Hessey, the proprietors of the *London Maga-zine*, he offered them some translations of German authors, who he thought should be better known to the English public. The shrewder publishers, however, saw a far greater "attraction" in De Quincey's own experiences; so it came to pass that in a little room in York Street, Covent Garden, De Quincey penned the *Confessions of an English Opium-Eater*. With the readers of the *Magazine*, to whom it came in 1821, the new classic eclipsed in interest the *Essays of Elia*, which were now appearing, and it was promptly published in book form. Curiosity soon discovered the shrinking author, and his circle of acquaintance grew rap-idly: Charles Knight has good stories to tell of him; Tom Hood, co-editor of the *London Magazine*, found the Opium-Eater "at home, quite at home in a German Ocean of

[1] See note 340 2.

literature, in a storm, flooding all the floor, the table and the chairs — billows of books," and "listened by the hour, whilst the philosopher, standing with his eyes fixed on one side of the room, seemed to be less speaking than reading from 'a handwriting on the wall.'" Richard Woodhouse, barrister of the Temple and the friend of Keats and Hunt, made his *Notes of Conversations with Thomas de Quincey*[1] at this time; and the following account of the Opium-Eater's appearance and learning, set down by Woodhouse in 1821, seems to have been composed with the greatest care:

"I had formed to myself the idea of a tall, thin, pale, gentlemanly-looking, courtier-like man; but I met a short, sallow-looking person, of a very peculiar cast of countenance, and apparently much an invalid. His demeanour was very gentle, modest and unassuming; and his conversation fully came up to the idea I had formed of the writer of those articles [the *Confessions*]. . . . The Opium-Eater appears to have read a great deal, and to have thought much more. I was astonished at the depth and *reality*, if I may so call it, of his knowledge. He seems to have passed nothing that occurred in the course of his study unreflected on or unremembered. His conversation appeared like the elaboration of a mine of results; and if at any time a general observation of his became matter of question or ulterior disquisition it was found that he had ready his reasons at a moment's notice; so that it was clear that his opinions were the fruits of his own reflections on what had come before him, and had not been taken up from others. Indeed, this last clearly appeared, since upon most of the topics that arose he was able to give a very satisfactory account, not merely of *what books* had been written upon those subjects, but of *what opinions* had been

---

[1] Published in Garnett's edition of the *Confessions* and in Hogg's *De Quincey and his Friends*.

entertained upon them, together with his own judgments of those opinions, his acquiescence in them, or qualifications of them. Upon almost every subject that was introduced he had not only that general information which is easily picked up in literary society or from books, but that minute and accurate acquaintance with the details that can be acquired only from personal investigation of a subject and reflection upon it at the same time. Taylor led him into political economy, into the Greek and Latin accents, into antiquities, Roman roads, old castles, the origin and analogy of languages; upon all these he was informed to considerable minuteness. The same with regard to Shakespeare's sonnets, Spenser's minor poems, and the great writers and characters of Elizabeth's age and those of Cromwell's time. His judgments of books, of writers, of politics, were particularly satisfactory and sound. He is a slight Danish scholar, a moderate Italian, a good Frenchman, exact as to pronunciation, and it seemed to me an excellent German scholar." [1]

In the *London Magazine* the *Confessions* was followed by De Quincey's *Richter* with *Analects*, and in 1823–24 by the *Letters to a Young Man whose Education has been Neglected*, *Herder*, *Knocking at the Gate in "Macbeth,"* *Rosicrucians and Free-Masons*, *German Tales*, etc. In 1824 his connection with the *London* ceased, apparently, and after that year he was reckoned by Knight as on the staff of his *Quarterly Magazine*, though he contributed to it only two translations from the German. In the meantime reputation and friends had not apparently bettered the Opium-Eater's financial condition. His mother is in despair about him: in February, 1822, she "sees not at the bottom of his calamities any better hope than that which has ever cheated her unfortunate children"; in January, 1825, she formally

---

[1] Garnett, pp. 192–196; Hogg, pp. 72–74.

divides her reduced income, allotting to Thomas de Quincey
£100, or one-sixth of the whole.

De Quincey was soon, however, to exchange London and
the Lakes — to which he apparently returned for several
months in 1826 or 1827 — for a literary centre more active
than either.   Shortly after he settled in Grasmere he had
been introduced by Wordsworth to their common neighbor,
John Wilson of Elleray.   Wilson had been a famous scholar
and great athlete at Oxford ; probably De Quincey was the
only man of Wilson's time that did not know him.   Now,
at all events, they became well acquainted, and through
many a long tramp among the hills De Quincey bravely
trotted by his big friend's side.   But Wilson lost his money
and was obliged to go to Edinburgh, where in 1813 he
took examinations for the bar.   In 1815 De Quincey visited him there, and made the acquaintance of Lockhart,
Gillies, the Hamiltons, and others of the literary *coterie* of
the "Modern Athens."   Soon after this, Blackwood's *Edinburgh Magazine* began its brilliant career as the great Tory
opponent of the *Edinburgh Review*.   While the proprietor
was really the only editor, Wilson was certainly, though
well seconded by Lockhart, the chief contributor, and possessed considerable editorial discretion.[1]   Naturally Wilson
sought very early to secure for "Maga," as he delighted
affectionately to term it, the services of the Opium-Eater.
In March, 1820, Wilson wrote with many protestations of
love to tell De Quincey of the impossibility of accepting

[1] Lockhart's description of Wilson in these days, in *Peter's Letters
to his Kinsfolk*, Letter XII, is perhaps the best pen-picture we have of
De Quincey's intimate friend : " In complexion, he is the best specimen
I have ever seen of the genuine or ideal *Goth*.   His hair is of the true
Sicambrian yellow ; his eyes are of the lightest, and at the same time of
the clearest blue, and the blood glows in his cheek with as firm a fer-
vour as it did, according to the description of Jornandes, in those of the
Bello gaudentes, praelio ridentes Teutones."

any more of the latter's drafts. Several years before De Quincey had lent his friend £200, which was paid; now Wilson was obliged to sell his books to meet the bills which the Opium-Eater was drawing upon him. In the same letter he continues thus: "Unless something has occurred to make it impossible for you to send y^r contribution as you so solemnly promised when we parted, no doubt you w^d have done so. But I can never again mention the subject to Mr. Blackwood, who delayed the printing of the work several days on my assurance of a packet coming from you. . . . Your assistance is becoming every day more desirable and I have only to add that payment at the rate of £10, 10s. a sheet shall be monthly transmitted for your communications. . . . Whatever and whenever you send, it shall be inserted, and nothing can ever come wrong." In August of the same year he writes: "In your letter of the 26th you proposed to send in a day or two your review of Malthus [this appeared in the *London Magazine* in 1823]. It is now the 5th of August, and I am beginning to fear that something has occurred to stop your composition. *Ebony* [*i.e.*, Mr. Blackwood], who is the child of Hope and Fear, and who has shown a face of smiles for some days, begins to droop excessively; and if the article does not come soon, no doubt he will commit suicide, which will be some considerable relief to me and many others of his well-wishers." And, further on: "I tried to convince Blackwood that you never *had engaged to* write for the Magazine [the year before De Quincey had counted this ten guineas a month as part of his income], and his face was worth ten pounds — for it was pale as a sheet. — I told him, however, that now you *were* engaged, so that if the articles don't come now, he will become a sceptic even in religion, and end in total disbelief in Earth, Heaven and Hell." In February, 1821, Wilson continues in a tone of quiet despair: "With respect to *Blackwood's Magazine*, I do not think I can press that subject upon you any more, for, if you c^d write for it, surely you would; . . . £120, £130, or even £150 per annum could be made by you in this way," etc.   In 1825, during which year "Maga" got nothing at all from De Quincey, Wilson is "looking out every day for your [De Quincey's] communications, which are much needed. . . . Remember that everything you think good, on whatever subject, original or translated, will answer our purpose."   It would appear that De Quincey's need was very great at this time.   Fox Ghyll, a cottage he had leased when Dove Cottage became too small, had been sold; his wife and children were with his father-in-law; he himself was in London, hiding from process for debt.   On the other hand, in a letter to Wilson in February, 1825, he pleads that opium has left his liver "subject to affections which are tremendous for the weight of wretchedness attached to them."   "To fence with these with the one hand," he continues, "and with the other to maintain the war with the wretched business of hack-author, with all its horrible degradations, is more than I am able to bear.   At this moment I have not a place to hide my head in.   Something I meditate — I know not what — '*Itaque e conspectu omnium abiit.*'   With a good publisher and leisure to premeditate what I write, I might yet liberate myself: after which, having paid everybody, I would slink into some dark corner — educate my children — and show my face in the world no more."

Finally Wilson's repeated assurances brought to *Blackwood* De Quincey's *Lessing*, which appeared in 1826–27. This was followed by the *Last Days of Immanuel Kant* and *Murder Considered as one of the Fine Arts* (first paper) in 1827, and the *Toilette of a Hebrew Lady* and *Rhetoric* in 1828.   His connections in London having now entirely ceased, De Quincey removed to Edinburgh and settled there for good ; by 1830 he had gathered his family again about him. From this time on we hear less of De Quincey's financial distresses, though he was obliged once to seek sanctuary within the precincts of Holyrood, where his wife loyally joined him. His literary production during this long period was great in amount, and, as there was a ready and good market for anything he had to offer, his income must have been by no means despicable. Within five years after his arrival in Edinburgh he had given the short-lived *Edinburgh Literary Gazette* his first sketch of *Professor Wilson* (1829) and had gratified " Ebony " with such articles as *Richard Bentley*, *Dr. Parr*, *The Cæsars*, and *Charlemagne*, while at the same time (in 1832) his remarkable mediæval romance, *Klosterheim*, appeared as an independent work. In 1834 a fruitful connection with *Tait's Edinburgh Magazine*, a Whig rival to *Blackwood*, began, and in this way appeared from time to time during the next six or seven years the *Autobiographic Sketches* and *Literary Reminiscences*. In 1837–38 he published in the *Encyclopædia Britannica* his articles on *Goethe*, *Pope*, and *Shakespeare*, while *Blackwood* secured the *Revolt of the Tartars*. In 1840–44 *The Essenes*, *Style*, *Homer and the Homeridæ*, and *Cicero* appeared in that magazine, while at the same time (1844) Messrs. Blackwood published separately De Quincey's *Logic of Political Economy*. In 1845–50 *Coleridge and Opium-Eating*, the *Suspiria de Profundis*, and *The English Mail-Coach* (originally assigned to the series of *Suspiria*) were brought out by *Blackwood*, while *Tait* gave to the world the *Notes on Literary Portraits*, *Joan of Arc*, *The Spanish Military Nun*, *Conversation*, *Protestantism*, etc. In 1847 some work was done by De Quincey on the *North British Daily Mail* in Glasgow; in 1849 articles on *Goldsmith*, *The Poetry of Pope*, and *Lamb* appeared in the *North British Review*. After 1850

De Quincey contributed chiefly to James Hogg's *Edinburgh Weekly Instructor* and its monthly successor, *Titan: Language*, *Sir William Hamilton*, and other pieces came out in this way. His connection with Hogg was in one way the most important of De Quincey's alliances with publishers, for to this intrepid Scotchman we owe the collective edition of the Opium-Eater's works, edited by himself, the first volume of which came out in Edinburgh in 1853. De Quincey, not knowing how far this edition might extend, prudently named it *Selections Grave and Gay*. These last years were one long struggle to provide copy for these volumes, with the result that they are almost all utterly heterogeneous as to contents. The fourteenth volume of this work was nearly ready for the press when De Quincey died.

We must not suppose that this " business of hack-author " took up all De Quincey's time during these thirty years ; some diversions he enjoyed of his own peculiar kind. He had, as has been said, many acquaintances in these Edinburgh days, and not a few friends. Carlyle — not yet famous — wrote from Craigenputtoch in December, 1828 : " Come and see us, for we often long after you. . . . Would *you* come hither and be king over us ; *then* indeed we had made a fair beginning, and the ' Bog School ' might snap its fingers at the ' Lake School ' itself, and hope to be one day recognised of all men." Professor Wilson he could see as often as he wished ; and our store of anecdotes of De Quincey in this period testifies to occasional meetings with many more recent acquaintances. His publisher, Mr. Hogg, saw a good deal of him in the last years of his life, and a younger man, Mr. J. R. Findlay, was often with him. To the latter we owe our most trustworthy description of the Opium-Eater's appearance as an old man : " He was a very little man (about 5 feet 3 or 4 inches) ; his countenance the most remarkable for its intellectual attractiveness that I have ever seen. His features, though not regular, were aristocratically fine, and an air of delicate breeding pervaded the face. His forehead was unusually high, square, and compact. At first sight his face appeared boyishly fresh and smooth, with a sort of hectic glow upon it that contrasted strangely with the evident appearances of age in the grizzled hair and dim-looking eyes. The flush or bloom on the cheeks was, I have no doubt, an effect of his constant use of opium ; and the apparent smoothness of the face disappeared upon examination." [1] But De Quincey's habit of executing mysterious disappearances from time to time would have interfered with the growth of friendship had the Opium-Eater been prepared to enter into really close relations with any man. It is clear, however, despite the courtesy with which he received his guests, that on the whole he preferred to be alone, and generally had his wish. So the Carlyle invitation came to nothing, and it is evident that neither Mr. Hogg nor Mr. Findlay was in any sense intimate with the celebrated author. After Mrs. de Quincey's death in 1837, while his family still remained in Edinburgh, he found it desirable to take separate lodgings in Lothian Street in the Old Town. When, in 1840, his elder daughters removed the rest of his family to Lasswade, a charming suburb of Edinburgh, he was still a very irregular resident of their pretty cottage. In 1841–43 he spent most of his time in Glasgow,—at first as a guest of Professor Nichol, the astronomer, or Professor Lushington ; afterwards in lodgings in Renfield Street. In 1843 and 1844 came the fourth — and perhaps the most terrible — of his great excesses in the use of opium. His sufferings during his heroic efforts to reduce the doses of

[1] Findlay, *Recollections*, pp. 2–3; reprinted in Hogg, *De Quincey and his Friends*, p. 125.

the drug were awful. " Eternally the words sounded in my ears : 'Suffered and was buried.' " This, however, was the end of the opium curse. The disease of the stomach we now hear no more of ; and, although De Quincey continued to drink laudanum to the end of his days, the great craving against which he had had continually to struggle seems now to have worn itself out. Relieved also of financial worries, the Opium-Eater was thus able to enjoy, after his own fashion, a serene old age. He made another visit to Glasgow in 1847, reëstablished himself in his lodgings in Renfield Street (which he had retained as a storehouse for his Glasgow accumulations of books and papers), and, in the intervals of composition, enjoyed himself in observing the people in the Market. Soon after his return to Edinburgh he settled himself again in his rooms at 42 Lothian Street, which he now retained — and frequently inhabited — until his death ; after *Selections Grave and Gay* began to appear he was permanently established in these quarters. Here, on the 8th of December, 1859, he died. A simple tablet marks the position of his rooms.

IV

De Quincey's later history carries out the tendencies so marked in his early years. Physical weakness, unhealthy sensibility, injudicious rearing, revolt, wanderings, opium-eating, ill-assorted marriage, had been the continuous chain of misfortune that not only determined the tenor of his life, but gave to his mind and character their peculiar bent. His chief resource first and always was solitude, — a solitude that was marked, however, by varying employment. Most of the time it was, as De Quincey says, "for intellectual purposes " ; and he is found immersed in those studies and speculations which have furnished the material for the bulk of his literary work. But there were other hours — few but long remembered — of which the strange results were the dreams and visions that distinguish the smaller but far more famous portion of his authorship. It is the common quality of both kinds of work that at no time do we find him in a wholesome, helpful relation to ordinary human life.

In his essay on *Rhetoric* De Quincey censures Junius for "lingering forever in the dust and rubbish of individuality, amongst the tangible realities of things and persons." Whatever may have been the result of this tendency in Junius, the want of it is the essential defect in De Quincey's work. To start away from the present fact that must be faced as a fact, and fix attention upon the distant set of facts that may be made the subject of speculation, was the ingrained habit of De Quincey's mind. We think we see here the not unnatural result of persistent solitude and musing. At all events De Quincey's power over a fact is in inverse ratio to its nearness. He is the farsighted man in literature, who cannot focus his mental vision upon anything near at hand. The Essenes are more interesting than the Methodists; the Cæsars for him displace Napoleon; Toryism and Whiggism he discusses with respect to the theories upon which the parties historically rest, and with specific disregard of their actions. As might be expected, De Quincey's own experiences, at one time so remarkable and so instructive, when absorbed into his mind, reappear chiefly in dream and vision. Ann of Oxford Street [1] does not set before this young philosopher the most difficult problem in the range of sociology; she only becomes his dream-companion in many an uneasy slumber. Thus it is with him always: equal to the most delicate analysis in matters of purely speculative

[1] See *Confessions*, below, pp. 176–195.

interest, in things of nearer personal concernment he is utterly helpless.

The man who cannot grasp and make his own the facts of daily life is, it need hardly be said, a man who cannot learn from experience. Intellectually this may be a serious shortcoming; it carries with it, however, a much greater moral defect. Character grows only as it is nourished through the doing and enduring of daily life. De Quincey was not properly a weak man, but he had the moral standing of a child. Efforts, like those of Miss Mitford and Dr. Japp, to exonerate De Quincey where the Words-worths or any others are concerned, are foredoomed to failure; had they any hope of success, — had they indeed been in place, — they would have been made long ago by the culprit himself. But it is useless to talk of our Opium-Eater as of one having full moral responsibility. Mr. Rae-Brown has spoken of De Quincey's extreme gentleness of manner as "almost that of a retiring yet high-bred child"; his discourtesy also, of which the attack on his Lake friends was an example, was likewise that of a presump-tuous boy. This presumption is mingled with not a little vanity, — the same childish self-conceit that speaks in the "I was right, as I always am," "I think I may claim to have studied this subject more than any other modern Englishman," and other familiar formulas. To the very end De Quincey cherished a youth's dreams of intellectual conquests of the world. When over seventy years of age he discussed with the elder Mr. Hogg a project for "the greatest work that had ever been done," — the "History of England" in twelve volumes; and he left not only notes endorsed "My History of England," but also others marked "My book on the Infinite" and "For my book on the Relations of Christianity to Man." One further profession of his sublime faith in himself is striking enough to bear citation here: "I hoped and have every year hoped with better grounds," he writes, "that (if I should be blessed with life sufficient) I should accomplish a great revolution in the intellectual condition of the world. That I should both as one cause and effect of that revolution place education upon a new footing throughout all civilized nations was but one part of the revolution. It was also but a part of this revolution; it was also but a part (though it may seem singly more than enough for a whole) to be the first founder of true philosophy. It was no more than a part that I hoped to be the re-establisher in England with accessions of Mathematics."

A man — nay, "every inch a king" — in the past and the speculative, De Quincey was a child in the moral, the practical, the present. Growing rapidly, abnormally, on the one side, he was quite "cheated of this fair proportion" on the other. It would seem that we may, without being too fanciful, trace this childish element in De Quincey's character through some features of his make-up as a writer. De Quincey, who thought that the young poet should be willing to pluck out his right eye if by such a sacrifice he could "attain to greater purity, precision, compass, or idiomatic energy of diction," [1] shows at times a child's love of slang. "A dangerous customer, but not a customer to be sneezed at," "a gone coon," "to call the whole kit of them monsters," are fair examples. This fondness for slang is closely connected with a flippant treatment of serious subjects where no humorous effect is apparently sought, as for instance of Socrates, — "the old gentleman himself, the founder of the concern." There is a touch of the self-confidence of youth about these expressions; they seem to be notes of that effervescence of

[1] Essay on Keats, in which Lucretius and Horace figure as "two old files."

childish vanity which adult humanity generally endeavors to conceal.

The struggle of child with man in De Quincey confronts us again in the difficulties which beset the question of his accuracy as a writer. We should not ordinarily expect an opium-eater and dreamer to be always quite sure of his ground, but our opium-eater is also a philosopher, likewise a rhetorician, and he prides himself upon a scrupulous precision in all his statements, — a quality of style which, as we have seen above, he strongly recommended to others. That De Quincey is apt, and so far exact, in his use of words no one will wish to deny; but his most devoted apologist must stand silent before the accumulating instances of his quiet neglect of facts. Whether the Malay of the *Confessions*, in whom Mr. Saintsbury has taken so great an interest, ever called upon the Opium-Eater or not, what is to be said of the long passages in the *Revolt of the Tartars* for which no original exists, and the culminating stroke by which the author erected two lofty columns in China with a magnificent De Quinceyan inscription, — all imaginary?[1] De Quincey's accuracy throughout is the choice of a phrase to correspond to a mental conception, which in turn, under the constant modification of a vivid imagination, may or may not coincide with actual fact. De Quincey seems to have retained that love of making a good story, and that sublime unconsciousness of the nature of the little step over the bounds of truth, which we find so frequently in children. At all events, a thoroughly childish negligence of fact contends with the philosopher's precision of statement again and again in his work.

[1] "Slightly altered in one or two phrases," says De Quincey's note. *Cf.* in De Quincey's *Flight of a Tartar Tribe* (Riverside Literature Series), notes to pp. 31, 33, 41, 55, 78. For some remarks upon De Quincey's statements about Coleridge, see notes to pp. 110–117, below.

Indeed, with his immaturity and lack of grasp on practical considerations we may connect the most serious of all limitations of De Quincey's style, — his diffuseness. He is without doubt the least concentrated of all who lay claim to a high place as masters of the language ; he is diffuse and wandering to an extent that discloses a complete ignorance of the existence of such a fault. After all, the saving of a reader's time and brain power are purely practical considerations for which it would be idle to expect to engage De Quincey's interest and effort. Occasionally, as in the revised *Confessions*, De Quincey expands purposely to fill a certain space, but ordinarily he merely gives way to his natural tendency to exhaust the manifold minor divisions and side issues of his subjects, as a sociable dog follows his master, with excursions into all the neighboring fields. De Quincey's *Story of a Libel*,[1] to cite some examples outside this volume, treats of Romish casuistry, of Wordsworth's imagery, of Paley's philosophy, of duelling, of the unpleasantness of being libelled, of courts of honor, and of several other matters. The account of London[2] is another good specimen of digression within digression.

But these comparisons need not always result to our author's disadvantage. The tendency of De Quincey's mind to hunt strange trails has no doubt secured us many a valuable paper from his pen, and the range and variety of his writings may well recompense us for the discomfort we suffer from the discursiveness of many single pieces. In another way too his weakness is closely allied to strength. If he lost much by failing to take his place on the solid ground of adult manhood, his residence in the cloudland

---

[1] *Cf. Works*, Masson's Ed., Vol. III, pp. 160 *et seq.*; Riverside Ed., Vol. III, pp. 661 *et seq.*

[2] *Cf. Works*, Masson's Ed., Vol. II, pp. 9 *et seq.*; Riverside Ed., Vol. II, pp. 499 *et seq.*

of children was not without its consolations. He alone —
at least among adult Englishmen — was able to preserve in
advanced years that glorious faculty of dreaming which is
the peculiar privilege of childhood.

V

In the essay on Pope, contributed by De Quincey to the
North British Review in 1858,[1] he elaborates with great
care the distinction, which he had drawn in his *Letters to
a Young Man*, between the "literature of *knowledge*" and
the "literature of *power*" : — "The function of the first is
— to *teach;* the function of the second is — to *move:* the
first is a rudder; the second, an oar or a sail. The first
speaks ultimately, it may happen, to the higher understanding or reason, but always *through* affections of pleasure or
sympathy. . . . What do you learn from ' Paradise Lost ' ?
Nothing at all. What do you learn from a cookery-
book? Something new. . . . What you owe to Milton
is not any knowledge, of which a million separate items
are still but a million advancing steps on the same earthly
level; what you owe is *power* — that is, exercise and expansion to your own latent capacity of sympathy with the
infinite, where every pulse and each separate influx is a
step upwards, a step ascending as upon a Jacob's ladder
from earth to mysterious altitudes above the earth." In
most history, biography, and miscellaneous essays, as
De Quincey takes pains to avow in a note, "threads of
direct *instruction* intermingle in the texture with these
threads of *power*," and a third and mixed form is produced in which the broad distinctions between his two
great classes are lost.

[1] *Works*, Masson's Ed., Vol. XI, pp. 54–59; Riverside Ed., Vol. V,
pp. 383–390.

These distinctions, beyond all doubt, furnished in De Quincey's mind the basis for the "wide general classification" of his works which he attempted in the General Preface to his own edition of them. He distributes them into three classes: "*First*, into that class which proposes primarily to amuse the reader, but which, in doing so, may or may not happen occasionally to reach a higher station, at which the amusement passes into an impassioned interest." The *Autobiographic Sketches* belong to this class. Into the second class he throws "those papers which address themselves purely to the understanding as an insulated faculty; or do so primarily." These essays must be judged, the author tells us, according to the character of the problem each undertakes, and the ability and success attained in the solution of that problem. From these "problem papers" he selects especially those on *The Essenes*, *The Cæsars*, and *Cicero* as examples. "Finally, as a third class, and, in virtue of their aim, as a far higher class of compositions" he ranks "*The Confessions of an Opium-Eater*, and also (but more emphatically) the *Suspiria de Profundis*." "On these," he continues, "as modes of impassioned prose ranging under no precedents that I am aware of in any literature, it is much more difficult to speak justly, whether in a hostile or a friendly character."

This classification is not perfect in point of accuracy, nor is it complete. It is clear that large portions of the *Confessions* are not to be distinguished in any way from the *Autobiographic Sketches*, while parts of these again run into the purely intellectual vein. But the arrangement is useful because it brings into prominence the two strongly contrasted sides of De Quincey, — the philosophical and what may be called the rhapsodical; it emphasizes his two great powers, — the faculty of acute analysis and the faculty of soaring imagination.

A subdivision of the second class of writings, to which we will now for a moment confine ourselves, is evidently necessary; the recent arrangement of Professor Masson is as follows:

(*a*) Biographies and Biographic Sketches, such as *Shakespeare, Goethe, Pope, Bentley*, and *Joan of Arc*.

(*b*) Historical Essays and Researches, such as *The Cæsars, Cicero, Homer and the Homeridæ*, and *The Essenes*.

(*c*) Speculative and Theological Essays, like *The System of the Heavens, Plato's Republic, Christianity as an Organ of Political Movement, Protestantism, Modern Superstition, Murder*, and *Suicide*.

(*d*) Essays in Political Economy and Politics, such as *The Logic of Political Economy, Dialogues of Three Templars*, and *A Tory's Account of Toryism, Whiggism, and Radicalism*.

(*e*) Papers of Literary Theory and Criticism, such as *Rhetoric, Style, Language, Conversation, Appraisal of Greek Literature, Poetry of Pope, Literary Portraits*, and the brief but noteworthy monograph *On the Knocking at the Gate in "Macbeth."*

A mere glance at the themes of this great mass of essay work imposes instant respect for the wide range of De Quincey's inquiring mind; even a complete list of his writings would give, however, a very inadequate idea of the scope of his investigations, for one essay, as we have observed, may deal with many topics besides that one to which its title points. We see that De Quincey loses force as an essayist by failing to keep his work within a field that he might hope with some adequacy to cover. Again, there is a tendency on his part, it appears, towards the choice of abstruse subjects for the sake of their abstruseness; the writer loves a topic for the amount of speculative exercise he can get out of it. The weakness that lies behind both these faults is the defect of

De Quincey's character, — the aloofness of the man from the world. The Opium-Eater talked, we are told, as if he were "reading from a handwriting on the wall"; he wrote with the same concentration of interest upon the subject and his speculations about it, and with the same slight consideration of the point of view and the advantage of his audience.[1] There are times when he seems fairly to turn his back upon his readers while he sits in entranced rumination upon some delicate morsel of speculation. There are other moments, too, in these purely intellectual writings when De Quincey the rhapsodist seems to be with us, and not for our good. He becomes interested — again forgetting us — in the flow of his own periods, and, before the impulse has ceased, a page or two of words have been added that cover magnificently a very slender thread of matter.

Beyond all cavil, however, De Quincey's analytical power was astonishing. His mind was, as he says, constitutionally apt to discover hidden analogies; it had been bent from very infancy upon intellectual pursuits, and through many years it had been nourished in solitude with a steadily increasing mass of miscellaneous knowledge. His power of analysis was therefore intense; it was an intellectual engine of incalculable power. Yet in its own way it would seem that De Quincey's use of this great endowment had its touch of that morbidness and excess which we have found ingrained in his character. Too often, as has been observed, however shrewd and however learned he may be, De Quincey is "as destitute of the true critical spirit, the sense of the actual, as anything can well be." That touch of hard-headedness, if we may so term it, which

---

[1] *Cf.* below, p. 231 : "But my way of writing is rather to think aloud, and follow my own humours, than much to consider who is listening to me."

cannot be gained from books or from solitary musing, but which is the endowment of a million common mortals of the uninspired world, — that little gift was denied to De Quincey. He is in his own way, to be sure, a most persistent investigator. Working in solitude, and wholly engrossed in his subject, he delights in supporting a theory with countless intellectual subtleties. Erudition and penetration he will display in abundance; but we cannot at all times expect from him good judgment in proportion to his critical insight and power.

There might then be some doubt about the life of these essays of De Quincey if they stood alone, unsupported by such clear candidates for immortality as the *Confessions* and *The Mail-Coach*. Ranging over so wide a field, it is evident that he cannot make a thorough study of his subjects. Indeed, for the dog's work of tracking a theme through a mass of uninteresting "material," De Quincey had no taste. It is unavoidable, therefore, that the weaker parts of his work should not rank above the quality of "respectable padding for magazines," and that not a little should be preserved in his *Works* that has in itself but slight claim to republication. To compare him with a great contemporary who also wrote much for magazines, his essays when collected want the solid front presented by Macaulay's articles. The reader of De Quincey cannot range through a series of coördinate efforts that really make a book; his interest in the *System of the Heavens* does not commend to him an account of *Plato's Republic*, nor a paper on *Modern Superstition*, nor articles on *Murder* and *Suicide*, — all included in the same volume; and the student of the *Logic of Political Economy* may view with some indifference its companion, *A Tory's Account of Toryism, Whiggism, and Radicalism*. Contributors are often but desultory beings, but none of them ever equalled

De Quincey in "scattering his fire." If Macaulay has no more of original thought to offer us, there are yet some solid reasons why his critical and miscellaneous essays may outweigh De Quincey's as an effective contribution to our supply of good reading.

To take up these writings of De Quincey in detail. I do not know that any of his speculative or theological essays, so called, has an important place in the literature of its subject to-day. His work in political economy, while esteemed at the time as a useful elucidation of Ricardo, no longer makes great claims upon the attention of the students of that science. He has left behind him hardly a fragment that might even preserve the memory of his deep interest in metaphysics and his considerable pretensions as a philosopher. His volumes of history, biography, and literary criticism, however, give us an impression of greater solidity and permanency. To speak first of the historical essays, *The Cæsars* was meant, to quote De Quincey, "as a specimen of fruits, gathered hastily and without effort, by a vagrant but thoughtful mind," with "so much, at least, of originality as ought *not* to have been left open to anybody in the nineteenth century." The *Cicero* is a "new reading of Roman history in the most dreadful and comprehensive of her convulsions," showing how Cicero was "governed in one half by his own private interest as a *novus homo* dependent upon a wicked oligarchy, and in the other half by his blind hatred of Caesar; the grandeur of whose nature he could not comprehend, and the real patriotism of whose policy could never be appreciated by one bribed to a selfish course." The article on the *Essenes* is an attempt in which the author took great interest and pride, to show that that sect was the "early Christians, locally in danger, and therefore locally putting themselves, with the wisdom of the serpent, under a cloud of disguise," — a theory which more recent investigations have not supported. In the *Revolt of the Tartars* De Quincey seizes an historical event of great scenic power and develops with brilliant success its dramatic capabilities; the essay exhibits in a high degree the Opium-Eater's tendency, not exactly to give a story a "cocked hat and cane," but at least to pass it through the crucible of his imagination without taking the trouble to note that the process has taken place. In many respects, however, this is the most attractive of De Quincey's historical writings, and there are passages of prose in it that vie with the "purple patches" of his professedly imaginative prose. Of the biographies we should probably select *Shakespeare*, *Richard Bentley*, and *Joan of Arc* as representing the high level of De Quincey's workmanship. The life of Shakspere has by no means lost its usefulness, even in this flood tide of Shakspere literature. The author at the outset puts his ban upon the notion that the great dramatist was little known throughout the seventeenth century; and he offers the Parliamentary War, the fact that Shakspere was a player, the burning of the Globe Theatre, etc., as explanations — not, of course, original — of the meagreness of our knowledge of the greatest figure in literature. His biography of Bentley is, in view of the comparative lack of attention to the subject on the part of others, probably the most useful of all his essays in this kind. He would have us know that the famous scholar was also a great man; and there are few more delightful stories than his account of the celebrated fight to oust his hero from the Mastership of Trinity, — how after twenty-nine years of legal effort on the part of his adversaries "the smoke of Bentley's pipe still ascended in Trinity Lodge," and "his enemies became finally satisfied that 'this world was made for Caesar.'" If the account of Joan of Arc is better known than any similar paper, it is for excellence of a special kind; merely as an adequate biography it can hardly vie with the life of Bentley. But it is a far more brilliant piece of English, because it possesses not only many touches of humor and pathos, but it displays an eloquence that here and there rises into the sublime. The life of *La Pucelle* seized upon De Quincey's imagination as did the migration of the Tartars, and the result is again a work that is by no means merely a contribution to the "literature of knowledge."

De Quincey's ventures in literary criticism were not always successful, but his efforts in the theory of prose-writing have apparently their assured place among the classics in their department. The essays on *Style*, *Rhetoric*, *Language*, and *Conversation* have all the value of the words of an expert. De Quincey's literary verdicts vary greatly in value. He failed surprisingly in his estimate of *Werther* as the best of Goethe's works, as well as in the dictum that the reputation of Goethe at his death "must decline for a generation or two, until it reaches its true level."[1] He seems to have been unable to appreciate rightly great humorists like Swift. He appeared to regard a preference for Thackeray over Dickens as simply "a crotchety illusion or a blind partiality."[2] Not many of us will be able to concur in his decided exaltation of Milton above Dante.[3] Yet there is much in De Quincey's literary

---

[1] These judgments occur in the life of *Goethe*, *Works*, Masson's Ed., Vol. IV, p. 421; Riverside Ed., Vol. VI, p. 442. *Cf.* close of *Reminiscences of Coleridge*, Masson's Ed., Vol. II, p. 225; Riverside Ed., Vol. III, p. 259.

[2] Rev. Francis Jacox, Page's *Life*, Vol. I, p. 386.

[3] This passage from the less accessible part of De Quincey's writings is worthy of quotation: "Nobody will pretend to show us in any Continental creation the least approach toward the colossal sublimities of

criticisms that is both wise and inspiring.   His estimate of
Lamb's works as "cabinet specimens which express the
utmost delicacy, purity and tenderness of the national
intellect, together with the rarest felicity of finish and
expression," is especially satisfying ; and as he has justly
claimed, he did his countrymen a great if unappreciated
service in pointing out even in the first decade of this century the true position of Wordsworth among our poets, and
defending that singular view with all the ardor of youthful
discipleship.   Finally, the little paper *On the Knocking at
the Gate in "Macbeth"* is interesting in several ways.   It is
a classical instance of the peculiar faculty of discovering
hidden analogies of which De Quincey boasts ; like Lamb's
essay on the tragedies of Shakspere considered as to their
fitness for stage representation, it is an early note of the
great burden of rational Shakspere appreciation that took
its rise, in England, in the lectures of Coleridge ; and it is
a contribution from one who does not rank among the
great commentators upon the Elizabethan drama, which
no such commentator can afford to neglect.   There is, in
fact, no part of De Quincey's additions to literature in
which he has more clearly redeemed for all time a bit
of the unknown.

the 'Paradise Lost.' . . . As to Dante, it is not awe and shadowy
terror which preside in *his* poetry, but carnal horror.   Like all those
who treat a dreadful theme, he was tempted by the serpent to eat from
the tree of fleshly horror ; he did eat ; and in that hour his poetry
became tainted with the principle of death.   Even for the present,
with national jealousy working through six centuries on its behalf, *live*
it does not.   It does not abide in the heart of man, nor domineer by
mighty shadows over the brains of men." — JAPP, *Eclectic Magazine*,
New Series, Vol. XLIV, p. 505.

VI

In a discussion of that part of De Quincey's work gathered in his first and third divisions a word may be spared to the Tales and Romances, which, partly through the author's own fault perhaps, are his least known works. Setting aside the mere translations, there are three original tales: *The Household Wreck*, a painful story of English domestic life; *The Avenger*, a very harrowing German tale; and *Klosterheim*. The last named is one of the two works of De Quincey that appeared originally in book form. It is a German story of some length, and it represents the best that De Quincey could accomplish in this direction. Like all his romances, it recalls Mrs. Baird Smith's avowal of her father's "demand for the excitement of fear." "When he was chilling our marrow with awesome stories of ghosts, murders and mysteries," she writes, "he only thought he was producing a luxurious excitement." If De Quincey as a novelist had a model, it is to be found in Charles Robert Maturin, the head of the School of Terror in the English novel. At all events, he did not conceal his admiration for such works as *The Family of Montorio* and *Melmoth*, greatly preferring them to Miss Edgeworth's novels of uneventful domestic life, with her array of "prudence, discretion and the like sober sisterhood." The story of *The Spanish Military Nun*, though not original, has been so De Quinceyfied that its literary parent would hardly recognize it; it is the pleasantest reading of all these tales, for it adds touches of real humor to the interest of situation and incident. This question of De Quincey's humor, which the story of the fighting nun brings before us, cannot be treated without drawing into the discussion his greatest effort in the humorous, the amazing lectures *On Murder Considered as one of the Fine Arts*. Critics have

differed on this point widely.   A Westminster reviewer in
1854 gave our author short shrift with the words: "Never
was there anyone with less humor, or except in merely
verbal matters less faculty of wit.   At times sarcastic pun-
gency and at times an amusing quaintness.   But that is
all."   That is not much, certainly ; yet such a censure,
though itself extreme, may indicate very well the limitation of De Quincey's powers.   No one would go to the
Opium-Eater, as nowadays we go to the theatre, to have a
hearty laugh.   He can compel no man to mirth by the
bubbling over of such a spontaneous fountain of humor
as we find in some famous Americans ; he has no vein of
veiled irony, delicate but certain of its effect, like Thackeray's ; nor, on the other hand, has he that feeling of the
helpless absurdity of little man out of which the satire of a
Swift might grow.   The humor of De Quincey is in its
nature conscious even to being strained ; it is generally
narrow in its object, — confined to the " art of telling a story
with quaint garnishings," or the scholarly and severe handling of some trifle.   To be sure he tells a story admirably
in this way.   There is nothing better of their kind than his
relation of a certain mishap of the elder Coleridge,[1] the
true narration of General William de Quincey and the
factory boys, and the veracious chronicles of the kingdoms of Gombroon and Tigrosylvania.[2]   And furthermore,
if the lectures on *Murder* suffer from being too evidently
the manufactured article, they are none the less a unique
creation.   It is likely that to people of delicate sensibilities
they will never be agreeable reading ; and, on the other
hand, to compare them with Swift's *Proposal* for cooking
the unused children of Ireland is to miss a fundamental

[1] See *Works*, Masson's Ed., Vol. II, p. 165 ; Riverside Ed., Vol. III,
p. 185.
[2] *Cf.* below, pp. 36 *et seq.*

part of the greatness of all Swift's work — the awful query
that suggests itself in this case whether the children are
likely to be better off if left to their miserable existence.
There is nothing of this sort behind De Quincey's papers;
they are pure extravaganzas existing only for their absurdity. But they are monumental essays in the incongruous,
and so long as boys and men love to break the prison of
convention — to shock propriety and defy probability, —
they will have their place — a singular but secure one —
in literary art.

The papers which readers of recent editions of De Quincey know as the *Autobiography* and *Literary Reminiscences*
have been gathered from many sources. The *Autobiography*
as far as the year 1803 was made up, with much cutting,
dovetailing, and refurbishing, by De Quincey himself for
his collective edition out of the original *Autobiographic
Sketches* in *Tait's Magazine*, some much later articles in
Hogg's Instructor, and certain fragments of the *Suspiria
de Profundis* that served his purpose. The rest of the autobiographic papers were left untouched by their author in
the pages of *Tait*, from which later editors have rescued
them. The *Reminiscences* of literary friends in London and
the Lakes, which had come out in *Tait* concurrently with
the *Autobiography*, — to which they are closely allied, —
must also for the most part be reprinted directly from the
Magazine; the chief Coleridge and Wordsworth papers,
however, were reproduced by De Quincey in his edition,
the former with extensive revision. It follows necessarily
that these papers as a whole present an extremely disjointed and formless appearance; even in the first part of
the *Autobiography*, which De Quincey revised, there seems
to have been no attempt to achieve artistic unity. But for
all that, these volumes contain a notable revelation of the
versatility — moral as well as intellectual — of the great

contributor. Where else in any document or collection of
cognate documents in modern literature are fine narrative, splendid prose-poetry, shrewd speculation, varied erudition, and incisive criticism so jumbled together, and only
to give place to mere trivial and ill-natured gossip in the
end!

To touch for a moment upon the *Reminiscences*. The
action of De Quincey as editor would seem to have evinced
some doubt of their permanent value. Many of them, as
he well knew, were written hastily as "potboilers," and
were felt, perhaps, to need more extensive rehandling than
he had time to give them. But there has been the widest
difference of opinion among later critics concerning those
papers upon which their author bestowed the deliberate
approval of republication. "Of Wordsworth's demeanour
and physical presence," writes Mr. John Morley, " De Quincey's account, silly, coxcombical and vulgar, is the worst."
Miss Mitford, on the other hand, found "the truth and
life of these Lake sketches something wonderful," and
Dr. Japp is sure that in this comment most readers will
find evidence of the lady's "singular impartiality and
good judgment." Sara Coleridge, even in complaining of
the harsh treatment of the character of the great poet-
philosopher by his disciple, feels constrained to add, "He
has characterized my father's genius and peculiar mode of
discourse with great eloquence and discrimination." Perhaps we have here a critical problem that no single formula
will solve ; the personal equation is very important. Were
De Quincey's accounts of the personality of these men of
letters the only descriptions of them we could receive,
we should certainly wish much added to them — and not a
little expunged ; yet even the worst of these papers, through
the writer's peculiar insight, — his power of investigation
and comparison, — adds something to our pictures of the

The *Confessions of an English Opium-Eater* is one of the few popular books that are candidates for favor in two greatly differing forms. After the two magazine articles of 1821, De Quincey had promised a third part, for which the edition of 1822 offered only a brief appendix. In this condition the book was a household companion in England and America for more than thirty years. In 1856, however, as Vol. V of De Quincey's *Selections Grave and Gay*, appeared a new version of the work, three times as large as the original form. It would seem that the reading public has never been willing to surrender the shorter form, and the American Riverside Edition has very wisely retained it. Professor Masson, however, in reëditing the English *Collected Works*, takes a decided position in favor of the later version in these words: "By his [De Quincey's] own act and deed the enlarged edition of 1856 was intended to be the final edition, superseding the other; and by *his* intention we are bound to abide."[1] The last part of this statement is surely open to question; it is not clear that De Quincey's readers are bound — even at his bidding — to discard a terse and powerful account of his opium experiences for a voluminous, wandering, and often conflicting *rifacimento* of his old age; and in this sense the 1856 edition certainly has not superseded the other. But did De Quincey intend this to be the final edition? As Vol. V was issuing from the press he wrote to his daughter Emily, in part, as follows: "Reviewing the volume as a *whole*, . . . greatly I doubt whether many readers will not prefer it in its original fragmentary state to its present full-blown development. But if so, why could I not have felt this objection many weeks since? . . . The truth is, I did feel it, but . . . a doubt had arisen whether . . . I could count upon bringing together enough of the 'Suspiria'

[1] De Quincey, *Works*, Masson's Ed., Vol. III, p. 9.

(yet unpublished) materially to enlarge the volume.[1] . . .
Such being the case, no remedy remained but that I should
doctor the book, and expand it into a portliness that might
countenance its price. . . . Hereafter it will travel into a
popular edition, priced suppose one half-crown instead of
three; and in that edition I can profit by the opinions
reported."[2] A letter of November, 1856, to his daughter
Margaret is even more explicit: "A copy of the 'Confessions' was sent to you on Tuesday. . . . Criticise furiously and without mercy. The next will be the *final*
edition, far different and far better."[3] It seems quite clear,
then, that De Quincey regarded these two versions of his
best known work as rival candidates for popular favor,
that he felt pretty sure that the public would prefer the
former, and that on the whole he was inclined to concur
in that opinion. Be that as it may, the edition "intended
to be final" was never prepared.

We have in the letters quoted above one among many
evidences of the pains that De Quincey was disposed to
spend upon these Confessions. There can be no doubt that
he viewed them, with their adjuncts, the *Suspiria*, as the
crown and glory of his authorship. The care bestowed, in
the revision, upon many of the minutest alterations not
only bespeaks the literary artist, but also displays the
intense ardor of a voluminous writer adorning his fancy's
favorite child.

The additions to the *Confessions*, when not merely pleasant phrase-making, are valuable chiefly as a running commentary on some of the incidents of the earlier version.
It may be, as the author assured his daughters at the
time, that in the edition of 1856 nothing was introduced

[1] See the first note on the *Suspiria*, below, pp. 470-473.
[2] See Page's *Life*, Vol. II, p. 110.
[3] *Ibid.*, Vol. II, p. 125.

that did not originally belong to his outline of the work; if so, we may the more abundantly rejoice that stern necessity and opium had left him in 1821 neither time nor energy to carry out that plan. As to the *Confessions* of 1821, it is doubtful if anything that followed it destroyed the primacy of this "first heir of his invention." Certainly no later effort has taken the same hold upon the popular mind. The intense interest aroused by the work at the time has never died out, and it has at this day many readers that hardly know who the Opium-Eater was or ever glance at his many volumes of classic prose. To this exclusive attachment, however, the author would certainly have demurred. De Quincey is accustomed to speak of the *Confessions* and *Suspiria* together as the acme of his literary achievements; whenever he distinguishes between them, however, he seems greatly to prefer the later work. "Whatever pleasure you may at any time have found in the original 'Confessions,'" he writes to Professor Lushington,[1] "will probably be trebled in this second series. . . . I, if at all I can pretend to judge in such a case, think them very greatly superior to the first." In point of style there can be little doubt that the best of the *Suspiria* excel the *Confessions:* they are more finished specimens of literary art; they are purer — and so far better — examples of De Quincey's peculiar mode of imaginative prose. On the other hand, these "Sighs from the Depths" can be termed *Confessions* only in a technical sense. It is true that they present "dreams and noon-day visions" that arose "under the latter stages of opium influence"; and that their material is not intrinsically different from that of the original

---

[1] Letter of February, 1845 (Page's *Life*, Vol. I, pp. 338–339). It is impossible to tell just what *Suspiria* were then in existence; for a discussion of the whole complicated question of the origin of these pieces, see the first note on the *Suspiria*, below, pp. 470–473.

work. But the treatment is radically changed. Deficient
as the *Confessions* may be in revealing the character of its
writer, the interest in that production is still centred upon
the sufferer, — upon the seer of visions and the dreamer of
terrible dreams. In the *Suspiria*, on the contrary, attention
is quite withdrawn from the Opium-Eater, to be fixed upon
the unearthly pictures made real by his glowing pen. It
was at all times, as has been intimated, De Quincey's dear
defect to theorize, subtilize, and endlessly refine until sorrow seems to vanish into the thin air of speculation or be
lost amid the mazes of brilliant rhetoric. But it is probable that in 1821 the pleasures and pains of opium were
too new and too real to be treated as objects of speculation
or studies in style. At all events we have here altogether
the most powerful record of actual personal experience that
De Quincey ever put upon paper, and it would seem that
this book, of all that he wrote, has the vitality that can
compel attention from many generations of readers.

The style of the *Confessions* and *Suspiria* has been the
theme of universal praise,[1] and critics have generally agreed
that it partakes somewhat of the peculiar beauty of poetry.
The great artist-poet of our day, we are told, in reciting
a brilliant passage[2] from the *Confessions*, characterized
De Quincey's prose as some of the finest in the English language, "not poetry, but as fine as any verse."[3] It will be
remembered, however, that a very unusual pretension was
made for these pieces by their author, who drew especial
attention to them as "modes of impassioned prose ranging
under no precedents in literature." What is this department of "impassioned prose" to which De Quincey lays

[1] Professor Minto's *Manual of English Prose Literature* provides an
admirable analysis of De Quincey's style, pp. 49–76.

[2] "Yet I knew ... legions." *Cf.* below, p. 241, lines 25–32.

[3] H. Tennyson, *Alfred Lord Tennyson*, Vol. II, p. 414.

exclusive claim? De Quincey has strangely neglected to reply to this natural query, and we are indebted for our answer to the efforts of his latest editor. By bringing together the sense of many scattered passages, Professor Masson has arrived at the following highly interesting result.

It appears that De Quincey considered three kinds of prose worthy of recognition as literary art: 1. *Rhetorical Prose.* What De Quincey meant by the name "rhetoric" or a rhetorical style was "the art of rich or ornate style, the art of conscious playing with a subject intellectually and inventively, and of never leaving it till it has been brocaded with the utmost possible amount of subsidiary thought, humour, fancy, ornamentation, and anecdote."[1] The first very eminent "rhetorician" in English literature, De Quincey tells us, is Donne; then come Burton, Milton, Jeremy Taylor, and Sir Thomas Browne.[2] To De Quincey himself belongs a very high place among representatives of this rich style in English prose, but evidently his writings in this kind are by no means unique. 2. *Eloquent Prose*, or *Prose Eloquence*. This is evidently oratory, the literature of strong emotion, of which we have many exemplars in English prose. That mode of prose eloquence, however, in which De Quincey could claim to stand alone was evidently, as Professor Masson suggests, "a kind of new lyrical prose that could undertake the expression of feelings till then supposed unutterable except in verse. Oratory in some of its extremes — as when the feeling to be expressed is peculiarly keen and ecstatic — does tend to pass into song or metrical lyric;

---

[1] This and the two succeeding quotations are from the preface to Vol. XIII of Masson's *De Quincey's Works.*

[2] *Essay on Rhetoric, Works*, Riverside Ed., Vol. IV, pp. 330–341; Masson's Ed., Vol. X, pp. 100–109.

and De Quincey, in order to extend the powers of prose in this extreme and difficult direction, proposed to institute, we may say, a new form of prose literature nameable as the prose-lyric." 3. *Prose Fantasy* or *Prose-Poetry*. "Not only is it certain that even such solid matter of phantasy or 'feigned history' as may be undertaken in prose receives incalculable modifications when it is lifted into verse; but it is also certain that there are peculiar kinds of phantasy for which Prose in all ages has felt itself incompetent, or which it has been too shamefaced to attempt. Such, in especial, are the visionary phantasies that form themselves in the poetic mind in its most profound fits of solitary self-musing, its hours of inventive day-dream in some sequestered nook of rocky sea-shore, or of long nocturnal reverie within-doors over the embers of a dying fire. Now, as De Quincey had been a dreamer all his life, with an abnormal faculty of dreaming at work in him constitution-ally from his earliest infancy, and with the qualification moreover that he had unlocked the terrific potencies of opium for the generation of dreams beyond the human, his idea seems to have been that, if prose would but exert itself, it could compass, almost equally with verse, or even better, the representation of some forms at least of dream-experience and dream-phantasmagory. Add this idea to that other of the possibility of a prose-lyric that should rival the verse-lyric in ability to express the keenest and rarest forms of human feeling, or suppose the two ideas combined, and De Quincey's conception of the exact nature of his service towards the extension of the liberties and powers of English prose will be fully apprehended."

It may be that there is no prose quite like the most bril-liant strains of De Quincey. Milton, Browne, and Taylor certainly influenced him, and the names of Jean Paul and Ruskin occur to us in this connection. But, whatever isolation may be claimed for him, let it be remembered that De Quincey's faculty was the gift of Heaven and not of opium. He possessed without other conspicuous poetical gifts a power of imagination generally restricted to poets; he had a command over prose expression so far denied to them: the combination of these powers in him was exercised very often upon the visions of his opium slumbers; it was developed, however, occasionally with great success in the treatment of other material. The narcotic could confer no such power; indeed, it was far more apt to deprive him of all powers.

VII

De Quincey's style, in whatever kind of writing he attempted, has now for many years been zealously bepraised, and he has suffered everything that academic analysis can do to make masterpieces commonplace. The extent of his vocabulary and the aptness with which it is used, the variety of his sentence structure and the ease and grace he lends to the weighty periodic form, his transparent clearness and his sympathetic tone, — these excellencies and superiorities have all been exploited again and again. And then we pass on to those special achievements of his in the small cabinet-piece — to the gorgeous imagery, the unique poetical quality of style — that have thrown a nimbus of glory about the "Ladies of Sorrow" and "Savannah-la-Mar."

Occasion has arisen already in these pages to speak of details in De Quincey's style that especially reveal the man, and his prose-poetry has just been treated at some length. One great quality, however, which has been touched upon but briefly, deserves in my opinion the position of emphasis in these closing paragraphs. Mr. Saintsbury has spoken of the strong appeal that De Quincey makes to boys.[1] It is not without significance that he mentions as especially attractive to the young only writings with a large narrative element.[2] Few boys read poetry, whether in verse or prose, and fewer still criticism or philosophy; to every normal boy the gate of good literature is the good story. It is the narrative skill of De Quincey that has secured for him, in preference to other writers of his class, the favor of youthful readers.

It would be too much to say that the talent that attracts the young to him must needs be the Opium-Eater's grand talent, though the notion is defensible, seeing that only salient qualities in good writing appeal to inexperienced readers. I believe, however, that this skill in narration is De Quincey's most persistent quality, — the golden thread that unites all his most distinguished and most enduring work. And it is with him a part of his genius for style. Creative power of the kind that goes to the making of plots De Quincey had not; he has proved that forever by the mediocrity of *Klosterheim*. Give him Bergmann's account of the Tartar Migration, or the story of the Fighting Nun, — give him the matter, — and a brilliant narrative will result. Indeed, De Quincey loved a story for its own sake; he rejoiced to see it extend its winding course before him; he delighted to follow it, touch it, color it, see it grow into body and being under his hand. That this enthusiasm should now and then tend to endanger the

---

[1] " Probably more boys have in the last forty years been brought to a love of literature proper by De Quincey than by any other writer whatever." — *History of Nineteenth Century Literature*, p. 198.

[2] " To read the *Essay on Murder*, the *English Mail Coach*, *The Spanish Nun*, *The Caesars*, and half a score other things at the age of about fifteen or sixteen is, or ought to be, to fall in love with them." — *Essays in English Literature, 1780–1860*, p. 307.

integrity of the facts need not surprise us; as I have said in another place, accuracy in these matters is hardly to be expected of De Quincey. And we can take our pleasure in the skillful unfolding of the dramatic narrative of the Tartar Flight — we can feel the author's joy in the scenic possibilities of his theme — even if we know that here and there an incident appears that is quite in its proper place — but is unknown to history.[1]

In his *Confessions* the same constructive power bears its part in the author's triumph. A peculiar end was to be reached in that narrative, — an end in which the writer had a deep personal interest. What is an opium-eater? Says a character in a recent work of fiction, of a social wreck: "If it isn't whiskey with him, it's opium; if it isn't opium, it's whiskey." This speech establishes the popular category in which De Quincey's habit had placed him. Our attention was to be drawn from these degrading connections. And this is done not merely by the correction of some widespread fallacies as to the effects of the drug; far more it is the result of narrative skill. As we follow with ever-increasing sympathy the lonely and sensitive child, the wandering youth, the neuralgic patient, into the terrible grasp of opium, who realizes, amid the gorgeous delights and the awful horrors of the tale, that the writer is after all the victim of the worst of bad habits? We can hardly praise too highly the art which even as we look beneath it throws its glamour over us still.

Nor is it only in this constructive power, in the selection and arrangement of details, that De Quincey excels as a narrator; a score of minor excellencies of his style, such as the fine Latin words or the sweeping periodic sentences, contribute to the effective progress of his narrative prose. Mr. Lowell has said that "there are no such vistas and

[1] *Cf.* above, p. xl.

avenues of verse as Milton's." The comparison with the great Puritan is somewhat hazardous for our author, still I should like to venture the parallel claim that there are no such streams of prose as De Quincey's. The movement of his discourse is that of the broad river, not in its weight or force perhaps, but in its easy flowing progress, in its serene, unhurried certainty of its end. To be sure, only too often the waters overflow their banks and run far afield in alien channels. Yet, when great power over the instrument of language is joined to so much constructive skill, the result is narrative art of high quality, — an achievement that must be in no small measure the solid basis of De Quincey's fame.

A word to sum up. One title all will concede to De Quincey; he was the "great contributor" of his day. No other man has won so important a place in literature merely through the magazine. His excellencies and his defects are in great measure those of his calling. His name cannot be said to be associated with any sustained effort of the intellect nor with any great and novel idea. Assuredly he was not capable of such prolonged endeavor, and it is doubtful if even necessity would have brought him to the exertions that he made, had not the modern magazines come into being just in time. Yet, not only were his attainments extensive, his powers of mind were undoubtedly very great; of De Quincey intellectually one may say — with a certain lowering of the scale — what he said of Burke: "His great and peculiar distinction was that he viewed all objects of the understanding under more relations than other men and under more complex relations."

The writer has ventured to express in these pages a preference for the *Confessions* over any of De Quincey's later work, because, in a word, there is more of De Quincey in it. The elusive personality of the opium sufferer is to me ever replete with interest and charm. It is a question, after all, in this case whether the man be not more interesting than his work; both are in the highest degree perplexing. Some of his critics have essayed to settle all problems concerning De Quincey with a few telling phrases. "Clever brains and shallow character" is one recent dictum. Surely the English Opium-Eater is not to be so readily stamped, sealed, and directed to Oblivion. A very high order of cleverness goes to the making of his fourteen volumes; and, as to his character, we have a quarrel again with the adjective employed. If De Quincey lived apart from the moral interests and enthusiasms of his generation, let us not forget that in many a solitary hour he fought his own bitter fight against the "unimaginable trance and agony that cannot be remembered." A child he was in practical affairs, but, as Carlyle reminds us: "*Eccovi*, this child has been in hell!" Let us admit, then, that there was a touch of greatness, if only that, upon the man and his work; and for the rest, — he had lofty visions of the possibilities of such a mind as his, granted only certain adult qualities of concentration and organization that he did not possess.

VIII

A BRIEF BIBLIOGRAPHY

I. WORKS

1. *Confessions of an English Opium-Eater.* London: Printed for Taylor and Hessey, Fleet Street, 1822. [An American edition, Philadelphia, 1823. There were six English issues before the enlarged edition of 1856, in *Selections Grave and Gay.*]

2. *Klosterheim; or The Masque. By the English Opium-Eater.* Edinburgh and London, 1832.

3. *The Logic of Political Economy, by Thomas De Quincey.* Edinburgh, 1844.

4. *De Quincey's Writings.* Boston: Ticknor & Fields, 1851–59. [22 vols., each with an independent title: 20 vols., 1851–56; 2 vols., 1859.]

5. *Selections, Grave and Gay, from Writings, published and unpublished, of Thomas de Quincey, revised and arranged by himself.* Edinburgh: J. Hogg, 1853–60. [14 vols.; the last was nearly ready when De Quincey died.]

6. *The Collected Works of Thomas de Quincey.* Author's Edition. With Portrait and Illustrations. Edinburgh: A. and C. Black, 1862–71. [14 vols. (1862–63), containing the pieces printed in the Hogg Ed., the ownership of which had passed to the Blacks, rearranged and with the addition of two treatises; 2 vols. (1863 and 1871) giving new matter.]

7. *The Works of Thomas de Quincey.* Riverside Edition. Boston: Houghton, Mifflin & Co., 1877. [12 vols., with notes and index. A reissue of the Fields Ed., with great improvements.]

8. *The Works of Thomas de Quincey*, " *The English Opium-Eater*," including all his contributions to Periodical Literature. Edinburgh : A. and C. Black, 1878. [No. 6, a little altered and enlarged. Reprinted in 1880.]

9. *Thomas de Quincey : Confessions of an English Opium-Eater.* Reprinted from the first edition, with Notes of De Quincey's Conversations by Richard Woodhouse, and other additions [in particular, Alfred de Musset's French continuation of the *Confessions*, with the Opium-Eater's second meeting with Anne]. Edited by Richard Garnett. London : Kegan Paul, Trench, Trübner & Co., Ltd., 1885.

10. *The Collected Writings of Thomas de Quincey.* New and enlarged edition by David Masson. Edinburgh : A. and C. Black, 1889–90. [14 vols., with footnotes, a preface to each volume, and index. Reissued in cheaper form.]

11. *The Uncollected Writings of Thomas de Quincey.* With a preface and annotations by James Hogg. In two volumes. London : Swan, Sonnenschein & Co., 1890.

12. *The Posthumous Works of Thomas de Quincey.* Edited from the Author's MSS., with introductions and notes, by A. H. Japp. London : W. Heinemann. [Vol. I, *Suspiria de Profundis, with other essays.* 1891. Vol. II, *Conversation and Coleridge, with other essays.* 1893.]

13. *Joan of Arc ; The English Mail-Coach, by Thomas De Quincey.* Edited with introduction and notes, by J. M. Hart. New York, 1893.

II. BIOGRAPHY AND CRITICISM

Four works are indispensable to the student of De Quincey's life and character.

14. H. A. PAGE [A. H. Japp]. *Thomas De Quincey : His Life and Writings. With unpublished Correspondence.* London, 1877. [2 vols. in one. New York : Scribner. This, though far from satisfactory, is still the standard life ; it contains valuable communications from De Quincey's

daughters, J. Hogg, Rev. F. Jacox, Professor Masson, and others ; but the material is not well digested.]

15. D. MASSON. *Thomas De Quincey.* English Men of Letters. London. [New York: Harper. An excellent brief biography.]

16. A. H. JAPP. *De Quincey Memorials. Being Letters and other Records, here first published. With Communications from Coleridge, the Wordsworths, Hannah More, Professor Wilson, and others.* 2 vols. London: W. Heinemann, 1891.

17. J. HOGG. *De Quincey and his Friends. Personal Recollections, Souvenirs, and Anecdotes* [including Woodhouse's Conversations, Findlay's Personal Recollections, Hodgson's On the Genius of De Quincey, and a mass of personal notes from a host of friends]. London: Sampson Low, Marston & Co., 1895.

Nearly all personal reminiscences of De Quincey have been included in the works just mentioned ; a few further citations, chiefly recent critical discussions, will suffice.

18. A. BIRRELL. *Essays about Men, Women and Books.* New York, 1892.

19. E. B. CHANCELLOR. *Literary Types.* New York, 1896.

20. E. DOWDEN. *How De Quincey worked.* In the *Saturday Review*, No. 2052, Vol. LXXIX (Feb. 23, 1895), p. 246.

21. C. M. INGLEBY. *Essays.* London, 1888.

22. G. P. LATHROP. *Some Aspects of De Quincey.* In the *Atlantic Monthly*, Vol. XL (November, 1877), p. 569.

23. E. T. MASON. *Personal Traits of British Authors.* New York, 1885. [4 vols. The volume sub-titled *Scott, Hogg,* etc., contains some accounts of De Quincey not included by Japp or Hogg.]

24. D. MASSON. *Wordsworth, Shelley, Keats,* etc. London, 1881.

25. W. MINTO. *Manual of English Prose Literature.* Boston, 1889.

26. C. POLLITT. *De Quincey's Editorship of the Westmoreland Gazette.* London, 1890.

27. G. Saintsbury. *Essays in English Literature.* 1780–1860. First Series. New York, 1893.

28. H. S. Salt. *Literary Sketches.* London, 1888.

29. Mrs. H. Sandford. *Thomas Poole and his Friends.* 2 vols. New York, 1888.

30. L. Stephen. *Hours in a Library.* Vol. I. New York, 1892.

31. J. H. Stirling. *Jerrold, Tennyson, Macaulay,* etc. Edinburgh, 1868.

SELECTIONS FROM DE QUINCEY

THE AFFLICTION OF CHILDHOOD

THE earliest incidents in my life, which left stings in my memory so as to be remembered at this day, were two, and both before I could have completed my second year; namely, 1st, a remarkable dream of terrific grandeur about a favourite nurse, which is interesting to myself for this reason — that it demonstrates my dreaming tendencies to have been constitutional, and not dependent upon laudanum;[1] and, 2dly, the fact of having connected a profound sense of pathos with the reappearance, very early in the spring, of some crocuses. This I mention as inexplicable; for such annual resurrections of plants and flowers affect us only as memorials, or suggestions of some higher change, and therefore in connection with the idea of death; yet of death I could, at that time, have had no experience whatever.

This, however, I was speedily to acquire. My two eldest sisters — eldest of three *then* living, and also elder than myself — were summoned to an early death. The first

[1] It is true that in those days *paregoric elixir* was occasionally given to children in colds; and in this medicine there is a small proportion of laudanum. But no medicine was ever administered to any member of our nursery except under medical sanction; and this, assuredly, would not have been obtained to the exhibition of laudanum in a case such as mine. For I was not more than twenty-one months old; at which age the action of opium is capricious, and therefore perilous.

who died was Jane, about two years older than myself.
She was three and a half, I one and a half, more or less by
some trifle that I do not recollect. But death was then
scarcely intelligible to me, and I could not so properly
5 be said to suffer sorrow as a sad perplexity. There was
another death in the house about the same time, namely,
of a maternal grandmother; but, as she had come to us for
the express purpose of dying in her daughter's society, and
from illness had lived perfectly secluded, our nursery circle
10 knew her but little, and were certainly more affected by
the death (which I witnessed) of a beautiful bird — viz., a
kingfisher, which had been injured by an accident. With
my sister Jane's death (though otherwise, as I have said,
less sorrowful than perplexing) there was, however, con-
15 nected an incident which made a most fearful impression
upon myself, deepening my tendencies to thoughtfulness and
abstraction beyond what would seem credible for my years.
If there was one thing in this world from which, more than
from any other, nature had forced me to revolt, it was bru-
20 tality and violence. Now, a whisper arose in the family
that a female servant, who by accident was drawn off from
her proper duties to attend my sister Jane for a day or two,
had on one occasion treated her harshly, if not brutally;
and as this ill-treatment happened within three or four
25 days of her death, so that the occasion of it must have
been some fretfulness in the poor child caused by her sufferings, naturally there was a sense of awe and indignation
diffused through the family. I believe the story never
reached my mother, and possibly it was exaggerated; but
30 upon me the effect was terrific. I did not often see the
person charged with this cruelty; but, when I did, my eyes
sought the ground; nor could I have borne to look her in
the face; not, however, in any spirit that could be called
anger. The feeling which fell upon me was a shuddering

horror, as upon a first glimpse of the truth that I was in a world of evil and strife. Though born in a large town (the town of Manchester, even then among the largest of the island), I had passed the whole of my childhood, except for the few earliest weeks, in a rural seclusion. With three innocent little sisters for playmates, sleeping always amongst them, and shut up for ever in a silent garden from all knowledge of poverty, or oppression, or outrage, I had not suspected until this moment the true complexion of the world in which myself and my sisters were living. Henceforward the character of my thoughts changed greatly; for so *representative* are some acts, that one single **case** of the class is sufficient to throw open before you the whole theatre of possibilities in that direction. I never heard that the woman accused of this cruelty took it at all to heart, even after the event which so immediately succeeded had reflected upon it a more painful emphasis. But for myself, that incident had a lasting revolutionary power in colouring my estimate of life.

So passed away from earth one of those three sisters that made up my nursery playmates; and so did my acquaintance (if such it could be called) commence with mortality. Yet, in fact, I knew little more of mortality than that Jane had disappeared. She had gone away; but, perhaps, she would come back. Happy interval of heaven-born ignorance! Gracious immunity of infancy from sorrow disproportioned to its strength! I was sad for Jane's absence. But still in my heart I trusted that she would come again. Summer and winter came again—crocuses and roses; why not little Jane?

Thus easily was healed, then, the first wound in my infant heart. Not so the second. For thou, dear, noble Elizabeth, around whose ample brow, as often as thy sweet countenance rises upon the darkness, I fancy a *tiara* of light or a gleaming

aureola[1] in token of thy premature intellectual grandeur
— thou whose head, for its superb developments, was the
astonishment of science [2] — thou next, but after an interval
of happy years, thou also wert summoned away from our
nursery; and the night which for me gathered upon that
event ran after my steps far into life; and perhaps at this
day I resemble little for good or for ill that which else I
should have been. Pillar of fire that didst go before me to
guide and to quicken — pillar of darkness, when thy countenance was turned away to God, that didst too truly reveal
to my dawning fears the secret shadow of death, by what
mysterious gravitation was it that *my* heart had been drawn

[1] " *Aureola* " : — The *aureola* is the name given in the " Legends of the
Christian Saints " to that golden diadem or circlet of supernatural light
(that *glory*, as it is commonly called in English) which, amongst the
great masters of painting in Italy, surrounded the heads of Christ and
of distinguished saints.

[2] " *The astonishment of science* " : — Her medical attendants were
Dr. Percival, a well-known literary physician, who had been a correspondent of Condorcet, D'Alembert, etc., and Mr. Charles White, the
most distinguished surgeon at that time in the North of England. It
was he who pronounced her head to be the finest in its development of
any that he had ever seen — an assertion which, to my own knowledge,
he repeated in after years, and with enthusiasm. That he had some
acquaintance with the subject may be presumed from this, that, at so
early a stage of such inquiries, he had published a work on human
craniology, supported by measurements of heads selected from all
varieties of the human species. Meantime, as it would grieve me that
any trait of what might seem vanity should creep into this record, I
will admit that my sister died of hydrocephalus; and it has been often
supposed that the premature expansion of the intellect in cases of that
class is altogether morbid — forced on, in fact, by the mere stimula-
tion of the disease. I would, however, suggest, as a possibility, the
very opposite order of relation between the disease and the intellectual
manifestations. Not the disease may always have caused the preternatural growth of the intellect; but, inversely, this growth of the
intellect coming on spontaneously, and outrunning the capacities of
the physical structure, may have caused the disease.

to thine? Could a child, six years old, place any special
value upon intellectual forwardness? Serene and capacious
as my sister's mind appeared to me upon after review, was
that a charm for stealing away the heart of an infant? Oh
no! I think of it *now* with interest, because it lends, in a
stranger's ear, some justification to the excess of my fondness. But then it was lost upon me; or, if not lost, was
perceived only through its effects. Hadst thou been an
idiot, my sister, not the less I must have loved thee, having
that capacious heart — overflowing, even as mine overflowed,
with tenderness, strung, even as mine was strung, by the
necessity of loving and being loved. This it was which
crowned thee with beauty and power: —

> "Love, the holy sense,
> Best gift of God, in thee was most intense."

That lamp of Paradise was, for myself, kindled by reflection
from the living light which burned so steadfastly in thee;
and never but to thee, never again since *thy* departure, had
I power or temptation, courage or desire, to utter the feelings which possessed me. For I was the shyest of children;
and, at all stages of life, a natural sense of personal dignity
held me back from exposing the least ray of feelings which
I was not encouraged *wholly* to reveal.

It is needless to pursue, circumstantially, the course of
that sickness which carried off my leader and companion.
She (according to my recollection at this moment) was just
as near to nine years as I to six. And perhaps this natural
precedency in authority of years and judgment, united to
the tender humility with which she declined to assert it, had
been amongst the fascinations of her presence. It was upon
a Sunday evening, if such conjectures can be trusted, that
the spark of fatal fire fell upon that train of predispositions
to a brain complaint which had hitherto slumbered within

her. She had been permitted to drink tea at the house of a labouring man, the father of a favourite female servant. The sun had set when she returned, in the company of this servant, through meadows reeking with exhalations after a
5 fervent day. From that day she sickened. In such circumstances, a child, as young as myself, feels no anxieties. Looking upon medical men as people privileged, and naturally commissioned, to make war upon pain and sickness, I never had a misgiving about the result. I grieved, indeed,
10 that my sister should lie in bed; I grieved still more to hear her moan. But all this appeared to me no more than as a night of trouble, on which the dawn would soon arise. O! moment of darkness and delirium, when the elder nurse awakened me from that delusion, and launched God's
15 thunderbolt at my heart in the assurance that my sister MUST die. Rightly it is said of utter, utter misery, that it "cannot be *remembered*."[1] Itself, as a remarkable thing, is swallowed up in its own chaos. Blank anarchy and confusion of mind fell upon me. Deaf and blind I was, as I
20 reeled under the revelation. I wish not to recall the circumstances of that time, when *my* agony was at its height, and hers, in another sense, was approaching. Enough it is to say, that all was soon over; and the morning of that day had at last arrived which looked down upon her inno-
25 cent face, sleeping the sleep from which there is no awaking, and upon me sorrowing the sorrow for which there is no consolation.

On the day after my sister's death, whilst the sweet temple of her brain was yet unviolated by human scrutiny,
30 I formed my own scheme for seeing her once more. Not for the world would I have made this known, nor have

---

[1] "I stood in unimaginable trance
And agony which cannot be remember'd."
Speech of Alhadra, in Coleridge's Remorse.

suffered a witness to accompany me. I had never heard of feelings that take the name of "sentimental," nor dreamed of such a possibility. But grief, even in a child, hates the light, and shrinks from human eyes. The house was large enough to have two staircases; and by one of these I 5 knew that about mid-day, when all would be quiet (for the servants dined at one o'clock), I could steal up into her chamber. I imagine that it was about an hour after high noon when I reached the chamber-door; it was locked, but the key was not taken away. Entering, I closed the door 10 so softly, that, although it opened upon a hall which ascended through all the storeys, no echo ran along the silent walls. Then, turning round, I sought my sister's face. But the bed had been moved, and the back was now turned towards myself. Nothing met my eyes but one large 15 window, wide open, through which the sun of midsummer at mid-day was showering down torrents of splendour. The weather was dry, the sky was cloudless, the blue depths seemed the express types of infinity; and it was not possible for eye to behold, or for heart to conceive, 20 any symbols more pathetic of life and the glory of life.

Let me pause for one instant in approaching a remembrance so affecting for my own mind, to mention that, in the "Opium Confessions," I endeavoured to explain the reason why death, other conditions remaining the same, is 25 more profoundly affecting in summer than in other parts of the year — so far, at least, as it is liable to any modification at all from accidents of scenery or season. The reason, as I there suggested, lies in the antagonism between the tropical redundancy of life in summer, and the frozen 30 sterilities of the grave. The summer we see, the grave we haunt with our thoughts; the glory is around us, the darkness is within us; and, the two coming into collision, each exalts the other into stronger relief. But, in my case, there

was even a subtler reason why the summer had this intense
power of vivifying the spectacle or the thoughts of death.
And, recollecting it, I am struck with the truth, that far
more of our deepest thoughts and feelings pass to us through
5 perplexed combinations of *concrete* objects, pass to us as
involutes (if I may coin that word) in compound experiences
incapable of being disentangled, than ever reach us *directly*,
and in their own abstract shapes. It had happened, that
amongst our vast nursery collection of books was the Bible
10 illustrated with many pictures. And in long dark evenings,
as my three sisters with myself sat by the firelight round
the *guard*[1] of our nursery, no book was so much in request
amongst us. It ruled us and swayed us as mysteriously as
music. Our younger nurse, whom we all loved, would some-
15 times, according to her simple powers, endeavour to explain
what we found obscure. We, the children, were all constitutionally touched with pensiveness; the fitful gloom and
sudden lambencies of the room by firelight suited our
evening state of feelings; and they suited, also, the divine
20 revelations of power and mysterious beauty which awed us.
Above all, the story of a just man — man and yet *not* man,
real above all things, and yet shadowy above all things —
who had suffered the passion of death in Palestine, slept
upon our minds like early dawn upon the waters. The
25 nurse knew and explained to us the chief differences in
oriental climates; and all these differences (as it happens)
express themselves, more or less, in varying relations to the
great accidents and powers of summer. The cloudless sunlights of Syria — those seemed to argue everlasting sum-
30 mer; the disciples plucking the ears of corn — that *must*

---

[1] "*The guard*" : — I know not whether the word is a local one in
this sense. What I mean is a sort of fender, four or five feet high,
which locks up the fire from too near an approach on the part of
children.

be summer; but, above all, the very name of Palm Sunday
(a festival in the English Church) troubled me like an
anthem. "Sunday!" what was *that?* That was the day
of peace which masked another peace deeper than the
heart of man can comprehend. "Palms!" what were 5
they? *That* was an equivocal word; palms, in the sense
of trophies, expressed the pomps of life; palms, as a
product of nature, expressed the pomps of summer. Yet
still even this explanation does not suffice; it was not
merely by the peace and by the summer, by the deep 10
sound of rest below all rest and of ascending glory, that
I had been haunted. It was also because Jerusalem stood
near to those deep images both in time and in place.
The great event of Jerusalem was at hand when Palm
Sunday came; and the scene of that Sunday was near in 15
place to Jerusalem. What then was Jerusalem? Did I
fancy it to be the *omphalos* (navel) or physical centre of
the earth? Why should *that* affect me? Such a pretension
had once been made for Jerusalem, and once for a Grecian
city; and both pretensions had become ridiculous, as the 20
figure of the planet became known. Yes; but if not of the
earth, yet of mortality, for earth's tenant, Jerusalem, had
now become the *omphalos* and absolute centre. Yet how?
There, on the contrary, it was, as we infants understood,
that mortality had been trampled under foot. True; but, 25
for that very reason, there it was that mortality had opened
its very gloomiest crater. There it was, indeed, that the
human had risen on wings from the grave; but, for that
reason, there also it was that the divine had been swallowed
up by the abyss; the lesser star could not rise, before the 30
greater should submit to eclipse. Summer, therefore, had
connected itself with death, not merely as a mode of antagonism, but also as a phenomenon brought into intricate
relations with death by scriptural scenery and events.

Out of this digression, for the purpose of showing how inextricably my feelings and images of death were entangled with those of summer, as connected with Palestine and Jerusalem, let me come back to the bedchamber of my sister. From the gorgeous sunlight I turned round to the corpse. There lay the sweet childish figure; there the angel face; and, as people usually fancy, it was said in the house that no features had suffered any change. Had they not? The forehead, indeed — the serene and noble forehead — *that* might be the same; but the frozen eyelids, the darkness that seemed to steal from beneath them, the marble lips, the stiffening hands, laid palm to palm, as if repeating the supplications of closing anguish — could these be mistaken for life? Had it been so, wherefore did I not spring to those heavenly lips with tears and never-ending kisses? But so it was *not*. I stood checked for a moment; awe, not fear, fell upon me; and, whilst I stood, a solemn wind began to blow — the saddest that ear ever heard. It was a wind that might have swept the fields of mortality for a thousand centuries. Many times since, upon summer days, when the sun is about the hottest, I have remarked the same wind arising and uttering the same hollow, solemn, Memnonian,[1] but saintly swell: it is

[1] "*Memnonian*" : — For the sake of many readers, whose hearts may go along earnestly with a record of infant sorrow, but whose course of life has not allowed them much leisure for study, I pause to explain — that the head of Memnon, in the British Museum, that sublime head which wears upon its lips a smile co-extensive with all time and all space, an Æonian smile of gracious love and Panlike mystery, the most diffusive and pathetically divine that the hand of man has created, is represented on the authority of ancient traditions to have uttered at sunrise, or soon after, as the sun's rays had accumulated heat enough to rarify the air within certain cavities in the bust, a solemn and dirge-like series of intonations; the simple explanation being, in its general outline, this — that sonorous currents of air were

in this world the one great *audible* symbol of eternity. And three times in my life have I happened to hear the same sound in the same circumstances — namely, when standing between an open window and a dead body on a summer day.

Instantly, when my ear caught this vast Æolian intonation, when my eye filled with the golden fulness of life, the pomps of the heavens above, or the glory of the flowers below, and turning when it settled upon the frost which overspread my sister's face, instantly a trance fell upon me. A vault seemed to open in the zenith of the far blue sky, a shaft which ran up for ever. I, in spirit, rose as if on

produced by causing chambers of cold and heavy air to press upon other collections of air, warmed, and therefore rarified, and therefore yielding readily to the pressure of heavier air. Currents being thus established, by artificial arrangements of tubes, a certain succession of notes could be concerted and sustained. Near the Red Sea lie a chain of sand hills, which, by a natural system of grooves inosculating with each other, become vocal under changing circumstances in the position of the sun, etc. I knew a boy who, upon observing steadily, and reflecting upon a phenomenon that met him in his daily experience — viz., that tubes, through which a stream of water was passing, gave out a very different sound according to the varying slenderness or fulness of the current — devised an instrument that yielded a rude hydraulic gamut of sounds ; and, indeed, upon this simple phenomenon is founded the use and power of the stethoscope. For exactly as a thin thread of water, trickling through a leaden tube, yields a stridulous and plaintive sound compared with the full volume of sound corresponding to the full volume of water — on parity of principles, nobody will doubt that the current of blood pouring through the tubes of the human frame will utter to the learned ear, when armed with the stethoscope, an elaborate gamut or compass of music, recording the ravages of disease, or the glorious plenitudes of health, as faithfully as the cavities within this ancient Memnonian bust reported this mighty event of sunrise to the rejoicing world of light and life — or, again, under the sad passion of the dying day, uttered the sweet requiem that belonged to its departure.

billows that also ran up the shaft for ever; and the billows seemed to pursue the throne of God; but *that* also ran before us and fled away continually. The flight and the pursuit seemed to go on for ever and ever. Frost gathering
5 frost, some Sarsar wind of death, seemed to repel me; some mighty relation between God and death dimly struggled to evolve itself from the dreadful antagonism between them; shadowy meanings even yet continue to exercise and torment, in dreams, the deciphering oracle within me. I slept
10 — for how long I cannot say; slowly I recovered my self-possession; and, when I woke, found myself standing, as before, close to my sister's bed.

I have reason to believe that a *very* long interval had elapsed during this wandering or suspension of my perfect
15 mind. When I returned to myself, there was a foot (or I fancied so) on the stairs. I was alarmed; for, if anybody had detected me, means would have been taken to prevent my coming again. Hastily, therefore, I kissed the lips that I should kiss no more, and slunk, like a guilty thing, with
20 stealthy steps from the room. Thus perished the vision, loveliest amongst all the shows which earth has revealed to me; thus mutilated was the parting which should have lasted for ever; tainted thus with fear was that farewell sacred to love and grief, to perfect love and to grief that
25 could not be healed.

O Ahasuerus, everlasting Jew![1] fable or not a fable, thou, when first starting on thy endless pilgrimage of woe — thou, when first flying through the gates of Jerusalem, and vainly yearning to leave the pursuing curse behind
30 thee — couldst not more certainly in the words of Christ have read thy doom of endless sorrow, than I when passing

---

[1] "*Everlasting Jew*": — *der ewige Jude* — which is the common German expression for "The Wandering Jew," and sublimer even than our own.

for ever from my sister's room. The worm was at my heart; and, I may say, the worm that could not die. Man is doubtless *one* by some subtle *nexus*, some system of links, that we cannot perceive, extending from the new-born infant to the superannuated dotard: but, as regards many affections and passions incident to his nature at different stages, he is *not* one, but an intermitting creature, ending and beginning anew; the unity of man, in this respect, is co-extensive only with the particular stage to which the passion belongs. Some passions, as that of sexual love, are celestial by one half of their origin, animal and earthly by the other half. These will not survive their own appropriate stage. But love, which is *altogether* holy, like that between two children, is privileged to revisit by glimpses the silence and the darkness of declining years; and, possibly, this final experience in my sister's bedroom, or some other in which her innocence was concerned, may rise again for me to illuminate the clouds of death.

On the day following this which I have recorded, came a body of medical men to examine the brain, and the particular nature of the complaint; for in some of its symptoms it had shown perplexing anomalies. An hour after the strangers had withdrawn, I crept again to the room; but the door was now locked, the key had been taken away — and I was shut out for ever.

Then came the funeral. I, in the ceremonial character of *mourner*, was carried thither. I was put into a carriage with some gentlemen whom I did not know. They were kind and attentive to me; but naturally they talked of things disconnected with the occasion, and their conversation was a torment. At the church, I was told to hold a white handkerchief to my eyes. Empty hypocrisy! What need had *he* of masks or mockeries, whose heart died within him at every word that was uttered? During that part of

the service which passed within the church, I made an
effort to attend; but I sank back continually into my own
solitary darkness, and I heard little consciously, except some
fugitive strains from the sublime chapter of St. Paul, which
5 in England is always read at burials.[1]

Lastly came that magnificent liturgical service which the
English Church performs at the side of the grave; for this
church does not forsake her dead so long as they continue
in the upper air, but waits for her last "sweet and solemn
10 farewell"[2] at the side of the grave. There is exposed once
again, and for the last time, the coffin. All eyes survey
the record of name, of sex, of age, and the day of departure
from earth — records how shadowy! and dropped into darkness as messages addressed to worms. Almost at the very
15 last comes the symbolic ritual, tearing and shattering the
heart with volleying discharges, peal after peal, from the
fine artillery of woe. The coffin is lowered into its home;
it has disappeared from all eyes but those that look down
into the abyss of the grave. The sacristan stands ready,
20 with his shovel of earth and stones. The priest's voice is
heard once more — *earth to earth* — and immediately the
dread rattle ascends from the lid of the coffin; *ashes to
ashes* — and again the killing sound is heard; *dust to dust*
— and the farewell volley announces that the grave, the
25 coffin, the face are sealed up for ever and ever.

Grief! thou art classed amongst the depressing passions.
And true it is that thou humblest to the dust, but also

---

[1] First Epistle to Corinthians, chap. xv., beginning at verse 20.
[2] This beautiful expression, I am pretty certain, must belong to
Mrs. Trollope; I read it, probably, in a tale of hers connected with
the backwoods of America, where the absence of such a farewell must
unspeakably aggravate the gloom at any rate belonging to a household
separation of that eternal character occurring amongst the shadows
of those mighty forests.

thou exaltest to the clouds. Thou shakest as with ague,
but also thou steadiest like frost. Thou sickenest the
heart, but also thou healest its infirmities. Among the
very foremost of mine was morbid sensibility to shame.
And, ten years afterwards, I used to throw my self-
reproaches with regard to that infirmity into this shape —
viz., that if I were summoned to seek aid for a perishing
fellow-creature, and that I could obtain that aid only by
facing a vast company of critical or sneering faces, I might,
perhaps, shrink basely from the duty. It is true that no
such case had ever actually occurred; so that it was a mere
romance of casuistry to tax myself with cowardice so shocking. But to feel a doubt was to feel condemnation; and
the crime that *might* have been, was in my eyes the crime
that *had* been. Now, however, all was changed; and, for
anything which regarded my sister's memory, in one hour
I received a new heart. Once in Westmoreland I saw a
case resembling it. I saw a ewe suddenly put off and abjure
her own nature, in a service of love — yes, slough it as com-
pletely as ever serpent sloughed his skin. Her lamb had
fallen into a deep trench, from which all escape was hopeless without the aid of man. And to a man she advanced,
bleating clamorously, until he followed her and rescued
her beloved. Not less was the change in myself. Fifty
thousand sneering faces would not have troubled me *now*
in any office of tenderness to my sister's memory. Ten
legions would not have repelled me from seeking her, if
there had been a chance that she could be found. Mockery!
it was lost upon me. Laughter! I valued it not. And when
I was taunted insultingly with "my girlish tears," that word
"*girlish*" had no sting for me, except as a verbal echo to
the one eternal thought of my heart — that a girl was
the sweetest thing which I, in my short life, had known
— that a girl it was who had crowned the earth with

beauty, and had opened to my thirst fountains of pure celestial love, from which, in this world, I was to drink no more.

Now began to unfold themselves the consolations of solitude, those consolations which only I was destined to taste; now, therefore, began to open upon me those fascinations of solitude, which, when acting as a co-agency with unresisted grief, end in the paradoxical result of making out of grief itself a luxury; such a luxury as finally becomes a snare, overhanging life itself, and the energies of life, with growing menaces. All deep feelings of a *chronic* class agree in this, that they seek for solitude, and are fed by solitude. Deep grief, deep love, how naturally do these ally themselves with religious feeling! and all three — love, grief, religion — are haunters of solitary places. Love, grief, and the mystery of devotion — what were these without solitude? All day long, when it was not impossible for me to do so, I sought the most silent and sequestered nooks in the grounds about the house, or in the neighbouring fields. The awful stillness oftentimes of summer noons, when no winds were abroad, the appealing silence of gray or misty afternoons — these were fascinations as of witchcraft. Into the woods, into the desert air, I gazed, as if some comfort lay hid in *them*. I wearied the heavens with my inquest of beseeching looks. Obstinately I tormented the blue depths with my scrutiny, sweeping them for ever with my eyes, and searching them for one angelic face that might, perhaps, have permission to reveal itself for a moment.

At this time, and under this impulse of rapacious grief, that grasped at what it could not obtain, the faculty of shaping images in the distance out of slight elements, and grouping them after the yearnings of the heart, grew upon me in morbid excess. And I recall at the present moment one instance of that sort, which may show how merely shadows, or a gleam of brightness, or nothing at all, could furnish a sufficient basis for this creative faculty.

On Sunday mornings I went with the rest of my family to church : it was a church on the ancient model of England, having aisles, galleries,[1] organ, all things ancient and venerable, and the proportions majestic. Here, whilst the congregation knelt through the long litany, as often as we came to that passage, so beautiful amongst many that are so, where God is supplicated on behalf of "all sick persons and young children," and that he would "show his pity upon all prisoners and captives," I wept in secret; and raising my streaming eyes to the upper windows of the galleries, saw, on days when the sun was shining, a spectacle as affecting as ever prophet can have beheld. The *sides* of the windows were rich with storied glass; through the deep purples and crimsons streamed the golden light; emblazonries of heavenly illumination (from the sun) mingling with the earthly emblazonries (from art and its gorgeous colouring) of what is grandest in man. *There* were the apostles that had trampled upon earth, and the glories of earth, out of celestial love to man. *There* were the martyrs that had borne witness to the truth through flames, through torments, and through armies of fierce, insulting faces. *There* were the saints who, under intolerable pangs, had glorified God by meek submission to his will. And all the time whilst this tumult of sublime memorials held on as the deep chords from some accompaniment in the bass, I saw through the wide central field of the window, where the glass was *un*coloured, white, fleecy clouds sailing over

[1] "*Galleries*" : — These, though condemned on some grounds by the restorers of authentic church architecture, have, nevertheless, this one advantage — that, when the *height* of a church is that dimension which most of all expresses its sacred character, galleries expound and interpret that height.

the azure depths of the sky; were it but a fragment or a
hint of such a cloud, immediately under the flash of my
sorrow-haunted eye, it grew and shaped itself into visions
of beds with white lawny curtains; and in the beds lay
5 sick children, dying children, that were tossing in anguish,
and weeping clamorously for death. God, for some mysterious reason, could not suddenly release them from their
pain; but he suffered the beds, as it seemed, to rise slowly
through the clouds; slowly the beds ascended into the
10 chambers of the air; slowly also his arms descended from
the heavens, that he and his young children, whom in
Palestine, once and for ever, he had blessed, though they
must pass slowly through the dreadful chasm of separation, might yet meet the sooner. These visions were self-
15 sustained. These visions needed not that any sound should
speak to me, or music mould my feelings. The hint from
the litany, the fragment from the clouds — those and the
storied windows were sufficient. But not the less the blare
of the tumultuous organ wrought its own separate creations.
20 And oftentimes in anthems, when the mighty instrument
threw its vast columns of sound, fierce yet melodious, over
the voices of the choir — high in arches, when it seemed to
rise, surmounting and overriding the strife of the vocal
parts, and gathering by strong coercion the total storm
25 into unity — sometimes I seemed to rise and walk trium-
phantly upon those clouds which, but a moment before, I
had looked up to as mementos of prostrate sorrow; yes,
sometimes under the transfigurations of music, felt of grief
itself as of a fiery chariot for mounting victoriously above
30 the causes of grief.

God speaks to children, also, in dreams, and by the
oracles that lurk in darkness. But in solitude, above all
things, when made vocal to the meditative heart by the
truths and services of a national church, God holds with

children "communion undisturbed." Solitude, though it may be silent as light, is, like light, the mightiest of agencies; for solitude is essential to man. All men come into this world *alone;* all leave it *alone.* Even a little child has a dread, whispering consciousness, that, if he should 5 be summoned to travel into God's presence, no gentle nurse will be allowed to lead him by the hand, nor mother to carry him in her arms, nor little sister to share his trepidations. King and priest, warrior and maiden, philosopher and child, all must walk those mighty galleries alone. The 10 solitude, therefore, which in this world appals or fascinates a child's heart, is but the echo of a far deeper solitude, through which already he has passed, and of another solitude, deeper still, through which he *has* to pass: reflex of one solitude — prefiguration of another. 15

Oh, burden of solitude, that cleavest to man through every stage of his being! in his birth, which *has* been — in his life, which *is* — in his death, which *shall* be — mighty and essential solitude! that wast, and art, and art to be; thou broodest, like the Spirit of God moving upon the sur- 20 face of the deeps, over every heart that sleeps in the nurseries of Christendom. Like the vast laboratory of the air, which, seeming to be nothing, or less than the shadow of a shade, hides within itself the principles of all things, solitude for the meditating child is the Agrippa's mirror of the 25 unseen universe. Deep is the solitude of millions who, with hearts welling forth love, have none to love them. Deep is the solitude of those who, under secret griefs, have none to pity them. Deep is the solitude of those who, fighting with doubts or darkness, have none to counsel them. But 30 deeper than the deepest of these solitudes is that which broods over childhood under the passion of sorrow — bringing before it, at intervals, the final solitude which watches for it, and is waiting for it within the gates of death. Oh, mighty and essential solitude, that wast, and art, and art to be! thy kingdom is made perfect in the grave; but even over those that keep watch outside the grave, like myself, an infant of six years old, thou stretchest out a sceptre of fascination.

INTRODUCTION TO THE WORLD OF STRIFE

So, then, one chapter in my life had finished. Already, before the completion of my sixth year, this first chapter had run its circle, had rendered up its music to the final chord — might seem even, like ripe fruit from a tree, to have detached itself for ever from all the rest of the arras that was shaping itself within my loom of life. No Eden of lakes and forest-lawns, such as the *mirage* suddenly evokes in Arabian sands — no pageant of air-built battlements and towers, that ever burned in dream-like silence amongst the vapours of summer sunsets, mocking and repeating with celestial pencil "the fuming vanities of earth" — could leave behind it the mixed impression of so much truth combined with so much absolute delusion. Truest of all things it seemed by the excess of that happiness which it had sustained: most fraudulent it seemed of all things, when looked back upon as some mysterious parenthesis in the current of life, "self-withdrawn into a wondrous depth," hurrying as if with headlong malice to extinction, and alienated by *every* feature from the new aspects of life that seemed to await me. Were it not in the bitter corrosion of heart that I was called upon to face, I should have carried over to the present no connecting link whatever from the past. Mere reality in this fretting it was, and the undeniableness of its too potent remembrances, that forbade me to regard this burnt-out inaugural chapter of my life as no chapter at all, but a pure exhalation of dreams. Misery is a guarantee of truth too substantial to be refused : else, by its determinate

evanescence, the total experience would have worn the
character of a fantastic illusion.

Well it was for me at this period, if well it were for me
to live at all, that from any continued contemplation of my
5 misery I was forced to wean myself, and suddenly to assume
the harness of life. Else, under the morbid languishing of
grief, and of what the Romans called *desiderium* (the yearning too obstinate after one irrecoverable face), too probably
I should have pined away into an early grave. Harsh was
10 my awaking; but the rough febrifuge which this awaking administered broke the strength of my sickly reveries
through a period of more than two years; by which time,
under the natural expansion of my bodily strength, the
danger had passed over.

15 In the first chapter I have rendered solemn thanks for
having been trained amongst the gentlest of sisters, and not
under "horrid pugilistic brothers." Meantime, one such
brother I had: senior by much to myself, and the stormiest
of his class; him I will immediately present to the reader;
20 for up to this point of my narrative he may be described as
a stranger even to myself. Odd as it sounds, I had at this
time both a brother and a father, neither of whom would
have been able to challenge me as a relative, nor I *him*, had
we happened to meet on the public roads.

25 In my father's case, this arose from the accident of his
having lived abroad for a space that, measured against *my*
life, was a very long one. First, he lived for months in
Portugal, at Lisbon, and at Cintra; next in Madeira; then
in the West Indies; sometimes in Jamaica, sometimes in St.
30 Kitt's; courting the supposed benefit of hot climates in his
complaint of pulmonary consumption. He had, indeed,
repeatedly returned to England, and met my mother at
watering-places on the south coast of Devonshire, etc.
But I, as a younger child, had not been one of the party

selected for such excursions from home. And now, at last, when all had proved unavailing, he was coming home to die amongst his family, in his thirty-ninth year. My mother had gone to await his arrival at the port (whatever port) to which the West India packet should bring him; and amongst the deepest recollections which I connect with that period, is one derived from the night of his arrival at Greenhay.

It was a summer evening of unusual solemnity. The servants, and four of us children, were gathered for hours, on the lawn before the house, listening for the sound of wheels. Sunset came — nine, ten, eleven o'clock, and nearly another hour had passed — without a warning sound; for Greenhay, being so solitary a house, formed a *terminus ad quem*, beyond which was nothing but a cluster of cottages, composing the little hamlet of Greenhill; so that any sound of wheels coming from the winding lane which then connected us with the Rusholme Road carried with it, of necessity, a warning summons to prepare for visitors at Greenhay. No such summons had yet reached us; it was nearly midnight; and, for the last time, it was determined that we should move in a body out of the grounds, on the chance of meeting the travelling party, if, at so late an hour, it could yet be expected to arrive. In fact, to our general surprise, we met it almost immediately, but coming at so slow a pace, that the fall of the horses' feet was not audible until we were close upon them. I mention the case for the sake of the undying impressions which connected themselves with the circumstances. The first notice of the approach was the sudden emerging of horses' heads from the deep gloom of the shady lane; the next was the mass of white pillows against which the dying patient was reclining. The hearse-like pace at which the carriage moved recalled the overwhelming spectacle of that funeral which had so lately formed part in the most memorable event of my

life. But these elements of awe, that might at any rate
have struck forcibly upon the mind of a child, were for
me, in my condition of morbid nervousness, raised into
abiding grandeur by the antecedent experiences of that
5 particular summer night. The listening for hours to the
sounds from horses' hoofs upon distant roads, rising and
falling, caught and lost, upon the gentle undulation of such
fitful airs as might be stirring — the peculiar solemnity of the
hours succeeding to sunset — the glory of the dying day —
10 the gorgeousness which, by description, so well I knew of
sunset in those West Indian islands from which my father
was returning — the knowledge that he returned only to die
— the almighty pomp in which this great idea of Death
apparelled itself to my young sorrowing heart — the corre-
15 sponding pomp in which the antagonistic idea, not less
mysterious, of life, rose, as if on wings, amidst tropic
glories and floral pageantries, that seemed even *more* solemn and pathetic than the vapoury plumes and trophies
of mortality — all this chorus of restless images, or of sug-
20 gestive thoughts, gave to my father's return, which else
had been fitted only to interpose one transitory red-letter
day in the calendar of a child, the shadowy power of an
ineffaceable agency among my dreams. This, indeed, was
the one sole memorial which restores my father's image to
25 me as a personal reality. Otherwise, he would have been
for me a bare *nominis umbra*. He languished, indeed, for
weeks upon a sofa; and during that interval, it happened
naturally, from my repose of manners, that I was a privileged visitor to him throughout his waking hours. I
30 was also present at his bedside in the closing hour of
his life, which exhaled quietly, amidst snatches of delirious
conversation with some imaginary visitors.

My brother was a stranger from causes quite as little to
be foreseen, but seeming quite as natural after they had

really occurred. In an early stage of his career, he had been found wholly unmanageable. His genius for mischief amounted to inspiration : it was a divine *afflatus* which drove him in that direction ; and such was his capacity for riding in whirlwinds and directing storms, that he made it his trade to create them, as a νεφεληγερετα Ζευς, a cloud-compelling Jove, in order that he *might* direct them. For this, and other reasons, he had been sent to the Grammar School of Louth, in Lincolnshire — one of those many old classic institutions which form the peculiar [1] glory of England. To box, and to box under the severest restraint of honourable laws, was in those days a mere necessity of schoolboy life at *public* schools ; and hence the superior manliness, generosity, and self-control, of those generally who had benefited by such discipline — so systematically hostile to all meanness, pusillanimity, or indirectness. Cowper, in his "Tyrocinium," is far from doing justice to our great public schools. Himself disqualified, by delicacy of temperament, for reaping the benefits from such a warfare, and having suffered too much in his own Westminster experience, he could not judge them from an impartial station ; but I, though ill enough adapted to an atmosphere so stormy, yet having tried both classes of schools, public and private, am compelled in mere conscience to give my vote (and if I had a thousand votes, to give *all* my votes) for the former.

[1] "*Peculiar*" : — viz., as *endowed* foundations to which those resort who are rich and pay, and those also who, being poor, or cannot pay so much. This most honourable distinction amongst the services of England from ancient times to the interests of education — a service absolutely unapproached by any one nation of Christendom — is amongst the foremost cases of that remarkable class which make England, while often the most aristocratic, yet also, for many noble purposes, the most democratic of lands.

Fresh from such a training as this, and at a time when his additional five or six years availed nearly to make *his* age the double of mine, my brother very naturally despised me ; and, from his exceeding frankness, he took no pains to
5 conceal that he did. Why should he ? Who was it that could have a right to feel aggrieved by his contempt ? Who, if not myself ? But it happened, on the contrary, that I had a perfect craze for being despised. I doted on it ; and considered contempt a sort of luxury that I was in
10 continual fear of losing. Why not ? Wherefore should any rational person shrink from contempt, if it happen to form the tenure by which he holds his repose in life ? The cases, which are cited from comedy, of such a yearning after contempt, stand upon a footing altogether different :
15 *there* the contempt is wooed as a serviceable ally and tool of religious hypocrisy. But, to me, at that era of life, it formed the main guarantee of an unmolested repose : and security there was not, on any lower terms, for the *latentis semita vitæ*. The slightest approach to any favourable
20 construction of my intellectual pretensions alarmed me beyond measure ; because it pledged me in a manner with the hearer to support this first attempt by a second, by a third, by a fourth — O heavens ! there is no saying how far the horrid man might go in his unreasonable
25 demands upon me. I groaned under the weight of his expectations ; and, if I laid but the first round of such a staircase, why, then, I saw in vision a vast Jacob's ladder towering upwards to the clouds, mile after mile, league after league ; and myself running up and down this ladder, like
30 any fatigue party of Irish hodmen, to the top of any Babel which my wretched admirer might choose to build. But I nipped the abominable system of extortion in the very bud, by refusing to take the first step. The man could have no pretence, you know, for expecting me to climb the third or

fourth round, when I had seemed quite unequal to the first. Professing the most absolute bankruptcy from the very beginning, giving the man no sort of hope that I would pay even one farthing in the pound, I never could be made miserable by unknown responsibilities.

Still, with all this passion for being despised, which was so essential to my peace of mind, I found at times an altitude — a starry altitude — in the station of contempt for me assumed by my brother that nettled me. Sometimes, indeed, the mere necessities of dispute carried me, before I was aware of my own imprudence, so far up the staircase of Babel, that my brother was shaken for a moment in the infinity of his contempt : and, before long, when my superiority in some bookish accomplishments displayed itself, by results that could not be entirely dissembled, mere foolish human nature forced me into some trifle of exultation at these retributory triumphs. But more often I was disposed to grieve over them. They tended to shake that solid foundation of utter despicableness upon which I relied so much for my freedom from anxiety ; and, therefore, upon the whole, it was satisfactory to my mind that my brother's opinion of me, after any little transient oscillation, gravitated determinately back towards that settled contempt which had been the result of his original inquest. The pillars of Hercules upon which rested the vast edifice of his scorn were these two — 1st, my physics : he denounced me for effeminacy; 2d, he assumed, and even postulated as a *datum*, which I myself could never have the face to refuse, my general idiocy. Physically, therefore, and intellectually, he looked upon me as below notice ; but, *morally*, he assured me that he would give me a written character of the very best description, whenever I chose to apply for it. "You're honest," he said ; "you're willing, though lazy ; you *would* pull, if you had the strength of a flea ; and, though a

monstrous coward, you don't run away." My own demurs
to these harsh judgments were not so many as they might
have been. The idiocy I confessed; because, though positive that I was not uniformly an idiot, I felt inclined to think
5 that, in a majority of cases, I really *was;* and there were
more reasons for thinking so than the reader is yet aware
of. But, as to the effeminacy, I denied it *in toto;* and
with good reason, as will be seen. Neither did my brother
pretend to have any experimental proofs of it. The ground
10 he went upon was a mere *a priori* one — viz., that I had
always been tied to the apron-string of women or girls;
which amounted at most to this — that, by training and
the natural tendency of circumstances, I *ought* to be effeminate: that is, there was reason to expect beforehand that
15 I *should* be so; but, then, the more merit in me, if, in spite
of such reasonable presumptions, I really were *not.* In fact,
my brother soon learned, by a daily experience, how entirely
he might depend upon me for carrying out the most audacious of his own warlike plans; such plans it is true that I
20 abominated; but *that* made no difference in the fidelity
with which I tried to fulfil them.

This eldest brother of mine was in all respects a remarkable boy. Haughty he was, aspiring, immeasurably active;
fertile in resources as Robinson Crusoe; but also full of
25 quarrel as it is possible to imagine; and, in default of any
other opponent, he would have fastened a quarrel upon his
own shadow for presuming to run before him when going
westwards in the morning, whereas, in all reason, a shadow,
like a dutiful child, ought to keep deferentially in rear of
30 that majestic substance which is the author of its existence.
Books he detested, one and all, excepting only such as he
happened to write himself. And these were not a few. On
all subjects known to man, from the Thirty-nine Articles of
our English Church, down to pyrotechnics, legerdemain,

magic, both black and white, thaumaturgy, and necromancy,
he favoured the world (which world was the nursery where
I lived amongst my sisters) with his select opinions. On
this last subject especially — of necromancy — he was very
great; witness his profound work, though but a fragment,
and, unfortunately, long since departed to the bosom of
Cinderella, entitled, "How to raise a Ghost; and when
you've got him down, how to keep him down." To which
work he assured us, that some most learned and enormous
man, whose name was a foot and a half long, had promised
him an appendix; which appendix treated of the Red Sea
and Solomon's signet-ring; with forms of *mittimus* for ghosts
that might be refractory; and probably a riot act, for any
émeute amongst ghosts inclined to raise barricades; since
he often thrilled our young hearts by supposing the case
(not at all unlikely, he affirmed), that a federation, a solemn
league and conspiracy, might take place amongst the infinite
generations of ghosts against the single generation of men
at any one time composing the garrison of earth. The
Roman phrase for expressing that a man had died — viz.,
"*Abiit ad plures*" (He has gone over to the majority) —
my brother explained to us; and we easily comprehended.
that any one generation of the living human race, even if
combined, and acting in concert, must be in a frightful
minority, by comparison with all the incalculable generations that had trod this earth before us. The Parliament
of living men, Lords and Commons united, what a miserable
array against the Upper and Lower House composing the
Parliament of ghosts! Perhaps the Pre-Adamites would
constitute one wing in such a ghostly army. My brother,
dying in his sixteenth year, was far enough from seeing or
foreseeing Waterloo; else he might have illustrated this
dreadful duel of the living human race with its ghostly predecessors, by the awful apparition which at three o'clock

in the afternoon, on the 18th of June, 1815, the mighty contest at Waterloo must have assumed to eyes that watched
over the trembling interests of man. The English army,
about that time in the great agony of its strife, was thrown
5 into squares; and under that arrangement, which con-
densed and contracted its apparent numbers within a few
black geometrical diagrams, how frightfully narrow — how
spectral did its slender quadrangles appear at a distance,
to any philosophic spectators that knew the amount of
10 human interests confided to that army, and the hopes for
Christendom that even were trembling in the balance!
Such a disproportion, it seems, might exist, in the case of
a ghostly war, between the harvest of possible results and
the slender band of reapers that were to gather it. And
15 there was even a worse peril than any analogous one that
has been *proved* to exist at Waterloo. A British surgeon,
indeed, in a work of two octavo volumes, has endeavoured
to show that a conspiracy was traced at Waterloo, between
two or three foreign regiments, for kindling a panic in the
20 heat of the battle, by flight, and by a sustained blowing up
of tumbrils, under the miserable purpose of shaking the
British steadiness. But the evidences are not clear;
whereas my brother insisted that the presence of sham
men, distributed extensively amongst the human race,
25 and meditating treason against us all, had been demonstrated to the satisfaction of all true philosophers. Who
were these shams and make-believe men? They were,
in fact, people that had been dead for centuries, but
that, for reasons best known to themselves, had returned
30 to this upper earth, walked about amongst us, and were
undistinguishable, except by the most learned of necro-
mancers, from authentic men of flesh and blood. I
mention this for the sake of illustrating the fact, of
which the reader will find a singular instance in the

foot-note attached, that the same crazes are everlastingly
revolving upon men.[1]

This hypothesis, however, like a thousand others, when
it happened that they engaged no durable sympathy from
his nursery audience, he did not pursue. For some time 5
he turned his thoughts to philosophy, and read lectures to
us every night upon some branch or other of physics.
This undertaking arose from some one of us envying or
admiring flies for their power of walking upon the ceiling.
" Pooh !" he said, "they are impostors ; they pretend to 10
do it, but they can't do it as it ought to be done. Ah !
you should see *me* standing upright on the ceiling, with
my head downwards, for half an hour together, meditating
profoundly." My sister Mary remarked, that we should all
be very glad to see him in that position. "If that's the 15

---

[1] Five years ago, during the carnival of universal anarchy equally
amongst doers and thinkers, a closely-printed pamphlet was published
with this title, "A New Revelation ; or the Communion of the Incarnate Dead with the Unconscious Living. Important Fact, without
trifling Fiction, by HIM." I have not the pleasure of knowing HIM ;
but certainly I must concede to HIM, that he writes like a man of
extreme sobriety, upon his extravagant theme. He is angry with
Swedenborg, as might be expected, for his chimeras ; some of which,
however, of late years have signally altered their aspect ; but as to
HIM, there is no chance that he should be occupied with chimeras,
because (p. 6) "he has met with some who have acknowledged the
fact of their having come from the dead " — *habes confitentem reum.*
Few, however, are endowed with so much candour ; and, in particular,
for the honour of literature, it grieves me to find, by p. 10, that the
largest number of these shams, and perhaps the most uncandid, are to
be looked for amongst "publishers and printers," of whom, it seems,
"the great majority" are mere forgeries ; a very few speak frankly
about the matter, and say they don't care who knows it, which, to
my thinking, is impudence ; but by far the larger section doggedly
deny it, and call a policeman, if you persist in charging them with
being shams. Some differences there are between my brother and
HIM, but in the great outline of their views they coincide.

case," he replied, "it's very well that all is ready, except as
to a strap or two." Being an excellent skater, he had first
imagined that, if held up until he had started, he might
then, by taking a bold sweep ahead, keep himself in posi-
5 tion through the continued impetus of skating. But this
he found not to answer; because, as he observed, "the
friction was too retarding from the plaster of Paris; but
the case would be very different if the ceiling were coated
with ice." As it was *not*, he changed his plan. The true
10 secret, he now discovered, was this: he would consider
himself in the light of a humming-top; he would make an
apparatus (and he made it) for having himself launched,
like a top, upon the ceiling, and regularly spun. Then the
vertiginous motion of the human top would overpower the
15 force of gravitation. He should, of course, spin upon his
own axis, and sleep upon his own axis — perhaps he might
even dream upon it; and he laughed at "those scoundrels,
the flies," that never improved in their pretended art, nor
made anything of it. The principle was now discovered;
20 "and, of course," he said, "if a man can keep it up for
five minutes, what's to hinder him from doing so for five
months?" "Certainly, nothing that I can think of," was
the reply of my sister, whose scepticism, in fact, had not
settled upon the five months, but altogether upon the five
25 minutes. The apparatus for spinning him, however, perhaps from its complexity, would not work; a fact evidently
owing to the stupidity of the gardener. On reconsidering
the subject, he announced, to the disappointment of some
amongst us, that, although the physical discovery was now
30 complete, he saw a moral difficulty. It was not a *humming-*
top that was required, but a *peg*-top. Now, this, in order
to keep up the *vertigo* at full stretch, without which, to a
certainty, gravitation would prove too much for him, needed
to be whipped incessantly. But that was precisely what a

gentleman ought not to tolerate; to be scourged uninter-
mittingly on the legs by any grub of a gardener, unless it
were Father Adam himself, was a thing he could not bring
his mind to face. However, as some compensation, he proposed to improve the art of flying, which was, as everybody 5
must acknowledge, in a condition disgraceful to civilised
society. As he had made many a fire balloon, and had
succeeded in some attempts at bringing down cats by *parachutes*, it was not very difficult to fly downwards from moderate elevations. But, as he was reproached by my sister 10
for never flying back again, which, however, was a far
different thing, and not even attempted by the philosopher
in "Rasselas" (for

> " Revocare gradum, et *superas* evadere ad auras,
>   Hic labor, hoc opus est "),
>
> 15

he refused, under such poor encouragement, to try his winged
parachutes any more, either "aloft or alow," till he had
thoroughly studied Bishop Wilkins[1] on the art of translating right reverend gentlemen to the moon; and, in the
meantime, he resumed his general lectures on physics. From 20
these, however, he was speedily driven, or one might say
shelled out, by a concerted assault of my sister Mary's. He

---

[1] *"Bishop Wilkins"* : — Dr. W., Bishop of Chester, in the reign of
Charles II, notoriously wrote a book on the possibility of a voyage to
the moon, which, in a bishop, would be called a translation to the moon,
and perhaps it was *his* name in combination with *his* book that suggested the "Adventures of Peter Wilkins." It is unfair, however, to
mention him in connection with that single one of his works which
announces an extravagant purpose. He was really a scientific man, and
already in the time of Cromwell (about 1656) had projected that Royal
Society of London which was afterwards realised and presided over
by Isaac Barrow and Isaac Newton. He was also a learned man, but
still with a vein of romance about him, as may be seen in his most
elaborate work — " The Essay towards a Philosophic or Universal
Language."

had been in the habit of lowering the pitch of his lectures
with ostentatious condescension to the presumed level of our
poor understandings. This superciliousness annoyed my
sister; and accordingly, with the help of two young female
5 visitors, and my next younger brother — in subsequent
times a little middy on board many a ship of H.M., and
the most predestined rebel upon earth against all assump-
tions, small or great, of superiority — she arranged a mutiny,
that had the unexpected effect of suddenly extinguishing
10 the lectures for ever. He had happened to say, what was
no unusual thing with him, that he flattered himself he
had made the point under discussion tolerably clear;
"clear," he added, bowing round the half-circle of us, the
audience, "to the meanest of capacities"; and then he
15 repeated, sonorously, "clear to the most excruciatingly
mean of capacities." Upon which a voice, a female voice
— but whose voice, in the tumult that followed, I did not
distinguish — retorted, "No, you haven't; it's as dark as
sin"; and then, without a moment's interval, a second
20 voice exclaimed, "Dark as night"; then came my younger
brother's insurrectionary yell, "Dark as midnight"; then
another female voice chimed in melodiously, "Dark as
pitch"; and so the peal continued to come round like a
catch, the whole being so well concerted, and the rolling
25 fire so well sustained, that it was impossible to make head
against it; whilst the abruptness of the interruption gave
to it the protecting character of an oral "round-robin," it
being impossible to challenge any one in particular as the
ringleader. Burke's phrase of "the swinish multitude,"
30 applied to mobs, was then in everybody's mouth; and,
accordingly, after my brother had recovered from his first
astonishment at this audacious mutiny, he made us several sweeping bows, that looked very much like tentative
rehearsals of a sweeping *fusillade*, and then addressed us

in a very brief speech, of which we could distinguish the words *pearls* and *swinish multitude*, but uttered in a very low key, perhaps out of some lurking consideration for the two young strangers. We all laughed in chorus at this parting salute ; my brother himself condescended at last to join us ; but there ended the course of lectures on natural philosophy.

As it was impossible, however, that he should remain quiet, he announced to us, that for the rest of his life he meant to dedicate himself to the intense cultivation of the tragic drama. He got to work instantly ; and very soon he had composed the first act of his " Sultan Selim " ; but, in defiance of the metre, he soon changed the title to " Sultan Amurath," considering *that* a much fiercer name, more be-whiskered and beturbaned. It was no part of his intention that we should sit lolling on chairs like ladies and gentlemen that had paid opera prices for private boxes. He expected every one of us, he said, to pull an oar. We were to *act* the tragedy. But, in fact, we had many oars to pull. There were so many characters, that each of us took four at the least, and the future middy had six. He, this wicked little middy,[1] caused the greatest affliction to Sultan Amurath, forcing him to order the amputation of his head six several times (that is, once in every one of his six parts) during the first act. In reality, the sultan, though otherwise a decent man, was too bloody. What by the bowstring, and what by the scimitar, he had so thinned the population with which

---

[1] " *Middy* " : — I call him so simply to avoid confusion, and by way of anticipation ; else he was too young at this time to serve in the navy. Afterwards he did so for many years, and saw every variety of service in every class of ships belonging to our navy. At one time, when yet a boy, he was captured by pirates, and compelled to sail with them ; and the end of his adventurous career was, that for many a year he has been lying at the bottom of the Atlantic.

he commenced business, that scarcely any of the characters remained alive at the end of act the first. Sultan Amurath found himself in an awkward situation. Large arrears of work remained, and hardly anybody to do it but the sultan
5 himself. In composing act the second, the author had to proceed like Deucalion and Pyrrha, and to create an entirely new generation. Apparently this young generation, that ought to have been so good, took no warning by what had happened to their ancestors in act the first ; one must con-
10 clude that they were quite as wicked, since the poor sultan had found himself reduced to order them all for execution in the course of this act the second. To the brazen age had succeeded an iron age, and the prospects were becoming sadder and sadder as the tragedy advanced. But here the
15 author began to hesitate. He felt it hard to resist the instinct of carnage. And was it right to do so ? Which of the felons whom he had cut off prematurely could pretend that a court of appeal would have reversed his sentence ? But the consequences were distressing. A new set of charac-
20 ters in every act brought with it the necessity of a new plot ; for people could not succeed to the arrears of old actions, or inherit ancient motives, like a landed estate. Five crops, in fact, must be taken off the ground in each separate tragedy, amounting, in short, to five tragedies
25 involved in one.

Such, according to the rapid sketch which at this moment my memory furnishes, was the brother who now first laid open to me the gates of war. The occasion was this. He had resented, with a shower of stones, an affront offered to
30 us by an individual boy, belonging to a cotton factory ; for more than two years afterwards this became the *teterrima causa* of a skirmish or a battle as often as we passed the factory ; and, unfortunately, *that* was twice a day on every day, except Sunday. Our situation in respect to the enemy

was as follows : — Greenhay, a country-house, newly built
by my father, at that time was a clear mile from the
outskirts of Manchester ; but in after years, Manchester,
throwing out the *tentacula* of its vast expansions, absolutely enveloped Greenhay ; and, for anything I know, the
grounds and gardens which then insulated the house may
have long disappeared.   Being a modest mansion, which
(including hot walls, offices, and gardener's house) had cost
only six thousand pounds, I do not know how it should
have risen to the distinction of giving name to a region of
that great town ; however, it *has* done so ;[1] and at this
time, therefore, after changes so great, it will be difficult
for the *habitué* of that region to understand how my brother
and myself could have a solitary road to traverse between
Greenhay and Princess Street, then the termination, on
that side, of Manchester.   But so it was.   Oxford *Street*,
like its namesake in London, was then called the Oxford
Road ; and during the currency of our acquaintance with it,
arose the first three houses in its neighbourhood ; of which
the third was built for the Rev. S. H., one of our guardians,
for whom his friends had also built the church of St. Peter's
— not a bowshot from the house.   At present, however, he
resided in Salford, nearly two miles from Greenhay ; and
to him we went over daily, for the benefit of his classical
instructions.   One sole cotton factory had then risen along
the line of Oxford Street ; and this was close to a bridge,
which also was a new creation ; for previously all passengers to Manchester went round by Garrat.   This factory
became to us the *officina gentium*, from which swarmed forth
those Goths and Vandals that continually threatened our

[1] " Green*heys*," with a slight variation in the spelling, is the name
given to that district, of which Greenhay formed the original nucleus.
Probably, it was the solitary situation of the house which (failing any
other grounds of denomination) raised it to this privilege.

steps; and this bridge became the eternal arena of combat,
we taking good care to be on the right side of the bridge
for retreat — *i.e.*, on the town side, or the country side,
accordingly as we were going out in the morning, or return
5 ing in the afternoon.   Stones were the implements of warfare; and by continual practice both parties became expert
in throwing them.

The origin of the feud it is scarcely requisite to rehearse,
since the particular accident which began it was not the
10 true efficient cause of our long warfare, but simply the
casual occasion.   The cause lay in our aristocratic dress.
As children of an opulent family, where all provisions were
liberal, and all appointments elegant, we were uniformly
well-dressed ; and, in particular, we wore trousers (at that
15 time unheard of, except among sailors), and we also wore
Hessian boots — a crime that could not be forgiven in the
Lancashire of that day, because it expressed the double
offence of being aristocratic and being outlandish.   We
were aristocrats, and it was vain to deny it; could we
20 deny our boots ? whilst our antagonists, if not absolutely
sansculottes, were slovenly and forlorn in their dress, often
unwashed, with hair totally neglected, and always covered
with flakes of cotton.   Jacobins they were not, as regarded
any sympathy with the Jacobinism that then desolated
25 France ; for, on the contrary, they detested everything
French, and answered with brotherly signals to the cry of
"Church and King," or "King and Constitution."   But,
for all that, as they were perfectly independent, getting
very high wages, and these wages in a mode of industry
30 that was then taking vast strides ahead, they contrived to
reconcile this patriotic anti-Jacobinism with a personal
Jacobinism of that sort which is native to the heart of
man, who is by natural impulse (and not without a root of
nobility, though also of base envy) impatient of inequality,

and submits to it only through a sense of its necessity, or under a long experience of its benefits.

It was on an early day of our new *tyrocinium*, or perhaps on the very first, that, as we passed the bridge, a boy happening to issue from the factory [1] sang out to us, derisively, "Holloa, Bucks!" In this the reader may fail to perceive any atrocious insult commensurate to the long war which followed. But the reader is wrong. The word "*dandies*," [2] which was what the villain meant, had not then been born, so that he could not have called us by that name, unless through the spirit of prophecy. *Buck* was the nearest word at hand in his Manchester vocabulary; he gave all he could, and let us dream the rest. But in the next moment he discovered our boots, and he consummated his crime by saluting us as "Boots! boots!" My brother made a dead stop, surveyed him with intense disdain, and bade him draw near, that he might "give his flesh to the fowls of the air." The boy declined to accept this liberal invitation, and conveyed his answer by a most contemptuous and plebeian gesture, [3] upon which my brother drove him in with a shower of stones.

During this inaugural flourish of hostilities, I, for my part, remained inactive, and therefore apparently neutral. But this was the last time that I did so: for the moment, indeed, I was taken by surprise. To be called a *buck* by

[1] "*Factory*" : — Such was the designation technically at that time. At present, I believe that a building of that class would be called a "mill."

[2] This word, however, exists in *Jack-a-dandy* — a very old English word. But what does *that* mean?

[3] Precisely, however, the same gesture, plebeian as it was, by which the English commandant at Heligoland replied to the Danes when civilly inviting him to surrender. Southey it was, on the authority of Lieutenant Southey, his brother, who communicated to me this anecdote.

one that had it in his choice to have called me a coward,
a thief, or a murderer, struck me as a most pardonable
offence; and as to *boots*, that rested upon a flagrant fact
that could not be denied; so that at first I was green
5 enough to regard the boy as very considerate and indulgent.
But my brother soon rectified my views; or, if any doubts
remained, he impressed me, at least, with a sense of my
paramount duty to himself, which was threefold.   First, it
seems that I owed military allegiance to *him*, as my com-
10 mander-in-chief, whenever we "took the field"; secondly,
by the law of nations, I, being a cadet of my house, owed
suit and service to him who was its head; and he assured
me, that twice in a year, on *my* birth-day and on *his*, he
had a right, strictly speaking, to make me lie down, and to
15 set his foot upon my neck; lastly, by a law not so rigorous,
but valid amongst gentlemen — viz., "by the *comity* of
nations" — it seems I owed eternal deference to one so
much older than myself, so much wiser, stronger, braver,
more beautiful, and more swift of foot.   Something like all
20 this in tendency I had already believed, though I had not
so minutely investigated the modes and grounds of my
duty.   By temperament, and through natural dedication to
despondency, I felt resting upon me always too deep and
gloomy a sense of obscure duties attached to life, that I
25 never *should* be able to fulfil; a burden which I could not
carry, and which yet I did not know how to throw off.
Glad, therefore, I was to find the whole tremendous weight
of obligations — the law and the prophets — all crowded
into this one pocket command, "Thou shalt obey thy
30 brother as God's vicar upon earth."   For now, if by any
future stone levelled at him who had called me a "buck,"
I should chance to draw blood — perhaps I might not have
committed so serious a trespass on any rights which he
could plead: but if I *had* (for on this subject my convictions

were still cloudy), at any rate the duty I might have violated in regard to this general brother, in right of Adam, was cancelled when it came into collision with my paramount duty to this liege brother of my own individual house.

From this day, therefore, I obeyed all my brother's military commands with the utmost docility; and happy it made me that every sort of doubt, or question or opening for demur, was swallowed up in the unity of this one papal principle, discovered by my brother — viz., that all rights and duties of casuistry were transferred from me to himself. *His* was the judgment — *his* was the responsibility; and to me belonged only the sublime obligation of unconditional faith in *him*. That faith I realised. It is true that he taxed me at times, in his reports of particular fights, with "horrible cowardice," and even with a "cowardice that seemed inexplicable, except on the supposition of treachery." But this was only a *façon de parler* with him : the idea of secret perfidy, that was constantly moving under-ground, gave an interest to the progress of the war, which else tended to the monotonous. It was a dramatic artifice for sustaining the interest, where the incidents might happen to be too slightly diversified. But that he did not believe his own charges was clear, because he never repeated them in his "General History of the Campaigns," which was a *résumé*, or recapitulating digest, of his daily reports.

We fought every day; and, generally speaking, *twice* every day ; and the result was pretty uniform — viz., that my brother and I terminated the battle by insisting upon our undoubted right to run away. *Magna Charta*, I should fancy, secures that great right to every man ; else, surely, it is sadly defective. But out of this catastrophe to most of our skirmishes, and to all our pitched battles except one, grew a standing schism between my brother and myself. My unlimited obedience had respect to action, but not to opinion. Loyalty to my brother did not rest upon hypocrisy; because I was faithful, it did not follow that I must be false in relation to his capricious opinions. And these opinions sometimes took the shape of acts. Twice, at the least, in every week, but sometimes every night, my brother insisted on singing "Te Deum" for supposed victories he had won; and he insisted also on my bearing a part in these "Te Deums." Now, as I knew of no such victories, but resolutely asserted the truth — viz., that we ran away — a slight jar was thus given to the else triumphal effect of these musical ovations. Once having uttered my protest, however, willingly I gave my aid to the chanting; for I loved unspeakably the grand and varied system of chanting in the Romish and English Churches. And, looking back at this day to the ineffable benefits which I derived from the church of my childhood, I account among the very greatest those which reached me through the various chants connected with the "O, Jubilate," the "Magnificat," the "Te Deum," the "Benedicite," etc. Through these chants it was that the sorrow which laid waste my infancy, and the devotion which nature had made a necessity of my being, were profoundly interfused: the sorrow gave reality and depth to the devotion; the devotion gave grandeur and idealisation to the sorrow. Neither was my love for chanting altogether without knowledge. A son of my reverend guardian, much older than myself, who possessed a singular faculty of producing a sort of organ accompaniment with one-half of his mouth, whilst he sang with the other half, had given me some instructions in the art of chanting: and, as to my brother, he, the hundred-handed Briareus, could do all things; of course, therefore, he could chant.

Once having begun, it followed naturally that the war should deepen in bitterness. Wounds that wrote memorials in the flesh, insults that rankled in the heart — these were not features of the case likely to be forgotten by our enemies, and far less by my fiery brother. I, for my part, entered not into any of the passions that war may be supposed to kindle, except only the chronic passion of anxiety. *Fear* it was not; for experience had taught me that, under the random firing of our undisciplined enemies, the chances were not many of being wounded. But the uncertainties of the war; the doubts in every separate action whether I could keep up the requisite connection with my brother; and, in case I could not, the utter darkness that surrounded my fate; whether, as a trophy won from Israel, I should be dedicated to the service of some Manchester Dagon, or pass through fire to Moloch; all these contingencies, for me that had no friend to consult, ran too violently into the master-current of my constitutional despondency, ever to give way under any casual elation of success. Success, however, we really had at times; in slight skirmishes pretty often; and once, at least, as the reader will find to his mortification, if he is wicked enough to take the side of the Philistines, a most smashing victory in a pitched battle. But even then, and whilst the hurrahs were yet ascending from our jubilating lips, the freezing remembrance came back to my heart of that deadly depression which, duly at the coming round of the morning and evening watches, travelled with me like my shadow on our approach to the memorable bridge. A bridge of sighs [1] too surely it was

---

[1] "*Bridge of Sighs*": — Two men of memorable genius, Hood last, and Lord Byron by many years previously, have so appropriated this phrase, and re-issued it as English currency, that many readers suppose it to be theirs. But the genealogies of fine expressions should be more carefully preserved. The expression belongs originally to Venice.

for me ; and even for my brother it formed an object of
fierce yet anxious jealousy, that he could not always disguise, as we first came in sight of it : for, if it happened to
be occupied in strength, there was an end of all hope that
5 we could attempt the passage ; and *that* was a fortunate
solution of the difficulty, as it imposed no evil beyond a
circuit ; which, at least, was safe, if the world should
choose to call it inglorious. Even this shade of ignominy,
however, my brother contrived to colour favourably, by
10 calling us — that is, me and himself — " a corps of observation " ; and he condescendingly explained to me, that,
although making " a lateral movement," he had his eye
upon the enemy, and " might yet come round upon his left

This *jus postliminii* becomes of real importance in many cases, but
especially in the case of Shakspere. Could one have believed it possible beforehand ? And yet it is a fact that he is made to seem a robber
of the lowest order, by mere dint of suffering robbery. Purely through
their own jewelly splendour have many hundreds of his phrases forced
themselves into usage so general, under the vulgar infirmity of seeking
to strengthen weak prose by shreds of poetic quotation, that at length
the majority of careless readers come to look upon these phrases as
belonging to the language, and traceable to no distinct proprietor any
more than proverbs : and thus, on afterwards observing them in
Shakspere, they regard him in the light of one accepting alms (like so
many meaner persons) from the common treasury of the universal
mind, on which treasury, meantime, he had himself conferred these
phrases as original donations of his own. Many expressions in the
" Paradise Lost," in " Il Penseroso," and in " L'Allegro," are in the
same predicament. And thus the almost incredible case is realised
which I have described — viz., that simply by having suffered a robbery
through two centuries (for the first attempt at plundering Milton was
made upon his juvenile poems), have Shakspere and Milton come to be
taxed as robbers. N.B. — In speaking of Hood as having appropriated
the phrase *Bridge of Sighs*, I would not be understood to represent him
as by possibility aiming at any concealment. He was far above such a
meanness by his nobility of heart, as he was raised above all need for it
by the overflowing opulence of his genius.

flank in a way that wouldn't, perhaps, prove very agreeable." This, from the nature of the ground, never happened. We crossed the river at Garrat, out of sight from
the enemy's position; and, on our return in the evening,
when we reached that point of our route from which the
retreat was secure to Greenhay, we took such revenge for
the morning insult as might belong to extra liberality in
our stone donations. On this line of policy there was,
therefore, no cause for anxiety; but the common case was,
that the numbers might not be such as to justify this caution, and yet quite enough for mischief. To my brother,
however, stung and carried headlong into hostility by the
martial instincts of his nature, the uneasiness of doubt or
insecurity was swallowed up by his joy in the anticipation
of victory, or even of contest; whilst to myself, whose exultation was purely official and ceremonial, as due by loyalty
from a cadet to the head of his house, no such compensation existed. The enemy was no enemy in *my* eyes; his
affronts were but retaliations; and his insults were so
inapplicable to my unworthy self, being of a calibre exclusively meant for the use of my brother, that from me they
recoiled, one and all, as cannon-shot from cotton bags.

The ordinary course of our day's warfare was this:
between nine and ten in the morning occurred our first
transit, and consequently our earliest opportunity for doing
business. But at this time the great sublunary interest of
breakfast, which swallowed up all nobler considerations of
glory and ambition, occupied the work-people of the factory (or what in the pedantic diction of this day are
termed the "operatives"), so that very seldom any serious
business was transacted. Without any formal armistice,
the paramount convenience of such an arrangement silently
secured its own recognition. Notice there needed none of
truce, when the one side yearned for breakfast, and the

other for a respite ; the groups, therefore, on or about the
bridge, if any at all, were loose in their array, and careless.
We passed through them rapidly, and, on my part, uneasily ;
exchanging a few snarls, perhaps, but seldom or never snap-
5 ping at each other. The tameness was almost shocking of
those who, in the afternoon, would inevitably resume their
natural characters of tiger-cats and wolves. Sometimes,
however, my brother felt it to be a duty that we should
fight in the morning; particularly when any expression of
10 public joy for a victory — bells ringing in the distance —
or when a royal birth-day, or some traditional commemoration of ancient feuds (such as the 5th of November), irritated
his martial propensities. Some of these, being religious festivals, seemed to require of us an *extra* homage, for which
15 we knew not how to find any natural or significant expression, except through sharp discharges of stones, that being
a language older than Hebrew or Sanscrit, and universally
intelligible. But, excepting these high days of religious
solemnity, when a man is called upon to show that he is not
20 a Pagan or a miscreant in the eldest of senses, by thump-
ing, or trying to thump, somebody who is accused or accus-
able of being heterodox, the great ceremony of breakfast
was allowed to sanctify the hour. Some natural growls we
uttered, but hushed them soon, regardless

25   " Of the sweeping whirlpool's sway,
        That, hush'd in grim repose, look'd for his evening prey."

That came but too surely. Yes, evening never forgot to
come ; this odious necessity of fighting never missed its road
back, or fell asleep, or loitered by the way, more than a bill
30 of exchange, or a tertian fever. Five times a week (Saturday sometimes, and Sunday always, were days of rest) the
same scene rehearsed itself in pretty nearly the same succession of circumstances. Between four and five o'clock we

course of lectures on the "dendrology" of Oxford Street)
— but, notwithstanding such little stumblings in my career,
I continued to ascend in the service; and I am sure it will
gratify my friendly readers to hear, that, before my eighth
birth-day, I was promoted to the rank of major-general. 5
Over this sunshine, however, soon swept a train of clouds.
Three times I was taken prisoner; and with different results.
The first time I was carried to the rear, and not molested
in any way. Finding myself thus ignominiously neglected,
I watched my opportunity; and, by making a wide circuit, 10
easily effected my escape. In the next case, a brief council
was held over me; but I was not allowed to hear the delib-
erations; the result only being communicated to me — which
result consisted in a message not very complimentary to my
brother, and a small present of kicks to myself. This pres- 15
ent was paid down without any discount, by means of a
general subscription amongst the party surrounding me —
that party, luckily, not being very numerous; besides which,
I must, in honesty, acknowledge myself, generally speaking,
indebted to their forbearance. They were not disposed to 20
be too hard upon me. But, at the same time, they clearly
did not think it right that I should escape altogether from
tasting the calamities of war. And this translated the estimate of my guilt from the public jurisdiction to that of the
individual, sometimes capricious and harsh, and carrying 25
out the public award by means of legs that ranged through
all gradations of weight and agility. One kick differed
exceedingly from another kick in dynamic value; and, in
some cases, this difference was so distressingly conspicuous,
as to imply special malice, unworthy, I conceive, of all 30
generous soldiership.

On returning to our own frontiers, I had an opportunity
of displaying my exemplary greenness. That message to
my brother, with all its *virus* of insolence, I repeated as

faithfully for the spirit, and as literally for the expressions,
as my memory allowed me to do : and in that troublesome
effort, simpleton that I was, fancied myself exhibiting a
soldier's loyalty to his commanding officer. My brother
5 thought otherwise : he was more angry with me than with
the enemy. I ought, he said, to have refused all partici-
pation in such *sansculottes'* insolence ; to carry it, was to
acknowledge it as fit to be carried. One grows wiser every
day ; and on this particular day I made a resolution that,
10 if again made prisoner, I would bring no more "jaw" (so
my brother called it) from the Philistines. If these people
would send "jaw," I settled that, henceforwards, it must go
through the post-office.

In my former captures, there had been nothing special or
15 worthy of commemoration in the circumstances. Neither
was there in the third, excepting that, by accident, in the
second stage of the case, I was delivered over to the custody
of young women and girls ; whereas the ordinary course
would have thrown me upon the vigilant attentions (relieved
20 from monotony by the experimental kicks) of boys. So far,
the change was very much for the better. I had a feeling
myself, on first being presented to my new young mistresses,
of a distressing sort. Having always, up to the completion
of my sixth year, been a privileged pet, and almost, I might
25 say, ranking amongst the sanctities of the household, with
all its female sections, whether young or old (an advantage
which I owed originally to a long illness, an ague, stretching
over two entire years of my infancy), naturally I had learned
to appreciate the indulgent tenderness of women ; and my
30 heart thrilled with love and gratitude, as often as they took
me up into their arms and kissed me. Here it would have
been as everywhere else ; but, unfortunately, my introduction to these young women was in the very worst of characters. I had been taken in arms — in arms against their own

brothers, cousins, sweethearts, and on pretexts too frivolous
to mention. If asked the question, it would be found that
I should not myself deny the fact of being at war with their
whole order. What was the meaning of *that?* What was
it to which war pledged a man? It pledged him, in case
of opportunity, to burn, ravage, and depopulate the houses
and lands of the enemy; which enemy was these fair girls.
The warrior stood committed to universal destruction.
Neither sex nor age; neither the smiles of unoffending
infancy nor the grey hairs of the venerable patriarch;
neither the sanctity of the matron nor the loveliness of
the youthful bride, would confer any privilege with the
warrior, consequently not with me.

Many other hideous features in the military character
will be found in books innumerable — levelled at those who
make war, and therefore at myself. And it appears finally
by these books — that, as one of my ordinary practices, I
make a wilderness, and call it a pacification; that I hold it
a duty to put people to the sword; which done, to plough
up the foundations of their hearths and altars, and then to
sow the ground with salt.

All this was passing through my brain, when suddenly
one young woman snatched me up in her arms, and kissed
me; from *her*, I was passed round to others of the party,
who all in turn caressed me, with no allusion to that warlike
mission, against them and theirs, which only had procured
me the honour of an introduction to themselves in the character of captive. The too palpable fact that I was not the
person meant by nature to exterminate their families, or to
make wildernesses and call them pacifications, had withdrawn from their minds the counter fact — that, whatever
had been my performances, my intentions had been hostile,
and that in such a character only I could have become their
prisoner. Not only did these young people kiss me, but I

(seeing no military reason against it) kissed *them*.   Really,
if young women will insist on kissing major-generals, they
must expect that the generals will retaliate.   One only of
the crowd adverted to the character in which I came before
them: to be a lawful prisoner, it struck her too logical
mind that I must have been caught in some aggressive
practices.   "Think," she said, "of this little dog fighting,
and fighting our Jack."   "But," said another, in a pro-
pitiatory tone, "perhaps he'll not do so any more."   I was
touched by the kindness of her suggestion, and the sweet,
merciful sound of that same "*Not do so any more*," which
really was prompted, I fear, much more by that charity in
her which hopeth all things, than by any signs of amendment in myself.   Well was it for me that no time was
allowed for investigation into my morals by point-blank
questions as to my future intentions.   In which case it
would have appeared too undeniably, that the same sad
necessity which had planted me hitherto in a position of
hostility to their estimable families, would continue to
persecute me; and that, on the very next day, duty to
my brother, howsoever it might struggle with gratitude
to themselves, would range me in martial attitude, with a
pocketful of stones, meant, alas! for the exclusive use of
their respectable kinsmen.   Whilst I was preparing myself,
however, for this painful exposition, my female friends
observed issuing from the factory a crowd of boys not
likely at all to improve my prospects.   Instantly setting
me down on my feet, they formed a sort of *cordon sanitaire*
behind me, by stretching out their petticoats or aprons, as
in dancing, so as to touch: and then, crying out, "Now,
little dog, run for thy life," prepared themselves (I doubt
not) for rescuing me, should my re-capture be effected.

But this was *not* effected, although attempted with an
energy that alarmed me, and even perplexed me with a

vague thought (far too ambitious for my years) that one
or two of the pursuing party might be possessed by some
demon of jealousy, as eyewitnesses to my revelling amongst
the lips of that fair girlish bevy, kissing and being kissed,
loving and being loved; in which case, from all that ever 5
I had read about jealousy (and I had read a great deal —
viz., "Othello," and Collins's "Ode to the Passions"), I was
satisfied that, if again captured, I had very little chance for
my life. That jealousy was a green-eyed monster, nobody
could know better than *I* did. "Oh, my lord, beware of 10
jealousy!" Yes; and my lord couldn't possibly have more
reason for bewaring of it than myself; indeed, well it would
have been had his lordship run away from all the ministers
of jealousy — Iago, Cassio, and embroidered handkerchiefs
— at the same pace of six miles an hour which kept me 15
ahead of my infuriated pursuers. Ah, that maniac, white
as a leper with flakes of cotton, can I ever forget him, *him*
that ran so far in advance of his party? What passion,
but jealousy, could have sustained him in so hot a chase?
There were some lovely girls in the fair company that had 20
so condescendingly caressed me; but, doubtless, upon that
sweet creature his love must have settled, who suggested,
in her soft, relenting voice, a penitence in me that, alas!
had not dawned, saying, "*Yes; but perhaps he will not do so
any more.*" Thinking, as I ran, of her beauty, I felt that 25
this jealous demoniac must fancy himself justified in com-
mitting seven times seven murders upon me, if he should
have it in his power. But, thank heaven, if jealousy can
run six miles an hour, there are other passions, as for
instance panic, that can run, upon occasion, six and a half; 30
so, as I had the start of him (you know, reader), and not a
very short start — thanks be to the expanded petticoats of
my dear female friends! — naturally it happened that the
green-eyed monster came in second best. Time luckily was

precious with *him;* and, accordingly, when he had chased me into the by-road leading down to Greenhay, he turned back. For the moment, therefore, I found myself suddenly released from danger. But this counted for nothing. The same
5 scene would probably revolve upon me continually; and, on the next rehearsal, Green-eyes might have better luck. It saddened me, besides, to find myself under the political necessity of numbering amongst the Philistines, and as daughters of Gath, so many kind-hearted girls, whom, by
10 personal proof, I knew to be such. In the profoundest sense I was unhappy; and not from any momentary accident of distress, but from deep glimpses which now, and heretofore, had opened themselves, as occasions arose, into the inevitable conflicts of life. One of the saddest among
15 such conflicts is the necessity, wheresoever it occurs, of adopting — though the heart should disown — the enmities of one's own family, or country, or religious sect. In forms how afflicting must that necessity have sometimes occurred during the Parliamentary War! And, in after
20 years, amongst our beautiful old English metrical romances, I found the same impassioned complaint uttered by a knight, Sir Ywain, as early as A.D. 1240 —

> "But now, where'er I stray or go,
> My heart SHE has that is my foe!"

25 I knew — I anticipated to a certainty — that my brother would not hear of any merit belonging to the factory population whom every day we had to meet in battle; on the contrary, even submission on *their* part, and willingness to walk penitentially through the *Furcæ Caudinæ*, would hardly
30 have satisfied his sense of their criminality. Often, indeed, as we came in view of the factory, he would shake his fist at it, and say, in a ferocious tone of voice, " *Delenda est Carthago!*" And certainly, I thought to myself, it must be

admitted by everybody, that the factory people are inex-
cusable in raising a rebellion against my brother. But still
rebels were men, and sometimes were women; and rebels
that stretch out their petticoats like fans for the sake of
screening one from the hot pursuit of enemies with fiery 5
eyes (green or otherwise) really are not the sort of people
that one wishes to hate.

Homewards, therefore, I drew in sadness, and little
doubting that *hereafter* I might have verbal feuds with my
brother on behalf of my fair friends, but not dreaming how 10
much displeasure I had already incurred by my treasonable
collusion with their caresses. That part of the affair he had
seen with his own eyes, from his position on the field; and
then it was that he left me indignantly to my fate, which, by
my first reception, it was easy to see would not prove very 15
gloomy. When I came into our own study, I found him
engaged in preparing a *bulletin* (which word was just then
travelling into universal use), reporting briefly the events
of the day. The art of drawing, as I shall again have
occasion to mention, was amongst his foremost accom- 20
plishments; and round the margin of the bulletin ran a
black border, ornamented with cypress, and other funereal
emblems. When finished, it was carried into the room of
Mrs. Evans. This Mrs. Evans was an important person in
our affairs. My mother, who never chose to have any 25
direct communication with her servants, always had a
housekeeper for the regulation of all domestic business;
and the housekeeper for some years was this Mrs. Evans.
Into her private parlour, where she sat aloof from the under
servants, my brother and I had the *entrée* at all times, but 30
upon very different terms of acceptance: he as a favourite
of the first class; *I*, by sufferance, as a sort of gloomy
shadow that ran after *his* person, and could not well be
shut out if *he* were let in. Him she admired in the very

highest degree; myself, on the contrary, she detested, — which made me unhappy. But then, in some measure, she made amends for this, by despising me in extremity; and for *that* I was truly thankful — I need not say *why*, as the reader already knows. Why she detested me, so far as I know, arose in part out of my thoughtfulness indisposed to garrulity, and in part out of my savage, Orson-like sincerity. I had a great deal to say, but then I could say it only to a very few people, amongst whom Mrs. Evans was certainly not one; and when I *did* say anything, I fear that dire ignorance prevented my laying the proper restraints upon my too liberal candour; and *that* could not prove acceptable to one who thought nothing of working for any purpose, or for no purpose, by petty tricks, or even falsehoods — all which I held in stern abhorrence, that I was at no pains to conceal. The *bulletin* on this occasion, garnished with its pageantry of woe, cypress wreaths, and arms reversed, was read aloud to Mrs. Evans, indirectly therefore to me. It communicated, with Spartan brevity, the sad intelligence (but not sad to Mrs. E.), "that the major-general had for ever disgraced himself, by submitting to the   caresses of the enemy." I leave a blank for the epithet affixed to "caresses," not because there *was* any blank, but, on the contrary, because my brother's wrath had boiled over in such a hubble-bubble of epithets, some only half erased, some doubtfully erased, that it was impossible, out of the various readings, to pick out the true classical text. "Infamous," "disgusting," and "odious," struggled for precedency; and *infamous* they might be; but on the other affixes I held my own private opinions. For some days, my brother's displeasure continued to roll in reverberating thunders; but at length it growled itself to rest; and at last he descended to mild expostulations with me, showing clearly, in a series of general orders, what frightful consequences must ensue, if major-generals (as a general principle) should allow themselves to be kissed by the enemy.

About this time, my brother began to issue, instead of occasional bulletins, through which hitherto he had breathed his opinions into the ear of the public (viz., of Mrs. Evans), a regular gazette, which, in imitation of the "London Gazette," was published twice a week. I suppose that no creature ever led such a life as *I* did in that gazette. Run up to the giddiest heights of promotion on one day, for merits which I could not myself discern, in a week or two I was brought to a court-martial for offences equally obscure. I was cashiered; I was restored "on the intercession of a distinguished lady" (Mrs. Evans, to wit); I was threatened with being drummed out of the army, to the music of the "Rogue's March"; and then, in the midst of all this misery and degradation, upon the discovery of some supposed energy that I had manifested, I was decorated with the Order of the Bath. My reading had been extensive enough to give me some vague aerial sense of the honour involved in such a decoration, whilst I was profoundly ignorant of the channels through which it could reach an individual, and of the sole fountain from which it could flow. But, in this enormity of disproportion between the cause and the effect, between the agency and the result, I saw nothing more astonishing than I had seen in many other cases confessedly true. Thousands of vast effects, by all that I had heard, linked themselves to causes apparently trivial. The dreadful taint of scrofula, according to the belief of all Christendom, fled at the simple touch of a Stuart sovereign[1]: no miracle in the Bible, from Jordan or from

---

[1] "*Of a Stuart sovereign*": — and by no means of a Stuart only. Queen Anne, the last Stuart who sat on the British throne, was the last of *our* princes who touched for the *king's evil* (as scrofula was

Bethesda, could be more sudden, or more astoundingly victorious. By my own experience, again, I knew that a *styan* (as it is called) upon the eyelid could be easily reduced, though not instantaneously, by the slight appli-
5 cation of any golden trinket. Warts upon the fingers of children I had myself known to vanish under the *verbal* charm of a gipsy woman, without any medicinal appli-cation whatever. And I well knew, that almost all nations believed in the dreadful mystery of the *evil eye;* some
10 requiring, as a condition of the evil agency, the co-presence of malice in the agent; but others, as appeared from my father's Portuguese recollections, ascribing the same horrid power to the eye of certain select persons, even though innocent of all malignant purpose, and absolutely uncon-
15 scious of their own fatal gift, until awakened to it by the results. Why, therefore, should there be anything to shock, or even to surprise, in the power claimed by my brother, as an attribute inalienable from primogeniture in certain select families, of conferring knightly honours?
20 The red riband of the Bath he certainly *did* confer upon me; and once, in a paroxysm of imprudent liberality, he promised me at the end of certain months, supposing that I swerved from my duty by no atrocious delinquency, the Garter itself. This, I knew, was a far loftier distinction
25 than the Bath. Even then it was so; and since those days it has become much more so; because the long roll of mar-tial services in the great war with Napoleon compelled our government greatly to widen the basis of the Bath. This

generally called until lately); but the Bourbon Houses, on the thrones of France, Spain, and Naples, as well as the House of Savoy, claimed and exercised the same supernatural privilege down to a much later period than the year 1714 — the last of Queen Anne: according to their own and the popular faith, they could have cleansed Naaman the Syrian, and Gehazi too.

promise was never fulfilled; but not for any want of clam-
orous persecution on my part addressed to my brother's
wearied ear, and somewhat callous sense of honour. Every
fortnight or so, I took care that he should receive a
"refresher," as lawyers call it — a new and revised brief — 5
memorialising my pretensions. These it was my brother's
policy to parry, by alleged instances of recent misconduct on my part. But all such offences, I insisted, were
thoroughly washed away by subsequent services in moments
of peril, such as he himself could not always deny. In 10
reality, I believe his real motive for withholding the Garter
was, that he had nothing better to bestow upon himself.

"Now, look here," he would say, appealing to Mrs. Evans;
"I suppose there's a matter of half a dozen kings on the
Continent that would consent to lose three of their fingers, 15
if by such a sacrifice they could purchase the blue riband;
and here is this little scamp, conceiting himself entitled to it
before he has finished two campaigns." But I was not the
person to be beaten off in this fashion. I took my stand
upon the promise. A promise *was* a promise, even if made 20
to a scamp; and then, besides —— but there I hesitated;
awful thoughts interposed to check me; else I wished to
suggest that, perhaps, some two or three among that half-
dozen kings might also be scamps. However, I reduced the
case to this plain dilemma: These six kings had received a 25
promise, or they had not. If they had not, my case was
better than theirs; if they *had*, then, said I, "all seven of
us" —— I was going to add, "are sailing in the same boat,"
or something to that effect, though not so picturesquely
expressed; but I was interrupted by his deadly frown at my 30
audacity in thus linking myself on as a seventh to this
attelage of kings; and that such an absolute grub should
dream of ranking as one in a bright pleiad of pretenders to
the Garter. I had not particularly thought of that; but,

now that such a demur was offered to my consideration, I
thought of reminding him that, in a certain shadowy sense,
I also might presume to class myself as a king. — the meaning of which was this: Both my brother and myself, for the
sake of varying our intellectual amusements, occupied ourselves at times in governing imaginary kingdoms. I do not
mention this as anything unusual; it is a common resource
of mental activity and of aspiring energies amongst boys.
Hartley Coleridge, for example, had a kingdom which he
governed for many years; whether well or ill, is more than
I can say. Kindly, I am sure, he would govern it; but, unless
a machine had been invented for enabling him to write without effort (as was really done for our Fourth George during
the pressure of illness), I fear that the public service must
have languished deplorably for want of the royal signature.
In sailing past his own dominions, what dolorous outcries
would have saluted him from the shore — "Holloa, royal
sir! here's the deuce to pay: a perfect lock there is, as tight
as locked jaw, upon the course of our public business; throats
there are to be cut, from the product of ten jail-deliveries,
and nobody dares to cut them, for want of the proper warrant; archbishoprics there are to be filled, and, because
they are *not* filled, the whole nation is running helter-skelter
into heresy; — and all in consequence of your majesty's
sacred laziness." *Our* governments were less remissly
administered; since each of us, by continued reports of
improvements and gracious concessions to the folly or the
weakness of our subjects, stimulated the zeal of his rival.
And here, at least, there seemed to be no reason why I
should come into collision with my brother. At any rate,
I took pains *not* to do so. But all was in vain. My destiny
was, to live in one eternal element of feud.

My own kingdom was an island called Gombroon. But
in what parallel of north or south latitude it lay, I concealed

for a time as rigorously as ancient Rome through every century concealed her real name.[1] The object in this provisional concealment was, to regulate the position of my own territory by that of my brother's; for I was determined to place a monstrous world of waters between us, as the only chance (and a very poor one it proved) for compelling my brother to keep the peace. At length, for some reason unknown to me, and much to my astonishment, he located his capital city in the high latitude of 65 deg. north. That fact being once published and settled, instantly I smacked my little kingdom of Gombroon down into the tropics, 10 deg., I think, south of the line. Now, at least, I was on the right side of the hedge, or so I flattered myself; for it struck me that my brother never would degrade himself by fitting out a costly nautical expedition against poor little Gombroon; and how else could he get at me? Surely the very fiend himself, if he happened to be in a high arctic latitude, would not indulge his malice so far as to follow its trail into the Tropic of Capricorn. And what was to be got by such a freak? There was no Golden Fleece in Gombroon. If the fiend or my brother fancied *that*, for once they were in the wrong box; and there was no variety of vegetable produce, for I never denied that the poor little island was only 270 miles in circuit. Think, then, of sailing through 75 deg. of latitude only to crack such a miserable little filbert as that. But my brother stunned me by explaining that, although his capital lay in lat. 65 deg. N., not the less

---

[1] One reason, I believe, why it was held a point of wisdom, in ancient days, that the metropolis of a warlike state should have a secret name hidden from the world, lay in the Pagan practice of *evocation*, applied to the tutelary deities of such a state. These deities might be lured by certain rites and briberies into a transfer of their favours to the besieging army. But, in order to make such an evocation effectual, it was necessary to know the original and secret name of the beleaguered city: and this, therefore, was religiously concealed.

his dominions swept southwards through a matter of 80 or 90 deg.; and, as to the Tropic of Capricorn, much of it was his own private property. I was aghast at hearing *that*. It seemed that vast horns and promontories ran down 5 from all parts of his dominions towards any country whatsoever, in either hemisphere — empire, or republic; monarchy, polyarchy, or anarchy — that he might have reasons for assaulting.

Here in one moment vanished all that I had relied on 10 for protection: distance I had relied on, and suddenly I was found in close neighbourhood to my most formidable enemy. Poverty I had relied on, and *that* was not denied; he granted the poverty, but it was dependent on the barbarism of the Gombroonians. It seems that in the central forests of 15 Gombroonia there were diamond mines, which my people, from their low condition of civilisation, did not value, nor had any means of working. Farewell, therefore, on *my* side, to all hopes of enduring peace, for here was established, in legal phrase, *a lien* for ever upon my island, and not upon 20 its margin, but its very centre, in favour of any invaders, better able than the natives to make its treasures available. For, of old, it was an article in my brother's code of morals — that, supposing a contest between any two parties, of which one possessed an article, whilst the other was better 25 able to use it, the rightful property vested in the latter. As if you met a man with a musket, then you might justly challenge him to a trial in the art of making gunpowder; which if you *could* make, and he could *not*, in that case the musket was *de jure* yours. For what shadow of a right 30 had the fellow to a noble instrument which he could not "maintain" in a serviceable condition, and "feed" with its daily rations of powder and shot? Still, it may be fancied that, since all the relations between us as independent sovereigns (whether of war, or peace, or treaty) rested upon our own representations and official reports, it was surely within my competence to deny or qualify, as much as within his to assert. But, in reality, the *law* of the contest between us, as suggested by some instinct of propriety in my own mind, would not allow me to proceed in such a method. What he said was like a move at chess or draughts, which it was childish to dispute. The move being made, my business was — to face it, to parry it, to evade it, and, if I could, to overthrow it. I proceeded as a lawyer who moves as long as he can, not by blank denial of facts (or *coming to an issue*), but by *demurring* (*i.e.*, admitting the allegations of fact, but otherwise interpreting their construction). It was the understood necessity of the case, that I must passively accept my brother's statements so far as regarded their verbal expression ; and, if I would extricate my poor islanders from their troubles, it must be by some distinction or evasion lying *within* this expression, or not blankly contradicting it.

"How, and to what extent," my brother asked, "did I raise taxes upon my subjects?" My first impulse was to say, that I did not tax them at all, for I had a perfect horror of doing so ; but prudence would not allow of my saying *that;* because it was too probable he would demand to know how, in that case, I maintained a standing army; and if I once allowed it to be supposed that I had none, there was an end for ever to the independence of my people. Poor things! they would have been invaded and dragooned in a month. I took some days, therefore, to consider that point, but at last replied, that my people, being maritime, supported themselves mainly by a herring fishery, from which I deducted a part of the produce, and afterwards sold it for manure to neighbouring nations. This last hint I borrowed from the conversation of a stranger who happened to dine one day at Greenhay, and mentioned that in

Devonshire, or at least on the western coast of that country, near Ilfracombe, upon any excessive take of herrings, beyond what the markets could absorb, the surplus was applied to the land as a valuable dressing. It might be
5 inferred from this account, however, that the arts must be in a languishing state, amongst a people that did not understand the process of salting fish; and my brother observed derisively, much to my grief, that a wretched ichthyophagous people must make shocking soldiers, weak
10 as water, and liable to be knocked over like nine-pins; whereas, in *his* army, not a man ever ate herrings, pilchards, mackerels, or, in fact, condescended to anything worse than sirloins of beef.

At every step I had to contend for the honour and
15 independence of my islanders; so that early I came to understand the weight of Shakspere's sentiment —

" Uneasy lies the head that wears a crown ! "

Oh, reader, do not laugh! I lived for ever under the terror of two separate wars in two separate worlds: one against
20 the factory boys, in a real world of flesh and blood, of stones and brickbats, of flight and pursuit, that were anything but figurative; the other in a world purely aerial, where all the combats and the sufferings were absolute moonshine. And yet the simple truth is — that, for anxiety
25 and distress of mind, the reality (which almost every morning's light brought round) was as nothing in comparison of that dream-kingdom which rose like a vapour from my own brain, and which apparently by the *fiat* of my will could be for ever dissolved. Ah! but no; I had contracted obliga-
30 tions to Gombroon; I had submitted my conscience to a yoke; and in secret truth my will had no such autocratic power. Long contemplation of a shadow, earnest study for the welfare of that shadow, sympathy with the wounded

sensibilities of that shadow under accumulated wrongs, these bitter experiences, nursed by brooding thought, had gradually frozen that shadow into a rigour of reality far denser than the material realities of brass or granite. Who builds the most durable dwellings? asks the labourer in "Hamlet"; 5 and the answer is, The gravedigger. He builds for corruption; and yet *his* tenements are incorruptible: "the houses which *he* makes last to doomsday."[1] Who is it that seeks for concealment? Let him hide himself[2] in the unsearch-

---

[1] "Hamlet," Act v. scene 1.

[2] "*Hide himself in — light*":— The greatest scholar, by far, that this island ever produced (viz., Richard Bentley) published (as is well known) a 4to volume that in some respects is the very worst 4to now extant in the world — viz., a critical edition of the "Paradise Lost." I observe, in the "Edinburgh Review" (July, 1851, No. 191, p. 15), that a learned critic supposes Bentley to have meant this edition as a "practical jest." Not at all. Neither could the critic have fancied such a possibility, if he had taken the trouble (which *I* did many a year back) to examine it. A jest-book it certainly is, and the most prosperous of jest-books, but undoubtedly never meant for such by the author. A man whose lips are livid with anger does not jest, and does not understand jesting. Still, the Edinburgh Reviewer is right about the proper functions of the book, though wrong about the intentions of the author. The fact is, the man was maniacally in error, and always in error, as regarded the ultimate or poetic truth of Milton; but, as regarded truth reputed and truth *apparent*, he often had the air of being furiously in the right; an example of which I will cite. Milton, in the First Book of the "Paradise Lost," had said —

> " That from the *secret* top
> Of Oreb or of Sinai didst inspire;"

upon which Bentley comments in effect thus: "How! — the exposed summit of a mountain *secret*? Why, it's like Charing Cross — always the least secret place in the whole county." So one might fancy: since the summit of a mountain, like Plinlimmon or Cader Idris in Wales, like Skiddaw or Helvellyn in England, constitutes a central object of attention and gaze for the whole circumjacent district, measured by a radius sometimes of 15 to 20 miles. Upon this consideration, Bentley

able chambers of light — of light which at noonday, more
effectually than any gloom, conceals the very brightest
stars, rather than in labyrinths of darkness the thickest.
What criminal is that who wishes to abscond from public
5 justice? Let him hurry into the frantic publicities of London, and by no means into the quiet privacies of the
country. So, and upon the analogy of these cases, we
may understand that, to make a strife overwhelming by a
thousandfold to the feelings, it must not deal with gross
10 material interests, but with such as rise into the world of
dreams, and act upon the nerves through spiritual, and not
through fleshly, torments. Mine, in the present case, rose
suddenly, like a rocket, into their meridian altitude, by
means of a hint furnished to my brother from a Scottish
15 advocate's reveries.

This advocate, who by his writings became the remote
cause of so much affliction to my childhood, and struck a
blow at the dignity of Gombroon that neither my brother
nor all the forces of Tigrosylvania (my brother's kingdom)
20 ever could have devised, was the celebrated James Burnett,
better known to the English public by his judicial title of
Lord Monboddo. The Burnetts of Monboddo, I have often
heard, were a race distinguished for their intellectual accomplishments through several successive generations; and the
25 judge in question was eminently so. It did him no injury

instructs us to substitute as the true reading — "That on the *sacred*
top," &c. Meantime, an actual experiment will demonstrate that there
is no place so absolutely secret and hidden as the exposed summit of a
mountain, 3500 feet high, in respect to an eye stationed in the valley
immediately below. A whole party of men, women, horses, and even
tents, looked at under those circumstances, is absolutely invisible unless
by the aid of glasses: and it becomes evident that a murder might be
committed on the bare open summit of such a mountain with more
assurance of absolute secrecy than anywhere else in the whole surrounding district.

that many people regarded him as crazy. In England, at
the beginning of the last century, we had a saying,[1] in reference to the Harveys of Lord Bristol's family, equally
distinguished for wit, beauty, and eccentricity, that at the
creation there had been three kinds of people made — viz.,
men, women, and Harveys; and by all accounts something
of the same kind might plausibly have been said in Scotland about the Burnetts. Lord Monboddo's nieces, of
whom one perished by falling from a precipice (and, as I
have heard, through mere absence of mind, whilst musing
upon a book which she carried in her hand), still survive in the affection of many friends, through the interest
attached to their intellectual gifts; and Miss Burnett, the
daughter of the judge, is remembered in all the memorials
of Burns the poet, as the most beautiful, and otherwise
the most interesting, of his female aristocratic friends
in Edinburgh. Lord Monboddo himself trod an eccentric path in literature and philosophy; and our tutor, who
spent his whole life in reading, withdrawing himself in that
way from the anxieties incident to a narrow income and a
large family, found, no doubt, a vast fund of interesting
suggestions in Lord M.'s "Dissertations on the Origin of
Language"; but to us he communicated only one section
of the work. It was a long passage, containing some very
useful illustrations of a Greek idiom; useful I call them,
because four years afterwards, when I had made great
advances in my knowledge of Greek, they so appeared to
me.[2] But then, being scarcely seven years old, as soon as

[1] Which "*saying*" is sometimes ascribed, I know not how truly, to
Lady Mary Wortley Montagu.

[2] It strikes me, upon second thoughts, that the particular idiom
which Lord Monboddo illustrated as regarded the Greek language
merits a momentary notice; and for this reason — that it plays a part
not at all less conspicuous or less delicate in the Latin. Here is an

our tutor had finished his long extract from the Scottish
judge's prelection, I could express my thankfulness for what
I had received only by composing my features to a deeper
solemnity and sadness than usual — no very easy task, I
5 have been told; otherwise, I really had not the remotest
conception of what his lordship meant.   I knew very well
the thing called a *tense;* I knew even then by name the
Aoristus Primus, as a respectable tense in the Greek

instance of its use in Greek, taken from the well-known Night-scene
in the "Iliad":—

$$\text{———}\gamma\eta\theta\eta\sigma\epsilon\ \delta\epsilon\ \pi\omega\mu\epsilon\nu\omega\varsigma\ \dot{\eta}\tau\omega\rho,$$

"and the heart of the shepherd *rejoices*"; where the verb γηθησε is in
the indefinite or aorist tense, and is meant to indicate a condition of
feeling not limited to any time whatever — past, present, or future.   In
Latin the force and elegance of this usage are equally impressive, if not
more so.   At this moment I remember two cases of this in Horace—

    1.   "Raro antecedentem scelestum
          Deseruit pede pœna claudo";
    2.   "sæpe Diespiter
          Neglectus incesto *addidit* integrum."

That is — "Oftentimes the Supreme Ruler, when treated with neglect,
confounds or unites (not *has united*, as the tyro might fancy) the
impure man with the upright in one common fate."

Exceedingly common is this usage in Latin poetry, when the object
is to generalise a remark — as not connected with one mode of time
more than another.   In reality, all three modes of time — past, present, future — are used (though not equally used) in all languages for
this purpose of generalisation.   Thus,

    1. The *future:* as, Sapiens dominabitur astris.
    2. The *present:* as, Fortes fortuna juvat.
    3. The *past:* as in the two cases cited from Horace.

But this practice holds equally in English: as to the future and
the present, nobody will doubt it; and here is a case from the past —
"The fool *hath said* in his heart, There is no God"; not meaning
that in some past time he hath said so, but that generally in all times
he *does* say so, and *will* say so.

language. It (or shall we say *he?*) was known to the whole
Christian world by this distinction of *Primus;* clearly,
therefore, there must be some low, vulgar tense in the background, pretending also to the name of Aorist, but universally scouted as the *Aoristus Secundus*, or Birmingham
counterfeit. So that, unable as I was, from ignorance, to
go along with Lord M.'s appreciation of his pretensions,
still, had it been possible to meet an Aoristus Primus in
the flesh, I should have bowed to him submissively, as
to one apparently endowed with the mysterious rights
of primogeniture. Not so my brother. Aorist, indeed!
Primus or Secundus, what mattered it? Paving-stones
were something, brickbats were something, but an old
superannuated tense! That any grown man should trouble
himself about *that!* Indeed, there *was* something extraordinary there. For it is not amongst the ordinary functions of lawyers to take charge of Greek; far less, one
might suppose, of lawyers in Scotland, where the *general*
system of education has moved for two centuries upon a
principle of slight regard to classical literature. Latin
literature was very much neglected, and Greek nearly
altogether. The more was the astonishment at finding a
rare delicacy of critical instinct, as well as of critical
sagacity, applied to the Greek idiomatic niceties by a
Scottish lawyer — viz., that same eccentric judge, first
made known to us by our tutor.

To the majority of readers, meantime, at this day, Lord
M. is memorable chiefly for his craze about the degeneracy
of us poor moderns, when compared with the men of Pagan
antiquity; which craze itself might possibly not have been
generally known, except in connection with the little skirmish between him and Dr. Johnson, noticed in Boswell's
account of the Doctor's Scottish tour. "Ah, doctor," said
Lord M., upon some casual suggestion of that topic, "poor

creatures are we of this eighteenth century; our fathers were better men than we!" "Oh no, my lord," was Johnson's reply; "we are quite as strong as our forefathers, and a great deal wiser!" Such a craze, however, is too widely diffused, and falls in with too obstinate a preconception [1]

[1] " *Too obstinate a preconception* " : — Until the birth of geology, and of fossil palæontology, concurring with vast strides ahead in the science of comparative anatomy, it is a well-established fact, that oftentimes the most scientific museum admitted as genuine fragments of the human osteology what in fact belonged to the gigantic brutes of our earth in her earliest stages of development. This mistake would go some way in accounting for the absurd disposition in all generations to view themselves as abridged editions of their forefathers. Added to which, as a separate cause of error, there can be little doubt, that intermingled with the human race there has at most periods of the world been a separate and Titanic race, such as the Anakim amongst the peoples of Palestine, the Cyclopean race diffused over the Mediterranean in the elder ages of Greece, and certain tribes amongst the Alps, known to Evelyn in his youth (about Cromwell's time) by an unpleasant travelling experience. These gigantic races, however, were no arguments for a degeneration amongst the rest of mankind. They were evidently a variety of man, co-existent with the ordinary races, but liable to be absorbed and gradually lost by intermarriage amongst other tribes of the ordinary standard. Occasional exhumations of such Titan skeletons would strengthen the common prejudice. They would be taken not for a local variety, but for an antediluvian or prehistoric type, from which the present races of man had arisen by gradual degeneration.

These cases of actual but misinterpreted experience, at the same time that they naturally must tend to fortify the popular prejudice, would also, by accounting for it, and engrafting it upon a reasonable origin, so far tend to take from it the reproach of a prejudice. Though erroneous, it would yet seem to us, in looking back upon it, a rational and even an inevitable opinion, having such plausible grounds to stand upon; plausible, I mean, until science and accurate examination of the several cases had begun to read them into a different construction. Yet, on the other hand, in spite of any colourable excuses that may be pleaded for this prejudice, it is pretty plain that, after all, there is in human nature a deep-laid predisposition to an obstinate

in the human race, which has in every age hypochondriacally regarded itself as under some fatal necessity of dwindling, much to have challenged public attention. As real para- doxes (spite of the idle meaning attached usually to the word *paradox*) have often no falsehood in them, so here, on 5 the contrary, was a falsehood which had in it nothing paradoxical. It contradicted all the indications of history and experience, which uniformly had pointed in the very opposite direction ; and so far it ought to have been para- doxical (that is, revolting to popular opinion) ; but was *not* 10

craze of this nature. Else why is it that, in every age alike, men have asserted or even assumed the downward tendency of the human race in all that regards *moral* qualities. For the *physical* degenera- tion of man there really were some apparent (though erroneous) arguments ; but for the moral degeneration, no argument at all, small or great. Yet, a bigotry of belief in this idle notion has always pre- vailed amongst moralists, Pagan alike and Christian. Horace, for example, informs us that

> " Aetas parentum, pejor avis, tulit
>   Nos nequiores — mox daturos
>   Progeniem vitiosiorem."

The last generation was worse, it seems, than the penultimate, as the present is worse than the last. We, however, of the present, bad as we may be, shall be kept in countenance by the coming generation, which will prove much worse than ourselves. On the same precedent, all the sermons through the three last centuries, if traced back through decennial periods, so as to form thirty successive strata, will be found regularly claiming the precedency in wickedness for the immediate period of the writer. Upon which theories, as men ought physically to have dwindled long ago into pigmies, so, on the other hand, morally they must by this time have left Sodom and Gomorrah far behind. What a strange animal must man upon this scheme offer to our con- templation ; shrinking in size, by graduated process, through every century, until at last he would not rise an inch from the ground · and, on the other hand, as regards villany, towering ever more and more up to the heavens. What a dwarf ! what a giant ! Why, the very crows would combine to destroy such a little monster.

so; for it fell in with prevailing opinions, with the oldest, blindest, and most inveterate of human superstitions. If extravagant, yet to the multitude it did not *seem* extravagant. So natural a craze, therefore, however baseless, would never 5 have carried Lord Monboddo's name into that meteoric notoriety and atmosphere of astonishment which soon invested it in England. And, in that case, my childhood would have escaped the deadliest blight of mortification and despondency that could have been incident to a most 10 morbid temperament concurring with a situation of visionary (yes! if you please, of fantastic) but still of most real distress.

How much it would have astonished Lord Monboddo to find himself made answerable — virtually made answerable, 15 by the evidence of secret tears — for the misery of an unknown child in Lancashire. Yet night and day these silent memorials of suffering were accusing him as the founder of a wound that could not be healed. It happened that the several volumes of his work lay for weeks in the 20 study of our tutor. Chance directed the eye of my brother, one day, upon that part of the work in which Lord M. unfolds his hypothesis that originally the human race had been a variety of the ape. On which hypothesis, by the way, Dr. Adam Clarke's substitution of *ape* for *serpent*, in 25 translating the word *nachash* (the brute tempter of Eve), would have fallen to the ground, since this would simply have been the case of one human being tempting another. It followed inevitably, according to Lord M., however painful it might be to human dignity, that, in this their early 30 stage of brutality, men must have had tails. My brother mused upon this reverie, and, in a few days, published an extract from some scoundrel's travels in Gombroon, according to which the Gombroonians had not yet emerged from this early condition of apedom. They, it seems, were still *homines caudati.* Overwhelming to me and stunning was the ignominy of this horrible discovery. Lord M. had not overlooked the natural question, In what way did men get rid of their tails? To speak the truth, they never *would* have got rid of them had they continued to run wild; but growing civilisation introduced arts, and the arts introduced sedentary habits. By these it was, by the mere necessity of continually sitting down, that men gradually wore off their tails! Well, and what should hinder the Gombroonians from sitting down? *Their* tailors and shoemakers would and could, I hope, sit down, as well as those of Tigrosylvania. Why not? Ay, but my brother had insisted already that they *had* no tailors, that they *had* no shoemakers; which, *then*, I did not care much about, as it merely put back the clock of our history — throwing us into an earlier, and therefore, perhaps, into a more warlike stage of society. But, as the case stood now, this want of tailors, &c., showed clearly that the process of sitting down, so essential to the ennobling of the race, had not commenced. My brother, with an air of consolation, suggested that I might even now, without an hour's delay, compel the whole nation to sit down for six hours a day, which would always "make a beginning." But the truth would remain as before — viz., that I was the king of a people that had tails; and the slow, slow process by which, in a course of many centuries, their posterity might rub them off, a hope of vintages never to be enjoyed by any generations that are yet heaving in sight — *that* was to me the worst form of despair.

Still there was one resource: if I "didn't like it" — meaning the state of things in Gombroon — I might "abdicate." Yes, I knew *that*. I might abdicate; and, once having cut the connection between myself and the poor abject islanders, I might seem to have no further interest in the degradation that affected them. After such a

disruption between us, what was it to me if they had even three tails apiece? Ah, *that* was fine talking; but this connection with my poor subjects had grown up so slowly and so genially, in the midst of struggles so constant against the
5 encroachments of my brother and his rascally people; we had suffered so much together; and the filaments connecting them with my heart were so aerially fine and fantastic, but for that reason so inseverable, that I abated nothing of my anxiety on their account; making this difference only in my
10 legislation and administrative cares, that I pursued them more in a spirit of despondency, and retreated more shyly from communicating them. It was in vain that my brother counselled me to dress my people in the Roman toga, as the best means of concealing their ignominious appendages: if
15 he meant this as comfort, it was none to me; the disgrace lay in the fact, not in its publication; and, in my heart, though I continued to honour Lord Monboddo (whom I heard my guardian also daily delighting to honour) as a good Grecian, yet secretly I cursed the Aoristus Primus, as
20 the indirect occasion of a misery which was not and could not be comprehended.

From this deep degradation of myself and my people, I was drawn off at intervals to contemplate a different mode of degradation affecting two persons, twin sisters, whom I
25 saw intermittingly; sometimes once a-week, sometimes frequently on each separate day. You have heard, reader, of pariahs. The pathos of that great idea possibly never reached you. Did it ever strike you how far that idea had extended? Do not fancy it peculiar to Hindostan. Before
30 Delhi was, before Agra, or Lahore, might the pariah say, I was. The most interesting, if only as the most mysterious, race of ancient days, the Pelasgi, that overspread, in early times of Greece, the total Mediterranean — a race distinguished for beauty and for intellect, and sorrowful beyond

all power of man to read the cause that could lie deep
enough for so imperishable an impression — *they* were
pariahs. The Jews that, in the twenty-eighth chapter of
Deuteronomy, were cursed in a certain contingency with a
sublimer curse than ever rang through the passionate wrath
of prophecy, and that afterwards, in Jerusalem, cursed themselves, voluntarily taking on their own heads, and on the
heads of their children's children for ever and ever, the
guilt of innocent blood — *they* are pariahs to this hour.
Yet for *them* there has ever shone a sullen light of hope.
The gipsies, for whom no conscious or acknowledged hope
burns through the mighty darkness that surrounds them —
they are pariahs of pariahs. Lepers were a race of mediæval pariahs, rejected of men, that now have gone to rest.
But travel into the forests of the Pyrenees, and there you
will find their modern representatives in the Cagots. Are
these Pyrenean Cagots Pagans? Not at all. They are
good Christians. Wherefore, then, that low door in the
Pyrenean churches, through which the Cagots are forced
to enter, and which, obliging them to stoop almost to the
ground, is a perpetual memento of their degradation?
Wherefore is it that men of pure Spanish blood will hold
no intercourse with the Cagot? Wherefore is it that even
the shadow of a Cagot, if it falls across a fountain, is held
to have polluted that fountain? All this points to some
dreadful taint of guilt, real or imputed, in ages far
remote.[1]

[1] The name and history of the Pyrenean Cagots are equally obscure.
Some have supposed that, during the period of the Gothic warfare with
the Moors, the Cagots were a Christian tribe that betrayed the Christian cause and interests at a critical moment. But all is conjecture.
As to the name, Southey has somewhere offered a possible interpretation of it; but it struck me as far from felicitous, and not what might
have been expected from Southey, whose vast historical research and
commanding talent should naturally have unlocked this most mysterious

But in ages far nearer to ourselves, nay, in our own
generation, and our own land, are many pariahs, sitting
amongst us all, nay, oftentimes sitting (yet not recognised
for what they really are) at good men's tables. How general is that sensuous dulness, that deafness of the heart,
which the Scriptures attribute to human beings! "Having
ears, they hear not; and, seeing, they do not understand."
In the very act of facing or touching a dreadful object,
they will utterly deny its existence. Men say to me daily,
when I ask them, in passing, "Anything in this morning's
paper?" "Oh no, nothing at all." And, as I never had
any other answer, I am bound to suppose that there never
was anything in a daily newspaper; and, therefore, that
the horrible burden of misery and of change which a century accumulates as its *facit* or total result, has not been
distributed at all amongst its thirty-six thousand five hundred and twenty-five days: every day, it seems, was separately a blank day, yielding absolutely nothing — what
children call a deaf nut, offering no kernel; and yet the
total product has caused angels to weep and tremble.
Meantime, when I come to look at the newspaper with my
own eyes, I am astonished at the misreport of my inform-
ants. Were there no other section in it than simply that
allotted to the police reports, oftentimes I stand aghast at
the revelations there made of human life and the human
heart — at its colossal guilt, and its colossal misery; at the
suffering which oftentimes throws its shadow over palaces,

of modern secrets, if any unlocking does yet lie within the resources of
human skill and combining power, now that so many ages divide
us from the original steps of the case. I may here mention, as a fact
accidentally made known to myself, and apparently not known to
Southey, that the Cagots, under a name very slightly altered, are
found in France also, as well as Spain; and in provinces of France
that have no connection at all with Spain.

and the grandeur of mute endurance which sometimes glori-
fies a cottage. Here transpires the dreadful truth of what
is going on for ever under the thick curtains of domestic
life, close behind us, and before us, and all around us.
Newspapers are evanescent, and are too rapidly recurrent,
and people see nothing great in what is familiar, nor can ever
be trained to read the silent and the shadowy in what, for
the moment, is covered with the babbling garrulity of daylight. I suppose now that, in the next generation after that
which is here concerned, had any neighbour of our tutor
been questioned on the subject of a domestic tragedy, which
travelled through its natural stages in a leisurely way, and
under the eyes of good Dr. S——, he would have replied,
"Tragedy! oh, sir, nothing of the kind! You have been
misled; the gentleman must lie under a mistake: perhaps it
was in the next street." No, it was *not* in the next street;
and the gentleman does not lie under a mistake, or, in fact,
lie at all. The simple truth is, blind old neighbour, that
you, being rarely in the house, and, *when* there, only in one
particular room, saw no more of what was hourly going on,
than if you had been residing with the Sultan of Bokhara.
But I, a child between seven and eight years old, had access
everywhere. I was privileged, and had the *entrée* even of
the female apartments; one consequence of which was, that
I put *this* and *that* together. A number of syllables, that
each for itself separately might have meant nothing at all,
did yet, when put together, through weeks and months, read
for *my* eyes into sentences as deadly and significant as *Tekel*,
Pharsin. And another consequence was, that being, on
account of my age, nobody at all, or very near it, I sometimes witnessed things that perhaps it had not been meant
for anybody to witness, or perhaps some half-conscious
negligence overlooked my presence. "Saw things! What
was it now? Was it a man at midnight, with a dark lantern

and a six-barrel revolver?" No *that* was not in the least
like what I saw: it was a great deal more like what I will
endeavour to describe. Imagine two young girls, of what
exact age I really do not know, but apparently from twelve
to fourteen, twins, remarkably plain in person and features,
unhealthy, and obscurely reputed to be idiots. Whether
they really were such was more than I knew, or could
devise any plan for learning. Without dreaming of anything unkind or uncourteous, my original impulse had
been to say, "If you please, are you idiots?" But I felt
that such a question had an air of coarseness about it,
though, for my own part, I had long reconciled myself
to being called an idiot by my brother. There was, however, a further difficulty: breathed as a gentle, murmuring
whisper, the question might possibly be reconciled to an
indulgent ear as confidential and tender. Even to take a
liberty with those you love, is to show your trust in their
affection; but, alas! these poor girls were deaf; and to
have shouted out, "Are you idiots, if you please?" in a
voice that would have rung down three flights of stairs,
promised (as I felt, without exactly seeing why) a dreadful
exaggeration to whatever incivility might, at any rate, attach
to the question; and some *did* attach, that was clear even
if warbled through an air of Cherubini's, and accompanied
on the flute. Perhaps they were *not* idiots, and only seemed
to be such from the slowness of apprehension naturally connected with deafness. That I saw them but seldom, arose
from their peculiar position in the family. Their father had
no private fortune; his income from the church was very
slender; and, though considerably increased by the allowance made for us, his two pupils, still, in a great town, and
with so large a family, it left him little room for luxuries.
Consequently, he never had more than two servants, and at
times only one. Upon this plea rose the scheme of the

mother for employing these two young girls in menial offices
of the household economy. One reason for that was, that
she thus indulged her dislike for them, which she took no
pains to conceal; and thus, also, she withdrew them from
the notice of strangers. In this way, it happened that I saw 5
them myself but at uncertain intervals. Gradually, however, I came to be aware of their forlorn condition, to pity
them, and to love them. The poor twins were undoubtedly
plain, to the degree which is called, by unfeeling people, ugli-
ness. They were also deaf, as I have said, and they were 10
scrofulous; one of them was disfigured by the small-pox;
they had glimmering eyes, red, like the eyes of ferrets, and
scarcely half-open; and they did not walk so much as
stumble along. There, you have the worst of them. Now,
hear something on the other side. What first won my pity 15
was, their affection for each other, united to their constant
sadness; secondly, a notion which had crept into my head,
probably derived from something said in my presence by
elder people, that they were destined to an early death;
and, lastly, the incessant persecutions of their mother. This 20
lady belonged, by birth, to a more elevated rank than that of
her husband, and she was remarkably well-bred as regarded
her manners. But she had probably a weak understanding:
she was shrewish in her temper; was a severe economist;
a merciless exactor of what she viewed as duty; and, in per- 25
secuting her two unhappy daughters, though she yielded
blindly to her unconscious dislike of them, as creatures that
disgraced her, she was not aware, perhaps, of ever having
put forth more expressions of anger and severity than were
absolutely required to rouse the constitutional torpor of 30
her daughters' nature; and where disgust has once rooted
itself, and been habitually expressed in tones of harshness,
the mere sight of the hateful object mechanically calls forth
the eternal tones of anger, without distinct consciousness

or separate intention in the speaker. Loud speaking, besides, or even shouting, was required by the deafness of the two girls. From anger so constantly discharging its thunders, naturally they did not show open signs of recoiling;
5 but that they felt it deeply, may be presumed from their sensibility to kindness. My own experience showed *that;* for, as often as I met them, we exchanged kisses; and my wish had always been to beg them, if they really *were* idiots, not to mind it, since I should not like them the less on that
10 account. This wish of mine never came to utterance; but not the less they were aware, by my manner of salutation, that one person at least, amongst those who might be considered strangers, did not find anything repulsive about them; and the pleasure they felt was expressed broadly
15 upon their kindly faces.

Such was the outline of their position; and, that being explained, what I saw was simply this; it composed a silent and symbolic scene, a momentary interlude in dumb show, which interpreted itself and settled for ever in my recollec-
20 tion, as if it had prophesied and interpreted the event which soon followed. They were resting from toil, and both sitting down. This had lasted for perhaps ten or fifteen minutes. Suddenly from below-stairs the voice of angry summons rang up to their ears. Both rose in an instant, as if the echoing
25 scourge of some avenging Tisiphone were uplifted above their heads; both opened their arms; flung them round each other's necks; and then, unclasping them, parted to their separate labours. This was my last rememberable interview with the two sisters; in a week both were corpses.
30 They had died, I believe, of scarlatina, and very nearly at the same moment.

But surely it was no matter for grief, that the two scrofulous idiots were dead and buried. Oh no! Call them

idiots at your pleasure, serfs, or slaves, strulbrugs [1] or pariahs
— *their* case was certainly not worsened by being booked for
places in the grave. Idiocy, for anything I know, may, in
that vast kingdom, enjoy a natural precedency ; scrofula and
leprosy may have some mystic privilege in a coffin ; and the 5
pariahs of the upper earth may form the aristocracy of the
dead. That the idiots, real or reputed, were at rest — that
their warfare was accomplished — might, if a man happened
to know enough, be interpreted as a glorious festival. The
sisters were seen no more upon staircases or in bedrooms, 10
and deadly silence had succeeded to the sound of continual
uproars. Memorials of *them* were none surviving on earth.

[1] "*Strulbrugs*" : — Hardly *strulbrugs*, will be the thought of the
learned reader, who knows that *young* women could not be strulbrugs ;
since the true strulbrug was one who, from base fear of dying, had
lingered on into an old age omnivorous of every genial or vital impulse.
The strulbrug of Swift (and Swift, being his horrid creator, ought to
understand his own horrid creation) was a wreck, a shell, that had
been burned hollow, and cancered by the fierce furnace of life. His
clock-work was gone, or carious ; only some miserable fragment of a
pendulum continued to oscillate paralytically from mere incapacity of
anything so abrupt, and therefore so vigorous, as a decided HALT !
However, the use of this dreadful word may be reasonably extended
to the young who happen to have become essentially old in misery.
Intensity of a suffering existence may compensate the want of extension ;
and a boundless depth of misery may be a transformed expression for a
boundless duration of misery. The most aged person, to all appearance, that ever came under my eyes, was an infant — hardly eight
months old. He was the illegitimate son of a poor idiot girl, who had
herself been shamefully ill-treated ; and the poor infant, falling under
the care of an enraged grandmother, who felt herself at once burdened
and disgraced, was certainly not better treated. He was dying, when I
saw him, of a lingering malady, with features expressive of frantic
misery ; and it seemed to me that he looked at least three centuries old.
One might have fancied him one of Swift's strulbrugs, that, through long
attenuation and decay, had dwindled back into infancy, with one organ
only left perfect — the organ of fear and misery.

Not *they* it was that furnished mementoes of themselves.
The mother it was, the father it was — that mother who by
persecution had avenged the wounds offered to her pride;
that father who had tolerated this persecution; — she it was,
5 he it was, that by the altered glances of her haunted eye,
that by the altered character of his else stationary habits,
had revived for *me* a spectacle, once real, of visionary twin
sisters, moving for ever up and down the stairs — sisters,
patient, humble, silent, that snatched convulsively at a
10 loving smile, or loving gesture, from a child, as at some
message of remembrance from God, whispering to them,
"You are not forgotten" — sisters born apparently for the
single purpose of suffering, whose trials, it is true, were
over, and could not be repeated; but (alas for her who had
15 been their cause!) could not be recalled. Her face grew
thin, her eye sunken and hollow, after the death of her
daughters; and, meeting her on the staircase, I sometimes
fancied that she did not see *me* so much as something
beyond me. Did any misfortune befall her after this
20 double funeral? Did the Nemesis that waits upon the
sighs of children pursue her steps? Not apparently: externally, things went well; her sons were reasonably prosperous; her handsome daughter — for she had a more
youthful daughter, who really *was* handsome — continued
25 to improve in personal attractions; and some years after,
I have heard, she married happily. But from herself, so
long as I continued to know her, the altered character of
countenance did not depart, nor the gloomy eye, that
seemed to converse with secret and visionary objects.

30   This result from the irrevocable past was not altogether
confined to herself. It is one evil attached to chronic and
domestic oppression, that it draws into its vortex, as unwilling, or even as loathing, co-operators, others who either see
but partially the wrong they are abetting, or, in cases where

they *do* see it, are unable to make head against it, through
the inertia of their own nature, or through the coercion of
circumstances. Too clearly, by the restless irritation of
his manner for some time after the children's death, their
father testified, in a language not fully, perhaps, perceived
by himself, or meant to be understood by others, that to his
inner conscience he also was not clear of blame. Had he
then in any degree sanctioned the injustice which sometimes he must have witnessed? Far from it: he had been
roused from his habitual indolence into energetic expressions of anger: he had put an end to the wrong, when it
came openly before him: I had myself heard him say on
many occasions, with patriarchal fervour, "Woman, they
are your children, and God made them. Show mercy to
them, as you expect it for yourself." But he must have
been aware, that, for any three instances of tyrannical
usage that fell under his notice, at least five hundred would
escape it. That was the sting of the case — that was its
poisonous aggravation. But with a nature that sought for
peace before all things, in this very worst of its aggra-
vations was found a morbid cure — the effectual temptation to wilful blindness and forgetfulness. The sting
became the palliation of the wrong, and the poison became
its anodyne. For together with the five hundred hidden
wrongs, arose the necessity that *must* be hidden. Could
he be pinned on, morning, noon, and night, to his wife's
apron? And if not, what else should he do by angry
interferences at chance times, than add special vindictive
impulses to those of general irritation and dislike? Some
truth there was in this, it cannot be denied: innumerable
cases arise, in which a man the most just is obliged, in some
imperfect sense, to connive at injustice; his chance experience must convince him that injustice is continually going
on; and yet, in any attempt to intercept it or to check it,

he is met and baffled by the insuperable obstacles of house
hold necessities. Dr. S——, therefore, surrendered himself, as under a coercion that was *none* of his creating, to
a passive acquiescence and a blindness that soothed his
5 constitutional indolence; and he reconciled his feelings
to a tyranny which he tolerated, under some self-flattering
idea of submitting with resignation to a calamity that he
suffered.

Some years after this, I read the "Agamemnon" of
10 Æschylus; and then, in the prophetic horror with which
Cassandra surveys the regal abode in Mycenæ, destined to
be the scene of murders so memorable through the long
traditions of the Grecian stage, murders that, many centuries
after all the parties to them — perpetrators, sufferers, aven-
15 gers — had become dust and ashes, kindled again into
mighty life through a thousand years upon the vast theatres
of Athens and Rome, I retraced the horrors, not prophetic
but memorial, with which I myself had invested that humble dwelling of Dr. S——; and read again, repeated in
20 visionary proportions, the sufferings which there had darkened the days of people known to myself through two distinct successions — not, as was natural to expect, of parents
first, and then of children, but inversely of children and
parents. Manchester was not Mycenæ. No, but by many
25 degrees nobler. In some of the features most favourable
to tragic effects, it was so; and wanted only those idealising advantages for withdrawing mean details which are in
the gift of distance and hazy antiquity. Even at that day,
Manchester was far larger, teeming with more and with
30 stronger hearts; and it contained a population the most
energetic even in the *modern* world — how much more so,
therefore, by comparison with any race in *ancient* Greece,
inevitably rendered effeminate by dependence too generally
upon slaves. Add to this superior energy in Lancashire,

the immeasurably profounder feelings generated by the
mysteries which stand behind Christianity, as compared
with the shallow mysteries that stood behind Paganism,
and it would be easy to draw the inference, that, in the
capacity for the infinite and the impassioned, for horror 5
and for pathos, Mycenæ could have had no pretensions to
measure herself against Manchester. Not that I had drawn
such an inference myself. Why should I? there being nothing to suggest the points in which the two cities differed,
but only the single one in which they agreed — viz., the 10
dusky veil that overshadowed in both the noonday tragedies haunting their household recesses; which veil was
raised only to the gifted eyes of a Cassandra, or to eyes
that, like my own, had experimentally become acquainted
with them as facts. Pitiably mean is he that measures the 15
relations of such cases by the scenical apparatus of purple
and gold. That which never *has* been apparelled in royal
robes, and hung with theatrical jewels, is but suffering from
an accidental fraud, having the same right to them that
any similar misery can have, or calamity upon an equal 20
scale. These proportions are best measured from the fathom-
ing ground of a real uncounterfeit sympathy.

I have mentioned already that we had four male guardians
(a fifth being my mother). These four were B., E., G., and
H. The two consonants, B. and G., gave us little trouble. 25
G., the wisest of the whole band, lived at a distance of
more than one hundred miles: him, therefore, we rarely
saw; but B., living within four miles of Greenhay, washed
his hands of us, by inviting us, every now and then, to
spend a few days at his house. 30
At this house, which stood in the country, there was a
family of amiable children, who were more skilfully trained
in their musical studies than at that day was usual. They

sang the old English glees and madrigals, and correctly
enough for me, who, having, even at that childish age, a
preternatural sensibility to music, had also, as may be supposed, the most entire want of musical knowledge. No
5 blunders could do much to mar *my* pleasure. There first I
heard the concertos of Corelli; but also, which far more
profoundly affected me, a few selections from Jomelli and
Cimarosa. With Handel I had long been familiar, for the
famous chorus-singers of Lancashire sang continually at
10 churches the most effective parts from his chief oratorios.
Mozart was yet to come; for, except perhaps at the opera
in London, even at this time his music was most imperfectly diffused through England. But, above all, a thing
which to my dying day I could never forget, at the house
15 of this guardian I heard sung a long canon of Cherubini's.
Forty years later, I heard it again, and better sung; but
at that time I needed nothing better. It was sung by four
male voices, and rose into a region of thrilling passion,
such as my heart had always dimly craved and hungered
20 after, but which now first interpreted itself, as a physical
possibility, to my ear.

My brother did not share my inexpressible delight; his
taste ran in a different channel; and the arrangements of
the house did not meet his approbation; particularly this,
25 that either Mrs. B. herself, or else the governess, was always
present when the young ladies joined our society, which my
brother considered particularly vulgar; since natural propriety and decorum should have whispered to an old lady
that a young gentleman might have " things " to say to her
30 daughters which he could not possibly intend for the general
ear of eavesdroppers — things tending to the confidential or
the sentimental, which none but a shameless old lady would
seek to participate; by that means compelling a young man
to talk as loud as if he were addressing a mob at Charing

Cross, or reading the Riot Act. There were other out-of-door amusements, amongst which a swing — which I mention for the sake of illustrating the passive obedience which my brother levied upon me, either through my conscience, as mastered by his doctrine of primogeniture, or, as in this case, through my sensibility to shame under his taunts of cowardice. It was a most ambitious swing, ascending to a height beyond any that I have since seen in fairs or public gardens. Horror was at my heart regularly as the swing reached its most aerial altitude; for the oily, swallow-like fluency of the swoop downwards threatened always to make me sick, in which case it is probable that I must have relaxed my hold of the ropes, and have been projected, with fatal violence, to the ground. But, in defiance of all this miserable panic, I continued to swing whenever he tauntingly invited me. It was well that my brother's path in life soon ceased to coincide with my own; else I should infallibly have broken my neck in confronting perils which brought me neither honour nor profit, and in accepting defiances which, issue how they might, won self-reproach from myself, and sometimes a gaiety of derision from *him*. One only of these defiances I declined. There was a horse of this same guardian B.'s, who always, after listening to Cherubini's music, grew irritable to excess; and, if anybody mounted him, would seek relief to his wounded feelings in kicking, more or less violently, for an hour. This habit endeared him to my brother, who acknowledged to a propensity of the same amiable kind ; protesting that an abstract desire of kicking seized him always after hearing good performers on particular instruments, especially the bagpipes. Of kicking? But of kicking what or *whom?* I fear of kicking the venerable public collectively, creditors without exception, but also as many of the debtors as might be found at large ; doctors of medicine more especially, but

with no absolute immunity for the majority of their patients,
Jacobins, but not the less Anti-Jacobins; every Calvinist,
which seems reasonable; but then also, which is intolerable,
every Arminian. Is philosophy able to account for this mor-
5 bid affection, and particularly when it takes the restricted
form (as sometimes it does, in the bagpipe case), of seeking
furiously to kick the piper, instead of paying him? In this
case, my brother was urgent with me to mount *en croupe*
behind himself. But, weak as I usually was, this proposal I
10 resisted as an immediate suggestion of the fiend; for I had
heard, and have since known proofs of it, that a horse, when
he is ingeniously vicious, sometimes has the power, in lashing
out, of curving round his hoofs, so as to lodge them, by way
of indorsement, in the small of his rider's back; and, of
15 course, he would have an advantage for such a purpose, in
the case of a rider sitting on the crupper. That sole invitation I persisted in declining.

A young gentleman had joined us as a fellow-student
under the care of our tutor. He was an only son; indeed,
20 the only child of an amiable widow, whose love and hopes
all centred in *him*. He was destined to inherit several separate estates, and a great deal had been done to spoil him by
indulgent aunts; but his good natural disposition defeated
all these efforts; and, upon joining us, he proved to be a
25 very amiable boy, clever, quick at learning, and abundantly
courageous. In the summer months, his mother usually took
a house out in the country, sometimes on one side of Manchester, sometimes on another. At these rusticating seasons,
he had often much further to come than ourselves, and on
30 that account he rode horseback. Generally it was a fierce
mountain-pony that he rode; and it was worth while to
cultivate the pony's acquaintance, for the sake of understanding the extent to which the fiend can sometimes incarnate
himself in a horse. I do not trouble the reader with any

account of his tricks, and drolleries, and scoundrelisms; but
this I may mention, that he had the propensity ascribed
many centuries ago to the Scandinavian horses for sharing
and practically asserting his share in the angry passions of
a battle. He would fight, or attempt to fight, on his rider's 5
side, by biting, rearing, and suddenly wheeling round, for
the purpose of lashing out when he found himself within
kicking range.[1] This little monster was coal-black; and, in
virtue of his carcase, would not have seemed very formidable; but his head made amends — it was the head of a 10
buffalo, or of a bison, and his vast jungle of mane was
the mane of a lion. His eyes, by reason of this intolerable and unshorn mane, one did not often see, except
as lights that sparkled in the rear of a thicket; but, once
seen, they were not easily forgotten, for their malignity was 15
diabolic. A few miles more or less being a matter of indifference to one who was so well mounted, O. would sometimes ride out with us to the field of battle; and, by
manœuvring so as to menace the enemy on the flanks,
in skirmishes he did good service. But at length came 20
a day of pitched battle. The enemy had mustered in
unusual strength, and would certainly have accomplished
the usual result of putting us to flight with more than
usual ease, but, under the turn which things took, their
very numbers aided their overthrow, by deepening their 25
confusion. O. had, on this occasion, accompanied us;
and, as he had hitherto taken no very decisive part in
the war, confining himself to distant "demonstrations,"
the enemy did not much regard his presence in the
field. This carelessness threw them into a dense mass, 30
upon which my brother's rapid eye saw instantly the

---

[1] This was a manœuvre regularly taught to the Austrian cavalry in
the middle of the last century, as a ready way of opening the doors of
cottages.

opportunity offered for operating most effectually by a
charge. O. saw it too; and happening to have his spurs
on, he complied cheerfully with my brother's suggestion.
He had the advantage of a slight descent: the wicked
5 pony went down "with a will": his echoing hoofs drew
the general gaze upon him: his head, his leonine mane,
his diabolic eyes, did the rest; and in a moment the
whole hostile array had broken, and was in rapid flight
across the brick-fields. I leave the reader to judge
10 whether "Te Deum" would be sung on that night. A
Gazette Extraordinary was issued; and my brother had
really some reason for his assertion, "that in conscience
he could not think of comparing Cannæ to this smashing
defeat"; since at Cannæ many brave men had refused
15 to fly—the consul himself, Terentius Varro, amongst
them; but, in the present rout, there was no Terentius
Varro—*everybody* fled.

The victory, indeed, considered in itself, was complete.
But it had consequences which we had not looked for. In
20 the ardour of our conflict, neither my brother nor myself
had remarked a stout, square-built man, mounted on an
uneasy horse, who sat quietly in his saddle as spectator
of the battle, and, in fact, as the sole non-combatant
present. This man, however, had been observed by O.,
25 both before and after his own brilliant charge; and, by
the description, there could be no doubt that it had
been our guardian B., as also, by the description of the
horse, we could as little doubt that he had been mounted
on Cherubini. My brother's commentary was in a tone
30 of bitter complaint, that so noble an opportunity should
have been lost for strengthening O.'s charge. But the
consequences of this incident were graver than we anticipated. A general board of our guardians, vowels and
consonants, was summoned to investigate the matter. The

origin of the feud, or "war," as my brother called it, was inquired into. As well might the war of Troy or the pur-ser's accounts from the Argonautic expedition have been overhauled. Ancient night and chaos had closed over the "incunabula belli"; and that point was given up in despair. 5 But what hindered a general pacification, no matter in how many wrongs the original dispute had arisen? Who stopped the way which led to peace? Not we, was our firm declara-tion; we were most pacifically inclined, and ever had been; we were, in fact, little saints. But the enemy could not be 10 brought to any terms of accommodation. "That we will try," said the vowel amongst our guardians, Mr. E. He, being a magistrate, had naturally some weight with the pro-prietors of the cotton factory. The foremen of the several floors were summoned, and gave it as their humble opinion 15 that we, the aristocratic party in the war, were as bad as the *sansculottes* — "not a pin to choose between us." Well, but no matter for the past: could any plan be devised for a pacific future? Not easily. The work-people were so thoroughly independent of their employers, and so careless 20 of their displeasure, that finally this only settlement was available, as wearing any promise of permanence — viz., that we should alter our hours, so as not to come into collision with the exits or returns of the boys.

Under this arrangement, a sort of hollow armistice pre- 25 vailed for some time; but it was beginning to give way, when suddenly an internal change in our own home put an end to the war for ever. My brother, amongst his many accomplishments, was distinguished for his skill in drawing. Some of his sketches had been shown to Mr. de Louther- 30 bourg, an academician well known in those days, esteemed even in these days, after he has been dead for forty or fifty years, and personally a distinguished favourite with the king (George III). He pronounced a very flattering opinion upon

my brother's promise of excellence.   This being known, a
fee of a thousand guineas was offered to Mr. L. by the
guardians; and finally that gentleman took charge of my
brother as a pupil.   Now, therefore, my brother, King of
Tigrosylvania, scourge of Gombroon, separated from me;
and, as it turned out, for ever.   I never saw him again;
and, at Mr. de L.'s house in Hammersmith, before he had
completed his sixteenth year, he died of typhus fever.   And
thus it happened that a little gold-dust skilfully applied put
an end to wars that else threatened to extend into a Carthaginian length.   In one week's time

> " Hi motus animorum atque hæc certamina tanta
>   Pulveris exigui jactu compressa quiêrunt."

A MEETING WITH LAMB

AMONGST the earliest literary acquaintances I made was
that with the inimitable Charles Lamb : inimitable, I say,
but the word is too limited in its meaning ; for, as is said
of Milton in that well-known life of him attached to all
common editions of the " Paradise Lost " (Fenton's, I think),   5
" in both senses he was above imitation."   Yes ; it was as
impossible to the moral nature of Charles Lamb that he
should imitate another as, in an intellectual sense, it was
impossible that any other should successfully imitate him.
To write with patience even, not to say genially, for Charles 10
Lamb it was a very necessity of his constitution that he
should write from his own wayward nature ; and that nature
was so peculiar that no other man, the ablest at mimicry,
could counterfeit its voice.   But let me not anticipate ; for
these were opinions about Lamb which I had not when I 15
first knew him, nor could have had by any reasonable title.
" Elia," be it observed, the exquisite " Elia," was then
unborn ; Lamb had as yet published nothing to the world
which proclaimed him in his proper character of a most
original man of genius[1]: at best, he could have been 20

---

[1] " *Man of genius* " . . . " *man of talent* " : — I have, in another
place, laid down what I conceive to be the true ground of distinction
between *genius* and *talent ;* which lies mainly in this — that genius is
intellectual power impregnated with the *moral* nature, and expresses a
synthesis of the active in man with his original organic capacity of
pleasure and pain.   Hence the very word *genius*, because the *genial*
nature in its whole organization is expressed and involved in it.

thought no more than a man of talent — and of talent
moving in a narrow path, with a power rather of mimick-
ing the quaint and the fantastic than any large grasp over
catholic beauty. And, therefore, it need not offend the most
5 doting admirer of Lamb as he is *now* known to us, a
brilliant star for ever fixed in the firmament of English
Literature, that I acknowledge myself to have sought his
acquaintance rather under the reflex honour he had enjoyed
of being known as Coleridge's friend than for any which
10 he yet held directly and separately in his own person. My
earliest advances towards this acquaintance had an inaus-
picious aspect; and it may be worth while reporting the
circumstances, for they were characteristic of Charles
Lamb; and the immediate result was — that we parted,
15 not perhaps (as Lamb says of his philosophic friend R.
and the Parisians) "with mutual contempt," but at least
with coolness ; and, on my part, with something that might
have even turned to disgust — founded, however, entirely
on my utter misapprehension of Lamb's character and his
20 manners — had it not been for the winning goodness of
Miss Lamb, before which all resentment must have melted
in a moment.

It was either late in 1804 or early in 1805, according to
my present computations, that I had obtained from a literary
25 friend a letter of introduction to Mr. Lamb. All that I
knew of his works was his play of " John Woodvil," which

Hence, also, arises the reason that genius is always peculiar and individual ; one man's genius never exactly repeats another man's. But
talent is the same in all men ; and that which is effected by talent can
never serve to identify or indicate its author. Hence, too, that, although
talent is the object of respect, it never conciliates love ; you love a man
of talent perhaps *in concreto*, but not talent ; whereas genius, even for
itself, is idolized. I am the more proud of this distinction since I have
seen the utter failure of Mr. Coleridge, judging from his attempt in his
" Table-Talk."

I had bought in Oxford, and perhaps *I* only had bought throughout that great University, at the time of my matriculation there, about the Christmas of 1803. Another book fell into my hands on that same morning, I recollect — the " Gebir " of Mr. Walter Savage Landor, which aston- 5 ished me by the splendour of its descriptions (for I had opened accidentally upon the sea-nymph's marriage with Tamor, the youthful brother of Gebir) — and I bought this also. Afterwards, when placing these two most unpopular of books on the same shelf with the other far holier 10 idols of my heart, the joint poems of Wordsworth and Coleridge as then associated in the " Lyrical Ballads " — poems not equally unknown, perhaps a *little* better known, but only with the result of being more openly scorned, rejected — I could not but smile internally at 15 the fair prospect I had of congregating a library which no man had read but myself. " John Woodvil " I had almost studied, and Miss Lamb's pretty " High-Born Helen," and the ingenious imitations of Burton; these I had read, and, to a certain degree, must have admired, for 20 some parts of them had settled without effort in my memory. I had read also the *Edinburgh* notice of them ; and with what contempt may be supposed from the fact that my veneration for Wordsworth transcended all that I felt for any created being, past or present ; insomuch that, 25 in the summer, or spring rather, of that same year, and full eight months before I first went to Oxford, I had ventured to address a letter to him, through his publishers, the Messrs. Longman (which letter, Miss Wordsworth in after years assured me they believed to be the production of 30 some person much older than I represented myself), and that in due time I had been honoured by a long answer from Wordsworth ; an honour which, I well remember, kept me awake, from mere excess of pleasure, through a long

night in June 1803. It was not to be supposed that the very feeblest of admirations could be shaken by mere scorn and contumely, unsupported by any shadow of a reason. Wordsworth, therefore, could not have suffered
5 in any man's opinion from the puny efforts of this new autocrat amongst reviewers; but what was said of Lamb, though not containing one iota of criticism, either good or bad, had certainly more point and cleverness. The supposition that "John Woodvil" might be a lost drama,
10 recovered from the age of Thespis, and entitled to the hircus, &c., must, I should think, have won a smile from Lamb himself; or why say "Lamb himself," which means "*even* Lamb," when he would have been the *very* first to laugh (as he was afterwards among the first to hoot at his
15 own farce), provided only he could detach his mind from the ill-nature and hard contempt which accompanied the wit. This wit had certainly not dazzled my eyes in the slightest degree. So far as I was left at leisure by a more potent order of poetry to think of the "John Woodvil" at
20 all, I had felt and acknowledged a delicacy and tenderness in the situations as well as the sentiments, but disfigured, as I thought, by quaint, grotesque, and *mimetic* phraseology. The main defect, however, of which I complained, was defect of power. I thought Lamb had no right to
25 take his station amongst the inspired writers who had just then risen to throw new blood into our literature, and to breathe a breath of life through the worn-out, or, at least, torpid organization of the national mind. He belonged, I thought, to the old literature; and, as a poet, he certainly
30 does. There were in his verses minute scintillations of genius — now and then, even a subtle sense of beauty; and there were shy graces, lurking half-unseen, like violets in the shade. But there was no power on a colossal scale; no breadth; no choice of great subjects; no wrestling

with difficulty; no creative energy. So I thought then;
and so I should think now, if Lamb were viewed chiefly as
a poet. Since those days he has established his right to a
seat in any company. But why? and in what character?
As "Elia":—the essays of "Elia" are as exquisite a gem
amongst the jewellery of literature as any nation can show.
They do not, indeed, suggest to the typifying imagination
a Last Supper of Da Vinci or a Group from the Sistine
Chapel; but they suggest some exquisite cabinet painting;
such, for instance, as that Carlo Dolce known to all who
have visited Lord Exeter's place of Burleigh (by the way,
I bar the allusion to *Charles* Lamb which a shameless
punster suggests in the name *Carlo Dolce*); and in this
also resembling that famous picture — that many critics
(Hazlitt amongst others) can see little or nothing in it.
Quam nihil ad genium, Papiniane, tuum! Those, therefore,
err, in my opinion who present Lamb to our notice
amongst the poets. Very pretty, very elegant, very tender,
very beautiful verses he has written; nay, twice he has
written verses of extraordinary force, almost demoniac
force — viz., "The Three Graves," and "The Gipsy's
Malison." But, speaking generally, he writes verses as
one to whom that function was a secondary and occasional function, not his original and natural vocation, —
not an ἔργον, but a παρέργον.

For the reasons, therefore, I have given, never thinking
of Charles Lamb as a poet, and, at that time, having no
means for judging of him in any other character, I had
requested the letter of introduction to him rather with a
view to some further knowledge of Coleridge (who was then
absent from England) than from any special interest about
Lamb himself. However, I felt the extreme discourtesy of
approaching a man and asking for his time and civility
under such an avowal: and the letter, therefore, as I

believe, or as I requested, represented me in the light of an
admirer. I hope it did; for that character might have
some excuse for what followed, and heal the unpleasant
impression likely to be left by a sort of *fracas* which
5 occurred at my first meeting with Lamb. This was so
characteristic of Lamb that I have often laughed at it
since I came to know what *was* characteristic of Lamb.

But first let me describe my brief introductory call upon
him at the India House. I had been told that he was
10 never to be found at home except in the evenings; and to
have called then would have been, in a manner, forcing
myself upon his hospitalities, and at a moment when
he might have confidential friends about him; besides
that, he was sometimes tempted away to the theatres. I
15 went, therefore, to the India House; made inquiries
amongst the servants; and, after some trouble (for *that*
was early in his Leadenhall Street career, and possibly he
was not much known), I was shown into a small room, or
else a small section of a large one (thirty-four years affects
20 one's remembrance of some circumstances), in which was a
very lofty writing-desk, separated by a still higher railing
from that part of the floor on which the profane — the
laity, like myself—were allowed to approach the *clerus*, or
clerkly rulers of the room. Within the railing sat, to the
25 best of my remembrance, six quill-driving gentlemen; not
gentlemen whose duty or profession it was merely to
drive the quill, but who were then driving it — *gens de
plume*, such *in esse*, as well as *in posse* — in act as well as
habit; for, as if they supposed me a spy sent by some
30 superior power to report upon the situation of affairs as
surprised by me, they were all too profoundly immersed
in their oriental studies to have any sense of my presence.
Consequently, I was reduced to a necessity of announcing
myself and my errand. I walked, therefore, into one of the

two open doorways of the railing, and stood closely by
the high stool of him who occupied the first place within
the little aisle. I touched his arm, by way of recalling
him from his lofty Leadenhall speculation to this sublunary world ; and, presenting my letter, asked if that gen- 5
tleman (pointing to the address) were really a citizen of
the present room ; for I had been repeatedly misled, by
the directions given me, into wrong rooms. The gentleman smiled ; it was a smile not to be forgotten. This was
Lamb. And here occurred a *very, very* little incident — 10
one of those which pass so fugitively that they are gone
and hurrying away into Lethe almost before your attention
can have arrested them; but it was an incident which,
to me, who happened to notice it, served to express the
courtesy and delicate consideration of Lamb's manners. 15
The seat upon which he sat was a very high one ; so
absurdly high, by the way, that I can imagine no possible
use or sense in such an altitude, unless it were to restrain
the occupant from playing truant at the fire by opposing
Alpine difficulties to his descent. 20

Whatever might be the original purpose of this aspiring
seat, one serious dilemma arose from it, and this it was
which gave the occasion to Lamb's act of courtesy. Somewhere there is an anecdote, meant to illustrate the ultra-
obsequiousness of the man, — either I have heard of it in 25
connexion with some actual man known to myself, or it is
told in a book of some historical coxcomb, — that, being
on horseback, and meeting some person or other whom it
seemed advisable to flatter, he actually dismounted, in
order to pay his court by a more ceremonious bow. In 30
Russia, as we all know, this was, at one time, upon meeting any of the Imperial family, an act of legal necessity :
and there, accordingly, but there only, it would have worn
no ludicrous aspect. Now, in this situation of Lamb's,

the act of descending from his throne, a very elaborate
process, with steps and stages analogous to those on
horseback — of slipping your right foot out of the stirrup,
throwing your leg over the crupper, &c. — was, to all
5 intents and purposes, the same thing as dismounting from
a great elephant of a horse. Therefore it both was, and
was felt to be by Lamb, supremely ludicrous. On the
other hand, to have sate still and stately upon this aerial
station, to have bowed condescendingly from this altitude,
10 would have been — not ludicrous indeed ; performed by a
very superb person and supported by a superb bow, it
might have been vastly fine, and even terrifying to many
young gentlemen under sixteen ; but it would have had an
air of ungentlemanly assumption. Between these extremes,
15 therefore, Lamb had to choose ;— between appearing ridiculous himself for a moment, by going through a ridiculous
evolution which no man could execute with grace ; or, on
the other hand, appearing lofty and assuming, in a degree
which his truly humble nature (for he was the humblest of
20 men in the pretensions which he put forward for himself)
must have shrunk from with horror. Nobody who knew
Lamb can doubt how the problem was solved : he began
to dismount instantly ; and, as it happened that the very
first *round* of his descent obliged him to turn his back
25 upon me as if for a sudden purpose of flight, he had an
excuse for laughing ; which he did heartily — saying, at the
same time, something to this effect : that I must not judge
from first appearances ; that he should revolve upon me ;
that he was not going to fly ; and other facetiæ, which
30 challenged a general laugh from the clerical brotherhood.

When he had reached the basis of terra firma on which
I was standing, naturally, as a mode of thanking him for
his courtesy, I presented my hand ; which, in a general case,
I should certainly not have done ; for I cherished, in an

ultra-English degree, the English custom (a wise custom)
of bowing in frigid silence on a first introduction to a
stranger; but, to a man of literary talent, and one who had
just practised so much kindness in my favour at so probable a hazard to himself of being laughed at for his pains,   5
I could not maintain that frosty reserve. Lamb took my
hand; did not absolutely reject it: but rather repelled my
advance by his manner. This, however, long afterwards I
found, was only a habit derived from his too great sensitiveness to the variety of people's feelings, which run   10
through a gamut so infinite of degrees and modes as to
make it unsafe for any man who respects himself to be
too hasty in his allowances of familiarity. Lamb had,
as he was entitled to have, a high self-respect; and me he
probably suspected (as a young Oxonian) of some aris-   15
tocratic tendencies. The letter of introduction, containing (I imagine) no matters of business, was speedily run
through; and I instantly received an invitation to spend
the evening with him. Lamb was not one of those who
catch at the chance of escaping from a bore by fixing some   20
distant day, when accidents (in duplicate proportion, perhaps, to the number of intervening days) may have carried
you away from the place: he sought to benefit by no luck
of that kind; for he was, with his limited income — and I
say it deliberately — positively the most hospitable man   25
I have known in this world. That night, the same night,
I was to come and spend the evening with him. I had
gone to the India House with the express purpose of
accepting whatever invitation he should give me; and,
therefore, I accepted this, took my leave, and left Lamb   30
in the act of resuming his aerial position.

I was to come so early as to drink tea with Lamb; and
the hour was seven. He lived in the Temple; and I, who
was not then, as afterwards I became, a student and

member of "the Honourable Society of the Middle
Temple," did not know much of the localities.   However, I found out his abode, not greatly beyond my time:
nobody had been asked to meet me, — which a little sur-
5 prised me, but I was glad of it; for, besides Lamb, there
was present his sister, Miss Lamb, of whom, and whose
talents and sweetness of disposition, I had heard.   I
turned the conversation, upon the first opening which
offered, to the subject of Coleridge ; and many of my ques-
10 tions were answered satisfactorily, because seriously, by
Miss Lamb.   But Lamb took a pleasure in baffling me, or
in throwing ridicule upon the subject.   Out of this grew
the matter of our affray.   We were speaking of "The
Ancient Mariner."*   Now, to explain what followed, and a
15 little to excuse myself, I must beg the reader to understand
that I was under twenty years of age, and that my admiration for Coleridge (as, in perhaps a still greater degree, for
Wordsworth) was literally in no respect short of a religious
feeling: it had, indeed, all the sanctity of religion, and
20 all the tenderness of a human veneration.   Then, also, to
imagine the strength which it would derive from circumstances that do not exist now, but did then, let the reader
further suppose a case — not such as he may have known
since that era about Sir Walter Scotts and Lord Byrons,
25 where every man you could possibly fall foul of, early or
late, night or day, summer or winter, was in perfect readi-
ness to feel and express his sympathy with the admirer
— but when no man, beyond one or two in each ten thousand, had so much as heard of either Coleridge or Words-
30 worth, and that one, or those two, knew them only to scorn
them, trample on them, spit upon them.   Men so abject in
public estimation, I maintain, as that Coleridge and that
Wordsworth, had not existed before, have not existed
since, will not exist again.   We have heard in old times of

donkeys insulting effete or dying lions by kicking them;
but in the case of Coleridge and Wordsworth it was effete
donkeys that kicked living lions. They, Coleridge and
Wordsworth, were the Pariahs of literature in those days:
as much scorned wherever they were known; but escaping
that scorn only because they were as little known as
Pariahs, and even more obscure.

Well, after this bravura, by way of conveying my sense
of the real position then occupied by these two authors —
a position which thirty and odd years have altered, by a
revolution more astonishing and total than ever before
happened in literature or in life — let the reader figure to
himself the sensitive horror with which a young person,
carrying his devotion about with him, of necessity, as the
profoundest of secrets, like a primitive Christian amongst
a nation of Pagans, or a Roman Catholic convert amongst
the bloody idolaters of Japan — in Oxford, above all
places, hoping for no sympathy, and feeling a daily grief,
almost a shame, in harbouring this devotion to that
which, nevertheless, had done more for the expansion
and sustenance of his own inner mind than all literature
besides — let the reader figure, I say, to himself, the shock
with which such a person must recoil from hearing the
very friend and associate of these authors utter what
seemed at that time a burning ridicule of all which belonged to them — their books, their thoughts, their places,
their persons. This had gone on for some time before we
came upon the ground of "The Ancient Mariner"; I had
been grieved, perplexed, astonished; and how else could I
have felt reasonably, knowing nothing of Lamb's propensity
to mystify a stranger; he, on the other hand, knowing
nothing of the depth of my feelings on these subjects,
and that they were not so much mere literary preferences
as something that went deeper than life or household

affections? At length, when he had given utterance to some
ferocious canon of judgment, which seemed to question
the entire value of the poem, I said, perspiring (I dare
say) in this detestable crisis — "But, Mr. Lamb, good
heavens! how is it possible you can allow yourself in such
opinions? What instance could you bring from the poem
that would bear you out in these insinuations?" "Instances?" said Lamb: "oh, I'll instance you, if you come
to that. Instance, indeed! Pray, what do you say to
this —

        'The many men so beautiful,
          And they all dead did lie'?

So beautiful, indeed! Beautiful! Just think of such a gang
of Wapping vagabonds, all covered with pitch, and chewing
tobacco; and the old gentleman himself — what do you
call him? — the bright-eyed fellow?" What more might
follow I never heard; for, at this point, in a perfect rapture of horror, I raised my hands — both hands — to both
ears; and, without stopping to think or to apologize, I
endeavoured to restore equanimity to my disturbed sensibilities by shutting out all further knowledge of Lamb's
impieties. At length he seemed to have finished; so I, on
my part, thought I might venture to take off the embargo:
and in fact he *had* ceased; but no sooner did he find me
restored to my hearing than he said with a most sarcastic
smile — which he could assume upon occasion — "If you
please, sir, we'll say grace before we begin." I know not
whether Lamb were really piqued or not at the mode by
which I had expressed my disturbance: Miss Lamb certainly was not; her goodness led her to pardon me, and to
treat me — in whatever light she might really view my
almost involuntary rudeness — as the party who had suffered wrong; and, for the rest of the evening, she was so
pointedly kind and conciliatory in her manner that I felt

greatly ashamed of my boyish failure in self-command.
Yet, after all, Lamb necessarily appeared so much worse,
in my eyes, as a traitor is worse than an open enemy.

Lamb, after this one visit — not knowing at that time
any particular reason for continuing to seek his acquaint- 5
ance — I did not trouble with my calls for some years. At
length, however, about the year 1808, and for the six or
seven following years, in my evening visits to Coleridge, I
used to meet him again ; not often, but sufficiently to
correct the altogether very false impression I had received 10
of his character and manners.

A MEETING WITH COLERIDGE

It was, I think, in the month of August, but certainly in the summer season, and certainly in the year 1807, that I first saw this illustrious man. My knowledge of him as a man of most original genius began about the year 1799. A little before that time Wordsworth had published the first edition (in a single volume) of the "Lyrical Ballads," and into this had been introduced Mr. Coleridge's poem of the "Ancient Mariner," as the contribution of an anonymous friend. It would be directing the reader's attention too much to myself if I were to linger upon this, the greatest event in the unfolding of my own mind. Let me say, in one word, that, at a period when neither the one nor the other writer was valued by the public — both having a long warfare to accomplish of contumely and ridicule before they could rise into their present estimation — I found in these poems "the ray of a new morning," and an absolute revelation of untrodden worlds teeming with power and beauty as yet unsuspected amongst men. I may here mention that, precisely at the same time, Professor Wilson, entirely unconnected with myself, and not even known to me until ten years later, received the same startling and profound impressions from the same volume. With feelings of reverential interest, so early and so deep, pointing towards two contemporaries, it may be supposed that I inquired eagerly after their names. But these inquiries were self-baffled; the same deep feelings which prompted my curiosity causing me to recoil from all

casual opportunities of pushing the inquiry, as too generally lying amongst those who gave no sign of partici-
pating in my feelings; and, extravagant as this may seem,
I revolted with as much hatred from coupling my question with any occasion of insult to the persons whom it 5
respected as a primitive Christian from throwing frankincense upon the altars of Cæsar, or a lover from giving
up the name of his beloved to the coarse license of a Bac-
chanalian party. It is laughable to record for how long
a period my curiosity in this particular was thus self- 10
defeated. Two years passed before I ascertained the two
names. Mr. Wordsworth published *his* in the second and
enlarged edition of the poems; and for Mr. Coleridge's
I was "indebted" to a private source; but I discharged
that debt ill, for I quarrelled with my informant for what 15
I considered his profane way of dealing with a subject
so hallowed in my own thoughts. After this I searched,
east and west, north and south, for all known works or
fragments of the same authors. I had read, therefore,
as respects Mr. Coleridge, the Allegory which he con- 20
tributed to Mr. Southey's "Joan of Arc." I had read
his fine Ode entitled "France," his Ode to the Duchess
of Devonshire, and various other contributions, more or
less interesting, to the two volumes of the "Anthology"
published at Bristol, about 1799–1800, by Mr. Southey; 25
and, finally, I had, of course, read the small volume of
poems published under his own name. These, however,
as a juvenile and immature collection, made expressly
with a view to pecuniary profit, and therefore courting
expansion at any cost of critical discretion, had in gen- 30
eral greatly disappointed me.

Meantime, it had crowned the interest which to me
invested his name, that about the year 1804 or 1805 I
had been informed by a gentleman from the English

Lakes, who knew him as a neighbour, that he had for some time applied his whole mind to metaphysics and psychology — which happened to be my own absorbing pursuit. From 1803 to 1808, I was a student at Oxford; and, on the first occasion when I could conveniently have sought for a personal knowledge of one whom I contemplated with so much admiration, I was met by a painful assurance that he had quitted England, and was then residing at Malta, in the quality of secretary to the Governor. I began to inquire about the best route to Malta; but, as any route at that time promised an inside place in a French prison, I reconciled myself to waiting; and at last, happening to visit the Bristol Hot-Wells in the summer of 1807, I had the pleasure to hear that Coleridge was not only once more upon English ground, but within forty and odd miles of my own station. In that same hour I bent my way to the south; and, before evening, reaching a ferry on the river Bridgewater, at a village called, I think, Stogursey (*i.e.*, Stoke de Courcy, by way of distinction from some other Stoke), I crossed it, and a few miles farther attained my object — viz., the little town of Nether Stowey, amongst the Quantock Hills. Here I had been assured that I should find Mr. Coleridge, at the house of his old friend Mr. Poole. On presenting myself, however, to that gentleman, I found that Coleridge was absent at Lord Egmont's, an elder brother (by the father's side) of Mr. Perceval, the Prime Minister, assassinated five years later; and, as it was doubtful whether he might not then be on the wing to another friend's in the town of Bridgewater, I consented willingly, until his motions should be ascertained, to stay a day or two with this Mr. Poole — a man on his own account well deserving a separate notice; for, as Coleridge afterwards remarked to me, he was almost an ideal model for a useful member of

Parliament. I found him a stout, plain-looking farmer, leading a bachelor life, in a rustic, old-fashioned house; the house, however, upon further acquaintance, proving to be amply furnished with modern luxuries, and especially with a good library, superbly mounted in all departments bearing at all upon political philosophy; and the farmer turning out a polished and liberal Englishman, who had travelled extensively, and had so entirely dedicated himself to the service of his humble fellow-countrymen — the hewers of wood and drawers of water in this southern part of Somersetshire — that for many miles round he was the general arbiter of their disputes, the guide and counsellor of their difficulties; besides being appointed executor and guardian to his children by every third man who died in or about the town of Nether Stowey.

The first morning of my visit, Mr. Poole was so kind as to propose, knowing my admiration of Wordsworth, that we should ride over to Alfoxton — a place of singular interest to myself, as having been occupied in his unmarried days by that poet, during the minority of Mr. St. Aubyn, its present youthful proprietor. At this delightful spot, the ancient residence of an ancient English family, and surrounded by those ferny Quantock Hills which are so beautifully glanced at in the poem of " Ruth," Wordsworth, accompanied by his sister, had passed a good deal of the interval between leaving the University (Cambridge) and the period of his final settlement amongst his native lakes of Westmoreland : some allowance, however, must be made — but how much I do not accurately know — for a long residence in France, for a short one in North Germany, for an intermitting one in London, and for a regular domestication with his sister at Race Down in Dorsetshire.

Returning late from this interesting survey, we found ourselves without company at dinner; and, being thus seated

tête-à-tête, Mr. Poole propounded the following question to me, which I mention because it furnished me with the first hint of a singular infirmity besetting Coleridge's mind: —
"Pray, my young friend, did you ever form any opinion,
5 or, rather, did it ever happen to you to meet with any rational opinion or conjecture of others, upon that most revolting dogma of Pythagoras about beans? You know what I mean: that monstrous doctrine in which he asserts that a man might as well, for the wickedness of the thing,
10 eat his own grandmother as meddle with beans."

"Yes," I replied; "the line is, I believe, in the Golden Verses. I remember it well."

P. — "True: now, our dear excellent friend Coleridge, than whom God never made a creature more divinely
15 endowed, yet, strange it is to say, sometimes steals from other people, just as you or I might do; I beg your pardon — just as a poor creature like myself might do, that sometimes have not wherewithal to make a figure from my own exchequer: and the other day, at a dinner party,
20 this question arising about Pythagoras and his beans, Coleridge gave us an interpretation which, from his manner, I suspect to have been not original. Think, therefore, if you have anywhere read a plausible solution."

"I have: and it was a German author. This German,
25 understand, is a poor stick of a man, not to be named on the same day with Coleridge: so that, if Coleridge should appear to have robbed him, be assured that he has done the scamp too much honour."

P. — "Well: what says the German?"
30 "Why, you know the use made in Greece of beans in voting and balloting? Well: the German says that Pythagoras speaks symbolically; meaning that electioneering, or, more generally, all interference with political intrigues, is fatal to a philosopher's pursuits and their appropriate

serenity. Therefore, says he, follower of mine, abstain
from public affairs as you would from parricide."

P. — " Well, then, Coleridge *has* done the scamp too
much honour : for, by Jove, that is the very explanation he
gave us ! "   5

Here was a trait of Coleridge's mind, to be first made
known to me by his best friend, and first published to
the world by me, the foremost of his admirers ! But both
of us had sufficient reasons : — Mr. Poole knew that, stum-
bled on by accident, such a discovery would be likely to 10
impress upon a man as yet unacquainted with Coleridge a
most injurious jealousy with regard to all he might write :
whereas, frankly avowed by one who knew him best, the
fact was disarmed of its sting ; since it thus became evident that, where the case had been best known and most 15
investigated, it had not operated to his serious disadvantage. On the same argument, — to forestall, that is to
say, other discoverers, who would make a more unfriendly
use of the discovery, — and also as matters of literary curiosity, I shall here point out a few others of Coleridge's 20
unacknowledged obligations, noticed by myself in a very
wide course of reading.

1. The Hymn to Chamouni is an expansion of a short
poem in stanzas, upon the same subject, by Frederica Brun,
a female poet of Germany, previously known to the world 25
under her maiden name of Münter. The mere framework
of the poem is exactly the same — an appeal to the most
impressive features of the regal mountain (Mont Blanc),
adjuring them to proclaim their author: the torrent, for
instance, is required to say by whom it had been arrested 30
in its headlong raving, and stiffened, as by the petrific
touch of Death, into everlasting pillars of ice; and the
answer to these impassioned apostrophes is made by the
same choral burst of rapture. In mere logic, therefore,

and even as to the choice of circumstances, Coleridge's poem is a translation. On the other hand, by a judicious amplification of some topics, and by its far deeper tone of lyrical enthusiasm, the dry bones of the German outline have been awakened by Coleridge into the fulness of life. It is not, therefore, a paraphrase, but a re-cast of the original. And how was this calculated, if frankly avowed, to do Coleridge any injury with the judicious?

2. A more singular case of Coleridge's infirmity is this: —In a very noble passage of "France," a fine expression or two occur from "Samson Agonistes." Now, to take a phrase or an inspiriting line from the great fathers of poetry, even though no marks of quotations should be added, carries with it no charge of plagiarism. Milton is justly presumed to be as familiar to the ear as nature to the eye; and to steal from him as impossible as to appropriate, or sequester to a private use, some "bright particular star." And there is a good reason for rejecting the typographical marks of quotation: they break the continuity of the passion, by reminding the reader of a printed book; on which account Milton himself (to give an instance) has not marked the sublime words, "tormented all the air" as borrowed; nor has Wordsworth, in applying to an unprincipled woman of commanding beauty the memorable expression "a weed of glorious feature," thought it necessary to acknowledge it as originally belonging to Spenser. Some dozens of similar cases might be adduced from Milton. But Coleridge, when saying of republican France that,

> "*Insupportably advancing,*
> Her arm made mockery of the warrior's tramp,*"

not satisfied with omitting the marks of acknowledgment, thought fit positively to deny that he was indebted to Milton. Yet who could forget that semi-chorus in the

"Samson" where the "bold Ascalonite" is described as having "fled from his lion ramp"? Or who, that was not in this
point liable to some hallucination of judgment, would have
ventured on a public challenge (for virtually it was that) to
produce from the "Samson" words so impossible to be 5
overlooked as those of "insupportably advancing the
foot"? The result was that one of the critical journals
placed the two passages in juxtaposition and left the reader
to his own conclusions with regard to the poet's veracity.
But, in this instance, it was common sense rather than 10
veracity which the facts impeach.

3. In the year 1810 I happened to be amusing myself
by reading, in their chronological order, the great classical
circumnavigations of the earth; and, coming to Shelvocke,
I met with a passage to this effect:—That Hatley, his 15
second captain (*i.e.*, lieutenant), being a melancholy man,
was possessed by a fancy that some long season of foul
weather, in the solitary sea which they were then traversing, was due to an albatross which had steadily pursued
the ship; upon which he shot the bird, but without mend- 20
ing their condition. There at once I saw the germ of the
"Ancient Mariner"; and I put a question to Coleridge
accordingly. Could it have been imagined that he would
see cause utterly to disown so slight an obligation to Shelvocke? Wordsworth, a man of stern veracity, on hearing 25
of this, professed his inability to understand Coleridge's
meaning; the fact being notorious, as he told me, that
Coleridge had derived from the very passage I had cited
the original hint for the action of the poem; though it is
very possible, from something which Coleridge said on 30
another occasion, that, before meeting a fable in which to
embody his ideas, he had meditated a poem on delirium,
confounding its own dream-scenery with external things,
and connected with the imagery of high latitudes.

4. All these cases amount to nothing at all as cases of plagiarism, and for this reason expose the more conspicuously that obliquity of feeling which could seek to decline the very slight acknowledgments required. But now I come to a case of real and palpable plagiarism; yet that, too, of a nature to be quite accountable in a man of Coleridge's attainments. It is not very likely that this particular case will soon be detected; but others will. Yet who knows? Eight hundred or a thousand years hence, some reviewer may arise who, having read the "Biographia Literaria" of Coleridge, will afterwards read the "Philosophical ——" [1] of Schelling, the great Bavarian professor — a man in some respects worthy to be Coleridge's assessor; and he will then make a singular discovery. In the "Biographia Literaria" occurs a dissertation upon the reciprocal relations of the *Esse* and the *Cogitare*, — that is, of the *objective* and the *subjective:* and an attempt is made, by inverting the postulates from which the argument starts, to show how each might arise as a product, by an intelligible genesis, from the other. It is a subject which, since the time of Fichte, has much occupied the German metaphysicians; and many thousands of essays have been written on it, or indirectly so, of which many hundreds have been read by many tens of persons. Coleridge's essay, in particular, is prefaced by a few words in which, aware of his coincidence with Schelling, he declares his willingness to acknowledge himself indebted to so great a man in any case where the truth would allow him to do so; but, in this particular case, insisting on the impossibility that he could have borrowed arguments which he had first seen some years after he had thought out the

---

[1] I forget the exact title, not having seen the book since 1823, and then only for one day; but I believe it was Schelling's "Kleine Philosophische Werke."

whole hypothesis *proprio marte*. After this, what was my astonishment to find that the entire essay, from the first word to the last, is a *verbatim* translation from Schelling, with no attempt in a single instance to appropriate the paper by developing the arguments or by diversifying the illustrations? Some other obligations to Schelling, of a slighter kind, I have met with in the "Biographia Lite- raria"; but this was a barefaced plagiarism, which could in prudence have been risked only by relying too much upon the slight knowledge of German literature in this country, and especially of that section of the German literature. Had, then, Coleridge any need to borrow from Schelling? Did he borrow *in forma pauperis?* Not at all: there lay the wonder. He spun daily, and at all hours, for mere amusement of his own activities, and from the loom of his own magical brain, theories more gorgeous by far, and supported by a pomp and luxury of images such as neither Schelling — no, nor any German that ever breathed, not John Paul — could have emulated in his dreams. With the riches of El Dorado lying about him, he would condescend to filch a handful of gold from any man whose purse he fancied, and in fact reproduced in a new form, applying itself to intellectual wealth, that maniacal propensity which is sometimes well known to attack enormous proprietors and millionaires for acts of petty larceny. The last Duke of Anc[aster] could not abstain from exercising his furtive mania upon articles so humble as silver spoons; and it was the nightly care of a pious daughter, watching over the aberrations of her father, to have his pockets searched by a confidential valet; and the claimants of the purloined articles traced out.

Many cases have crossed me in life of people, otherwise not wanting in principle, who had habits, or at least hankerings, of the same kind. And the phrenologists, I

believe, are well acquainted with the case, its signs, its progress, and its history.   Dismissing, however, this subject,
which I have at all noticed only that I might anticipate,
and (in old English) that I might *prevent*, the uncandid
interpreter of its meaning, I will assert finally that, after
having read for thirty years in the same track as Coleridge
— that track in which few of any age will ever follow us,
such as German metaphysicians, Latin schoolmen, thau-
maturgic Platonists, religious Mystics — and having thus
discovered a large variety of trivial thefts, I do, nevertheless, most heartily believe him to have been as entirely
original in all his capital pretensions as any one man that
ever has existed ; as Archimedes in ancient days, or as
Shakspere in modern.   Did the reader ever see Milton's
account of the rubbish contained in the Greek and Latin
Fathers ?   Or did he ever read a statement of the monstrous chaos with which an African Obeah man stuffs his
enchanted scarecrows ?   Or, take a more common illustration, did he ever amuse himself by searching the pockets
of a child — three years old, suppose — when buried in
slumber after a long summer's day of out-o'-doors intense
activity ?   I have done this ; and, for the amusement of the
child's mother, have analyzed the contents, and drawn up
a formal register of the whole.   Philosophy is puzzled,
conjecture and hypothesis are confounded, in the attempt
to explain the law of selection which *can* have presided in
the child's labours ; stones remarkable only for weight, old
rusty hinges, nails, crooked skewers stolen when the cook
had turned her back, rags, broken glass, tea-cups having
the bottom knocked out, and loads of similar jewels, were
the prevailing articles in this *procès-verbal*.   Yet, doubtless,
much labour had been incurred, some sense of danger
perhaps had been faced, and the anxieties of a conscious
robber endured, in order to amass this splendid treasure.

Such in value were the robberies of Coleridge; such their usefulness to himself or anybody else; and such the circumstances of uneasiness under which he had committed them. I return to my narrative.

Two or three days had slipped away in waiting for Coleridge's re-appearance at Nether Stowey, when suddenly Lord Egmont called upon Mr. Poole, with a present for Coleridge: it was a canister of peculiarly fine snuff, which Coleridge now took profusely. Lord Egmont, on this occasion, spoke of Coleridge in the terms of excessive admiration, and urged Mr. Poole to put him upon undertaking some great monumental work, that might furnish a sufficient arena for the display of his various and rare accomplishments; for his multiform erudition on the one hand, for his splendid power of theorizing and combining large and remote notices of facts on the other. And he suggested, judiciously enough, as one theme which offered a field at once large enough and indefinite enough to suit a mind that could not show its full compass of power unless upon very plastic materials — a History of Christianity, in its progress and in its chief divarications into Church and Sect, with a continual reference to the relations subsisting between Christianity and the current philosophy; their occasional connexions or approaches, and their constant mutual repulsions. "But, at any rate, let him do something," said Lord Egmont; "for at present he talks very much like an angel, and does nothing at all." Lord Egmont I understood from everybody to be a truly good and benevolent man; and on this occasion he spoke with an earnestness which agreed with my previous impression. Coleridge, he said, was now in the prime of his powers — uniting something of youthful vigour with sufficient experience of life; having the benefit, beside, of vast meditation, and of reading unusually discursive. No man had ever

been better qualified to revive the heroic period of literature in England, and to give a character of weight to the
philosophic erudition of the country upon the Continent.
"And what a pity," he added, "if this man were, after all,
to vanish like an apparition, and you, I, and a few others,
who have witnessed his grand *bravuras* of display, were to
have the usual fortune of ghost-seers, in meeting no credit
for any statements that we might vouch on his behalf!"

On this occasion we learned, for the first time, that
Lord Egmont's carriage had, some days before, conveyed
Coleridge to Bridgewater, with a purpose of staying one
single day at that place, and then returning to Mr. Poole's.
From the sort of laugh with which Lord Egmont taxed
his own simplicity, in having confided at all in the sta-
bility of any Coleridgian plan, I now gathered that procrastination in excess was, or had become, a marking
feature in Coleridge's daily life. Nobody who knew him
ever thought of depending on any appointment he might
make: spite of his uniformly honourable intentions, nobody
attached any weight to his assurances *in re futura :* those
who asked him to dinner or any other party, as a matter
of course, sent a carriage for him, and went personally
or by proxy to fetch him ; and, as to letters, unless the
address were in some female hand that commanded his
affectionate esteem, he tossed them all into one general
dead-letter bureau, and rarely, I believe, opened them at
all. Bourrienne mentions a mode of abridging the trouble
attached to a very extensive correspondence, by which
infinite labour was saved to himself, and to Napoleon,
when First Consul. Nine out of ten letters, supposing
them letters of business with official applications of a
special kind, he contends, answer themselves : in other
words, time alone must soon produce events which virtually contain the answer. On this principle the letters

were opened periodically, after intervals, suppose, of six weeks; and, at the end of that time, it was found that not many remained to require any further more particular answer. Coleridge's plan, however, was shorter: he opened none, I understood, and answered none. At least such was his habit at that time. But, on that same day, all this, which I heard now for the first time, and with much concern, was fully explained; for already he was under the full dominion of opium, as he himself revealed to me, and with a deep expression of horror at the hideous bond- age, in a private walk of some length which I took with him about sunset.

Lord Egmont's information, and the knowledge now gained of Coleridge's habits, making it very uncertain when I might see him in my present hospitable quarters, I immediately took my leave of Mr. Poole, and went over to Bridgewater. I had received directions for finding out the house where Coleridge was visiting; and, in riding down a main street of Bridgewater, I noticed a gateway corresponding to the description given me. Under this was standing, and gazing about him, a man whom I will describe. In height he might seem to be about five feet eight (he was, in reality, about an inch and a-half taller, but his figure was of an order which drowns the height); his person was broad and full, and tended even to corpu- lence; his complexion was fair, though not what painters technically style fair, because it was associated with black hair; his eyes were large, and soft in their expression; and it was from the peculiar appearance of haze or dreami- ness which mixed with their light that I recognised my object. This was Coleridge. I examined him steadfastly for a minute or more; and it struck me that he saw neither myself nor any other object in the street. He was in a deep reverie; for I had dismounted, made two or three

trifling arrangements at an inn-door, and advanced close
to him, before he had apparently become conscious of my
presence. The sound of my voice, announcing my own
name, first awoke him; he started, and for a moment
5 seemed at a loss to understand my purpose or his own
situation; for he repeated rapidly a number of words
which had no relation to either of us. There was no
mauvaise honte in his manner, but simple perplexity, and
an apparent difficulty in recovering his position amongst
10 daylight realities. This little scene over, he received me
with a kindness of manner so marked that it might be
called gracious. The hospitable family with whom he was
domesticated were distinguished for their amiable manners
and enlightened understandings: they were descendants
15 from Chubb, the philosophic writer, and bore the same
name. For Coleridge they all testified deep affection
and esteem — sentiments in which the whole town of
Bridgewater seemed to share; for in the evening, when
the heat of the day had declined, I walked out with him;
20 and rarely, perhaps never, have I seen a person so much
interrupted in one hour's space as Coleridge, on this occasion, by the courteous attentions of young and old.

All the people of station and weight in the place, and
apparently all the ladies, were abroad to enjoy the lovely
25 summer evening; and not a party passed without some
mark of smiling recognition, and the majority stopping to
make personal inquiries about his health, and to express
their anxiety that he should make a lengthened stay
amongst them. Certain I am, from the lively esteem
30 expressed towards Coleridge at this time by the people
of Bridgewater, that a very large subscription might, in
that town, have been raised to support him amongst them,
in the character of a lecturer, or philosophical professor.
Especially I remarked that the young men of the place

manifested the most liberal interest in all that concerned him; and I can add my attestation to that of Mr. Coleridge himself, when describing an evening spent amongst the enlightened tradesmen of Birmingham, that nowhere is more unaffected good sense exhibited, and particularly nowhere more elasticity and *freshness* of mind, than in the conversation of the reading men in manufacturing towns. In Kendal, especially, in Bridgewater, and in Manchester, I have witnessed more interesting conversations, as much information, and more natural eloquence in conveying it, than usually in literary cities, or in places professedly learned. One reason for this is that in trading towns the time is more happily distributed; the day given to business and active duties — the evening to relaxation; on which account, books, conversation, and literary leisure are more cordially enjoyed: the same satiation never can take place which too frequently deadens the genial enjoyment of those who have a surfeit of books and a monotony of leisure. Another reason is that more simplicity of manner may be expected, and more natural picturesqueness of conversation, more open expression of character, in places where people have no previous name to support. Men in trading towns are not afraid to open their lips for fear they should disappoint your expectations, nor do they strain for showy sentiments that they may meet them. But, elsewhere, many are the men who stand in awe of their own reputation: not a word which is unstudied, not a movement in the spirit of natural freedom, dare they give way to, because it might happen that on review something would be seen to retract or to qualify — something not properly planed and chiselled to build into the general architecture of an artificial reputation. But to return: —

Coleridge led me to a drawing-room, rang the bell for refreshments, and omitted no point of a courteous reception.

He told me that there would be a very large dinner party on that day, which, perhaps, might be disagreeable to a perfect stranger; but, if not, he could assure me of a most hospitable welcome from the family. I was too
5 anxious to see him under all aspects to think of declining this invitation. That point being settled, Coleridge, like some great river, the Orellana, or the St. Lawrence, that, having been checked and fretted by rocks and thwarting islands, suddenly recovers its volume of waters and its
10 mighty music, swept at once, as if returning to his natural business, into a continuous strain of eloquent dissertation, certainly the most novel, the most finely illustrated, and traversing the most spacious fields of thought by transitions the most just and logical, that it was possible to
15 conceive. What I mean by saying that his transitions were "just" is by way of contradistinction to that mode of conversation which courts variety through links of *verbal* connexions. Coleridge, to many people, and often I have heard the complaint, seemed to wander; and he
20 seemed then to wander the most when, in fact, his resistance to the wandering instinct was greatest — viz., when the compass and huge circuit by which his illustrations moved travelled farthest into remote regions before they began to revolve. Long before this coming round com-
25 menced most people had lost him, and naturally enough supposed that he had lost himself. They continued to admire the separate beauty of the thoughts, but did not see their relations to the dominant theme. Had the conversation been thrown upon paper, it might have been
30 easy to trace the continuity of the links; just as in Bishop Berkeley's "Siris," [1] from a pedestal so low and abject, so

---

[1] *Siris* ought to have been the title — *i.e.*, Σειρις, a chain. From this defect in the orthography, I did not in my boyish days perceive, nor could obtain any light upon, its meaning.

culinary, as Tar Water, the method of preparing it, and
its medicinal effects, the dissertation ascends, like Jacob's
ladder, by just gradations, into the Heaven of Heavens
and the thrones of the Trinity.   But Heaven is there
connected with earth by the Homeric chain of gold;   5
and, being subject to steady examination, it is easy to
trace the links; whereas, in conversation, the loss of a
single word may cause the whole cohesion to disappear
from view.   However, I can assert, upon my long and
intimate knowledge of Coleridge's mind, that logic the   10
most severe was as inalienable from his modes of thinking
as grammar from his language.

RECOLLECTIONS OF WORDSWORTH

In 1807 it was, at the beginning of winter, that I first saw William Wordsworth. I have already mentioned that I had introduced myself to his notice by letter as early as the spring of 1803. To this hour it has continued, I believe, a mystery to Wordsworth why it was that I suffered an interval of four and a half years to slip away before availing myself of the standing invitation with which I had been honoured to the poet's house. Very probably he accounted for this delay by supposing that the new-born liberty of an Oxford life, with its multiplied enjoyments, acting upon a boy just emancipated from the restraints of a school, and, in one hour, elevated into what we Oxonians so proudly and so exclusively denominate "a man,"[1] might have tempted me into pursuits alien from the pure intellectual passions which had so powerfully mastered my youthful heart some years before. Extinguished such a passion could not be; nor could he think so, if remembering the fervour with which I had expressed it, the sort of "nympholepsy" which had seized upon me, and which, in some imperfect way, I had avowed with reference to the very lakes and mountains amongst which the scenery of this most original poetry had chiefly

---

[1] At the Universities of Oxford and Cambridge, where the town is viewed as a mere ministerial appendage to the numerous colleges — the civic Oxford, for instance, existing for the sake of the academic Oxford, and not *vice versâ* — it has naturally happened that the students honour with the name of "*a man*" him only who wears a cap and gown.

grown up and moved. The very names of the ancient hills
— Fairfield, Seat Sandal, Helvellyn, Blencathara, Glara-
mara ; the names of the sequestered glens — such as Bor-
rowdale, Martindale, Mardale, Wasdale, and Ennerdale ;
but, above all, the shy pastoral recesses, not garishly in
the world's eye, like Windermere or Derwentwater, but
lurking half unknown to the traveller of that day — Grasmere, for instance, the lovely abode of the poet himself,
solitary, and yet sowed, as it were, with a thin diffusion
of humble dwellings — here a scattering, and there a clustering, as in the starry heavens — sufficient to afford, at
every turn and angle, human remembrances and memorials of time-honoured affections, or of passions (as the
"Churchyard amongst the Mountains" will amply demonstrate) not wanting even in scenic and tragical interest :
these were so many local spells upon me, equally poetic
and elevating with the Miltonic names of Valdarno and
Vallombrosa.

Deep are the voices which seem to call, deep is the
lesson which would be taught, even to the most thoughtless of men —

> " Could field, or grove, or any spot of earth,
>   Show to his eye an image of the pangs
>   Which it hath witnessed ; render back an echo
>   Of the sad steps by which it hath been trod."[1]

Meantime, my delay was due to anything rather than to
waning interest. On the contrary, the real cause of my delay
was the too great profundity, and the increasing profundity,
of my interest in this regeneration of our national poetry,
and the increasing awe, in due proportion to the decaying
thoughtlessness of boyhood, which possessed me for the

---

[1] See the divine passage (in the Sixth Book of "The Excursion")
beginning —   " Ah, what a lesson to a thoughtless man," &c.

character of its author. So far from neglecting Wordsworth, it is a fact that twice I had undertaken a long
journey expressly for the purpose of paying my respects
to Wordsworth; twice I came so far as the little rustic
5 inn (then the sole inn of the neighbourhood) at Church
Coniston; and on neither occasion could I summon confidence enough to present myself before him. It was not
that I had any want of proper boldness for facing the
most numerous company of a mixed or ordinary char-
10 acter: reserved, indeed, I was, perhaps even shy — from
the character of my mind, so profoundly meditative, and
the character of my life, so profoundly sequestered —
but still, from counteracting causes, I was not deficient
in a reasonable self-confidence towards the world gener-
15 ally. But the very image of Wordsworth, as I prefigured
it to my own planet-struck eye, crushed my faculties as
before Elijah or St. Paul. Twice, as I have said, did I
advance as far as the Lake of Coniston; which is about
eight miles from the church of Grasmere, and once I abso-
20 lutely went forwards from Coniston to the very gorge of
Hammerscar, from which the whole Vale of Grasmere suddenly breaks upon the view in a style of almost theatrical
surprise, with its lovely valley stretching before the eye
in the distance, the lake lying immediately below, with
25 its solemn ark-like island of four and a half acres in size
seemingly floating on its surface, and its exquisite outline on the opposite shore, revealing all its little bays[1]
and wild sylvan margin, feathered to the edge with wild
flowers and ferns. In one quarter, a little wood, stretch-
30 ing for about half a mile towards the outlet of the lake;

[1] All which inimitable graces of nature have, by the hands of
mechanic art, by solid masonry, by whitewashing, &c., been extermi-
nated, as a growth of weeds and nuisances, for thirty years. — *August*
17, 1853.

more directly in opposition to the spectator, a few green
fields; and beyond them, just two bowshots from the
water, a little white cottage gleaming from the midst of
trees, with a vast and seemingly never-ending series of
ascents rising above it to the height of more than three
thousand feet. That little cottage was Wordsworth's from
the time of his marriage, and earlier; in fact, from the
beginning of the century to the year 1808. Afterwards,
for many a year, it was mine. Catching one hasty glimpse
of this loveliest of landscapes, I retreated like a guilty
thing, for fear I might be surprised by Wordsworth, and
then returned faintheartedly to Coniston, and so to Oxford,
re infecta.

This was in 1806. And thus far, from mere excess of
nervous distrust in my own powers for sustaining a conversation with Wordsworth, I had for nearly five years
shrunk from a meeting for which, beyond all things
under heaven, I longed. In early youth I laboured under
a peculiar embarrassment and penury of words, when I
sought to convey my thoughts adequately upon interesting subjects: neither was it words only that I wanted;
but I could not unravel, I could not even make perfectly
conscious to myself, the subsidiary thoughts into which
one leading thought often radiates; or, at least, I could
not do this with anything like the rapidity requisite for
conversation. I laboured like a sibyl instinct with the
burden of prophetic woe, as often as I found myself dealing with any topic in which the understanding combined
with deep feelings to suggest mixed and tangled thoughts:
and thus partly — partly also from my invincible habit
of reverie — at that era of my life, I had a most distinguished talent "*pour le silence.*" Wordsworth, from something of the same causes, suffered (by his own report to
myself) at the same age from pretty much the same

infirmity.   And yet, in more advanced years — probably
about twenty-eight or thirty — both of us acquired a
remarkable fluency in the art of unfolding 'our thoughts
colloquially.   However, at that period my deficiencies
5 were what I have described.   And, after all, though I
had no absolute cause for anticipating contempt, I was
so far right in my fears, that since that time I have
had occasion to perceive a worldly tone of sentiment in
Wordsworth, not less than in Mrs. Hannah More and
10 other literary people, by which they were led to set a
higher value upon a limited respect from a person high
in the world's esteem than upon the most lavish spirit of
devotion from an obscure quarter.   Now, in that point,
my feelings are far otherwise.

15   Meantime, the world went on; events kept moving;
and, amongst them, in the course of 1807, occurred the
event of Coleridge's return to England from his official
station in the Governor's family at Malta.   At Bridgewater, as I have already recorded, in the summer of 1807,
20 I was introduced to him.   Several weeks after he came
with his family to the Bristol Hot-Wells, at which, by
accident, I was then visiting.   On calling upon him, I
found that he had been engaged by the Royal Institution to lecture at their theatre in Albemarle Street dur-
25 ing the coming winter of 1807–8, and, consequently, was
embarrassed about the mode of conveying his family to
Keswick.   Upon this, I offered my services to escort them
in a post-chaise.   This offer was cheerfully accepted;
and at the latter end of October we set forwards — Mrs.
30 Coleridge, viz., with her two sons — Hartley, aged nine,
Derwent, about seven — her beautiful little daughter,[1]

----

[1] That most accomplished, and to Coleridge most pious daughter,
whose recent death afflicted so very many who knew her only by her
writings.   She had married her cousin, Mr. Serjeant Coleridge, and

about five, and, finally, myself.   Going by the direct
route through Gloucester, Bridgenorth, &c., on the third
day we reached Liverpool, where I took up my quarters
at a hotel, whilst Mrs. Coleridge paid a visit of a few days
to a very interesting family, who had become friends of 5
Southey during his visit to Portugal.   These were the
Misses Koster, daughters of an English gold-merchant
of celebrity, who had recently quitted Lisbon on the
approach of the French army under Junot.   Mr. Koster
did me the honour to call at my quarters, and invite me 10
to his house; an invitation which I very readily accepted,
and had thus an opportunity of becoming acquainted with
a family the most accomplished I had ever known.   At
dinner there appeared only the family party — several
daughters, and one son, a fine young man of twenty, 15
but who was *consciously* dying of asthma.   Mr. Koster,
the head of the family, was distinguished for his good
sense and practical information; but, in Liverpool, even
more so by his eccentric and obstinate denial of certain
notorious events; in particular, some two years later, he 20
denied that any such battle as Talavera had ever been
fought, and had a large wager depending upon the deci-
sion.   His house was the resort of distinguished foreigners; and, on the first evening of my dining there, as
well as afterwards, I there met that marvel of women, 25
Madame Catalani.   I had heard her repeatedly; but
never before been near enough to see her smile and converse — even to be honoured with a smile myself.   She
and Lady Hamilton were the most effectively brilliant

in that way retained her illustrious maiden name as a wife. At seventeen, when last I saw her, she was the most perfect of all pensive,
nun-like, intellectual beauties that I have seen in real breathing life.
The upper parts of her face were verily divine. See, for an artist's
opinion, the Life of that admirable man Collins, by his son.

women I ever saw. However, on this occasion, the
Misses Koster outshone even La Catalani; to her they
talked in the most fluent Italian; to some foreign men,
in Portuguese; to one in French; and to most of the
party in English; and each, by turns, seemed to be their
native tongue. Nor did they shrink, even in the presence
of the mighty enchantress, from exhibiting their musical
skill.

Leaving Liverpool, after about a week's delay, we pursued our journey northwards. We had slept on the first
day at Lancaster. Consequently, at the rate of motion
which then prevailed throughout England — which, however, was rarely equalled on that western road, where all
things were in arrear by comparison with the eastern and
southern roads of the kingdom — we found ourselves, about
three o'clock in the afternoon, at Ambleside, fourteen miles
to the north-west of Kendal, and thirty-six from Lancaster.
There, for the last time, we stopped to change horses; and
about four o'clock we found ourselves on the summit of
the White Moss, a hill which rises between the second and
third milestones on the stage from Ambleside to Keswick,
and which then retarded the traveller's advance by a full
fifteen minutes, but is now evaded by a lower line of road.
In ascending this hill, from weariness of moving so slowly,
I, with the two Coleridges, had alighted; and, as we all
chose to refresh ourselves by running down the hill into
Grasmere, we had left the chaise behind us, and had even
lost the sound of the wheels at times, when all at once
we came, at an abrupt turn of the road, in sight of a white
cottage, with two yew-trees breaking the glare of its white
walls. A sudden shock seized me on recognising this
cottage, of which, in the previous year, I had gained a
momentary glimpse from Hammerscar, on the opposite
side of the lake. I paused, and felt my old panic returning

upon me; but just then, as if to take away all doubt upon the subject, I saw Hartley Coleridge, who had gained upon me considerably, suddenly turn in at a garden gate; this motion to the right at once confirmed me in my belief that here at last we had reached our port; that this little cottage was tenanted by that man whom, of all the men from the beginning of time, I most fervently desired to see; that in less than a minute I should meet Wordsworth face to face. Coleridge was of opinion that, if a man were really and *consciously* to see an apparition, in such circumstances death would be the inevitable result; and, if so, the wish which we hear so commonly expressed for such experience is as thoughtless as that of Semele in the Grecian Mythology, so natural in a female, that her lover should visit her *en grand costume* — presumptuous ambition, that unexpectedly wrought its own ruinous chastisement! Judged by Coleridge's test, my situation could not have been so terrific as *his* who anticipates a ghost; for, certainly, I survived this meeting; but at that instant it seemed pretty much the same to my own feelings.

Never before or since can I reproach myself with having trembled at the approaching presence of any creature that is born of woman, excepting only, for once or twice in my life, woman herself. Now, however, I *did* tremble; and I forgot, what in no other circumstances I could have forgotten, to stop for the coming up of the chaise, that I might be ready to hand Mrs. Coleridge out. Had Charlemagne and all his peerage been behind me, or Cæsar and his equipage, or Death on his pale horse, I should have forgotten them at that moment of intense expectation, and of eyes fascinated to what lay before me, or what might in a moment appear. Through the little gate I pressed forward; ten steps beyond it lay the principal door of the house. To this, no longer clearly conscious of my own

feelings, I passed on rapidly; I heard a step, a voice, and, like a flash of lightning, I saw the figure emerge of a tallish man, who held out his hand, and saluted me with most cordial expressions of welcome. The chaise, how-
5 ever, drawing up to the gate at that moment, he (and there needed no Roman nomenclator to tell me that this *he* was Wordsworth) felt himself summoned to advance and receive Mrs. Coleridge. I, therefore, stunned almost with the actual accomplishment of a catastrophe so long anticipated
10 and so long postponed, mechanically went forward into the house. A little semi-vestibule between two doors prefaced the entrance into what might be considered the principal room of the cottage. It was an oblong square, not above eight and a half feet high, sixteen feet long, and twelve
15 broad; very prettily wainscoted from the floor to the ceiling with dark polished oak, slightly embellished with carving. One window there was — a perfect and unpretending cottage window, with little diamond panes, embowered at almost every season of the year with roses, and in the
20 summer and autumn with a profusion of jasmine and other fragrant shrubs. From the exuberant luxuriance of the vegetation around it, and from the dark hue of the wainscoting, this window, though tolerably large, did not furnish a very powerful light to one who entered from the open air.
25 However, I saw sufficiently to be aware of two ladies just entering the room, through a doorway opening upon a little staircase. The foremost, a tallish young woman, with the most winning expression of benignity upon her features, advanced to me, presenting her hand with so frank an air
30 that all embarrassment must have fled in a moment before the native goodness of her manner. This was Mrs. Wordsworth, cousin of the poet, and, for the last five years or more, his wife. She was now mother of two children, a son and a daughter; and she furnished a remarkable proof

how possible it is for a woman neither handsome nor even
comely according to the rigour of criticism — nay, generally
pronounced very plain — to exercise all the practical fascination of beauty, through the mere compensatory charms
of sweetness all but angelic, of simplicity the most entire, 5
womanly self-respect and purity of heart speaking through
all her looks, acts, and movements. *Words*, I was going
to have added; but her words were few. In reality, she
talked so little that Mr. Slave-Trade Clarkson used to
allege against her that she could only say " *God bless* 10
you!" Certainly, her intellect was not of an active order;
but, in a quiescent, reposing, meditative way, she appeared
always to have a genial enjoyment from her own thoughts;
and it would have been strange, indeed, if she, who enjoyed
such eminent advantages of training, from the daily society 15
of her husband and his sister, failed to acquire some power
of judging for herself, and putting forth some functions of
activity. But undoubtedly that was not her element : to
feel and to enjoy in a luxurious repose of mind — there
was her *forte* and her peculiar privilege ; and how much 20
better this was adapted to her husband's taste, how much
more adapted to uphold the comfort of his daily life, than
a blue-stocking loquacity, or even a legitimate talent for
discussion, may be inferred from his verses, beginning —

> " She was a phantom of delight,
> When first she gleam'd upon my sight." 25

Once for all,[1] these exquisite lines were dedicated to Mrs.
Wordsworth ; were understood to describe her — to have
been prompted by the feminine graces of her character ;

---

[1] *Once for all*, I say — on recollecting that Coleridge's verses to
Sara were made transferable to any Sara who reigned at the time.
At least three Saras appropriated them; all three long since in the
grave.

hers they are, and will remain for ever.   To these, therefore,
I may refer the reader for an idea of what was most important in the partner and second self of the poet.   And I will
add to this abstract of her *moral* portrait these few con-
5 cluding traits of her appearance in a physical sense.   Her
figure was tolerably good.   In complexion she was fair,
and there was something peculiarly pleasing even in this
accident of the skin, for it was accompanied by an animated expression of health, a blessing which, in fact, she
10 possessed uninterruptedly.   Her eyes, the reader may
already know, were

> " Like stars of twilight fair ;
>   Like twilight, too, her dark brown hair ;
>   But all things else about her drawn
15   From May-time and the cheerful dawn."

Yet strange it is to tell that, in these eyes of vesper gentleness, there was a considerable obliquity of vision ; and
much beyond that slight obliquity which is often supposed
to be an attractive foible in the countenance: this *ought* to
20 have been displeasing or repulsive ; yet, in fact, it was not.
Indeed all faults, had they been ten times more and
greater, would have been neutralized by that supreme
expression of her features to the unity of which every
lineament in the fixed parts, and every undulation in the
25 moving parts, of her countenance, concurred, viz., a sunny
benignity — a radiant graciousness — such as in this
world I never saw surpassed.

Immediately behind her moved a lady, shorter, slighter,
and perhaps, in all other respects, as different from her
30 in personal characteristics as could have been wished for
the most effective contrast.   " Her face was of Egyptian
brown "; rarely, in a woman of English birth, had I seen
a more determinate gipsy tan.   Her eyes were not soft, as

Mrs. Wordsworth's, nor were they fierce or bold; but they were wild and startling, and hurried in their motion. Her manner was warm and even ardent; her sensibilities seemed constitutionally deep; and some subtle fire of impassioned intellect apparently burned within her, which, being alternately pushed forward into a conspicuous expression by the irrepressible instincts of her temperament, and then immediately checked, in obedience to the decorum of her sex and age, and her maidenly condition, gave to her whole demeanour, and to her conversation, an air of embarrassment, and even of self-conflict, that was almost distressing to witness. Even her very utterance and enunciation often suffered, in point of clearness and steadiness, from the agitation of her excessive organic sensibility. At times, the self-counteraction and self-baffling of her feelings caused her even to stammer, and so determinately to stammer that a stranger who should have seen her and quitted her in that state of feeling would certainly set her down for one plagued with that infirmity of speech as distressingly as Charles Lamb himself. This was Miss Wordsworth, the only sister of the poet — his "Dorothy"; who naturally owed so much to the lifelong intercourse with her great brother in his most solitary and sequestered years; but, on the other hand, to whom he has acknowledged obligations of the profoundest nature; and, in particular, this mighty one, through which we also, the admirers and the worshippers of this great poet, are become equally her debtors — that, whereas the intellect of Wordsworth was, by its original tendency, too stern, too austere, too much enamoured of an ascetic harsh sublimity, she it was — the lady who paced by his side continually through sylvan and mountain tracks, in Highland glens, and in the dim recesses of German charcoal-burners— that first *couched* his eye to the sense of beauty, humanised him by the gentler charities, and engrafted, with her delicate female touch, those graces upon the ruder growths of his nature which have since clothed the forest of his genius with a foliage correspond-ing in loveliness and beauty to the strength of its boughs and the massiness of its trunks. The greatest deductions from Miss Wordsworth's attractions, and from the exceed-ing interest which surrounded her in right of her character, of her history, and of the relation which she fulfilled towards her brother, were the glancing quickness of her motions, and other circumstances in her deportment (such as her stooping attitude when walking), which gave an ungraceful, and even an unsexual character to her appear-ance when out-of-doors. She did not cultivate the graces which preside over the person and its carriage. But, on the other hand, she was a person of very remarkable endowments intellectually; and, in addition to the other great services which she rendered to her brother, this I may mention, as greater than all the rest, and it was one which equally operated to the benefit of every casual com-panion in a walk — viz., the exceeding sympathy, always ready and always profound, by which she made all that one could tell her, all that one could describe, all that one could quote from a foreign author, reverberate, as it were, à *plusieurs reprises*, to one's own feelings, by the manifest impression it made upon *hers*. The pulses of light are not more quick or more inevitable in their flow and undulation, than were the answering and echoing movements of her sympathising attention. Her knowledge of literature was irregular, and thoroughly unsystematic. She was content to be ignorant of many things; but what she knew and had really mastered lay where it could not be disturbed — in the temple of her own most fervid heart.

Such were the two ladies who, with himself and two children, and at that time one servant, composed the poet's household. They were both, I believe, about twenty-eight years old; and, if the reader inquires about the single point which I have left untouched in their portraiture—viz., the style of their manners—I may say that it was, in *some* points, naturally of a plain household simplicity, but every way pleasing, unaffected, and (as respects Mrs. Wordsworth) even dignified. Few persons had seen so little as this lady of the world. She had seen nothing of high life, for she had seen little of any. Consequently, she was unacquainted with the conventional modes of behaviour, prescribed in particular situations by high breeding. But, as these modes are little more than the product of dispassionate good sense, applied to the circumstances of the case, it is surprising how few deficiencies are perceptible, even to the most vigilant eye — or, at least, essential deficiencies — in the general demeanour of any unaffected young woman, acting habitually under a sense of sexual dignity and natural courtesy. Miss Wordsworth had seen more of life, and even of good company; for she had lived, when quite a girl, under the protection of Dr. Cookson, a near relative, canon of Windsor, and a personal favourite of the Royal Family, especially of George III. Consequently, she ought to have been the more polished of the two; and yet, from greater natural aptitudes for refinement of manner in her sister-in-law, and partly, perhaps, from her more quiet and subdued manner, Mrs. Wordsworth would have been pronounced very much the more lady-like person.

From the interest which attaches to anybody so nearly connected as these two ladies with a great poet, I have allowed myself a larger latitude than else might have been justifiable in describing them. I now go on with my narrative: —

I was ushered up a little flight of stairs, fourteen in all, to a little drawing-room, or whatever the reader chooses to

call it.   Wordsworth himself has described the fireplace or
this room as his

> " Half-kitchen and half-parlour fire."

It was not fully seven feet six inches high, and, in other
respects, pretty nearly of the same dimensions as the rustic
hall below.   There was, however, in a small recess, a
library of perhaps three hundred volumes, which seemed
to consecrate the room as the poet's study and composing
room ; and such occasionally it was.   But far oftener he
both studied, as I found, and composed, on the high road.
I had not been two minutes at the fireside, when in came
Wordsworth, returning from his friendly attentions to the
travellers below, who, it seemed, had been over-persuaded
by hospitable solicitations to stay for this night in Grasmere, and to make out the remaining thirteen miles o
their road to Keswick on the following day.   Wordsworth
entered.   And "*what-like*" — to use a Westmoreland a
well as a Scottish expression — "*what-like*" was Wordsworth ?   A reviewer in "Tait's Magazine," noticing som
recent collection of literary portraits, gives it as his opinio
that Charles Lamb's head was the finest among them
This remark may have been justified by the engraved po-
traits ; but, certainly, the critic would have cancelled it, ha
he seen the original heads — at least, had he seen them i
youth or in maturity ; for Charles Lamb bore age with le-
disadvantage to the intellectual expression of his appea-
ance than Wordsworth, in whom a sanguine complexion ha-
of late years, usurped upon the original bronze-tint ; and th-
change of hue, and change in the quality of skin, had bee-
made fourfold more conspicuous, and more unfavourab-
in its general effect, by the harsh contrast of grizzled ha-
which had displaced the original brown.   No change

1 Vol. iv. p. 793 (Dec. 1837).

personal appearance ever can have been so unfortunate; for, generally speaking, whatever other disadvantages old age may bring along with it, one effect, at least in male subjects, has a compensating tendency — that it removes any tone of vigour too harsh, and mitigates the expression of power too unsubdued. But, in Wordsworth, the effect of the change has been to substitute an air of animal vigour, or, at least, hardiness, as if derived from constant exposure to the wind and weather, for the fine sombre complexion which he once wore, resembling that of a Venetian senator or a Spanish monk.

Here, however, in describing the personal appearance of Wordsworth, I go back, of course, to the point of time at which I am speaking. He was, upon the whole, not a well-made man. His legs were pointedly condemned by all female connoisseurs in legs; not that they were bad in any way which *would* force itself upon your notice — there was no absolute deformity about them; and undoubtedly they had been serviceable legs beyond the average standard of human requisition; for I calculate, upon good data, that with these identical legs Wordsworth must have traversed a distance of 175,000 to 180,000 English miles — a mode of exertion which, to him, stood in the stead of alcohol and all other stimulants whatsoever to the animal spirits; to which, indeed, he was indebted for a life of unclouded happiness, and we for much of what is most excellent in his writings. But, useful as they have proved themselves, the Wordsworthian legs were certainly not ornamental; and it was really a pity, as I agreed with a lady in thinking, that he had not another pair for evening dress parties — when no boots lend their friendly aid to mask our imperfections from the eyes of female rigorists — those *elegantes formarum spectatrices*. A sculptor would certainly have disapproved of their contour. But the worst part of Wordsworth's person was

the bust; there was a narrowness and a droop about the shoulders which became striking, and had an effect of meanness, when brought into close juxtaposition with a figure of a more statuesque build. Once on a summer evening, walk-
5 ing in the Vale of Langdale with Wordsworth, his sister, and Mr. J——, a native Westmoreland clergyman, I remember that Miss Wordsworth was positively mortified by the peculiar illustration which settled upon this defective conformation. Mr. J——, a fine towering figure, six feet high, massy
10 and columnar in his proportions, happened to be walking, a little in advance, with Wordsworth; Miss Wordsworth and myself being in the rear; and from the nature of the conversation which then prevailed in our front rank, something or other about money, devises, buying and selling,
15 we of the rear-guard thought it requisite to preserve this arrangement for a space of three miles or more; during which time, at intervals, Miss Wordsworth would exclaim, in a tone of vexation, "Is it possible, — can that be William? How very mean he looks!" And she did not conceal a
20 mortification that seemed really painful, until I, for my part, could not forbear laughing outright at the serious interest which she carried into this trifle. She was, however, right, as regarded the mere visual judgment. Wordsworth's figure, with all its defects, was brought into powerful relief by one
25 which had been cast in a more square and massy mould; and in such a case it impressed a spectator with a sense of absolute meanness, more especially when viewed from behind and not counteracted by his countenance; and yet Wordsworth was of a good height (five feet ten), and not a slender
30 man; on the contrary, by the side of Southey, his limbs looked thick, almost in a disproportionate degree. But the total effect of Wordsworth's person was always worst in a state of motion. Meantime, his face — that was one which would have made amends for greater defects of figure.

Many such, and finer, I have seen amongst the portraits of Titian, and, in a later period, amongst those of Vandyke, from the great era of Charles I, as also from the court of Elizabeth and of Charles II, but none which has more impressed me in my own time.

Haydon, in his great picture of "Christ's Entry into Jerusalem," has introduced Wordsworth in the character of a disciple attending his Divine Master, and Voltaire in the character of a sneering Jewish elder. This fact is well known; and, as the picture itself is tolerably well known to the public eye, there are multitudes now living who will have seen a very impressive likeness of Wordsworth — some consciously, some not suspecting it. There will, however, always be many who have *not* seen any portrait at all of Wordsworth; and therefore I will describe its general outline and effect. It was a face of the long order, often falsely classed as oval: but a greater mistake is made by many people in supposing the long face which prevailed so remarkably in the Elizabethan and Carolinian periods to have become extinct in our own. Miss Ferrier, in one of her novels ("Marriage," I think), makes a Highland girl protest that "no Englishman *with his round face*" shall ever wean her heart from her own country; but England is not the land of round faces; and those have observed little, indeed, who think so: France it is that grows the round face, and in so large a majority of her provinces that it has become one of the national characteristics. And the remarkable impression which an Englishman receives from the eternal recurrence of the orbicular countenance proves of itself, without any *conscious* testimony, how the fact stands; in the blind sense of a monotony, not felt elsewhere, lies involved an argument that cannot be gainsaid. Besides, even upon an *a priori* argument, how is it possible that the long face so prevalent in England, by all confession, in certain splendid eras of our history, should have had time, in some five or six generations, to grow extinct? Again, the character of face varies essentially in different provinces. Wales has no connexion in this respect with Devonshire, nor Kent with Yorkshire, nor either with West-moreland. England, it is true, tends, beyond all known examples, to a general amalgamation of differences, by means of its unrivalled freedom of intercourse. Yet, even in England, law and necessity have opposed as yet such and so many obstacles to the free diffusion of labour that every generation occupies, by at least five-sixths of its numbers, the ground of its ancestors.

The movable part of a population is chiefly the higher part; and it is the lower classes that, in every nation, com-pose the *fundus*, in which lies latent the national face, as well as the national character. Each exists here in racy purity and integrity, not disturbed in the one by alien intermarriages, nor in the other by novelties of opinion, or other casual effects, derived from education and reading. Now, look into this *fundus*, and you will find, in many dis-tricts, no such prevalence of the round orbicular face as some people erroneously suppose; and in Westmoreland, especially, the ancient long face of the Elizabethan period, powerfully resembling in all its lineaments the ancient Roman face, and often (though not so uniformly) the face of northern Italy in modern times. The face of Sir Walter Scott, as Irving, the pulpit orator, once remarked to me, was the indigenous face of the Border: the mouth, which was bad, and the entire lower part of the face, are seen repeated in thousands of working-men; or, as Irving chose to illustrate his position, "in thousands of Border horse-jockeys." In like manner, Wordsworth's face was, if not absolutely the indigenous face of the Lake district, at any rate a variety of that face, a modification of that original type. The head was well filled out; and there, to begin with, was a great advantage over the head of Charles Lamb, which was absolutely truncated in the posterior region — sawn off, as it were, by no timid sawyer. The forehead was not remarkably lofty — and, by the way, some artists, in their ardour for realising their phrenological preconceptions, not suffering nature to surrender quietly and by slow degrees her real alphabet of signs and hieroglyphic characters, but forcing her language prematurely into conformity with their own crude speculations, have given to Sir Walter Scott a pile of forehead which is unpleasing and cataphysical, in fact, a caricature of anything that is ever seen in nature, and would (if real) be esteemed a deformity; in one instance — that which was introduced in some animal or other — the forehead makes about two-thirds of the entire face. Wordsworth's forehead is also liable to caricature misrepresentations in these days of phrenology: but, whatever it may appear to be in any man's fanciful portrait, the real living forehead, as I have been in the habit of seeing it for more than five-and-twenty years, is not remarkable for its height; but it *is*, perhaps, remarkable for its breadth and expansive development. Neither are the eyes of Wordsworth "large," as is erroneously stated somewhere in "Peter's Letters"; on the contrary, they are (I think) rather small; but *that* does not interfere with their effect, which at times is fine, and suitable to his intellectual character. At times, I say, for the depth and subtlety of eyes, even their colouring (as to condensation or dilation), varies exceedingly with the state of the stomach; and, if young ladies were aware of the magical transformations which can be wrought in the depth and sweetness of the eye by a few weeks' walking exercise, I fancy we should see their habits in this point altered greatly for the better. I have seen Wordsworth's eyes oftentimes affected powerfully in this respect; his

eyes are not, under any circumstances, bright, lustrous, or
piercing; but, after a long day's toil in walking, I have
seen them assume an appearance the most solemn and
spiritual that it is possible for the human eye to wear.
5 The light which resides in them is at no time a superficial
light; but, under favourable accidents, it is a light which
seems to come from unfathomed depths: in fact, it is more
truly entitled to be held "the light that never was on land
or sea," a light radiating from some far spiritual world,
10 than any the most idealising that ever yet a painter's hand
created.   The nose, a little arched, is large; which, by the
way (according to a natural phrenology, existing centuries
ago amongst some of the lowest amongst the human species), has always been accounted an unequivocal expression
15 of animal appetites organically strong. And that expressed
the simple truth: Wordsworth's intellectual passions were
fervent and strong: but they rested upon a basis of preternatural animal sensibility diffused through *all* the animal
passions (or appetites); and something of that will be found
20 to hold of all poets who have been great by original force
and power, not (as Virgil) by means of fine management
and exquisite artifice of composition applied to their con-
ceptions.   The mouth, and the whole circumjacencies of
the mouth, composed the strongest feature in Wordsworth's
25 face; there was nothing specially to be noticed that I know
of in the mere outline of the lips; but the swell and pro-
trusion of the parts above and around the mouth are both
noticeable in themselves, and also because they remind me
of a very interesting fact which I discovered about three
30 years after this my first visit to Wordsworth.

Being a great collector of everything relating to Milton,
I had naturally possessed myself, whilst yet very young, of
Richardson the painter's thick octavo volume of notes on
the "Paradise Lost."   It happened, however, that my copy,

in consequence of that mania for portrait collecting which has stripped so many English classics of their engraved portraits, wanted the portrait of Milton. Subsequently I ascertained that it ought to have had a very good likeness of the great poet; and I never rested until I procured a copy of the book which had not suffered in this respect by the fatal admiration of the amateur. The particular copy offered to me was one which had been priced unusually high, on account of the unusually fine specimen which it contained of the engraved portrait. This, for a particular reason, I was exceedingly anxious to see; and the reason was — that, according to an anecdote reported by Richardson himself, this portrait, of all that were shown to her, was the only one acknowledged by Milton's last surviving daughter to be a strong likeness of her father. And her involuntary gestures concurred with her deliberate words: — for, on seeing all the rest, she was silent and inanimate; but the very instant she beheld that crayon drawing from which is derived the engraved head in Richardson's book, she burst out into a rapture of passionate recognition; exclaiming — " That is my father! that is my dear father!" Naturally, therefore, after such a testimony, so much stronger than any other person in the world could offer to the authentic value of this portrait, I was eager to see it.

Judge of my astonishment when, in this portrait of Milton, I saw a likeness nearly perfect of Wordsworth, better by much than any which I have since seen of those expressly painted for himself. The likeness is tolerably preserved in that by Carruthers, in which one of the little Rydal waterfalls, &c., composes a background; yet this is much inferior, as a mere portrait of Wordsworth, to the Richardson head of Milton; and this, I believe, is the last which represents Wordsworth in the vigour of his power.

The rest, which I have not seen, may be better as works of art (for anything I know to the contrary), but they must labour under the great disadvantage of presenting the features when "defeatured," in the degree and the way I have described, by the peculiar ravages of old age, as it affects this family; for it is noticed of the Wordsworths, by those who are familiar with their peculiarities, that in their very blood and constitutional differences lie hidden causes that are able, in some mysterious way,

> "Those shocks of passion to prepare
> That kill the bloom before its time,
> And blanch, without the owner's crime,
> The most resplendent hair."

Some people, it is notorious, live faster by much than others; the oil is burned out sooner in one constitution than another: and the cause of this may be various; but in the Wordsworths one part of the cause is, no doubt, the secret fire of a temperament too fervid; the self-consuming energies of the brain, that gnaw at the heart and life-strings for ever. In that account which "The Excursion" presents to us of an imaginary Scotsman who, to still the tumult of his heart, when visiting the cataracts of a mountainous region, obliges himself to study the laws of light and colour as they affect the rainbow of the stormy waters, vainly attempting to mitigate the fever which consumed him by entangling his mind in profound speculations; raising a cross-fire of artillery from the subtilising intellect, under the vain conceit that in this way he could silence the mighty battery of his impassioned heart: there we read a picture of Wordsworth and his own youth. In Miss Wordsworth every thoughtful observer might read the same self-consuming style of thought. And the effect upon each was so powerful for the promotion of a pre-

mature old age, and of a premature expression of old age,
that strangers invariably supposed them fifteen to twenty
years older than they were. And I remember Wordsworth
once laughingly reporting to me, on returning from a short
journey in 1809, a little personal anecdote, which sufficiently showed what was the spontaneous impression upon
that subject of casual strangers, whose feelings were not
confused by previous knowledge of the truth. He was
travelling by a stage-coach, and seated outside, amongst a
good half-dozen of fellow-passengers. One of these, an
elderly man, who confessed to having passed the grand
climacterical year (9 multiplied into 7) of 63, though he did
not say precisely by how many years, said to Wordsworth,
upon some anticipations which they had been mutually discussing of changes likely to result from enclosures, &c.,
then going on or projecting — "Ay, ay, another dozen of
years will show us strange sights ; but you and I can hardly
expect to see them." — "How so?" said Wordsworth.
"How so, my friend ? How old do you take me to be?"
— "Oh, I beg pardon," said the other ; "I meant no
offence — but what?" looking at Wordsworth more atten-
tively — "you'll never see threescore, I'm of opinion" ;
meaning to say that Wordsworth *had* seen it already.
And, to show that he was not singular in so thinking, he
appealed to all the other passengers ; and the motion
passed (*nem. con.*) that Wordsworth was rather over than
under sixty. Upon this he told them the literal truth —
that he had not yet accomplished his thirty-ninth year.
"God bless me ! " said the climacterical man ; "so then,
after all, you'll have a chance to see your childer get up
like, and get settled ! Only to think of that ! " And so
closed the conversation, leaving to Wordsworth an unde-
niable record of his own prematurely expressed old age in
this unaffected astonishment, amongst a whole party of

plain men, that he could really belong to a generation of the forward-looking, who live by hope; and might reasonably expect to see a child of seven years old matured into a man. And yet, as Wordsworth lived into his 82d year, 5 it is plain that the premature expression of decay does not argue any real decay.

Returning to the question of portraits, I would observe that this Richardson engraving of Milton has the advantage of presenting, not only by far the best likeness of Words- 10 worth, but of Wordsworth in the prime of his powers — a point essential in the case of one so liable to premature decay. It may be supposed that I took an early opportunity of carrying the book down to Grasmere, and calling for the opinions of Wordsworth's family upon this most 15 remarkable coincidence. Not one member of that family but was as much impressed as myself with the accuracy of the likeness. All the peculiarities even were retained — a drooping appearance of the eyelids, that remarkable swell which I have noticed about the mouth, the way in which 20 the hair lay upon the forehead. In two points only there was a deviation from the rigorous truth of Wordsworth's features — the face was a little too short and too broad, and the eyes were too large. There was also a wreath of laurel about the head, which (as Wordsworth remarked) disturbed 25 the natural expression of the whole picture; else, and with these few allowances, he also admitted that the resemblance was, *for that period of his life*, perfect, or as nearly so as art could accomplish.

I have gone into so large and circumstantial a review of 30 my recollections on this point as would have been trifling and tedious in excess, had these recollections related to a less important man; but I have a certain knowledge that the least of them will possess a lasting and a growing interest in connexion with William Wordsworth. How

peculiar, how different from the interest which we grant
to the ideas of a great philosopher, a great mathematician,
or a great reformer, is that burning interest which settles
on the great poets who have made themselves necessary to
the human heart; who have first brought into conscious- 5
ness, and have clothed in words, those grand catholic feelings that belong to the grand catholic situations of life
through all its stages; who have clothed them in such
words that human wit despairs of bettering them! Mighty
were the powers, solemn and serene is the memory, of 10
Archimedes; and Apollonius shines like "the starry
Galileo" in the firmament of human genius; yet how frosty
is the feeling associated with these names by comparison
with that which, upon every sunny lawn, by the side of
every ancient forest, even in the farthest depths of Canada, 15
many a young innocent girl, perhaps at this very moment
— looking now with fear to the dark recesses of the infinite
forest, and now with love to the pages of the infinite poet,
until the fear is absorbed and forgotten in the love — cher-
ishes in her heart for the name and person of Shakspere! 20

The English language is travelling fast towards the fulfilment of its destiny. Through the influence of the dreadful Republic[1] that within the thirty last years has run

---

[1] Not many months ago, the blind hostility of the Irish newspaper
editors in America forged a ludicrous estimate of the Irish numerical
preponderance in the United States, from which it was inferred, as at
least a possibility, that the Irish Celtic language might come to dispute
the pre-eminence with the English. Others anticipated the same
destiny for the German. But, in the meantime, the unresting career of
the law-courts, of commerce, and of the national senate, that cannot sus-
pend themselves for an hour, reduce the case to this dilemma: If the
Irish and the Germans in the United States adapt their general schemes
of education to the service of their public ambition, they must begin by
training themselves to the use of the language now prevailing on all the
available stages of ambition. On the other hand, by refusing to do

through all the stages of infancy into the first stage of
maturity, and through the English colonies — African,
Canadian, Indian, Australian — the English language
(and, therefore, the English literature) is running forward
5 towards its ultimate mission of eating up, like Aaron's rod,
all other languages. Even the German and the Spanish
will inevitably sink before it; perhaps within 100 or 150
years. In the recesses of California, in the vast solitudes
of Australia, *The Churchyard amongst the Mountains*, from
10 Wordsworth's " Excursion," and many a scene of his
shorter poems, will be read, even as now Shakspere is read
amongst the forests of Canada. All which relates to the
writer of these poems will then bear a value of the same
kind as that which attaches to our personal memorials
15 (unhappily so slender) of Shakspere.

this, they lose in the very outset every point of advantage. In other
words, adopting the English, they renounce the contest — *not* adopting
it, they disqualify themselves for the contest.

CONFESSIONS OF AN ENGLISH OPIUM-EATER

To the Reader.

I HERE present you, courteous reader, with the record of a remarkable period in my life: according to my application of it, I trust that it will prove, not merely an interesting record, but, in a considerable degree, useful and instructive. In *that* hope it is, that I have drawn it 5 up: and *that* must be my apology for breaking through that delicate and honourable reserve, which, for the most part, restrains us from the public exposure of our own errors and infirmities. Nothing, indeed, is more revolting to English feelings, than the spectacle of a human being 10 obtruding on our notice his moral ulcers and scars, and tearing away that 'decent drapery,' which time, or indulgence to human frailty, may have drawn over them: accordingly, the greater part of *our* confessions (that is, spontaneous and extra-judicial confessions) proceed from 15 demireps, adventurers, or swindlers: and for any such acts of gratuitous self-humiliation from those who can be supposed in sympathy with the decent and self-respecting part of society, we must look to French literature, or to that part of the German which is tainted with the spurious and 20 defective sensibility of the French. All this I feel so forcibly, and so nervously am I alive to reproach of this tendency, that I have for many months hesitated about the propriety of allowing this, or any part of my narrative, to come before the public eye, until after my death, 25 when, for many reasons, the whole will be published: and it is not without an anxious review of the reasons for and against this step that I have, at last, concluded on taking it.

Guilt and misery shrink, by a natural instinct, from public notice : they court privacy and solitude : and, even in their choice of a grave, will sometimes sequester themselves from the general population of the churchyard, as if declining to claim fellowship with the great family of man; and wishing (in the affecting language of Mr. Wordsworth)

> " — humbly to express
> A penitential loneliness."

It is well, upon the whole, and for the interest of us all, that it should be so : nor would I willingly, in my own person, manifest a disregard of such salutary feelings ; nor in act or word do anything to weaken them.   But, on the one hand, as my self-accusation does not amount to a confession of guilt, so, on the other, it is possible that, if it *did*, the benefit resulting to others from the record of an experience purchased at so heavy a price, might compensate, by a vast overbalance, for any violence done to the feelings I have noticed, and justify a breach of the general rule.   Infirmity and misery do not, of necessity, imply guilt.   They approach, or recede from, the shades of that dark alliance, in proportion to the probable motives and prospects of the offender, and the palliations, known or secret, of the offence : in proportion as the temptations to it were potent from the first, and the resistance to it, in act or in effort, was earnest to the last.   For my own part, without breach of truth or modesty, I may affirm, that my life has been, on the whole, the life of a philosopher : from my birth I was made an intellectual creature : and intellectual in the highest sense my pursuits and pleasures have been, even from my schoolboy days.   If opium-eating be a sensual pleasure, and if I am bound to confess that I have indulged in it to an excess not yet recorded[1] of any other man, it is no less true that I have struggled against this fascinating enthralment with a religious zeal, and have, at length, accomplished what I never yet heard attributed to any other man — have untwisted, almost to its final links, the accursed chain which fettered me. Such a self-conquest may reasonably be set off in counterbalance to any kind or degree of self-indulgence. Not to insist that, in my case, the self-conquest was unquestionable, the self-indulgence open to doubts of casuistry, according as that name shall be extended to acts aiming at the bare relief of pain, or shall be restricted to such as aim at the excitement of positive pleasure.

Guilt, therefore, I do not acknowledge: and, if I did, it is possible that I might still resolve on the present act of confession, in consideration of the service which I may thereby render to the whole class of opium-eaters. But who are they? Reader, I am sorry to say, a very numerous class indeed. Of this I became convinced some years ago, by computing, at that time, the number of those in one small class of English society — the class of men distinguished for talents, or of eminent station, — who were known to me, directly or indirectly, as opium-eaters; such, for instance, as the eloquent and benevolent [William Wilberforce]; the late dean of [Carlisle, Dr. Isaac Milner]; Lord [Erskine]; Mr. ——, the philosopher; the late under-secretary of state [Mr. Addington, brother to the late Lord Sidmouth] (who described to me the sensation which first drove him to the use of opium, in the very same words as the Dean of [Carlisle], viz., "that he felt as though rats were gnawing and abrading the coats of his stomach");

[1] "Not yet *recorded*," I say: for there is one celebrated man of the present day, who, if all be true which is reported of him, has greatly exceeded me in quantity.

Mr. [Coleridge]; and many others, hardly less known, whom it would be tedious to mention. Now, if one class, comparatively so limited, could furnish so many scores of cases (and *that* within the knowledge of one single 5 inquirer), it was a natural inference that the entire population of England would furnish a proportionable number. The soundness of this inference, however, I doubted, until some facts became known to me, which satisfied me that it was not incorrect. I will mention two: 1. Three 10 respectable London druggists, in widely remote quarters of London, from whom I happened lately to be purchasing small quantities of opium, assured me, that the number of *amateur* opium-eaters (as I may term them) was, at this time, immense; and that the difficulty of distinguishing 15 these persons, to whom habit had rendered opium necessary, from such as were purchasing it with a view to suicide, occasioned them daily trouble and disputes. This evidence respected London only. But, 2. (which will possibly surprise the reader more) some years ago, on 20 passing through Manchester, I was informed by several cotton-manufacturers that their work-people were rapidly getting into the practice of opium-eating; so much so, that on a Saturday afternoon the counters of the druggists were strewed with pills of one, two, or three grains, in 25 preparation for the known demand of the evening. The immediate occasion of this practice was the lowness of wages, which, at that time, would not allow them to indulge in ale or in spirits: and, wages rising, it may be thought that this practice would cease: but, as I do not 30 readily believe that any man, having once tasted the divine luxuries of opium, will afterwards descend to the gross and mortal enjoyments of alcohol, I take it for granted,

> " That those eat now, who never ate before ;
> And those who always ate, now eat the more."

Indeed the fascinating powers of opium are admitted, even by medical writers, who are its greatest enemies : thus, for instance, Awsiter, apothecary to Greenwich Hospital, in his " Essay on the Effects of Opium " (published in the year 1763), when attempting to explain, why Mead had not been sufficiently explicit on the properties, counteragents, etc., of this drug, expresses himself in the following myste-rious terms (φωναντα συνετοισι) : "perhaps he thought the subject of too delicate a nature to be made common ; and as many people might then indiscriminately use it, it would take from that necessary fear and caution, which should prevent their experiencing the extensive power of this drug : *for there are many properties in it, if universally known, that would habituate the use, and make it more in request with us than the Turks themselves :* the result of which knowl-edge," he adds, "must prove a general misfortune." In the necessity of this conclusion I do not altogether con-cur : but upon that point I shall have occasion to speak at the close of my confessions, where I shall present the reader with the *moral* of my narrative.

PRELIMINARY CONFESSIONS

THESE preliminary confessions, or introductory narrative of the youthful adventures which laid the foundation of the writer's habit of opium-eating in after-life, it has been judged proper to premise, for three several reasons :

1. As forestalling that question, and giving it a satis-factory answer, which else would painfully obtrude itself in the course of the Opium Confessions — " How came any reasonable being to subject himself to such a yoke of misery, voluntarily to incur a captivity so servile, and knowingly to fetter himself with such a sevenfold chain ? " — a question which, if not somewhere plausibly resolved,

could hardly fail, by the indignation which it would be apt to raise as against an act of wanton folly, to interfere with that degree of sympathy which is necessary in any case to an author's purposes.

5   2. As furnishing a key to some parts of that tremendous scenery which afterwards peopled the dreams of the opium-eater.

3. As creating some previous interest of a personal sort in the confessing subject, apart from the matter of the confessions, which cannot fail to render the confessions themselves more interesting. If a man, "whose talk is of oxen," should become an opium-eater, the probability is, that (if he is not too dull to dream at all) — he will dream about oxen : whereas, in the case before him, the reader will find that the opium-eater boasteth himself to be a philosopher ; and accordingly, that the phantasmagoria of *his* dreams (waking or sleeping, day-dreams or night-dreams) is suitable to one who in that character,

"Humani nihil a se alienum putat."

20   For amongst the conditions which he deems indispensable to the sustaining of any claim to the title of philosopher, is not merely the possession of a superb intellect in its *analytic* functions — in which part of the pretension, however, England can for some generations show but few claimants ; at least, he is not aware of any known candidate for this honour, who can be styled emphatically *a subtle thinker*, with the exception of *Samuel Taylor Coleridge*, and, in a narrower department of thought, with the recent illustrious exception [1] of *David Ricardo* — but also such a

---

[1] A third exception might perhaps have been added ; and my reason for not adding that exception is chiefly because it was only in his juvenile efforts that the writer whom I allude to expressly addressed himself to philosophical themes ; his riper powers having been all

constitution of the *moral* faculties as shall give him an inner eye and power of intuition for the vision and the mysteries of our human nature : *that* constitution of faculties, in short, which, amongst all the generations of men that from the beginning of time have deployed into life, as it were, upon this planet, our English poets have possessed in the highest degree, and Scottish[1] professors in the lowest.

I have often been asked how I came to be a regular opium-eater ; and have suffered, very unjustly, in the opinion of my acquaintance, from being reputed to have brought upon myself all the sufferings which I shall have to record, by a long course of indulgence in this practice purely for the sake of creating an artificial state of pleasurable excitement. This, however, is a misrepresentation of my case. True it is, that for nearly ten years I did occasionally take opium for the sake of the exquisite pleasure it gave me : but, so long as I took it with this view, I was effectually protected from all material bad consequences by the necessity of interposing long intervals between the several acts of indulgence, in order to renew the pleasurable sensations. It was not for the purpose of creating pleasure, but of mitigating pain in the severest degree, that I first

dedicated (on very excusable and very intelligible grounds, under the present direction of the popular mind in England) to criticism and the Fine Arts. This reason apart, however, I doubt whether he is not rather to be considered an acute thinker than a subtle one. It is, besides, a great drawback on his mastery over philosophical subjects, that he has obviously not had the advantage of a regular scholastic education : he has not read Plato in his youth (which most likely was only his misfortune) ; but neither has he read Kant in his manhood (which is his fault).

[1] I disdain any allusion to *existing* professors, of whom indeed I know only one.

began to use opium as an article of daily diet. In the twenty-eighth year of my age, a most painful affection of the stomach, which I had first experienced about ten years before, attacked me in great strength. This affection had originally been caused by extremities of hunger, suffered in my boyish days. During the season of hope and redundant happiness which succeeded (that is, from eighteen to twenty-four) it had slumbered: for the three following years it had revived at intervals: and now, under unfavourable circumstances, from depression of spirits, it attacked me with a violence that yielded to no remedies but opium. As the youthful sufferings which first produced this derangement of the stomach, were interesting in themselves, and in the circumstances that attended them, I shall here briefly retrace them.

My father died when I was about seven years old, and left me to the care of four guardians. I was sent to various schools, great and small; and was very early distinguished for my classical attainments, especially for my knowledge of Greek. At thirteen I wrote Greek with ease; and at fifteen my command of that language was so great that I not only composed Greek verses in lyric metres, but could converse in Greek fluently, and without embarrassment — an accomplishment which I have not since met with in any scholar of my times, and which, in my case, was owing to the practice of daily reading off the newspapers into the best Greek I could furnish *extempore:* for the necessity of ransacking my memory and invention for all sorts and combinations of periphrastic expressions, as equivalents for modern ideas, images, relations of things, etc., gave me a compass of diction which would never have been called out by a dull translation of moral essays, etc. "That boy," said one of my masters, pointing the attention of a stranger to me, "that boy could harangue an

Athenian mob better than you or I could address an English one." He who honoured me with this eulogy, was a scholar, "and a ripe and good one": and, of all my tutors, was the only one whom I loved or reverenced. Unfortunately for me (and, as I afterwards learned, to this worthy man's great indignation), I was transferred to the care, first of a blockhead, who was in a perpetual panic lest I should expose his ignorance; and finally, to that of a respectable scholar, at the head of a great school on an ancient foundation. This man had been appointed to his situation by [Brasenose] College, Oxford; and was a sound, well-built scholar, but, like most men whom I have known from that college, coarse, clumsy, and inelegant. A miserable contrast he presented, in my eyes, to the Etonian brilliancy of my favourite master: and, besides, he could not disguise from my hourly notice the poverty and meagreness of his understanding. It is a bad thing for a boy to be, and to know himself, far beyond his tutors, whether in knowledge or in power of mind. This was the case, so far as regarded knowledge at least, not with myself only: for the two boys, who jointly with myself composed the first form, were better Grecians than the head-master, though not more elegant scholars, nor at all more accustomed to sacrifice to the graces. When I first entered, I remember that we read Sophocles; and it was a constant matter of triumph to us, the learned triumvirate of the first form, to see our 'Archididascalus,' as he loved to be called, conning our lesson before we went up, and laying a regular train, with lexicon and grammar, for blowing up and blasting, as it were, any difficulties he found in the choruses; whilst *we* never condescended to open our books until the moment of going up, and were generally employed in writing epigrams upon his wig, or some such important matter. My two class-fellows were poor, and dependent for their future

prospects at the university, on the recommendation of the
head-master : but I, who had a small patrimonial property,
the income of which was sufficient to support me at college,
wished to be sent thither immediately.   I made earnest
5 representations on the subject to my guardians, but all
to no purpose.   One, who was more reasonable, and had
more knowledge of the world than the rest, lived at a distance : two of the other three resigned all their authority
into the hands of the fourth ; and this fourth, with whom I
10 had to negotiate, was a worthy man in his way, but
haughty, obstinate, and intolerant of all opposition to his
will.   After a certain number of letters and personal inter-
views, I found that I had nothing to hope for, not even a
compromise of the matter, from my guardian : unconditional
15 submission was what he demanded : and I prepared myself, therefore, for other measures.   Summer was now coming on with hasty steps, and my seventeenth birthday was
fast approaching ; after which day I had sworn within
myself that I would no longer be numbered amongst
20 schoolboys.   Money being what I chiefly wanted, I wrote
to a woman of high rank, who, though young herself, had
known me from a child, and had latterly treated me with
great distinction, requesting that she would 'lend' me five
guineas.   For upwards of a week no answer came ; and I
25 was beginning to despond, when, at length, a servant put
into my hands a double letter, with a coronet on the seal.
The letter was kind and obliging : the fair writer was on
the sea-coast, and in that way the delay had arisen : she
enclosed double of what I had asked, and good-naturedly
30 hinted that if I should *never* repay her it would not absolutely ruin her.   Now then, I was prepared for my scheme :
ten guineas, added to about two which I had remaining
from my pocket money, seemed to me sufficient for an
indefinite length of time : and at that happy age, if no

definite boundary can be assigned to one's power, the spirit of hope and pleasure makes it virtually infinite.

It is a just remark of Dr. Johnson's, and, what cannot often be said of his remarks, it is a very feeling one, that we never do anything consciously for the last time — of things, that is, which we have long been in the habit of doing — without sadness of heart. This truth I felt deeply, when I came to leave [Manchester], a place which I did not love, and where I had not been happy. On the evening before I left [Manchester] for ever, I grieved when the ancient and lofty school-room resounded with the evening service, performed for the last time in my hearing; and at night, when the muster-roll of names was called over, and mine, as usual, was called first, I stepped forward, and, passing the head-master, who was standing by, I bowed to him, and looked earnestly in his face, thinking to myself, "He is old and infirm, and in this world I shall not see him again." I was right: I never *did* see him again, nor ever shall. He looked at me complacently, smiled good-naturedly, returned my salutation, or rather my valediction, and we parted, though he knew it not, for ever. I could not reverence him intellectually: but he had been uniformly kind to me, and had allowed me many indulgences: and I grieved at the thought of the mortification I should inflict upon him.

The morning came which was to launch me into the world, and from which my whole succeeding life has, in many important points, taken its colouring. I lodged in the head-master's house, and had been allowed, from my first entrance, the indulgence of a private room, which I used both as a sleeping-room and as a study. At half after three I rose, and gazed with deep emotion at the ancient towers of [the Collegiate Church], "drest in earliest light," and beginning to crimson with the radiant lustre of a

cloudless July morning. I was firm and immovable in my
purpose : but yet agitated by anticipation of uncertain danger and troubles ; and, if I could have foreseen the hurricane and perfect hail-storm of affliction which soon fell
5 upon me, well might I have been agitated. To this agitation the deep peace of the morning presented an affecting
contrast, and in some degree a medicine. The silence was
more profound than that of midnight : and to me the
silence of a summer morning is more touching than all
10 other silence, because, the light being broad and strong, as
that of noon-day at other seasons of the year, it seems to
differ from perfect day chiefly because man is not yet
abroad ; and thus the peace of nature, and of the innocent
creatures of God, seems to be secure and deep, only so long
15 as the presence of man, and his restless and unquiet spirit,
are not there to trouble its sanctity. I dressed myself,
took my hat and gloves, and lingered a little in the room.
For the last year and a half this room had been my " pensive citadel " : here I had read and studied through all the
20 hours of night : and, though true it was that for the latter
part of this time I, who was framed for love and gentle
affections, had lost my gaiety and happiness, during the
strife and fever of contention with my guardian ; yet, on
the other hand, as a boy so passionately fond of books, and
25 dedicated to intellectual pursuits, I could not fail to have
enjoyed many happy hours in the midst of general dejection. I wept as I looked round on the chair, hearth,
writing-table, and other familiar objects, knowing too certainly that I looked upon them for the last time. Whilst
30 I write this, it is eighteen years ago : and yet, at this
moment, I see distinctly as if it were yesterday the lineaments and expression of the object on which I fixed my
parting gaze : it was a picture of the lovely ——, which
hung over the mantle-piece ; the eyes and mouth of which

were so beautiful, and the whole countenance so radiant with benignity and divine tranquillity, that I had a thousand times laid down my pen or my book, to gather consolation from it, as a devotee from his patron saint. Whilst I was yet gazing upon it, the deep tones of [Manchester] clock proclaimed that it was four o'clock. I went up to the picture, kissed it, and then gently walked out, and closed the door for ever!

*   *   *   *   *

So blended and intertwisted in this life are occasions of laughter and of tears, that I cannot yet recall, without smiling, an incident which occurred at that time, and which had nearly put a stop to the immediate execution of my plan. I had a trunk of immense weight; for, besides my clothes, it contained nearly all my library. The difficulty was to get this removed to a carrier's: my room was at an aerial elevation in the house, and (what was worse) the staircase, which communicated with this angle of the building, was accessible only by a gallery, which passed the head-master's chamber-door. I was a favourite with all the servants; and, knowing that any of them would screen me, and act confidentially, I communicated my embarrassment to a groom of the head-master's. The groom swore he would do anything I wished; and, when the time arrived, went up stairs to bring the trunk down. This I feared was beyond the strength of any one man: however, the groom was a man —

> " Of Atlantean shoulders, fit to bear
> The weight of mightiest monarchies ";

and had a back as spacious as Salisbury plain. Accordingly he persisted in bringing down the trunk alone, whilst I stood waiting at the foot of the last flight, in anxiety for the event. For some time I heard him descending with

slow and firm steps: but, unfortunately, from his trepidation
as he drew near the dangerous quarter, within a few steps
of the gallery, his foot slipped; and the mighty burden,
falling from his shoulders, gained such increase of impetus
5 at each step of the descent, that, on reaching the bottom,
it tumbled, or rather leaped, right across, with the noise
of twenty devils, against the very bedroom door of the
Archididascalus.   My first thought was, that all was lost;
and that my only chance for executing a retreat was to sac-
10 rifice my baggage.   However, on reflection, I determined
to abide the issue.   The groom was in the utmost alarm,
both on his own account and on mine: but, in spite of
this, so irresistibly had the sense of the ludicrous, in this
unhappy *contretemps*, taken possession of his fancy, that he
15 sang out a long, loud, and canorous peal of laughter, that
might have wakened the Seven Sleepers.   At the sound of
this resonant merriment, within the very ears of insulted
authority, I could not myself forbear joining in it: subdued
to this, not so much by the unhappy *étourderie* of the trunk,
20 as by the effect it had upon the groom.   We both expected,
as a matter of course, that Dr. [Lawson] would sally out
of his room: for, in general, if but a mouse stirred, he
sprang out like a mastiff from his kennel.   Strange to say,
however, on this occasion, when the noise of laughter had
25 ceased, no sound, or rustling even, was to be heard in the
bedroom.   Dr. [Lawson] had a painful complaint, which,
sometimes keeping him awake, made his sleep, perhaps,
when it *did* come, the deeper.   Gathering courage from the
silence, the groom hoisted his burden again, and accom-
30 plished the remainder of his descent without accident.
I waited until I saw the trunk placed on a wheel-barrow,
and on its road to the carrier's: then, "with Providence
my guide," I set off on foot, — carrying a small parcel, with
some articles of dress, under my arm; a favourite English

poet in one pocket; and a small 12mo volume, containing about nine plays of Euripides, in the other.

It had been my intention originally to proceed to Westmoreland, both from the love I bore to that country, and on other personal accounts. Accident, however, gave a different direction to my wanderings, and I bent my steps towards North Wales.

After wandering about for some time in Denbighshire, Merionethshire, and Caernarvonshire, I took lodgings in a small neat house in B[angor]. Here I might have staid with great comfort for many weeks; for provisions were cheap at B[angor], from the scarcity of other markets for the surplus produce of a wide agricultural district. An accident, however, in which, perhaps, no offence was designed, drove me out to wander again. I know not whether my reader may have remarked, but *I* have often remarked, that the proudest class of people in England, or, at any rate, the class whose pride is most apparent, are the families of bishops. Noblemen and their children carry about with them, in their very titles, a sufficient notification of their rank. Nay, their very names, and this applies also to the children of many untitled houses, are often to the English ear adequate exponents of high birth or descent. Sackville, Manners, Fitzroy, Paulet, Cavendish, and scores of others, tell their own tale. Such persons, therefore, find everywhere a due sense of their claims already established, except among those who are ignorant of the world by virtue of their own obscurity: " Not to know *them*, argues one's self unknown." Their manners take a suitable tone and colouring; and, for once that they find it necessary to impress a sense of their consequence upon others, they meet with a thousand occasions for moderating and tempering this sense by acts of courteous condescension. With the families of bishops it is otherwise: with them it is all uphill work to make known

their pretensions : for the proportion of the episcopal bench
taken from noble families is not at any time very large ; and
the succession to these dignities is so rapid that the public
ear seldom has time to become familiar with them, unless
5 where they are connected with some literary reputation.
Hence it is, that the children of bishops carry about with
them an austere and repulsive air, indicative of claims not
generally acknowledged, a sort of *noli me tangere* manner,
nervously apprehensive of too familiar approach, and shrink-
10 ing with the sensitiveness of a gouty man, from all contact
with the οἱ πολλοί. Doubtless, a powerful understanding,
or unusual goodness of nature, will preserve a man from
such weakness : but, in general, the truth of my representation will be acknowledged : pride, if not of deeper root
15 in such families, appears, at least, more upon the surface of
their manners. This spirit of manners naturally communicates itself to their domestics and other dependents. Now,
my landlady had been a lady's maid, or a nurse, in the
family of the Bishop of [Bangor]; and had but lately
20 married away and "settled" (as such people express it) for
life. In a little town like B[angor] merely to have lived
in the bishop's family conferred some distinction : and my
good landlady had rather more than her share of the pride
I have noticed on that score. What "my lord" said, and
25 what "my lord" did, how useful he was in parliament, and
how indispensable at Oxford, formed the daily burden of
her talk. All this I bore very well : for I was too good-
natured to laugh in anybody's face, and I could make an
ample allowance for the garrulity of an old servant. Of
30 necessity, however, I must have appeared in her eyes very
inadequately impressed with the bishop's importance : and,
perhaps, to punish me for my indifference, or possibly by
accident, she one day repeated to me a conversation in
which I was indirectly a party concerned. She had been

to the palace to pay her respects to the family; and, dinner being over, was summoned into the dining-room. In giving an account of her household economy, she happened to mention that she had let her apartments. Thereupon the good bishop (it seemed) had taken occasion to caution her as to her selection of inmates: "for," said he, "you must recollect, Betty, that this place is in the high road to the Head; so that multitudes of Irish swindlers, running away from their debts into England — and of English swindlers, running away from their debts to the Isle of Man, are likely to take this place in their route." This advice was certainly not without reasonable grounds: but rather fitted to be stored up for Mrs. Betty's private meditations, than specially reported to me. What followed, however, was somewhat worse:— "Oh, my lord," answered my landlady (according to her own representation of the matter), "I really don't think this young gentleman is a swindler; because——:" "You don't *think* me a swindler?" said I, interrupting her, in a tumult of indignation: "for the future I shall spare you the trouble of thinking about it." And without delay I prepared for my departure. Some concessions the good woman seemed disposed to make: but a harsh and contemptuous expression which I fear that I applied to the learned dignitary himself, roused *her* indignation in turn: and reconciliation then became impossible. I was, indeed, greatly irritated at the bishop's having suggested any grounds of suspicion, however remotely, against a person whom he had never seen: and I thought of letting him know my mind in Greek: which, at the same time that it would furnish some presumption that I was no swindler, would also, I hoped, compel the bishop to reply in the same language; in which case, I doubted not to make it appear, that if I was not so rich as his lordship, I was a better Grecian. Calmer thoughts, however, drove this boyish design out of my mind: for I considered that the bishop was in the right to counsel an old servant; that he could not have designed that his advice should be reported to me; and that the same coarseness of mind which had led Mrs. Betty to repeat the advice at all might have coloured it in a way more agreeable to her own style of thinking than to the actual expressions of the worthy bishop.

I left the lodgings the same hour; and this turned out a very unfortunate occurrence for me: because, living henceforward at inns, I was drained of my money very rapidly. In a fortnight I was reduced to short allowance; that is, I could allow myself only one meal a day. From the keen appetite produced by constant exercise and mountain air acting on a youthful stomach, I soon began to suffer greatly on this slender regimen; for the single meal which I could venture to order was coffee or tea. Even this, however, was at length withdrawn: and afterwards, so long as I remained in Wales, I subsisted either on blackberries, hips, haws, etc., or on the casual hospitalities which I now and then received, in return for such little services as I had an opportunity of rendering. Sometimes I wrote letters of business for cottagers, who happened to have relatives in Liverpool, or in London: more often I wrote love-letters to their sweethearts for young women who had lived as servants in Shrewsbury, or other towns on the English border. On all such occasions I gave great satisfaction to my humble friends, and was generally treated with hospitality: and once, in particular, near the village of Llan-y-styndw (or some such name), in a sequestered part of Merionethshire, I was entertained for upwards of three days by a family of young people, with an affectionate and fraternal kindness that left an impression upon my heart not yet impaired. The family consisted, at that time, of four sisters and three brothers, all grown up, and

all remarkable for elegance and delicacy of manners. So
much beauty, and so much native good-breeding and
refinement, I do not remember to have seen before or
since in any cottage, except once or twice in Westmoreland
and Devonshire. They spoke English: an accomplishment not often met with in so many members of one
family, especially in villages remote from the high road.
Here I wrote, on my first introduction, a letter about prize-
money, for one of the brothers, who had served on board
an English man-of-war; and more privately, two love-
letters for two of the sisters. They were both interesting
looking girls, and one of uncommon loveliness. In the
midst of their confusion and blushes, whilst dictating, or
rather giving me general instructions, it did not require
any great penetration to discover that what they wished
was, that their letters should be as kind as was consistent
with proper maidenly pride. I contrived so to temper my
expressions as to reconcile the gratification of both feelings : and they were as much pleased with the way in
which I had expressed their thoughts, as, in their simplicity, they were astonished at my having so readily discovered them. The reception one meets with from the
women of a family generally determines the tenour of one's
whole entertainment. In this case I had discharged my
confidential duties as secretary so much to the general
satisfaction, perhaps also amusing them with my conversation, that I was pressed to stay with a cordiality which I
had little inclination to resist. I slept with the brothers,
the only unoccupied bed standing in the apartment of the
young women: but in all other points, they treated me
with a respect not usually paid to purses as light as mine;
as if my scholarship were sufficient evidence that I was of
"gentle blood." Thus I lived with them for three days,
and a greater part of a fourth: and from the undiminished

kindness which they continued to show me, I believe I might have staid with them up to this time, if their power had corresponded with their wishes.   On the last morning, however, I perceived upon their countenances, as they sat
5 at breakfast, the expression of some unpleasant communication which was at hand; and soon after one of the brothers explained to me, that their parents had gone, the day before my arrival, to an annual meeting of Methodists, held at Caernarvon, and were that day expected to return;
10 " and if they should not be so civil as they ought to be," he begged, on the part of all the young people, that I would not take it amiss.   The parents returned, with churlish faces, and "*Dym Sassenach*" (*no English*), in answer to all my addresses.   I saw how matters stood; and so, tak-
15 ing an affectionate leave of my kind and interesting young hosts, I went my way.   For, though they spoke warmly to their parents in my behalf, and often excused the manner of the old people, by saying that it was "only their way," yet I easily understood that my talent for writing love-
20 letters would do as little to recommend me with two grave sexagenarian Welsh Methodists, as my Greek Sapphics or Alcaics: and what had been hospitality, when offered to me with the gracious courtesy of my young friends, would become charity, when connected with the harsh demeanour
25 of these old people.   Certainly, Mr. Shelley is right in his notions about old age: unless powerfully counteracted by all sorts of opposite agencies, it is a miserable corrupter and blighter to the genial charities of the human heart.

    Soon after this, I contrived, by means which I must
30 omit for want of room, to transfer myself to London.   And now began the latter and fiercer stage of my long sufferings; without using a disproportionate expression, I might say, of my agony.   For I now suffered, for upwards of sixteen weeks, the physical anguish of hunger in various degrees

of intensity; but as bitter, perhaps, as ever any human being can have suffered who has survived it. I would not needlessly harass my reader's feelings by a detail of all that I endured: for extremities such as these, under any circumstances of heaviest misconduct or guilt, cannot be contemplated even in description without a rueful pity that is painful to the natural goodness of the human heart. Let it suffice, at least on this occasion, to say that a few fragments of bread from the breakfast-table of one individual, who supposed me to be ill, but did not know of my being in utter want, and these at uncertain intervals, constituted my whole support. During the former part of my sufferings, that is, generally in Wales, and always for the first two months in London, I was houseless, and very seldom slept under a roof. To this constant exposure to the open air I ascribe it mainly that I did not sink under my torments. Latterly, however, when colder and more inclement weather came on, and when, from the length of my sufferings, I had begun to sink into a more languishing condition, it was, no doubt, fortunate for me that the same person to whose breakfast-table I had access allowed me to sleep in a large unoccupied house, of which he was tenant. Unoccupied, I call it, for there was no household or establishment in it; nor any furniture indeed, except a table and a few chairs. But I found, on taking possession of my new quarters, that the house already contained one single inmate, a poor friendless child, apparently ten years old; but she seemed hunger-bitten; and sufferings of that sort often make children look older than they are. From this forlorn child I learned that she had slept and lived there alone for some time before I came: and great joy the poor creature expressed, when she found that I was, in future, to be her companion through the hours of darkness. The house was large; and, from the want of furniture, the noise

of the rats made a prodigious echoing on the spacious stair
case and hall; and, amidst the real fleshly ills of cold, and,
I fear, hunger, the forsaken child had found leisure to suffer
still more, it appeared, from the self-created one of ghosts.
5 I promised her protection against all ghosts whatsoever:
but, alas! I could offer her no other assistance. We lay
upon the floor, with a bundle of cursed law papers for a
pillow: but with no other covering than a sort of large
horseman's cloak: afterwards, however, we discovered, in
10 a garret, an old sofa-cover, a small piece of rug, and some
fragments of other articles, which added a little to our
warmth. The poor child crept close to me for warmth,
and for security against her ghostly enemies. When I was
not more than usually ill, I took her into my arms, so that,
15 in general, she was tolerably warm, and often slept when I
could not: for, during the last two months of my sufferings,
I slept much in the day-time, and was apt to fall into transient dozings at all hours. But my sleep distressed me more
than my watching: for, besides the tumultuousness of my
20 dreams, which were only not so awful as those which I shall
have to describe hereafter as produced by opium, my sleep
was never more than what is called *dog-sleep;* so that I
could hear myself moaning, and was often, as it seemed to
me, wakened suddenly by my own voice; and, about this
25 time, a hideous sensation began to haunt me as soon as I
fell into a slumber, which has since returned upon me at
different periods of my life, viz., a sort of twitching, I know
not where, but apparently about the region of the stomach,
which compelled me violently to throw out my feet for the
30 sake of relieving it. This sensation coming on as soon
as I began to sleep, and the effort to relieve it constantly
awaking me, at length I slept only from exhaustion; and
from increasing weakness, as I said before, I was constantly
falling asleep, and constantly awaking. Meantime, the

master of the house sometimes came in upon us suddenly, and very early, sometimes not till ten o'clock, sometimes not at all. He was in constant fear of bailiffs: improving on the plan of Cromwell, every night he slept in a different quarter of London; and I observed that he never failed to examine through a private window the appearance of those who knocked at the door, before he would allow it to be opened. He breakfasted alone: indeed, his tea equipage would hardly have admitted of his hazarding an invitation to a second person — any more than the quantity of esculent *matériel*, which, for the most part, was little more than a roll, or a few biscuits, which he had bought on his road from the place where he had slept. Or, if he *had* asked a party, as I once learnedly and facetiously observed to him — the several members of it must have *stood* in the relation to each other (not *sat* in any relation whatever) of succession, as the metaphysicians have it, and not of co-existence; in the relation of the parts of time, and not of the parts of space. During his breakfast, I generally contrived a reason for lounging in; and, with an air of as much indifference as I could assume, took up such fragments as he had left — sometimes, indeed, there were none at all. In doing this, I committed no robbery except upon the man himself, who was thus obliged, I believe, now and then to send out at noon for an extra biscuit; for, as to the poor child, *she* was never admitted into his study, if I may give that name to his chief depository of parchments, law writings, etc.; that room was to her the Blue-beard room of the house, being regularly locked on his departure to dinner, about six o'clock, which usually was his final departure for the night. Whether this child were an illegitimate daughter of Mr. [Brunell], or only a servant, I could not ascertain; she did not herself know; but certainly she was treated altogether as a menial servant. No sooner did Mr. [Brunell] make

his appearance, than she went below stairs, brushed his
shoes, coat, etc. ; and, except when she was summoned to
run an errand, she never emerged from the dismal Tartarus
of the kitchens, etc., to the upper air, until my welcome
knock at night called up her little trembling footsteps to
the front door. Of her life during the day-time, however,
I knew little but what I gathered from her own account at
night ; for, as soon as the hours of business commenced, I
saw that my absence would be acceptable ; and, in general,
therefore, I went off, and sat in the parks, or elsewhere,
until night-fall.

But who, and what, meantime, was the master of the
house himself ? Reader, he was one of those anomalous
practitioners in lower departments of the law, who —
what shall I say ? — who, on prudential reasons, or from
necessity, deny themselves all indulgence in the luxury of
too delicate a conscience : (a periphrasis which might be
abridged considerably, but *that* I leave to the reader's
taste :) in many walks of life, a conscience is a more expensive encumbrance, than a wife or a carriage ; and just as
people talk of "laying down" their carriages, so I suppose
my friend, Mr. [Brunell], had "laid down" his conscience
for a time ; meaning, doubtless, to resume it as soon as he
could afford it. The inner economy of such a man's daily
life would present a most strange picture, if I could allow
myself to amuse the reader at his expense. Even with my
limited opportunities for observing what went on, I saw
many scenes of London intrigues, and complex chicanery
"cycle and epicycle, orb in orb," at which I sometimes
smile to this day — and at which I smiled then, in spite of
my misery. My situation, however, at that time, gave me
little experience, in my own person, of any qualities in Mr.
[Brunell]'s character but such as did him honour ; and of
his whole strange composition I must forget everything

but that towards me he was obliging, and to the extent of his power, generous.

That power was not, indeed, very extensive ; however, in common with the rats, I sat rent free ; and, as Dr. Johnson has recorded, that he never but once in his life had as much wall-fruit as he could eat, so let me be grateful, that on that single occasion I had as large a choice of apartments in a London mansion as I could possibly desire. Except the Blue-beard room, which the poor child believed to be haunted, all others, from the attics to the cellars, were at our service ; "the world was all before us " ; and we pitched our tent for the night in any spot we chose. This house I have already described as a large one ; it stands in a conspicuous situation, and in a well-known part of London. Many of my readers will have passed it, I doubt not, within a few hours of reading this. For myself, I never fail to visit it when business draws me to London ; about ten o'clock, this very night, August 15, 1821, being my birthday, — I turned aside from my evening walk, down Oxford Street, purposely to take a glance at it : it is now occupied by a respectable family ; and, by the lights in the front drawing-room, I observed a domestic party, assembled perhaps at tea, and apparently cheerful and gay. Marvellous contrast in my eyes to the darkness — cold — silence — and desolation of that same house eighteen years ago, when its nightly occupants were one famishing scholar, and a neglected child. — Her, by the bye, in after years, I vainly endeavoured to trace. Apart from her situation, she was not what would be called an interesting child : she was neither pretty, nor quick in understanding, nor remarkably pleasing in manners. But, thank God ! even in those years I needed not the embellishments of novel accessaries to conciliate my affections ; plain human nature, in its humblest and most homely apparel, was enough for me : and I loved

the child because she was my partner in wretchedness. If
she is now living, she is probably a mother, with children
of her own ; but, as I have said, I could never trace her.

This I regret, but another person there was at that time,
whom I have since sought to trace with far deeper earnestness, and with far deeper sorrow at my failure. This person was a young woman, and one of that unhappy class who
subsist upon the wages of prostitution. I feel no shame,
nor have any reason to feel it, in avowing, that I was then
on familiar and friendly terms with many women in that
unfortunate condition. The reader needs neither smile at
this avowal, nor frown. For, not to remind my classical
readers of the old Latin proverb — "*Sine Cerere*," etc., it
may well be supposed that in the existing state of my purse
my connexion with such women could not have been an
impure one. But the truth is, that at no time of my life
have I been a person to hold myself polluted by the touch
or approach of any creature that wore a human shape : on
the contrary, from my very earliest youth it has been my
pride to converse familiarly, *more Socratico*, with all human
beings, man, woman, and child, that chance might fling in
my way : a practice which is friendly to the knowledge of
human nature, to good feelings, and to that frankness of
address which becomes a man who would be thought a philosopher. For a philosopher should not see with the eyes of
the poor limitary creature, calling himself a man of the world,
and filled with narrow and self-regarding prejudices of birth
and education, but should look upon himself as a catholic
creature, and as standing in an equal relation to high and
low — to educated and uneducated, to the guilty and the
innocent. Being myself at that time of necessity a peripa-
tetic, or a walker of the streets, I naturally fell in more
frequently with those female peripatetics who are technically called street-walkers. Many of these women had

occasionally taken my part against watchmen who wished to drive me off the steps of houses where I was sitting. But one amongst them, the one on whose account I have at all introduced this subject — yet no! let me not class thee, oh noble-minded Ann ——, with that order of women; let me find, if it be possible, some gentler name to designate the condition of her to whose bounty and compassion, ministering to my necessities when all the world had forsaken me, I owe it that I am at this time alive. — For many weeks I had walked at nights with this poor friendless girl up and down Oxford Street, or had rested with her on steps and under the shelter of porticoes. She could not be so old as myself: she told me, indeed, that she had not completed her sixteenth year. By such questions as my interest about her prompted, I had gradually drawn forth her simple history. Hers was a case of ordinary occurrence (as I have since had reason to think), and one in which, if London beneficence had better adapted its arrangements to meet it, the power of the law might oftener be interposed to protect, and to avenge. But the stream of London charity flows in a channel which, though deep and mighty, is yet noiseless and under-ground; not obvious or readily accessible to poor houseless wanderers: and it cannot be denied that the outside air and frame-work of London society is harsh, cruel, and repulsive. In any case, however, I saw that part of her injuries might easily have been redressed; and I urged her often and earnestly to lay her complaint before a magistrate: friendless as she was, I assured her that she would meet with immediate attention; and that English justice, which was no respecter of persons, would speedily and amply avenge her on the brutal ruffian who had plundered her little property. She promised me often that she would; but she delayed taking the steps I pointed out from time to time: for she was timid and dejected to a degree which showed how deeply sorrow had taken hold of her young heart : and perhaps she thought justly that the most upright judge, and the most righteous tribunals, could do nothing to repair her heaviest 5 wrongs. Something, however, would perhaps have been done : for it had been settled between us at length, but unhappily on the very last time but one that I was ever to see her, that in a day or two we should go together before a magistrate, and that I should speak on her behalf. This 10 little service it was destined, however, that I should never realise. Meantime, that which she rendered to me, and which was greater than I could ever have repaid her, was this : — One night, when we were pacing slowly along Oxford Street, and after a day when I had felt more than 15 usually ill and faint, I requested her to turn off with me into Soho Square : thither we went ; and we sat down on the steps of a house, which, to this hour, I never pass without a pang of grief, and an inner act of homage to the spirit of that unhappy girl, in memory of the noble action 20 which she there performed. Suddenly, as we sat, I grew much worse : I had been leaning my head against her bosom ; and all at once I sank from her arms and fell backwards on the step. From the sensations I then had, I felt an inner conviction of the liveliest kind that without some 25 powerful and reviving stimulus, I should either have died on the spot — or should at least have sunk to a point of exhaustion from which all re-ascent under my friendless circumstances would soon have become hopeless. Then it was, at this crisis of my fate, that my poor orphan com-30 panion — who had herself met with little but injuries in this world — stretched out a saving hand to me. Uttering a cry of terror, but without a moment's delay, she ran off into Oxford Street, and in less time than could be imagined, returned to me with a glass of port wine and spices, that acted upon my empty stomach (which at that time would have rejected all solid food) with an instantaneous power of restoration : and for this glass the generous girl without a murmur paid out of her own humble purse at a time — be it remembered ! — when she had scarcely wherewithal to 5 purchase the bare necessaries of life, and when she could have no reason to expect that I should ever be able to reimburse her. ——— Oh ! youthful benefactress ! how often in succeeding years, standing in solitary places, and think- ing of thee with grief of heart and perfect love, how often 10 have I wished that, as in ancient times the curse of a father was believed to have a supernatural power, and to pursue its object with a fatal necessity of self-fulfilment, — even so the benediction of a heart oppressed with gratitude might have a like prerogative; might have power given it 15 from above to chase — to haunt — to way-lay — to overtake — to pursue thee into the central darkness of a London brothel, or, if it were possible, into the darkness of the grave — there to awaken thee with an authentic message of peace and forgiveness, and of final reconciliation ! 20

I do not often weep : for not only do my thoughts on subjects connected with the chief interests of man daily, nay hourly, descend a thousand fathoms "too deep for tears"; not only does the sternness of my habits of thought present an antagonism to the feelings which prompt tears 25 — wanting of necessity to those who, being protected usually by their levity from any tendency to meditative sorrow, would by that same levity be made incapable of resisting it on any casual access of such feelings : — but also, I believe that all minds which have contemplated 30 such objects as deeply as I have done, must, for their own protection from utter despondency, have early encouraged and cherished some tranquillising belief as to the future balances and the hieroglyphic meanings of human sufferings.

On these accounts, I am cheerful to this hour; and, as I have said, I do not often weep. Yet some feelings, though not deeper or more passionate, are more tender than others; and often, when I walk at this time in Oxford Street by dreamy lamp-light, and hear those airs played on a barrel-organ which years ago solaced me and my dear companion, as I must always call her, I shed tears, and muse with myself at the mysterious dispensation which so suddenly and so critically separated us for ever. How it happened, the reader will understand from what remains of this introductory narration.

Soon after the period of the last incident I have recorded, I met, in Albemarle Street, a gentleman of his late majesty's household. This gentleman had received hospitalities, on different occasions, from my family: and he challenged me upon the strength of my family likeness. I did not attempt any disguise: I answered his questions ingenuously, — and, on his pledging his word of honour that he would not betray me to my guardians, I gave him an address to my friend the attorney's. The next day I received from him a £10 Bank-note. The letter enclosing it was delivered with other letters of business to the attorney; but, though his look and manner informed me that he suspected its contents, he gave it up to me honourably and without demur.

This present, from the particular service to which it was applied, leads me naturally to speak of the purpose which had allured me up to London, and which I had been (to use a forensic word) *soliciting* from the first day of my arrival in London, to that of my final departure.

In so mighty a world as London, it will surprise my readers that I should not have found some means of staving off the last extremities of penury: and it will strike them that two resources at least must have been open to me, — viz., either to seek assistance from the friends of my family, or to turn my youthful talents and attainments into some channel of pecuniary emolument. As to the first course, I may observe, generally, that what I dreaded beyond all other evils was the chance of being reclaimed by my guardians; not doubting that whatever power the law gave them would have been enforced against me to the utmost; that is, to the extremity of forcibly restoring me to the school which I had quitted : a restoration which as it would in my eyes have been a dishonour, even if submitted to voluntarily, could not fail, when extorted from me in contempt and defiance of my known wishes and efforts, to have been a humiliation worse to me than death, and which would indeed have terminated in death. I was, therefore, shy enough of applying for assistance even in those quarters where I was sure of receiving it — at the risk of furnishing my guardians with any clue for recovering me.   But, as to London in particular, though, doubtless, my father had in his life-time had many friends there, yet, as ten years had passed since his death, I remembered few of them even by name : and never having seen London before, except once for a few hours, I knew not the address of even those few.   To this mode of gaining help, therefore, in part the difficulty, but much more the paramount fear which I have mentioned, habitually indisposed me. In regard to the other mode, I now feel half inclined to join my reader in wondering that I should have overlooked it.   As a corrector of Greek proofs, if in no other way, I might doubtless have gained enough for my slender wants. Such an office as this I could have discharged with an exemplary and punctual accuracy that would soon have gained me the confidence of my employers.   But it must not be forgotten that, even for such an office as this, it was necessary that I should first of all have an introduction to

some respectable publisher : and this I had no means of
obtaining. To say the truth, however, it had never once
occurred to me to think of literary labours as a source of
profit. No mode sufficiently speedy of obtaining money
had ever occurred to me, but that of borrowing it on the
strength of my future claims and expectations. This mode
I sought by every avenue to compass, and amongst other
persons I applied to a Jew named D[ell].[1]

To this Jew, and to other advertising money-lenders,
some of whom were, I believe, also Jews, I had introduced
myself with an account of my expectations ; which account,

[1] To this same Jew, by the way, some eighteen months afterwards,
I applied again on the same business ; and, dating at that time from
a respectable college, I was fortunate enough to gain his serious attention to my proposals. My necessities had not arisen from any extravagance or youthful levities (these my habits and the nature of my
pleasures raised me far above), but simply from the vindictive malice
of my guardian, who, when he found himself no longer able to prevent
me from going to the university, had, as a parting token of his good
nature, refused to sign an order for granting me a shilling beyond the
allowance made to me at school — viz., £100 per annum. Upon this
sum it was, in my time, barely possible to have lived in college, and
not possible to a man who, though above the paltry affectation of
ostentatious disregard for money, and without any expensive tastes,
confided nevertheless rather too much in servants, and did not delight
in the petty details of minute economy. I soon, therefore, became
embarrassed ; and at length, after a most voluminous negotiation with
the Jew (some parts of which, if I had leisure to rehearse them, would
greatly amuse my readers), I was put in possession of the sum I asked
for, on the "regular" terms of paying the Jew seventeen and a-half per
cent. by way of annuity on all the money furnished ; Israel, on his part,
graciously resuming no more than about ninety guineas of the said
money, on account of an attorney's bill (for what services, to whom
rendered, and when, whether at the siege of Jerusalem — at the building of the Second Temple — or on some earlier occasion, I have not
yet been able to discover). How many perches this bill measured I
really forget ; but I still keep it in a cabinet of natural curiosities, and
sometime or other I believe I shall present it to the British Museum.

on examining my father's will at Doctor's Commons, they had ascertained to be correct. The person there mentioned as the second son of ——, was found to have all the claims, or more than all, that I had stated : but one question still remained, which the faces of the Jews pretty significantly suggested, — was *I* that person ? This doubt had never occurred to me as a possible one : I had rather feared, whenever my Jewish friends scrutinized me keenly, that I might be too well known to be that person — and that some scheme might be passing in their minds for entrapping me, and selling me to my guardians. It was strange to me to find my own self, *materialiter* considered (so I expressed it, for I doted on logical accuracy of distinctions), accused, or at least suspected, of counterfeiting my own self, *formaliter* considered. However, to satisfy their scruples, I took the only course in my power. Whilst I was in Wales, I had received various letters from young friends : these I produced : for I carried them constantly in my pocket — being, indeed, by this time, almost the only relics of my personal incumbrances (excepting the clothes I wore) which I had not in one way or other disposed of. Most of these letters were from the Earl of [Altamont], who was at that time my chief, or rather only, confidential friend. These letters were dated from Eton. I had also some from the Marquess of [Sligo], his father, who, though absorbed in agricultural pursuits, yet having been an Etonian himself, and as good a scholar as a nobleman needs to be — still retained an affection for classical studies, and for youthful scholars. He had, accordingly, from the time that I was fifteen, corresponded with me ; sometimes upon the great improvements which he had made, or was meditating, in the counties of M[ayo] and Sl[igo] since I had been there; sometimes upon the merits of a Latin poet ; at other times suggesting subjects to me on which he wished me to write verses.

On reading the letters, one of my Jewish friends agreed
to furnish two or three hundred pounds on my personal
security — provided I could persuade the young Earl, who
was, by the way, not older than myself, to guarantee the
5 payment on our coming of age: the Jew's final object
being, as I now suppose, not the trifling profit he could
expect to make by me, but the prospect of establishing a connexion with my noble friend, whose immense expectations
were well known to him.   In pursuance of this proposal on
10 the part of the Jew, about eight or nine days after I had
received the £10, I prepared to go down to Eton.   Nearly
£3 of the money I had given to my money-lending friend,
on his alleging that the stamps must be bought, in order
that the writings might be preparing whilst I was away
15 from London.   I thought in my heart that he was lying;
but I did not wish to give him any excuse for charging his
own delays upon me.   A smaller sum I had given to my
friend the attorney, who was connected with the money-
lenders as their lawyer, to which, indeed, he was entitled
20 for his unfurnished lodgings.   About fifteen shillings I had
employed in re-establishing, though in a very humble way,
my dress.   Of the remainder I gave one-quarter to Ann,
meaning on my return to have divided with her whatever
might remain.   These arrangements made, — soon after six
25 o'clock, on a dark winter evening, I set off, accompanied
by Ann, towards Piccadilly; for it was my intention to go
down as far as Salt Hill on the Bath or Bristol mail.   Our
course lay through a part of the town which has now all
disappeared, so that I can no longer retrace its ancient
30 boundaries: Swallow Street, I think it was called.   Having
time enough before us, however, we bore away to the
left until we came into Golden Square: there, near the
corner of Sherrard Street, we sat down; not wishing to
part in the tumult and blaze of Piccadilly.   I had told her

of my plans some time before: and I now assured her again that she should share in my good fortune, if I met with any; and that I would never forsake her, as soon as I had power to protect her. This I fully intended, as much from inclination as from a sense of duty: for, setting aside gratitude, which in any case must have made me her debtor for life, I loved her as affectionately as if she had been my sister: and at this moment, with sevenfold tenderness, from pity at witnessing her extreme dejection. I had, apparently, most reason for dejection, because I was leaving the saviour of my life: yet I, considering the shock my health had received, was cheerful and full of hope. She, on the contrary, who was parting with one who had little means of serving her, except by kindness and brotherly treatment, was overcome by sorrow; so that, when I kissed her at our final farewell, she put her arms about my neck, and wept without speaking a word. I hoped to return in a week at farthest, and I agreed with her that on the fifth night from that, and every night afterwards, she should wait for me at six o'clock near the bottom of Great Titchfield Street, which had been our customary haven, as it were, of rendezvous, to prevent our missing each other in the great Mediterranean of Oxford Street. This, and other measures of precaution I took: one only I forgot. She had either never told me, or (as a matter of no great interest) I had forgotten, her surname. It is a general practice, indeed, with girls of humble rank in her unhappy condition, not (as novel-reading women of higher pretensions) to style themselves — *Miss Douglas*, *Miss Montague*, etc., but simply by their Christian names, *Mary*, *Jane*, *Frances*, etc. Her surname, as the surest means of tracing her hereafter, I ought now to have inquired: but the truth is, having no reason to think that our meeting could, in consequence of a short interruption, be more difficult or

uncertain than it had been for so many weeks, I had scarcely for a moment adverted to it as necessary, or placed it amongst my memoranda against this parting interview: and, my final anxieties being spent in comfort-
5 ing her with hopes, and in pressing upon her the necessity of getting some medicines for a violent cough and hoarse-ness with which she was troubled, I wholly forgot it until it was too late to recall her.

It was past eight o'clock when I reached the Gloucester
10 coffee-house: and, the Bristol mail being on the point of going off, I mounted on the outside. The fine fluent motion[1] of this mail soon laid me asleep: it is somewhat remarkable that the first easy or refreshing sleep which I had enjoyed for some months was on the outside of a mail-
15 coach—a bed which, at this day, I find rather an uneasy one. Connected with this sleep was a little incident, which served, as hundreds of others did at that time, to convince me how easily a man who has never been in any great distress may pass through life without knowing, in his
20 own person at least, anything of the possible goodness of the human heart—or, as I must add with a sigh, of its possible vileness. So thick a curtain of *manners* is drawn over the features and expression of men's *natures*, that to the ordinary observer the two extremities, and the infinite
25 field of varieties which lie between them, are all con-founded—the vast and multitudinous compass of their several harmonies reduced to the meagre outline of differ-ences expressed in the gamut or alphabet of elementary sounds. The case was this: for the first four or five miles
30 from London, I annoyed my fellow-passenger on the roof by occasionally falling against him when the coach gave a

---

[1] The Bristol mail is the best appointed in the kingdom—owing to the double advantages of an unusually good road, and of an extra sum for expenses subscribed by the Bristol merchants.

lurch to his side; and indeed, if the road had been less smooth and level than it is, I should have fallen off from weakness. Of this annoyance he complained heavily, as perhaps in the same circumstances most people would; he expressed his complaint, however, more morosely than the occasion seemed to warrant; and, if I had parted with him at that moment, I should have thought of him, if I had considered it worth while to think of him at all, as a surly and almost brutal fellow. However, I was conscious that I had given him some cause for complaint: and, therefore, I apologised to him, and assured him that I would do what I could to avoid falling asleep for the future; and, at the same time, in as few words as possible, I explained to him that I was ill and in a weak state from long suffering; and that I could not afford at that time to take an inside place. The man's manner changed, upon hearing this explanation, in an instant: and when I next woke for a minute from the noise and lights of Hounslow (for in spite of my wishes and efforts I had fallen asleep again within two minutes from the time I had spoken to him), I found that he had put his arm around me to protect me from falling off: and for the rest of my journey he behaved to me with the gentleness of a woman, so that, at length, I almost lay in his arms: and this was the more kind, as he could not have known that I was not going the whole way to Bath or Bristol. Unfortunately, indeed, I *did* go rather farther than I intended: for so genial and refreshing was my sleep, that the next time after leaving Hounslow that I fully awoke, was upon the sudden pulling up of the mail, possibly at a post-office; and on inquiry, I found that we had reached Maidenhead — six or seven miles, I think, ahead of Salt Hill. Here I alighted: and for the half-minute that the mail stopped, I was entreated by my friendly companion, who, from the transient glimpse

I had had of him in Piccadilly, seemed to me to be a gentleman's butler — or person of that rank, to go to bed without delay. .This I promised, though with no intention of
doing so: and in fact, I immediately set forward, or rather
backward, on foot. It must then have been nearly midnight: but so slowly did I creep along, that I heard a clock
in a cottage strike four before I turned down the lane from
Slough to Eton. The air and the sleep had both refreshed
me; but I was weary nevertheless. I remember a thought,
obvious enough, and which has been prettily expressed by
a Roman poet, which gave me some consolation at that
moment under my poverty. There had been some time
before a murder committed on or near Hounslow Heath.
I think I cannot be mistaken when I say that the name of
the murdered person was Steele, and that he was the owner
of a lavender plantation in that neighbourhood. Every
step of my progress was bringing me nearer to the heath:
and it naturally occurred to me that I and the accursed
murderer, if he were that night abroad, might at every
instant be unconsciously approaching each other through
the darkness: in which case, said I, — supposing that I,
instead of being, as indeed I am, little better than an
outcast, —

"Lord of my learning and no land beside,"

were, like my friend, Lord [Altamont], heir by general
repute to £70,000 per ann., what a panic should I be
under at this moment about my throat ! — indeed, it was not
likely that Lord [Altamont] should ever be in my situation.
But nevertheless, the spirit of the remark remains true —
that vast power and possessions make a man shamefully
afraid of dying: and I am convinced that many of the
most intrepid adventurers who, by fortunately being poor,
enjoy the full use of their natural courage, would, if at the

very instant of going into action news were brought to them that they had unexpectedly succeeded to an estate in England of £50,000 a year, feel their dislike to bullets considerably sharpened [1] — and their efforts at perfect equanimity and self-possession proportionably difficult. So true it is, in the language of a wise man whose own experience had made him acquainted with both fortunes, that riches are better fitted —

> " To slacken virtue, and abate her edge,
> Than tempt her to do aught may merit praise."
>
> *Paradise Regained.*

I dally with my subject because, to myself, the remembrance of these times is profoundly interesting. But my reader shall not have any further cause to complain : for I now hasten to its close. — In the road between Slough and Eton, I fell asleep : and, just as the morning began to dawn, I was awakened by the voice of a man standing over me and surveying me. I know not what he was : he was an ill-looking fellow — but not therefore of necessity an ill-meaning fellow : or, if he were, I suppose he thought that no person sleeping out-of-doors in winter would be worth robbing. In which conclusion, however, as it regarded myself, I beg to assure him, if he should be among my readers, that he was mistaken. After a slight remark he passed on : and I was not sorry at his disturbance, as it enabled me to pass through Eton before people were generally up. The night had been heavy and lowering : but towards the morning it had changed to a slight frost :

---

[1] It will be objected that many men, of the highest rank and wealth, have in our own day, as well as throughout our history, been amongst the foremost in courting danger in battle. True ; but this is not the case supposed ; long familiarity with power has to them deadened its effect and attractions.

and the ground and the trees were now covered with rime.
I slipped through Eton unobserved; washed myself, and, as
far as possible, adjusted my dress at a little public-house
in Windsor; and about eight o'clock went down towards
5 Pote's.   On my road I met some junior boys of whom I
made inquiries: an Etonian is always a gentleman; and,
in spite of my shabby habiliments, they answered me
civilly.   My friend, Lord [Altamont], was gone to the
University of [Cambridge].   "Ibi omnis effusus labor!"
10 I had, however, other friends at Eton: but it is not to all
who wear that name in prosperity that a man is willing to
present himself in distress.   On recollecting myself, however, I asked for the Earl of D[esart] to whom (though my
acquaintance with him was not so intimate as with some
15 others) I should not have shrunk from presenting myself
under any circumstances.   He was still at Eton, though I
believe on the wing for Cambridge.   I called, was received
kindly, and asked to breakfast.

Here let me stop for a moment to check my reader from
20 any erroneous conclusions: because I have had occasion
incidentally to speak of various patrician friends, it must
not be supposed that I have myself any pretensions to
rank or high blood.   I thank God that I have not:—I am
the son of a plain English merchant, esteemed during his
25 life for his great integrity, and strongly attached to literary
pursuits; indeed, he was himself, anonymously, an author:
if he had lived, it was expected that he would have been
very rich; but, dying prematurely, he left no more than
about £30,000 amongst seven different claimants.   My
30 mother I may mention with honour, as still more highly
gifted.   For, though unpretending to the name and honours
of a *literary* woman, I shall presume to call her (what many
literary women are not) an *intellectual* woman: and I believe
that if ever her letters should be collected and published,

they would be thought generally to exhibit as much strong and masculine sense, delivered in as pure "mother English," racy and fresh with idiomatic graces, as any in our language — hardly excepting those of Lady M. W. Montague. — These are my honours of descent : I have no others : and I have thanked God sincerely that I have not, because, in my judgment, a station which raises a man too eminently above the level of his fellow-creatures is not the most favourable to moral, or to intellectual qualities.

Lord D[esart] placed before me a most magnificent breakfast. It was really so ; but in my eyes it seemed trebly magnificent — from being the first regular meal, the first "good man's table," that I had sat down to for months. Strange to say, however, I could scarcely eat anything. On the day when I first received my £10 Bank-note, I had gone to a baker's shop and bought a couple of rolls : this very shop I had two months or six weeks before surveyed with an eagerness of desire which it was almost humiliating to me to recollect. I remembered the story about Otway ; and feared that there might be danger in eating too rapidly. But I had no need for alarm, my appetite was quite sunk, and I became sick before I had eaten half of what I had bought. This effect from eating what approached to a meal, I continued to feel for weeks : or, when I did not experience any nausea, part of what I ate was rejected, sometimes with acidity, sometimes immediately, and without any acidity. On the present occasion, at Lord D[esart]'s table, I found myself not at all better than usual : and, in the midst of luxuries, I had no appetite. I had, however, unfortunately, at all times a craving for wine : I explained my situation, therefore, to Lord D[esart], and gave him a short account of my late sufferings, at which he expressed great compassion, and called for wine. This gave me a momentary relief and pleasure ; and on all occasions when I had an

opportunity, I never failed to drink wine — which I worshipped then as I have since worshipped opium. I am
convinced, however, that this indulgence in wine contributed to strengthen my malady; for the tone of my
5 stomach was apparently quite sunk; but by a better regimen it might sooner, and perhaps effectually, have been
revived. I hope that it was not from this love of wine
that I lingered in the neighbourhood of my Eton friends:
I persuaded myself *then* that it was from reluctance to ask
10 of Lord D[esart], on whom I was conscious I had not
sufficient claims, the particular service in quest of which I
had come down to Eton. I was, however, unwilling to lose
my journey, and — I asked it. Lord D[esart], whose good
nature was unbounded, and which, in regard to myself
15 had been measured rather by his compassion perhaps for
my condition, and his knowledge of my intimacy with
some of his relatives, than by an over-rigorous inquiry into
the extent of my own direct claims, faltered, nevertheless, at
this request. He acknowledged that he did not like to
20 have any dealings with money-lenders, and feared lest such
a transaction might come to the ears of his connexions.
Moreover, he doubted whether *his* signature, whose expectations were so much more bounded than those of [his
cousin], would avail with my unchristian friends. How-
25 ever, he did not wish, as it seemed, to mortify me by
an absolute refusal: for after a little consideration, he
promised, under certain conditions which he pointed out,
to give his security. Lord D[esart] was at this time not
eighteen years of age: but I have often doubted, on recol-
30 lecting since the good sense and prudence which on this
occasion he mingled with so much urbanity of manner, an
urbanity which in him wore the grace of youthful sincerity,
whether any statesman — the oldest and the most accomplished in diplomacy — could have acquitted himself better

under the same circumstances. Most people, indeed, cannot be addressed on such a business without surveying you with looks as austere and unpropitious as those of a Saracen's head.

Recomforted by this promise, which was not quite equal to the best, but far above the worst that I had pictured to myself as possible, I returned in a Windsor coach to London three days after I had quitted it. And now I come to the end of my story : — the Jews did not approve of Lord D[esart]'s terms ; whether they would in the end have acceded to them, and were only seeking time for making due inquiries, I know not ; but many delays were made — time passed on — the small fragment of my Banknote had just melted away ; and before any conclusion could have been put to the business, I must have relapsed into my former state of wretchedness. Suddenly, however, at this crisis, an opening was made, almost by accident, for reconciliation with my friends. I quitted London, in haste, for a remote part of England : after some time, I proceeded to the university ; and it was not until many months had passed away that I had it in my power again to revisit the ground which had become so interesting to me, and to this day remains so, as the chief scene of my youthful sufferings.

Meantime, what had become of poor Ann ? For her I have reserved my concluding words : according to our agreement, I sought her daily, and waited for her every night, so long as I staid in London, at the corner of Titchfield Street. I inquired for her of every one who was likely to know her ; and during the last hours of my stay in London I put into activity every means of tracing her that my knowledge of London suggested, and the limited extent of my power made possible. The street where she had lodged I knew, but not the house ; and I remembered at last some account which she had given me of ill treatment from her landlord, which made it probable that she had quitted those lodgings before we parted. She had few acquaintance; most people, besides, thought that the earnestness 5 of my inquiries arose from motives which moved their laughter, or their slight regard; and others, thinking I was in chase of a girl who had robbed me of some trifles, were naturally and excusably indisposed to give me any clue to her, if, indeed, they had any to give. Finally, as my 10 despairing resource, on the day I left London I put into the hands of the only person who (I was sure) must know Ann by sight, from having been in company with us once or twice, an address to —— in ——shire, at that time the residence of my family. But, to this hour, I have never 15 heard a syllable about her. This, amongst such troubles as most men meet with in this life, has been my heaviest affliction. — If she lived, doubtless we must have been sometimes in search of each other, at the very same moment, through the mighty labyrinths of London; per- 20 haps even within a few feet of each other — a barrier no wider in a London street often amounting in the end to a separation for eternity! During some years, I hoped that she *did* live; and I suppose that, in the literal and unrhetorical use of the word *myriad*, I may say that on 25 my different visits to London, I have looked into many, many myriads of female faces, in the hope of meeting her. I should know her again amongst a thousand, if I saw her for a moment; for, though not handsome, she had a sweet expression of countenance, and a peculiar and graceful 30 carriage of the head. — I sought her, I have said, in hope. So it was for years; but now I should fear to see her; and her cough, which grieved me when I parted with her, is now my consolation. I now wish to see her no longer; but think of her, more gladly, as one long since laid in the grave ; in the grave, I would hope, of a Magdalen ; taken away, before injuries and cruelty had blotted out and transfigured her ingenuous nature, or the brutalities of ruffians had completed the ruin they had begun.

So then, Oxford Street, stony-hearted step-mother ! thou that listenest to the sighs of orphans, and drinkest the tears of children, at length I was dismissed from thee : the time was come at last that I no more should pace in anguish thy never-ending terraces ; no more should dream, and wake in captivity to the pangs of hunger. Successors, too many, to myself and Ann, have, doubtless, since trodden in our foot-steps,— inheritors of our calamities : other orphans than Ann have sighed : tears have been shed by other children : and thou, Oxford Street, hast since, doubtless, echoed to the groans of innumerable hearts. For myself, however, the storm which I had outlived seemed to have been the pledge of a long fair-weather ; the premature sufferings which I had paid down to have been accepted as a ransom for many years to come, as a price of long immunity from sorrow : and if again I walked in London, a solitary and contemplative man (as oftentimes I did), I walked for the most part in serenity and peace of mind. And, although it is true that the calamities of my noviciate in London had struck root so deeply in my bodily constitution that afterwards they shot up and flourished afresh, and grew into a noxious umbrage that has overshadowed and darkened my latter years, yet these second assaults of suffering were met with a fortitude more confirmed, with the resources of a maturer intellect, and with alleviations from sympathising affection — how deep and tender !

Thus, however, with whatsoever alleviations, years that were far asunder were bound together by subtle links of suffering derived from a common root. And herein I notice

an instance of the short-sightedness of human desires, that
oftentimes on moonlight nights, during my first mournful
abode in London, my consolation was (if such it could be
thought) to gaze from Oxford Street up every avenue in
5 succession which pierces through the heart of Marylebone
to the fields and the woods; and *that*, said I, travelling with
my eyes up the long vistas which lay part in light and part
in shade, "*that* is the road to the north, and therefore to
[Grasmere], and if I had the wings of a dove, *that* way I
10 would fly for comfort." Thus I said, and thus I wished,
in my blindness; yet, even in that very northern region it
was, even in that very valley, nay, in that very house to
which my erroneous wishes pointed, that this second birth
of my sufferings began; and that they again threatened to
15 besiege the citadel of life and hope. There it was, that for
years I was persecuted by visions as ugly, and as ghastly
phantoms as ever haunted the couch of an Orestes: and in
this unhappier than he, that sleep which comes to all as a
respite and a restoration, and to him especially, as a blessed[1]
20 balm for his wounded heart and his haunted brain, visited
me as my bitterest scourge. Thus blind was I in my desires;
yet, if a veil interposes between the dim-sightedness of man
and his future calamities, the same veil hides from him their
alleviations; and a grief which had not been feared is met
25 by consolations which had not been hoped. I, therefore, who
participated, as it were, in the troubles of Orestes (excepting only in his agitated conscience), participated no less
in all his supports: my Eumenides, like his, were at my
bed-feet, and stared in upon me through the curtains: but,
30 watching by my pillow, or defrauding herself of sleep to
bear me company through the heavy watches of the night,
sat my Electra: for thou, beloved [Margaret], dear companion of my later years, thou wast my Electra! and neither

[1] Φίλον ὕπνη θελγητρον ἐπικουρον νοσου.

in nobility of mind nor in long-suffering affection, wouldst permit that a Grecian sister should excel an English wife. For thou thoughtest not much to stoop to humble offices of kindness, and to servile [1] ministrations of tenderest affection ; — to wipe away for years the unwholesome dews upon the forehead, or to refresh the lips when parched and baked with fever ; nor, even when thy own peaceful slumbers had by long sympathy become infected with the spectacle of my dread contest with phantoms and shadowy enemies that oftentimes bade me "sleep no more!" — not even then, didst thou utter a complaint or any murmur, nor withdraw thy angelic smiles, nor shrink from thy service of love more than Electra did of old. For she too, though she was a Grecian woman, and the daughter of the king [2] of men, yet wept sometimes, and hid her face [3] in her robe.

But these troubles are past ; and thou wilt read these records of a period so dolorous to us both as the legend of some hideous dream that can return no more. Meantime, I am again in London: and again I pace the terraces of Oxford Street by night: and oftentimes, when I am oppressed by anxieties that demand all my philosophy and the comfort of thy presence to support, and yet remember that I am separated from thee by three hundred miles, and the length of three dreary months, — I look up the streets that

---

[1] ἡδὺ δούλευμα. *Eurip. Orest.*

[2] ἄναξ ἀνδρῶν ᾿Αγαμεμνων.

[3] ὄμμα θεισ᾿ ἔισω πεπλων. The scholar will know that throughout this passage I refer to the earlier scenes of the "Orestes"; one of the most beautiful exhibitions of the domestic affections which even the dramas of Euripides can furnish. To the English reader, it may be necessary to say, that the situation at the opening of the drama is that of a brother attended only by his sister during the demoniacal possession of a suffering conscience (or, in the mythology of the play, haunted by the furies), and in circumstances of immediate danger from enemies, and of desertion or cold regard from nominal friends.

run northwards from Oxford Street, upon moonlight nights,
and recollect my youthful ejaculation of anguish; — and
remembering that thou art sitting alone in that same valley,
and mistress of that very house to which my heart turned
5 in its blindness nineteen years ago, I think that, though
blind indeed, and scattered to the winds of late, the prompt-
ings of my heart may yet have had reference to a remoter
time, and may be justified if read in another meaning: —
and, if I could allow myself to descend again to the impo-
10 tent wishes of childhood, I should again say to myself, as
I look to the north, "Oh, that I had the wings of a dove — "
and with how just a confidence in thy good and gracious
nature might I add the other half of my early ejaculation
— "And *that* way I would fly for comfort."

The Pleasures of Opium

15 It is so long since I first took opium that if it had been
a trifling incident in my life I might have forgotten its date:
but cardinal events are not to be forgotten; and from circumstances connected with it I remember that it must be
referred to the autumn of 1804. During that season I was
20 in London, having come thither for the first time since my
entrance at college. And my introduction to opium arose
in the following way. From an early age I had been accustomed to wash my head in cold water at least once a day:
being suddenly seized with toothache, I attributed it to
25 some relaxation caused by an accidental intermission of
that practice; jumped out of bed; plunged my head into
a basin of cold water; and with hair thus wetted went to
sleep. The next morning, as I need hardly say, I awoke
with excruciating rheumatic pains of the head and face,
30 from which I had hardly any respite for about twenty days.
On the twenty-first day, I think it was, and on a Sunday,

that I went out into the streets; rather to run away, if possible, from my torments, than with any distinct purpose. By accident I met a college acquaintance who recommended opium. Opium! dread agent of unimaginable pleasure and pain! I had heard of it as I had of manna or of ambrosia, but no further: how unmeaning a sound was it at that time! what solemn chords does it now strike upon my heart! what heart-quaking vibrations of sad and happy remembrances! Reverting for a moment to these, I feel a mystic importance attached to the minutest circumstances connected with the place and the time, and the man, if man he was, that first laid open to me the Paradise of Opium-eaters. It was a Sunday afternoon, wet and cheerless: and a duller spectacle this earth of ours has not to show than a rainy Sunday in London. My road homewards lay through Oxford Street; and near "the *stately* Pantheon," as Mr. Wordsworth has obligingly called it, I saw a druggist's shop. The druggist, unconscious minister of celestial pleasures!—as if in sympathy with the rainy Sunday, looked dull and stupid, just as any mortal druggist might be expected to look on a Sunday: and, when I asked for the tincture of opium, he gave it to me as any other man might do: and furthermore, out of my shilling, returned me what seemed to be real copper halfpence, taken out of a real wooden drawer. Nevertheless, in spite of such indications of humanity, he has ever since existed in my mind as the beatific vision of an immortal druggist, sent down to earth on a special mission to myself. And it confirms me in this way of considering him, that, when I next came up to London, I sought him near the stately Pantheon, and found him not: and thus to me, who knew not his name (if indeed he had one), he seemed rather to have vanished from Oxford Street than to have removed in any bodily fashion. The reader may choose to think of him as, possibly, no more than a sublunary

druggist: it may be so: but my faith is better: I believe him to have evanesced,[1] or evaporated. So unwillingly would I connect any mortal remembrances with that hour, and place, and creature, that first brought me acquainted
5 with the celestial drug.

Arrived at my lodgings, it may be supposed that I lost not a moment in taking the quantity prescribed. I was necessarily ignorant of the whole art and mystery of opium-taking: and, what I took, I took under every disadvantage.
10 But I took it:—and in an hour, oh! heavens! what a revulsion! what an upheaving, from its lowest depths, of the inner spirit! what an apocalypse of the world within me! That my pains had vanished, was now a trifle in my eyes:—this negative effect was swallowed up in
15 the immensity of those positive effects which had opened before me — in the abyss of divine enjoyment thus suddenly revealed. Here was a panacea — a φαρμακον νηπενθες for all human woes: here was the secret of happiness, about which philosophers had disputed for so many ages, at once dis-
20 covered: happiness might now be bought for a penny, and carried in the waistcoat pocket: portable ecstasies might be had corked up in a pint bottle: and peace of mind could be sent down in gallons by the mail-coach. But, if I talk in this way, the reader will think I am laughing: and I can

---

[1] *Evanesced:* — This way of going off the stage of life appears to have been well known in the seventeenth century, but at that time to have been considered a peculiar privilege of blood-royal, and by no means to be allowed to druggists. For about the year 1686, a poet of rather ominous name (and who, by the by, did ample justice to his name) — viz., Mr. *Flat-man*, in speaking of the death of Charles II, expresses his surprise that any prince should commit so absurd an act as dying because, says he,

"Kings should disdain to die, and only *disappear*."

They should *abscond*, that is, into the other world.

assure him, that nobody will laugh long who deals much with opium : its pleasures even are of a grave and solemn complexion ; and in his happiest state, the opium-eater cannot present himself in the character of "L'Allegro": even then, he speaks and thinks as becomes "Il Penseroso." 5 Nevertheless, I have a very reprehensible way of jesting at times in the midst of my own misery : and, unless when I am checked by some more powerful feelings, I am afraid I shall be guilty of this indecent practice even in these annals of suffering or enjoyment. The reader must allow a little to 10 my infirm nature in this respect : and with a few indulgences of that sort, I shall endeavour to be as grave, if not drowsy, as fits a theme like opium, so anti-mercurial as it really is, and so drowsy as it is falsely reputed.

And, first, one word with respect to its bodily effects : 15 for upon all that has been hitherto written on the subject of opium, whether by travellers in Turkey, who may plead their privilege of lying as an old immemorial right, or by professors of medicine, writing *ex cathedra*, — I have but one emphatic criticism to pronounce — Lies ! lies ! lies ! I 20 remember once, in passing a book-stall, to have caught these words from a page of some satiric author : — "By this time I became convinced that the London newspapers spoke truth at least twice a week, viz., on Tuesday and Saturday, and might safely be depended upon for —— the list of 25 bankrupts." In like manner, I do by no means deny that some truths have been delivered to the world in regard to opium : thus it has been repeatedly affirmed by the learned that opium is a dusky brown in colour ; and this, take notice, I grant : secondly, that it is rather dear ; which I 30 also grant : for in my time, East-India opium has been three guineas a pound, and Turkey eight : and, thirdly, that if you eat a good deal of it, most probably you must do what is particularly disagreeable to any man of regular habits,

viz., die.[1]   These weighty propositions are, all and singular, true : I cannot gainsay them : and truth ever was,
and will be, commendable.   But in these three theorems, I
believe we have exhausted the stock of knowledge as yet
accumulated by man on the subject of opium.   And therefore, worthy doctors, as there seems to be room for further
discoveries, stand aside, and allow me to come forward and
lecture on this matter.

   First, then, it is not so much affirmed as taken for granted
by all who ever mention opium, formally or incidentally,
that it does, or can, produce intoxication.   Now, reader,
assure yourself, *meo periculo*, that no quantity of opium ever
did, or could intoxicate.   As to the tincture of opium (commonly called laudanum) *that* might certainly intoxicate if
a man could bear to take enough of it ; but why ? because
it contains so much proof spirit, and not because it contains
so much opium.   But crude opium, I affirm peremptorily, is
incapable of producing any state of body at all resembling
that which is produced by alcohol : and not in *degree* only
incapable, but even in *kind :* it is not in the quantity of its
effects merely, but in the quality, that it differs altogether.
The pleasure given by wine is always mounting, and tending
to a crisis, after which it declines : that from opium, when
once generated, is stationary for eight or ten hours : the
first, to borrow a technical distinction from medicine, is a
case of acute — the second, of chronic pleasure ; the one
is a flame, the other a steady and equable glow.   But the

----

[1] Of this, however, the learned appear latterly to have doubted : for
in a pirated edition of Buchan's " Domestic Medicine," which I once saw
in the hands of a farmer's wife who was studying it for the benefit of
her health, the Doctor was made to say — " Be particularly careful never
to take above five-and-twenty *ounces* of laudanum at once " ; the true
reading being probably five-and-twenty *drops*, which are held equal to
about one grain of crude opium.

main distinction lies in this, and whereas wine disorders the mental faculties, opium, on the contrary, if taken in a proper manner, introduces amongst them the most exquisite order, legislation, and harmony. Wine robs a man of his self-possession: opium greatly invigorates it. Wine unsettles and clouds the judgment, and gives a preternatural bright-ness and a vivid exaltation to the contempts and the admi-rations, the loves and the hatreds, of the drinker: opium on the contrary communicates serenity and equipoise to all the faculties, active or passive: and with respect to the temper and moral feelings in general, it gives simply that sort of vital warmth which is approved by the judgment, and which would probably always accompany a bodily constitution of primeval or antediluvian health. Thus, for instance, opium, like wine, gives an expansion to the heart and the benevo-lent affections: but then, with this remarkable difference, that in the sudden development of kind-heartedness which accompanies inebriation, there is always more or less of a maudlin character, which exposes it to the contempt of the by-stander. Men shake hands, swear eternal friendship, and shed tears — no mortal knows why: and the sensual creature is clearly uppermost. But the expansion of the benigner feelings incident to opium, is no febrile access, but a healthy restoration to that state which the mind would naturally recover upon the removal of any deep-seated irritation of pain that had disturbed and quarrelled with the impulses of a heart originally just and good. True it is, that even wine, up to a certain point, and with certain men, rather tends to exalt and to steady the intel-lect: I myself, who have never been a great wine-drinker, used to find that half a dozen glasses of wine advanta-geously affected the faculties — brightened and intensified the consciousness — and gave to the mind a feeling of being " ponderibus librata suis ": and certainly it is most absurdly

said in popular language of any man that he is *disguised*
in liquor : for, on the contrary, most men are disguised by
sobriety ; and it is when they are drinking (as some old
gentleman says in Athenæus), that men ἑαυτοὺς ἐμφανίζουσιν
5 οἵτινες εἰσιν — display themselves in their true complexion of
character ; which surely is not disguising themselves. But
still, wine constantly leads a man to the brink of absurdity
and extravagance ; and, beyond a certain point, it is sure to
volatilise and to disperse the intellectual energies : whereas
10 opium always seems to compose what had been agitated,
and to concentrate what had been distracted. In short, to
sum up all in one word, a man who is inebriated, or tending
to inebriation, is, and feels that he is, in a condition which
calls up into supremacy the merely human, too often the
15 brutal, part of his nature : but the opium-eater (I speak of
him who is not suffering from any disease, or other remote
effects of opium) feels that the diviner part of his nature is
paramount ; that is, the moral affections are in a state of
cloudless serenity ; and over all is the great light of the
20 majestic intellect.

This is the doctrine of the true church on the subject of
opium : of which church I acknowledge myself to be the
only member — the alpha and the omega : but then it is to
be recollected that I speak from the ground of a large and
25 profound personal experience : whereas most of the unscien-
tific [1] authors who have at all treated of opium, and even of

---

[1] Amongst the great herd of travellers, etc., who show sufficiently by
their stupidity that they never held any intercourse with opium, I must
caution my readers especially against the brilliant author of " Anastasius." This gentleman, whose wit would lead one to presume him an
opium-eater, has made it impossible to consider him in that character
from the grievous misrepresentation which he gives of its effects, at
pp. 215–17 of vol. i. Upon consideration, it must appear such to the
author himself ; for, waiving the errors I have insisted on in the text,
which (and others) are adopted in the fullest manner, he will himself

those who have written expressly on the materia medica, make it evident, from the horror they express of it, that their experimental knowledge of its action is none at all. I will, however, candidly acknowledge that I have met with one person who bore evidence to its intoxicating power, such as staggered my own incredulity : for he was a surgeon, and had himself taken opium largely. I happened to say to him that his enemies, as I had heard, charged him with talking nonsense on politics, and that his friends apologized for him by suggesting that he was constantly in a state of intoxication from opium. Now the accusation, said I, is not *prima facie*, and of necessity, an absurd one : but the defence *is*. To my surprise, however, he insisted that both his enemies and his friends were in the right : " I will maintain," said he, " that I *do* talk nonsense ; and secondly, I will maintain that I do not talk nonsense upon principle, or with any view to profit, but solely and simply," said he, " solely and simply, — solely and simply " (repeating it three times over), " because I am drunk with opium ; and *that* daily." I replied that, as to the allegation of his enemies, as it seemed to be established upon such respectable testimony, seeing that the three parties concerned all

admit, that an old gentleman, "with a snow-white beard," who eats "ample doses of opium," and is yet able to deliver what is meant and received as very weighty counsel on the bad effects of that practice, is but an indifferent evidence that opium either kills people prematurely, or sends them into a mad-house. But for my part, I see into this old gentleman and his motives ; the fact is, he was enamoured of "the little golden receptacle of the pernicious drug " which Anastasius carried about him ; and no way of obtaining it so safe and so feasible occurred as that of frightening its owner out of his wits (which, by the by, are none of the strongest). This commentary throws a new light upon the case, and greatly improves it as a story; for the old gentleman's speech, considered as a lecture on pharmacy, is highly absurd, but, considered as a hoax on Anastasius, it reads excellently.

agreed in it, it did not become me to question it; but the defence set up I must demur to. He proceeded to discuss the matter, and to lay down his reasons; but it seemed to me so impolite to pursue an argument which must have presumed a man mistaken in a point belonging to his own profession, that I did not press him even when his course of argument seemed open to objection: not to mention that a man who talks nonsense, even though "with no view to profit," is not altogether the most agreeable partner in a dispute, whether as opponent or respondent. I confess, however, that the authority of a surgeon, and one who was reputed a good one, may seem a weighty one to my prejudice: but still I must plead my experience, which was greater than his greatest by 7000 drops a day; and, though it was not possible to suppose a medical man unacquainted with the characteristic symptoms of vinous intoxication, it yet struck me that he might proceed on a logical error of using the word intoxication with too great latitude, and extending it generally to all modes of nervous excitement, instead of restricting it as the expression for a specific sort of excitement, connected with certain diagnostics. Some people have maintained, in my hearing, that they have been drunk upon green tea: and a medical student in London, for whose knowledge in his profession I have reason to feel great respect, assured me, the other day, that a patient, in recovering from an illness, had got drunk on a beef-steak.

Having dwelt so much on this first and leading error in respect to opium, I shall notice very briefly a second and a third; which are, that the elevation of spirits produced by opium is necessarily followed by a proportionate depression, and that the natural and even immediate consequence of opium is torpor and stagnation, animal and mental. The first of these errors I shall content myself with simply denying, assuring my reader, that for ten years, during which I took opium at intervals, the day succeeding to that on which I allowed myself this luxury was always a day of unusually good spirits.

With respect to the torpor supposed to follow, or rather, if we were to credit the numerous pictures of Turkish opium-eaters, to accompany the practice of opium-eating, I deny that also. Certainly, opium is classed under the head of narcotics; and some such effect it may produce in the end: but the primary effects of opium are always, and in the highest degree, to excite and stimulate the system: this first stage of its action always lasted with me, during my noviciate, for upwards of eight hours; so that it must be the fault of the opium-eater himself if he does not so time his exhibition of the dose, to speak medically, as that the whole weight of its narcotic influence may descend upon his sleep. Turkish opium-eaters, it seems, are absurd enough to sit, like so many equestrian statues, on logs of wood as stupid as themselves. But that the reader may judge of the degree in which opium is likely to stupify the faculties of an Englishman, I shall, by way of treating the question illustratively, rather than argumentatively, describe the way in which I myself often passed an opium evening in London, during the period between 1804 and 1812. It will be seen, that at least opium did not move me to seek solitude, and much less to seek inactivity, or the torpid state of self-involution ascribed to the Turks. I give this account at the risk of being pronounced a crazy enthusiast or visionary: but I regard *that* little: I must desire my reader to bear in mind that I was a hard student, and at severe studies for all the rest of my time: and certainly I had a right occasionally to relaxations as well as other people: these, however, I allowed myself but seldom.

The late Duke of [Norfolk] used to say, "Next Friday, by the blessing of Heaven, I purpose to be drunk": and in like manner I used to fix beforehand how often, within a given time, and when, I would commit a debauch of opium. This was seldom more than once in three weeks: for at that time I could not have ventured to call every day (as I did afterwards) for "*a glass of laudanum negus, warm, and without sugar.*" No: as I have said, I seldom drank laudanum, at that time, more than once in three weeks: this was usually on a Tuesday or a Saturday night; my reason for which was this. In those days Grassini sang at the Opera: and her voice was delightful to me beyond all that I had ever heard. I know not what may be the state of the Opera-house now, having never been within its walls for seven or eight years, but at that time it was by much the most pleasant place of public resort in London for passing an evening. Five shillings admitted one to the gallery, which was subject to far less annoyance than the pit of the theatres: the orchestra was distinguished by its sweet and melodious grandeur from all English orchestras, the composition of which, I confess, is not acceptable to my ear, from the predominance of the clangorous instruments, and the absolute tyranny of the violin. The choruses were divine to hear: and when Grassini appeared in some interlude, as she often did, and poured forth her passionate soul as Andromache at the tomb of Hector, etc., I question whether any Turk, of all that ever entered the paradise of opium-eaters, can have had half the pleasure I had. But, indeed, I honour the Barbarians too much by supposing them capable of any pleasures approaching to the intellectual ones of an Englishman. For music is an intellectual or a sensual pleasure, according to the temperament of him who hears it. And, by the by, with the exception of the fine extravaganza on that subject in "Twelfth Night," I do not recollect more than one thing said adequately on the subject of music in all literature: it is a passage in the

"Religio Medici"[1] of Sir T. Brown; and, though chiefly remarkable for its sublimity, has also a philosophic value, inasmuch as it points to the true theory of musical effects. The mistake of most people is to suppose that it is by the ear they communicate with music, and, therefore, that they are purely passive to its effects. But this is not so : it is by the reaction of the mind upon the notices of the ear, (the *matter* coming by the senses, the *form* from the mind) that the pleasure is constructed : and therefore it is that people of equally good ear differ so much in this point from one another. Now opium, by greatly increasing the activity of the mind generally, increases, of necessity, that particular mode of its activity by which we are able to construct out of the raw material of organic sound an elaborate intellectual pleasure. But, says a friend, a succession of musical sounds is to me like a collection of Arabic characters : I can attach no ideas to them. Ideas ! my good sir ? there is no occasion for them : all that class of ideas which can be available in such a case has a language of representative feelings. But this is a subject foreign to my present purposes : it is sufficient to say, that a chorus, etc., of elaborate harmony, displayed before me, as in a piece of arras work, the whole of my past life — not as if recalled by an act of memory, but as if present and incarnated in the music : no longer painful to dwell upon : but the detail of its incidents removed, or blended in some hazy abstraction ; and its passions exalted, spiritualised, and sublimed. All this was to be had for five shillings. And over and above the music of the stage and the orchestra, I had all around me, in the intervals of the performance, the music of the Italian language talked by Italian women : for the gallery was usually

---

[1] I have not the book at this moment to consult ; but I think the passage begins — "And even that tavern music, which makes one man merry, another mad, in me strikes a deep fit of devotion," etc.

crowded with Italians : and I listened with a pleasure such
as that with which Weld the traveller lay and listened, in
Canada, to the sweet laughter of Indian women ; for the
less you understand of a language the more sensible you
5 are to the melody or harshness of its sounds : for such a
purpose, therefore, it was an advantage to me that I was a
poor Italian scholar, reading it but little, and not speaking
it at all, nor understanding a tenth part of what I heard
spoken.

10   These were my Opera pleasures : but another pleasure I
had which, as it could be had only on a Saturday night,
occasionally struggled with my love of the Opera ; for, at
that time, Tuesday and Saturday were the regular Opera
nights. On this subject I am afraid I shall be rather
15 obscure, but, I can assure the reader, not at all more so
than Marinus in his life of Proclus, or many other biographers and autobiographers of fair reputation. This
pleasure, I have said, was to be had only on a Saturday
night. What then was Saturday night to me more than
20 any other night ? I had no labours that I rested from ;
no wages to receive : what needed I to care for Saturday
night, more than as it was a summons to hear Grassini?
True, most logical reader : what you say is unanswerable.
And yet so it was and is, that, whereas different men throw
25 their feelings into different channels, and most are apt to
show their interest in the concerns of the poor, chiefly by
sympathy, expressed in some shape or other, with their
distresses and sorrows, I, at that time, was disposed to
express my interest by sympathising with their pleasures.
30 The pains of poverty I had lately seen too much of ; more
than I wished to remember : but the pleasures of the poor,
their consolations of spirit, and their reposes from bodily
toil, can never become oppressive to contemplate. Now
Saturday night is the season for the chief, regular, and

periodic return of rest to the poor : in this point the most hostile sects unite, and acknowledge a common link of brotherhood : almost all Christendom rests from its labours. It is a rest introductory to another rest : and divided by a whole day and two nights from the renewal of toil. On this account I feel always, on a Saturday night, as though I also were released from some yoke of labour, had some wages to receive, and some luxury of repose to enjoy. For the sake, therefore, of witnessing, upon as large a scale as possible, a spectacle with which my sympathy was so entire, I used often, on Saturday nights, after I had taken opium, to wander forth, without much regarding the direction or the distance, to all the markets and other parts of London to which the poor resort on a Saturday night for laying out their wages. Many a family party, consisting of a man, his wife, and sometimes one or two of his children, have I listened to, as they stood consulting on their ways and means, or the strength of their exchequer, or the price of household articles. Gradually I became familiar with their wishes, their difficulties, and their opinions. Sometimes there might be heard murmurs of discontent : but far oftener expressions on the countenance, or uttered in words, of patience, hope, and tranquillity. And taken generally, I must say, that, in this point at least, the poor are far more philosophic than the rich — that they show a more ready and cheerful submission to what they consider as irremediable evils, or irreparable losses. Whenever I saw occasion, or could do it without appearing to be intrusive, I joined their parties ; and gave my opinion upon the matter in discussion, which, if not always judicious, was always received indulgently. If wages were a little higher, or expected to be so, or the quartern loaf a little lower, or it was reported that onions and butter were expected to fall, I was glad : yet, if the

contrary were true, I drew from opium some means of con-
soling myself.   For opium, like the bee, that extracts its
materials indiscriminately from roses and from the soot of
chimneys, can overrule all feelings into a compliance with
5 the master key.   Some of these rambles led me to great
distances : for an opium-eater is too happy to observe
the motion of time.   And sometimes in my attempts to
steer homewards upon nautical principles, by fixing my
eye on the pole-star, and seeking ambitiously for a north-
10 west passage, instead of circumnavigating all the capes
and headlands I had doubled in my outward voyage, I
came suddenly upon such knotty problems of alleys, such
enigmatical entries, and such sphinx's riddles of streets
without thoroughfares, as must, I conceive, baffle the
15 audacity of porters, and confound the intellects of hackney-
coachmen.   I could almost have believed, at times, that I
must be the first discoverer of some of these *terræ incog-
nitæ*, and doubted whether they had yet been laid down
in the modern charts of London.   For all this, however, I
20 paid a heavy price in distant years, when the human face
tyrannised over my dreams, and the perplexities of my
steps in London came back and haunted my sleep with the
feeling of perplexities moral or intellectual, that brought
confusion to the reason, or anguish and remorse to the
25 conscience.

Thus I have shown that opium does not, of necessity,
produce inactivity or torpor ; but that, on the contrary, it
often led me into markets and theatres.   Yet, in candour,
I will admit that markets and theatres are not the appro-
30 priate haunts of the opium-eater, when in the divinest state
incident to his enjoyment.   In that state, crowds become
an oppression to him ; music even, too sensual and gross.
He naturally seeks solitude and silence, as indispensable
conditions of those trances and profoundest reveries which

are the crown or consummation of what opium can do for human nature. I, whose disease it was to meditate too much, and to observe too little, and who upon my first entrance at college was nearly falling into a deep melancholy from brooding too much on the sufferings which I had 5 witnessed in London, was sufficiently aware of the tendencies of my own thoughts to do all I could to counteract them. — I was, indeed, like a person who, according to the old legend, had entered the cave of Trophonius: and the remedies I sought were to force myself into society, and to 10 keep my understanding in continual activity upon matters of science. But for these remedies, I should certainly have become hypochondriacally melancholy. In after years, however, when my cheerfulness was more fully re-established, I yielded to my natural inclination for a solitary life. And, 15 at that time, I often fell into these reveries upon taking opium; and more than once it has happened to me, on a summer night, when I have been at an open window, in a room from which I could overlook the sea at a mile below me, and could command a view of the great town of 20 L[iverpool], at about the same distance, that I have sat, from sun-set to sun-rise, motionless, and without wishing to move.

I shall be charged with mysticism, Behmenism, quietism, etc., but *that* shall not alarm me. Sir H. Vane, the younger, 25 was one of our wisest men: and let my readers see if he, in his philosophical works, be half as unmystical as I am. — I say, then, that it has often struck me that the scene itself was somewhat typical of what took place in such a reverie. The town of L[iverpool] represented the earth, 30 with its sorrows and its graves left behind, yet not out of sight, nor wholly forgotten. The ocean, in everlasting but gentle agitation, and brooded over by a dove-like calm, might not unfitly typify the mind and the mood which then

swayed it.   For it seemed to me as if then first I stood at
a distance, and aloof from the uproar of life, as if the
tumult, the fever, and the strife, were suspended ; a respite
granted from the secret burthens of the heart ; a sabbath
5 of repose ; a resting from human labours.   Here were the
hopes which blossom in the paths of life, reconciled with
the peace which is in the grave ; motions of the intellect
as unwearied as the heavens, yet for all anxieties a halcyon
calm : a tranquillity that seemed no product of inertia, but
10 as if resulting from mighty and equal antagonisms ; infinite
activities, infinite repose.

Oh ! just, subtle, and mighty opium ! that to the hearts
of poor and rich alike, for the wounds that will never heal,
and for "the pangs that tempt the spirit to rebel," bring-
15 est an assuaging balm ; eloquent opium ! that with thy
potent rhetoric stealest away the purposes of wrath ; and
to the guilty man for one night givest back the hopes of
his youth, and hands washed pure from blood ; and to the
proud man a brief oblivion for

20   " Wrongs unredress'd and insults unavenged ";

that summonest to the chancery of dreams, for the triumphs of suffering innocence, false witnesses ; and con-
foundest perjury ; and dost reverse the sentences of
unrighteous judges : — thou buildest upon the bosom of
25 darkness, out of the fantastic imagery of the brain, cities
and temples beyond the art of Phidias and Praxiteles —
beyond the splendour of Babylon and Hekatompylos : and
"from the anarchy of dreaming sleep," callest into sunny
light the faces of long-buried beauties, and the blessed
30 household countenances, cleansed from the "dishonours
of the grave."   Thou only givest these gifts to man ; and
thou hast the keys of Paradise, oh, just, subtle, and mighty
opium !

INTRODUCTION TO THE PAINS OF OPIUM

COURTEOUS, and, I hope, indulgent reader — for all *my* readers must be indulgent ones, or else, I fear, I shall shock them too much to count on their courtesy — having accompanied me thus far, now let me request you to move onwards for about eight years ; that is to say, from 1804, when I have said that my acquaintance with opium first began, to 1812. The years of academic life are now over and gone — almost forgotten : — the student's cap no longer presses my temples ; if my cap exist at all, it presses those of some youthful scholar, I trust, as happy as myself, and as passionate a lover of knowledge. My gown is, by this time, I dare to say, in the same condition with many thousands of excellent books in the Bodleian, viz., diligently perused by certain studious moths and worms : or departed, however, which is all that I know of its fate, to that great reservoir of *somewhere*, to which all the tea-cups, tea-caddies, tea-pots, tea-kettles, etc., have departed (not to speak of still frailer vessels, such as glasses, decanters, bed-makers, etc.) which occasional resemblances in the present generation of tea-cups, etc., remind me of having once possessed, but of whose departure and final fate I, in common with most gownsmen of either university, could give, I suspect, but an obscure and conjectural history. The persecution of the chapel-bell, sounding its unwelcome summons to six o'clock matins, interrupts my slumbers no longer : the porter who rang it, upon whose beautiful nose (bronze, inlaid with copper) I wrote, in retaliation, so many Greek epigrams whilst I was dressing, is dead, and has ceased to disturb anybody : and I and many others who suffered much from his tintinnabulous propensities, have now agreed to overlook his errors, and have forgiven him. Even with the bell I am now in charity : it rings, I

suppose, as formerly, thrice a day : and cruelly annoys, I
doubt not, many worthy gentlemen, and disturbs their
peace of mind : but as to me, in this year 1812, I regard
its treacherous voice no longer — treacherous, I call it, for,
5 by some refinement of malice, it spoke in as sweet and
silvery tones as if it had been inviting one to a party — its
tones have no longer, indeed, power to reach me, let the
wind sit as favourable as the malice of the bell itself could
wish : for I am two hundred and fifty miles away from it, and
10 buried in the depth of mountains.   And what am I doing
amongst the mountains ?   Taking opium.   Yes, but what
else ?   Why, reader, in 1812, the year we are now arrived at,
as well as for some years previous, I have been chiefly studying German metaphysics, in the writings of Kant, Fichte,
15 Schelling, etc.   And how, and in what manner, do I live ?
in short, what class or description of men do I belong to ?
I am at this period, viz., in 1812, living in a cottage ; and
with a single female servant (*honi soit qui mal y pense*),
who, amongst my neighbours, passes by the name of my
20 "housekeeper."   And, as a scholar and a man of learned
education, and in that sense a gentleman, I may presume
to class myself as an unworthy member of that indefinite body called *gentlemen.*   Partly on the ground I have
assigned, perhaps ; partly because, from my having no
25 visible calling or business, it is rightly judged that I must
be living on my private fortune ; I am so classed by my
neighbours : and, by the courtesy of modern England, I
am usually addressed on letters, etc., *esquire,* though having, I fear, in the rigorous construction of heralds, but
30 slender pretensions to that distinguished honour : yes, in
popular estimation, I am X. Y. Z., esquire, but not Justice
of the Peace, nor Custos Rotulorum.   Am I married ?
Not yet.   And I still take opium ?   On Saturday nights.
And, perhaps, have taken it unblushingly ever since "the

rainy Sunday," and "the stately Pantheon," and "the beatific druggist" of 1804? — Even so. And how do I find my health after all this opium-eating? in short, how do I do? Why, pretty well, I thank you, reader: in the phrase of ladies in the straw, "as well as can be expected." 5 In fact, if I dared to say the real and simple truth, though, to satisfy the theories of medical men, I *ought* to be ill, I never was better in my life than in the spring of 1812; and I hope sincerely, that the quantity of claret, port, or "particular Madeira," which, in all probability, you, good 10 reader, have taken, and design to take, for every term of eight years, during your natural life, may as little disorder your health as mine was disordered by the opium I had taken for the eight years between 1804 and 1812. Hence you may see again the danger of taking any medical advice 15 from "Anastasius"; in divinity, for aught I know, or law, he may be a safe counsellor; but not in medicine. No: it is far better to consult Dr. Buchan; as I did: for I never forgot that worthy man's excellent suggestion: and I was "particularly careful not to take above five-and-twenty 20 ounces of laudanum." To this moderation and temperate use of the article, I may ascribe it, I suppose, that as yet, at least, (*i.e.*, in 1812) I am ignorant and unsuspicious of the avenging terrors which opium has in store for those who abuse its lenity. At the same time, it must not be 25 forgotten, that hitherto I have been only a dilettante eater of opium: eight years' practice even, with the single pre-caution of allowing sufficient intervals between every indul-gence, has not been sufficient to make opium necessary to me as an article of daily diet. But now comes a different 30 era. Move on, if you please, reader, to 1813. In the summer of the year we have just quitted, I had suffered much in bodily health from distress of mind connected with a very melancholy event. This event, being no ways

related to the subject now before me, further than through the bodily illness which it produced, I need not more particularly notice. Whether this illness of 1812 had any share in that of 1813, I know not: but so it was, that in the latter
5 year I was attacked by a most appalling irritation of the stomach, in all respects the same as that which had caused me so much suffering in youth, and accompanied by a revival of all the old dreams. This is the point of my narrative on which, as respects my own self-justification, the
10 whole of what follows may be said to hinge. And here I find myself in a perplexing dilemma : — Either, on the one hand, I must exhaust the reader's patience, by such a detail of my malady, and of my struggles with it, as might suffice to establish the fact of my inability to wrestle any
15 longer with irritation and constant suffering : or, on the other hand, by passing lightly over this critical part of my story, I must forego the benefit of a stronger impression left on the mind of the reader, and must lay myself open to the misconstruction of having slipped by the easy and
20 gradual steps of self-indulging persons, from the first to the final stage of opium-eating, a misconstruction to which there will be a lurking predisposition in most readers, from my previous acknowledgments. This is the dilemma : the first horn of which would be sufficient to toss and gore any
25 column of patient readers, though drawn up sixteen deep and constantly relieved by fresh men: consequently *that* is not to be thought of. It remains then, that I *postulate* so much as is necessary for my purpose. And let me take as full credit for what I postulate as if I had demonstrated it,
30 good reader, at the expense of your patience and my own. Be not so ungenerous as to let me suffer in your good opinion through my own forbearance and regard for your comfort. No: believe all that I ask of you, viz., that I could resist no longer; believe it liberally, and as an act

of grace : or else in mere prudence : for, if not, then in the next edition of my Opium Confessions revised and enlarged, I will make you believe and tremble: and *à force d'ennuyer*, by mere dint of pandiculation I will terrify all readers of mine from ever again questioning any postulate that I shall 5 think fit to make.

This then, let me repeat, I postulate — that, at the time I began to take opium daily, I could not have done otherwise. Whether, indeed, afterwards I might not have succeeded in breaking off the habit, even when it seemed to 10 me that all efforts would be unavailing, and whether many of the innumerable efforts which I *did* make might not have been carried much further, and my gradual re-conquests of ground lost might not have been followed up much more energetically — these are questions which I must decline. 15 Perhaps I might make out a case of palliation , but, shall I speak ingenuously ? I confess it, as a besetting infirmity of mine, that I am too much of an Eudæmonist: I hanker too much after a state of happiness, both for myself and others : I cannot face misery, whether my own or not, with 20 an eye of sufficient firmness : and am little capable of encountering present pain for the sake of any reversionary benefit. On some other matters, I can agree with the gentlemen in the cotton-trade [1] at Manchester in affecting the Stoic philosophy : but not in this. Here I take the liberty 25 of an Eclectic philosopher, and I look out for some courteous and considerate sect that will condescend more to the infirm condition of an opium-eater ; that are 'sweet men,' as Chaucer says, 'to give absolution,' and will show some

---

[1] A handsome news-room, of which I was very politely made free in passing through Manchester by several gentlemen of that place, is called, I think, *The Porch ;* whence I, who am a stranger in Manchester, inferred that the subscribers meant to profess themselves followers of Zeno. But I have been since assured that this is a mistake.

conscience in the penances they inflict, and the efforts of
abstinence they exact from poor sinners like myself. An
inhuman moralist I can no more endure in my nervous
state than opium that has not been boiled. At any rate,
5 he, who summons me to send out a large freight of self-
denial and mortification upon any cruising voyage of moral
improvement, must make it clear to my understanding that
the concern is a hopeful one. At my time of life (six and
thirty years of age) it cannot be supposed that I have much
10 energy to spare: in fact, I find it all little enough for the
intellectual labours I have on my hands: and, therefore, let
no man expect to frighten me by a few hard words into embark-
ing any part of it upon desperate adventures of morality.

Whether desperate or not, however, the issue of the
15 struggle in 1813 was what I have mentioned; and from
this date, the reader is to consider me as a regular and confirmed opium-eater, of whom to ask whether on any particular day he had or had not taken opium, would be to ask
whether his lungs had performed respiration, or the heart
20 fulfilled its functions. — You understand now, reader, what
I am: and you are by this time aware, that no old gentleman, "with a snow-white beard," will have any chance of
persuading me to surrender "the little golden receptacle
of the pernicious drug." No: I give notice to all, whether
25 moralists or surgeons, that, whatever be their pretensions
and skill in their respective lines of practice, they must not
hope for any countenance from me, if they think to begin
by any savage proposition for a Lent or Ramadan of abstinence from opium. This then being all fully understood
30 between us, we shall in future sail before the wind. Now
then, reader, from 1813, where all this time we have been
sitting down and loitering — rise up, if you please, and
walk forward about three years more. Now draw up the
curtain, and you shall see me in a new character.

If any man, poor or rich, were to say that he would tell us what had been the happiest day in his life, and the why, and the wherefore, I suppose that we should all cry out — Hear him! Hear him! — As to the happiest *day*, that must be very difficult for any wise man to name: because any event, that could occupy so distinguished a place in a man's retrospect of his life, or be entitled to have shed a special felicity on any one day, ought to be of such an enduring character, as that, accidents apart, it should have continued to shed the same felicity, or one not distinguishably less, on many years together. To the happiest *lustrum*, however, or even to the happiest *year*, it may be allowed to any man to point without discountenance from wisdom. This year, in my case, reader, was the one which we have now reached; though it stood, I confess, as a parenthesis between years of a gloomier character. It was a year of brilliant water, to speak after the manner of jewellers, set as it were, and insulated, in the gloom and cloudy melancholy of opium. Strange as it may sound, I had a little before this time descended suddenly, and without any considerable effort, from 320 grains of opium (*i.e.*, eight [1] thousand drops of laudanum) per day, to forty grains, or one-eighth part. Instantaneously, and as if by magic, the cloud of profoundest melancholy which rested upon my brain, like some black vapours that I have seen roll away from the summits of mountains, drew off in one day (νυχθημερον); passed off with its murky banners as

[1] I here reckon twenty-five drops of laudanum as equivalent to one grain of opium, which, I believe, is the common estimate. However, as both may be considered variable quantities (the crude opium varying much in strength, and the tincture still more), I suppose that no infinitesimal accuracy can be had in such a calculation. Tea-spoons vary as much in size as opium in strength. Small ones hold about 100 drops; so that 8000 drops are about eighty times a tea-spoonful. The reader sees how much I kept within Dr. Buchan's indulgent allowance.

simultaneously as a ship that has been stranded, and is floated off by a spring tide —

"That moveth altogether, if it move at all."

Now, then, I was again happy: I now took only 1000
5 drops of laudanum per day: and what was that? A latter spring had come to close up the season of youth: my brain performed its functions as healthily as ever before: I read Kant again; and again I understood him, or fancied that I did. Again my feelings of pleasure expanded them-
10 selves to all around me: and if any man from Oxford or Cambridge, or from neither, had been announced to me in my unpretending cottage, I should have welcomed him with as sumptuous a reception as so poor a man could offer. Whatever else was wanting to a wise man's happiness, —
15 of laudanum I would have given him as much as he wished, and in a golden cup. And, by the way, now that I speak of giving laudanum away, I remember, about this time, a little incident, which I mention, because, trifling as it was, the reader will soon meet it again in my dreams, which it
20 influenced more fearfully than could be imagined. One day a Malay knocked at my door. What business a Malay could have to transact amongst English mountains, I cannot conjecture: but possibly he was on his road to a seaport about forty miles distant.

25 The servant who opened the door to him was a young girl born and bred amongst the mountains, who had never seen an Asiatic dress of any sort: his turban, therefore, confounded her not a little: and, as it turned out that his attainments in English were exactly of the same extent as
30 hers in the Malay, there seemed to be an impassable gulf fixed between all communication of ideas, if either party had happened to possess any. In this dilemma, the girl, recollecting the reputed learning of her master, and

doubtless giving me credit for a knowledge of all the languages of the earth, besides, perhaps, a few of the lunar ones,
came and gave me to understand that there was a sort
of demon below, whom she clearly imagined that my art
could exorcise from the house. I did not immediately go 5
down : but, when I did, the group which presented itself,
arranged as it was by accident, though not very elaborate,
took hold of my fancy and my eye in a way that none of
the statuesque attitudes exhibited in the ballets at the
Opera-house, though so ostentatiously complex, had ever 10
done. In a cottage kitchen, but panelled on the wall with
dark wood that from age and rubbing resembled oak, and
looking more like a rustic hall of entrance than a kitchen,
stood the Malay — his turban and loose trousers of **dingy**
white relieved upon the dark panelling : he had placed him- 15
self nearer to the girl than she seemed to relish ; though
her native spirit of mountain intrepidity contended with
the feeling of simple awe which her countenance expressed
as she gazed upon the tiger-cat before her. And a more
striking picture there could not be imagined, than the beau- 20
tiful English face of the girl, and its exquisite fairness, together with her erect and independent attitude, contrasted
with the sallow and bilious skin of the Malay, enamelled or
veneered with mahogany, by marine air, his small, fierce,
restless eyes, thin lips, slavish gestures and adorations. 25
Half-hidden by the ferocious looking Malay was a little
child from a neighbouring cottage who had crept in after
him, and was now in the act of reverting its head, and gazing upwards at the turban and the fiery eyes beneath it,
whilst with one hand he caught at the dress of the young 30
woman for protection. My knowledge of the Oriental
tongues is not remarkably extensive, being indeed confined
to two words — the Arabic word for barley, and the
Turkish for opium (madjoon), which I have learnt from

Anastasius. And, as I had neither a Malay dictionary, nor even Adelung's "Mithridates," which might have helped me to a few words, I addressed him in some lines from the Iliad; considering that, of such languages as I possessed,
5 Greek, in point of longitude, came geographically nearest to an Oriental one. He worshipped me in a most devout manner, and replied in what I suppose was Malay. In this way I saved my reputation with my neighbours: for the Malay had no means of betraying the secret. He lay
10 down upon the floor for about an hour, and then pursued his journey. On his departure, I presented him with a piece of opium. To him, as an Orientalist, I concluded that opium must be familiar: and the expression of his face convinced me that it was. Nevertheless, I was struck
15 with some little consternation when I saw him suddenly raise his hand to his mouth, and, in the schoolboy phrase, bolt the whole, divided into three pieces, at one mouthful. The quantity was enough to kill three dragoons and their horses: and I felt some alarm for the poor creature: but
20 what could be done? I had given him the opium in compassion for his solitary life, on recollecting that if he had travelled on foot from London it must be nearly three weeks since he could have exchanged a thought with any human being. I could not think of violating the laws of
25 hospitality by having him seized and drenched with an emetic, and thus frightening him into a notion that we were going to sacrifice him to some English idol. No: there was clearly no help for it: — he took his leave: and for some days I felt anxious: but as I never heard of any
30 Malay being found dead, I became convinced that he was used[1] to opium: and that I must have done him the service

[1] This, however, is not a necessary conclusion; the varieties of effect produced by opium on different constitutions are infinite. A London Magistrate (Harriott's "Struggles through Life," vol. iii, p. 391, Third

I designed, by giving him one night of respite from the pains of wandering.

This incident I have digressed to mention, because this Malay, partly from the picturesque exhibition he assisted to frame, partly from the anxiety I connected with his image for some days, fastened afterwards upon my dreams, and brought other Malays with him worse than himself, that ran "a-muck"[1] at me, and led me into a world of troubles. — But to quit this episode, and to return to my intercalary year of happiness. I have said already, that on a subject so important to us all as happiness, we should listen with pleasure to any man's experience or experiments, even though he were but a plough-boy, who cannot be supposed to have ploughed very deep into such an intractable soil as that of human pains and pleasures, or to have conducted his researches upon any very enlightened principles. But I, who have taken happiness, both in a solid and a liquid shape, both boiled and unboiled, both East India and Turkey — who have conducted my experiments upon this interesting subject with a sort of galvanic battery — and have, for the general benefit of the world, inoculated myself, as it were, with the poison of 8000 drops of laudanum per day (just for the same reason as a French surgeon inoculated himself lately with cancer — an English one, twenty

Edition) has recorded that, on the first occasion of his trying laudanum for the gout, he took *forty* drops, the next night *sixty*, and on the fifth night *eighty*, without any effect whatever; and this at an advanced age. I have an anecdote from a country surgeon, however, which sinks Mr. Harriott's case into a trifle; and in my projected medical treatise on opium, which I will publish, provided the College of Surgeons will pay me for enlightening their benighted understandings upon this subject, I will relate it; but it is far too good a story to be published gratis.

[1] See the common accounts in any Eastern traveller or voyager of the frantic excesses committed by Malays who have taken opium, or are reduced to desperation by ill luck at gambling.

years ago, with plague — and a third, I know not of what
nation, with hydrophobia), — *I*, it will be admitted, must
surely know what happiness is, if anybody does.   And,
therefore, I will here lay down an analysis of happiness;
and as the most interesting mode of communicating it, I
will give it, not didactically, but wrapt up and involved
in a picture of one evening, as I spent every evening
during the intercalary year when laudanum, though taken
daily, was to me no more than the elixir of pleasure.   This
done, I shall quit the subject of happiness altogether, and
pass to a very different one — the *pains of opium*.

   Let there be a cottage, standing in a valley, eighteen
miles from any town — no spacious valley, but about two
miles long, by three-quarters of a mile in average width;
the benefit of which provision is that all the families resident within its circuit will compose, as it were, one larger
household personally familiar to your eye, and more or less
interesting to your affections.   Let the mountains be real
mountains, between three and four thousand feet high;
and the cottage, a real cottage; not, as a witty author has
it, "a cottage with a double coach-house": let it be, in fact
— for I must abide by the actual scene — a white cottage,
embowered with flowering shrubs, so chosen as to unfold a
succession of flowers upon the walls, and clustering round
the windows through all the months of spring, summer, and
autumn — beginning, in fact, with May roses, and ending
with jasmine.   Let it, however, *not* be spring, nor summer,
nor autumn — but winter, in his sternest shape.   This is a
most important point in the science of happiness.   And I
am surprised to see people overlook it, and think it matter
of congratulation that winter is going; or, if coming, is
not likely to be a severe one.   On the contrary, I put up a
petition annually for as much snow, hail, frost, or storm,
of one kind or other, as the skies can possibly afford us.

Surely everybody is aware of the divine pleasures which attend a winter fire-side: candles at four o'clock, warm hearth-rugs, tea, a fair tea-maker, shutters closed, curtains flowing in ample draperies on the floor, whilst the wind and rain are raging audibly without, 5

> "And at the doors and windows seemed to call,
> As heav'n and earth they would together mell;
> Yet the least entrance find they none at all;
> Whence sweeter grows our rest secure in massy hall."

> *Castle of Indolence.*

All these are items in the description of a winter evening, 10 which must surely be familiar to everybody born in a high latitude. And it is evident, that most of these delicacies, like ice-cream, require a very low temperature of the atmosphere to produce them: they are fruits which cannot be ripened without weather stormy or inclement, in some way 15 or other. I am not "*particular*," as people say, whether it be snow, or black frost, or wind so strong, that (as Mr. [Anti-Slavery Clarkson] says) "you may lean your back against it like a post." I can put up even with rain, provided it rains cats and dogs: but something of the sort I 20 must have: and, if I have it not, I think myself in a manner ill-used: for why am I called on to pay so heavily for winter, in coals, and candles, and various privations that will occur even to gentlemen, if I am not to have the article good of its kind? No: a Canadian winter for my money: or a 25 Russian one, where every man is but a co-proprietor with the north wind in the fee-simple of his own ears. Indeed, so great an epicure am I in this matter, that I cannot relish a winter night fully if it be much past St. Thomas's day, and have degenerated into disgusting tendencies to vernal 30 appearances: no: it must be divided by a thick wall of dark nights from all return of light and sunshine. — From

the latter weeks of October to Christmas-eve, therefore, is
the period during which happiness is in season, which, in
my judgment, enters the room with the tea-tray: for tea,
though ridiculed by those who are naturally of coarse nerves,
5 or are become so from wine-drinking, and are not suscep-
tible of influence from so refined a stimulant, will always
be the favourite beverage of the intellectual: and, for my
part, I would have joined Dr. Johnson in a *bellum inter-
necinum* against Jonas Hanway, or any other impious per-
10 son who should presume to disparage it. — But here, to save
myself the trouble of too much verbal description, I will
introduce a painter; and give him directions for the rest
of the picture.   Painters do not like white cottages, unless
a good deal weather-stained: but as the reader now under-
15 stands that it is a winter night, his services will not be
required, except for the inside of the house.

Paint me, then, a room seventeen feet by twelve, and
not more than seven and a half feet high.   This, reader, is
somewhat ambitiously styled, in my family, the drawing-
20 room: but, being contrived "a double debt to pay," it is
also, and more justly, termed the library; for it happens
that books are the only article of property in which I am
richer than my neighbours.   Of these, I have about five
thousand, collected gradually since my eighteenth year.
25 Therefore, painter, put as many as you can into this room.
Make it populous with books: and, furthermore, paint me
a good fire; and furniture, plain and modest, befitting the
unpretending cottage of a scholar.   And, near the fire, paint
me a tea-table; and, as it is clear that no creature can come
30 to see one such a stormy night, place only two cups and
saucers on the tea-tray: and, if you know how to paint such
a thing symbolically, or otherwise, paint me an eternal teapot — eternal *a parte ante*, and *a parte post;* for I usually
drink tea from eight o'clock at night to four o'clock in the

morning. And, as it is very unpleasant to make tea, or to pour it out for oneself, paint me a lovely young woman, sitting at the table. Paint her arms like Aurora's, and her smiles like Hebe's: — But no, dear M[argaret], not even in jest let me insinuate that thy power to illuminate my cottage rests upon a tenure so perishable as mere personal beauty; or that the witchcraft of angelic smiles lies within the empire of any earthly pencil. Pass, then, my good painter, to something more within its power: and the next article brought forward should naturally be myself — a picture of the Opium-eater with his "little golden receptacle of the pernicious drug," lying beside him on the table. As to the opium, I have no objection to see a picture of *that*, though I would rather see the original: you may paint it, if you choose; but I apprise you, that no "little" receptacle would, even in 1816, answer *my* purpose, who was at a distance from the "stately Pantheon," and all druggists (mortal or otherwise). No: you may as well paint the real receptacle, which was not of gold, but of glass, and as much like a wine-decanter as possible. Into this you may put a quart of ruby-coloured laudanum: that, and a book of German metaphysics placed by its side, will sufficiently attest my being in the neighbourhood; but, as to myself, — there I demur. I admit that, naturally, I ought to occupy the foreground of the picture; that being the hero of the piece, or (if you choose) the criminal at the bar, my body should be had into court. This seems reasonable: but why should I confess, on this point, to a painter? or why confess at all? If the public (into whose private ear I am confidentially whispering my confessions, and not into any painter's) should chance to have framed some agreeable picture for itself, of the Opium-eater's exterior, — should have ascribed to him, romantically, an elegant person, or a handsome face, why should I barbarously tear from it so pleasing a delusion —

pleasing both to the public and to me? No: paint me, if at all, according to your own fancy; and, as a painter's fancy should teem with beautiful creations, I cannot fail, in that way, to be a gainer. And now, reader, we have run 5 through all the ten categories of my condition, as it stood about 1816–17: up to the middle of which latter year I judge myself to have been a happy man: and the elements of that happiness I have endeavoured to place before you, in the above sketch of the interior of a scholar's library, in 10 a cottage among the mountains, on a stormy winter evening.

But now farewell — a long farewell to happiness — winter or summer! farewell to smiles and laughter! farewell to peace of mind! farewell to hope and to tranquil dreams, and to the blessed consolations of sleep! for more than 15 three years and a half I am summoned away from these: I am now arrived at an Iliad of woes: for I have now to record

THE PAINS OF OPIUM

" ———— as when some great painter dips
His pencil in the gloom of earthquake and eclipse."

Shelley's Revolt of Islam.

20   READERS, who have thus far accompanied me, I must request your attention to a brief explanatory note on three points:

1. For several reasons, I have not been able to compose the notes for this part of my narrative into any regular 25 and connected shape. I give the notes disjointed as I find them, or have now drawn them up from memory. Some of them point to their own date; some I have dated; and some are undated. Whenever it could answer my purpose to transplant them from the natural or chronological order, 30 I have not scrupled to do so. Sometimes I speak in the

present, sometimes in the past tense. Few of the notes, perhaps, were written exactly at the period of time to which they relate; but this can little affect their accuracy; as the impressions were such that they can never fade from my mind. Much has been omitted. I could not, without effort, constrain myself to the task of either recalling, or constructing into a regular narrative, the whole burthen of horrors which lies upon my brain. This feeling partly I plead in excuse, and partly that I am now in London, and am a helpless sort of person, who cannot even arrange his own papers without assistance; and I am separated from the hands which are wont to perform for me the offices of an amanuensis.

2. You will think, perhaps, that I am too confidential and communicative of my own private history. It may be so. But my way of writing is rather to think aloud, and follow my own humours, than much to consider who is listening to me; and, if I stop to consider what is proper to be said to this or that person, I shall soon come to doubt whether any part at all is proper. The fact is, I place myself at a distance of fifteen or twenty years ahead of this time, and suppose myself writing to those who will be interested about me hereafter; and wishing to have some record of a time, the entire history of which no one can know but myself, I do it as fully as I am able with the efforts I am now capable of making, because I know not whether I can ever find time to do it again.

3. It will occur to you often to ask, why did I not release myself from the horrors of opium, by leaving it off, or diminishing it? To this I must answer briefly: it might be supposed that I yielded to the fascinations of opium too easily; it cannot be supposed that any man can be charmed by its terrors. The reader may be sure, therefore, that I made attempts innumerable to reduce the quantity. I add,

that those who witnessed the agonies of those attempts, and not myself, were the first to beg me to desist. But could not I have reduced it a drop a day, or by adding water, have bisected or trisected a drop? A thousand drops bisected would thus have taken nearly six years to reduce; and that way would certainly not have answered. But this is a common mistake of those who know nothing of opium experimentally; I appeal to those who do, whether it is not always found that down to a certain point it can be reduced with ease and even pleasure, but that, after that point, further reduction causes intense suffering. Yes, say many thoughtless persons, who know not what they are talking of, you will suffer a little low spirits and dejection for a few days. I answer, no; there is nothing like low spirits; on the contrary, the mere animal spirits are uncommonly raised: the pulse is improved: the health is better. It is not there that the suffering lies. It has no resemblance to the sufferings caused by renouncing wine. It is a state of unutterable irritation of stomach (which surely is not much like dejection), accompanied by intense perspirations, and feelings such as I shall not attempt to describe without more space at my command.

I shall now enter *in medias res*, and shall anticipate, from a time when my opium pains might be said to be at their *acme*, an account of their palsying effects on the intellectual faculties.

My studies have now been long interrupted. I cannot read to myself with any pleasure, hardly with a moment's endurance. Yet I read aloud sometimes for the pleasure of others; because reading is an accomplishment of mine; and, in the slang use of the word *accomplishment* as a superficial and ornamental attainment, almost the only one I

possess: and formerly, if I had any vanity at all connected
with any endowment or attainment of mine, it was with
this ; for I had observed that no accomplishment was so rare.
Players are the worst readers of all : John Kemble reads
vilely : and Mrs. Siddons, who is so celebrated, can read
nothing well but dramatic compositions : Milton she cannot read sufferably. People in general either read poetry
without any passion at all, or else overstep the modesty of
nature, and read not like scholars. Of late, if I have felt
moved by anything in books, it has been by the grand
lamentations of Samson Agonistes, or the great harmonies
of the Satanic speeches in "Paradise Regained," when
read aloud by myself. A young lady sometimes comes and
drinks tea with us : at her request and M[argaret]'s I now
and then read Wordsworth's poems to them. (Wordsworth, by the by, is the only poet I ever met who could
read his own verses : often indeed he reads admirably.)

For nearly two years I believe that I read no book but
one : and I owe it to the author, in discharge of a great
debt of gratitude, to mention what that was. The sublimer
and more passionate poets I still read, as I have said, by
snatches, and occasionally. But my proper vocation, as I
well knew, was the exercise of the analytic understanding.
Now, for the most part, analytic studies are continuous,
and not to be pursued by fits and starts, or fragmentary
efforts. Mathematics, for instance, intellectual philosophy,
etc., were all become insupportable to me ; and I shrunk
from them with a sense of powerless and infantine feeble-
ness that gave me an anguish the greater from remembering the time when I grappled with them to my own hourly
delight ; and for this further reason, because I had devoted
the labour of my whole life, and had dedicated my intellect,
blossoms and fruits, to the slow and elaborate toil of constructing one single work, to which I had presumed to give

the title of an unfinished work of Spinoza's; viz., *De emendatione humani intellectus.* This was now lying locked up, as by frost, like any Spanish bridge or aqueduct, begun upon too great a scale for the resources of the architect; 5 and, instead of surviving me as a monument of wishes at least, and aspirations, and a life of labour dedicated to the exaltation of human nature in that way in which God had best fitted me to promote so great an object, it was likely to stand a memorial to my children of hopes defeated, 10 of baffled efforts, of materials uselessly accumulated, of foundations laid that were never to support a super-structure, — of the grief and the ruin of the architect. In this state of imbecility, I had, for amusement, turned my attention to political economy; my understanding, which 15 formerly had been as active and restless as a hyena, could not, I suppose (so long as I lived at all), sink into utter lethargy; and political economy offers this advantage to a person in my state, that though it is eminently an organic science (no part, that is to say, but what acts on the whole, 20 as the whole again reacts on each part), yet the several parts may be detached and contemplated singly. Great as was the prostration of my powers at this time, yet I could not forget my knowledge; and my understanding had been for too many years intimate with severe thinkers, 25 with logic, and the great masters of knowledge, not to be aware of the utter feebleness of the main herd of modern economists. I had been led in 1811 to look into loads of books and pamphlets on many branches of economy; and, at my desire, M[argaret] sometimes read to me chapters 30 from more recent works, or parts of parliamentary debates. I saw that these were generally the very dregs and rinsings of the human intellect: and that any man of sound head, and practised in wielding logic with a scholastic adroitness, might take up the whole academy of modern economists, and throttle them between heaven and earth with his finger and thumb, or bray their fungus heads to powder with a lady's fan. At length, in 1819, a friend in Edinburgh sent me down Mr. Ricardo's book : and recurring to my own prophetic anticipation of the advent of some legislator for this science, I said, before I had finished the first chapter, "Thou art the man!" Wonder and curiosity were emotions that had long been dead in me. Yet I wondered once more : I wondered at myself that I could once again be stimulated to the effort of reading : and much more I wondered at the book. Had this profound work been really written in England during the nineteenth century? Was it possible? I supposed thinking [1] had been extinct in England. Could it be that an Englishman, and he not in academic bowers, but oppressed by mercantile and sena-torial cares, had accomplished what all the universities of Europe, and a century of thought, had failed even to advance by one hair's breadth? All other writers had been crushed and overlaid by the enormous weight of facts and documents ; Mr. Ricardo had deduced, *a priori*, from the understanding itself, laws which first gave a ray of light into the unwieldy chaos of materials, and had constructed what had been but a collection of tentative discussions into a science of regular proportions, now first standing on an eternal basis.

Thus did one single work of a profound understanding avail to give me a pleasure and an activity which I had not

---

[1] The reader must remember what I here mean by *thinking ;* because else this would be a very presumptuous expression. England, of late, has been rich to excess in fine thinkers, in the departments of creative and combining thought; but there is a sad dearth of masculine thinkers in any analytic path. A Scotchman of eminent name has lately told us, that he is obliged to quit even mathematics for want of encouragement.

known for years : — it roused me even to write, or, at least, to dictate what M[argaret] wrote for me. It seemed to me that some important truths had escaped even "the inevitable eye" of Mr. Ricardo: and, as these were, for 5 the most part, of such a nature that I could express or illustrate them more briefly and elegantly by algebraic symbols than in the usual clumsy and loitering diction of economists, the whole would not have filled a pocket-book; and being so brief, with M[argaret] for my amanuensis, 10 even at this time, incapable as I was of all general exertion, I drew up my "Prolegomena to all Future Systems of Political Economy." I hope it will not be found redolent of opium; though, indeed, to most people, the subject itself is a sufficient opiate.

15   This exertion, however, was but a temporary flash; as the sequel showed — for I designed to publish my work: arrangements were made at a provincial press, about eighteen miles distant, for printing it. An additional compositor was retained, for some days, on this account. The work 20 was even twice advertised : and I was, in a manner, pledged to the fulfilment of my intention. But I had a preface to write; and a dedication, which I wished to make a splendid one, to Mr. Ricardo. I found myself quite unable to accomplish all this. The arrangements were 25 countermanded : the compositor dismissed : and my "Prolegomena" rested peacefully by the side of its elder and more dignified brother.

I have thus described and illustrated my intellectual torpor, in terms that apply, more or less, to every part of 30 the four years during which I was under the Circean spells of opium. But for misery and suffering, I might, indeed, be said to have existed in a dormant state. I seldom could prevail on myself to write a letter; an answer of a few words, to any that I received, was the utmost that I could accomplish ; and often *that* not until the letter had lain weeks, or even months, on my writing table. Without the aid of M[argaret] all records of bills paid, or *to be* paid, must have perished : and my whole domestic economy, whatever became of Political Economy, must have gone into irretrievable confusion. I shall not afterwards allude to this part of the case : it is one, however, which the opium-eater will find, in the end, as oppressive and torment-ing as any other, from the sense of incapacity and feeble-ness, from the direct embarrassments incident to the neglect or procrastination of each day's appropriate duties, and from the remorse which must often exasperate the stings of these evils to a reflective and conscientious mind. The opium-eater loses none of his moral sensibilities, or aspirations : he wishes and longs, as earnestly as ever, to realise what he believes possible, and feels to be exacted by duty ; but his intellectual apprehension of what is possible infinitely outruns his power, not of execution only, but even of power to attempt. He lies under the weight of incubus and night-mare : he lies in the sight of all that he would fain perform, just as a man forcibly confined to his bed by the mortal languor of a relaxing disease, who is compelled to witness injury or outrage offered to some object of his tenderest love : — he curses the spells which chain him down from motion : — he would lay down his life if he might but get up and walk ; but he is powerless as an infant, and cannot even attempt to rise.

I now pass to what is the main subject of these latter confessions, to the history and journal of what took place in my dreams ; for these were the immediate and proximate cause of my acutest suffering.

The first notice I had of any important change going on in this part of my physical economy, was from the reawak-ening of a state of eye generally incident to childhood, or exalted states of irritability. I know not whether my reader is aware that many children, perhaps most, have a power of painting, as it were, upon the darkness, all sorts of phantoms; in some, that power is simply a mechanic 5 affection of the eye; others have a voluntary, or a semi-voluntary power to dismiss or to summon them; or, as a child once said to me when I questioned him on this matter, "I can tell them to go, and they go; but sometimes they come when I don't tell them to come." Whereupon 10 I told him that he had almost as unlimited command over apparitions as a Roman centurion over his soldiers. — In the middle of 1817, I think it was, that this faculty became positively distressing to me: at night, when I lay awake in bed, vast processions passed along in mournful pomp; 15 friezes of never-ending stories, that to my feelings were as sad and solemn as if they were stories drawn from times before Œdipus or Priam — before Tyre — before Memphis. And, at the same time, a corresponding change took place in my dreams; a theatre seemed suddenly opened and 20 lighted up within my brain, which presented nightly spectacles of more than earthly splendour. And the four following facts may be mentioned, as noticeable at this time:

1. That, as the creative state of the eye increased, a sympathy seemed to arise between the waking and the 25 dreaming states of the brain in one point — that whatsoever I happened to call up and to trace by a voluntary act upon the darkness was very apt to transfer itself to my dreams; so that I feared to exercise this faculty; for, as Midas turned all things to gold, that yet baffled his hopes 30 and defrauded his human desires, so whatsoever things capable of being visually represented I did but think of in the darkness, immediately shaped themselves into phantoms of the eye; and, by a process apparently no less inevitable, when thus once traced in faint and visionary

colours, like writings in sympathetic ink, they were drawn out by the fierce chemistry of my dreams, into insufferable splendour that fretted my heart.

2. For this, and all other changes in my dreams, were accompanied by deep-seated anxiety and gloomy melancholy, such as are wholly incommunicable by words. I seemed every night to descend, not metaphorically, but literally to descend, into chasms and sunless abysses, depths below depths, from which it seemed hopeless that I could ever reascend. Nor did I, by waking, feel that I *had* reascended. This I do not dwell upon; because the state of gloom which attended these gorgeous spectacles, amounting at least to utter darkness, as of some suicidal despondency, cannot be approached by words.

3. The sense of space, and in the end, the sense of time, were both powerfully affected. Buildings, landscapes, etc., were exhibited in proportions so vast as the bodily eye is not fitted to receive. Space swelled, and was amplified to an extent of unutterable infinity. This, however, did not disturb me so much as the vast expansion of time; I sometimes seemed to have lived for 70 or 100 years in one night; nay, sometimes had feelings representative of a millennium passed in that time, or, however, of a duration far beyond the limits of any human experience.

4. The minutest incidents of childhood, or forgotten scenes of later years, were often revived: I could not be said to recollect them; for if I had been told of them when waking, I should not have been able to acknowledge them as parts of my past experience. But placed as they were before me, in dreams like intuitions, and clothed in all their evanescent circumstances and accompanying feelings, I *recognised* them instantaneously. I was once told by a near relative of mine, that having in her childhood fallen into a river, and being on the very verge of death

but for the critical assistance which reached her, she saw
in a moment her whole life, in its minutest incidents,
arrayed before her simultaneously as in a mirror; and she
had a faculty developed as suddenly for comprehending
5 the whole and every part.   This, from some opium experiences of mine, I can believe; I have, indeed, seen the
same thing asserted twice in modern books, and accompanied by a remark which I am convinced is true; viz.,
that the dread book of account which the Scriptures speak
10 of is, in fact, the mind itself of each individual.   Of this,
at least, I feel assured, that there is no such thing as *forgetting* possible to the mind; a thousand accidents may
and will interpose a veil between our present consciousness and the secret inscriptions on the mind; accidents of
15 the same sort will also rend away this veil; but alike,
whether veiled or unveiled, the inscription remains for
ever; just as the stars seem to withdraw before the common light of day, whereas, in fact, we all know that it is the
light which is drawn over them as a veil—and that they
20 are waiting to be revealed, when the obscuring daylight
shall have withdrawn.

Having noticed these four facts as memorably distinguishing my dreams from those of health, I shall now cite a case
illustrative of the first fact; and shall then cite any others
25 that I remember, either in their chronological order, or any
other that may give them more effect as pictures to the reader.

I had been in youth, and even since, for occasional amusement, a great reader of Livy, whom I confess that I prefer,
both for style and matter, to any other of the Roman his-
30 torians; and I had often felt as most solemn and appalling
sounds, and most emphatically representative of the majesty
of the Roman people, the two words so often occurring in
Livy — *Consul Romanus;* especially when the consul is
introduced in his military character.   I mean to say, that

the words king — sultan — regent, etc., or any other titles of those who embody in their own persons the collective majesty of a great people, had less power over my reverential feelings. I had also, though no great reader of history, made myself minutely and critically familiar with one period of English history, viz., the period of the Parliamentary War, having been attracted by the moral grandeur of some who figured in that day, and by the many interesting memoirs which survive those unquiet times. Both these parts of my lighter reading, having furnished me often with matter of reflection, now furnished me with matter for my dreams. Often I used to see, after painting upon the blank darkness a sort of rehearsal whilst waking, a crowd of ladies, and perhaps a festival, and dances. And I heard it said, or I said to myself, "These are English ladies from the unhappy times of Charles I. These are the wives and the daughters of those who met in peace, and sat at the same tables, and were allied by marriage or by blood; and yet, after a certain day in August, 1642, never smiled upon each other again, nor met but in the field of battle; and at Marston Moor, at Newbury, or at Naseby, cut asunder all ties of love by the cruel sabre, and washed away in blood the memory of ancient friendship." — The ladies danced, and looked as lovely as the court of George IV. Yet I knew, even in my dream, that they had been in the grave for nearly two centuries. — This pageant would suddenly dissolve: and, at a clapping of hands, would be heard the heart-quaking sound of *Consul Romanus:* and immediately came "sweeping by," in gorgeous paludaments, Paulus, or Marius, girt round by a company of centurions, with the crimson tunic hoisted on a spear, and followed by the *alalagmos* of the Roman legions.

Many years ago, when I was looking over Piranesi's Antiquities of Rome, Mr. Coleridge, who was standing by,

described to me a set of plates by that artist, called his *Dreams*, and which record the scenery of his own visions during the delirium of a fever : some of them (I describe only from memory of Mr. Coleridge's account) representing
5 vast Gothic halls : on the floor of which stood all sorts of engines and machinery, wheels, cables, pulleys, levers, catapults, etc., etc., expressive of enormous power put forth, and resistance overcome.   Creeping along the sides of the walls, you perceived a staircase ; and upon it, groping his
10 way upwards, was Piranesi himself : follow the stairs a little further, and you perceive it come to a sudden abrupt termination, without any balustrade, and allowing no step onwards to him who had reached the extremity, except into the depths below.   Whatever is to become of poor
15 Piranesi, you suppose, at least, that his labours must in some way terminate here.   But raise your eyes, and behold a second flight of stairs still higher : on which again Piranesi is perceived, but this time standing on the very brink of the abyss.   Again elevate your eye, and a still
20 more aerial flight of stairs is beheld : and again is poor Piranesi busy on his aspiring labours : and so on, until the unfinished stairs and Piranesi both are lost in the upper gloom of the hall. — With the same power of endless growth and self-reproduction did my architecture proceed in dreams.
25 In the early stage of my malady, the splendours of my dreams were indeed chiefly architectural : and I beheld such pomp of cities and palaces as was never yet beheld by the waking eye, unless in the clouds.   From a great modern poet I cite part of a passage which describes, as
30 an appearance actually beheld in the clouds, what in many of its circumstances I saw frequently in sleep :

> " The appearance, instantaneously disclosed,
>   Was of a mighty city — boldly say
>   A wilderness of building, sinking far

And self-withdrawn into a wondrous depth,
Far sinking into splendour — without end !
Fabric it seem'd of diamond, and of gold,
With alabaster domes, and silver spires,
And blazing terrace upon terrace, high   5
Uplifted ; here, serene pavilions bright
In avenues disposed ; there towers begirt
With battlements that on their restless fronts
Bore stars — illumination of all gems !
By earthly nature had the effect been wrought   10
Upon the dark materials of the storm
Now pacified : on them, and on the coves,
And mountain-steeps and summits, whereunto
The vapours had receded, — taking there
Their station under a cerulean sky," etc., etc.   15

The sublime circumstance — "battlements that on their
restless fronts bore stars," — might have been copied from
my architectural dreams, for it often occurred. — We hear
it reported of Dryden, and of Fuseli in modern times, that
they thought proper to eat raw meat for the sake of obtain-   20
ing splendid dreams : how much better for such a purpose
to have eaten opium, which yet I do not remember that
any poet is recorded to have done, except the dramatist
Shadwell : and in ancient days, Homer is, I think, rightly
reputed to have known the virtues of opium.   25

To my architecture succeeded dreams of lakes and silvery
expanses of water : — these haunted me so much that I
feared, though possibly it will appear ludicrous to a medical
man, that some dropsical state or tendency of the brain
might thus be making itself, to use a metaphysical word,   30
objective; and the sentient organ *project* itself as its own
object. — For two months I suffered greatly in my head —
a part of my bodily structure which had hitherto been so
clear from all touch or taint of weakness, physically, I mean,
that I used to say of it, as the last Lord Orford said of his   35

stomach, that it seemed likely to survive the rest of my person. — Till now I had never felt headache even, or any the slightest pain, except rheumatic pains caused by my own folly. However, I got over this attack, though it must have been verging on something very dangerous.

The waters now changed their character, — from translucent lakes, shining like mirrors, they now became seas and oceans. And now came a tremendous change, which, unfolding itself slowly like a scroll, through many months, promised an abiding torment; and, in fact, never left me until the winding up of my case. Hitherto the human face had mixed often in my dreams, but not despotically, nor with any special power of tormenting. But now that which I have called the tyranny of the human face began to unfold itself. Perhaps some part of my London life might be answerable for this. Be that as it may, now it was that upon the rocking waters of the ocean the human face began to appear: the sea appeared paved with innumerable faces, upturned to the heavens: faces, imploring, wrathful, despairing, surged upwards by thousands, by myriads, by generations, by centuries:—my agitation was infinite, — my mind tossed—and surged with the ocean.

May, 1818.

The Malay has been a fearful enemy for months. I have been every night, through his means, transported into Asiatic scenes. I know not whether others share in my feelings on this point; but I have often thought that if I were compelled to forego England, and to live in China, and among Chinese manners and modes of life and scenery, I should go mad. The causes of my horror lie deep; and some of them must be common to others. Southern Asia, in general, is the seat of awful images and associations. As the cradle of the human race, it would alone have a dim and reverential feeling connected with it. But there are other reasons. No man can pretend that the wild, barbarous, and capricious superstitions of Africa, or of savage tribes elsewhere, affect him in the way that he is affected by the ancient, monumental, cruel, and elaborate religions of Indostan, etc. The mere antiquity of Asiatic things, of their institutions, histories, modes of faith, etc., is so impressive, that to me the vast age of the race and name overpowers the sense of youth in the individual. A young Chinese seems to me an antediluvian man renewed. Even Englishmen, though not bred in any knowledge of such institutions, cannot but shudder at the mystic sublimity of *castes* that have flowed apart, and refused to mix, through such immemorial tracts of time; nor can any man fail to be awed by the names of the Ganges or the Euphrates. It contributes much to these feelings that southern Asia is, and has been for thousands of years, the part of the earth most swarming with human life; the great *officina gentium*. Man is a weed in those regions. The vast empires also, into which the enormous population of Asia has always been cast, give a further sublimity to the feelings associated with all Oriental names or images. In China, over and above what it has in common with the rest of southern Asia, I am terrified by the modes of life, by the manners, and the barrier of utter abhorrence, and want of sympathy, placed between us by feelings deeper than I can analyze. I could sooner live with lunatics, or brute animals. All this, and much more than I can say, or have time to say, the reader must enter into before he can comprehend the unimaginable horror which these dreams of Oriental imagery, and mythological tortures, impressed upon me. Under the connecting feeling of tropical heat and vertical sunlights, I brought together all creatures, birds, beasts, reptiles, all trees and plants, usages and appearances, that are found in all tropical

regions, and assembled them together in China or Indostan. From kindred feelings, I soon brought Egypt and
all her gods under the same law. I was stared at, hooted
at, grinned at, chattered at, by monkeys, by paroquets,
by cockatoos. I ran into pagodas: and was fixed for
centuries at the summit, or in secret rooms; I was the
idol; I was the priest; I was worshipped; I was sacrificed.
I fled from the wrath of Brama through all the forests of
Asia: Vishnu hated me: Seeva laid wait for me. I came
suddenly upon Isis and Osiris: I had done a deed, they
said, which the ibis and the crocodile trembled at. I was
buried for a thousand years in stone coffins, with mum-
mies and sphinxes, in narrow chambers at the heart of
eternal pyramids. I was kissed, with cancerous kisses, by
crocodiles; and laid, confounded with all unutterable slimy
things, amongst reeds and Nilotic mud.

I thus give the reader some slight abstraction of my Oriental dreams, which always filled me with such amazement
at the monstrous scenery, that horror seemed absorbed,
for a while, in sheer astonishment. Sooner or later, came
a reflux of feeling that swallowed up the astonishment, and
left me, not so much in terror, as in hatred and abomina-
tion of what I saw. Over every form, and threat, and
punishment, and dim sightless incarceration, brooded a
sense of eternity and infinity that drove me into an oppression as of madness. Into these dreams only, it was, with
one or two slight exceptions, that any circumstances of
physical horror entered. All before had been moral and
spiritual terrors. But here the main agents were ugly
birds, or snakes, or crocodiles; especially the last. The
cursed crocodile became to me the object of more horror
than almost all the rest. I was compelled to live with him;
and (as was always the case almost in my dreams) for centuries. I escaped sometimes, and found myself in Chinese

houses, with cane tables, etc. All the feet of the tables, sofas, etc., soon became instinct with life : the abominable head of the crocodile, and his leering eyes, looked out at me, multiplied into a thousand repetitions : and I stood loathing and fascinated. And so often did this hideous reptile haunt my dreams, that many times the very same dream was broken up in the very same way : I heard gentle voices speaking to me (I hear everything when I am sleeping) ; and instantly I awoke : it was broad noon ; and my children were standing, hand in hand, at my bedside ; come to show me their coloured shoes, or new frocks, or to let me see them dressed for going out. I protest that so awful was the transition from the damned crocodile, and the other unutterable monsters and abortions of my dreams, to the sight of innocent *human* natures and of infancy, that, in the mighty and sudden revulsion of mind, I wept, and could not forbear it, as I kissed their faces.

June, 1819.

I have had occasion to remark, at various periods of my life, that the deaths of those whom we love, and indeed the contemplation of death generally, is (*cæteris paribus*) more affecting in summer than in any other season óf the year. And the reasons are these three, I think : first, that the visible heavens in summer appear far higher, more distant, and (if such a solecism may be excused) more infinite ; the clouds, by which chiefly the eye expounds the distance of the blue pavilion stretched over our heads, are in summer more voluminous, massed, and accumulated in far grander and more towering piles : secondly, the light and the appearances of the declining and the setting sun are much more fitted to be types and characters of the Infinite : and, thirdly, which is the main reason, the exuberant and riotous prodigality of life naturally forces the mind more powerfully upon the antagonist thought of death, and the wintry sterility of the grave. For it may be observed, generally, that wherever two thoughts stand related to each other by a law of antagonism, and exist, as it were, by mutual repulsion, they are apt to suggest each 5 other. On these accounts it is that I find it impossible to banish the thought of death when I am walking alone in the endless days of summer; and any particular death, if not more affecting, at least haunts my mind more obstinately and besiegingly in that season. Perhaps this cause, 10 and a slight incident which I omit, might have been the immediate occasions of the following dream; to which, however, a predisposition must always have existed in my mind; but having been once roused, it never left me, and split into a thousand fantastic varieties, which often sud- 15 denly reunited, and composed again the original dream.

I thought that it was a Sunday morning in May, that it was Easter Sunday, and as yet very early in the morning. I was standing, as it seemed to me, at the door of my own cottage. Right before me lay the very scene which could 20 really be commanded from that situation, but exalted, as was usual, and solemnised by the power of dreams. There were the same mountains, and the same lovely valley at their feet; but the mountains were raised to more than Alpine height, and there was interspace far larger between 25 them of meadows and forest lawns; the hedges were rich with white roses; and no living creature was to be seen, excepting that in the green churchyard there were cattle tranquilly reposing upon the verdant graves, and particularly round about the grave of a child whom I had tenderly loved, 30 just as I had really beheld them, a little before sunrise in the same summer, when that child died. I gazed upon the well-known scene, and I said aloud (as I thought) to myself, "It yet wants much of sunrise; and it is Easter Sunday; and that is the day on which they celebrate the first-fruits of resurrection. I will walk abroad; old griefs shall be forgotten to-day; for the air is cool and still, and the hills are high, and stretch away to heaven; and the forest-glades are as quiet as the churchyard; and with the dew I can wash the fever from my forehead, and then I shall be unhappy no longer." And I turned, as if to open my garden gate; and immediately I saw upon the left a scene far different; but which yet the power of dreams had reconciled into harmony with the other. The scene was an Oriental one; and there also it was Easter Sunday, and very early in the morning. And at a vast distance were visible, as a stain upon the horizon, the domes and cupolas of a great city — an image or faint abstraction, caught perhaps in childhood from some picture of Jerusalem. And not a bowshot from me, upon a stone, and shaded by Judean palms, there sat a woman; and I looked; and it was — Ann! She fixed her eyes upon me earnestly; and I said to her at length: " So then I have found you at last." I waited: but she answered me not a word. Her face was the same as when I saw it last, and yet again how different! Seventeen years ago, when the lamplight fell upon her face, as for the last time I kissed her lips (lips, Ann, that to me were not polluted), her eyes were streaming with tears: the tears were now wiped away; she seemed more beautiful than she was at that time, but in all other points the same, and not older. Her looks were tranquil, but with unusual solemnity of expression; and I now gazed upon her with some awe, but suddenly her countenance grew dim, and, turning to the mountains, I perceived vapours rolling between us; in a moment, all had vanished; thick darkness came on; and, in the twinkling of an eye, I was far away from mountains, and by lamplight in Oxford Street, walking again with Ann — just as we walked seventeen years before, when we were both children.

As a final specimen, I cite one of a different character, from 1820.

The dream commenced with a music which now I often heard in dreams — a music of preparation and of awaken-ing suspense; a music like the opening of the Coronation Anthem, and which, like *that*, gave the feeling of a vast march — of infinite cavalcades filing off — and the tread of innumerable armies. The morning was come of a mighty day — a day of crisis and of final hope for human nature, then suffering some mysterious eclipse, and labouring in some dread extremity. Somewhere, I knew not where — somehow, I knew not how — by some beings, I knew not whom — a battle, a strife, an agony, was conducting, — was evolving like a great drama, or piece of music; with which my sympathy was the more insupportable from my confusion as to its place, its cause, its nature, and its possible issue. I, as is usual in dreams (where, of necessity, we make ourselves central to every movement), had the power, and yet had not the power, to decide it. I had the power, if I could raise myself, to will it, and yet again had not the power, for the weight of twenty Atlantics was upon me, or the oppression of inexpiable guilt. "Deeper than ever plummet sounded," I lay inactive. Then, like a chorus, the passion deepened. Some greater interest was at stake; some mightier cause than ever yet the sword had pleaded, or trumpet had proclaimed. Then came sudden alarms: hurryings to and fro: trepidations of innumerable fugitives, I knew not whether from the good cause or the bad: darkness and lights: tempest and human faces: and at last, with the sense that all was lost, female forms, and the features that were worth all the world to me, and but a moment allowed, — and clasped hands, and heart-breaking partings, and then — everlasting farewells! and with a sigh, such as the caves of hell sighed when the incestuous mother uttered the abhorred name of death, the sound was reverberated — everlasting farewells! and again, and yet again reverberated — everlasting farewells!

And I awoke in struggles, and cried aloud — "I will sleep no more!"

5

But I am now called upon to wind up a narrative which has already extended to an unreasonable length. Within more spacious limits, the materials which I have used might have been better unfolded; and much which I have not used might have been added with effect. Perhaps, however, enough has been given. It now remains that I should say something of the way in which this conflict of horrors was finally brought to its crisis. The reader is already aware (from a passage near the beginning of the introduction to the first part) that the opium-eater has, in some way or other, "unwound, almost to its final links, the accursed chain which bound him." By what means? To have narrated this, according to the original intention, would have far exceeded the space which can now be allowed. It is fortunate, as such a cogent reason exists for abridging it, that I should, on a maturer view of the case, have been exceedingly unwilling to injure, by any such unaffecting details, the impression of the history itself, as an appeal to the prudence and the conscience of the yet unconfirmed opium-eater — or even, though a very inferior consideration, to injure its effect as a composition. The interest of the judicious reader will not attach itself chiefly to the subject of the fascinating spells, but to the fascinating power. Not the opium-eater, but the opium, is the true hero of the tale; and the legitimate centre on which the interest revolves. The object was to display the marvellous agency of opium, whether for pleasure or for pain: if that is done, the action of the piece has closed.

However, as some people, in spite of all laws to the contrary, will persist in asking what became of the opium-eater, and in what state he now is, I answer for him thus: The reader is aware that opium had long ceased to found 5 its empire on spells of pleasure; it was solely by the tortures connected with the attempt to abjure it, that it kept its hold. Yet, as other tortures, no less it may be thought, attended the non-abjuration of such a tyrant, a choice only of evils was left; and *that* might as well have 10 been adopted, which, however terrific in itself, held out a prospect of final restoration to happiness. This appears true; but good logic gave the author no strength to act upon it. However, a crisis arrived for the author's life, and a crisis for other objects still dearer to him — and 15 which will always be far dearer to him than his life, even now that it is again a happy one. — I saw that I must die if I continued the opium: I determined, therefore, if that should be required, to die in throwing it off. How much I was at that time taking I cannot say; for the opium 20 which I used had been purchased for me by a friend who afterwards refused to let me pay him; so that I could not ascertain even what quantity I had used within the year. I apprehend, however, that I took it very irregularly: and that I varied from about fifty or 25 sixty grains, to 150 a day. My first task was to reduce it to forty, to thirty, and, as fast as I could, to twelve grains.

I triumphed: but think not, reader, that therefore my sufferings were ended; nor think of me as of one sitting 30 in a *dejected* state. Think of me as of one, even when four months had passed, still agitated, writhing, throbbing, palpitating, shattered; and much, perhaps, in the situation of him who has been racked, as I collect the torments of that state from the affecting account of them left by the most innocent sufferer [1] of the times of James I. Meantime, I derived no benefit from any medicine, except one prescribed to me by an Edinburgh surgeon of great eminence, viz., ammoniated tincture of valerian. Medical account, therefore, of my emancipation I have not much to give: and even that little, as managed by a man so ignorant of medicine as myself, would probably tend only to mislead. At all events, it would be misplaced in this situation. The moral of the narrative is addressed to the opium-eater; and therefore, of necessity, limited in its application. If he is taught to fear and tremble, enough has been effected. But he may say, that the issue of my case is at least a proof that opium, after a seventeen years' use, and an eight years' abuse of its powers, may still be renounced: and that *he* may chance to bring to the task greater energy than I did, or that with a stronger constitution than mine he may obtain the same results with less. This may be true: I would not presume to measure the efforts of other men by my own: I heartily wish him more energy: I wish him the same success. Nevertheless, I had motives external to myself which he may unfortunately want: and these supplied me with conscientious supports which mere personal interests might fail to supply to a mind debilitated by opium.

Jeremy Taylor conjectures that it may be as painful to be born as to die: I think it probable: and, during the whole period of diminishing the opium, I had the torments of a man passing out of one mode of existence into another. The issue was not death, but a sort of physical regeneration: and I may add, that ever since, at intervals, I have had a restoration of more than youthful spirits, though under the pressure of difficulties, which, in a less happy state of mind, I should have called misfortunes.

[1] William Lithgow: his book ("Travels," etc.) is ill and pedantically written: but the account of his own sufferings on the rack at Malaga is overpoweringly affecting.

One memorial of my former condition still remains: my dreams are not yet perfectly calm: the dread swell and agitation of the storms have not wholly subsided: the legions that encamped in them are drawing off, but not all departed: my sleep is still tumultuous, and, like the gates of Paradise to our first parents when looking back from afar, it is still, in the tremendous line of Milton —

"With dreadful faces throng'd and fiery arms."

APPENDIX

THE proprietors of this little work having determined on reprinting it, some explanation seems called for, to account for the non-appearance of a Third Part promised in the "London Magazine" of December last; and the more so, because the proprietors, under whose guarantee that promise was issued, might otherwise be implicated in the blame — little or much — attached to its non-fulfilment. This blame, in mere justice, the author takes wholly upon himself. What may be the exact amount of the guilt which he thus appropriates, is a very dark question to his own judgment, and not much illuminated by any of the masters in casuistry whom he has consulted on the occasion. On the one hand it seems generally agreed that a promise is binding in the *inverse* ratio of the numbers to whom it is made: for which reason it is that we see many persons break promises without scruple that are made to a whole nation, who keep their faith religiously in all private engagements, —breaches of promise towards the stronger party being committed at a man's own peril: on the other hand, the only parties interested in the promises of an author are his readers; and these it is a point of modesty in any author to believe as few as possible; or perhaps only one, in which case any promise imposes a sanctity of moral obligation which it is shocking to think of. Casuistry dismissed however, — the author throws himself on the indulgent consideration of all who may conceive themselves aggrieved by his delay — in the following account of his own condition from the end of last year, when the engagement was made, up nearly to the present time. For any purpose of self-excuse, it might be sufficient to say that intolerable bodily suffering had totally disabled him for almost any exertion of mind, more especially for such as demand and presuppose a pleasurable and genial state of feeling: but, as a case that may by possibility contribute a trifle to the medical history of opium in a further stage of its action than can often have been brought under the notice of professional men, he has judged that it might be acceptable to some readers to have it described more at length. *Fiat experimentum in corpore vili* is a just rule where there is any reasonable presumption of benefit to arise on a large scale; what the benefit may be, will admit of a doubt: but there can be none as to the value of the body: for a more worthless body than his own, the author is free to confess, cannot be: it is his pride to believe — that it is the very ideal of a base, crazy, despicable human system — that hardly ever could have been meant to be sea-worthy for two days under the ordinary storms and wear-and-tear of life: and indeed, if that were the creditable way of disposing of human bodies, he must own that he should almost be ashamed to bequeath his wretched structure to any respectable dog. — But now to the case; which, for the sake of avoiding the constant recurrence of a cumbersome periphrasis, the author will take the liberty of giving in the first person.

Those who have read the Confessions will have closed them with the impression that I had wholly renounced the use of opium. This impression I meant to convey: and

that for two reasons: first, because the very act of deliberately recording such a state of suffering necessarily presumes in the recorder a power of surveying his own case
as a cool spectator, and a degree of spirits for adequately
describing it, which it would be inconsistent to suppose in
any person speaking from the station of an actual sufferer;
secondly, because I, who had descended from so large a
quantity as 8000 drops to so small a one (comparatively
speaking) as a quantity ranging between 300 and 160 drops,
might well suppose that the victory was in effect achieved.
In suffering my readers therefore to think of me as of a
reformed opium-eater, I left no impression but what I shared
myself; and, as may be seen, even this impression was left
to be collected from the general tone of the conclusion, and
not from any specific words — which are in no instance at
variance with the literal truth. — In no long time after that
paper was written, I became sensible that the effort which
remained would cost me far more energy than I had anticipated: and the necessity for making it was more apparent
every month.   In particular I became aware of an increasing callousness or defect of sensibility in the stomach; and
this I imagined might imply a scirrhous state of that organ
either formed or forming.   An eminent physician, to whose
kindness I was at that time deeply indebted, informed me
that such a termination of my case was not impossible,
though likely to be forestalled by a different termination,
in the event of my continuing the use of opium.   Opium
therefore I resolved wholly to abjure, as soon as I should
find myself at liberty to bend my undivided attention and
energy to this purpose.   It was not however until the 24th
of June last that any tolerable concurrence of facilities for
such an attempt arrived.   On that day I began my experiment, having previously settled in my own mind that I
would not flinch, but would "stand up to the scratch" —

under any possible "punishment." I must premise that about 170 or 180 drops had been my ordinary allowance for many months: occasionally I had run up as high as 500; and once nearly to 700: in repeated preludes to my final experiment I had also gone as low as 100 drops; but had found it impossible to stand it beyond the 4th day — which, by the way, I have always found more difficult to get over than any of the preceding three. I went off under easy sail — 130 drops a day for 3 days: on the 4th I plunged at once to 80: the misery which I now suffered "took the conceit" out of me at once: and for about a month I continued off and on about this mark: then I sunk to 60: and the next day to —— none at all. This was the first day for nearly ten years that I had existed without opium. I persevered in my abstinence for 90 hours; *i.e.*, upwards of half a week. Then I took —— ask me not how much: say, ye severest, what would ye have done? then I abstained again: then took about 25 drops: then abstained: and so on.

Meantime the symptoms which attended my case for the first six weeks of the experiment were these: — enormous irritability and excitement of the whole system: the stomach in particular restored to a full feeling of vitality and sensibility; but often in great pain: unceasing restlessness night and day: sleep —— I scarcely knew what it was: three hours out of the twenty-four was the utmost I had, and that so agitated and shallow that I heard every sound that was near me: lower jaw constantly swelling: mouth ulcerated: and many other distressing symptoms that would be tedious to repeat; amongst which however I must mention one, because it had never failed to accompany any attempt to renounce opium — viz., violent sternutation: this now became exceedingly troublesome: sometimes lasting for two hours at once, and recurring at least twice or three times a day. I was not much surprised at this, on

recollecting what I had somewhere heard or read, that the
membrane which lines the nostrils is a prolongation of that
which lines the stomach; whence I believe are explained
the inflammatory appearances about the nostrils of dram-
drinkers.   The sudden restoration of its original sensibility
to the stomach expressed itself, I suppose, in this way.   It
is remarkable also that, during the whole period of years
through which I had taken opium, I had never once caught
cold (as the phrase is), nor even the slightest cough.   But
now a violent cold attacked me, and a cough soon after.
In an unfinished fragment of a letter begun about this time
to ——— I find these words: "You ask me to write the ———
———.   Do you know Beaumont and Fletcher's play of
Thierry and Theodoret?   There you will see my case as to
sleep: nor is it much of an exaggeration in other features.
— I protest to you that I have a greater influx of thoughts
in one hour at present than in a whole year under the reign
of opium.   It seems as though all the thoughts which had
been frozen up for a decad of years by opium, had now
according to the old fable been thawed at once — such a
multitude stream in upon me from all quarters.   Yet such
is my impatience and hideous irritability — that, for one
which I detain and write down, fifty escape me: in spite
of my weariness from suffering and want of sleep, I cannot
stand still or sit for two minutes together.   '*I nunc, et versus
tecum meditare canoros.*'"

At this stage of my experiment I sent to a neighbouring
surgeon, requesting that he would come over to see me.   In
the evening he came: and after briefly stating the case to
him, I asked this question: — Whether he did not think
that the opium might have acted as a stimulus to the diges-
tive organs; and that the present state of suffering in the
stomach, which manifestly was the cause of the inability to
sleep, might arise from indigestion?   His answer was — No:

on the contrary he thought that the suffering was caused
by digestion itself — which should naturally go on below
the consciousness, but which from the unnatural state of
the stomach, vitiated by so long a use of opium, was become
distinctly perceptible. This opinion was plausible: and the
unintermitting nature of the suffering disposes me to think
that it was true: for, if it had been any mere *irregular*
affection of the stomach, it should naturally have inter-
mitted occasionally, and constantly fluctuated as to degree.
The intention of nature, as manifested in the healthy
state, obviously is to withdraw from our notice all the vital
motions, such as the circulation of the blood, the expansion
and contraction of the lungs, the peristaltic action of the
stomach, etc. ; and opium, it seems, is able in this as in
other instances to counteract her purposes. — By the advice
of the surgeon I tried *bitters :* for a short time these greatly
mitigated the feelings under which I laboured: but about
the forty-second day of the experiment the symptoms already
noticed began to retire, and new ones to arise of a different
and far more tormenting class: under these, but with a
few intervals of remission, I have since continued to suffer.
But I dismiss them undescribed for two reasons: 1st,
because the mind revolts from retracing circumstantially
any sufferings from which it is removed by too short or by
no interval: to do this with minuteness enough to make
the review of any use — would be indeed " *infandum renovare
dolorem*," and possibly without a sufficient motive: for 2dly,
I doubt whether this latter state be any way referable to
opium — positively considered, or even negatively ; that is,
whether it is to be numbered amongst the last evils from
the direct action of opium, or even amongst the earliest
evils consequent upon a *want* of opium in a system long
deranged by its use. Certainly one part of the symptoms
might be accounted for from the time of year (August): for,

though the summer was not a hot one, yet in any case the
sum of all the heat *funded*, if one may say so, during the
previous months, added to the existing heat of that month,
naturally renders August in its better half the hottest part
5 of the year: and it so happened that the excessive perspi-
ration, which even at Christmas attends any great reduction in the daily quantum of opium — and which in July
was so violent as to oblige me to use a bath five or six times
a day, had about the setting in of the hottest season wholly
10 retired: on which account any bad effect of the heat might
be the more unmitigated.   Another symptom, viz., what in
my ignorance I call internal rheumatism, sometimes affecting the shoulders, etc., but more often appearing to be
seated in the stomach, seemed again less probably attribu-
15 table to the opium or the want of opium than to the damp-
ness of the house [1] which I inhabit, which had about that
time attained its maximum — July having been, as usual, a
month of incessant rain in our most rainy part of England.

Under these reasons for doubting whether opium had
20 any connexion with the latter stage of my bodily wretchedness — except indeed as an occasional cause, as having left
the body weaker and more crazy, and thus pre-disposed to
any mal-influence whatever, — I willingly spare my reader
all description of it: let it perish to him: and would that I
25 could as easily say, let it perish to my own remembrances:
that any future hours of tranquillity may not be disturbed
by too vivid an ideal of possible human misery!

[1] In saying this I mean no disrespect to the individual house, as the
reader will understand when I tell him that, with the exception of one
or two princely mansions, and some few inferior ones that have been
coated with Roman cement, I am not acquainted with any house in this
mountainous district which is wholly waterproof. The architecture of
books, I flatter myself, is conducted on just principles in this country;
but for any other architecture — it is in a barbarous state, and what is
worse, in a retrograde state.

So much for the sequel of my experiment: as to the former stage, in which properly lies the experiment and its application to other cases, I must request my reader not to forget the reasons for which I have recorded it : these were two: 1st, a belief that I might add some trifle to the 5 history of opium as a medical agent: in this I am aware that I have not at all fulfilled my own intentions, in consequence of the torpor of mind — pain of body — and extreme disgust to the subject which besieged me whilst writing that part of my paper ; which part, being immedi- 10 ately sent off to the press (distant about five degrees of latitude), cannot be corrected or improved. But from this account, rambling as it may be, it is evident that thus much of benefit may arise to the persons most interested in such a history of opium — viz., to opium-eaters in general 15 — that it establishes, for their consolation and encouragement, the fact that opium may be renounced ; and without greater sufferings than an ordinary resolution may support ; and by a pretty rapid course [1] of descent.

[1] On which last notice I would remark that mine was *too* rapid, and the suffering therefore needlessly aggravated; or rather, perhaps, it was not sufficiently continuous and equably graduated. But that the reader may judge for himself, and above all that the opium-eater, who is preparing to retire from business, may have every sort of information before him, I subjoin my diary : —

FIRST WEEK	Drops of Laud.		THIRD WEEK	Drops of Laud.
Mond. June 24	130		Mond. July 8	300
" 25	140		" 9	50
" 26	130		" 10	
" 27	80		" 11	
" 28	80		" 12	Hiatus in MS.
" 29	80		" 13	
" 30	80		" 14	76

SECOND WEEK			FOURTH WEEK	
Mond. July 1	80		Mond. July 15	76
" 2	80		" 16	73½
" 3	90		" 17	73½
" 4	100		" 18	70
" 5	80		" 19	240
" 6	80		" 20	80
" 7	80		" 21	350

To communicate this result of my experiment — was my foremost purpose. 2dly, as a purpose collateral to this, I wished to explain how it had become impossible for me to compose a Third Part in time to accompany this repub-
5 lication: for during the very time of this experiment, the proof sheets of this reprint were sent to me from London : and such was my inability to expand or to improve them, that I could not even bear to read them over with attention enough to notice the press errors, or to correct any verbal
10 inaccuracies. These were my reasons for troubling my reader with any record, long or short, of experiments relating to so truly base a subject as my own body: and I am earnest with the reader that he will not forget them, or so far misapprehend me as to believe it possible that I would
15 condescend to so rascally a subject for its own sake, or indeed for any less object than that of general benefit to others. Such an animal as the self-observing valetudi-narian — I know there is: I have met him myself occa-sionally : and I know that he is the worst imaginable
20 *heautontimoroumenos;* aggravating and sustaining, by call-ing into distinct consciousness, every symptom that would

FIFTH WEEK

	Drops of Laud.		Drops of Laud.
Mond. July 22	60	July 25	none
" 23	none	" 26	200
" 24	none	" 27	none

What mean these abrupt relapses, the reader will ask perhaps, to such numbers as 300, 350, &c. ? The *impulse* to these relapses was mere infirmity of purpose ; the *motive*, where any motive blended with this impulse, was either the principle of "*reculer pour mieux sauter*" (for under the torpor of a large dose, which lasted for a day or two, a less quantity satisfied the stomach, which on awakening found itself partly accustomed to this new ration) ; or else it was this principle — that of sufferings otherwise equal, those will be borne best which meet with a mood of anger. Now, whenever I ascended to my large dose I was furiously incensed on the following day, and could then have borne anything.

else perhaps—under a different direction given to the thoughts—become evanescent. But as to myself, so profound is my contempt for this undignified and selfish habit, that I could as little condescend to it as I could to spend my time in watching a poor servant girl—to whom at this moment I hear some lad or other making love at the back of my house. Is it for a Transcendental Philosopher to feel any curiosity on such an occasion? Or can I, whose life is worth only $8\frac{1}{2}$ years' purchase, be supposed to have leisure for such trivial employments?—However, to put this out of question, I shall say one thing, which will perhaps shock some readers: but I am sure it ought not to do so, considering the motives on which I say it. No man, I suppose, employs much of his time on the phenomena of his own body without some regard for it; whereas the reader sees that, so far from looking upon mine with any complacency or regard, I hate it and make it the object of my bitter ridicule and contempt: and I should not be displeased to know that the last indignities which the law inflicts upon the bodies of the worst malefactors might hereafter fall upon it. And, in testification of my sincerity in saying this, I shall make the following offer. Like other men, I have particular fancies about the place of my burial: having lived chiefly in a mountainous region, I rather cleave to the conceit that a grave in a green churchyard amongst the ancient and solitary hills will be a sublimer and more tranquil place of repose for a philosopher than any in the hideous Golgothas of London. Yet if the gentlemen of Surgeons' Hall think that any benefit can redound to their science from inspecting the appearances in the body of an opium-eater, let them speak but a word, and I will take care that mine shall be legally secured to them——*i.e.*, as soon as I have done with it myself. Let them not hesitate to express their wishes upon any

scruples of false delicacy, and consideration for my feelings : I assure them they will do me too much honour by
'demonstrating' on such a crazy body as mine: and it will
give me pleasure to anticipate this posthumous revenge
5 and insult inflicted upon that which has caused me so
much suffering in this life.   Such bequests are not common : reversionary benefits contingent upon the death of
the testator are indeed dangerous to announce in many
cases : of this we have a remarkable instance in the habits
10 of a Roman prince — who used, upon any notification made
to him by rich persons that they had left him a handsome
estate in their wills, to express his entire satisfaction at
such arrangements, and his gracious acceptance of those
loyal legacies : but then, if the testators neglected to give
15 him immediate possession of the property, if they traitor-
ously 'persisted in living' (*si vivere perseverarent*, as Suetonius expresses it), he was highly provoked, and took his measures accordingly. — In those times, and from one of the
worst of the Cæsars, we might expect such conduct : but I
20 am sure that from English surgeons at this day I need look
for no expressions of impatience, or of any other feelings
but such as are answerable to that pure love of science and
all its interests which induces me to make such an offer.

Sept. 30th, 1822.

FROM THE *SUSPIRIA DE PROFUNDIS*

LEVANA AND OUR LADIES OF SORROW

OFTENTIMES at Oxford I saw Levana in my dreams. I knew her by her Roman symbols. Who is Levana? Reader, that do not pretend to have leisure for very much scholarship, you will not be angry with me for telling you. Levana was the Roman goddess that performed for the new-born infant the earliest office of ennobling kindness, — typical, by its mode, of that grandeur which belongs to man everywhere, and of that benignity in powers invisible which even in Pagan worlds sometimes descends to sustain it. At the very moment of birth, just as the infant tasted for the first time the atmosphere of our troubled planet, it was laid on the ground. *That* might bear different interpretations. But immediately, lest so grand a creature should grovel there for more than one instant, either the paternal hand, as proxy for the goddess Levana, or some near kinsman, as proxy for the father, raised it upright, bade it look erect as the king of all this world, and presented its forehead to the stars, saying, perhaps, in his heart, "Behold what is greater than yourselves!" This symbolic act represented the function of Levana. And that mysterious lady, who never revealed her face (except to me in dreams), but always acted by delegation, had her name from the Latin verb (as still it is the Italian verb) *levare*, to raise aloft.

This is the explanation of Levana. And hence it has arisen that some people have understood by Levana the tutelary power that controls the education of the nursery.

She, that would not suffer at his birth even a prefigurative or mimic degradation for her awful ward, far less could be supposed to suffer the real degradation attaching to the non-development of his powers. She therefore watches over human education. Now, the word *edŭco*, with the penultimate short, was derived (by a process often exemplified in the crystallisation of languages) from the word *edūco*, with the penultimate long. Whatsoever *educes*, or develops, *educates*. By the education of Levana, therefore, is meant, — not the poor machinery that moves by spelling-books and grammars, but that mighty system of central forces hidden in the deep bosom of human life, which by passion, by strife, by temptation, by the energies of resistance, works for ever upon children, — resting not day or night, any more than the mighty wheel of day and night themselves, whose moments, like restless spokes, are glimmering [1] for ever as they revolve.

If, then, *these* are the ministries by which Levana works, how profoundly must she reverence the agencies of grief! But you, reader, think that children generally are not liable to grief such as mine. There are two senses in the word *generally*, — the sense of Euclid, where it means *universally*

---

[1] As I have never allowed myself to covet any man's ox nor his ass, nor anything that is his, still less would it become a philosopher to covet other people's images or metaphors. Here, therefore, I restore to Mr. Wordsworth this fine image of the revolving wheel and the glimmering spokes, as applied by him to the flying successions of day and night. I borrowed it for one moment in order to point my own sentence ; which being done, the reader is witness that I now pay it back instantly by a note made for that sole purpose. On the same principle I often borrow their seals from young ladies, when closing my letters, because there is sure to be some tender sentiment upon them about " memory," or " hope," or " roses," or "reunion," and my correspondent must be a sad brute who is not touched by the eloquence of the seal, even if his taste is so bad that he remains deaf to mine.

(or in the whole extent of the *genus*), and a foolish sense of this word, where it means *usually*. Now, I am far from saying that children universally are capable of grief like mine. But there are more than you ever heard of who die of grief in this island of ours. I will tell you a common case. The rules of Eton require that a boy on the *foundation* should be there twelve years: he is superannuated at eighteen; consequently he must come at six. Children torn away from mothers and sisters at that age not unfrequently die. I speak of what I know. The complaint is not entered by the registrar as grief; but *that* it is. Grief of that sort, and at that age, has killed more than ever have been counted amongst its martyrs.

Therefore it is that Levana often communes with the powers that shake man's heart; therefore it is that she dotes upon grief. "These ladies," said I softly to myself, on seeing the ministers with whom Levana was conversing, "these are the Sorrows; and they are three in number: as the *Graces* are three, who dress man's life with beauty; the *Parcæ* are three, who weave the dark arras of man's life in their mysterious loom always with colours sad in part, sometimes angry with tragic crimson and black; the *Furies* are three, who visit with retributions called from the other side of the grave offences that walk upon this; and once even the *Muses* were but three, who fit the harp, the trumpet, or the lute, to the great burdens of man's impassioned creations. These are the Sorrows; all three of whom I know." The last words I say *now;* but in Oxford I said, "one of whom I know, and the others too surely I *shall* know." For already, in my fervent youth, I saw (dimly relieved upon the dark background of my dreams) the imperfect lineaments of the awful Sisters.

These Sisters — by what name shall we call them? If I say simply "The Sorrows," there will be a chance of

mistaking the term; it might be understood of individual
sorrow, — separate cases of sorrow, — whereas I want a term
expressing the mighty abstractions that incarnate themselves in all individual sufferings of man's heart, and I wish
to have these abstractions presented as impersonations, —
that is, as clothed with human attributes of life, and with
functions pointing to flesh.   Let us call them, therefore,
Our Ladies of Sorrow.

I know them thoroughly, and have walked in all their
kingdoms.   Three sisters they are, of one mysterious household; and their paths are wide apart; but of their dominion
there is no end.   Them I saw often conversing with Levana,
and sometimes about myself.   Do they talk, then?   O no!
Mighty phantoms like these disdain the infirmities of language.   They may utter voices through the organs of man
when they dwell in human hearts, but amongst themselves
is no voice nor sound; eternal silence reigns in *their*
kingdoms.   They spoke not as they talked with Levana;
they whispered not; they sang not; though oftentimes
methought they *might* have sung: for I upon earth had
heard their mysteries oftentimes deciphered by harp and
timbrel, by dulcimer and organ.   Like God, whose servants
they are, they utter their pleasure not by sounds that
perish, or by words that go astray, but by signs in heaven,
by changes on earth, by pulses in secret rivers, heraldries
painted on darkness, and hieroglyphics written on the
tablets of the brain.   *They* wheeled in mazes; *I* spelled
the steps.   *They* telegraphed from afar; *I* read the signals.
They conspired together; and on the mirrors of darkness
my eye traced the plots.   *Theirs* were the symbols; *mine*
are the words.

What is it the Sisters are?   What is it that they do?
Let me describe their form and their presence, if form it
were that still fluctuated in its outline, or presence it were

that for ever advanced to the front or for ever receded amongst shades.

The eldest of the three is named *Mater Lachrymarum*, Our Lady of Tears. She it is that night and day raves and moans, calling for vanished faces. She stood in Rama, where a voice was heard of lamentation, — Rachel weeping for her children, and refusing to be comforted. She it was that stood in Bethlehem on the night when Herod's sword swept its nurseries of Innocents, and the little feet were stiffened for ever which, heard at times as they trotted along floors overhead, woke pulses of love in household hearts that were not unmarked in heaven. Her eyes are sweet and subtle, wild and sleepy, by turns; oftentimes rising to the clouds, oftentimes challenging the heavens. She wears a diadem round her head. And I knew by child-ish memories that she could go abroad upon the winds, when she heard the sobbing of litanies, or the thundering of organs, and when she beheld the mustering of summer clouds. This Sister, the elder, it is that carries keys more than papal at her girdle, which open every cottage and every palace. She, to my knowledge, sat all last summer by the bedside of the blind beggar, him that so often and so gladly I talked with, whose pious daughter, eight years old, with the sunny countenance, resisted the temptations of play and village mirth, to travel all day long on dusty roads with her afflicted father. For this did God send her a great reward. In the spring time of the year, and whilst yet her own spring was budding, He recalled her to himself. But her blind father mourns for ever over *her:* still he dreams at midnight that the little guiding hand is locked within his own; and still he wakens to a darkness that is *now* within a second and a deeper darkness. This *Mater Lachrymarum* also has been sitting all this winter of 1844–5 within the bedchamber of the Czar, bringing before his

eyes a daughter (not less pious) that vanished to God not less suddenly, and left behind her a darkness not less profound. By the power of the keys it is that Our Lady of Tears glides, a ghostly intruder, into the chambers of sleep-
5 less men, sleepless women, sleepless children, from Ganges to the Nile, from Nile to Mississippi. And her, because she is the first-born of her house, and has the widest empire, let us honour with the title of " Madonna."

The second Sister is called *Mater Suspiriorum*, Our Lady
10 of Sighs. She never scales the clouds, nor walks abroad upon the winds. She wears no diadem. And her eyes, if they were ever seen, would be neither sweet nor subtle; no man could read their story; they would be found filled with perishing dreams, and with wrecks of forgotten delirium.
15 But she raises not her eyes; her head, on which sits a dilapidated turban, droops for ever, for ever fastens on the dust. She weeps not. She groans not. But she sighs inaudibly at intervals. Her sister, Madonna, is oftentimes stormy and frantic, raging in the highest against heaven,
20 and demanding back her darlings. But Our Lady of Sighs never clamours, never defies, dreams not of rebellious aspirations. She is humble to abjectness. Hers is the meekness that belongs to the hopeless. Murmur she may, but it is in her sleep. Whisper she may, but it is to herself in
25 the twilight. Mutter she does at times, but it is in solitary places that are desolate as she is desolate, in ruined cities, and when the sun has gone down to his rest. This Sister is the visitor of the Pariah, of the Jew, of the bondsman to the oar in the Mediterranean galleys ; of the English crim-
30 inal in Norfolk Island, blotted out from the books of remembrance in sweet far-off England ; of the baffled penitent reverting his eyes for ever upon a solitary grave, which to him seems the altar overthrown of some past and bloody sacrifice, on which altar no oblations can now be availing,

whether towards pardon that he might implore, or towards reparation that he might attempt. Every slave that at noonday looks up to the tropical sun with timid reproach, as he points with one hand to the earth, our general mother, but for *him* a stepmother, as he points with the other hand to the Bible, our general teacher, but against *him* sealed and sequestered;[1] every woman sitting in darkness, without love to shelter her head, or hope to illumine her solitude, because the heaven-born instincts kindling in her nature germs of holy affections, which God implanted in her womanly bosom, having been stifled by social necessities, now burn sullenly to waste, like sepulchral lamps amongst the ancients; every nun defrauded of her unreturning Maytime by wicked kinsman, whom God will judge; every captive in every dungeon; all that are betrayed, and all that are rejected; outcasts by traditionary law, and children of *hereditary* disgrace: all these walk with Our Lady of Sighs. She also carries a key; but she needs it little. For her kingdom is chiefly amongst the tents of Shem, and the houseless vagrant of every clime. Yet in the very highest ranks of man she finds chapels of her own; and even in glorious England there are some that, to the world, carry their heads as proudly as the reindeer, who yet secretly have received her mark upon their foreheads.

But the third Sister, who is also the youngest——! Hush! whisper whilst we talk of *her!* Her kingdom is not large, or else no flesh should live; but within that kingdom all power is hers. Her head, turreted like that of Cybele, rises almost beyond the reach of sight. She

[1] This, the reader will be aware, applies chiefly to the cotton and tobacco States of North America; but not to them only: on which account I have not scrupled to figure the sun which looks down upon slavery as *tropical*, — no matter if strictly within the tropics, or simply so near to them as to produce a similar climate.

droops not; and her eyes, rising so high, *might* be hidden
by distance.   But, being what they are, they cannot be
hidden: through the treble veil of crape which she wears
the fierce light of a blazing misery, that rests not for
5 matins or for vespers, for noon of day or noon of night,
for ebbing or for flowing tide, may be read from the very
ground.   She is the defier of God.   She also is the mother
of lunacies, and the suggestress of suicides.   Deep lie
the roots of her power; but narrow is the nation that she
10 rules.   For she can approach only those in whom a profound nature has been upheaved by central convulsions;
in whom the heart trembles and the brain rocks under
conspiracies of tempest from without and tempest from
within.   Madonna moves with uncertain steps, fast or
15 slow, but still with tragic grace.   Our Lady of Sighs
creeps timidly and stealthily.   But this youngest Sister
moves with incalculable motions, bounding, and with
tiger's leaps.   She carries no key; for, though coming
rarely amongst men, she storms all doors at which she is
20 permitted to enter at all.   And *her* name is *Mater Tenebrarum,* — Our Lady of Darkness.

These were the *Semnai Theai* or Sublime Goddesses,[1]
these were the *Eumenides* or Gracious Ladies (so called
by antiquity in shuddering propitiation), of my Oxford
25 dreams.   Madonna spoke.   She spoke by her mysterious
hand.   Touching my head, she beckoned to Our Lady of
Sighs; and *what* she spoke, translated out of the signs
which (except in dreams) no man reads, was this: —

"Lo! here is he whom in childhood I dedicated to my
30 altars.   This is he that once I made my darling.   Him I

---

[1] *"Sublime Goddesses":* — The word σεμνος is usually rendered *venerable* in dictionaries, — not a very flattering epithet for females.   But I
am disposed to think that it comes nearest to our idea of the *sublime,*
— as near as a Greek word *could* come.

led astray, him I beguiled; and from heaven I stole away
his young heart to mine. Through me did he become
idolatrous; and through me it was, by languishing desires,
that he worshipped the worm, and prayed to the wormy
grave. Holy was the grave to him; lovely was its dark- 5
ness; saintly its corruption. Him, this young idolater, I
have seasoned for thee, dear gentle Sister of Sighs! Do
thou take him now to *thy* heart, and season him for our
dreadful sister. And thou," — turning to the *Mater Tene-*
brarum, she said, — "wicked sister, that temptest and 10
hatest, do thou take him from *her*. See that thy sceptre
lie heavy on his head. Suffer not woman and her tenderness to sit near him in his darkness. Banish the frailties
of hope; wither the relenting of love; scorch the fountains
of tears; curse him as only *thou* canst curse. So shall he 15
be accomplished in the furnace; so shall he see the things
that ought *not* to be seen, sights that are abominable, and
secrets that are unutterable. So shall he read elder truths,
sad truths, grand truths, fearful truths. So shall he rise
again *before* he dies. And so shall our commission be 20
accomplished which from God we had, — to plague his
heart until we had unfolded the capacities of his spirit."

SAVANNAH-LA-MAR

God smote Savannah-la-mar, and in one night, by earthquake, removed her, with all her towers standing and
population sleeping, from the steadfast foundations of the 25
shore to the coral floors of ocean. And God said, —
" Pompeii did I bury and conceal from men through seventeen centuries: this city I will bury, but not conceal. She
shall be a monument to men of my mysterious anger, set
in azure light through generations to come; for I will 30
enshrine her in a crystal dome of my tropic seas." This

city, therefore, like a mighty galleon with all her apparel mounted, streamers flying, and tackling perfect, seems floating along the noiseless depths of ocean ; and oftentimes in glassy calms, through the translucid atmosphere of water
5 that now stretches like an air-woven awning above the silent encampment, mariners from every clime look down into her courts and terraces, count her gates, and number the spires of her churches. She is one ample cemetery, and *has* been for many a year ; but, in the mighty calms that
10 brood for weeks over tropic latitudes, she fascinates the eye with a *Fata-Morgana* revelation, as of human life still subsisting in submarine asylums sacred from the storms that torment our upper air.

Thither, lured by the loveliness of cerulean depths, by
15 the peace of human dwellings privileged from molestation, by the gleam of marble altars sleeping in everlasting sanctity, oftentimes in dreams did I and the Dark Interpreter cleave the watery veil that divided us from her streets. We looked into the belfries, where the pendulous
20 bells were waiting in vain for the summons which should awaken their marriage peals ; together we touched the mighty organ-keys, that sang no *jubilates* for the ear of heaven, that sang no requiems for the ear of human sorrow ; together we searched the silent nurseries, where the chil-
25 dren were all asleep, and *had* been asleep through five generations. "They are waiting for the heavenly dawn," whispered the Interpreter to himself: "and, when *that* comes, the bells and organs will utter a *jubilate* repeated by the echoes of Paradise." Then, turning to me, he
30 said, — "This is sad, this is piteous ; but less would not have sufficed for the purpose of God. Look here. Put into a Roman clepsydra one hundred drops of water ; let these run out as the sands in an hour-glass, every drop measuring the hundredth part of a second, so that each

shall represent but the three-hundred-and-sixty-thousandth
part of an hour. Now, count the drops as they race
along ; and, when the fiftieth of the hundred is passing,
behold ! forty-nine are not, because already they have
perished, and fifty are not, because they are yet to come. 5
You see, therefore, how narrow, how incalculably narrow, is the true and actual present. Of that time which
we call the present, hardly a hundredth part but belongs
either to a past which has fled, or to a future which is still
on the wing. It has perished, or it is not born. It was, 10
or it is not. Yet even this approximation to the truth is
infinitely false. For again subdivide that solitary drop,
which only was found to represent the present, into a
lower series of similar fractions, and the actual present
which you arrest measures now but the thirty-sixth-mil- 15
lionth of an hour ; and so by infinite declensions the true
and very present, in which only we live and enjoy, will
vanish into a mote of a mote, distinguishable only by a
heavenly vision. Therefore the present, which only man
possesses, offers less capacity for his footing than the 20
slenderest film that ever spider twisted from her womb.
Therefore, also, even this incalculable shadow from the
narrowest pencil of moonlight is more transitory than
geometry can measure, or thought of angel can overtake.
The time which *is* contracts into a mathematic point ; and 25
even that point perishes a thousand times before we can
utter its birth. All is finite in the present ; and even that
finite is infinite in its velocity of flight towards death. But
in God there is nothing finite ; but in God there is nothing
transitory ; but in God there *can* be nothing that tends to 30
death. Therefore it follows that for God there can be no
present. The future is the present of God, and to the
future it is that he sacrifices the human present. Therefore it is that he works by earthquake. Therefore it is

that he works by grief.   O, deep is the ploughing of earthquake!   O, deep " — (and his voice swelled like a *sanctus*
rising from a choir of a cathedral) — "O, deep is the
ploughing of grief!   But oftentimes less would not suffice
5 for the agriculture of God.   Upon a night of earthquake
he builds a thousand years of pleasant habitations for
man.   Upon the sorrow of an infant he raises oftentimes
from human intellects glorious vintages that could not else
have been.   Less than these fierce ploughshares would not
10 have stirred the stubborn soil.   The one is needed for Earth,
our planet, — for Earth itself as the dwelling-place of man ;
but the other is needed yet oftener for God's mightiest
instrument, — yes " (and he looked solemnly at myself),
"is needed for the mysterious children of the Earth ! "

THE ENGLISH MAIL–COACH

Section I — The Glory of Motion

Some twenty or more years before I matriculated at
Oxford, Mr. Palmer, at that time M.P. for Bath, had
accomplished two things, very hard to do on our little
planet, the Earth, however cheap they may be held by
eccentric people in comets : he had invented mail-coaches, 5
and he had married the daughter of a duke. He was,
therefore, just twice as great a man as Galileo, who did
certainly invent (or, which is the same thing,[1] discover)
the satellites of Jupiter, those very next things extant to
mail-coaches in the two capital pretensions of speed and 10
keeping time, but, on the other hand, who did *not* marry
the daughter of a duke.

These mail-coaches, as organised by Mr. Palmer, are
entitled to a circumstantial notice from myself, having had
so large a share in developing the anarchies of my subse- 15
quent dreams : an agency which they accomplished, 1st,
through velocity at that time unprecedented — for they first
revealed the glory of motion ; 2dly, through grand effects
for the eye between lamplight and the darkness upon solitary roads ; 3dly, through animal beauty and power so often 20
displayed in the class of horses selected for this mail service ;

---

[1] " *The same thing* " : — Thus, in the calendar of the Church Festivals, the discovery of the true cross (by Helen, the mother of
Constantine) is recorded (and, one might think, with the express
consciousness of sarcasm) as the *Invention* of the Cross.

4thly, through the conscious presence of a central intellect, that, in the midst of vast distances [1]— of storms, of darkness, of danger— overruled all obstacles into one steady co-opera-
tion to a national result.   For my own feeling, this post-office
5 service spoke as by some mighty orchestra, where a thousand instruments, all disregarding each other, and so far in dan-ger of discord, yet all obedient as slaves to the supreme *baton* of some great leader, terminate in a perfection of harmony like that of heart, brain, and lungs in a healthy animal organ-
10 isation.   But, finally, that particular element in this whole combination which most impressed myself, and through which it is that to this hour Mr. Palmer's mail-coach system tyrannises over my dreams by terror and terrific beauty, lay in the awful *political* mission which at that time it fulfilled.
15 The mail-coach it was that distributed over the face of the land, like the opening of apocalyptic vials, the heart-shaking news of Trafalgar, of Salamanca, of Vittoria, of Waterloo. These were the harvests that, in the grandeur of their reaping, redeemed the tears and blood in which they
20 had been sown.   Neither was the meanest peasant so much below the grandeur and the sorrow of the times as to con-found battles such as these, which were gradually moulding the destinies of Christendom, with the vulgar conflicts of ordinary warfare, so often no more than gladiatorial trials
25 of national prowess.   The victories of England in this stupendous contest rose of themselves as natural *Te Deums* to heaven; and it was felt by the thoughtful that such victories, at such a crisis of general prostration, were not more beneficial to ourselves than finally to France, our
30 enemy, and to the nations of all western or central Europe,

---

[1] " *Vast distances* " : — One case was familiar to mail-coach travellers where two mails in opposite directions, north and south, starting at the same minute from points six hundred miles apart, met almost con-stantly at a particular bridge which bisected the total distance.

through whose pusillanimity it was that the French domina-
tion had prospered.

The mail-coach, as the national organ for publishing
these mighty events, thus diffusively influential, became
itself a spiritualised and glorified object to an impassioned
heart; and naturally, in the Oxford of that day, *all* hearts
were impassioned, as being all (or nearly all) in *early* manhood. In most universities there is one single college; in
Oxford there were five-and-twenty, all of which were peopled
by young men, the *élite* of their own generation; not boys,
but men: none under eighteen. In some of these many
colleges the custom permitted the student to keep what are
called "short terms"; that is, the four terms of Michaelmas, Lent, Easter, and Act, were kept by a residence, in
the aggregate, of ninety-one days, or thirteen weeks. Under
this interrupted residence, it was possible that a student
might have a reason for going down to his home four
times in the year. This made eight journeys to and fro.
But, as these homes lay dispersed through all the shires of
the island, and most of us disdained all coaches except his
Majesty's mail, no city out of London could pretend to so
extensive a connexion with Mr. Palmer's establishment as
Oxford. Three mails, at the least, I remember as passing
every day through Oxford, and benefiting by my personal
patronage — viz., the Worcester, the Gloucester, and the
Holyhead mail. Naturally, therefore, it became a point of
some interest with us, whose journeys revolved every six
weeks on an average, to look a little into the executive
details of the system. With some of these Mr. Palmer had
no concern; they rested upon bye-laws enacted by posting-
houses for their own benefit, and upon other bye-laws,
equally stern, enacted by the inside passengers for the
illustration of their own haughty exclusiveness. These last
were of a nature to rouse our scorn; from which the

transition was not very long to systematic mutiny. Up to
this time, say 1804, or 1805 (the year of Trafalgar), it had
been the fixed assumption of the four inside people (as an
old tradition of all public carriages derived from the reign of
5 Charles II) that they, the illustrious quaternion, constituted
a porcelain variety of the human race, whose dignity would
have been compromised by exchanging one word of civility
with the three miserable delf-ware outsides. Even to have
kicked an outsider might have been held to attaint the foot
10 concerned in that operation, so that, perhaps, it would have
required an act of Parliament to restore its purity of blood.
What words, then, could express the horror, and the sense
of treason, in that case, which *had* happened, where all three
outsides (the trinity of Pariahs) made a vain attempt to sit
15 down at the same breakfast-table or dinner-table with the
consecrated four ? I myself witnessed such an attempt ; and
on that occasion a benevolent old gentleman endeavoured
to soothe his three holy associates, by suggesting that, if
the outsides were indicted for this criminal attempt at the
20 next assizes, the court would regard it as a case of lunacy
or *delirium tremens* rather than of treason. England owes
much· of her grandeur to the depth of the aristocratic
element in her social composition, when pulling against
her strong democracy. I am not the man to laugh at it.
25 But sometimes, undoubtedly, it expressed itself in comic
shapes. The course taken with the infatuated outsiders,
in the particular attempt which I have noticed, was that
the waiter, beckoning them away from the privileged *salle-
à-manger*, sang out, " This way, my good men," and then
30 enticed these good men away to the kitchen. But that plan
had not always answered. Sometimes, though rarely, cases
occurred where the intruders, being stronger than usual, or
more vicious than usual, resolutely refused to budge, and so
far carried their point as to have a separate table arranged

for themselves in a corner of the general room. Yet, if an Indian screen could be found ample enough to plant them out from the very eyes of the high table, or *dais*, it then became possible to assume as a fiction of law that the three delf fellows, after all, were not present. They could be ignored by the porcelain men, under the maxim that objects not appearing and objects not existing are governed by the same logical construction.[1]

Such being, at that time, the usage of mail-coaches, what was to be done by us of young Oxford? We, the most aristocratic of people, who were addicted to the practice of looking down superciliously even upon the insides themselves as often very questionable characters — were we, by voluntarily going outside, to court indignities? If our dress and bearing sheltered us generally from the suspicion of being " raff " (the name at that period for "snobs"[2]), we really *were* such constructively by the place we assumed. If we did not submit to the deep shadow of eclipse, we entered at least the skirts of its penumbra. And the analogy of theatres was valid against us, — where no man can complain of the annoyances incident to the pit or gallery, having his instant remedy in paying the higher price of the boxes. But the soundness of this analogy we disputed. In the case of the theatre, it cannot be pretended that the inferior situations have any separate attractions, unless the pit may be supposed to have an advantage for the purposes of the critic or the dramatic reporter. But the critic or reporter is a rarity. For most

---

[1] *De non apparentibus*, etc.

[2] " *Snobs*," and its antithesis, " *nobs*," arose among the internal factions of shoemakers perhaps ten years later. Possibly enough, the terms may have existed much earlier; but they were then first made known, picturesquely and effectively, by a trial at some assizes which happened to fix the public attention.

people, the sole benefit is in the price. Now, on the contrary, the outside of the mail had its own incommunicable advantages. These we could not forego. The higher price we would willingly have paid, but not the price
5 connected with the condition of riding inside; which condition we pronounced insufferable. The air, the freedom of prospect, the proximity to the horses, the elevation of seat: these were what we required; but, above all, the certain anticipation of purchasing occasional opportunities
10 of driving.

Such was the difficulty which pressed us; and under the coercion of this difficulty we instituted a searching inquiry into the true quality and valuation of the different apartments about the mail. We conducted this inquiry on meta-
15 physical principles; and it was ascertained satisfactorily that the roof of the coach, which by some weak men had been called the attics, and by some the garrets, was in reality the drawing-room; in which drawing-room the box was the chief ottoman or sofa; whilst it appeared that the
20 *inside*, which had been traditionally regarded as the only room tenantable by gentlemen, was, in fact, the coal-cellar in disguise.

Great wits jump. The very same idea had not long before struck the celestial intellect of China. Amongst the
25 presents carried out by our first embassy to that country was a state-coach. It had been specially selected as a personal gift by George III; but the exact mode of using it was an intense mystery to Pekin. The ambassador, indeed (Lord Macartney), had made some imperfect expla-
30 nations upon this point; but, as His Excellency communicated these in a diplomatic whisper at the very moment of his departure, the celestial intellect was very feebly illuminated, and it became necessary to call a cabinet council on the grand state question, "Where was the Emperor to

sit?" The hammer-cloth happened to be unusually gorgeous; and, partly on that consideration, but partly also because the box offered the most elevated seat, was nearest to the moon, and undeniably went foremost, it was resolved by acclamation that the box was the imperial throne, and, for the scoundrel who drove, — he might sit where he could find a perch. The horses, therefore, being harnessed, solemnly his imperial majesty ascended his new English throne under a flourish of trumpets, having the first lord of the treasury on his right hand, and the chief jester on his left. Pekin gloried in the spectacle; and in the whole flowery people, constructively present by representation, there was but one discontented person, and *that* was the coachman. This mutinous individual audaciously shouted, "Where am *I* to sit?" But the privy council, incensed by his disloyalty, unanimously opened the door, and kicked him into the inside. He had all the inside places to himself; but such is the rapacity of ambition that he was still dissatisfied. "I say," he cried out in an extempore petition addressed to the Emperor through the window — "I say, how am I to catch hold of the reins?" — "Anyhow," was the imperial answer; "don't trouble *me*, man, in my glory. How catch the reins? Why, through the windows, through the keyholes—*any*how." Finally this contumacious coachman lengthened the check-strings into a sort of jury-reins communicating with the horses; with these he drove as steadily as Pekin had any right to expect. The Emperor returned after the briefest of circuits; he descended in great pomp from his throne, with the severest resolution never to remount it. A public thanksgiving was ordered for his majesty's happy escape from the disease of a broken neck; and the state-coach was dedicated thenceforward as a votive offering to the god Fo Fo — whom the learned more accurately called Fi Fi.

A revolution of this same Chinese character did young Oxford of that era effect in the constitution of mail-coach society. It was a perfect French Revolution; and we had good reason to say, *ça ira*. In fact, it soon became *too*
5 popular. The "public" — a well-known character, particularly disagreeable, though slightly respectable, and notorious for affecting the chief seats in synagogues — had at first loudly opposed this revolution; but, when the opposition showed itself to be ineffectual, our disagreeable
10 friend went into it with headlong zeal. At first it was a sort of race between us; and, as the public is usually from thirty to fifty years old, naturally we of young Oxford, that averaged about twenty, had the advantage. Then the public took to bribing, giving fees to horse-keepers, &c.,
15 who hired out their persons as warming-pans on the box seat. *That*, you know, was shocking to all moral sensibilities. Come to bribery, said we, and there is an end to all morality, — Aristotle's, Zeno's, Cicero's, or anybody's. And, besides, of what use was it? For *we* bribed also.
20 And, as our bribes, to those of the public, were as five shillings to sixpence, here again young Oxford had the advantage. But the contest was ruinous to the principles of the stables connected with the mails. This whole corporation was constantly bribed, rebribed, and often sur-
25 rebribed; a mail-coach yard was like the hustings in a contested election; and a horse-keeper, ostler, or helper, was held by the philosophical at that time to be the most corrupt character in the nation.

There was an impression upon the public mind, natural
30 enough from the continually augmenting velocity of the mail, but quite erroneous, that an outside seat on this class of carriages was a post of danger. On the contrary, I maintained that, if a man had become nervous from some gipsy prediction in his childhood, allocating to a particular

moon now approaching some unknown danger, and he
should inquire earnestly, "Whither can I fly for shelter?
Is a prison the safest retreat? or a lunatic hospital? or the
British Museum?" I should have replied, "Oh no; I'll
tell you what to do. Take lodgings for the next forty days 5
on the box of his Majesty's mail. Nobody can touch you
there. If it is by bills at ninety days after date that you
are made unhappy — if noters and protesters are the sort
of wretches whose astrological shadows darken the house
of life — then note you what I vehemently protest: viz., 10
that, no matter though the sheriff and under-sheriff in every
county should be running after you with his *posse*, touch a
hair of your head he cannot whilst you keep house and
have your legal domicile on the box of the mail. It is
felony to stop the mail; even the sheriff cannot do that. 15
And an *extra* touch of the whip to the leaders (no great
matter if it grazes the sheriff) at any time guarantees your
safety." In fact, a bedroom in a quiet house seems a
safe enough retreat; yet it is liable to its own notorious
nuisances — to robbers by night, to rats, to fire. But the 20
mail laughs at these terrors. To robbers, the answer is
packed up and ready for delivery in the barrel of the guard's
blunderbuss. Rats again! there *are* none about mail-
coaches any more than snakes in Von Troil's Iceland [1];
except, indeed, now and then a parliamentary rat, who 25
always hides his shame in what I have shown to be the
"coal-cellar." And, as to fire, I never knew but one in a
mail-coach; which was in the Exeter mail, and caused by
an obstinate sailor bound to Devonport. Jack, making
light of the law and the lawgiver that had set their faces 30

---

[1] "*Von Troil's Iceland*": — The allusion is to a well-known chapter
in Von Troil's work, entitled, "Concerning the Snakes of Iceland."
The entire chapter consists of these six words — "*There are no snakes
in Iceland.*"

against his offence, insisted on taking up a forbidden seat [1] in the rear of the roof, from which he could exchange his own yarns with those of the guard. No greater offence was then known to mail-coaches ; it was treason, it was
5 *læsa majestas*, it was by tendency arson ; and the ashes of Jack's pipe, falling amongst the straw of the hinder boot, containing the mail-bags, raised a flame which (aided by the wind of our motion) threatened a revolution in the republic of letters. Yet even this left the sanctity of the
10 box unviolated. In dignified repose, the coachman and myself sat on, resting with benign composure upon our knowledge that the fire would have to burn its way through four inside passengers before it could reach ourselves. I remarked to the coachman, with a quotation from Virgil's
15 " Æneid " really too hackneyed—

> " Jam proximus ardet
> Ucalegon."

[1] *" Forbidden seat" : —* The very sternest code of rules was enforced upon the mails by the Post-office. Throughout England, only three outsides were allowed, of whom one was to sit on the box, and the other two immediately behind the box ; none, under any pretext, to come near the guard ; an indispensable caution ; since else, under the guise of a passenger, a robber might by any one of a thousand advantages — which sometimes are created, but always are favoured, by the animation of frank social intercourse — have disarmed the guard. Beyond the Scottish border, the regulation was so far relaxed as to allow of *four* outsides, but not relaxed at all as to the mode of placing them. One, as before, was seated on the box, and the other three on the front of the roof, with a determinate and ample separation from the little insulated chair of the guard. This relaxation was conceded by way of compensating to Scotland her disadvantages in point of population. England, by the superior density of her population, might always count upon a large fund of profits in the fractional trips of chance passengers riding for short distances of two or three stages. In Scotland this chance counted for much less. And therefore, to make good the deficiency, Scotland was allowed a compensatory profit upon one *extra* passenger.

But, recollecting that the Virgilian part of the coachman's education might have been neglected, I interpreted so far as to say that perhaps at that moment the flames were catching hold of our worthy brother and inside passenger, Ucalegon. The coachman made no answer, — which is my own way when a stranger addresses me either in Syriac or in Coptic; but by his faint sceptical smile he seemed to insinuate that he knew better, — for that Ucalegon, as it happened, was not in the way-bill, and therefore could not have been booked.

No dignity is perfect which does not at some point ally itself with the mysterious. The connexion of the mail with the state and the executive government — a connexion obvious, but yet not strictly defined — gave to the whole mail establishment an official grandeur which did us service on the roads, and invested us with seasonable terrors. Not the less impressive were those terrors because their legal limits were imperfectly ascertained. Look at those turn-pike gates: with what deferential hurry, with what an obedient start, they fly open at our approach! Look at that long line of carts and carters ahead, audaciously usurping the very crest of the road. Ah! traitors, they do not hear us as yet; but, as soon as the dreadful blast of our horn reaches them with proclamation of our approach, see with what frenzy of trepidation they fly to their horses' heads, and deprecate our wrath by the precipitation of their crane-neck quarterings. Treason they feel to be their crime; each individual carter feels himself under the ban of confiscation and attainder; his blood is attainted through six generations; and nothing is wanting but the headsman and his axe, the block and the sawdust, to close up the vista of his horrors. What! shall it be within benefit of clergy to delay the king's message on the high road? — to interrupt the great respirations, ebb and flood, *systole*

and *diastole*, of the national intercourse ? — to endanger the
safety of tidings running day and night between all nations
and languages ? Or can it be fancied, amongst the weakest
of men, that the bodies of the criminals will be given up to
5 their widows for Christian burial ? Now, the doubts which
were raised as to our powers did more to wrap them in
terror, by wrapping them in uncertainty, than could have
been effected by the sharpest definitions of the law from
the Quarter Sessions. We, on our parts (we, the collective
10 mail, I mean), did our utmost to exalt the idea of our
privileges by the insolence with which we wielded them.
Whether this insolence rested upon law that gave it a sanction, or upon conscious power that haughtily dispensed with
that sanction, equally it spoke from a potential station ;
15 and the agent, in each particular insolence of the moment,
was viewed reverentially, as one having authority.

Sometimes after breakfast his Majesty's mail would
become frisky ; and, in its difficult wheelings amongst the
intricacies of early markets, it would upset an apple-cart, a
20 cart loaded with eggs, &c.   Huge was the affliction and
dismay, awful was the smash.   I, as far as possible, endeavoured in such a case to represent the conscience and moral
sensibilities of the mail ; and, when wildernesses of eggs
were lying poached under our horses' hoofs, then would I
25 stretch forth my hands in sorrow, saying (in words too
celebrated at that time, from the false echoes [1] of Marengo),
" Ah ! wherefore have we not time to weep over you ? " —
which was evidently impossible, since, in fact, we had not

---

[1] "*False echoes*" : — Yes, false ! for the words ascribed to Napoleon,
as breathed to the memory of Desaix, never were uttered at all.   They
stand in the same category of theatrical fictions as the cry of the
foundering line-of-battle ship *Vengeur*, as the vaunt of General Cam
bronne at Waterloo, " La Garde meurt, mais ne se rend pas," or as the
repartees of Talleyrand.

time to laugh over them. Tied to post-office allowance in
some cases of fifty minutes for eleven miles, could the royal
mail pretend to undertake the offices of sympathy and con-
dolence? Could it be expected to provide tears for the
accidents of the road? If even it seemed to trample on 5
humanity, it did so, I felt, in discharge of its own more
peremptory duties.

Upholding the morality of the mail, *a fortiori* I upheld
its rights; as a matter of duty, I stretched to the utter-
most its privilege of imperial precedency, and astonished 10
weak minds by the feudal powers which I hinted to be
lurking constructively in the charters of this proud establishment. Once I remember being on the box of the
Holyhead mail, between Shrewsbury and Oswestry, when
a tawdry thing from Birmingham, some "Tallyho" or 15
"Highflyer," all flaunting with green and gold, came up
alongside of us. What a contrast to our royal simplicity
of form and colour in this plebeian wretch! The single
ornament on our dark ground of chocolate colour was the
mighty shield of the imperial arms, but emblazoned in pro- 20
portions as modest as a signet-ring bears to a seal of office.
Even this was displayed only on a single panel, whispering,
rather than proclaiming, our relations to the mighty state;
whilst the beast from Birmingham, our green-and-gold friend
from false, fleeting, perjured Brummagem, had as much 25
writing and painting on its sprawling flanks as would have
puzzled a decipherer from the tombs of Luxor. For some
time this Birmingham machine ran along by our side — a
piece of familiarity that already of itself seemed to me
sufficiently jacobinical. But all at once a movement of 30
the horses announced a desperate intention of leaving us
behind. "Do you see *that?*" I said to the coachman. —
"I see," was his short answer. He was wide awake, — yet
he waited longer than seemed prudent; for the horses of

our audacious opponent had a disagreeable air of freshness
and power.   But his motive was loyal; his wish was that
the Birmingham conceit should be full-blown before he
froze it.   When *that* seemed right, he unloosed, or, to speak
5 by a stronger word, he *sprang*, his known resources: he
slipped our royal horses like cheetahs, or hunting-leopards,
after the affrighted game.   How they could retain such a
reserve of fiery power after the work they had accomplished
seemed hard to explain.   But on our side, besides the physical
10 superiority, was a tower of moral strength, namely the king's
name, "which they upon the adverse faction wanted."
Passing them without an effort, as it seemed, we threw
them into the rear with so lengthening an interval
between us as proved in itself the bitterest mockery of
15 their presumption; whilst our guard blew back a shattering blast of triumph that was really too painfully full of
derision.

I mention this little incident for its connexion with what
followed.   A Welsh rustic, sitting behind me, asked if I had
20 not felt my heart burn within me during the progress of
the race?   I said, with philosophic calmness, *No;* because
we were not racing with a mail, so that no glory could be
gained.   In fact, it was sufficiently mortifying that such a
Birmingham thing should dare to challenge us.   The Welsh-
25 man replied that he didn't see *that;* for that a cat might
look at a king, and a Brummagem coach might lawfully
race the Holyhead mail.   "*Race* us, if you like," I replied,
"though even *that* has an air of sedition; but not *beat* us.
This would have been treason; and for its own sake I am
30 glad that the 'Tallyho' was disappointed."   So dissatisfied
did the Welshman seem with this opinion that at last I was
obliged to tell him a very fine story from one of our elder
dramatists: viz., that once, in some far Oriental kingdom,
when the sultan of all the land, with his princes, ladies, and

chief omrahs, were flying their falcons, a hawk suddenly
flew at a majestic eagle, and, in defiance of the eagle's natural advantages, in contempt also of the eagle's traditional
royalty, and before the whole assembled field of astonished
spectators from Agra and Lahore, killed the eagle on the   5
spot. Amazement seized the sultan at the unequal contest,
and burning admiration for its unparalleled result. He commanded that the hawk should be brought before him; he
caressed the bird with enthusiasm; and he ordered that,
for the commemoration of his matchless courage, a diadem 10
of gold and rubies should be solemnly placed on the hawk's
head, but then that, immediately after this solemn coronation, the bird should be led off to execution, as the most
valiant indeed of traitors, but not the less a traitor, as
having dared to rise rebelliously against his liege lord   15
and anointed sovereign, the eagle. "Now," said I to the
Welshman, "to you and me, as men of refined sensibilities,
how painful it would have been that this poor Brummagem
brute, the 'Tallyho,' in the impossible case of a victory
over us, should have been crowned with Birmingham tinsel, 20
with paste diamonds and Roman pearls, and then led off
to instant execution." The Welshman doubted if that
could be warranted by law. And, when I hinted at the 6th
of Edward Longshanks, chap. 18, for regulating the precedency of coaches, as being probably the statute relied   25
on for the capital punishment of such offences, he replied
drily that, if the attempt to pass a mail really were treasonable, it was a pity that the "Tallyho" appeared to have so
imperfect an acquaintance with law.

The modern modes of travelling cannot compare with 30
the old mail-coach system in grandeur and power. They
boast of more velocity, — not, however, as a consciousness,
but 'as a fact of our lifeless knowledge, resting upon *alien*
evidence: as, for instance, because somebody *says* that we

have gone fifty miles in the hour, though we are far from feeling it as a personal experience; or upon the evidence of a result, as that actually we find ourselves in York four hours after leaving London. Apart from such an assertion, or such a result, I myself am little aware of the pace. But, seated on the old mail-coach, we needed no evidence out of ourselves to indicate the velocity. On this system the word was not *magna loquimur*, as upon railways, but *vivimus*. Yes, "magna *vivimus*"; we do not make verbal ostentation of our grandeurs, we realise our grandeurs in act, and in the very experience of life. The vital experience of the glad animal sensibilities made doubts impossible on the question of our speed; we heard our speed, we saw it, we felt it as a thrilling; and this speed was not the product of blind insensate agencies, that had no sympathy to give, but was incarnated in the fiery eyeballs of the noblest amongst brutes, in his dilated nostril, spasmodic muscles, and thunder-beating hoofs. The sensibility of the horse, uttering itself in the maniac light of his eye, might be the last vibration of such a movement; the glory of Salamanca might be the first. But the intervening links that connected them, that spread the earthquake of battle into the eyeballs of the horse, were the heart of man and its electric thrillings— kindling in the rapture of the fiery strife, and then propagating its own tumults by contagious shouts and gestures to the heart of his servant the horse. But now, on the new system of travelling, iron tubes and boilers have disconnected man's heart from the ministers of his locomotion. Nile nor Trafalgar has power to raise an extra bubble in a steam-kettle. The galvanic cycle is broken up for ever; man's imperial nature no longer sends itself forward through the electric sensibility of the horse; the inter-agencies are gone in the mode of communication between the horse and his master out of which grew so many aspects of sublimity under accidents of mists that hid, or sudden blazes that revealed, of mobs that agitated, or midnight solitudes that awed. Tidings fitted to convulse all nations must henceforwards travel by culinary process; and the trumpet that once announced from afar the laurelled mail, heart-shaking when heard screaming on the wind and proclaiming itself through the darkness to every village or solitary house on its route, has now given way for ever to the pot-wallopings of the boiler. Thus have perished multiform openings for public expressions of interest, scenical yet natural, in great national tidings, — for revelations of faces and groups that could not offer themselves amongst the fluctuating mobs of a railway station. The gatherings of gazers about a laurelled mail had one centre, and acknowledged one sole interest. But the crowds attending at a railway station have as little unity as running water, and own as many centres as there are separate carriages in the train.

How else, for example, than as a constant watcher for the dawn, and for the London mail that in summer months entered about daybreak amongst the lawny thickets of Marlborough forest, couldst thou, sweet Fanny of the Bath road, have become the glorified inmate of my dreams? Yet Fanny, as the loveliest young woman for face and person that perhaps in my whole life I have beheld, merited the station which even now, from a distance of forty years, she holds in my dreams; yes, though by links of natural association she brings along with her a troop of dreadful creatures, fabulous and not fabulous, that are more abominable to the heart than Fanny and the dawn are delightful.

Miss Fanny of the Bath road, strictly speaking, lived at a mile's distance from that road, but came so continually to meet the mail that I on my frequent transits rarely missed her, and naturally connected her image with the

great thoroughfare where only I had ever seen her.   Why
she came so punctually I do not exactly know ; but I
believe with some burden of commissions, to be executed
in Bath, which had gathered to her own residence as a cen-
5 tral rendezvous for converging them.   The mail-coachman
who drove the Bath mail and wore the royal livery [1] happened to be Fanny's grandfather.   A good man he was,
that loved his beautiful granddaughter, and, loving her
wisely, was vigilant over her deportment in any case where
10 young Oxford might happen to be concerned.   Did my
vanity then suggest that I myself, individually, could fall
within the line of his terrors ?   Certainly not, as regarded
any physical pretensions that I could plead ; for Fanny (as
a chance passenger from her own neighbourhood once told
15 me) counted in her train a hundred and ninety-nine professed admirers, if not open aspirants to her favour ; and
probably not one of the whole brigade but excelled myself
in personal advantages.   Ulysses even, with the unfair
advantage of his accursed bow, could hardly have under-
20 taken that amount of suitors.   So the danger might have
seemed slight — only that woman is universally aristocratic ;
it is amongst her nobilities of heart that she *is* so.   Now,
the aristocratic distinctions in my favour might easily with
Miss Fanny have compensated my physical deficiencies.
25 Did I then make love to Fanny ?   Why, yes ; about as

---

[1] " *Wore the royal livery* " : — The general impression was that the
royal livery belonged of right to the mail-coachmen as their professional dress.   But that was an error.   To the guard it *did* belong, I
believe, and was obviously essential as an official warrant, and as a
means of instant identification for his person, in the discharge of his
important public duties.   But the coachman, and especially if his
place in the series did not connect him immediately with London
and the General Post-Office, obtained the scarlet coat only as an
honorary distinction after long (or, if not long, trying and special)
service.

much love as one *could* make whilst the mail was changing horses — a process which, ten years later, did not occupy above eighty seconds; but *then*, — viz., about Waterloo — it occupied five times eighty. Now, four hundred seconds offer a field quite ample enough for whispering into a young 5 woman's ear a great deal of truth, and (by way of parenthesis) some trifle of falsehood. Grandpapa did right, therefore, to watch me. And yet, as happens too often to the grandpapas of earth in a contest with the admirers of granddaughters, how vainly would he have watched me had I 10 meditated any evil whispers to Fanny! She, it is my belief, would have protected herself against any man's evil suggestions. But he, as the result showed, could not have intercepted the opportunities for such suggestions. Yet, why not? Was he not active? Was he not blooming? 15 Blooming he was as Fanny herself.

> " Say, all our praises why should lords —— "

Stop, that's not the line.

> " Say, all our roses why should girls engross? "

The coachman showed rosy blossoms on his face deeper 20 even than his granddaughter's — *his* being drawn from the ale-cask, Fanny's from the fountains of the dawn. But, in spite of his blooming face, some infirmities he had; and one particularly in which he too much resembled a crocodile. This lay in a monstrous inaptitude for turning round. 25 The crocodile, I presume, owes that inaptitude to the absurd *length* of his back; but in our grandpapa it arose rather from the absurd *breadth* of his back, combined, possibly, with some growing stiffness in his legs. Now, upon this crocodile infirmity of his I planted a human advantage for ten- 30 dering my homage to Miss Fanny. In defiance of all his honourable vigilance, no sooner had he presented to us his

mighty Jovian back (what a field for displaying to mankind his royal scarlet!), whilst inspecting professionally
the buckles, the straps, and the silvery turrets [1] of his harness, than I raised Miss Fanny's hand to my lips, and, by
5 the mixed tenderness and respectfulness of my manner,
caused her easily to understand how happy it would make
me to rank upon her list as No. 10 or 12 : in which case a
few casualties amongst her lovers (and, observe, they *hanged*
liberally in those days) might have promoted me speedily
10 to the top of the tree; as, on the other hand, with how
much loyalty of submission I acquiesced by anticipation
in her award, supposing that she should plant me in the
very rearward of her favour, as No. 199 + 1.   Most truly
I loved this beautiful and ingenuous girl; and, had it not
15 been for the Bath mail, timing all courtships by post-office
allowance, heaven only knows what might have come of it.
People talk of being over head and ears in love; now, the
mail was the cause that I sank only over ears in love, —
which, you know, still left a trifle of brain to overlook the
20 whole conduct of the affair.

Ah, reader! when I look back upon those days, it seems
to me that all things change — all things perish.   " Perish
the roses and the palms of kings " : perish even the crowns
and trophies of Waterloo : thunder and lightning are not
25 the thunder and lightning which I remember.   Roses are
degenerating.   The Fannies of our island — though this I
say with reluctance — are not visibly improving; and the

---

[1] " *Turrets* " : — As one who loves and venerates Chaucer for his
unrivalled merits of tenderness, of picturesque characterisation, and
of narrative skill, I noticed with great pleasure that the word *torrettes*
is used by him to designate the little devices through which the reins
are made to pass.   This same word, in the same exact sense, I heard
uniformly used by many scores of illustrious mail-coachmen to whose
confidential friendship I had the honour of being admitted in my
younger days.

Bath road is notoriously superannuated. Crocodiles, you will say, are stationary. Mr. Waterton tells me that the crocodile does *not* change, — that a cayman, in fact, or an alligator, is just as good for riding upon as he was in the time of the Pharaohs. *That* may be; but the reason is that the crocodile does not live fast — he is a slow coach. I believe it is generally understood among naturalists that the crocodile is a blockhead. It is my own impression that the Pharaohs were also blockheads. Now, as the Pharaohs and the crocodile domineered over Egyptian society, this accounts for a singular mistake that prevailed through innumerable generations on the Nile. The crocodile made the ridiculous blunder of supposing man to be meant chiefly for his own eating. Man, taking a different view of the subject, naturally met that mistake by another: he viewed the crocodile as a thing sometimes to worship, but always to run away from. And this continued till Mr. Waterton [1] changed the relations between the animals. The mode of escaping from the reptile he showed to be not by running away, but by leaping on its back booted and spurred. The two animals had misunderstood each other. The use of the crocodile has now been cleared up — viz., to be ridden; and the final cause of man is that he may improve the health of the crocodile by riding him

[1] *"Mr. Waterton"*: — Had the reader lived through the last generation, he would not need to be told that, some thirty or thirty-five years back, Mr. Waterton, a distinguished country gentleman of ancient family in Northumberland, publicly mounted and rode in top-boots a savage old crocodile, that was restive and very impertinent, but all to no purpose. The crocodile jibbed and tried to kick, but vainly. He was no more able to throw the squire than Sinbad was to throw the old scoundrel who used his back without paying for it, until he discovered a mode (slightly immoral, perhaps, though some think not) of murdering the old fraudulent jockey, and so circuitously of unhorsing him.

a-fox-hunting before breakfast. And it is pretty certain that any crocodile who has been regularly hunted through the season, and is master of the weight he carries, will take a six-barred gate now as well as ever he would have done in the infancy of the pyramids.

If, therefore, the crocodile does *not* change, all things else undeniably *do :* even the shadow of the pyramids grows less. And often the restoration in vision of Fanny and the Bath road makes me too pathetically sensible of that truth. Out of the darkness, if I happen to call back the image of Fanny, up rises suddenly from a gulf of forty years a rose in June ; or, if I think for an instant of the rose in June, up rises the heavenly face of Fanny. One after the other, like the antiphonies in the choral service, rise Fanny and the rose in June, then back again the rose in June and Fanny. Then come both together, as in a chorus — roses and Fannies, Fannies and roses, without end, thick as blossoms in paradise. Then comes a venerable crocodile, in a royal livery of scarlet and gold, with sixteen capes ; and the crocodile is driving four-in-hand from the box of the Bath mail. And suddenly we upon the mail are pulled up by a mighty dial, sculptured with the hours, that mingle with the heavens and the heavenly host. Then all at once we are arrived at Marlborough forest, amongst the lovely households [1] of the roe-deer ; the deer and their fawns retire into the dewy thickets ; the thickets are rich with roses ; once again the roses call up the sweet countenance of Fanny ; and she,

---

[1] "*Households*" : — Roe-deer do not congregate in herds like the fallow or the red deer, but by separate families, parents and children ; which feature of approximation to the sanctity of human hearths, added to their comparatively miniature and graceful proportions, conciliates to them an interest of peculiar tenderness, supposing even that this beautiful creature is less characteristically impressed with the grandeurs of savage and forest life.

being the granddaughter of a crocodile, awakens a dreadful host of semi-legendary animals — griffins, dragons, basilisks, sphinxes — till at length the whole vision of fighting images crowds into one towering armorial shield, a vast emblazonry of human charities and human loveliness that have perished, but quartered heraldically with unutterable and demoniac natures, whilst over all rises, as a surmounting crest, one fair female hand, with the forefinger pointing, in sweet, sorrowful admonition, upwards to heaven, where is sculptured the eternal writing which proclaims the frailty of earth and her children.

Going Down with Victory

But the grandest chapter of our experience within the whole mail-coach service was on those occasions when we went down from London with the news of victory. A period of about ten years stretched from Trafalgar to Waterloo; the second and third years of which period (1806 and 1807) were comparatively sterile; but the other nine (from 1805 to 1815 inclusively) furnished a long succession of victories, the least of which, in such a contest of Titans, had an inappreciable value of position: partly for its absolute interference with the plans of our enemy, but still more from its keeping alive through central Europe the sense of a deep-seated vulnerability in France. Even to tease the coasts of our enemy, to mortify them by continual blockades, to insult them by capturing if it were but a baubling schooner under the eyes of their arrogant armies, repeated from time to time a sullen proclamation of power lodged in one quarter to which the hopes of Christendom turned in secret. How much more loudly must this proclamation have spoken in the audacity[1] of having bearded the

---

[1] *"Audacity":* — Such the French accounted it; and it has struck me that Soult would not have been so popular in London, at the period

élite of their troops, and having beaten them in pitched battles! Five years of life it was worth paying down for the privilege of an outside place on a mail-coach, when carrying down the first tidings of any such event. And it
5 is to be noted that, from our insular situation, and the multitude of our frigates disposable for the rapid transmission of intelligence, rarely did any unauthorised rumour steal away a prelibation from the first aroma of the regular despatches. The government news was generally the
10 earliest news.

From eight P.M. to fifteen or twenty minutes later imagine the mails assembled on parade in Lombard Street; where, at that time,[1] and not in St. Martin's-le-Grand, was seated the General Post-Office. In what exact strength we mus-
15 tered I do not remember; but, from the length of each separate *attelage*, we filled the street, though a long one, and though we were drawn up in double file. On *any* night the spectacle was beautiful. The absolute perfection of all the appointments about the carriages and the harness, their
20 strength, their brilliant cleanliness, their beautiful simplicity — but, more than all, the royal magnificence of the horses — were what might first have fixed the attention.

of her present Majesty's coronation, or in Manchester, on occasion of his visit to that town, if they had been aware of the insolence with which he spoke of us in notes written at intervals from the field of Waterloo. As though it had been mere felony in our army to look a French one in the face, he said in more notes than one, dated from two to four P.M. on the field of Waterloo, " Here are the English — we have them ; they are caught *en flagrant delit*." Yet no man should have known us better; no man had drunk deeper from the cup of humiliation than Soult had in 1809, when ejected by us with headlong violence from Oporto, and pursued through a long line of wrecks to the frontier of Spain ; and subsequently at Albuera, in the bloodiest of recorded battles, to say nothing of Toulouse, he should have learned our pretensions.

1 " *At that time* " : — I speak of the era previous to Waterloo.

Every carriage on every morning in the year was taken down to an official inspector for examination : wheels, axles, linchpins, pole, glasses, lamps, were all critically probed and tested.   Every part of every carriage had been cleaned, every horse had been groomed, with as much rigour as if they belonged to a private gentleman ; and that part of the spectacle offered itself always.   But the night before us is a night of victory ; and, behold ! to the ordinary display what a heart-shaking addition ! — horses, men, carriages, all are dressed in laurels and flowers, oak-leaves and ribbons.   The guards, as being officially his Majesty's servants, and of the coachmen such as are within the privilege of the post-office, wear the royal liveries of course ; and, as it is summer (for all the *land* victories were naturally won in summer), they wear, on this fine evening, these liveries exposed to view, without any covering of upper coats. Such a costume, and the elaborate arrangement of the laurels in their hats, dilate their hearts, by giving to them openly a personal connexion with the great news in which already they have the general interest of patriotism.   That great national sentiment surmounts and quells all sense of ordinary distinctions.   Those passengers who happen to be gentlemen are now hardly to be distinguished as such except by dress ; for the usual reserve of their manner in speaking to the attendants has on this night melted away. One heart, one pride, one glory, connects every man by the transcendent bond of his national blood.   The spectators, who are numerous beyond precedent, express their sympathy with these fervent feelings by continual hurrahs. Every moment are shouted aloud by the post-office servants, and summoned to draw up, the great ancestral names of cities known to history through a thousand years — Lincoln, Winchester, Portsmouth, Gloucester, Oxford, Bristol, Manchester, York, Newcastle, Edinburgh, Glasgow,

Perth, Stirling, Aberdeen — expressing the grandeur of the empire by the antiquity of its towns, and the grandeur of the mail establishment by the diffusive radiation of its separate missions. Every moment you hear the thunder of lids locked down upon the mail-bags. That sound to each individual mail is the signal for drawing off ; which process is the finest part of the entire spectacle. Then come the horses into play. Horses ! can these be horses that bound off with the action and gestures of leopards ? What stir ! — what sea-like ferment ! — what a thundering of wheels ! — what a trampling of hoofs ! — what a sounding of trumpets ! — what farewell cheers — what redoubling peals of brotherly congratulation, connecting the name of the particular mail — "Liverpool for ever ! " — with the name of the particular victory — "Badajoz for ever ! " or "Salamanca for ever ! " The half-slumbering consciousness that all night long, and all the next day — perhaps for even a longer period — many of these mails, like fire racing along a train of gunpowder, will be kindling at every instant new successions of burning joy, has an obscure effect of multiplying the victory itself, by multiplying to the imagination into infinity the stages of its progressive diffusion. A fiery arrow seems to be let loose, which from that moment is destined to travel, without intermission, westwards for three hundred [1] miles

---

[1] "*Three hundred*" : — Of necessity, this scale of measurement, to an American, if he happens to be a thoughtless man, must sound ludicrous. Accordingly, I remember a case in which an American writer indulges himself in the luxury of a little fibbing, by ascribing to an Englishman a pompous account of the Thames, constructed entirely upon American ideas of grandeur, and concluding in something like these terms : — " And, sir, arriving at London, this mighty father of rivers attains a breadth of at least two furlongs, having, in its winding course, traversed the astonishing distance of one hundred and seventy miles." And this the candid American thinks it fair to contrast with the scale of the Mississippi. Now, it is hardly worth while to answer

— northwards for six hundred; and the sympathy of our
Lombard Street friends at parting is exalted a hundredfold
by a sort of visionary sympathy with the yet slumbering
sympathies which in so vast a succession we are going to
awake.

Liberated from the embarrassments of the city, and
issuing into the broad uncrowded avenues of the northern
suburbs, we soon begin to enter upon our natural pace of
ten miles an hour. In the broad light of the summer evening, the sun, perhaps, only just at the point of setting, we
are seen from every storey of every house. Heads of every
age crowd to the windows; young and old understand the
language of our victorious symbols; and rolling volleys of
sympathising cheers run along us, behind us, and before us.
The beggar, rearing himself against the wall, forgets his

a pure fiction gravely; else one might say that no Englishman out of
Bedlam ever thought of looking in an island for the rivers of a continent, nor, consequently, could have thought of looking for the peculiar
grandeur of the Thames in the length of its course, or in the extent of
soil which it drains. Yet, if he *had* been so absurd, the American might
have recollected that a river, not to be compared with the Thames even
as to volume of water — viz., the Tiber — has contrived to make itself
heard of in this world for twenty-five centuries to an extent not reached
as yet by any river, however corpulent, of his own land. The glory of
the Thames is measured by the destiny of the population to which it
ministers, by the commerce which it supports, by the grandeur of the
empire in which, though far from the largest, it is the most influential
stream. Upon some such scale, and not by a transfer of Columbian
standards, is the course of our English mails to be valued. The
American may fancy the effect of his own valuations to our English
ears by supposing the case of a Siberian glorifying his country in these
terms : — "These wretches, sir, in France and England, cannot march
half a mile in any direction without finding a house where food can be
had and lodging; whereas such is the noble desolation of our magnificent country that in many a direction for a thousand miles I will engage
that a dog shall not find shelter from a snow-storm, nor a wren find an
apology for breakfast."

lameness — real or assumed — thinks not of his whining
trade, but stands erect, with bold exulting smiles, as we
pass him. The victory has healed him, and says, Be thou
whole! Women and children, from garrets alike and cellars,
5 through infinite London, look down or look up with loving
eyes upon our gay ribbons and our martial laurels; sometimes kiss their hands; sometimes hang out, as signals of
affection, pocket-handkerchiefs, aprons, dusters, anything
that, by catching the summer breezes, will express an aerial
10 jubilation. On the London side of Barnet, to which we
draw near within a few minutes after nine, observe that
private carriage which is approaching us. The weather
being so warm, the glasses are all down; and one may read,
as on the stage of a theatre, everything that goes on within.
15 It contains three ladies — one likely to be "mamma,"
and two of seventeen or eighteen, who are probably her
daughters. What lovely animation, what beautiful unpre-
meditated pantomime, explaining to us every syllable that
passes, in these ingenuous girls! By the sudden start
20 and raising of the hands on first discovering our laurelled
equipage, by the sudden movement and appeal to the elder
lady from both of them, and by the heightened colour on
their animated countenances, we can almost hear them
saying, "See, see! Look at their laurels! Oh, mamma!
25 there has been a great battle in Spain; and it has been a
great victory." In a moment we are on the point of passing them. We passengers — I on the box, and the two
on the roof behind me — raise our hats to the ladies; the
coachman makes his professional salute with the whip; the
30 guard even, though punctilious on the matter of his dignity
as an officer under the crown, touches his hat. The ladies
move to us, in return, with a winning graciousness of
gesture; all smile on each side in a way that nobody could
misunderstand, and that nothing short of a grand national

sympathy could so instantaneously prompt. Will these ladies say that we are nothing to *them*? Oh no; they will not say *that*. They cannot deny — they do not deny — that for this night they are our sisters; gentle or simple, scholar or illiterate servant, for twelve hours to come, we on the outside have the honour to be their brothers. Those poor women, again, who stop to gaze upon us with delight at the entrance of Barnet, and seem, by their air of weariness, to be returning from labour — do you mean to say that they are washerwomen and charwomen? Oh, my poor friend, you are quite mistaken. I assure you they stand in a far higher rank; for this one night they feel themselves by birthright to be daughters of England, and answer to no humbler title.

Every joy, however, even rapturous joy — such is the sad law of earth — may carry with it grief, or fear of grief, to some. Three miles beyond Barnet, we see approaching us another private carriage, nearly repeating the circumstances of the former case. Here, also, the glasses are all down; here, also, is an elderly lady seated; but the two daughters are missing; for the single young person sitting by the lady's side seems to be an attendant — so I judge from her dress, and her air of respectful reserve. The lady is in mourning; and her countenance expresses sorrow. At first she does not look up; so that I believe she is not aware of our approach, until she hears the measured beating of our horses' hoofs. Then she raises her eyes to settle them painfully on our triumphal equipage. Our decorations explain the case to her at once; but she beholds them with apparent anxiety, or even with terror. Some time before this, I, finding it difficult to hit a flying mark when embarrassed by the coach-man's person and reins intervening, had given to the guard a "Courier" evening paper, containing the gazette, for the next carriage that might pass. Accordingly he tossed it

in, so folded that the huge capitals expressing some such
legend as GLORIOUS VICTORY might catch the eye at once.
To see the paper, however, at all, interpreted as it was by
our ensigns of triumph, explained everything; and, if the
5 guard were right in thinking the lady to have received it
with a gesture of horror, it could not be doubtful that she
had suffered some deep personal affliction in connexion with
this Spanish war.

Here, now, was the case of one who, having formerly
10 suffered, might, erroneously perhaps, be distressing herself
with anticipations of another similar suffering. That same
night, and hardly three hours later, occurred the reverse
case. A poor woman, who too probably would find herself, in
a day or two, to have suffered the heaviest of afflictions by
15 the battle, blindly allowed herself to express an exultation
so unmeasured in the news and its details as gave to her the
appearance which amongst Celtic Highlanders is called *fey*.
This was at some little town where we changed horses an
hour or two after midnight. Some fair or wake had kept
20 the people up out of their beds, and had occasioned a partial
illumination of the stalls and booths, presenting an unusual
but very impressive effect. We saw many lights moving
about as we drew near; and perhaps the most striking scene
on the whole route was our reception at this place. The
25 flashing of torches and the beautiful radiance of blue lights
(technically, Bengal lights) upon the heads of our horses;
the fine effect of such a showery and ghostly illumination
falling upon our flowers and glittering laurels [1]; whilst all
around ourselves, that formed a centre of light, the darkness
30 gathered on the rear and flanks in massy blackness: these
optical splendours, together with the prodigious enthusiasm

---

[1] "*Glittering laurels*": — I must observe that the colour of *green*
suffers almost a spiritual change and exaltation under the effect of
Bengal lights.

of the people, composed a picture at once scenical and affecting, theatrical and holy. As we staid for three or four
minutes, I alighted; and immediately from a dismantled
stall in the street, where no doubt she had been presiding
through the earlier part of the night, advanced eagerly a 5
middle-aged woman. The sight of my newspaper it was
that had drawn her attention upon myself. The victory
which we were carrying down to the provinces on *this*
occasion was the imperfect one of Talavera — imperfect for
its results, such as the virtual treachery of the Spanish 10
general, Cuesta, but not imperfect in its ever-memorable
heroism. I told her the main outline of the battle. The
agitation of her enthusiasm had been so conspicuous when
listening, and when first applying for information, that I
could not but ask her if she had not some relative in the 15
Peninsular army. Oh yes; her only son was there. In
what regiment? He was a trooper in the 23d Dragoons.
My heart sank within me as she made that answer. This
sublime regiment, which an Englishman should never mention without raising his hat to their memory, had made the 20
most memorable and effective charge recorded in military
annals. They leaped their horses — *over* a trench where
they could; *into* it, and with the result of death or muti-
lation, when they could *not*. What proportion cleared the
trench is nowhere stated. Those who *did* closed up and 25
went down upon the enemy with such divinity of fervour
(I use the word *divinity* by design : the inspiration of God
must have prompted this movement for those whom even
then He was calling to His presence) that two results followed. As regarded the enemy, this 23d Dragoons, not, I 30
believe, originally three hundred and fifty strong, paralysed
a French column six thousand strong, then ascended the
hill, and fixed the gaze of the whole French army. As
regarded themselves, the 23d were supposed at first to have

been barely not annihilated ; but eventually, I believe, about
one in four survived.   And this, then, was the regiment —
a regiment already for some hours glorified and hallowed
to the ear of all London, as lying stretched, by a large
5 majority, upon one bloody aceldama — in which the young
trooper served whose mother was now talking in a spirit
of such joyous enthusiasm.   Did I tell her the truth ? Had
I the heart to break up her dreams ? No.   To-morrow, said
I to myself — to-morrow, or the next day, will publish the
10 worst.   For one night more wherefore should she not sleep
in peace ?   After to-morrow the chances are too many that
peace will forsake her pillow.   This brief respite, then, let
her owe to *my* gift and *my* forbearance.   But, if I told her
not of the bloody price that had been paid, not therefore
15 was I silent on the contributions from her son's regiment
to that day's service and glory.   I showed her not the
funeral banners under which the noble regiment was sleeping.   I lifted not the overshadowing laurels from the bloody
trench in which horse and rider lay mangled together.   But
20 I told her how these dear children of England, officers and
privates, had leaped their horses over all obstacles as gaily
as hunters to the morning's chase.   I told her how they
rode their horses into the midst of death, — saying to
myself, but not saying to *her*, " and laid down their young
25 lives for thee, O mother England ! as willingly — poured
out their noble blood as cheerfully — as ever, after a long
day's sport, when infants, they had rested their weary heads
upon their mother's knees, or had sunk to sleep in her arms."
Strange it is, yet true, that she seemed to have no fears for
30 her son's safety, even after this knowledge that the 23d
Dragoons had been memorably engaged ; but so much was
she enraptured by the knowledge that *his* regiment, and
therefore that *he*, had rendered conspicuous service in the
dreadful conflict — a service which had actually made them,

within the last twelve hours, the foremost topic of conversation in London — so absolutely was fear swallowed up in
joy — that, in the mere simplicity of her fervent nature, the
poor woman threw her arms round my neck, as she thought
of her son, and gave to *me* the kiss which secretly was meant 5
for *him*.

Section II — The Vision of Sudden Death

What is to be taken as the predominant opinion of man,
reflective and philosophic, upon SUDDEN DEATH ? It is
remarkable that, in different conditions of society, sudden
death has been variously regarded as the consummation 10
of an earthly career most fervently to be desired, or, again,
as that consummation which is with most horror to be
deprecated. Cæsar the Dictator, at his last dinner-party
(*cœna*), on the very evening before his assassination, when
the minutes of his earthly career were numbered, being 15
asked what death, in *his* judgment, might be pronounced
the most eligible, replied "That which should be most
sudden." On the other hand, the divine Litany of our
English Church, when breathing forth supplications, as if
in some representative character, for the whole human race 20
prostrate before God, places such a death in the very van
of horrors: "From lightning and tempest; from plague,
pestilence, and famine; from battle and murder, and from
SUDDEN DEATH — *Good Lord, deliver us.*" Sudden death is
here made to crown the climax in a grand ascent of calam- 25
ities; it is ranked among the last of curses; and yet by the
noblest of Romans it was ranked as the first of blessings.
In that difference most readers will see little more than the
essential difference between Christianity and Paganism.
But this, on consideration, I doubt. The Christian Church 30
may be right in its estimate of sudden death; and it is a

natural feeling, though after all it may also be an infirm
one, to wish for a quiet dismissal from life, as that which
seems most reconcilable with meditation, with penitential
retrospects, and with the humilities of farewell prayer.
5 There does not, however, occur to me any direct scriptural
warrant for this earnest petition of the English Litany,
unless under a special construction of the word "sudden."
It seems a petition indulged rather and conceded to human
infirmity than exacted from human piety. It is not so much
10 a doctrine built upon the eternities of the Christian system as a plausible opinion built upon special varieties of
physical temperament. Let that, however, be as it may,
two remarks suggest themselves as prudent restraints upon
a doctrine which else *may* wander, and *has* wandered, into
15 an uncharitable superstition. The first is this : that many
people are likely to exaggerate the horror of a sudden death
from the disposition to lay a false stress upon words or acts
simply because by an accident they have become *final* words
or acts. If a man dies, for instance, by some sudden death
20 when he happens to be intoxicated, such a death is falsely
regarded with peculiar horror; as though the intoxication
were suddenly exalted into a blasphemy. But *that* is
unphilosophic. The man was, or he was not, *habitually* a
drunkard. If not, if his intoxication were a solitary acci-
25 dent, there can be no reason for allowing special emphasis
to this act simply because through misfortune it became
his final act. Nor, on the other hand, if it were no accident, but one of his *habitual* transgressions, will it be the
more habitual or the more a transgression because some
30 sudden calamity, surprising him, has caused this habitual
transgression to be also a final one. Could the man have
had any reason even dimly to foresee his own sudden death,
there would have been a new feature in his act of intem-
perance — a feature of presumption and irreverence, as in

one that, having known himself drawing near to the presence of God, should have suited his demeanour to an
expectation so awful. But this is no part of the case
supposed. And the only new element in the man's act
is not any element of special immorality, but simply of   5
special misfortune.

The other remark has reference to the meaning of the
word *sudden*. Very possibly Cæsar and the Christian
Church do not differ in the way supposed, — that is, do
not differ by any difference of doctrine as between Pagan 10
and Christian views of the moral temper appropriate to
death ; but perhaps they are contemplating different cases.
Both contemplate a violent death, a Βιαθανατος — death
that is βιαιος, or, in other words, death that is brought
about, not by internal and spontaneous change, but by 15
active force having its origin from without. In this
meaning the two authorities agree. Thus far they are in
harmony. But the difference is that the Roman by the
word "sudden" means *unlingering*, whereas the Christian
Litany by "sudden death" means a death *without warning*, 20
consequently without any available summons to religious
preparation. The poor mutineer who kneels down to gather
into his heart the bullets from twelve firelocks of his pitying comrades dies by a most sudden death in Cæsar's sense ;
one shock, one mighty spasm, one (possibly *not* one) groan, 25
and all is over. But, in the sense of the Litany, the mutineer's death is far from sudden : his offence originally, his
imprisonment, his trial, the interval between his sentence
and its execution, having all furnished him with separate
warnings of his fate — having all summoned him to meet 30
it with solemn preparation.

Here at once, in this sharp verbal distinction, we
comprehend the faithful earnestness with which a holy
Christian Church pleads on behalf of her poor departing

children that God would vouchsafe to them the last great
privilege and distinction possible on a death-bed, viz.,
the opportunity of untroubled preparation for facing this
mighty trial. Sudden death, as a mere variety in the modes
5 of dying where death in some shape is inevitable, proposes
a question of choice which, equally in the Roman and the
Christian sense, will be variously answered according to
each man's variety of temperament. Meantime, one aspect
of sudden death there is, one modification, upon which no
10 doubt can arise, that of all martyrdoms it is the most agi-
tating — viz., where it surprises a man under circumstances
which offer (or which seem to offer) some hurrying, flying,
inappreciably minute chance of evading it. Sudden as the
danger which it affronts must be any effort by which such
15 an evasion can be accomplished. Even *that*, even the sickening necessity for hurrying in extremity where all hurry
seems destined to be vain, — even that anguish is liable to
a hideous exasperation in one particular case : viz., where
the appeal is made not exclusively to the instinct of self-
20 preservation, but to the conscience, on behalf of some other
life besides your own, accidentally thrown upon *your* protection. To fail, to collapse in a service merely your own,
might seem comparatively venial ; though, in fact, it is far
from venial. But to fail in a case where Providence has
25 suddenly thrown into your hands the final interests of
another, — a fellow-creature shuddering between the gates
of life and death : this, to a man of apprehensive conscience,
would mingle the misery of an atrocious criminality with
the misery of a bloody calamity. You are called upon, by
30 the case supposed, possibly to die, but to die at the very
moment when, by any even partial failure or effeminate
collapse of your energies, you will be self-denounced as a
murderer. You had but the twinkling of an eye for your
effort, and that effort might have been unavailing ; but **to**

have risen to the level of such an effort would have rescued you, though not from dying, yet from dying as a traitor to your final and farewell duty.

The situation here contemplated exposes a dreadful ulcer, lurking far down in the depths of human nature. It is not that men generally are summoned to face such awful trials. But potentially, and in shadowy outline, such a trial is moving subterraneously in perhaps all men's natures. Upon the secret mirror of our dreams such a trial is darkly projected, perhaps, to every one of us. That dream, so familiar to childhood, of meeting a lion, and, through languishing prostration in hope and the energies of hope, that constant sequel of lying down before the lion publishes the secret frailty of human nature — reveals its deep-seated falsehood to itself — records its abysmal treachery. Perhaps not one of us escapes that dream; perhaps, as by some sorrowful doom of man, that dream repeats for every one of us, through every generation, the original temptation in Eden. Every one of us, in this dream, has a bait offered to the infirm places of his own individual will; once again a snare is presented for tempting him into captivity to a luxury of ruin; once again, as in aboriginal Paradise, the man falls by his own choice; again, by infinite iteration, the ancient earth groans to Heaven, through her secret caves, over the weakness of her child. "Nature, from her seat, sighing through all her works," again "gives signs of woe that all is lost"; and again the counter-sigh is repeated to the sorrowing heavens for the endless rebellion against God. It is not without probability that in the world of dreams every one of us ratifies for himself the original transgression. In dreams, perhaps under some secret conflict of the midnight sleeper, lighted up to the consciousness at the time, but darkened to the memory as soon as all is finished, each several child of our mysterious race completes for himself the treason of the aboriginal fall.

The incident, so memorable in itself by its features of horror, and so scenical by its grouping for the eye, which furnished the text for this reverie upon *Sudden Death* occurred to myself in the dead of night, as a solitary spec-
5 tator, when seated on the box of the Manchester and Glasgow mail, in the second or third summer after Waterloo. I find it necessary to relate the circumstances, because they are such as could not have occurred unless under a singular combination of accidents. In those days, the oblique and
10 lateral communications with many rural post-offices were so arranged, either through necessity or through defect of system, as to make it re̷ ̷uisite f̷ ̷the main north-western mail (*i.e.*, the *down* mail) o̷ ̷re̷ ̷ ̷ ̷ Manchester to halt for a number of hours; how ṁ̷ ̷ ̷ , I do not remember; six or
15 seven, I think; but the re̷ ult was that, in the ordinary course, the mail recommenc̷ ̷d its journey northwards about midnight. Wearied with the long detention at a gloomy hotel, I walked out about eleven o'clock at night for the sake of fresh air; meaning to fall in with the mail and
20 resume my seat at the post-office. The night, however, being yet dark, as the moon had scarcely risen, and the streets being at that hour empty, so as to offer no opportunities for asking the road, I lost my way, and did not reach the post-office until it was considerably past mid-
25 night; but, to my great relief (as it was important for me to be in Westmoreland by the morning), I saw in the huge saucer eyes of the mail, blazing through the gloom, an evidence that my chance was not yet lost. Past the time it was; but, by some rare accident, the mail was not even
30 yet ready to start. I ascended to my seat on the box, where my cloak was still lying as it had lain at the Bridgewater Arms. I had left it there in imitation of a nautical discoverer, who leaves a bit of bunting on the shore of his discovery, by way of warning off the ground the whole

human race, and notifying to the Christian and the heathen
worlds, with his best compliments, that he has hoisted his
pocket-handkerchief once and for ever upon that virgin
soil: thenceforward claiming the *jus dominii* to the top of
the atmosphere above it, and also the right of driving   5
shafts to the centre of the earth below it; so that all
people found after this warning either aloft in upper chambers of the atmosphere, or groping in subterraneous shafts,
or squatting audaciously on the surface of the soil, will be
treated as trespassers — kicked, that is to say, or decap-   10
itated, as circumstances may suggest, by their very faithful
servant, the owner of the said pocket-handkerchief. In the
present case, it is probable that my cloak might not have
been respected, and the *jus gentium* might have been cruelly
violated in my person — for, in the dark, people commit   15
deeds of darkness, gas being a great ally of morality; but
it so happened that on this night there was no other outside passenger; and thus the crime, which else was but
too probable, missed fire for want of a criminal.

Having mounted the box, I took a small quantity of   20
laudanum, having already travelled two hundred and fifty
miles — viz., from a point seventy miles beyond London. In
the taking of laudanum there was nothing extraordinary.
But by accident it drew upon me the special attention of my
assessor on the box, the coachman. And in *that* also there   25
was nothing extraordinary. But by accident, and with great
delight, it drew my own attention to the fact that this
coachman was a monster in point of bulk, and that he had
but one eye. In fact, he had been foretold by Virgil as

" Monstrum horrendum, informe, ingens, cui lumen ademptum."   30

He answered to the conditions in every one of the items:
— 1, a monster he was; 2, dreadful; 3, shapeless; 4, huge;
5, who had lost an eye. But why should *that* delight me?

Had he been one of the Calendars in the "Arabian Nights," and had paid down his eye as the price of his criminal curiosity, what right had *I* to exult in his misfortune? I did *not* exult; I delighted in no man's punishment, though it were even merited. But these personal distinctions (Nos. 1, 2, 3, 4, 5) identified in an instant an old friend of mine whom I had known in the south for some years as the most masterly of mail-coachmen. He was the man in all Europe that could (if *any* could) have driven six-in-hand full gallop over *Al Sirat* — that dreadful bridge of Mahomet, with no side battlements, and of *extra* room not enough for a razor's edge — leading right across the bottomless gulf. Under this eminent man, whom in Greek I cognominated Cyclops *Diphrélates* (Cyclops the Charioteer), I, and others known to me, studied the diphrelatic art.. Excuse, reader, a word too elegant to be pedantic. As a pupil, though I paid extra fees, it is to be lamented that I did not stand high in his esteem. It showed his dogged honesty (though, observe, not his discernment) that he could not see my merits. Let us excuse his absurdity in this particular by remembering his want of an eye. Doubtless *that* made him blind to my merits. In the art of conversation, however, he admitted that I had the whip-hand of him. On the present occasion great joy was at our meeting. But what was Cyclops doing here? Had the medical men recommended northern air, or how? I collected, from such explanations as he volunteered, that he had an interest at stake in some suit-at-law now pending at Lancaster; so that probably he had got himself transferred to this station for the purpose of connecting with his professional pursuits an instant readiness for the calls of his lawsuit.

Meantime, what are we stopping for? Surely we have now waited long enough. Oh, this procrastinating mail, and this procrastinating post-office! Can't they take a lesson

upon that subject from *me*? Some people have called *me*
procrastinating. Yet you are witness, reader, that I was
here kept waiting for the post-office. Will the post-office lay
its hand on its heart, in its moments of sobriety, and assert
that ever it waited for me? What are they about? The 5
guard tells me that there is a large extra accumulation of
foreign mails this night, owing to irregularities caused by
war, by wind, by weather, in the packet service, which as
yet does not benefit at all by steam. For an *extra* hour, it
seems, the post-office has been engaged in threshing out the 10
pure wheaten correspondence of Glasgow, and winnowing
it from the chaff of all baser intermediate towns. But at
last all is finished. Sound your horn, guard! Manchester,
good-bye! we've lost an hour by your criminal conduct at
the post-office: which, however, though I do not mean to 15
part with a serviceable ground of complaint, and one which
really *is* such for the horses, to me secretly is an advantage,
since it compels us to look sharply for this lost hour
amongst the next eight or nine, and to recover it (if we
can) at the rate of one mile extra per hour. Off we are at 20
last, and at eleven miles an hour; and for the moment I
detect no changes in the energy or in the skill of Cyclops.

From Manchester to Kendal, which virtually (though not
in law) is the capital of Westmoreland, there were at this
time seven stages of eleven miles each. The first five of 25
these, counting from Manchester, terminate in Lancaster;
which is therefore fifty-five miles north of Manchester, and
the same distance exactly from Liverpool. The first three
stages terminate in Preston (called, by way of distinction
from other towns of that name, *Proud* Preston); at which 30
place it is that the separate roads from Liverpool and from
Manchester to the north become confluent.[1] Within these

---

[1] "*Confluent*" : — Suppose a capital Y (the Pythagorean letter):
Lancaster is at the foot of this letter; Liverpool at the top of the

first three stages lay the foundation, the progress, and termination of our night's adventure.   During the first stage, I
found out that Cyclops was mortal : he was liable to the
shocking affection of sleep — a thing which previously I had
5 never suspected.   If a man indulges in the vicious habit of
sleeping, all the skill in aurigation of Apollo himself, with
the horses of Aurora to execute his notions, avails him nothing.   "Oh, Cyclops ! " I exclaimed, "thou art mortal.   My
friend, thou snorest."   Through the first eleven miles, how-
10 ever, this infirmity — which I grieve to say that he shared
with the whole Pagan Pantheon — betrayed itself only by
brief snatches.   On waking up, he made an apology for
himself which, instead of mending matters, laid open a
gloomy vista of coming disasters.   The summer assizes, he
15 reminded me, were now going on at Lancaster : in consequence of which for three nights and three days he had
not lain down on a bed.   During the day he was waiting
for his own summons as a witness on the trial in which
he was interested, or else, lest he should be missing at the
20 critical moment, was drinking with the other witnesses
under the pastoral surveillance of the attorneys.   During
the night, or that part of it which at sea would form the
middle watch, he was driving.   This explanation certainly
accounted for his drowsiness, but in a way which made it
25 much more alarming ; since now, after several days' resistance to this infirmity, at length he was steadily giving way.
Throughout the second stage he grew more and more
drowsy.   In the second mile of the third stage he surrendered himself finally and without a struggle to his

right branch ; Manchester at the top of the *left ;* Proud Preston at
the centre, where the two branches unite.   It is thirty-three miles
along either of the two branches ; it is twenty-two miles along the
stem, — viz., from Preston in the middle to Lancaster at the root.
There's a lesson in geography for the reader !

perilous temptation. All his past resistance had but deepened the weight of this final oppression. Seven atmospheres of sleep rested upon him; and, to consummate the case, our worthy guard, after singing "Love amongst the Roses" for perhaps thirty times, without invitation and without applause, had in revenge moodily resigned himself to slumber — not so deep, doubtless, as the coachman's, but deep enough for mischief. And thus at last, about ten miles from Preston, it came about that I found myself left in charge of his Majesty's London and Glasgow mail, then running at the least twelve miles an hour.

What made this negligence less criminal than else it must have been thought was the condition of the roads at night during the assizes. At that time, all the law business of populous Liverpool, and also of populous Manchester, with its vast cincture of populous rural districts, was called up by ancient usage to the tribunal of Lilliputian Lancaster. To break up this old traditional usage required, 1, a conflict with powerful established interests, 2, a large system of new arrangements, and 3, a new parliamentary statute. But as yet this change was merely in contemplation. As things were at present, twice in the year [1] so vast a body of business rolled northwards from the southern quarter of the county that for a fortnight at least it occupied the severe exertions of two judges in its despatch. The consequence of this was that every horse available for such a service, along the whole line of road, was exhausted in carrying down the multitudes of people who were parties to the different suits. By sunset, therefore, it usually happened that, through utter exhaustion amongst men and horses, the road sank into profound silence. Except the

---

[1] *"Twice in the year":* — There were at that time only two assizes even in the most populous counties — viz., the Lent Assizes and the Summer Assizes.

exhaustion in the vast adjacent county of York from a contested election, no such silence succeeding to no such fiery uproar was ever witnessed in England.

On this occasion the usual silence and solitude prevailed along the road. Not a hoof nor a wheel was to be heard. And, to strengthen this false luxurious confidence in the noiseless roads, it happened also that the night was one of peculiar solemnity and peace. For my own part, though slightly alive to the possibilities of peril, I had so far yielded to the influence of the mighty calm as to sink into a profound reverie. The month was August; in the middle of which lay my own birthday — a festival to every thoughtful man suggesting solemn and often sigh-born[1] thoughts. The county was my own native county — upon which, in its southern section, more than upon any equal area known to man past or present, had descended the original curse of labour in its heaviest form, not mastering the bodies only of men, as of slaves, or criminals in mines, but working through the fiery will. Upon no equal space of earth was, or ever had been, the same energy of human power put forth daily. At this particular season also of the assizes, that dreadful hurricane of flight and pursuit, as it might have seemed to a stranger, which swept to and from Lancaster all day long, hunting the county up and down, and regularly subsiding back into silence about sunset, could not fail (when united with this permanent distinction of Lancashire as the very metropolis and citadel of labour) to point the thoughts pathetically upon that counter-vision of rest, of saintly repose from strife and sorrow, towards which, as to their secret haven, the profounder aspirations of man's heart are in solitude continually

---

[1] *"Sigh-born"* : — I owe the suggestion of this word to an obscure remembrance of a beautiful phrase in "Giraldus Cambrensis" — viz., *suspiriosæ cogitationes.*

travelling. Obliquely upon our left we were nearing the sea; which also must, under the present circumstances, be repeating the general state of halcyon repose. The sea, the atmosphere, the light, bore each an orchestral part in this universal lull. Moonlight and the first timid trem- 5 blings of the dawn were by this time blending; and the blendings were brought into a still more exquisite state of unity by a slight silvery mist, motionless and dreamy, that covered the woods and fields, but with a veil of equable transparency. Except the feet of our own horses, — which, 10 running on a sandy margin of the road, made but little disturbance, — there was no sound abroad. In the clouds and on the earth prevailed the same majestic peace; and, in spite of all that the villain of a schoolmaster has done for the ruin of our sublimer thoughts, which are the thoughts 15 of our infancy, we still believe in no such nonsense as a limited atmosphere. Whatever we may swear with our false feigning lips, in our faithful hearts we still believe, and must for ever believe, in fields of air traversing the total gulf between earth and the central heavens. Still, in the con- 20 fidence of children that tread without fear *every* chamber in their father's house, and to whom no door is closed, we, in that Sabbatic vision which sometimes is revealed for an hour upon nights like this, ascend with easy steps from the sorrow-stricken fields of earth upwards to the sandals 25 of God.

Suddenly, from thoughts like these I was awakened to a sullen sound, as of some motion on the distant road. It stole upon the air for a moment; I listened in awe; but then it died away. Once roused, however, I could not but 30 observe with alarm the quickened motion of our horses. Ten years' experience had made my eye learned in the valuing of motion; and I saw that we were now running thirteen miles an hour. I pretend to no presence of mind.

On the contrary, my fear is that I am miserably and shame-fully deficient in that quality as regards action. The palsy of doubt and distraction hangs like some guilty weight of dark unfathomed remembrances upon my energies when
5 the signal is flying for *action*. But, on the other hand, this accursed gift I have, as regards *thought*, that in the first step towards the possibility of a misfortune I see its total evolution; in the radix of the series I see too certainly and too instantly its entire expansion; in the first syllable
10 of the dreadful sentence I read already the last. It was not that I feared for ourselves. *Us* our bulk and impetus charmed against peril in any collision. And I had ridden through too many hundreds of perils that were frightful to approach, that were matter of laughter to look back upon,
15 the first face of which was horror, the parting face a jest — for any anxiety to rest upon *our* interests. The mail was not built, I felt assured, nor bespoke, that could betray *me* who trusted to its protection. But any carriage that we could meet would be frail and light in comparison of our-
20 selves. And I remarked this ominous accident of our situation, — we were on the wrong side of the road. But then, it may be said, the other party, if other there was, might also be on the wrong side; and two wrongs might make a right. *That* was not likely. The same motive which
25 had drawn *us* to the right-hand side of the road — viz., the luxury of the soft beaten sand as contrasted with the paved centre — would prove attractive to others. The two adverse carriages would therefore, to a certainty, be travelling on the same side; and from this side, as not being ours in
30 law, the crossing over to the other would, of course, be looked for from *us*.[1] Our lamps, still lighted, would give

---

[1] It is true that, according to the law of the case as established by legal precedents, all carriages were required to give way before royal equipages, and therefore before the mail as one of them. But this

the impression of vigilance on our part. And every creature that met us would rely upon *us* for quartering.[1] All
this, and if the separate links of the anticipation had been
a thousand times more, I saw, not discursively, or by effort,
or by succession, but by one flash of horrid simultaneous 5
intuition.

Under this steady though rapid anticipation of the evil
which *might* be gathering ahead, ah! what a sullen mystery
of fear, what a sigh of woe, was that which stole upon the
air, as again the far-off sound of a wheel was heard! A 10
whisper it was — a whisper from, perhaps, four miles off —
secretly announcing a ruin that, being foreseen, was not the
less inevitable ; that, being known, was not therefore healed.
What could be done — who was it that could do it — to check
the storm-flight of these maniacal horses? Could I not 15
seize the reins from the grasp of the slumbering coachman?
You, reader, think that it would have been in *your* power to
do so. And I quarrel not with your estimate of yourself.
But, from the way in which the coachman's hand was viced
between his upper and lower thigh, this was impossible. 20
Easy was it? See, then, that bronze equestrian statue. The
cruel rider has kept the bit in his horse's mouth for two centuries. Unbridle him for a minute, if you please, and wash
his mouth with water. Easy was it? Unhorse me, then,
that imperial rider ; knock me those marble feet from those 25
marble stirrups of Charlemagne.

The sounds ahead strengthened, and were now too clearly
the sounds of wheels. Who and what could it be? Was it
industry in a taxed cart? Was it youthful gaiety in a gig?

only increased the danger, as being a regulation very imperfectly made
known, very unequally enforced, and therefore often embarrassing the
movements on both sides.

[1] "*Quartering*" : — This is the technical word, and, I presume, derived
from the French *cartayer*, to evade a rut or any obstacle.

Was it sorrow that loitered, or joy that raced? For as yet the snatches of sound were too intermitting, from distance, to decipher the character of the motion. Whoever were the travellers, something must be done to warn them. Upon 5 the other party rests the active responsibility, but upon *us* — and, woe is me! that *us* was reduced to my frail opium-shattered self — rests the responsibility of warning. Yet, how should this be accomplished? Might I not sound the guard's horn? Already, on the first thought, I was making 10 my way over the roof of the guard's seat. But this, from the accident which I have mentioned, of the foreign mails being piled upon the roof, was a difficult and even danger-ous attempt to one cramped by nearly three hundred miles of outside travelling. And, fortunately, before I had lost 15 much time in the attempt, our frantic horses swept round an angle of the road which opened upon us that final stage where the collision must be accomplished and the catas-trophe sealed. All was apparently finished. The court was sitting; the case was heard; the judge had finished; and 20 only the verdict was yet in arrear.

Before us lay an avenue straight as an arrow, six hundred yards, perhaps, in length; and the umbrageous trees, which rose in a regular line from either side, meeting high over-head, gave to it the character of a cathedral aisle. These 25 trees lent a deeper solemnity to the early light; but there was still light enough to perceive, at the further end of this Gothic aisle, a frail reedy gig, in which were seated a young man, and by his side a young lady. Ah, young sir! what are you about? If it is requisite that you should whisper 30 your communications to this young lady — though really I see nobody, at an hour and on a road so solitary, likely to overhear you — is it therefore requisite that you should carry your lips forward to hers? The little carriage is creeping on at one mile an hour; and the parties within it, being thus tenderly engaged, are naturally bending down their heads. Between them and eternity, to all human calculation, there is but a minute and a half. Oh heavens! what is it that I shall do? Speaking or acting, what help can I offer? Strange it is, and to a mere auditor of the tale might seem laughable, that I should need a suggestion from the "Iliad" to prompt the sole resource that remained. Yet so it was. Suddenly I remembered the shout of Achilles, and its effect. But could I pretend to shout like the son of Peleus, aided by Pallas? No: but then I needed not the shout that should alarm all Asia militant; such a shout would suffice as might carry terror into the hearts of two thoughtless young people and one gig-horse. I shouted — and the young man heard me not. A second time I shouted — and now he heard me for now he raised his head.

Here, then, all had been done that, by me, *could* be done; more on *my* part was not possible. Mine had been the first step; the second was for the young man; the third was for God. If, said I, this stranger is a brave man, and if indeed he loves the young girl at his side — or, loving her not, if he feels the obligation, pressing upon every man worthy to be called a man, of doing his utmost for a woman confided to his protection — he will at least make some effort to save her. If *that* fails, he will not perish the more, or by a death more cruel, for having made it; and he will die as a brave man should, with his face to the danger, and with his arm about the woman that he sought in vain to save. But, if he makes no effort, — shrinking without a struggle from his duty, — he himself will not the less certainly perish for this baseness of poltroonery. He will die no less: and why not? Wherefore should we grieve that there is one craven less in the world? No; *let* him perish, without a pitying thought of ours wasted upon him; and, in that case, all our grief will be reserved for the fate of the helpless girl who now, upon the least shadow of failure in *him*, must by the fiercest of translations — must without time for a prayer — must within seventy seconds—stand before the judgment-seat of God.

5 But craven he was not: sudden had been the call upon him, and sudden was his answer to the call. He saw, he heard, he comprehended, the ruin that was coming down : already its gloomy shadow darkened above him; and already he was measuring his strength to deal with it. Ah! what a 10 vulgar thing does courage seem when we see nations buying it and selling it for a shilling a-day : ah! what a sublime thing does courage seem when some fearful summons on the great deeps of life carries a man, as if running before a hurricane, up to the giddy crest of some tumultuous crisis 15 from which lie two courses, and a voice says to him audibly, "One way lies hope; take the other, and mourn for ever!" How grand a triumph if, even then, amidst the raving of all around him, and the frenzy of the danger, the man is able to confront his situation — is able to retire for a moment into 20 solitude with God, and to seek his counsel from *Him!*

For seven seconds, it might be, of his seventy, the stranger settled his countenance steadfastly upon us, as if to search and value every element in the conflict before him. For five seconds more of his seventy he sat immovably, like one 25 that mused on some great purpose. For five more, perhaps, he sat with eyes upraised, like one that prayed in sorrow, under some extremity of doubt, for light that should guide him to the better choice. Then suddenly he rose; stood upright; and, by a powerful strain upon the reins, raising 30 his horse's fore-feet from the ground, he slewed him round on the pivot of his hind-legs, so as to plant the little equipage in a position nearly at right angles to ours. Thus far his condition was not improved; except as a first step had been taken towards the possibility of a second. If no more were done, nothing was done; for the little carriage still occupied the very centre of our path, though in an altered direction. Yet even now it may not be too late: fifteen of the seventy seconds may still be unexhausted; and one almighty bound may avail to clear the ground. Hurry, then, hurry! for the flying moments — *they* hurry. Oh, hurry, hurry, my brave young man! for the cruel hoofs of our horses — *they* also hurry! Fast are the flying moments, faster are the hoofs of our horses. But fear not for *him*, if human energy can suffice; faithful was he that drove to his terrific duty; faithful was the horse to *his* command. One blow, one impulse given with voice and hand, by the stranger, one rush from the horse, one bound as if in the act of rising to a fence, landed the docile creature's fore-feet upon the crown or arching centre of the road. The larger half of the little equipage had then cleared our over-towering shadow: *that* was evident even to my own agitated sight. But it mattered little that one wreck should float off in safety if upon the wreck that perished were embarked the human freightage. The rear part of the carriage — was *that* certainly beyond the line of absolute ruin? What power could answer the question? Glance of eye, thought of man, wing of angel, which of these had speed enough to sweep between the question and the answer, and divide the one from the other? Light does not tread upon the steps of light more indivisibly than did our all-conquering arrival upon the escaping efforts of the gig. *That* must the young man have felt too plainly. His back was now turned to us; not by sight could he any longer communicate with the peril; but, by the dreadful rattle of our harness, too truly had his ear been instructed that all was finished as regarded any effort of *his*. Already in resignation he had rested from his struggle; and perhaps in his heart he was whispering, "Father, which art in heaven, do Thou finish above what I on earth have attempted." Faster than ever mill-race we ran past them in our inexorable flight. Oh, raving of hurricanes that must have sounded in their young ears at the moment of our transit! Even in that moment the thunder of collision spoke aloud. Either with the swingle-bar, or with the haunch of our near leader, we had struck the off-wheel of the little gig; which stood rather obliquely, and not quite so far advanced as to be accurately parallel with the near-wheel. The blow, from the fury of our passage, resounded terrifically. I rose in horror, to gaze upon the ruins we might have caused. From my elevated station I looked down, and looked back upon the scene; which in a moment told its own tale, and wrote all its records on my heart for ever.

Here was the map of the passion that now had finished. The horse was planted immovably, with his fore-feet upon the paved crest of the central road. He of the whole party might be supposed untouched by the passion of death. The little cany carriage — partly, perhaps, from the violent torsion of the wheels in its recent movement, partly from the thundering blow we had given to it — as if it sympathised with human horror, was all alive with tremblings and shiverings. The young man trembled not, nor shivered. He sat like a rock. But *his* was the steadiness of agitation frozen into rest by horror. As yet he dared not to look round; for he knew that, if anything remained to do, by him it could no longer be done. And as yet he knew not for certain if their safety were accomplished. But the lady ——

But the lady ——! Oh, heavens! will that spectacle ever depart from my dreams, as she rose and sank upon her seat, sank and rose, threw up her arms wildly to heaven, clutched at some visionary object in the air, fainting, praying, raving, despairing? Figure to yourself, reader, the elements of the case; suffer me to recall before your mind the circumstances of that unparalleled situation. From the silence and deep peace of this saintly summer night — from the pathetic blending of this sweet moonlight, dawnlight, dreamlight — from the manly tenderness of this flattering, whispering, murmuring love — suddenly as from the woods and fields — suddenly as from the chambers of the air opening in revelation — suddenly as from the ground yawning at her feet, leaped upon her, with the flashing of cataracts, Death the crowned phantom, with all the equipage of his terrors, and the tiger roar of his voice.

The moments were numbered; the strife was finished; the vision was closed. In the twinkling of an eye, our flying horses had carried us to the termination of the umbrageous aisle; at the right angles we wheeled into our former direction; the turn of the road carried the scene out of my eyes in an instant, and swept it into my dreams for ever.

SECTION III — DREAM-FUGUE:

FOUNDED ON THE PRECEDING THEME OF SUDDEN DEATH

> " Whence the sound
> Of instruments, that made melodious chime,
> Was heard, of harp and organ ; and who moved
> Their stops and chords was seen; his volant touch
> Instinct through all proportions, low and high,
> Fled and pursued transverse the resonant fugue."

Par. Lost, Bk. XI.

Tumultuosissimamente

Passion of sudden death! that once in youth I read and interpreted by the shadows of thy averted signs[1]! — rapture

[1] *"Averted signs"*: — I read the course and changes of the lady's agony in the succession of her involuntary gestures; but it must be remembered that I read all this from the rear, never once catching the lady's full face, and even her profile imperfectly.

of panic taking the shape (which amongst tombs in churches
I have seen) of woman bursting her sepulchral bonds — of
woman's Ionic form bending forward from the ruins of her
grave with arching foot, with eyes upraised, with clasped
5 adoring hands — waiting, watching, trembling, praying for
the trumpet's call to rise from dust for ever! Ah, vision
too fearful of shuddering humanity on the brink of almighty
abysses! — vision that didst start back, that didst reel away,
like a shrivelling scroll from before the wrath of fire racing
10 on the wings of the wind! Epilepsy so brief of horror,
wherefore is it that thou canst not die? Passing so suddenly into darkness, wherefore is it that still thou shed-
dest thy sad funeral blights upon the gorgeous mosaics of
dreams? Fragment of music too passionate, heard once,
15 and heard no more, what aileth thee, that thy deep rolling
chords come up at intervals through all the worlds of sleep,
and after forty years have lost no element of horror?

I

Lo, it is summer — almighty summer! The everlasting
gates of life and summer are thrown open wide; and on the
20 ocean, tranquil and verdant as a savannah, the unknown
lady from the dreadful vision and I myself are floating —
she upon a fairy pinnace, and I upon an English three-
decker. Both of us are wooing gales of festal happiness
within the domain of our common country, within that
25 ancient watery park, within the pathless chase of ocean,
where England takes her pleasure as a huntress through
winter and summer, from the rising to the setting sun.
Ah, what a wilderness of floral beauty was hidden, or was
suddenly revealed, upon the tropic islands through which
30 the pinnace moved! And upon her deck what a bevy of
human flowers: young women how lovely, young men how

noble, that were dancing together, and slowly drifting towards *us* amidst music and incense, amidst blossoms from forests and gorgeous corymbi from vintages, amidst natural carolling, and the echoes of sweet girlish laughter. Slowly the pinnace nears us, gaily she hails us, and silently 5 she disappears beneath the shadow of our mighty bows. But then, as at some signal from heaven, the music, and the carols, and the sweet echoing of girlish laughter — all are hushed. What evil has smitten the pinnace, meeting or overtaking her ? Did ruin to our friends couch within 10 our own dreadful shadow ? Was our shadow the shadow of death ? I looked over the bow for an answer, and, behold ! the pinnace was dismantled ; the revel and the revellers were found no more ; the glory of the vintage was dust ; and the forests with their beauty were left without a 15 witness upon the seas. " But where," and I turned to our crew — " where are the lovely women that danced beneath the awning of flowers and clustering corymbi ? Whither have fled the noble young men that danced with *them* ? " Answer there was none. But suddenly the man at the 20 mast-head, whose countenance darkened with alarm, cried out, " Sail on the weather beam ! Down she comes upon us : in seventy seconds she also will founder."

II

I looked to the weather side, and the summer had departed. The sea was rocking, and shaken with gather- 25 ing wrath. Upon its surface sat mighty mists, which grouped themselves into arches and long cathedral aisles. Down one of these, with the fiery pace of a quarrel from a cross-bow, ran a frigate right athwart our course. " Are they mad ? " some voice exclaimed from our deck. " Do 30 they woo their ruin ? " But in a moment, as she was close

upon us, some impulse of a heady current or local vortex
gave a wheeling bias to her course, and off she forged without a shock.   As she ran past us, high aloft amongst the
shrouds stood the lady of the pinnace.   The deeps opened
5 ahead in malice to receive her, towering surges of foam
ran after her, the billows were fierce to catch her.   But
far away she was borne into desert spaces of the sea:
whilst still by sight I followed her, as she ran before the
howling gale, chased by angry sea-birds and by madden-
10 ing billows; still I saw her, as at the moment when she
ran past us, standing amongst the shrouds, with her white
draperies streaming before the wind.   There she stood,
with hair dishevelled, one hand clutched amongst the tackling — rising, sinking, fluttering, trembling, praying; there
15 for leagues I saw her as she stood, raising at intervals one
hand to heaven, amidst the fiery crests of the pursuing
waves and the raving of the storm; until at last, upon a
sound from afar of malicious laughter and mockery, all
was hidden for ever in driving showers; and afterwards,
20 but when I knew not, nor how,

III

Sweet funeral bells from some incalculable distance, wail-
ing over the dead that die before the dawn, awakened me
as I slept in a boat moored to some familiar shore.   The
morning twilight even then was breaking; and, by the
25 dusky revelations which it spread, I saw a girl, adorned
with a garland of white roses about her head for some
great festival, running along the solitary strand in extremity of haste.   Her running was the running of panic; and
often she looked back as to some dreadful enemy in the
30 rear.   But, when I leaped ashore, and followed on her steps
to warn her of a peril in front, alas! from me she fled as

from another peril, and vainly I shouted to her of quick-sands that lay ahead.   Faster and faster she ran ; round a promontory of rocks she wheeled out of sight ; in an instant I also wheeled round it, but only to see the treacherous sands gathering above her head.   Already her person was buried ; only the fair young head and the diadem of white roses around it were still visible to the pitying heavens ; and, last of all, was visible one white marble arm.   I saw by the early twilight this fair young head, as it was sinking down to darkness — saw this marble arm, as it rose above her head and her treacherous grave, tossing, faltering, ris-ing, clutching, as at some false deceiving hand stretched out from the clouds — saw this marble arm uttering her dying hope, and then uttering her dying despair.   The head, the diadem, the arm — these all had sunk ; at last over these also the cruel quicksand had closed ; and no memorial of the fair young girl remained on earth, except my own solitary tears, and the funeral bells from the desert seas, that, rising again more softly, sang a requiem over the grave of the buried child, and over her blighted dawn.

I sat, and wept in secret the tears that men have ever given to the memory of those that died before the dawn, and by the treachery of earth, our mother.   But suddenly the tears and funeral bells were hushed by a shout as of many nations, and by a roar as from some great king's artillery, advancing rapidly along the valleys, and heard afar by echoes from the mountains.   "Hush!" I said, as I bent my ear earthwards to listen — "hush! — this either is the very anarchy of strife, or else" — and then I listened more profoundly, and whispered as I raised my head — "or else, oh heavens! it is *victory* that is final, victory that swallows up all strife."

IV

Immediately, in trance, I was carried over land and sea to some distant kingdom, and placed upon a triumphal car, amongst companions crowned with laurel. The darkness of gathering midnight, brooding over all the land, hid from us the mighty crowds that were weaving restlessly about ourselves as a centre: we heard them, but saw them not. Tidings had arrived, within an hour, of a grandeur that measured itself against centuries; too full of pathos they were, too full of joy, to utter themselves by other language than by tears, by restless anthems, and *Te Deums* reverberated from the choirs and orchestras of earth. These tidings we that sat upon the laurelled car had it for our privilege to publish amongst all nations. And already, by signs audible through the darkness, by snortings and tramplings, our angry horses, that knew no fear or fleshly weariness, upbraided us with delay. Wherefore *was* it that we delayed? We waited for a secret word, that should bear witness to the hope of nations as now accomplished for ever. At midnight the secret word arrived; which word was — *Waterloo and Recovered Christendom!* The dreadful word shone by its own light; before us it went; high above our leaders' heads it rode, and spread a golden light over the paths which we traversed. Every city, at the presence of the secret word, threw open its gates. The rivers were conscious as we crossed. All the forests, as we ran along their margins, shivered in homage to the secret word. And the darkness comprehended it.

Two hours after midnight we approached a mighty Minster. Its gates, which rose to the clouds, were closed. But, when the dreadful word that rode before us reached them with its golden light, silently they moved back upon their hinges; and at a flying gallop our equipage entered the grand aisle of the cathedral. Headlong was our pace; and at every altar, in the little chapels and oratories to the right hand and left of our course, the lamps, dying or sickening, kindled anew in sympathy with the secret word that was flying past. Forty leagues we might have run in the 5 cathedral, and as yet no strength of morning light had reached us, when before us we saw the aerial galleries of organ and choir. Every pinnacle of fretwork, every station of advantage amongst the traceries, was crested by white-robed choristers that sang deliverance; that wept 10 no more tears, as once their fathers had wept; but at intervals that sang together to the generations, saying,

"Chant the deliverer's praise in every tongue,"

and receiving answers from afar,

"Such as once in heaven and earth were sung." 15

And of their chanting was no end; of our headlong pace was neither pause nor slackening.

Thus as we ran like torrents — thus as we swept with bridal rapture over the Campo Santo[1] of the cathedral graves — suddenly we became aware of a vast necropolis 20 rising upon the far-off horizon — a city of sepulchres, built within the saintly cathedral for the warrior dead that

---

[1] *"Campo Santo"*: — It is probable that most of my readers will be acquainted with the history of the Campo Santo (or cemetery) at Pisa, composed of earth brought from Jerusalem from a bed of sanctity as the highest prize which the noble piety of crusaders could ask or imagine. To readers who are unacquainted with England, or who (being English) are yet unacquainted with the cathedral cities of England, it may be right to mention that the graves within-side the cathedrals often form a flat pavement over which carriages and horses *might* run; and perhaps a boyish remembrance of one particular cathedral, across which I had seen passengers walk and burdens carried, as about two centuries back they were through the middle of St. Paul's in London, may have assisted my dream.

rested from their feuds on earth.   Of purple granite was
the necropolis ; yet, in the first minute, it lay like a purple
stain upon the horizon, so mighty was the distance.   In
the second minute it trembled through many changes,
5 growing into terraces and towers of wondrous altitude,
so mighty was the pace.   In the third minute already, with
our dreadful gallop, we were entering its suburbs.   Vast
sarcophagi rose on every side, having towers and turrets
that, upon the limits of the central aisle, strode forward
10 with haughty intrusion, that ran back with mighty shadows into answering recesses.   Every sarcophagus showed
many bas-reliefs — bas-reliefs of battles and of battle-fields;
battles from forgotten ages, battles from yesterday; battle-
fields that, long since, nature had healed and reconciled to
15 herself with the sweet oblivion of flowers; battle-fields that
were yet angry and crimson with carnage.   Where the
terraces ran, there did *we* run ; where the towers curved,
there did *we* curve.   With the flight of swallows our horses
swept round every angle.   Like rivers in flood wheeling
20 round headlands, like hurricanes that ride into the secrets
of forests, faster than ever light unwove the mazes of darkness, our flying equipage carried earthly passions, kindled
warrior instincts, amongst the dust that lay around us —
dust oftentimes of our noble fathers that had slept in God
25 from Crécy to Trafalgar.   And now had we reached the
last sarcophagus, now were we abreast of the last bas-relief,
already had we recovered the arrow-like flight of the illim-
itable central aisle, when coming up this aisle to meet us
we beheld afar off a female child, that rode in a carriage
30 as frail as flowers.   The mists which went before her hid
the fawns that drew her, but could not hide the shells and
tropic flowers with which she played — but could not hide
the lovely smiles by which she uttered her trust in the
mighty cathedral, and in the cherubim that looked down

upon her from the mighty shafts of its pillars. Face to
face she was meeting us; face to face she rode, as if danger
there were none. "Oh, baby!" I exclaimed, "shalt thou
be the ransom for Waterloo? Must we, that carry tidings
of great joy to every people, be messengers of ruin to 5
thee!" In horror I rose at the thought; but then also, in
horror at the thought, rose one that was sculptured on a
bas-relief — a Dying Trumpeter. Solemnly from the field
of battle he rose to his feet; and, unslinging his stony
trumpet, carried it, in his dying anguish, to his stony lips 10
— sounding once, and yet once again; proclamation that,
in *thy* ears, oh baby! spoke from the battlements of death.
Immediately deep shadows fell between us, and aboriginal
silence. The choir had ceased to sing. The hoofs of
our horses, the dreadful rattle of our harness, the groan- 15
ing of our wheels, alarmed the graves no more. By horror
the bas-relief had been unlocked unto life. By horror we,
that were so full of life, we men and our horses, with their
fiery fore-legs rising in mid air to their everlasting gallop,
were frozen to a bas-relief. Then a third time the trumpet 20
sounded; the seals were taken off all pulses; life, and the
frenzy of life, tore into their channels again; again the
choir burst forth in sunny grandeur, as from the muffling
of storms and darkness; again the thunderings of our
horses carried temptation into the graves. One cry burst 25
from our lips, as the clouds, drawing off from the aisle,
showed it empty before us. — "Whither has the infant
fled? — is the young child caught up to God?" Lo! afar
off, in a vast recess, rose three mighty windows to the
clouds; and on a level with their summits, at height 30
insuperable to man, rose an altar of purest alabaster.
On its eastern face was trembling a crimson glory. A
glory was it from the reddening dawn that now streamed
through the windows? Was it from the crimson robes of

the martyrs painted *on* the windows? Was it from the
bloody bas-reliefs of earth? There, suddenly, within that
crimson radiance, rose the apparition of a woman's head,
and then of a woman's figure. The child it was — grown
5 up to woman's height. Clinging to the horns of the altar,
voiceless she stood — sinking, rising, raving, despairing;
and behind the volume of incense that, night and day,
streamed upwards from the altar, dimly was seen the fiery
font, and the shadow of that dreadful being who should
10 have baptized her with the baptism of death. But by her
side was kneeling her better angel, that hid his face with
wings; that wept and pleaded for *her;* that prayed when
she could *not;* that fought with Heaven by tears for *her*
deliverance; which also, as he raised his immortal counte-
15 nance from his wings, I saw, by the glory in his eye, that
from Heaven he had won at last.

V

Then was completed the passion of the mighty fugue.
The golden tubes of the organ, which as yet had but mut-
tered at intervals — gleaming amongst clouds and surges
20 of incense — threw up, as from fountains unfathomable,
columns of heart-shattering music. Choir and anti-choir
were filling fast with unknown voices. Thou also, Dying
Trumpeter, with thy love that was victorious, and thy
anguish that was finishing, didst enter the tumult; trum-
25 pet and echo — farewell love, and farewell anguish — rang
through the dreadful *sanctus*. Oh, darkness of the grave!
that from the crimson altar and from the fiery font wert
visited and searched by the effulgence in the angel's eye —
were these indeed thy children? Pomps of life, that, from
30 the burials of centuries, rose again to the voice of perfect
joy, did ye indeed mingle with the festivals of Death? Lo!

as I looked back for seventy leagues through the mighty
cathedral, I saw the quick and the dead that sang together
to God, together that sang to the generations of man. All
the hosts of jubilation, like armies that ride in pursuit,
moved with one step. Us, that, with laurelled heads, were 5
passing from the cathedral, they overtook, and, as with a
garment, they wrapped us round with thunders greater than
our own. As brothers we moved together ; to the dawn
that advanced, to the stars that fled ; rendering thanks to
God in the highest — that, having hid His face through 10
one generation behind thick clouds of War, once again
was ascending, from the Campo Santo of Waterloo was
ascending, in the visions of Peace ; rendering thanks for
thee, young girl! whom having overshadowed with His
ineffable passion of death, suddenly did God relent, suffered 15
thy angel to turn aside His arm, and even in thee, sister
unknown! shown to me for a moment only to be hidden
for ever, found an occasion to glorify His goodness. A
thousand times, amongst the phantoms of sleep, have I
seen thee entering the gates of the golden dawn, with the 20
secret word riding before thee, with the armies of the
grave behind thee, — seen thee sinking, rising, raving,
despairing ; a thousand times in the worlds of sleep have I
seen thee followed by God's angel through storms, through
desert seas, through the darkness of quicksands, through 25
dreams and the dreadful revelations that are in dreams ;
only that at the last, with one sling of His victorious arm,
He might snatch thee back from ruin, and might emblazon
in thy deliverance the endless resurrections of His love !

ON MURDER CONSIDERED AS ONE OF THE FINE ARTS

A GOOD many years ago, the reader may remember that I came forward in the character of a *dilettante* in murder. Perhaps *dilettante* is too strong a word. *Connoisseur* is better suited to the scruples and infirmity of public taste. I sup-
5 pose there is no harm in *that*, at least. A man is not bound to put his eyes, ears, and understanding into his breeches pocket when he meets with a murder. If he is not in a downright comatose state, I suppose that he must see that one murder is better or worse than another, in point of
10 good taste. Murders have their little differences and shades of merit, as well as statues, pictures, oratorios, cameos, intaglios, or what not. You may be angry with the man for talking too much, or too publicly (as to the too much, that I deny — a man can never cultivate his
15 taste too highly); but you must allow him to think, at any rate. Well, would you believe it? all my neighbours came to hear of that little æsthetic essay which I had published; and, unfortunately, hearing at the very same time of a club that I was connected with, and a dinner at which I pre-
20 sided — both tending to the same little object as the essay, viz., the diffusion of a just taste among Her Majesty's sub·jects[1] — they got up the most barbarous calumnies against me. In particular, they said that I, or that the club (which

---

[1] *Her* Majesty : — In the lecture, having occasion to refer to the reigning sovereign, I said " *His* Majesty "; for at that time William IV was on the throne; but between the lecture and this supplement had occurred the accession of our present Queen.

comes to the same thing), had offered bounties on well-conducted homicides — with a scale of drawbacks, in case of any one defect or flaw, according to a table issued to private friends. Now, let me tell the whole truth about the dinner and the club, and it will be seen how malicious the world is. But, first, confidentially, allow me to say what my real principles are upon the matter in question.

As to murder, I never committed one in my life. It's a well-known thing amongst all my friends. I can get a paper to certify as much, signed by lots of people. Indeed, if you come to that, I doubt whether many people could produce as strong a certificate. Mine would be as big as a breakfast tablecloth. There is indeed one member of the club who pretends to say he caught me once making too free with his throat on a club night, after everybody else had retired. But, observe, he shuffles in his story according to his state of civilation. When not far gone, he contents himself with saying that he caught me ogling his throat, and that I was melancholy for some weeks after, and that my voice sounded in a way expressing, to the nice ear of a connoisseur, *the sense of opportunities lost;* but the club all know that he is a disappointed man himself, and that he speaks querulously at times about the fatal neglect of a man's coming abroad without his tools. Besides, all this is an affair between two amateurs, and everybody makes allowances for little asperities and fibs in such a case. "But," say you, "if no murderer, you may have encouraged, or even have bespoken, a murder." No, upon my honour — no. And that was the very point I wished to argue for your satisfaction. The truth is, I am a very particular man in everything relating to murder ; and perhaps I carry my delicacy too far. The Stagirite most justly, and possibly with a view to my case, placed virtue in the το μεσον, or middle point between two extremes. A golden mean is certainly what every man should aim at. But it is easier talking than doing; and, my infirmity being notoriously too much milkiness of heart, I find it difficult to maintain that steady equatorial line between the two poles of too much murder on the one hand 5 and too little on the other. I am too soft; and people get excused through me — nay, go through life without an attempt made upon them — that ought *not* to be excused. I believe, if I had the management of things, there would hardly be a murder from year's end to year's end. In fact, 10 I'm for peace, and quietness, and fawningness, and what may be styled *knocking-underness*. A man came to me as a candidate for the place of my servant, just then vacant. He had the reputation of having dabbled a little in our art; some said, not without merit. What startled me, however, 15 was, that he supposed this art to be part of his regular duties in my service, and talked of having it considered in his wages. Now, that was a thing I would not allow; so I said at once, "Richard (or James, as the case might be), you misunderstand my character. If a man will and must 20 practise this difficult (and, allow me to add, dangerous) branch of art — if he has an overruling genius for it — why, in that case, all I say is that he might as well pursue his studies whilst living in my service as in another's. And also I may observe that it can do no harm either to him-25 self or to the subject on whom he operates that he should be guided by men of more taste than himself. Genius may do much, but long study of the art must always entitle a man to offer advice. So far I will go — general principles I will suggest. But, as to any particular case, once for all 30 I will have nothing to do with it. Never tell me of any special work of art you are meditating — I set my face against it *in toto*. For, if once a man indulges himself in murder, very soon he comes to think little of robbing, and from robbing he comes next to drinking and Sabbath-breaking,

and from that to incivility and procrastination. Once
begin upon this downward path, you never know where you
are to stop. Many a man dated his ruin from some murder
or other that perhaps he thought little of at the time.
Principiis obsta — that's my rule." Such was my speech,   5
and I have always acted up to it; so, if that is not being
virtuous, I should be glad to know what is.

But now about the dinner and the club. The club was
not particularly of my creation; it arose, — pretty much as
other similar associations for the propagation of truth and 10
the communication of new ideas, — rather from the necessities of things than upon any one man's suggestion. As
to the dinner, if any man more than another could be held
responsible for that, it was a member known amongst us
by the name of *Toad-in-the-hole*. He was so called from 15
his gloomy misanthropical disposition, which led him into
constant disparagements of all modern murders as vicious
abortions, belonging to no authentic school of art. The
finest performances of our own age he snarled at cynically;
and at length this querulous humour grew upon him so 20
much, and he became so notorious as a *laudator temporis
acti*, that few people cared to seek his society. This made
him still more fierce and truculent. He went about muttering and growling; wherever you met him, he was soliloquis-
ing, and saying "Despicable pretender — without grouping 25
— without two ideas upon handling — without —— "; and
there you lost him. At length existence seemed to be painful to him; he rarely spoke; he seemed conversing with
phantoms in the air; his housekeeper informed us that his
reading was nearly confined to "God's Revenge upon 30
Murder" by Reynolds, and a more ancient book of the
same title, noticed by Sir Walter Scott in his "Fortunes of
Nigel." Sometimes, perhaps, he might read in the "Newgate Calendar" down to the year 1788; but he never looked

into a book more recent. In fact, he had a theory with regard to the French Revolution, as having been the great cause ot degeneration in murder. "Very soon, sir," he used to say, "men will have lost the art of killing poultry:
5 the very rudiments of the art will have perished!" In the year 1811 he retired from general society. Toad-in-the-hole was no more seen in any public resort. We missed him from his wonted haunts: "Nor up the lawn, nor at the wood was he." By the side of the main conduit his listless
10 length at noontide he would stretch, and pore upon the filth that muddled by. "Even dogs," this pensive moralist would say, "are not what they were, sir — not what they should be. I remember in my grandfather's time that some dogs had an idea of murder. I have known a mastiff, sir,
15 that lay in ambush for a rival, — yes, sir, and finally murdered him, with pleasing circumstances of good taste. I also was on intimate terms of acquaintance with a tom-cat that was an assassin. But now ——"; and then, the subject growing too painful, he dashed his hand to his forehead,
20 and went off abruptly in a homeward direction towards his favourite conduit; where he was seen by an amateur in such a state that he thought it dangerous to address him. Soon after Toad shut himself entirely up; it was understood that he had resigned himself to melancholy; and at length
25 the prevailing notion was that Toad-in-the-hole had hanged himself.

The world was wrong *there*, as it had been on some other questions. Toad-in-the-hole might be sleeping, but dead he was not; and of that we soon had ocular proof. One morn-
30 ing in 1812, an amateur surprised us with the news that he had seen Toad-in-the-hole brushing with hasty steps the dews away, to meet the postman by the conduit side. Even that was something: how much more, to hear that he had shaved his beard — had laid aside his sad-coloured clothes,

and was adorned like a bridegroom of ancient days. What
could be the meaning of all this? Was Toad-in-the-hole
mad? or how? Soon after the secret was explained: in
more than a figurative sense "the murder was out." For
in came the London morning papers, by which it appeared   5
that, but three days before, a murder the most superb of
the century by many degrees had occurred in the heart of
London. I need hardly say that this was the great exterminating *chef-d'œuvre* of Williams at Mr. Marr's, No. 29
Ratcliffe Highway. That was the *début* of the artist; at 10
least for anything the public knew. What occurred at Mr.
Williamson's twelve nights afterwards — the second work
turned out from the same chisel — some people pronounced
even superior. But Toad-in-the-hole always "reclaimed,"
he was even angry, at such comparisons. "This vulgar 15
gout de comparaison, as La Bruyère calls it," he would often
remark, "will be our ruin; each work has its own separate
characteristics — each in and for itself is incomparable.
One, perhaps, might suggest the 'Iliad' — the other the
'Odyssey': but what do you get by such comparisons? 20
Neither ever was or will be surpassed; and, when you've
talked for hours, you must still come back to that." Vain,
however, as all criticism might be, he often said that volumes might be written on each case for itself; and he even
proposed to publish a quarto on the subject.   25

Meantime, how had Toad-in-the-hole happened to hear of
this great work of art so early in the morning? He had
received an account by express, despatched by a correspondent in London who watched the progress of art on
Toad's behalf, with a general commission to send off a 30
special express, at whatever cost, in the event of any estimable works appearing. The express arrived in the night-
time; Toad-in-the-hole was then gone to bed; he had been
muttering and grumbling for hours; but of course he was

called up. On reading the account, he threw his arms
round the express, declared him his brother and his pre-
server, and expressed his regret at not having it in his
power to knight him. We amateurs, having heard that he
was abroad, and therefore had *not* hanged himself, made
sure of soon seeing him amongst us. Accordingly he soon
arrived ; seized every man's hand as he passed him —
wrung it almost frantically, and kept ejaculating, "Why,
now, here's something like a murder! — this is the real
thing — this is genuine — this is what you can approve,
can recommend to a friend : this — says every man, on
reflection — this is the thing that ought to be! Such
works are enough to make us all young." And in fact
the general opinion is that Toad-in-the-hole would have
died but for this regeneration of art, which he called a
second age of Leo the Tenth ; and it was our duty, he
said, solemnly to commemorate it. At present, and *en
attendant*, he proposed that the club should meet and dine
together. A dinner, therefore, was given by the club ;
to which all amateurs were invited from a distance of
one hundred miles.

Of this dinner there are ample shorthand notes amongst
the archives of the club. But they are not "extended," to
speak diplomatically ; and the reporter who only could give
the whole report *in extenso* is missing — I believe, murdered.
Meantime, in years long after that day, and on an occasion
perhaps equally interesting, viz., the turning up of Thugs
and Thuggism, another dinner was given. Of this I myself
kept notes, for fear of another accident to the shorthand
reporter. And I here subjoin them.

Toad-in-the-hole, I must mention, was present at this
dinner. In fact, it was one of its sentimental incidents.
Being as old as the valleys at the dinner of 1812, naturally
he was as old as the hills at the Thug dinner of 1838. He

again challenged with shouts the stormiest for the new glee. I foresaw a tempestuous evening; and I ordered myself to be strengthened with three waiters on each side, — the vice-president with as many. Symptoms of unruly enthusiasm were beginning to show out; and I own that I myself was considerably excited as the orchestra opened with its storm of music and the impassioned glee began — " Et interrogatum est a Toad-in-the-hole — Ubi est ille Reporter ? " And the frenzy of the passion became absolutely convulsing as the full chorus fell in — " Et iteratum est ab omnibus — *Non est inventus.*"

The next toast was — *The Jewish Sicarii.*

Upon which I made the following explanation to the company : — "Gentlemen, I am sure it will interest you all to hear that the Assassins, ancient as they were, had a race of predecessors in the very same country. All over Syria, but particularly in Palestine, during the early years of the Emperor Nero, there was a band of murderers, who prosecuted their studies in a very novel manner. They did not practise in the night-time, or in lonely places ; but, justly considering that great crowds are in themselves a sort of darkness by means of the dense pressure, and the impossibility of finding out who it was that gave the blow, they mingled with mobs everywhere ; particularly at the great paschal feast in Jerusalem ; where they actually had the audacity, as Josephus assures us, to press into the temple — and whom should they choose for operating upon but Jonathan himself, the Pontifex Maximus ? They murdered him, gentlemen, as beautifully as if they had had him alone on a moonless night in a dark lane. And, when it was asked who was the murderer, and where he was——"

"Why, then, it was answered," interrupted Toad-in-the-hole, " ' *Non est inventus.*' " And then, in spite of all I

could do or say, the orchestra opened, and the whole
company began — " Et interrogatum est a Toad-in-the-
hole — Ubi est ille Sicarius ? Et responsum est ab omnibus — *Non est inventus.*"

5   When the tempestuous chorus had subsided, I began
again : — "Gentlemen, you will find a very circumstantial
account of the Sicarii in at least three different parts of
Josephus : once in Book XX, sec. v, c. viii, of his 'Antiquities ' ; once in Book I of his 'Wars': but in sec. x of
10 the chapter first cited you will find a particular description
of their tooling. This is what he says : — ' They tooled
with small scimitars not much different from the Persian
acinacæ, but more curved, and for all the world most like
the Roman semi-lunar *sicæ.*' It is perfectly magnificent,
15 gentlemen, to hear the sequel of their history. Perhaps
the only case on record where a regular army of murderers was assembled, a *justus exercitus,* was in the case of
these *Sicarii.* They mustered in such strength in the
wilderness that Festus himself was obliged to march
20 against them with the Roman legionary force. A pitched
battle ensued ; and this army of amateurs was all cut to
pieces in the desert. Heavens, gentlemen, what a sublime picture ! The Roman legions — the wilderness —
Jerusalem in the distance — an army of murderers in the
25 foreground ! "

The next toast was — "To the further improvement
of Tooling, and thanks to the Committee for their services."

Mr. L., on behalf of the Committee who had reported
30 on that subject, returned thanks. He made an interesting
extract from the report, by which it appeared how very
much stress had been laid formerly on the mode of tooling
by the Fathers, both Greek and Latin. In confirmation of
this pleasing fact, he made a very striking statement in

reference to the earliest work of antediluvian art. Father Mersenne, that learned French Roman Catholic, in page one thousand four hundred and thirty-one of his operose Commentary on Genesis, mentions, on the authority of several rabbis, that the quarrel of Cain with Abel was about a young woman; that, according to various accounts, Cain had tooled with his teeth (Abelem fuisse *morsibus* dilaceratum a Cain); according to many others, with the jawbone of an ass, — which is the tooling adopted by most painters. But it is pleasing to the mind of sensibility to know that, as science expanded, sounder views were adopted. One author contends for a pitchfork, St. Chrysostom for a sword, Irenæus for a scythe, and Prudentius, the Christian poet of the fourth century, for a hedging-bill. This last writer delivers his opinion thus: —

" Frater, probatæ sanctitatis æmulus,
    Germana curvo colla frangit sarculo " :

i.e., his brother, jealous of his attested sanctity, fractures his fraternal throat with a curved hedging-bill. "All which is respectfully submitted by your committee, not so much as decisive of the question (for it is not), but in order to impress upon the youthful mind the importance which has ever been attached to the quality of the tooling by such men as Chrysostom and Irenæus."

"Irenæus be hanged!" said Toad-in-the-hole, who now rose impatiently to give the next toast: — "Our Irish friends; wishing them a speedy revolution in their mode of tooling, as well as in everything else connected with the art!"

"Gentlemen, I'll tell you the plain truth. Every day of the year when we take up a paper we read the opening of a murder. We say, This is good, this is charming, this is excellent! But, behold you! scarcely have we read

a little farther before the word Tipperary or Ballina-some-
thing betrays the Irish manufacture. Instantly we loathe
it; we call to the waiter; we say, 'Waiter, take away this
paper; send it out of the house; it is absolutely a scandal
5 in the nostrils of all just taste.' I appeal to every man
whether, on finding a murder (otherwise perhaps promising enough) to be Irish, he does not feel himself as much
insulted as when, Madeira being ordered, he finds it to be
Cape, or when, taking up what he takes to be a mushroom,
10 it turns out what children call a toad-stool? Tithes,
politics, something wrong in principle, vitiate every Irish
murder. Gentlemen, this must be reformed, or Ireland
will not be a land to live in; at least, if we do live there,
we must import all our murders, that's clear." Toad-in-
15 the-hole sat down, growling with suppressed wrath; and
the uproarious "Hear, hear!" clamorously expressed the
general concurrence.

The next toast was — "The sublime epoch of Burkism
and Harism!"

20 This was drunk with enthusiasm; and one of the members who spoke to the question made a very curious communication to the company :— "Gentlemen, we fancy
Burkism to be a pure invention of our own times; and in
fact no Pancirollus has ever enumerated this branch of art
25 when writing *de rebus deperditis*. Still, I have ascertained
that the essential principle of this variety in the art *was*
known to the ancients; although, like the art of painting
upon glass, of making the myrrhine cups, etc., it was lost
in the dark ages for want of encouragement. In the famous
30 collection of Greek epigrams made by Planudes is one
upon a very fascinating case of Burkism: it is a perfect
little gem of art. The epigram itself I cannot lay my hand
upon at this moment; but the following is an abstract of it
by Salmasius, as I find it in his notes on Vopiscus: 'Est

et elegans epigramma Lucilii,[1] ubi medicus et pollinctor de compacto sic egerunt ut medicus ægros omnes curæ suæ commissos occideret.' This was the basis of the contract, you see, — that on the one part the doctor, for himself and his assigns, doth undertake and contract duly and truly to murder all the patients committed to his charge : but why ? There lies the beauty of the case — 'Et ut pollinctori amico suo traderet pollingendos.' The *pollinctor*, you are aware, was a person whose business it was to dress and prepare dead bodies for burial. The original ground of the transaction appears to have been sentimental : 'He was my friend,' says the murderous doctor, — 'he was dear to me,' — in speaking of the pollinctor. But the law, gentlemen, is stern and harsh : the law will not hear of these tender motives : to sustain a contract of this nature in law, it is essential that a 'consideration' should be given. Now, what *was* the consideration ? For thus far all is on the side of the pollinctor : he will be well paid for his services ; but meantime the generous, the noble-minded doctor gets nothing. What *was* the equivalent, again I ask, which the law would insist on the doctor's taking, in order to establish that 'consideration' without which the contract had no force ? You shall hear : 'Et ut pollinctor vicissim τελαμωνας quos fura- 'batur de pollinctione mortuorum medico mitteret donis ad 'alliganda vulnera eorum quos curabat' ; *i.e.*, and that reciprocally the pollinctor should transmit to the physician, as free gifts for the binding up of wounds in those whom he treated medically, the belts or trusses (τελαμωνας)

---

[1] The epigram, which had been preserved by Planudes in its Greek form, is here attributed by Salmasius to the Latin satirical poet, Caius Lucilius, who was born about B.C. 148, and died about B.C. 103. It is not found, however, among the preserved fragments of Lucilius ; and the Greek form of the epigram is anonymous.

which he had succeeded in purloining in the course of his functions about the corpses.

"Now the case is clear: the whole went on a principle of reciprocity which would have kept up the trade for ever. The doctor was also a surgeon: he could not murder *all* his patients: some of the patients must be retained intact. For these he wanted linen bandages.   But, unhappily, the Romans wore woollen; on which account it was that they bathed so often.   Meantime, there *was* linen to be had in Rome; but it was monstrously dear; and the τελαμωνες, or linen swathing bandages, in which superstition obliged them to bind up corpses, would answer capitally for the surgeon. The doctor, therefore, contracts to furnish his friend with a constant succession of corpses, — provided, and be it understood always, that his sad friend, in return, should supply him with one-half of the articles he would receive from the friends of the parties murdered or to be murdered. The doctor invariably recommended his invaluable friend the pollinctor (whom let us call the undertaker); the undertaker, with equal regard to the sacred rights of friendship, uniformly recommended the doctor.   Like Pylades and Orestes, they were models of a perfect friendship: in their lives they were lovely; and on the gallows, it is to be hoped, they were not divided.

"Gentlemen, it makes me laugh horribly when I think of those two friends drawing and re-drawing on each other: 'Pollinctor in account with Doctor, debtor by sixteen corpses: creditor by forty-five bandages, two of which damaged.'   Their names unfortunately are lost; but I conceive they must have been Quintus Burkius and Publius Harius.   By the way, gentlemen, has anybody heard lately of Hare?   I understand he is comfortably settled in Ireland, considerably to the west, and does a little business now and then; but, as he observes with a sigh, only as a

retailer — nothing like the fine thriving wholesale concern
so carelessly blown up at Edinburgh. 'You see what comes
of neglecting business' — is the chief moral, the ἐπιμνθιον,
as Æsop would say, which Hare draws from his past
experience." 5

At length came the toast of the day — *Thugdom in all its
branches.*

The speeches *attempted* at this crisis of the dinner were
past all counting. But the applause was so furious, the
music so stormy, and the crashing of glasses so incessant, 10
from the general resolution never again to drink an inferior
toast from the same glass, that I am unequal to the task of
reporting. Besides which, Toad-in-the-hole now became
ungovernable. He kept firing pistols in every direction;
sent his servant for a blunderbuss, and talked of loading 15
with ball-cartridge. We conceived that his former madness
had returned at the mention of Burke and Hare; or that,
being again weary of life, he had resolved to go off in a
general massacre. This we could not think of allowing;
it became indispensable, therefore, to kick him out; which 20
we did with universal consent, the whole company·lending
their toes *uno pede*, as I may say, though pitying his gray
hairs and his angelic smile. During the operation the
orchestra poured in their old chorus. The universal company sang, and (what surprised us most of all) Toad-in-the- 25
hole joined us furiously in singing —

"Et interrogatum est ab omnibus — Ubi est ille Toad-in-the-hole?
Et responsum est ab omnibus — *Non est inventus.*"

JOAN OF ARC[1]

WHAT is to be thought of *her?* What is to be thought of the poor shepherd girl from the hills and forests of Lorraine, that — like the Hebrew shepherd boy from the hills and forests of Judea — rose suddenly out of the quiet, out 5 of the safety, out of the religious inspiration, rooted in deep pastoral solitudes, to a station in the van of armies, and to the more perilous station at the right hand of kings? The Hebrew boy inaugurated his patriotic mission by an *act,* by a victorious *act,* such as no man could deny. But so did 10 the girl of Lorraine, if we read her story as it was read by those who saw her nearest. Adverse armies bore witness

---

[1] *" Arc " :* — Modern France, that should know a great deal better than myself, insists that the name is not D'Arc — *i.e.,* of Arc — but *Darc.* Now it happens sometimes that, if a person whose position guarantees his access to the best information will content himself with gloomy dogmatism, striking the table with his fist, and saying in a terrific voice, " It *is* so, and there's an end of it," one bows deferentially, and submits. But, if, unhappily for himself, won by this docility, he relents too amiably into reasons and arguments, probably one raises an insurrection against him that may never be crushed; for in the fields of logic one can skirmish, perhaps, as well as he. Had he confined himself to dogmatism, he would have intrenched his position in darkness, and have hidden his own vulnerable points. But coming down to base reasons he lets in light, and one sees where to plant the blows. Now, the worshipful reason of modern France for disturbing the old received spelling is that Jean Hordal, a descendant of La Pucelle's brother, spelled the name *Darc* in 1612. But what of that? It is notorious that what small matter of spelling Providence had thought fit to disburse amongst man in the seventeenth century was all monopolised by printers; now, M. Hordal was *not* a printer.

to the boy as no pretender; but so they did to the gentle girl. Judged by the voices of all who saw them *from a station of good will*, both were found true and loyal to any promises involved in their first acts. Enemies it was that made the difference between their subsequent fortunes. The boy rose to a splendour and a noonday prosperity, both personal and public, that rang through the records of his people, and became a byword among his posterity for a thousand years, until the sceptre was departing from Judah. The poor, forsaken girl, on the contrary, drank not herself from that cup of rest which she had secured for France. She never sang together with the songs that rose in her native Domrémy as echoes to the departing steps of invaders. She mingled not in the festal dances at Vaucouleurs which celebrated in rapture the redemption of France. No! for her voice was then silent; no! for her feet were dust. Pure, innocent, noble-hearted girl! whom, from earliest youth, ever I believed in as full of truth and self-sacrifice, this was amongst the strongest pledges for *thy* truth, that never once — no, not for a moment of weakness — didst thou revel in the vision of coronets and honour from man. Coronets for thee! Oh, no! Honours, if they come when all is over, are for those that share thy blood.[1] Daughter of Domrémy, when the gratitude of thy king shall awaken, thou wilt be sleeping the sleep of the dead. Call her, King of France, but she will not hear thee. Cite her by the apparitors to come and receive a robe of honour, but she will be found *en contumace*. When the thunders of universal France, as even yet may happen, shall proclaim the grandeur of the poor shepherd girl that gave up all for her country, thy ear, young shepherd girl, will have been deaf for five centuries. To suffer and to do, that was thy

---

[1] "*Those that share thy blood*" : — A collateral relative of Joanna's was subsequently ennobled by the title of *Du Lys*.

358 SELECTIONS FROM DE QUINCEY

portion in this life; that was thy destiny; and not for a
moment was it hidden from thyself. Life, thou saidst, is
short; and the sleep which is in the grave is long; let me
use that life, so transitory, for the glory of those heavenly
5 dreams destined to comfort the sleep which is so long!
This pure creature — pure from every suspicion of even a
visionary self-interest, even as she was pure in senses more
obvious — never once did this holy child, as regarded herself, relax from her belief in the darkness that was travel-
10 ling to meet her. She might not prefigure the very manner
of her death; she saw not in vision, perhaps, the aerial
altitude of the fiery scaffold, the spectators without end,
on every road, pouring into Rouen as to a coronation, the
surging smoke, the volleying flames, the hostile faces all
15 around, the pitying eye that lurked but here and there,
until nature and imperishable truth broke loose from artificial restraints — these might not be apparent through the
mists of the hurrying future. But the voice that called
her to death, *that* she heard for ever.

20 Great was the throne of France even in those days, and
great was He that sat upon it; but well Joanna knew that
not the throne, nor he that sat upon it, was for *her;* but,
on the contrary, that she was for *them;* not she by them,
but they by her, should rise from the dust. Gorgeous were
25 the lilies of France, and for centuries had the privilege to
spread their beauty over land and sea, until, in another
century, the wrath of God and man combined to wither
them; but well Joanna knew, early at Domrémy she had
read that bitter truth, that the lilies of France would
30 decorate no garland for *her.* Flower nor bud, bell nor
blossom, would ever bloom for *her!*

. . . . . .

But stay. What reason is there for taking up this subject of Joanna precisely in the spring of 1847? Might it

not have been left till the spring of 1947, or, perhaps, left
till called for? Yes, but it *is* called for, and clamorously.
You are aware, reader, that amongst the many original
thinkers whom modern France has produced, one of the
reputed leaders is M. Michelet. All these writers are of
a revolutionary cast; not in a political sense merely, but
in all senses; mad, oftentimes, as March hares; crazy
with the laughing gas of recovered liberty; drunk with the
wine cup of their mighty Revolution, snorting, whinnying,
throwing up their heels, like wild horses in the boundless
pampas, and running races of defiance with snipes, or with
the winds, or with their own shadows, if they can find nothing else to challenge. Some time or other, I, that have
leisure to read, may introduce *you*, that have not, to two
or three dozen of these writers; of whom I can assure
you beforehand that they are often profound, and at intervals are even as impassioned as if they were come of our
best English blood. But now, confining our attention to
M. Michelet, we in England — who know him best by his
worst book, the book against priests, etc. — know him dis-
advantageously. That book is a rhapsody of incoherence.
But his "History of France" is quite another thing. A
man, in whatsoever craft he sails, cannot stretch away out
of sight when he is linked to the windings of the shore by
towing-ropes of History. Facts, and the consequences
of facts, draw the writer back to the falconer's lure from
the giddiest heights of speculation. Here, therefore — in
his "France" — if not always free from flightiness, if now
and then off like a rocket for an airy wheel in the clouds,
M. Michelet, with natural politeness, never forgets that
he has left a large audience waiting for him on earth, and
gazing upward in anxiety for his return; return, therefore,
he does. But History, though clear of certain temptations
in one direction, has separate dangers of its own. It is

impossible so to write a history of France, or of England
— works becoming every hour more indispensable to the
inevitably political man of this day — without perilous
openings for error. If I, for instance, on the part of
England, should happen to turn my labours into that
channel, and (on the model of Lord Percy going to
Chevy Chase)

> "A vow to God should make
>   My pleasure in the Michelet woods
>   Three summer days to take,"

probably, from simple delirium, I might hunt M. Michelet
into *delirium tremens*. Two strong angels stand by the side
of History, whether French history or English, as heraldic
supporters: the angel of research on the left hand, that
must read millions of dusty parchments, and of pages
blotted with lies; the angel of meditation on the right
hand, that must cleanse these lying records with fire, even
as of old the draperies of *asbestos* were cleansed, and must
quicken them into regenerated life. Willingly I acknowledge that no man will ever avoid innumerable errors of
detail; with so vast a compass of ground to traverse,
this is impossible; but such errors (though I have a
bushel on hand, at M. Michelet's service) are not the
game I chase; it is the bitter and unfair spirit in which
M. Michelet writes against England. Even *that*, after all,
is but my secondary object; the real one is Joanna, the
Pucelle d'Orléans herself.

I am not going to write the history of La Pucelle: to do
this, or even circumstantially to report the history of her
persecution and bitter death, of her struggle with false
witnesses and with ensnaring judges, it would be necessary to have before us *all* the documents, and therefore

the collection only now forthcoming in Paris.[1] But *my* purpose is narrower. There have been great thinkers, disdaining the careless judgments of contemporaries, who have thrown themselves boldly on the judgment of a far posterity, that should have had time to review, to ponder, to compare. There have been great actors on the stage of tragic humanity that might, with the same depth of confidence, have appealed from the levity of compatriot friends — too heartless for the sublime interest of their story, and too impatient for the labour of sifting its perplexities — to the magnanimity and justice of enemies. To this class belongs the Maid of Arc. The ancient Romans were too faithful to the ideal of grandeur in themselves not to relent, after a generation or two, before the grandeur of Hannibal. Mithridates, a more doubtful person, yet, merely for the magic perseverance of his indomitable malice, won from the same Romans the only real honour that ever he received on earth. And we English have ever shown the same homage to stubborn enmity. To work unflinchingly for the ruin of England; to say through life, by word and by deed, *Delenda est Anglia Victrix!* — that one purpose of malice, faithfully pursued, has quartered some people upon our national funds of homage as by a perpetual annuity. Better than an inheritance of service rendered to England herself has sometimes proved the most insane hatred to England. Hyder Ali, even his son Tippoo, though so far inferior, and Napoleon, have all benefited by this disposition among ourselves to exaggerate the merit of diabolic enmity. Not one of these men was ever capable, in a solitary instance, of praising an enemy (what do you say

---

[1] *"Only now forthcoming"* : — In 1847 *began* the publication (from official records) of Joanna's trial. It was interrupted, I fear, by the convulsions of 1848 ; and whether even yet finished I do not know.

to *that*, reader?); and yet in *their* behalf, we consent to
forget, not their crimes only, but (which is worse) their
hideous bigotry and anti-magnanimous egotism — for
nationality it was not.   Suffren, and some half dozen of
5 other French nautical heroes, because rightly they did
us all the mischief they could (which was really great),
are names justly reverenced in England.   On the same
principle, La Pucelle d'Orléans, the victorious enemy of
England, has been destined to receive her deepest com-
10 memoration from the magnanimous justice of Englishmen.

Joanna, as we in England should call her, but according
to her own statement, Jeanne (or, as M. Michelet asserts,
Jean[1]) D'Arc was born at Domrémy, a village on the
marches of Lorraine and Champagne, and dependent upon
15 the town of Vaucouleurs.   I have called her a Lorrainer,
not simply because the word is prettier, but because
Champagne too odiously reminds us English of what are
for *us* imaginary wines — which, undoubtedly, La Pucelle
tasted as rarely as we English: we English, because the
20 champagne of London is chiefly grown in Devonshire; La
Pucelle, because the champagne of Champagne never, by any

---

[1] "*Jean*": — M. Michelet asserts that there was a mystical meaning
at that era in calling a child *Jean ;* it implied a secret commendation of
a child, if not a dedication, to St. John the evangelist, the beloved
disciple, the apostle of love and mysterious visions.   But, really, as the
name was so exceedingly common, few people will detect a mystery in
calling a *boy* by the name of Jack, though it *does* seem mysterious to call
a girl Jack.   It may be less so in France, where a beautiful practice
has always prevailed of giving a boy his mother's name—preceded and
strengthened by a male name, as *Charles Anne, Victor Victoire*.   In
cases where a mother's memory has been unusually dear to a son, this
vocal memento of her, locked into the circle of his own name, gives to
it the tenderness of a testamentary relic, or a funeral ring.   I presume,
therefore, that La Pucelle must have borne the baptismal name of
Jeanne Jean; the latter with no reference, perhaps, to so sublime a
person as St. John, but simply to some relative.

chance, flowed into the fountain of Domrémy, from which only she drank. M. Michelet will have her to be a *Champenoise*, and for no better reason than that she "took after her father," who happened to be a *Champenois*.

These disputes, however, turn on refinements too nice. Domrémy stood upon the frontiers, and, like other frontiers, produced a *mixed* race, representing the *cis* and the *trans*. A river (it is true) formed the boundary line at this point — the river Meuse; and *that*, in old days, might have divided the populations; but in these days it did not; there were bridges, there were ferries, and weddings crossed from the right bank to the left. Here lay two great roads, not so much for travellers that were few, as for armies that were too many by half. These two roads, one of which was the great highroad between France and Germany, *decussated* at this very point; which is a learned way of saying that they formed a St. Andrew's Cross, or letter X. I hope the compositor will choose a good large X; in which case the point of intersection, the *locus* of conflux and intersection for these four diverging arms, will finish the reader's geographical education, by showing him to a hair's-breadth where it was that Domrémy stood. These roads, so grandly situated, as great trunk arteries between two mighty realms,[1] and haunted for ever by wars or rumours of wars, decussated (for anything I know to the contrary) absolutely under Joanna's bedroom window; one rolling away to the right, past M. D'Arc's old barn, and the other unaccountably preferring to sweep round that odious man's pig-sty to the left.

On whichever side of the border chance had thrown Joanna, the same love to France would have been nurtured.

---

[1] And reminding one of that inscription, so justly admired by Paul Richter, which a Russian Czarina placed on a guide-post near Moscow: *This is the road that leads to Constantinople.*

For it is a strange fact, noticed by M. Michelet and others, that the Dukes of Bar and Lorraine had for generations pursued the policy of eternal warfare with France on their own account, yet also of eternal amity and league with France in case anybody else presumed to attack her. Let peace settle upon France, and before long you might rely upon seeing the little vixen Lorraine flying at the throat of France. Let France be assailed by a formidable enemy, and instantly you saw a Duke of Lorraine insisting on having his own throat cut in support of France; which favour accordingly was cheerfully granted to him in three great successive battles: twice by the English, viz., at Crécy and Agincourt, once by the Sultan at Nicopolis.

This sympathy with France during great eclipses, in those that during ordinary seasons were always teasing her with brawls and guerilla inroads, strengthened the natural piety to France of those that were confessedly the children of her own house. The outposts of France, as one may call the great frontier provinces, were of all localities the most devoted to the Fleurs de Lys. To witness, at any great crisis, the generous devotion to these lilies of the little fiery cousin that in gentler weather was for ever tilting at the breast of France, could not but fan the zeal of France's legitimate daughters; while to occupy a post of honour on the frontiers against an old hereditary enemy of France would naturally stimulate this zeal by a sentiment of martial pride, by a sense of danger always threatening, and of hatred always smouldering. That great four-headed road was a perpetual memento to patriotic ardour. To say "This way lies the road to Paris, and that other way to Aix-la-Chapelle; this to Prague, that to Vienna," nourished the warfare of the heart by daily ministrations of sense. The eye that watched for the gleams

of lance or helmet from the hostile frontier, the ear that
listened for the groaning of wheels, made the highroad
itself, with its relations to centres so remote, into a
manual of patriotic duty.

The situation, therefore, *locally*, of Joanna was full of
profound suggestions to a heart that listened for the
stealthy steps of change and fear that too surely were
in motion. But, if the place were grand, the time, the
burden of the time, was far more so. The air overhead
in its upper chambers was *hurtling* with the obscure sound;
was dark with sullen fermenting of storms that had been
gathering for a hundred and thirty years. The battle of
Agincourt in Joanna's childhood had reopened the wounds
of France. Crécy and Poictiers, those withering over-
throws for the chivalry of France, had, before Agincourt
occurred, been tranquilised by more than half a century;
but this resurrection of their trumpet wails made the whole
series of battles and endless skirmishes take their stations
as parts in one drama. The graves that had closed sixty
years ago seemed to fly open in sympathy with a sorrow
that echoed their own. The monarchy of France laboured
in extremity, rocked and reeled like a ship fighting with
the darkness of monsoons. The madness of the poor king
(Charles VI), falling in at such a crisis, like the case of
women labouring in child-birth during the storming of a
city, trebled the awfulness of the time. Even the wild
story of the incident which had immediately occasioned
the explosion of this madness — the case of a man unknown, gloomy, and perhaps maniacal himself, coming out
of a forest at noonday, laying his hand upon the bridle of
the king's horse, checking him for a moment to say, "Oh,
king, thou art betrayed," and then vanishing, no man knew
whither, as he had appeared for no man knew what — fell
in with the universal prostration of mind that laid France

on her knees, as before the slow unweaving of some ancient prophetic doom. The famines, the extraordinary diseases, the insurrections of the peasantry up and down Europe — these were chords struck from the same mysterious harp; but these were transitory chords. There had been others of deeper and more ominous sound. The termination of the Crusades, the destruction of the Templars, the Papal interdicts, the tragedies caused or suffered by the house of Anjou, and by the Emperor — these were full of a more permanent significance. But, since then, the colossal figure of feudalism was seen standing, as it were on tiptoe, at Crécy, for flight from earth: that was a revolution unparalleled; yet *that* was a trifle by comparison with the more fearful revolutions that were mining below the Church. By her own internal schisms, by the abominable spectacle of a double Pope — so that no man, except through political bias, could even guess which was Heaven's vicegerent, and which the creature of Hell — the Church was rehearsing, as in still earlier forms she had already rehearsed, those vast rents in her foundations which no man should ever heal.

These were the loftiest peaks of the cloudland in the skies that to the scientific gazer first caught the colors of the *new* morning in advance. But the whole vast range alike of sweeping glooms overhead dwelt upon all meditative minds, even upon those that could not distinguish the tendencies nor decipher the forms. It was, therefore, not her own age alone, as affected by its immediate calamities, that lay with such weight upon Joanna's mind, but her own age as one section in a vast mysterious drama, unweaving through a century back, and drawing nearer continually to some dreadful crisis. Cataracts and rapids were heard roaring ahead; and signs were seen far back, by help of old men's memories, which answered secretly to signs now coming forward on the eye, even as locks answer to keys. It was not wonderful that in such a haunted solitude, with such a haunted heart, Joanna should see angelic visions, and hear angelic voices. These voices whispered to her for ever the duty, self-imposed, of delivering France. Five years she listened to these monitory voices with internal struggles. At length she could resist no longer. Doubt gave way; and she left her home for ever in order to present herself at the dauphin's court.

The education of this poor girl was mean according to the present standard: was ineffably grand, according to a purer philosophic standard: and only not good for our age because for us it would be unattainable. She read nothing, for she could not read; but she had heard others read parts of the Roman martyrology. She wept in sympathy with the sad " Misereres " of the Romish Church; she rose to heaven with the glad triumphant " Te Deums " of Rome; she drew her comfort and her vital strength from the rites of the same Church. But, next after these spiritual advantages, she owed most to the advantages of her situation. The fountain of Domrémy was on the brink of a boundless forest; and it was haunted to that degree by fairies that the parish priest (*curé*) was obliged to read mass there once a year, in order to keep them in any decent bounds. Fairies are important, even in a statistical view: certain weeds mark poverty in the soil; fairies mark its solitude. As surely as the wolf retires before cities does the fairy sequester herself from the haunts of the licensed victualer. A village is too much for her nervous delicacy; at most, she can tolerate a distant view of a hamlet. We may judge, therefore, by the uneasiness and extra trouble which they gave to the parson, in what strength the fairies mustered at Domrémy, and, by a satisfactory consequence, how thinly sown with men and women must have been that region even in its inhabited spots. But the forests of Domrémy — those were the glories of the land: for in them abode mysterious powers and ancient secrets that towered into tragic strength. "Abbeys there were, and abbey windows" — "like Moorish temples of the Hindoos" — that exercised even princely power both in Lorraine and in the German Diets. These had their sweet bells that pierced the forests for many a league at matins or vespers, and each its own dreamy legend. Few enough, and scattered enough, were these abbeys, so as in no degree to disturb the deep solitude of the region; yet many enough to spread a network or awning of Christian sanctity over what else might have seemed a heathen wilderness. This sort of religious talisman being secured, a man the most afraid of ghosts (like myself, suppose, or the reader) becomes armed into courage to wander for days in their sylvan recesses. The mountains of the Vosges, on the eastern frontier of France, have never attracted much notice from Europe, except in 1813–14 for a few brief months, when they fell within Napoleon's line of defence against the Allies. But they are interesting for this among other features, that they do not, like some loftier ranges, repel woods; the forests and the hills are on sociable terms. "Live and let live" is their motto. For this reason, in part, these tracts in Lorraine were a favourite hunting-ground with the Carlovingian princes. About six hundred years before Joanna's childhood, Charlemagne was known to have hunted there. That, of itself, was a grand incident in the traditions of a forest or a chase. In these vast forests, also, were to be found (if anywhere to be found) those mysterious fawns that tempted solitary hunters into visionary and perilous pursuits. Here was seen (if anywhere seen) that ancient stag who was already nine hundred years old, but possibly a hundred or two more, when met by Charlemagne ; and the thing was put beyond doubt by the inscription upon his golden collar.   I believe Charlemagne knighted the stag ; and, if ever he is met again by a king, he ought to be made an earl, or, being upon the marches of France, a marquis.   Observe, I don't absolutely 5 vouch for all these things : my own opinion varies.   On a fine breezy forenoon I am audaciously sceptical ; but as twilight sets in my credulity grows steadily, till it becomes equal to anything that could be desired.   And I have heard candid sportsmen declare that, outside of these very forests, 10 they laughed loudly at all the dim tales connected with their haunted solitudes, but, on reaching a spot notoriously eighteen miles deep within them, they agreed with Sir Roger de Coverley that a good deal might be said on both sides. 15

Such traditions, or any others that (like the stag) connect distant generations with each other, are, for that cause, sublime ; and the sense of the shadowy, connected with such appearances that reveal themselves or not according to circumstances, leaves a colouring of sanctity over 20 ancient forests, even in those minds that utterly reject the legend as a fact.

But, apart from all distinct stories of that order, in any solitary frontier between two great empires — as here, for instance, or in the desert between Syria and the Euphrates 25 — there is an inevitable tendency, in minds of any deep sensibility, to people the solitudes with phantom images of powers that were of old so vast.   Joanna, therefore, in her quiet occupation of a shepherdess, would be led continually to brood over the political condition of her country by the 30 traditions of the past no less than by the mementoes of the local present.

M. Michelet, indeed, says that La Pucelle was *not* a shepherdess.   I beg his pardon ; she *was*.   What he rests upon I guess pretty well: it is the evidence of a woman called Haumette, the most confidential friend of Joanna. Now, she is a good witness, and a good girl, and I like her; for she makes a natural and affectionate report of Joanna's ordinary life. But still, however good she may be as a witness, Joanna is better; and she, when speaking to the dauphin, calls herself in the Latin report *Bergereta.* Even Haumette confesses that Joanna tended sheep in her girlhood. And I believe that, if Miss Haumette were taking coffee along with me this very evening (February 12, 1847) — in which there would be no subject for scandal or for maiden blushes, because I am an intense philosopher, and Miss H. would be hard upon 450 years old — she would admit the following comment upon her evidence to be right. A Frenchman, about forty years ago — M. Simond, in his "Travels" — mentions accidentally the following hideous scene as one steadily observed and watched by himself in chivalrous France not very long before the French Revolution: A peasant was plowing; and the team that drew his plow was a donkey and a woman. Both were regularly harnessed; both pulled alike. This is bad enough; but the Frenchman adds that, in distributing his lashes, the peasant was obviously desirous of being impartial; or, if either of the yokefellows had a right to complain, certainly it was not the donkey. Now, in any country where such degradation of females could be tolerated by the state of manners, a woman of delicacy would shrink from acknowledging, either for herself or her friend, that she had ever been addicted to any mode of labour not strictly domestic; because, if once owning herself a prædial servant, she would be sensible that this confession extended by probability in the hearer's thoughts to the having incurred indignities of this horrible kind. Haumette clearly thinks it more dignified for Joanna to have been darning the stockings of her horny-hoofed father, M. D'Arc, than keeping sheep, lest she might then be suspected of having ever done something worse. But, luckily, there was no danger of *that*: Joanna never was in service; and my opinion is that her father should have mended his own stockings, since probably he was the party to make the holes in them, as many a better man than D'Arc does — meaning by *that* not myself, because, though probably a better man than D'Arc, I protest against doing anything of the kind. If I lived even with Friday in Juan Fernandez, either Friday must do all the darning, or else it must go undone. The better men that I meant were the sailors in the British navy, every man of whom mends his own stockings. Who else is to do it? Do you suppose, reader, that the junior lords of the admiralty are under articles to darn for the navy?

The reason, meantime, for my systematic hatred of D'Arc is this: There was a story current in France before the Revolution, framed to ridicule the pauper aristocracy, who happened to have long pedigrees and short rent rolls : viz., that a head of such a house, dating from the Crusades, was overheard saying to his son, a Chevalier of St. Louis, " *Chevalier, as-tu donné au cochon à manger?*" Now, it is clearly made out by the surviving evidence that D'Arc would much have preferred continuing to say, " *Ma fille, as-tu donné au cochon à manger?*" to saying, " *Pucelle d'Orléans, as-tu sauvé les fleurs-de-lys?*" There is an old English copy of verses which argues thus:

> " If the man that turnips cries
> Cry not when his father dies,
> Then 'tis plain the man had rather
> Have a turnip than his father."

I cannot say that the logic of these verses was ever *entirely* to my satisfaction. I do not see my way through it as clearly as could be wished. But I see my way most clearly through D'Arc; and the result is — that he would greatly have preferred not merely a turnip to his father, but the saving a pound or so of bacon to saving the Oriflamme of France.

It is probable (as M. Michelet suggests) that the title of Virgin or Pucelle had in itself, and apart from the miraculous stories about her, a secret power over the rude soldiery and partisan chiefs of that period; for in such a person they saw a representative manifestation of the Virgin Mary, who, in a course of centuries, had grown steadily upon the popular heart.

As to Joanna's supernatural detection of the dauphin (Charles VII) among three hundred lords and knights, I am surprised at the credulity which could ever lend itself to that theatrical juggle. Who admires more than myself the sublime enthusiasm, the rapturous faith in herself, of this pure creature? But I am far from admiring stage artifices which not La Pucelle, but the court, must have arranged; nor can surrender myself to the conjurer's leger-demain, such as may be seen every day for a shilling. Southey's "Joan of Arc" was published in 1796. Twenty years after, talking with Southey, I was surprised to find him still owning a secret bias in favor of Joan, founded on her detection of the dauphin. The story, for the benefit of the reader new to the case, was this: La Pucelle was first made known to the dauphin, and presented to his court, at Chinon; and here came her first trial. By way of testing her supernatural pretensions, she was to find out the royal personage amongst the whole ark of clean and unclean creatures. Failing in this *coup d'essai*, she would not simply disappoint many a beating heart in the glittering crowd that on different motives yearned for her success, but she would ruin herself, and, as the oracle within had told her, would, by ruining herself, ruin France. Our own Sovereign Lady Victoria rehearses annually a trial not so severe in degree, but the same in kind. She "pricks" for sheriffs. Joanna pricked for a king. But observe the difference: our own Lady pricks for two men out of three; 5 Joanna for one man out of three hundred. Happy Lady of the Islands and the Orient! — she *can* go astray in her choice only by one-half: to the extent of one-half she *must* have the satisfaction of being right. And yet, even with these tight limits to the misery of a boundless discretion, 10 permit me, Liege Lady, with all loyalty, to submit that now and then you prick with your pin the wrong man. But the poor child from Domrémy, shrinking under the gaze of a dazzling court — not *because* dazzling (for in visions she had seen those that were more so), but because 15 some of them wore a scoffing smile on their features — how should *she* throw her line into so deep a river to angle for a king, where many a gay creature was sporting that masqueraded as kings in dress! Nay, even more than any true king would have done: for, in Southey's version of 20 the story, the dauphin says, by way of trying the virgin's magnetic sympathy with royalty,

> "On the throne,
> I the while mingling with the menial throng,
> Some courtier shall be seated."
>
> 25

This usurper is even crowned: "the jeweled crown shines on a menial's head." But, really, that is "*un peu fort*"; and the mob of spectators might raise a scruple whether our friend the jackdaw upon the throne, and the dauphin himself, were not grazing the shins of treason. For the dau- 30 phin could not lend more than belonged to him. According to the popular notion, he had no crown for himself; consequently none to lend, on any pretence whatever, until

the consecrated Maid should take him to Rheims. This
was the *popular* notion in France. But certainly it was
the dauphin's interest to support the popular notion, as he
meant to use the services of Joanna. For if he were king
already, what was it that she could do for him beyond
Orléans? That is to say, what more than a merely *military*
service could she render him? And, above all, if he were
king without a coronation, and without the oil from the
sacred ampulla, what advantage was yet open to him by
celerity above his competitor, the English boy? Now was
to be a race for a coronation: he that should win *that*
race carried the superstition of France along with him: he
that should first be drawn from the ovens of Rheims was
under that superstition baked into a king.

La Pucelle, before she could be allowed to practise as a
warrior, was put through her manual and platoon exercise,
as a pupil in divinity, at the bar of six eminent men in
wigs. According to Southey (v. 393, bk. iii., in the original
edition of his "Joan of Arc,") she "appalled the doctors."
It's not easy to do *that:* but they had some reason to feel
bothered, as that surgeon would assuredly feel bothered
who, upon proceeding to dissect a subject, should find the
subject retaliating as a dissector upon himself, especially
if Joanna ever made the speech to them which occupies
v. 354–391, bk. iii. It is a double impossibility: 1st,
because a piracy from Tindal's "Christianity as old as the
Creation" — a piracy *a parte ante,* and by three centuries;
2d, it is quite contrary to the evidence on Joanna's trial.
Southey's "Joan" of A.D. 1796 (Cottle, Bristol) tells the
doctors, among other secrets, that she never in her life
attended — 1st, Mass; nor 2d, the Sacramental Table; nor
3d, Confession. In the meantime, all this deistical confession of Joanna's, besides being suicidal for the interest
of her cause, is opposed to the depositions upon *both* trials.

The very best witness called from first to last deposes that Joanna attended these rites of her Church even too often; was taxed with doing so; and, by blushing, owned the charge as a fact, though certainly not as a fault. Joanna was a girl of natural piety, that saw God in forests and hills and fountains, but did not the less seek him in chapels and consecrated oratories.

This peasant girl was self-educated through her own natural meditativeness. If the reader turns to that divine passage in "Paradise Regained" which Milton has put into the mouth of our Saviour when first entering the wilderness, and musing upon the tendency of those great impulses growing within himself——

> " Oh, what a multitude of thoughts at once
>   Awakened in me swarm, while I consider
>   What from within I feel myself, and hear
>   What from without comes often to my ears,
>   Ill sorting with my present state compared !
>   When I was yet a child, no childish play
>   To me was pleasing; all my mind was set
>   Serious to learn and know, and thence to do,
>   What might be public good; myself I thought
>   Born to that end—— "

ne will have some notion of the vast reveries which brooded over the heart of Joanna in early girlhood, when the wings were budding that should carry her from Orléans to Rheims; when the golden chariot was dimly revealing itself that should carry her from the kingdom of *France Delivered* to the Eternal Kingdom.

It is not requisite for the honour of Joanna, nor is there in this place room, to pursue her brief career of *action*. That, though wonderful, forms the earthly part of her story; the spiritual part is the saintly passion of her

imprisonment, trial, and execution. It is unfortunate, therefore, for Southey's "Joan of Arc" (which, however, should
always be regarded as a *juvenile* effort), that precisely when
her real glory begins the poem ends. But this limitation
5 of the interest grew, no doubt, from the constraint insep-
arably attached to the law of epic unity. Joanna's history
bisects into two opposite hemispheres, and both could not
have been presented to the eye in one poem, unless by sac-
rificing all unity of theme, or else by involving the earlier
10 half, as a narrative episode, in the latter; which, however,
might have been done, for it might have been communicated to a fellow-prisoner, or a confessor, by Joanna herself.
It is sufficient, as concerns *this* section of Joanna's life, to
say that she fulfilled, to the height of her promises, the
15 restoration of the prostrate throne. France had become
a province of England, and for the ruin of both, if such a
yoke could be maintained. Dreadful pecuniary exhaustion
caused the English energy to droop; and that critical
opening La Pucelle used with a corresponding felicity of
20 audacity and suddenness (that were in themselves porten-
tous) for introducing the wedge of French native resources,
for rekindling the national pride, and for planting the dauphin once more upon his feet. When Joanna appeared, he
had been on the point of giving up the struggle with the
25 English, distressed as they were, and of flying to the
south of France. She taught him to blush for such abject
counsels. She liberated Orleans, that great city, so decisive by its fate for the issue of the war, and then beleaguered
by the English with an elaborate application of engineer-
30 ing skill unprecedented in Europe. Entering the city after
sunset on the 29th of April, she sang mass on Sunday, May
8th, for the entire disappearance of the besieging force.
On the 29th of June she fought and gained over the English
the decisive battle of Patay; on the 9th of July she took

Troyes by a *coup-de-main* from a mixed garrison of English and Burgundians; on the 15th of that month she carried the dauphin into Rheims; on Sunday the 17th she crowned him; and there she rested from her labour of triumph. All that was to be *done* she had now accomplished; what remained was — to *suffer*.

All this forward movement was her own; excepting one man, the whole council was against her. Her enemies were all that drew power from earth. Her supporters were her own strong enthusiasm, and the headlong contagion by which she carried this sublime frenzy into the hearts of women, of soldiers, and of all who lived by labour. Henceforward she was thwarted; and the worst error that she committed was to lend the sanction of her presence to counsels which she had ceased to approve. But she had now accomplished the capital objects which her own visions had dictated. These involved all the rest. Errors were now less important; and doubtless it had now become more difficult for herself to pronounce authentically what *were* errors. The noble girl had achieved, as by a rapture of motion, the capital end of clearing out a free space around her sovereign, giving him the power to move his arms with effect, and, secondly, the inappreciable end of winning for that sovereign what seemed to all France the heavenly ratification of his rights, by crowning him with the ancient solemnities. She had made it impossible for the English now to step before her. They were caught in an irretrievable blunder, owing partly to discord among the uncles of Henry VI, partly to a want of funds, but partly to the very impossibility which they believed to press with tenfold force upon any French attempt to forestall theirs. They laughed at such a thought; and, while they laughed, she *did* it. Henceforth the single redress for the English of this capital oversight, but which never

could have redressed it effectually, was to vitiate and taint
the coronation of Charles VII as the work of a witch.
That policy, and not malice (as M. Michelet is so happy
to believe), was the moving principle in the subsequent
5 prosecution of Joanna.   Unless they unhinged the force of
the first coronation in the popular mind by associating
it with power given from hell, they felt that the sceptre of
the invader was broken.

But she, the child that, at nineteen, had wrought wonders
10 so great for France, was she not elated ?   Did she not lose,
as men so often *have* lost, all sobriety of mind when standing upon the pinnacle of success so giddy?   Let her
enemies declare.   During the progress of her movement,
and in the centre of ferocious struggles, she had mani-
15 fested the temper of her feelings by the pity which she
had everywhere expressed for the suffering enemy.   She
forwarded to the English leaders a touching invitation
to unite with the French, as brothers, in a common cru-
sade against infidels — thus opening the road for a soldierly
20 retreat.   She interposed to protect the captive or the
wounded ; she mourned over the excesses of her countrymen ; she threw herself off her horse to kneel by the
dying English soldier, and to comfort him with such ministrations, physical or spiritual, as his situation allowed.
25 "Nolebat," says the evidence, "uti ense suo, aut quem-
quam interficere."   She sheltered the English that invoked
her aid in her own quarters.   She wept as she beheld,
stretched on the field of battle, so many brave enemies
that had died without confession.   And, as regarded her-
30 self, her elation expressed itself thus: on the day when she
had finished her work, she wept ; for she knew that, when
her *triumphal* task was done, her end must be approaching.   Her aspirations pointed only to a place which seemed
to her more than usually full of natural piety, as one in

which it would give her pleasure to die. And she uttered, between smiles and tears, as a wish that inexpressibly fascinated her heart, and yet was half fantastic, a broken prayer that God would return her to the solitudes from which he had drawn her, and suffer her to become a shepherdess once more. It was a natural prayer, because nature has laid a necessity upon every human heart to seek for rest and to shrink from torment. Yet, again, it was a half-fantastic prayer, because, from childhood upward, visions that she had no power to mistrust, and the voices which sounded in her ear for ever, had long since persuaded her mind that for *her* no such prayer could be granted. Too well she felt that her mission must be worked out to the end, and that the end was now at hand. All went wrong from this time. She herself had created the *funds* out of which the French restoration should grow; but she was not suffered to witness their development or their prosperous application. More than one military plan was entered upon which she did not approve. But she still continued to expose her person as before. Severe wounds had not taught her caution. And at length, in a sortie from Compiègne (whether through treacherous collusion on the part of her own friends is doubtful to this day), she was made prisoner by the Burgundians, and finally surrendered to the English.

Now came her trial. This trial, moving of course under English influence, was conducted in chief by the Bishop of Beauvais. He was a Frenchman, sold to English interests, and hoping, by favour of the English leaders, to reach the highest preferment. " Bishop that art, Archbishop that shalt be, Cardinal that mayest be," were the words that sounded continually in his ear; and doubtless a whisper of visions still higher, of a triple crown, and feet upon the necks of kings, sometimes stole into his heart. M. Michelet is anxious to keep us in mind that this bishop was but an agent of the English. True. But it does not better the case for his countryman that, being an accomplice in the crime, making himself the leader in the persecution against the helpless girl, he was willing to be all this in the spirit, and with the conscious vileness of a cat's-paw. Never from the foundations of the earth was there such a trial as this, if it were laid open in all its beauty of defence and all its hellishness of attack. Oh, child of France! shepherdess, peasant girl! trodden under foot by all around thee, how I honour thy flashing intellect, quick as God's lightning, and true as God's lightning to its mark, that ran before France and laggard Europe by many a century, confounding the malice of the ensnarer, and making dumb the oracles of falsehood! Is it not scandalous, is it not humiliating to civilization, that, even at this day, France exhibits the horrid spectacle of judges examining the prisoner against himself; seducing him, by fraud, into treacherous conclusions against his own head; using the terrors of their power for extorting confessions from the frailty of hope; nay (which is worse), using the blandishments of condescension and snaky kindness for thawing into compliances of gratitude those whom they had failed to freeze into terror? Wicked judges! barbarian jurisprudence!—that, sitting in your own conceit on the summits of social wisdom, have yet failed to learn the first principles of criminal justice—sit ye humbly and with docility at the feet of this girl from Domrémy, that tore your webs of cruelty into shreds and dust. "Would you examine me as a witness against myself?" was the question by which many times she defied their arts. Continually she showed that their interrogations were irrelevant to any business before the court, or that entered into the ridiculous charges against her. General questions were proposed to her on points of casuistical

divinity; two-edged questions, which not one of themselves could have answered, without, on the one side, land-
ing himself in heresy (as then interpreted), or, on the
other, in some presumptuous expression of self-esteem.
Next came a wretched Dominican, that pressed her with 5
an objection, which, if applied to the Bible, would tax
every one of its miracles with unsoundness. The monk
had the excuse of never having read the Bible. M. Michelet
has no such excuse; and it makes one blush for him, as a
philosopher, to find him describing such an argument as 10
"weighty," whereas it is but a varied expression of rude
Mahometan metaphysics. Her answer to this, if there
were room to place the whole in a clear light, was as shattering as it was rapid. Another thought to entrap her by
asking what language the angelic visitors of her solitude 15
had talked — as though heavenly counsels could want
polyglot interpreters for every word, or that God needed
language at all in whispering thoughts to a human heart.
Then came a worse devil, who asked her whether the Arch-
angel Michael had appeared naked. Not comprehending 20
the vile insinuation, Joanna, whose poverty suggested to her
simplicity that it might be the *costliness* of suitable robes
which caused the demur, asked them if they fancied God,
who clothed the flowers of the valleys, unable to find
raiment for his servants. The answer of Joanna moves a 25
smile of tenderness, but the disappointment of her judges
makes one laugh exultingly. Others succeeded by troops,
who upbraided her with leaving her father; as if that greater
Father, whom she believed herself to have been serving, did
not retain the power of dispensing with his own rules, or 30
had not said that for a less cause than martyrdom man and
woman should leave both father and mother.

On Easter Sunday, when the trial had been long proceeding, the poor girl fell so ill as to cause a belief that

she had been poisoned. It was not poison. Nobody had any interest in hastening a death so certain. M. Michelet, whose sympathies with all feelings are so quick that one would gladly see them always as justly directed, reads the case most truly. Joanna had a twofold malady. She was visited by a paroxysm of the complaint called *homesickness*. The cruel nature of her imprisonment, and its length, could not but point her solitary thoughts, in darkness and in chains (for chained she was), to Domrémy. And the season, which was the most heavenly period of the spring, added stings to this yearning. That was one of her maladies — *nostalgia*, as medicine calls it; the other was weariness and exhaustion from daily combats with malice. She saw that everybody hated her and thirsted for her blood; nay, many kind-hearted creatures that would have pitied her profoundly, as regarded all political charges, had their natural feelings warped by the belief that she had dealings with fiendish powers. She knew she was to die; that was *not* the misery! the misery was that this consummation could not be reached without so much intermediate strife, as if she were contending for some chance (where chance was none) of happiness, or were dreaming for a moment of escaping the inevitable. Why, then, *did* she contend? Knowing that she would reap nothing from answering her persecutors, why did she not retire by silence from the superfluous contest? It was because her quick and eager loyalty to truth would not suffer her to see it darkened by frauds which *she* could expose, but others, even of candid listeners, perhaps, could not; it was through that imperishable grandeur of soul which taught her to submit meekly and without a struggle to her punishment, but taught her *not* to submit — no, not for a moment — to calumny as to facts, or to misconstruction as to motives. Besides, there were secretaries all around the court taking down her words.

That was meant for no good to *her*. But the end does not always correspond to the meaning. And Joanna might say to herself, " These words that will be used against me to-morrow and the next day, perhaps, in some nobler generation, may rise again for my justification." Yes, Joanna, they *are* rising 5 even now in Paris, and for more than justification !

Woman, sister, there are some things which you do not execute as well as your brother, man ; no, nor ever will. Pardon me if I doubt whether you will ever produce a great poet from your choirs, or a Mozart, or a Phidias, or 10 a Michael Angelo, or a great philosopher, or a great scholar. By which last is meant — not one who depends simply on an infinite memory, but also on an infinite and electrical power of combination ; bringing together from the four winds, like the angel of the resurrection, what else were 15 dust from dead men's bones, into the unity of breathing life. If you *can* create yourselves into any of these great creators, why have you not ?

Yet, sister woman, though I cannot consent to find a Mozart or a Michael Angelo in your sex, cheerfully, and 20 with the love that burns in depths of admiration, I acknowledge that you can do one thing as well as the best of us men — a greater thing than even Milton is known to have done, or Michael Angelo ; you can die grandly, and as goddesses would die, were goddesses mortal. If any dis- 25 tant worlds (which *may* be the case) are so far ahead of us Tellurians in optical resources as to see distinctly through their telescopes all that we do on earth, what is the grandest sight to which we ever treat them ? St. Peter's at Rome, do you fancy, on Easter Sunday, or Luxor, or 30 perhaps the Himalayas ? Oh, no ! my friend ; suggest something better ; these are baubles to *them ;* they see in other worlds, in their own, far better toys of the same kind. These, take my word for it, are nothing. Do you give it

up? The finest thing, then, we have to show them is a
scaffold on the morning of execution. I assure you there
is a strong muster in those far telescopic worlds, on any
such morning, of those who happen to find themselves
5 occupying the right hemisphere for a peep at *us*. How,
then, if it be announced in some such telescopic world by
those who make a livelihood of catching glimpses at our
newspapers, whose language they have long since deciphered, that the poor victim in the morning's sacrifice is a
10 woman? How, if it be published in that distant world
that the sufferer wears upon her head, in the eyes of many,
the garlands of martyrdom? How, if it should be some
Marie Antoinette, the widowed queen, coming forward on
the scaffold, and presenting to the morning air her head,
15 turned gray by sorrow — daughter of Cæsars kneeling down
humbly to kiss the guillotine, as one that worships death?
How, if it were the noble Charlotte Corday, that in the
bloom of youth, that with the loveliest of persons, that
with homage waiting upon her smiles wherever she turned
20 her face to scatter them — homage that followed those
smiles as surely as the carols of birds, after showers in
spring, follow the reappearing sun and the racing of sun-
beams over the hills — yet thought all these things cheaper
than the dust upon her sandals, in comparison of deliver-
25 ance from hell for her dear suffering France! Ah! these
were spectacles indeed for those sympathising people in
distant worlds; and some, perhaps, would suffer a sort of
martyrdom themselves, because they could not testify their
wrath, could not bear witness to the strength of love and to
30 the fury of hatred that burned within them at such scenes,
could not gather into golden urns some of that glorious
dust which rested in the catacombs of earth.

On the Wednesday after Trinity Sunday in 1431, being
then about nineteen years of age, the Maid of Arc under-

went her martyrdom. She was conducted before mid-day, guarded by eight hundred spearmen, to a platform of pro-digious height, constructed of wooden billets supported by occasional walls of lath and plaster, and traversed by hollow spaces in every direction for the creation of air currents. 5 The pile "struck terror," says M. Michelet, "by its height"; and, as usual, the English purpose in this is viewed as one of pure malignity. But there are two ways of explaining all that. It is probable that the purpose was merciful. On the circumstances of the execution I shall not linger. 10 Yet, to mark the almost fatal felicity of M. Michelet in finding out whatever may injure the English name, at a moment when every reader will be interested in Joanna's personal appearance, it is really edifying to notice the inge-nuity by which he draws into light from a dark corner a 15 very unjust account of it, and neglects, though lying upon the highroad, a very pleasing one. Both are from English pens. Grafton, a chronicler, but little read, being a stiff-necked John Bull, thought fit to say that no wonder Joanna should be a virgin, since her "foule face" was a satis- 20 factory solution of that particular merit. Holinshead, on the other hand, a chronicler somewhat later, every way more important, and at one time universally read, has given a very pleasing testimony to the interesting character of Joanna's person and engaging manners. Neither of these 25 men lived till the following century, so that personally this evidence is none at all. Grafton sullenly and carelessly believed as he wished to believe; Holinshead took pains to inquire, and reports undoubtedly the general impression of France. But I cite the case as illustrating M. Michelet's 30 candour.[1]

---

[1] Amongst the many ebullitions of M. Michelet's fury against us poor English are four which will be likely to amuse the reader; and they are the more conspicuous in collision with the justice which he

The circumstantial incidents of the execution, unless with more space than I can now command, I should be unwilling to relate. I should fear to injure, by imperfect report, a martyrdom which to myself appears so unspeak-
5 ably grand. Yet, for a purpose, pointing not at Joanna,

sometimes does us, and the very indignant admiration which, under some aspects, he grants to us.

1. Our English literature he admires with some gnashing of teeth. He pronounces it "fine and sombre," but, I lament to add, "skeptical, Judaic, Satanic — in a word, antichristian." That Lord Byron should figure as a member of this diabolical corporation will not surprise men. It *will* surprise them to hear that Milton is one of its Satanic leaders. Many are the generous and eloquent Frenchmen, besides Chateaubriand, who have, in the course of the last thirty years, nobly suspended their own burning nationality, in order to render a more rapturous homage at the feet of Milton ; and some of them have raised Milton almost to a level with angelic natures. Not one of them has thought of looking for him *below* the earth. As to Shakspere, M. Michelet detects in him a most extraordinary mare's nest. It is this : he does "not recollect to have seen the name of God" in any part of his works. On reading such words, it is natural to rub one's eyes, and suspect that all one has ever seen in this world may have been a pure ocular delusion. In particular, I begin myself to suspect that the word "*la gloire*" never occurs in any Parisian journal. "The great English nation," says M. Michelet, "has one immense profound vice" — to wit, "pride." Why, really, that may be true; but we have a neighbour not absolutely clear of an "immense profound vice," as like ours in colour and shape as cherry to cherry. In short, M. Michelet thinks us, by fits and starts, admirable — only that we are detestable ; and he would adore some of our authors, were it not that so intensely he could have wished to kick them.

2. M. Michelet thinks to lodge an arrow in our sides by a very odd remark upon Thomas à Kempis : which is, that a man of any conceivable European blood — a Finlander, suppose, or a Zantiote — might have written Tom ; only not an Englishman. Whether an Englishman could have forged Tom must remain a matter of doubt, unless the thing had been tried long ago. That problem was intercepted for ever by Tom's perverseness in choosing to manufacture himself. Yet, since nobody is better aware than M. Michelet that this very point of Kempis

but at M. Michelet — viz., to convince him that an Englishman is capable of thinking more highly of La Pucelle than
even her admiring countrymen — I shall, in parting, allude
to one or two traits in Joanna's demeanour on the scaffold,
and to one or two in that of the bystanders, which authorise   5

having manufactured Kempis is furiously and hopelessly litigated, three
or four nations claiming to have forged his work for him, the shocking
old doubt will raise its snaky head once more — whether this forger,
who rests in so much darkness, might not, after all, be of English
blood. Tom, it may be feared, is known to modern English literature
chiefly by an irreverent mention of his name in a line of Peter Pindar's
(Dr. Wolcot) fifty years back, where he is described as

> "Kempis Tom,
> Who clearly shows the way to Kingdom Come."

Few in these days can have read him, unless in the Methodist version of
John Wesley. Among those few, however, happens to be myself;
which arose from the accident of having, when a boy of eleven, received
a copy of the "De Imitatione Christi" as a bequest from a relation
who died very young; from which cause, and from the external pretti-
ness of the book — being a Glasgow reprint by the celebrated Foulis,
and gaily bound — I was induced to look into it, and finally read it
many times over, partly out of some sympathy which, even in those
days, I had with its simplicity and devotional fervour, but much more
from the savage delight I found in laughing at Tom's Latinity. *That,* I
freely grant to M. Michelet, is inimitable. Yet, after all, it is not certain whether the original *was* Latin. But, however *that* may have
been, if it is possible that M. Michelet * can be accurate in saying that
there are no less than *sixty* French versions (not editions, observe, but
separate versions) existing of the "De Imitatione," how prodigious

---

* "*If M. Michelet can be accurate*" : — However, on consideration, this statement
does not depend on Michelet. The bibliographer Barbier has absolutely *specified*
sixty in a separate dissertation, *soixante traductions*, among those even that have not
escaped the search. The Italian translations are said to be thirty. As to mere
editions, not counting the early MSS. for half a century before printing was introduced,
those in Latin amount to 2000, and those in French to 1000. Meantime, it is very clear
to me that this astonishing popularity, so entirely unparalleled in literature, could not
have existed except in Roman Catholic times, nor subsequently have lingered in any
Protestant land. It was the denial of Scripture fountains to thirsty lands which made
this slender rill of Scripture truth so passionately welcome.

me in questioning an opinion of his upon this martyr's firmness. The reader ought to be reminded that Joanna D'Arc
was subjected to an unusually unfair trial of opinion. Any
of the elder Christian martyrs had not much to fear of *per-*
5 *sonal* rancour. The martyr was chiefly regarded as the

must have been the adaptation of the book to the religious heart of the
fifteenth century! Excepting the Bible, but excepting *that* only in
Protestant lands, no book known to man has had the same distinction.
It is the most marvellous bibliographical fact on record.

3. Our English girls, it seems, are as faulty in one way as we English
males in another. None of us men could have written the *Opera Omnia*
of Mr. à Kempis; neither could any of our girls have assumed male
attire like La Pucelle. But why? Because, says Michelet, English
girls and German think so much of an indecorum. Well, that is a
good fault, generally speaking. But M. Michelet ought to have remembered a fact in the martyrologies which justifies both parties — the
French heroine for doing, and the general choir of English girls for
not doing. A female saint, specially renowned in France, had, for a
reason as weighty as Joanna's — viz., expressly to shield her modesty
among men — worn a male military harness. That reason and that
example authorised La Pucelle; but our English girls, as a body, have
seldom any such reason, and certainly no such saintly example, to
plead. This excuses *them*. Yet, still, if it is indispensable to the
national character that our young women should now and then trespass over the frontier of decorum, it then becomes a patriotic duty in
me to assure M. Michelet that we *have* such ardent females among us,
and in a long series; some detected in naval hospitals when too sick to
remember their disguise; some on fields of battle; multitudes never
detected at all; some only suspected; and others discharged without
noise by war offices and other absurd people. In our navy, both royal
and commercial, and generally from deep remembrances of slighted
love, women have sometimes served in disguise for many years, taking
contentedly their daily allowance of burgoo, biscuit, or cannon-balls —
anything, in short, digestible or indigestible, that it might please Providence to send. One thing, at least, is to their credit: never any of
these poor masks, with their deep silent remembrances, have been
detected through murmuring, or what is nautically understood by
"skulking." So, for once, M. Michelet has an *erratum* to enter upon
the fly-leaf of his book in presentation copies.

enemy of Cæsar; at times, also, where any knowledge of the Christian faith and morals existed, with the enmity that arises spontaneously in the worldly against the spiritual. But the martyr, though disloyal, was not supposed to be therefore anti-national; and still less was *individually* 5 hateful. What was hated (if anything) belonged to his class, not to himself separately. Now, Joanna, if hated at all, was hated personally, and in Rouen on national grounds.

4. But the last of these ebullitions is the most lively. We English, at Orleans, and after Orleans (which is not quite so extraordinary, if all were told), fled before the Maid of Arc. Yes, says M. Michelet, you *did:* deny it, if you can. Deny it, *mon cher?* I don't mean to deny it. Running away, in many cases, is a thing so excellent that no philosopher would, at times, condescend to adopt any other step. All of us nations in Europe, without one exception, have shown our philosophy in that way at times. Even people *"qui ne se rendent pas"* have deigned both to run and to shout, *"Sauve qui peut!"* at odd times of sunset; though, for my part, I have no pleasure in recalling unpleasant remembrances to brave men; and yet, really, being so philosophic, they ought *not* to be unpleasant. But the amusing feature in M. Michelet's reproach is the way in which he *improves* and varies against us the charge of running, as if he were singing a catch. Listen to him: They *"showed their backs,"* did these English. (Hip, hip, hurrah! three times three!) *"Behind good walls they let themselves be taken."* (Hip, hip! nine times nine!) They *"ran as fast as their legs could carry them."* (Hurrah! twenty-seven times twenty-seven!) They *"ran before a girl";* they did. (Hurrah! eighty-one times eighty-one!) This reminds one of criminal indictments on the old model in English courts, where (for fear the prisoner should escape) the crown lawyer varied the charge perhaps through forty counts. The law laid its guns so as to rake the accused at every possible angle. While the indictment was reading, he seemed a monster of crime in his own eyes; and yet, after all, the poor fellow had but committed one offence, and not always *that.* N. B. — Not having the French original at hand, I make my quotations from a friend's copy of Mr. Walter Kelly's translation; which seems to me faithful, spirited, and idiomatically English — liable, in fact, only to the single reproach of occasional provincialisms.

Hence there would be a certainty of calumny arising against *her* such as would not affect martyrs in general. That being the case, it would follow of necessity that some people would impute to her a willingness to recant. No
5 innocence could escape *that*. Now, had she really testified this willingness on the scaffold, it would have argued nothing at all but the weakness of a genial nature shrinking from the instant approach of torment. And those will often pity that weakness most who, in their own persons,
10 would yield to it least. Meantime, there never was a calumny uttered that drew less support from the recorded circumstances. It rests upon no *positive* testimony, and it has a weight of contradicting testimony to stem. And yet, strange to say, M. Michelet, who at times seems to
15 admire the Maid of Arc as much as I do, is the one sole writer among her *friends* who lends some countenance to this odious slander. His words are that, if she did not utter this word *recant* with her lips, she uttered it in her heart. "Whether she *said* the word is uncertain; but I
20 affirm that she *thought* it."

Now, I affirm that she did not; not in any sense of the word "*thought*" applicable to the case. Here is France calumniating La Pucelle; here is England defending her. M. Michelet can only mean that, on *a priori* principles,
25 every woman must be presumed liable to such a weakness; that Joanna was a woman; *ergo*, that she was liable to such a weakness. That is, he only supposes her to have uttered the word by an argument which presumes it impossible for anybody to have done otherwise. I, on the
30 contrary, throw the onus of the argument not on presumable tendencies of nature, but on the known facts of that morning's execution, as recorded by multitudes. What else, I demand, than mere weight of metal, absolute nobility of deportment, broke the vast line of battle then

arrayed against her? What else but her meek, saintly demeanour won, from the enemies that till now had believed her a witch, tears of rapturous admiration? "Ten thousand men," says M. Michelet himself — "ten thousand men wept"; and of these ten thousand the majority were political enemies knitted together by cords of superstition. What else was it but her constancy, united with her angelic gentleness, that drove the fanatic English soldier — who had sworn to throw a fagot on her scaffold as *his* tribute of abhorrence, that *did* so, that fulfilled his vow — suddenly to turn away à penitent for life, saying everywhere that he had seen a dove rising upon wings to heaven from the ashes where she had stood? What else drove the executioner to kneel at every shrine for pardon to *his* share in the tragedy? And, if all this were insufficient, then I cite the closing act of her life as valid on her behalf, were all other testimonies against her. The executioner had been directed to apply his torch from below. He did so. The fiery smoke rose upward in billowing volumes. A Dominican monk was then standing almost at her side. Wrapped up in his sublime office, he saw not the danger, but still persisted in his prayers. Even then, when the last enemy was racing up the fiery stairs to seize her, even at that moment did this noblest of girls think only for *him*, the one friend that would not forsake her, and not for herself; bidding him with her last breath to care for his own preservation, but to leave *her* to God. That girl, whose latest breath ascended in this sublime expression of self-oblivion, did not utter the word *recant* either with her lips or in her heart. No; she did not, though one should rise from the dead to swear it.

·   ·   ·   ·   ·   ·   ·

Bishop of Beauvais! thy victim died in fire upon a scaffold — thou upon a down bed. But, for the departing

minutes of life, both are oftentimes alike. At the farewell crisis, when the gates of death are opening, and flesh is resting from its struggles, oftentimes the tortured and the torturer have the same truce from carnal torment; both
5 sink together into sleep; together both sometimes kindle into dreams. When the mortal mists were gathering fast upon you two, bishop and shepherd girl — when the pavilions of life were closing up their shadowy curtains about you — let us try, through the gigantic glooms, to decipher
10 the flying features of your separate visions.

The shepherd girl that had delivered France — she, from her dungeon, she, from her baiting at the stake, she, from her duel with fire, as she entered her last dream — saw Domrémy, saw the fountain of Domrémy, saw the pomp of
15 forests in which her childhood had wandered. That Easter festival which man had denied to her languishing heart — that resurrection of springtime, which the darkness of dungeons had intercepted from *her*, hungering after the glorious liberty of forests — were by God given back into her hands
20 as jewels that had been stolen from her by robbers. With those, perhaps (for the minutes of dreams can stretch into ages), was given back to her by God the bliss of childhood. By special privilege for *her* might be created, in this farewell dream, a second childhood, innocent as the first; but
25 not, like *that*, sad with the gloom of a fearful mission in the rear. This mission had now been fulfilled. The storm was weathered; the skirts even of that mighty storm were drawing off. The blood that she was to reckon for had been exacted; the tears that she was to shed in secret had
30 been paid to the last. The hatred to herself in all eyes had been faced steadily, had been suffered, had been survived. And in her last fight upon the scaffold she had triumphed gloriously; victoriously she had tasted the stings of death. For all, except this comfort from her

farewell dream, she had died — died amid the tears of ten thousand enemies — died amid the drums and trumpets of armies — died amid peals redoubling upon peals, volleys upon volleys, from the saluting clarions of martyrs.

Bishop of Beauvais! because the guilt-burdened man is in dreams haunted and waylaid by the most frightful of his crimes, and because upon that fluctuating mirror — rising (like the mocking mirrors of *mirage* in Arabian deserts) from the fens of death — most of all are reflected the sweet countenances which the man has laid in ruins; therefore I know, bishop, that you also, entering your final dream, saw Domrémy. That fountain, of which the witnesses spoke so much, showed itself to your eyes in pure morning dews; but neither dews, nor the holy dawn, could cleanse away the bright spots of innocent blood upon its surface. By the fountain, bishop, you saw a woman seated, that hid her face. But, as *you* draw near, the woman raises her wasted features. Would Domrémy know them again for the features of her child? Ah, but *you* know them, bishop, well! Oh, mercy! what a groan was *that* which the servants, waiting outside the bishop's dream at his bedside, heard from his labouring heart, as at this moment he turned away from the fountain and the woman, seeking rest in the forests afar off. Yet not *so* to escape the woman, whom once again he must behold before he dies. In the forests to which he prays for pity, will he find a respite? What a tumult, what a gathering of feet is there! In glades where only wild deer should run armies and nations are assembling; towering in the fluctuating crowd are phantoms that belong to departed hours. There is the great English Prince, Regent of France. There is my Lord of Winchester, the princely cardinal, that died and made no sign. There is the bishop of Beauvais, clinging to the shelter of thickets. What building is that which hands so rapid are

raising? Is it a martyr's scaffold? Will they burn the child of Domrémy a second time? No; it is a tribunal that rises to the clouds; and two nations stand around it, waiting for a trial. Shall my Lord of Beauvais sit again
5 upon the judgment-seat, and again number the hours for the innocent? Ah, no! he is the prisoner at the bar. Already all is waiting: the mighty audience is gathered, the Court is hurrying to their seats, the witnesses are arrayed, the trumpets are sounding, the judge is taking his
10 place. Oh, but this is sudden! My lord, have you no counsel? "Counsel I have none; in heaven above, or on earth beneath, counsellor there is none now that would take a brief from *me:* all are silent." Is it, indeed, come to this? Alas! the time is short, the tumult is wondrous, the crowd
15 stretches away into infinity; but yet I will search in it for somebody to take your brief; I know of somebody that will be your counsel. Who is this that cometh from Domrémy? Who is she in bloody coronation robes from Rheims? Who is she that cometh with blackened flesh from walking the
20 furnaces of Rouen? This is she, the shepherd girl, counsellor that had none for herself, whom I choose, bishop, for yours. She it is, I engage, that shall take my lord's brief. She it is, bishop, that would plead for you; yes, bishop, *she*
— when heaven and earth are silent.

ON THE KNOCKING AT THE GATE IN
"MACBETH"

From my boyish days I had always felt a great perplexity on one point in "Macbeth." It was this : — the knocking at the gate which succeeds to the murder of Duncan produced to my feelings an effect for which I never could account. The effect was that it reflected back upon the murderer a 5 peculiar awfulness and a depth of solemnity ; yet, however obstinately I endeavoured with my understanding to comprehend this, for many years I never could see *why* it should produce such an effect.

Here I pause for one moment to exhort the reader never 10 to pay any attention to his understanding when it stands in opposition to any other faculty of his mind. The mere understanding, however useful and indispensable, is the meanest faculty in the human mind and the most to be distrusted ; and yet the great majority of people trust to 15 nothing else, — which may do for ordinary life, but not for philosophical purposes. Of this, out of ten thousand instances that I might produce, I will cite one. Ask of any person whatsoever who is not previously prepared for the demand by a knowledge of perspective, to draw in the 20 rudest way the commonest appearance which depends upon the laws of that science — as, for instance, to represent the effect of two walls standing at right angles to each other, or the appearance of the houses on each side of a street, as seen by a person looking down the street from one 25 extremity. Now, in all cases, unless the person has happened to observe in pictures how it is that artists produce

these effects, he will be utterly unable to make the smallest approximation to it.   Yet why?   For he has actually seen the effect every day of his life.   The reason is that he allows his understanding to overrule his eyes.   His under-
5 standing, which includes no intuitive knowledge of the laws of vision, can furnish him with no reason why a line which is known and can be proved to be a horizontal line should not *appear* a horizontal line : a line that made any angle with the perpendicular less than a right angle would seem
10 to him to indicate that his houses were all tumbling down together.   Accordingly he makes the line of his houses a horizontal line, and fails of course to produce the effect demanded.   Here then is one instance out of many, in which not only the understanding is allowed to overrule
15 the eyes, but where the understanding is positively allowed to obliterate the eyes, as it were ; for not only does the man believe the evidence of his understanding in opposition to that of his eyes, but (which is monstrous) the idiot is not aware that his eyes ever gave such evidence.   He does not
20 know that he has seen (and therefore *quoad* his conscious-ness has *not* seen) that which he *has* seen every day of his life.   But to return from this digression, — my understand-ing could furnish no reason why the knocking at the gate in "Macbeth" should produce any effect, direct or reflected.
25 In fact, my understanding said positively that it could *not* produce any effect.   But I knew better ; I felt that it did ; and I waited and clung to the problem until further knowl-edge should enable me to solve it.   At length, in 1812, Mr. Williams made his *début* on the stage of Ratcliffe Highway,
30 and executed those unparalleled murders which have pro-cured for him such a brilliant and undying reputation.   On which murders, by the way, I must observe, that in one respect they have had an ill effect, by making the connois-seur in murder very fastidious in his taste, and dissatisfied

with anything that has been since done in that line. All other murders look pale by the deep crimson of his; and, as an amateur once said to me in a querulous tone, "There has been absolutely nothing *doing* since his time, or nothing that's worth speaking of." But this is wrong, for it is unreasonable to expect all men to be great artists, and born with the genius of Mr. Williams. Now it will be remembered that in the first of these murders (that of the Marrs) the same incident (of a knocking at the door soon after the work of extermination was complete) did actually occur which the genius of Shakspere has invented; and all good judges, and the most eminent dilettanti, acknowledged the felicity of Shakspere's suggestion as soon as it was actually realised. Here then was a fresh proof that I had been right in relying on my own feeling in opposition to my understanding; and again I set myself to study the problem. At length I solved it to my own satisfaction; and my solution is this: — Murder, in ordinary cases, where the sympathy is wholly directed to the case of the murdered person, is an incident of coarse and vulgar horror; and for this reason — that it flings the interest exclusively upon the natural but ignoble instinct by which we cleave to life: an instinct which, as being indispensable to the primal law of self-preservation, is the same in kind (though different in degree) amongst all living creatures. This instinct, therefore, because it annihilates all distinctions, and degrades the greatest of men to the level of "the poor beetle that we tread on," exhibits human nature in its most abject and humiliating attitude. Such an attitude would little suit the purposes of the poet. What then must he do? He must throw the interest on the murderer. Our sympathy must be with *him* (of course I mean a sympathy of comprehension, a sympathy by which we enter into his feelings, and are made to understand them — not a sympathy of pity or

approbation).[1]   In the murdered person all strife of thought,
all flux and reflux of passion and of purpose, are crushed
by one overwhelming panic; the fear of instant death
smites him " with its petrific mace."   But in the murderer,
5 such a murderer as a poet will condescend to, there must
be raging some great storm of passion — jealousy, ambition,
vengeance, hatred — which will create a hell within him;
and into this hell we are to look.

In "Macbeth," for the sake of gratifying his own enormous
10 and teeming faculty of creation, Shakspere has introduced
two murderers : and, as usual in his hands, they are remarkably discriminated : but — though in Macbeth the strife
of mind is greater than in his wife, the tiger spirit not so
awake, and his feelings caught chiefly by contagion from
15 her — yet, as both were finally involved in the guilt of
murder, the murderous mind of necessity is finally to be
presumed in both.   This was to be expressed; and on its
own account, as well as to make it a more proportionable
antagonist to the unoffending nature of their victim, "the
20 gracious Duncan," and adequately to expound " the deep
damnation of his taking off," this was to be expressed with
peculiar energy.   We were to be made to feel that the
human nature — i.e., the divine nature of love and mercy,
spread through the hearts of all creatures, and seldom
25 utterly withdrawn from man — was gone, vanished, extinct,
and that the fiendish nature had taken its place.   And, as

---

[1] It seems almost ludicrous to guard and explain my use of a word
in a situation where it would naturally explain itself. But it has
become necessary to do so, in consequence of the unscholar-like use of
the word sympathy, at present so general, by which, instead of taking
it in its proper sense, as the act of reproducing in our minds the
feelings of another, whether for hatred, indignation, love, pity, or
approbation, it is made a mere synonyme of the word, pity; and
hence, instead of saying, " sympathy with another," many writers
adopt the monstrous barbarism of " sympathy for another."

this effect is marvellously accomplished in the *dialogues* and
soliloquies themselves, so it is finally consummated by the
expedient under consideration ; and it is to this that I now
solicit the reader's attention. If the reader has ever witnessed a wife, daughter, or sister, in a fainting fit, he may
chance to have observed that the most affecting moment
in such a spectacle is *that* in which a sigh and a stirring
announce the recommencement of suspended life. Or, if
the reader has ever been present in a vast metropolis on
the day when some great national idol was carried in
funeral pomp to his grave, and, chancing to walk near
the course through which it passed, has felt powerfully, in
the silence and desertion of the streets and in the stagnation of ordinary business, the deep interest which at that
moment was possessing the heart of man — if all at once
he should hear the death-like stillness broken up by the
sound of wheels rattling away from the scene, and making
known that the transitory vision was dissolved, he will be
aware that at no moment was his sense of the complete
suspension and pause in ordinary human concerns so full
and affecting as at that moment when the suspension
ceases, and the goings-on of human life are suddenly
resumed. All action in any direction is best expounded,
measured, and made apprehensible, by reaction. Now
apply this to the case in " Macbeth." Here, as I have said,
the retiring of the human heart and the entrance of the
fiendish heart was to be expressed and made sensible.
Another world has stepped in ; and the murderers are
taken out of the region of human things, human purposes,
human desires. They are transfigured : Lady Macbeth
is "unsexed "; Macbeth has forgot that he was born of
woman ; both are conformed to the image of devils ; and
the world of devils is suddenly revealed. But how shall
this be conveyed and made palpable ? In order that a new

world may step in, this world must for a time disappear. The murderers, and the murder, must be insulated — cut off by an immeasurable gulf from the ordinary tide and succession of human affairs — locked up and sequestered

5 in some deep recess; we must be made sensible that the world of ordinary life is suddenly arrested — laid asleep — tranced — racked into a dread armistice; time must be annihilated; relation to things without abolished; and all must pass self-withdrawn into a deep syncope and sus-

10 pension of earthly passion. Hence it is that, when the deed is done, when the work of darkness is perfect, then the world of darkness passes away like a pageantry in the clouds: the knocking at the gate is heard, and it makes known audibly that the reaction has commenced; the

15 human has made its reflux upon the fiendish: the pulses of life are beginning to beat again; and the re-establish-ment of the goings-on of the world in which we live first makes us profoundly sensible of the awful parenthesis that had suspended them.

20   O mighty poet! Thy works are not as those of other men, simply and merely great works of art, but are also like the phenomena of nature, like the sun and the sea, the stars and the flowers, like frost and snow, rain and dew, hail-storm and thunder, which are to be studied

25 with entire submission of our own faculties, and in the perfect faith that in them there can be no too much or too little, nothing useless or inert, but that, the farther we press in our discoveries, the more we shall see proofs of design and self-supporting arrangement where the care-

30 less eye had seen nothing but accident!

NOTES

THE AFFLICTION OF CHILDHOOD

This selection is mainly a reproduction, with considerable alterations, of portions of the *Suspiria de Profundis* articles in *Blackwood* for 1845; but the last part of it is a revision of the beginning of the first autobiographic sketch in *Hogg's Instructor* and *Harper's Magazine* for January, 1851. The title is taken from *Blackwood*. Several pages of prefatory matter are omitted; our selection occupies pp. 32–49 in Vol. I of the *Works*, Masson's Ed., and pp. 32–51 in Vol. II of the Riverside Ed.

1 16. **My two eldest sisters.** De Quincey appends to the first paragraph (omitted) of this chapter of his autobiography the following note: " As occasions arise in these Sketches, when, merely for the purposes of intelligibility, it becomes requisite to call into notice such personal distinctions in my family as otherwise might be unimportant, I here record the entire list of my brothers and sisters, according to their order of succession; and Miltonically I include myself; having surely as much logical right to count myself in the series of my own brothers as Milton could have to pronounce Adam the goodliest of his own sons. [*Cf. Paradise Lost*, Book IV, lines 323–324: " Adam the goodliest man of men since born His sons."] First and last, we counted as eight children — *viz.*, four brothers and four sisters, though never counting more than six living at once — *viz.*, 1. *William*, older than myself by more than five years; 2. *Elizabeth*; 3. *Jane*, who died in her 4th year; 4. *Mary;* 5. myself, certainly not the goodliest man of men since born my brothers; 6. *Richard*, known to us all by the household name of *Pink*, who in his after years tilted up and down what might then be called his Britannic Majesty's Oceans (*viz.*, the Atlantic and Pacific) in the quality of midshipman, until Waterloo in one day put an extinguisher on that whole generation of midshipmen, by extinguishing all further call for their services; 7. a second *Jane;* 8. *Henry*, a posthumous child, who belonged to Brasenose College, Oxford, and died about his 26th year." But *cf.* next following note.

2 2. **She was three and a half, I one and a half.** "The same grave-stone, in St. Anne's Churchyard, Manchester, which recorded the date of the death of De Quincey's father in 1793, recorded the dates of the deaths of the two sisters. The words are : ' Also of Jane Quincey, daughter of Thomas and Elizabeth Quincey, born September 18, 1786, died March 1790. Also of Elizabeth Quincey, their daughter, who died June 2, 1792, aged 9 years.' If this is correct, De Quincey, though right in giving the age of his sister Jane, at the time of her death, as three and a half years, seems to be wrong in making her older than himself. She was younger than himself by a whole year, — he being in the fifth year of his age when she died. His memory here seems to have reversed their relations of age." — MASSON. Apart from the fact that De Quincey makes such mistakes as this elsewhere, there can be little doubt that he has made an error here. De Quincey was nearly seven when his sister Elizabeth died at the age of nine ; his sister Mary, who survived till 1821, was undoubtedly between Elizabeth and Thomas in age ; this makes it, without the testimony of the grave-stone, likely that Jane was a younger sister, and that her death occurred when De Quincey was four and a half years old. This conclusion adds greatly to the credibility of the narrative as a recollection of childhood.

3 4. **I had passed ... my childhood ... in a rural seclusion.** "De Quincey was born in Manchester on the 15th of August 1785, and was baptized on the 23d of September, as appears from the Register of Baptisms in St. Anne's Church of that city. ' September 23, Thomas, son of Thomas and Elizabeth Quincey,' is the record, showing that his surname in his infancy, and for an indefinite period afterwards, was simply Quincey. Though he was born, as he here distinctly tells us, *in* Manchester (particular street now unknown, though there have been attempts to identify it, and even the particular house in it), the fact, also distinctly mentioned here, that he spent all his infancy, after the first few weeks, in 'a rural seclusion' has to be borne in mind. Till 1791 the family residence was a rustic cottage, called *The Farm*, some little way out of Manchester ; after which it was *Greenhay*, a mansion or villa which his father had built about a mile out of Manchester, in what was then a rural suburb, though it has long been absorbed into the great town, and now forms a district of the town itself, called commonly *Greenheys*, derived by extension of the name apparently from its original application to one notable mansion. Biographers of De Quincey have till lately been strangely unanimous in the blunder of making him born at Greenhay, — a blunder from which even his

tombstone in St. Cuthbert's Churchyard, Edinburgh, is not free. 'Born at Greenhay, near Manchester,' is part of the inscription." — MASSON.

5 14. **"Love, the holy sense,"** etc. This is an earlier version of the lines in Wordsworth's *Tribute to the Memory of the Same Dog*:

> " For love, that comes wherever life and sense
> Are given by God, in thee was most intense."

5 27. **As near to nine years as I to six.** For *six* De Quincey should have written *seven*. See note 2 2. De Quincey's tendency throughout seems to be to exaggerate his youth at the time of these occurrences.

7 25. **Why death ... is more profoundly affecting in summer.** In the *Pains of Opium*, below, p. 247, De Quincey gives three reasons for this, of which that mentioned here is the last.

8 16. **Constitutionally touched with pensiveness.** An expression of great importance in De Quincey's biography. *Cf.* Introduction, p. xvii; also p. 213.

9 18. **Such a pretension had once been made for Jerusalem, and once for a Grecian city.** As to Jerusalem, *cf.* Ezekiel, v, 5. In the Church of the Holy Sepulchre, in the Catholicon or main Chapel of the Greeks, the exact centre of the world is still indicated by a rounded stone, covered with netting and lifted from the floor on a low stand. (See Wallace's *Jerusalem the Holy*.) Delphi, or rather the round stone on which the Pythian Apollo sat in the adytum of the Delphic temple, was called ὀμφαλός, as marking the middle point of the earth, first in Pindar, *Pythian Odes*, IV, 74 (131); VI, 3; in Æschylus, *Eumenides*, 40, 160, etc.

12 4. **Frost gathering frost, some Sarsar wind of death.** The word *Sarsar* is Arabic and is thus defined by Freytag, *Lexicon Arabico-Latinum*: "A cold, or, as others have it, a loudly-sounding wind." It also means (1) "extreme cold," and (2) "a loud noise." The present context of itself fixes the meaning here as "a cold wind." The word is found in no English dictionary, however, and some explanation is necessary of De Quincey's use of an Arabic term without the apology of italics, — the more since in a passage of the *Confessions* (p. 223), reprinted without change in 1856, he declares his utter ignorance of all Oriental tongues. The whole phrase, it appears, is a quotation from a contemporary. Southey, *Thalaba*, Book I, in a note on line 36, quotes Lamai, and says of a building, "the foundation is not good nor the walls sufficiently strong, so that Azrael can enter on every side and the Sarsar can easily pass through "; and this the poet works into the verse.

In line 44, however, occurs the undoubted original of De Quincey's whole phrase:

> " The Sarsar from its womb went forth,
>   The Icey wind of death ! "

I owe these references to Southey to the kindness of Prof. W. C. Thayer, of Lehigh University.

12 **31.** **Thy doom of endless sorrow.** There are several different legends of the "Wandering Jew." According to that which De Quincey adopts, he was a cobbler who refused Christ permission to rest at his house when our Lord was on his way to Calvary. The "words of Christ" were: "Thou shalt wander on the earth till I return." Since then the "everlasting Jew" has toiled from land to land, longing for the grave that is nowhere ready for him. The story has repeatedly been used in art and literature, notably in two novels of this century,—George Croly's *Salathiel* (1827) and Eugène Sue's *Le Juif Errant* (1844–45).

13 **2.** **The worm that could not die.** The last verse of Isaiah reads: "And they shall go forth, and look upon the carcases of the men that have transgressed against me : for their worm shall not die, neither shall their fire be quenched ; and they shall be an abhorring unto all flesh." *Cf.* Mark, ix, 44, 46, 48; also Milton, *Paradise Lost*, Book VI, line 739. This phrase seems to have taken hold of De Quincey's imagination; he uses it repeatedly.

15 **34.** **A girl . . . had opened to my thirst fountains of pure celestial love.** This passage, also, is of biographical interest, showing what elsewhere is attested, that De Quincey's mother did not occupy the place in his young life that naturally fell to her.

16 **19.** **The awful stillness, etc.** In *Notes for Suspiria* (*cf.* following note) De Quincey refers to Wordsworth's *Hartleap Well* and *The Danish Boy* as expressing this feeling.

18 **31.** **God speaks to children, etc.** This famous passage is the fitting culmination of the striking description of De Quincey's visions in the church. If we are to believe this account to be a pure recollection uninfluenced by subsequent experiences, then it is of course conclusive proof of De Quincey's claim — which, after all, except for the magnificence of his visions, is not remarkable — that his power to see visions and dream dreams antedated his acquaintance with opium. In the *Suspiria* recovered by Dr. Japp and reprinted by him in *De Quincey's Posthumous Works*, Vol. I, there is, pp. 13–15, a brief treatment of *The Solitude of Childhood :* "As nothing which is impassioned escapes the eye of poetry, neither has this escaped it — that there is, or may be,

through solitude, ' sublime attractions of the grave.' But even poetry
has not perceived that these attractions may arise for a child. Not
indeed a passion for the grave *as* the grave —from *that* a child revolts;
but a passion for the grave as the portal through which it may recover
some heavenly countenance, mother or sister, that has vanished," etc.
In the same piece he speaks of "the breathless, mysterious, Pan-like
silence that haunts the noon-day . . . If this dead silence haunted the
air, then the peace which was in nature echoed another peace which lay
in graves, and I fell into a sick languishing for things which a voice
from heaven seemed to say '*cannot* be granted.'" (*Cf.* below, p. 16,
lines 19 *et seq.*) In the *Notes for Suspiria*, printed by Dr. Japp,
pp. 27–28, there seem to be suggestions for the present passage.
"God takes care for the religion of little children wheresoever His
Christianity exists," the note begins; and then further on : "Even by
solitude does God speak to little children, when made vocal by the services of Christianity, as also he does by darkness wheresoever it is
peopled with visions of his almighty power." See also the first note
on the *Suspiria*, below, pp. 470–473.

19 1. **"Communion undisturbed."** *Cf.* Wordsworth's *Excursion*,
Book IV, near the beginning :

> " Thou, who didst wrap the cloud
> Of infancy around us, that thyself,
> Therein, with our simplicity awhile
> Might'st hold, on earth, communion undisturbed."

19 24. **Solitude . . . is the Agrippa's mirror of the unseen universe.** Cornelius Heinrich Agrippa von Nettesheim, born 1486, died
1535, was a nobleman, philosopher, and student of alchemy and magic.
He produced among other works a treatise *Concerning Occult Philosophy*.
He became doctor of divinity, law, and medicine; and later historiog-
rapher to the Emperor Charles V, at whose court he resided for some
time. A very good account of his fame and alleged marvellous deeds
is given by Nash in *The Unfortunate Traveller, or The Life of Jack
Wilton* (1594). Wilton, journeying towards Italy with his master, the
Earl of Surrey (the poet), found at Wittenberg "that abundant scholler
Cornelius Agrippa," who at that time "bare the fame to be the greatest
coniurer in Christendome." Having seen some instances of his skill,
they accompanied him on his return to the Emperor's court. There
" some courtiers to wearie out time woulde tell vs further tales of *Cornelius Agrippa*, and how when sir *Thomas Moore* our countrieman was
there, hee shewed him the whole destruction of Troy in a dreame.

How the Lorde *Cromwell* being the kings Embassadour there, in lyke case, in a perspectiue glasse he set before his eyes, King *Henrie* the eight with all his Lordes hunting in his forrest at Windsore.... To *Charles* the fifte then Emperour, they reported how he shewed the nine worthies, *Dauid, Salomon, Gedeon,* and the rest, in that similitude and lykenesse that they liued vpon earth. My master and I hauing by the high waie side gotten some reasonable familiarities with him, vpon this accesse of myracles imputed to him, resolued to request him something in our owne behalfes. I because I was his suborned Lorde and master [master and man had changed places for the nonce], desired him to see the liuely image of *Geraldine* his loue in the glasse, and what at that instant she did, and with whom shee was talking. Hee shewed her vs without more adoe, sicke weeping on her bedde, and resolued all into deuoute religion for the absence of her Lorde." — NASH's *Unfortunate Traveller*, ed. E. Gosse, London, 1892, pp. 86–90. For similar exhi- bitions of magic power, see the account of the exploits of Dr. Faustus before the great Emperor; *Faust Volksbuch,* 1587.

INTRODUCTION TO THE WORLD OF STRIFE

A recast, with abridgments and alterations, of the matter of a series of articles in *Hogg's Instructor* for 1851 and 1852, all under the title of "A Sketch from Childhood" (Masson). A portion of these articles appeared also in *Harper's Magazine,* January and February, 1851. This selection, which is practically a continuation of that preceding it, is found in *Works,* Masson's Ed., Vol. I, pp. 55–114; Riverside Ed., Vol. II, pp. 58–130.

21 2. **My sixth year.** Seventh. *Cf.* note 2 2.

21 17. **"Self-withdrawn into a wondrous depth."** From Words- worth's *Excursion,* Book II, near the end; for *wondrous* read *boundless. Cf.* pp. 242–243 and note 242 28.

22 15. **I have rendered solemn thanks.** See Riverside Ed., Vol. II, p. 32; Masson's Ed., Vol. I, p. 32.

22 17. **One such brother.** William Quincey. See note 1 16.

23 7. **Greenhay.** See note 3 4.

24 30. **The closing hour of his life.** Though De Quincey speaks of his father (concerning whom see Introduction, p. xvi) as having died "in his thirty-ninth year," the inscription on his tombstone in the church- yard of St. Anne's, Manchester, reads: "Thomas Quincey, merchant, who died July 18, 1793, aged 40 years."

25 5. **Riding in whirlwinds.** *Cf.* Addison's *Campaign*. After describing Marlborough's calm direction of the Battle of Blenheim the poet (lines 287–292) uses this comparison :

> "So when an angel by divine command
> With rising tempests shakes a guilty land,
> Such as of late o'er pale Britannia past,
> Calm and serene he drives the furious blast;
> And pleas'd the Almighty's orders to perform,
> Rides in the whirlwind, and directs the storm."

25 6. **Cloud-compelling Jove.** See *Iliad*, I, 511 ; *Odyssey*, I, 63.

25 8. **Grammar School of Louth.** The school at which, some twenty years later, Tennyson suffered for four years, under a "tempestuous, flogging master of the old stamp." "How I did hate that school!" he said later in life. "The only good I ever got from it was the memory of the words, 'sonus desilientis aquae,' and of an old wall covered with wild weeds opposite the school windows." — *Alfred Lord Tennyson. A Memoir by his Son*, Vol. I, p. 7.

25 13. **Public schools.** The great preparatory schools in England are so called, in distinction from the private schools, which are collections of a few pupils under the roof of a master who superintends their education. Cowper's *Tirocinium* (*tirocinium*, "first military service," from *tiro*, a "recruit"), *or A Review of Schools* (dated Nov. 6, 1784), was a long poem "recommending Private Tuition in preference to an Education at School." It is worth noting here that Professor Benham asserts that Cowper's life at Westminster School (one of the great public schools, founded by Henry VIII in Westminster Abbey) seems to have been a very happy one. *Cf.* Cowper's *Works* (ed. Benham), p. xxiv.

26 2. **His age the double of mine.** If De Quincey refers to the time of Elizabeth's death (June, 1792), as seems probable, this statement is unusually accurate.

26 13. **Cases . . . cited from comedy, of such a yearning after contempt, . . . tool of religious hypocrisy.** Professor Winchester suggests as a famous example — though not from comedy — Swift's *Tale of a Tub*, sec. 11.

26 18. **Latentis semita vitæ.** Horace, *Epistles*, I, 18, 103, has *fallentis semita vitae*, which is probably the passage in De Quincey's mind, though no variant *latentis* has been found. That word has like associations, however, elsewhere ; as Ovid, *Tristia*, III, 4, 25 : "Crede mihi, bene qui latuit, bene vixit."

29 6. **Departed to the bosom of Cinderella.** That is, burned to ashes. Cinderella (French *Cendrillon*) is the "ash-maiden." Perhaps a parody on "going to Abraham's bosom." *Cf.* Luke, xvi, 22.

29 12. **Solomon's signet-ring.** Solomon, no doubt because of the tales of his remarkable wisdom, became in time by repute a great magician. In particular the Arabians and afterward western nations told of the ring with which Solomon accomplished marvels in the suppression of wicked genii.

30 16. **A British surgeon.** I have expended much effort fruitlessly in endeavoring to locate this surgeon and his octavos. Who is he?

31 14. **My sister Mary.** This sister (see note 2 2) was married in 1819 to the Rev. Philip Serle, and died early in 1821, just before the appearance of her brother as author.

33 12. **The philosopher in "Rasselas."** In the beginning of Dr. Johnson's novel *Rasselas* (1759), the Prince of Abyssinia seeks to escape from the Happy Valley, in which he is confined in the midst of luxury. In Chap. VI one of the (mechanical) artists offers to teach the Prince to fly out of the Valley. "In a year the wings were finished ; and, on a morning appointed, the maker appeared furnished for flight on a little promontory : he waved his pinions awhile to gather air, then leaped from his stand, and in an instant dropped into the lake."

33 14. **"Revocare gradum," etc.** From Virgil, *Æneid*, VI, 128–129. Here again De Quincey seems to misquote; "hoc opus, hic labor est" is the only reading.

33 18. **Bishop Wilkins** (1614–72), Master of Trinity College, Cambridge, as well as Bishop of Chester, published, when he was but twenty-four years old, his *The Discovery of a New World; or, a Discourse tending to prove that it is probable there may be another habitable World in the Moon; with a Discourse concerning the possibility of a passage thither*. His writings are said to have aided greatly in spreading in England a belief in the Copernican system.

The Adventures of Peter Wilkins (1751), by Robert Paltock, brings a supernatural element into the *Robinson Crusoe* type of novel. The hero is brought among a race of human beings provided with wings, but otherwise not greatly differing from good English folk. The book was a favorite, alongside of Defoe's great work, with boys a hundred years ago. *Cf.* Raleigh's *English Novel*, p. 219.

34 5. **My next younger brother.** Richard Quincey, known in the household as "Pink," and "younger by about four years" than the writer. De Quincey writes of him as "My Brother." (See Riverside Ed., Vol. II, p. 332; Masson's Ed., Vol. I, p. 287.) He ran away from excessive flogging at school, went to sea, returned after a time, departed again, and finally died at the age of twenty-five, probably while on a hunting expedition in the Blue Mountains of Jamaica. But *cf.* De Quincey's footnote to the following paragraph.

34 27. **"Round-robin."** *Cf.* in Boswell's *Life*, Temple Ed., Vol. IV, p. 88, the round-robin addressed to Johnson concerning his epitaph on Goldsmith.

34 29. **Burke's phrase of " the swinish multitude."** In the *French Revolution* (*Select Works*, ed. Payne, Vol. II, p. 93): "Along with its natural protectors and guardians, learning will be cast into the mire, and trodden down under the hoofs of a swinish multitude." It seems that Burke was actually accused by his political opponents, on account of this phrase, of having said that the common people were no better than swine.

35 12. **"Sultan Selim" . . . "Sultan Amurath."** Selim III was Sultan of Turkey at this time. In 1792 he concluded peace with Austria and Russia, with which states he had been at war since his accession in 1789. The first Sultan Selim (1512–20) annexed Syria, Palestine, and Egypt to his dominions. Amurath I (1359–89) was the first of the Ottoman sultans to make conquests in Europe.

36 6. **Deucalion and Pyrrha.** Deucalion, a king of Phthia in Thessaly, and his wife Pyrrha having been saved from a general deluge renewed the race by throwing stones behind them, which became men and women according to the sex of the thrower. *Cf.* Ovid, *Metamorphoses*, I, 244 *et seq.* For a study of Flood Traditions, see Worcester, *Genesis in the Light of Modern Knowledge*, New York, 1901, pp. 360 *et seq.*

36 13. **An iron age.** *Cf.* Ovid, *Metamorphoses*, I, 89–150, where the four ages of man, golden, silver, brazen, and iron, are described. Hesiod, *Works and Days*, 109 *et seq.*, gives the same scheme with a heroic age, that of the Trojan War, interposed between the ages of brass and iron.

37 8. **Hot walls.** Walls enclosing hot-air flues, used to keep trees, etc., warm.

37 20. **The Rev. S. H.** See note 85 24 and p. 160, line 9, and note.

38 16. **Hessian boots.** Long boots, which first appeared as a part of the uniform of Hessian troops.

38 21. **Sansculottes . . . Jacobins.** The *Sansculottes* (lit. " without breeches," *i.e.*, wearing trousers instead of the aristocratic knee-breeches) of the French Revolution were the violent Republicans of the Paris mob. The Jacobins, the extreme party in republican France to which the *Sansculottes* attached themselves, took their names from the revolutionary Jacobin Society, organized in 1789, which in turn had been

named from its meeting place, an ancient convent of monks of St. Jacques, *i.e.*, Dominicans. The cries which De Quincey here mentions expressed the Tory or conservative sentiment in opposition to the sympathy felt by many Englishmen (often called *Jacobins*) for the French Revolution.

39 3. Tyrocinium. *Cf.* note 25 13.

39 6. "Bucks" . . . "dandies." In the eighteenth century, according to the *New English Dictionary*, *buck* "indicated rather the assumption of 'spirit' or gaiety of conduct than elegance of dress; the latter notion comes forward early in the present century." *Dandy* was "in use on the Scottish Border in the end of the eighteenth century; and about 1813–19 in vogue in London, for the 'exquisite' or 'swell' of the period." The origin of the word is still unknown; *Jack-a-dandy* is perhaps the full form, and it is worth notice that in Scotland, where the term arose, *Dandy* is a nickname for *Andrew*.

43 15. Dagon . . . Moloch. *Dagon* is mentioned in the Old Testament as the national god of the Philistines. See Judges, xvi, 23, and 1 Samuel, v. *Moloch* is referred to in 1 Kings, xi, 7. Human sacrifices were offered to him.

43 29. The Bridge of Sighs in Venice connects the ducal palace with the prisons; through its two enclosed passages prisoners were led for trial or judgment.

44, footnote. Jus postliminii is "the right of return behind one's threshold" (*post-limen*), hence "the right of recovery, reprisal."

46 12. The 5th of November. Guy Fawkes Day, when the discovery of the Gunpowder Plot, by which Fawkes and his accomplices would have blown up the Parliament on Nov. 5, 1605, is celebrated after the fashion of an American Fourth of July.

46 23. Some natural growls, etc. This parodies Milton, *Paradise Lost*, Book XII, line 645:

> "Some natural tears they dropp'd, but wip'd them soon."

46 25. "Of the sweeping whirlpool's sway," etc. The lines in Gray's *Bard* read:

> "Youth on the prow, and Pleasure at the helm;
> Regardless of the sweeping Whirlwind's sway,
> That, hush'd in grim repose, expects his evening-prey."

47 26. Preternaturally keen for flaws of language, etc. Here, as often, De Quincey makes his niceness in the choice of words the evidence of a care for accuracy of statement with which no candid reader can accredit him. *Cf.* following note.

48 24. **Von Troil's famous chapter on the snakes of Lapland.**
There is great confusion in this reference. In the first place, *Lapland* is
an error for *Iceland*. *Cf.* p. 285, and footnote, written some years before
the present passage. The *Letters on Iceland* (Pinkerton's *Voyages and
Travels*, Vol. I, p. 621), *containing observations . . . made during a voyage undertaken in the year 1772*, by Uno Von Troil, D.D., of Stockholm,
contains no chapter of the kind. Such a chapter had appeared, however, in N. Horrebow's (Danish, 1758) *Natural History of Iceland :*
"Chap. LXXII. *Concerning snakes.* No snakes of any kind are to be
met with throughout the whole island." In Boswell's *Johnson*, Vol. IV,
p. 314, Temple Ed., there is a much more correct allusion, which
may have been in De Quincey's mind : "Langton said very well to me
afterwards, that he could repeat Johnson's conversation before dinner,
as Johnson had said that he could repeat a complete chapter of
The Natural History of Iceland, from the Danish of Horrebow,
the whole of which was exactly thus : 'Chap. LXXII. *Concerning
Snakes.* There are no snakes to be met with throughout the whole
island.'"

49 5. **I was promoted to the rank of major-general.** Page (Japp)
prints from De Quincey's papers, in the *Life*, Vol. I, p. 30, a dialogue
between the "reverend guardian" (Samuel Hall) and the major-general
when under arrest.

51 17. **I make a wilderness, etc.** The speech of Calgacus to the
Caledonians, Tacitus, *Agricola*, 30, uses concerning the Romans this
famous phrase : " Atque ubi solitudinem faciunt, pacem appellant."

54 22. **Sir Ywain** was one of the knights of Arthur's court, who
was the subject of a romance by Chrétien de Troyes (*Chevalier au
Lyon*), afterwards reproduced in an English metrical romance, *Ywaine
and Gawin*, which De Quincey read, no doubt, in Joseph Ritson's
Ancient Engleish Metrical Romanceës, London, 1802. There lines 869–
878 (Vol. I, p. 37) are :

> " Now lat we the lady be,
> And of sir Ywaine speke we.
> Luf that es so mekil of mayne,
> Sar had wownded sir Ywayne,
> That whareso he sal ride or ga
> His hert sho has that es his fa,
> His hert he has set albydene
> Whar him self dar noght be sene ;
> Bot thus in langing bides he,
> And hopes that it sal better be."

54 28. **To walk penitentially through the Furcæ Caudinæ.** *Furcae Caudinae* is found in Lucan, *Pharsalia*, II, 138; Livy uses the diminutive *Furculae Caudinae*. *Furca* denotes literally a two-pronged fork, and the two passes in the mountains near Caudium were thought to resemble such a fork. Here the Romans were entrapped and defeated by the Samnites in 321 B.C. *Cf.* Mommsen, *History of Rome*, Vol. I, p. 471 (new ed.).

54 33. **"Delenda est Carthago!"** "Carthage must be destroyed!" *Delenda est Karthago* is the version of Florus (II, 15) of the words used by Cato the Censor, just before the Third Punic War, whenever he was called upon to record his vote in the Senate on any subject under discussion.

55 17. **Bulletin.** The word *bulletino, bolletine*, from the Italian, had been in use during the seventeenth century, but the earliest instances given by Murray of *bulletin* (from the French) are: (1) 1765, H. Walpole's *Correspondence*, where it means a statement as to health; and (2) 1791, Burke's *Appeal from the New to the Old Whigs*, where it appears in De Quincey's sense.

56 7. **My savage, Orson-like sincerity.** *Valentine and Orson* is one of the romances clustering about the Emperor Charlemagne, as the mediæval romancers knew him. The two were twins, born in a forest. Orson was carried off by a bear and became rough and uncouth, while Valentine was brought up as a courtier.

57 19. **Order of the Bath.** This Order is supposed to have been founded by Henry IV in 1399. The candidates were put into a bath the evening before their reception into the Order, to symbolize their purification from all stain. The present Order, however, was instituted by George I in 1725 and has been considerably extended since.

58 3. **Styan.** De Quincey's use of this archaic form of *sty* or *stye*, when it must have been long obsolete in literary English, is odd. Perhaps he was familiar with it as a dialectal form.

58 11. **My father's Portuguese recollections.** *Cf. ante*, p. 22.

58 23. **The Garter itself.** The Order of the Garter is the highest Order in Great Britain; it consists of the king and twenty-five knights companions, to which number may be added foreign sovereigns and occasionally extra companions. The garter is a band of blue velvet worn about the left leg. The motto of the Order is: "Honi soit qui mal y pense." It was instituted by Edward III between 1344 and 1350.

60 9. **Hartley Coleridge,** born 1796, died 1849, eldest son of S. T. Coleridge, was very interesting as a child, and was celebrated by his

father (Sonnets, Campbell's *Coleridge*, p. 66) and by Wordsworth (*To H. C. Six Years Old*) in verse; as a man he showed considerable poetical talent, and he was the best beloved of all the "Lakers"; but his life was an unfortunate one, on account of his exceptionally sensitive and indolent nature.

61 1. **As rigorously as ancient Rome through every century concealed her real name.** In Pliny's (A.D. 23–79) *Natural History*, Book III, Chap. IX, appears apparently for the first time the statement as to Rome's secret name. He says there that Valerius Soranus suffered death for divulging the name. He also speaks (XXVIII, 4) of the practice of "evocation" to which De Quincey refers in his footnote (which see) and of the necessity of keeping secret on this account the name of the tutelary deity of the city (not the name of the city). Plutarch, a generation later than Pliny, says in his *Roman Questions* (61) that Valerius Soranus was killed for divulging the name of the tutelary deity. Solinus (third century) in his *Collectanea*, I, 5, repeats Pliny's remarks. Macrobius (fifth century) in his *Saturnalia*, III, 9, speaks of the matter of "evocation," and concludes with the general statement that on this account the Romans do not wish to have their tutelary god or the Latin name of the city known. On this probably De Quincey's remark is based. The other name is said to have been *Valentia*.

63 27. **They would have been invaded and dragooned in a month.** *Dragoon* here seems to have its specific sense of "persecute by military force." At one time in France dragoons were quartered upon Protestants, with the purpose of persecuting them into a change of faith.

64 17. **"Uneasy lies the head," etc.** Shakspere, *2 Henry IV*, Act iii, sc. 1, line 31.

66 16. **This advocate, etc.** The following pages, 66–72, are a good example of De Quinceyan divagation; a second and longer digression begins at p. 74.

66 22. **Lord Monboddo.** James Burnett was born at Monboddo, Kincardineshire, 1714, died 1799. He published the first volume of his work *Of the Origin and Progress of Language* in 1773. The passage referred to is Vol. I, Book II, Chap. III, especially pp. 234–239.

67 3. **The Harveys of Lord Bristol's family.** See under "Hervey" in *Dictionary of National Biography*. Lord John Hervey (1696–1743), second son of the first Earl of Bristol, is the best known of the race; his wife was the famous court beauty, celebrated by Pope, Gay, and Voltaire, Mary Lepell. Lord John was a friend of Lady Mary Wortley

Montagu (*cf.* note 191 4), and with her suffered the hostility of Pope, who virulently attacked him (and not without retort): as "Narcissus" in the *Dunciad* (IV, 103); in the first *Satire*, as "Lord Fanny"; as "Sporus" in the *Epistle to Dr. Arbuthnot*, and as "H—vy" in the Epilogue to the *Satires;* not to mention his prose *Letter to a Noble Lord.*

69 5. **Birmingham counterfeit.** Birmingham became early the chief place of manufacture of cheap wares. Hence the name *Brummagem*, a vulgar pronunciation of the name of the city, has become in England a common name for cheap tawdry jewelry.

69 31. **The little skirmish, etc.** See Boswell, *Journal of a Tour to the Hebrides with Samuel Johnson, LL.D.*, Temple Ed., p. 61: "Lord Monboddo received us at his gate most courteously; pointed to the Douglas arms upon his house, and told us that his great-grandmother was of that family. 'In such houses (said he,) our ancestors lived, who were better men than we.'—'No, no, my lord (said Dr. Johnson). We are as strong as they, and a great deal wiser.'"

72 24. **Dr. Adam Clarke** (1762–1832) was a Methodist preacher, commentator, and voluminous theological writer, of high repute. His most important work was his *Holy Bible*, . . . *with a Commentary and Critical Notes* (1810–26, 8 vols.), in which, in a long note to Genesis, iii, 1, the opinion mentioned by De Quincey is stated.

74 27. **Pariahs.** The fate of social outcasts seems to have taken early and strong hold upon De Quincey's mind; one of the *Suspiria* was to have enlarged upon this theme. Strictly speaking, the Pariahs is that one of the lower castes of Hindu society of which foreigners have seen most; it is not in all districts the lowest caste, however.

76 24. **Police reports.** This highly characteristic passage should be compared with the quotation of Mr. Pollitt from De Quincey's editorial article in the *Westmoreland Gazette* for Aug. 8, 1818, note 340 2.

80 25. **Some avenging Tisiphone.** Tisiphone, the "Blood-avenger," was one of the Furies; the others were Alecto, the "Unceasing," and Megæra, the "Envious." These deities were called euphemistically *Eumenides*, the "Well-wishers." *Cf.* p. 196.

81 1. **Strulbrugs.** See Swift, *Gulliver's Travels*, Part III, Chap. X.

84 11. **Cassandra surveys the regal abode.** *Cf.* Æschylus, *Agamemnon*, 1072 *et seq.*

85 24. **These four were B., E., G., and H.** Mr. B. was a merchant, like De Quincey's father; Mr. E. was a rural magistrate, in a populous district close upon Manchester; these were both too busy to attend much to the children's affairs. Mr. G. was a banker in Lincolnshire.

To H., therefore, the Rev. Samuel Hall, with Mrs. de Quincey, fell the active charge of the children. S. H. was curate at Salford, practically a part of Manchester.

86 6. **Corelli . . . Jomelli . . . Cimarosa.** Arcangelo Corelli (1653–1713) was a celebrated Italian violin player and a composer for the violin. His first success was made at Paris at the age of nineteen. Niccolo Jomelli (1714–74) was another famous Italian composer; he produced several successful operas. Domenico Cimarosa (1749–1801), also an Italian, composed a very large number of dramatic pieces.

88 2. **Jacobins, but not the less Anti-Jacobins.** See note 38 21. These names were freely used in England for sympathizers with French revolutionary ideas, and their opponents. *The Anti-Jacobin*, a weekly, founded in 1797, was famous in the hands of Canning and Frere. There was also an *Anti-Jacobin Review*, which ran from 1798 to 1821.

88 2. **Every Calvinist, . . . every Arminian.** All Protestant opponents of Calvinism are often called Arminians. Strictly these latter are the followers of James Arminius, a divine of Leyden (1560–1609). The original Arminians separated from the Calvinists because of their objection to Calvin's doctrine of predestination.

90 13. **Cannæ.** A town in Apulia, Italy, where in 216 B.C. Hannibal, the great Carthaginian general, nearly annihilated the Roman army under Terentius Varro and Æmilius Paulus. The story of the battle is told by Livy in Book XXII of his history.

91 30. **Mr. de Loutherbourg.** Philip James de Loutherbourg (1740–1812) was a highly respected painter of landscape, marine pieces, etc., and a member of the Royal Academy. He was of German birth and Polish ancestry. He settled in London in 1771. Later, in 1783, he established himself at 13 Hammersmith Terrace, Chiswick (London). He now took up mysticism, mesmerism, and healing by prayer and faith. In 1794 he gave a special exhibition of his great battle-piece, "Earl Howe's Victory," which may have drawn the attention of the De Quinceys to him, if his faith cures did not.

92 10. **Carthaginian length.** The Punic wars (between Rome and Carthage) were begun in 264 B.C., and extended over a period of 118 years.

92 12. **"Hi motus animorum," etc.** "These stirrings of spirits and these mighty strifes, restrained by the throwing of a little dust, were quiet." Virgil, *Georgics*, IV, 86–87 (*quiescunt* for *quiêrunt*). The lines are mock-heroic where they originally stand.

A MEETING WITH LAMB

This selection is the first part of an article which appeared in *Tait's Magazine* for April and June, 1838, Vol. V. It is found in *Works*, Masson's Ed., Vol. III, pp. 34–44; Riverside Ed., Vol. III, pp. 64–76. For other personal recollections of Lamb and his contemporaries, see Mason's *Personal Traits of British Authors*, in one volume of which Wordsworth, Coleridge, and Lamb occupy pp. 1–173. *Cf.* also De Quincey's paper on Lamb, Masson's Ed., Vol. V, pp. 215–258.

93 17. **"Elia."** Over this pseudonym Lamb published the delightful essays which appeared in the *London Magazine* in 1820–23, and which are said to have been exceeded in popularity at the time only by the *Opium Confessions*, which came out in the same magazine during the same period. The name *Elia* is said to have been that of an obscure clerk in the old South Sea House, in which office Lamb was before he entered that of the East India Company.

93, footnote. **In another place.** *Cf. Works*, Riverside Ed., Vol. II, p. 223, note; Vol. VI, p. 324; Masson's Ed., Vol. I, p. 194, note; Vol. XI, p. 382.

94, footnote. **The utter failure of Mr. Coleridge, judging from his attempt in his "Table-Talk."** In the *Table-Talk* (Coleridge's *Works*, Vol. VI, p. 319) we read: "Talent, lying in the understanding, is often inherited; genius, being the action of reason and imagination, rarely or never." Also (p. 481): "Genius must have talent for its complement and implement, just as, in like manner, imagination must have fancy."

94 21. **Miss Lamb.** Mary Lamb (1764–1847) was the sister of Charles, whom she assisted in the production of *Tales from Shakespeare* (1807), and who included some of her poems in his own publications. She is often referred to in the *Essays* as "my cousin Bridget Elia." Mary Lamb was subject to attacks of insanity, in one of which she killed her mother.

94 26. **His play of "John Woodvil."** Lamb published this drama in the Elizabethan style in 1802. In treatment of the emotions it was not deficient, but in plot and character it was decidedly weak.

95 5. **The "Gebir" of Mr. Walter Savage Landor.** The *Gebir* appeared in 1798, and established its author's position in English letters. Its character is well indicated by De Quincey.

95 12. **"Lyrical Ballads"** also appeared in 1798; it included the *Tintern Abbey Lines* of Wordsworth, and the *Ancient Mariner* of

Coleridge, and was, beyond doubt, an epoch-making work in English poetry.

95 16. **A library which no man had read but myself.** De Quincey often dwells proudly upon his early adherence to the views and the poetry of Wordsworth and Coleridge; but perhaps he somewhat overstates the general ignorance concerning them. In the article on *Oxford* in the *Autobiography* (Riverside Ed., Vol. II, p. 569; Masson's Ed., Vol. II, p. 60) he says: "In 1803, when I entered at Oxford, that name [Wordsworth] was absolutely unknown; and the finger of scorn, pointed at it in 1802 by the first or second number of the *Edinburgh Review*, failed to reach its mark from absolute defect of knowledge in the public mind. Some fifty besides myself knew who was meant by 'that poet who had cautioned his friend against growing double,' etc.; to all others it was a profound secret." *Cf.* also note 242 28. Yet in this very article (a review of Southey's *Thalaba, the Destroyer*, in *Edinburgh Review*, October, 1802, Vol. I, No. 1, pp. 63–83), in which Jeffrey pays his respects (p. 68) to "that poet who commemorates, with so much effect, the chatterings of Harry Gill's teeth, tells the tale of the one-eyed huntsman 'who had a cheek like a cherry,' and beautifully warns his studious friend of the risk he ran of 'growing double'" (see Wordsworth's *The Tables Turned*, 1798), — in this same article (p. 64) we read: "The authors of whom we are now speaking [Wordsworth, Coleridge, and Southey], have, among them, unquestionably, a very considerable portion of poetical talent, and have, consequently, been enabled to seduce many into an admiration of the false taste (as it appears to us) in which most of these productions are composed. They constitute, at present, the most formidable conspiracy that has lately been formed against sound judgment in matters poetical; and are entitled to a larger share of our censorial notice, than could be spared for an individual delinquent." Concerning the controversy itself, see Vaughan's *English Literary Criticism*, Introduction, or Courthope's *The Liberal Movement in English Literature*.

95 18. **"High-Born Helen."** This can be found as *Helen* in most collections of Charles Lamb's works. It is entirely in the romantic vein.

95 19. **The ingenious imitations of Burton.** "Curious Fragments, extracted from a common-place book, which belonged to Robert Burton, the famous author of the Anatomy of Melancholy" is the full title of these three "extracts," which came out with *John Woodvil* in 1802. Burton published his great work in 1621.

95 22. **The Edinburgh notice of them.** This notice is Article VII in the third number of the *Review* (April, 1803, Vol. II, pp. 90–98). Its character is accurately indicated by De Quincey's remarks below.

96 10. **From the age of Thespis,** *i.e.*, from the rudest age of the drama. Thespis, who lived in the sixth century B.C., was the reputed founder of tragedy.

96 10. **Entitled to the hircus.** De Quincey here follows the Edinburgh reviewers (p. 91) in using the Latin rather than the English word. The goat is said to have been made the prize of tragedy in Thespis' time.

96 14. **As he was afterwards among the first to hoot at his own farce.** Lamb's farce, *Mr. H.*, appeared in 1806 and was hooted off the stage the first night.

97 8. **Last Supper of Da Vinci.** A famous painting by Leonardo da Vinci (1452–1519) on the wall of the refectory in the Convent of Santa Maria delle Grazie in Milan, Italy; finished in 1498. It is well known in the engraving of Morghen.

97 8. **Group from the Sistine Chapel.** The Sistine, or Sixtine, Chapel is the papal private chapel, built in 1473 by Pope Sixtus IV. Its walls and ceilings are covered by magnificent paintings, of which the most celebrated are the pictures by Michelangelo of the Creation, the Deluge, and the Judgment.

97 10. **Carlo Dolce,** or Dolci (1616–86), was a Florentine painter, of good execution but inferior genius, who is best known through his Madonnas. The painting referred to by De Quincey, in the collection of the Marquis of Exeter, is a fine picture of "Christ breaking the Bread."

97 12. **Charles Lamb . . . Carlo Dolce.** The latter name in Italian might mean 'sweet Charles.'

97 15. **Hazlitt amongst others.** William Hazlitt (1778–1830) was a famous English critic and a friend — more or less steadfast — of Wordsworth, Lamb, and Coleridge.

97 16. **Quam nihil ad genium, Papiniane, tuum!** "How altogether little to your taste, Papinian!" This passage occurs on the title-page of the *Lyrical Ballads*, second, third, and fourth editions, and thence no doubt De Quincey took it. The earlier history of the expression, as Professor Dowden has kindly pointed out to me, is traced in Hutchinson's Edition of *Lyrical Ballads*, London, 1898, p. lix: "Coleridge found the line in Anderson's *British Poets*, Vol. III, p. 238, where it occurs in the foreword from the author [Selden] of the *Illustrations* prefixed to Drayton's *Polyolbion*." Æmilius Papinianus, A.D. 175–212, was a Roman lawyer of great distinction and probity. After having enjoyed the confidence of Septimius Severus, he lost his life for refusing to justify Caracalla's murder of his brother Geta. Papinian's

opinions retained great weight as precedents, and the Roman law students were called Papinianists when they had reached the third year of their five years' course. Hutchinson asserts that Papinianus, in the case of the *Lyrical Ballads*, "is no other than that 'counsellor keen,' Sir James Mackintosh, for whom Coleridge nursed a ludicrously vehement antipathy." De Quincey, apparently, addresses Hazlitt.

97 25. **Not an ἔργον, but a παρεργον.** "Not a vocation, but an avocation." Lamb has given us a few poems, such as *Hester* and *The Old Familiar Faces*, that are really immortal; those mentioned by De Quincey are certainly not among the number.

102 1. **Member of "the Honourable Society of the Middle Temple."** The Temple was originally a lodge (in the Strand) of the mediæval religious order of Knights Templars (so called from their early headquarters in the Crusaders' Palace, or Temple of Solomon, in Jerusalem). When this order was dissolved, its property passed to the crown and later to the Knights Hospitalers. In 1346 they leased part of it to students of the law, and on its site now stand the two Inns of Court known as the Inner and the Middle Temple. These have ever since been used by barristers, and are the property of the Societies of the Inner and Middle Temple, who have the right of calling students to the bar. The Inner Temple was so termed because it was within the old city of London; the Middle Temple was between the Inner and the Outer, which latter, the part not leased to the lawyers, was eventually converted into Exeter Buildings and lost its ancient name. De Quincey was a student of the Middle Temple, "eating terms," in a very desultory De Quinceyan way, for a while in 1808.

103 16. **A Roman Catholic convert amongst the bloody idolaters of Japan.** Jesuit missionaries came early to Japan and had considerable success. A violent persecution of Christians was undertaken by the Tokugawa dynasty; Christianity was proscribed; the missionaries were expelled by decree. In 1637 the peasantry of a convert district rose in rebellion, whereupon they were all massacred. It was not until after the overthrow of the Tokugawa dynasty and the introduction of foreign influence — about the time of De Quincey's death — that the proclamations against Christianity disappeared.

104 5. **Allow yourself in such opinions.** This use of *allow* as "permit (oneself) to indulge (in)" is certainly not common; but compare (from the *Murray Dictionary*) Paley's *Sermons* (1815), Vol. VII, p. 126: "The true child of God allows himself in no sin whatever." Also Ruskin's *Modern Painters* (1860), Vol. V, Part IX, Chap. V, sec. 5: "It refuses to allow itself in any violent or 'spasmodic' passion."

104 11. **" The many men so beautiful,"** etc. From Part IV of *The Ancient Mariner*.

104 13. **A gang of Wapping vagabonds.** Wapping is a quarter of London, along the north bank of the Thames, below the Tower. It is the haunt of sailors.

A MEETING WITH COLERIDGE

Under the title " Samuel Taylor Coleridge : By the English Opium-Eater," De Quincey contributed four articles to *Tait's Edinburgh Magazine* for September, October, and November, 1834, and January, 1835. Three of these articles De Quincey revised and made into one paper for *Selections Grave and Gay*, Vol. II, which was published in 1854. What is here included is therefore the beginning of the revised paper ; it is found in *Works*, Masson's Ed., Vol. II, pp. 138–153 ; Riverside Ed., Vol. III, pp. 153–170. For other personal accounts of Coleridge, see Mason, *Personal Traits of British Authors*.

106 6. **" Lyrical Ballads."** See p. 95, and notes 95 12, 16, 22.

106 19. **Professor Wilson, etc.** John Wilson is best known by the *Noctes Ambrosianæ* — dialogues on popular topics — which he contributed to *Blackwood*, over the pseudonym Christopher North, in 1822–35. *Cf.* Introduction, p. xxx, and De Quincey on *Oxford*, Riverside Ed., Vol. II, pp. 567–570 ; Masson's Ed., Vol. II, pp. 59–61.

107 6. **Throwing frankincense upon the altars of Cæsar.** *Cf.* Bryce's *Holy Roman Empire*, pp. 22–23 : " From the time of Julius and Augustus his [the Emperor's ; Cæsar's] person had been hallowed by the office of chief pontiff and the tribunician power ; to swear by his head was considered the most solemn of all oaths ; his effigy was sacred, even on a coin ; to him or to his Genius temples were erected and divine honours paid while he lived ; and when, as it was expressed, he ceased to be among men, the title of Divus was accorded to him, after a solemn consecration. In the confused multiplicity of mythologies, the worship of the Emperor was the only worship common to the whole Roman world, and was therefore that usually proposed as a test to the Christians on their trial."

107 13. **Enlarged edition of the poems.** Published in 1800.

107 21. **" Joan of Arc."** The first edition was published in 1796, the second, greatly altered, in 1798. *Cf.* De Quincey's *Joan of Arc*, and notes.

107 22. **Ode entitled " France."** Published, with other political

pieces, in 1798, after having appeared in the *Morning Post* newspaper (Masson).

107 24. **"Anthology."** *English Anthology* for 1799–1800, in 2 vols., published at Bristol and edited by Southey.

107 26. **The small volume of poems, etc.** The first edition, entitled *Poems on Various Subjects, by S. T. Coleridge, late of Jesus College, Cambridge,* was published at Bristol in 1796 ; the second at London in 1797 ; the third at London in 1803 (Masson).

108 8. **Was then residing at Malta.** Coleridge was private secretary to the governor of Malta, Vice-Admiral Sir Alexander Ball, from July, 1804, to January, 1805, and acting public secretary till September, 1805.

108 11. **An inside place in a French prison.** England had declared war against Napoleon in 1803.

108 24. **Mr. Poole.** Thomas Poole (1765–1837) was a Bristol man who has become famous for his kindness to authors and his friendships among them. See the delightful biography by his daughter, Mrs. Henry Sandford : *Thomas Poole and his Friends,* 2 vols., 1888. There we read (Vol. II, p. 190) that, on July 26, Cottle, the Bristol publisher and authors' friend, " was writing to Tom Poole a note of introduction, describing 'the bearer, Mr. De Quincey,' as 'a Gentleman of Oxford, a scholar and a man of genius,' who felt 'a high admiration for Coleridge's character,' and desired to make his acquaintance."

108 26. **Lord Egmont's, etc.** This, the third Earl of Egmont, was the first who took no prominent place in English affairs. Spencer Perceval, however, his younger brother, was a distinguished lawyer, Chancellor of the Exchequer (1807), and Prime Minister (1809). He was assassinated May 11, 1812, in the lobby of the House of Commons, by a man who believed he had a grievance against the government.

109 18. **Alfoxton.** More correctly spelled *Alfoxden*.

109 19. **Occupied . . . by that poet.** Wordsworth lived at Alfoxden in 1797–98, in order to be near Coleridge, who was then living in the little cottage of Tom Poole at Nether Stowey, three miles from Alfoxden. For a full account of his occupancy of the cottage, see *Letters of Samuel Taylor Coleridge,* edited by Ernest Hartley Coleridge, 1895, Vol. I, pp. 185 ff. *Cf.* also Hazlitt's charming account of his visit to Nether Stowey (*My First Acquaintance with Poets*), which should be compared with De Quincey's.

109 24. **Glanced at in the poem of "Ruth."** The allusions are less considerable than De Quincey would lead us to expect ; in an earlier version *glanced at* read *sketched,* an utter exaggeration.

109 25. **The interval, etc.** Wordsworth left Cambridge in 1791, and settled at Grasmere in 1799. He lived in France, 1791–92; settled at Racedown, Dorsetshire, in 1795; Alfoxden, 1797; Goslar, in the Harz, North Germany, in 1798–99. De Quincey gives an entirely false impression as to the length of Wordsworth's stay in Alfoxden; he did not spend a "good deal" of the eight years there. Important as the Alfoxden period was in Wordsworth's poetic development, its duration was only eleven months.

110 7. **Pythagoras** was born about 582 B.C., at Samos, Greece, and died about 500 B.C., at Metapontum, Magna Græcia. "At Crotona, in Lower Italy, where he settled in 529 B.C., he founded a society whose aims and character were at once political, philosophical, and religious. All that can be traced back with certainty to Pythagoras himself is the doctrine of metempsychosis and the institution of certain religious and ethical regulations, and perhaps also the commencement of that mathematico-theological form of speculation, which was subsequently carried to a high degree of development." — UEBERWEG's *History of Philosophy*, transl. Morris, Vol. I, p. 42. The *Golden Verses*, in which the doctrine about beans occurs, are certainly spurious.

110 15. **Yet, strange it is to say, sometimes, etc.** The grammar seems dubious here.

111 4. **"That is the very explanation he gave us."** H. N. Coleridge, Samuel Taylor Coleridge's nephew and son-in-law, published his famous uncle's *Table-Talk*. In his Preface, dated May 11, 1835, he takes up at length this and the following accusations of plagiarism (Coleridge's *Works*, ed. Shedd, Vol. VI, pp. 241 *et seq.*). After quoting this alleged conversation he makes a pretty conclusive defence (p. 243) : "I was a little boy at Eton in the fifth form, some six or seven years after this dialogue is said to have taken place, and I can testify, what I am sure I could bring fifty of my contemporaries at a week's notice to corroborate, that this solution of the Pythagorean abstinence from beans was regularly taught us in school, as a matter of course, whenever occasion arose." H. N. Coleridge also cites from "Lucian's *Vitarum auctio*, a favorite school treatise of ours," an explanation, identical with the unknown German's, about Pythagoras and beans. But Mr. Tom Poole had also an objection to make. In a letter to H. N. Coleridge, dated June 22, 1835, he writes : "As for the conversation he [De Quincey] states as having had with me, I am sure *it must be incorrect ;* for as I never considered Coleridge as a Plagiarist, I never could have said what he has given me, as cited in your Preface. I have no recollection of the conversation which passed between me

and De Quincey, but I should indeed be sorry if the *whole Tone of his report* is not unlike my general mode of expressing myself. I might among other things have said that I had heard Coleridge explain Pythagoras's prohibiting his Disciples the use of Beans, in the manner mentioned, as in fact I had done ; *but I never heard him pretend that the solution was his*, and therefore I could not have said that he took credit for the discovery." — SANDFORD'S *Thomas Poole and his Friends*, Vol. II, pp. 305-306. De Quincey, in a note to the Collective Edition of his works, makes some reply to H. N. Coleridge's Preface, saying that the explanation about Pythagoras was well known only locally ; but were his accusations based on this instance alone, no reasonable man could notice them.

111 8. **But both of us had sufficient reasons.** " For what ? " writes Poole. " For charging Coleridge with Plagiarism ? *I beg leave to say, I had no reason whatever*."— *Op. cit.*, p. 306. De Quincey's defence, in the note referred to, runs thus : (1) "*I* certainly was the first person to point out the plagiarisms of Coleridge." (2) "I greatly understated the case." (3) "In stating it at all, I did so in pure kindness. Well I knew that sooner or later these appropriations must be detected, and I felt that it would break the force of the discovery, as an unmitigated sort of police detection, if first of all it had been announced by one who, in the same breath, was professing an unshaken faith in Coleridge's philosophic powers." — Masson's Ed., Vol. II, pp. 226-227 ; Riverside Ed., Vol. III, pp. 705-709. It may be added that there is about as little doubt of the fact of Coleridge's plagiarizing as there is of the impropriety of De Quincey's lengthened disquisition on the subject, under the guise of friendship. See Sara Coleridge's introduction to the *Biographia Literaria* for a full discussion of the matter.

111 23. **The Hymn to Chamouni.** "What Mr. Dequincey says about the Hymn in the vale of Chamouni is just." — H. N. COLE-RIDGE's Preface, *op. cit.*, p. 245.

112 17. **Some "bright particular star."** *Cf.* Shakspere, *All's Well that Ends Well*, Act i, sc. 1, line 80.

112 22. **"Tormented all the air."** Milton uses this phrase in *Paradise Lost*, Book VI, line 244.

112 24. **"A weed of glorious feature."** Wordsworth uses this expression in his *Beggars*. Spenser has it in *Muiopotmos : or the Fate of a Butterfly*, line 213 :

> " What more felicitie can fall to creature
> Than to enjoy delight with libertie, . . .
> To feed on flowres and weeds of glorious feature."

112 27. **Coleridge . . . thought fit . . . to deny.** "If, therefore, Mr. Coleridge denied that he was *indebted* to Milton for them, I believe that he meant to deny any distinct consciousness of their Miltonic origin, at the moment of his using them in his Ode." — H. N. COLE-RIDGE's Preface, *op. cit.*, p. 244.

113 6. **"Insupportably advancing the foot."** The quotation is not correct. The passage (*Samson Agonistes*, lines 135–140) reads :

> " But safest he who stood aloof,
>   When insupportably his foot advanc't,
>   In scorn of their proud arms and warlike tools,
>   Spurn'd them to death by troops.   The bold Ascalonite
>   Fled from his lion ramp, old warriors turn'd
>   Their plated backs under his heel ;
>   Or groveling soil'd their crested helmets in the dust."

Ascalon was one of the five cities of the Philistines, against whom Samson was fighting.

113 7. **One of the critical journals placed the two passages in juxtaposition.** This seems a little inconsistent with De Quincey's claim (see note 111 8 above) to forestall discovery by his present disclosures.

113 14. **Coming to Shelvocke.** George Shelvocke, *Voyage round the World, by the Way of the Great South Sea*, 1719–22. London, 1726.

113 24. **To disown so slight an obligation to Shelvocke.** "If he did I firmly believe he had no recollection of it." — H. N. COLE-RIDGE's Preface, *op. cit.*, p. 245. As to the fact of this obligation, see Wordsworth's positive statement in the preface to his *We are Seven*.

114 12. **"Philosophical —— "** of Schelling. *Kleine Philosophische Schriften* was the actual title. Schelling was born in Würtemberg, 1775, died 1854. He was at Munich, Bavaria, 1806–41.

114 21. **Fichte** was born 1762, died 1814. He became professor of philosophy at the University of Berlin when it was opened in 1810.

114 24. **Coleridge's essay . . . is prefaced, etc.** This statement is discussed by Julius Hare, *British Magazine*, January, 1835. See the extract from Hare's article in H. N. Coleridge's Preface, *op. cit.*, pp. 246 *et seq.* Hare shows that De Quincey is distinctly unfair to Coleridge. While the latter deprecates the notion that " an identity of thought, or even similarity of phrase " indicates indebtedness to Schelling, and claims " all the main and fundamental ideas " as his own, yet he in the same passage gives his readers permission to attribute to his German predecessor " whatever shall be found in this or any future

work of mine, that resembles or coincides with" his doctrines. That Coleridge translated several pages from Schelling without acknowledgment all must admit. But Hare believes him to have been ignorant of the origin of the passage; he suggests that Coleridge must have placed the translated extract, without Schelling's name, in a notebook among observations and dissertations of his own, and then, years afterward, printed it innocently as his own.

115 18. **Not John Paul.** Some translations from the writings of John Paul Richter (1763–1825) were among the first of De Quincey's publications after the *Confessions*. Richter's style is not unlike De Quincey's in the *Suspiria*.

116 14. **Milton's account, etc.** "Whatever Time, or the heedless hand of blind Chance, hath drawn down from of old to this present in her huge drag-net, whether fish, or seaweed, shells or shrubs, unpicked, unchosen, these are the Fathers."— MILTON's Tract *Of Prelatical Episcopacy*, published in 1641 (Masson).

116 16. **The monstrous chaos with which an African Obeah man stuffs his enchanted scarecrows.** Obi, or obeah, is a kind of magic or sorcery practised by the African negroes and their descendants in America. Bones, feathers, rags, and such trash are the charms used; and a scarecrow thus prepared by the obi-man is supposed to possess peculiar defensive power. The negroes still look to the obi for the cure of disease, the satisfaction of revenge or spite, the discovery of theft, etc. It is held, however, that the power of the obi over the negro mind is due to the furtive and skillful use of poison.

116 31. **Procès-verbal.** In French law, this is a legal instrument in which some qualified officer sets down an infringement of the law, with all its circumstances ; in this case the stones, hinges, nails, etc., would fill up the *procès-verbal* of this child's misdemeanor.

117 26. **"He talks very much like an angel, and does nothing at all."** *Cf.* David Garrick's humorous epitaph on Goldsmith (1774) :

> "Here lies Poet Goldsmith, for shortness called Noll,
> Who wrote like an angel, and talked like poor Poll."

118 26. **Rarely . . . opened them at all.** As Masson remarks, this is a pretty accurate description of De Quincey's own practice in later years, if not throughout his life.

118 27. **Bourrienne mentions, etc.** Louis Antoine Fauvelet de Bourrienne (1769–1834) was Napoleon's private secretary in Egypt and during the consulate, which lasted from 1799 to 1804. He had been Napoleon's friend at the military school. He published his extensive

Memoirs of Napoleon in 1829; at the beginning of Chap. VI, under date of 1797 (when Napoleon was General-in-Chief under the Directory) we read : " To satisfy himself that people wrote too much, and lost, in trifling and useless answers, valuable time, he told me to open only the letters which came by extraordinary couriers, and to leave all the rest for three weeks in the basket. At the end of that time it was unnecessary to reply to four-fifths of these communications."

119 10. **The hideous bondage.** As to Coleridge and opium-eating, *cf.* De Quincey's essay on that subject, his *Confessions*, edition of 1856, Introduction, and Campbell's *Life of Coleridge*, London, 1894.

119 21. **A man whom I will describe.** Coleridge was nearly thirty-seven years old at this time, his visitor being fifteen years younger. *Cf.* Wordsworth's description of Coleridge in *Stanzas written in my Pocket-Copy of Thomson's Castle of Indolence.*

120 15. **Chubb, the philosophic writer** (1679–1747), was a mechanic who took a place among the eighteenth-century deists by various tracts.

122 7. **The Orellana.** A name formerly frequently given to the Amazon River, from its discoverer, Francisco de Orellana (1490–1546).

122 30. **Bishop Berkeley's " Siris."** George Berkeley (1685–1753) became Bishop of Cloyne, in Ireland, in 1734. As a philosopher he was an extreme idealist. In 1744 he published *A Chain of Philosophical Reflections and Inquiries concerning the Virtues of Tar-Water*, etc., to which in the next edition he gave the name *Siris*. He devoted much time during his later years to the propagation of knowledge concerning tar-water as a panacea.

123 5. **The Homeric chain of gold.** See *Iliad*, Book VIII, line 19.

RECOLLECTIONS OF WORDSWORTH

De Quincey published three articles on Wordsworth in *Tait's Magazine* for January, February, and April, 1839, Vol. VI; these, revised and enlarged, he republished in the Collective Edition in 1854. Our present extract is the introduction to the formal biography of the poet. It is found in *Works*, Masson's Ed., Vol. II, pp. 229–252 ; Riverside Ed., Vol. III, pp. 260–293. For other accounts of Wordsworth, — and better in some respects, — see Mason, *Personal Traits of British Authors*.

124 2. **I have already mentioned.** *Cf.* p. 95; also De Quincey's *Works*, Riverside Ed., Vol. II, p. 567 ; Masson's Ed., Vol. II, p. 59.

125 13. **The " Churchyard amongst the Mountains."** Books VI-VII of Wordsworth's *Excursion*.

125 17. **The Miltonic names of Valdarno and Vallombrosa.** See *Paradise Lost*, Book I, lines 290, 303. The Val' d'Arno is the valley (of the river Arno) in which Florence is situated. Vallombrosa ("shady valley") is eighteen miles from Florence. *Cf.* Wordsworth's *At Vallombrosa* (*Memorials of a Tour in Italy*, XVIII).

125 22. **"Could field, or grove," etc.** These five lines from the latter part of the sixth book of the *Excursion*, somewhat differently quoted by De Quincey in the text and footnote, now read thus :

> "Ah! what a warning for a thoughtless man,
> Could field or grove, could any spot of earth,
> Show to his eye an image of the pangs
> Which it hath witnessed; render back an echo
> Of the sad steps by which it hath been trod!"

127 3. **A little white cottage.** Dove Cottage, as it is called, — because once the Dove and Olive Bough Inn — is now the property of the English nation and is kept open to visitors. Wordsworth occupied it from 1799 to 1808 ; De Quincey, or his family, from 1809 to 1830. *Cf.* De Quincey's description in the *Confessions*, p. 226, also note 226 12.

127 18. **In early youth I laboured, etc.** This is a highly interesting confession, if we may accept it as an entirely accurate one. Beyond question, De Quincey became in time, as he here intimates, preëminently able to "follow out the subsidiary thoughts into which one leading thought often radiates," and extraordinarily fond of that exercise.

128 8. **A worldly tone of sentiment in Wordsworth.** This is certainly, as Professor Winchester has suggested, a good example of the strain of malice in De Quincey's notices of Wordsworth. There seems to be no ground for this charge.

128 9. **Mrs. Hannah More** (1745–1833) was an English religious writer of the so-called ultra-evangelical school. In her youth she knew Garrick, Dr. Johnson, Burke, and Reynolds. She was interested in establishing schools for the poor as an antidote to atheism. She wrote many tracts, voicing her rather severe views as to conduct, such as *The Shepherd of Salisbury Plain*, as well as other works, like *Cœlebs in Search of a Wife ;* all these were much read in the early part of this century, and some are still freely circulated. Mrs. de Quincey, our author's mother, not only subscribed to Mrs. More's opinions, but also enjoyed her friendship and very frequently sought her advice. *Cf.* Mrs. Baird Smith's remarks in Japp, *De Quincey Memorials*, Vol. I, p. 13; also De Quincey's account, *Works*, Riverside Ed., Vol. III, pp. 584–594 ; Masson's Ed., Vol. II, pp. 446–454.

128 16. **In the course of 1807, etc.** Coleridge arrived in England from Italy Aug. 11, 1806. He had left Malta Sept. 21, 1805. See note 108 8.

128 19. **Already recorded.** See pp. 106 *et seq.*

128 23. **Engaged by the Royal Institution to lecture.** These lectures, Coleridge's first course, were delivered in the months February to June, 1808. They were on the " Principles of Poetry." Sixteen were contracted for, and were probably all delivered.

128 26. **Conveying his family to Keswick,** where Mrs. Coleridge's sister, Mrs. Southey, resided (at Greta Hall). From this time on Coleridge did not spend more than a few days under the same roof with his wife. His entire family lived with Southey, who, with some coöperation from other relatives and friends, educated the children and provided for them all.

128 30. **Hartley, aged nine, Derwent, about seven.** As to the former, see note 60 9. "The career of Derwent," writes Mr. J. D. Campbell, "both as to the conduct of life and its rewards, was in marked contrast to his brother's. His bent was to be a student, but he was forced into action, partly by circumstance, partly by an honorable ambition. During a long and useful life . . . he did signal service to the cause of national education. He cannot be said to have left his mark on literature, but his chief work, *The Scriptural Character of the English Church*, won the admiration of F. D. Maurice for 'its calm scholarlike tone and careful English style.' " He died in 1883.

128 31. **Her beautiful little daughter.** Sara Coleridge (1802–52) married her cousin Henry Nelson Coleridge, and succeeded him, after his death, as editor of her father's works. *Cf.* De Quincey's footnote, and note 111 8.

129 26. **Madame Catalani.** Angelica Catalani, an Italian singer, was born in 1779, made her first appearance in Venice in 1795, and had a successful career for thirty years. She died at Paris in 1849. She had been married three years before De Quincey met her.

129 29. **Lady Hamilton** (1761–1815), wife of Sir William Hamilton (1730–1803), English ambassador at Naples, is notorious as the mistress of the great Lord Nelson. She was of mean birth and hopelessly illiterate. In early years she had a beautiful face, but later in life she grew very stout. She was undoubtedly a woman of considerable power of mind, and she retained her pernicious influence over Lord Nelson till his death.

130 20. **White Moss.** This name for a hill points to the fact that its flat top was covered with a " moss," or swamp.

131 13. Semele in the Grecian Mythology. The allusion is to the familiar story how Semele, the human maiden, wooed by Jupiter in shape of man, was persuaded by Juno's jealous machinations to insist upon his appearance to her in divine apparel. He came, and she perished in the flames caused by his lightnings.

131 27. Charlemagne and all his peerage. Charlemagne and his twelve paladins, or attendant peers, became the centre of a great number of poems in the Middle Ages, of which *The Song of Roland* is the most important representative.

131 28. Cæsar and his equipage. Cæsar's retinue was always of peculiar size and splendor.

131 29. Death on his pale horse. *Cf.* Revelations, vi, 8. About 1815 Benjamin West painted a famous picture on the subject "Death on the Pale Horse," which is now in Philadelphia.

132 6. No Roman nomenclator. In ancient Rome candidates canvassing for office were attended in public by a nomenclator (*i.e.*, name-caller), who informed the candidate of the names of persons they met.

132 31. Mrs. Wordsworth, etc. Mary Hutchinson, who became Wordsworth's wife in October, 1802, had been known to him since 1777, when she was his fellow-pupil in a dame's school at Penrith (Masson).

133 9. Mr. Slave-Trade Clarkson. Thomas Clarkson (1760–1846) was an English abolitionist, who published in 1808 a *History of the Abolition of the Slave-Trade*, whence he gained the appellation bestowed upon him here. This book Coleridge, who was a friend of the author, reviewed in the *Edinburgh Review*, having before begged the editor "to be merciful to an imperfect book for the sake of the almost perfect character of the author." *Cf.* p. 227.

134 12. Like stars, etc. The authoritative text reads :

> " Her eyes as stars of Twilight fair;
> Like Twilight's, too, her dusky hair ";

but De Quincey is quoting from an earlier version. The lines, like those above, are from *She was a Phantom of Delight* (1804).

134 31. "Her face was of Egyptian brown." From Wordsworth's *Beggars*. *Egyptian* means "gipsy" here (*cf.* Shakspere, *Othello*, Act iii, sc. 4, line 56; Longfellow, *Spanish Student*, Act iii, sc. 2, line 13); the latter word is a shortening of the former, the gipsies being popularly supposed to come from Egypt. Really they are, by the testimony of their speech, of a Hindu race.

135 1. They were wild and startling. *Cf.* Wordsworth, *Tintern Abbey* (to Dorothy Wordsworth) :

> " And read
> My former pleasures in the shooting lights
> Of thy wild eyes."

> " Nor catch from thy wild eyes these gleams
> Of past existence."

135 33. German charcoal-burners. Referring to their experiences in the Harz mountain district.

135 33. Couched his eye, etc. De Quincey seems fond of this word. *Cf.* article on *Oxford* (Riverside Ed., Vol. II, p. 561; Masson's Ed., Vol. II, p. 55): " My eye had been couched into a secondary power of vision," etc. *Cf.* also Chaucer, *Parliament of Birds*, lines 215–217 :

> " And with hir wyle
> She couched hem after as they shuld serve,
> Som for to slee, and som to wounde and kerve."

138 3. "Half-kitchen and half-parlour fire." The first of the sonnets headed *Personal Talk* (last four lines) now reads :

> " To sit without emotion, hope, or aim,
> In the loved presence of my cottage-fire,
> And listen to the flapping of the flame,
> Or kettle whispering its faint undersong."

In his prefatory note, however, Wordsworth says : " The last line but two stood, at first, better and more characteristically, thus :

> ' By my half-kitchen and half-parlour fire.' "

138 17. "What-like." A provincial word, as De Quincey intimates, meaning, "of what appearance." *Century Dictionary* quotes from Dickens, *Our Mutual Friend*, Book III, Chap. II : " What-like the home and what-like the friend."

138 19. A reviewer in "Tait's Magazine," etc. As Masson adds to De Quincey's footnote, " the paper in *Tait* referred to was a Review of Books of the Season, one of them being ' Tilt's Medallion Portraits of Modern English Authors, with illustrative notices by H. F. Chorley.' The reviewer's words were : ' The finest head, in every way, in the series, is that of Charles Lamb.' "

139 32. Elegantes formarum spectatrices. " Elegant critics of beauty." *Cf.* Terence, *Eunuchus*, III, 5, 18 :

> " Quom ipsus me noris, quam elegans formarum spectator siem? "

141 8. **Voltaire . . . a sneering Jewish elder.** François Marie Arouet, who assumed the name "de Voltaire" (1694–1778), the world-famous French dramatist, novelist, and reformer, exhibited the characteristics which Hayden thus emphasized best, perhaps, in his letters. "His immense energy and versatility, his adroit and unhesitating flattery when he chose to flatter, his ruthless sarcasm when he chose to be sarcastic, his rather unscrupulous business faculty, his rather more than unscrupulous resolve to double and twist in any fashion so as to escape his enemies, — all these things appear throughout the whole mass of letters." — SAINTSBURY.

141 20. **Miss Ferrier, in one of her novels.** Susan Ferrier (1782–1854) was a Scottish novelist whose material, like that of her more brilliant predecessor, Miss Austen, was drawn from domestic life. Her first novel, *Marriage* (1818), contains, on page 170 of the recent Routledge Edition, the passage referred to : " No Englishman, with his round face and trim meadows, shall ever captivate me. Heath-covered hills, and high cheek-bones, are the charms that must win my heart."

142 27. **Irving, the pulpit orator.** Edward Irving (1792–1834), Scotch preacher and friend of Carlyle, had a brilliant career until his curious religious notions called down the censure of the Scotch clergy, and brought about his condemnation for heresy. The Irvingite Church, founded on his doctrine, has elaborate orders and liturgy, and lays especial stress upon the continuance of prophecy and the gift of tongues.

143 23. **"Peter's Letters."** Lockhart's well-known publication, *Peter's Letters to his Kinsfolk* (1819), was a compend of most that was interesting in the *personalia* and literary talk of Edinburgh, Glasgow, and thereabouts at the time. In Letter LI, in an account of Wordsworth, Lockhart writes: " The large, dim, pensive eye, that dwells almost forever upon the ground, and the smile of placid abstraction, that clothes his long, tremulous, melancholy lips, complete a picture of solemn, wrapped-up, contemplative genius."

144 8. **"The light that never was on land or sea."** *Cf.* Wordsworth's *Elegiac Stanzas, suggested by a picture of Peele Castle, in a storm, painted by Sir George Beaumont:*

> "Ah! THEN, if mine had been the Painter's hand,
> To express what then I saw; and add the gleam,
> The light that never was, on sea or land,
> The consecration, and the Poet's dream."

144 33. **Richardson the painter's, etc.** "Jonathan Richardson (born about 1665, died 1745) published in 1734 a volume of Explanatory

Notes and Remarks on *Paradise Lost*, with a Life of Milton, containing particulars which Richardson had collected about Milton personally." — MASSON.

145 13. **This portrait was the only one, etc.** " It was between 1721 and 1725, when Mrs. Deborah Clarke, Milton's youngest and only surviving daughter, was living in old age and in very humble circumstances in Moorfields, London, that the engraver Vertue and others went to see her for the special purpose of consulting her about portraits of her father. Some that were shown her she rejected at once ; but one 'crayon drawing' moved her in the manner which De Quincey reports. This is the portrait which came into Richardson's possession; and after Richardson's death in 1745 it was acquired by Jacob Tonson tertius, of the Tonson publishing family. There seems to be little doubt that it was a drawing of Milton from the life by Faithorne about 1670, when Milton's *History of Britain* appeared with that portrait of him by Faithorne which is the only authentic print of him in later life, and worth all the other current portraits put together. Faithorne seems to have made two drawings, closely resembling each other, of Milton, — that (now lost) from which the engraving was made for the *History of Britain*, and this other 'crayon drawing' which Richardson possessed. Richardson's reproduction of it in his book is spoilt by a laureate wreath and other flummery about the head; and the only genuine copy of it known to me is a beautiful one prefixed to Mr. Leigh Sotheby's sumptuous volume entitled *Ramblings in Elucidation of the Autograph of Milton*, published in 1871. The face there is identically the same in essentials as that in the Faithorne engraving of 1670, though somewhat less sad in expression ; and the two drawings must have been by the same hand." — MASSON.

146 20. **In that account which " The Excursion" presents, etc.** A comparison of De Quincey's paraphrase with the original in Wordsworth's *Excursion*, Book I, near the beginning, is interesting :

> " From his intellect
> And from the stillness of abstracted thought
> He asked repose ; and, failing oft to win
> The peace required, he scanned the laws of light
> Amid the roar of torrents, where they send
> From hollow clefts up to the clearer air
> A cloud of mist that, smitten by the sun,
> Varies its rainbow hues. But vainly thus,
> And vainly by all other means, he strove
> To mitigate the fever of his heart."

147 11. **The grand climacterical year.** "The climacteric years or critical periods have been supposed to be the years ending the third, fifth, seventh, and ninth period of seven years, to which some add the eighty-first year. The sixty-third year was called the *grand* or *great climacteric*. It has been believed that each of these periods is attended with some remarkable change in respect to health, life, or fortune." — *Century Dictionary*. The derivation is from Greek κλιμακτήρ, "a step of a ladder," "a dangerous period of life."

147 30. "**Childer.**" Familiar dialectal plural of *child*; historically more correct than the standard form. *Cf. cildru* in oldest English.

148 4. **Into his 82d year.** Into his 81st only.

148 23. **There was also a wreath of laurel.** See note 145 13.

149 11. "**The starry Galileo.**" From Byron's *Childe Harold's Pilgrimage*, Canto IV, stanza 54:

> "The starry Galileo, with his woes."

150 6. **The German and the Spanish will inevitably sink, etc.** This preposterous statement can only be explained by recognizing the coincidence in De Quincey of a considerable ignorance of philology with a John-Bullish view of things foreign, hardly excused by comparison with that of Doctor Johnson.

150 14. **Our personal memorials (unhappily so slender) of Shakspere.** In his article on Shakspere in *Encyclopædia Britannica* (1837) (Riverside Ed., Vol. VI, p. 9; Masson's Ed., Vol. IV, p. 17) De Quincey goes at length into the question of the dearth of knowledge about Shakspere's life.

CONFESSIONS OF AN ENGLISH OPIUM-EATER

The first publication in book form (1822) was prefaced by the following notice:

"NOTICE TO THE READER: The incidents recorded in the Preliminary Confessions lie within a period of which the earlier extreme is now rather more, and the latter extreme less, than nineteen years ago: consequently, in a popular way of computing dates, many of the incidents might be indifferently referred to a distance of eighteen or of nineteen years; and, as the notes and memoranda for this narrative were drawn up originally about last Christmas, it seemed most natural in all cases to prefer the former date. In the hurry of composing the narrative, though some months had then elapsed, this date was everywhere retained: and, in many cases, perhaps, it leads to no error, or to none of importance. But in one instance, viz. where the author speaks of his own birth-day, this adoption of one uniform date has led to a positive inaccuracy of an entire year: for, during the very time of composition, the *nineteenth* year from the earlier term of the whole period revolved to its close. It is, therefore, judged proper to mention, that the period of that narrative lies between the early part of July, 1802, and the beginning or middle of March, 1803.

Oct. 1, 1821."

The full title in the magazine was *Confessions of an English Opium-Eater: Being an Extract from the Life of a Scholar.*

152 1. **I have, at last, concluded on taking it.** To this account from within of the origin of the *Confessions* may be added this external information from Page's *Life:* " He had intended unambitiously to begin [his contributions to the *London Magazine*] with translations from the German ; but his opium experiences, and his resolute efforts to escape from the thraldom of the drug, had of course been the subject of conversation on his first introduction to the circle [surrounding Taylor and Hessey, the publishers of the magazine], which was so impressed by his recitals, that he was asked to inaugurate his connection with the Magazine by a record of his opium experiences. Accordingly, there appeared in the 'London Magazine' for October and November, 1821, the 'Confessions of an English Opium-Eater.'" The *Confessions* appeared in September and October, 1821, Appendix in December, 1822. The following note from the hand of Mr. H. G. Bohn appears in Lowndes' *Bibliographer's Manual:* "These 'Confessions' were written in a little room at the back of [what later became] Mr. H. G. Bohn's premises No. 4, York Street, Covent Garden, where Mr. De Quincey resided, in comparative seclusion, for several years."

152 9. **"Humbly to express,"** etc. *Cf.* Wordsworth, *White Doe of Rylstone*, Canto I, lines 176–177 (of the grave where the doe made "her sabbath couch ") :

> " That humbly would express
> A penitential loneliness."

153, footnote. **There is one celebrated man.** "*23rd November, 1821.* I dined at Taylor's with Dr. Darling, Percival and the Opium-Eater. In the course of the evening the latter mentioned that the person he alluded to in his Confessions as far exceeding himself in the quantity of opium taken is Coleridge. The Opium-Eater was speaking to a surgeon in the north, a neighbour of Coleridge's, who supplied Coleridge with laudanum, and who, upon a calculation made as to the quantity consumed by Coleridge, found it to amount to 80,000 drops per day. The first time Coleridge went to the house of this surgeon, he was not at home, but his wife supplied Coleridge, and she saw him at once fill out a large wineglassful and drink it off. She was astonished, and in much alarm explained to him what the medicine was, as she imagined he had made a mistake. Very soon afterwards he drank off another glassful, and before he left the house he had emptied a half-pint bottle in addition."— WOODHOUSE'S *Notes of Conversations with De Quincey*, in *Confessions*, ed. Garnett, pp. 206–207, and HOGG'S *De Quincey and his Friends*, p. 83. This statement can hardly be credited ; yet Cottle, the Bristol publisher, and friend of Coleridge, states, "from an undoubted source," that the latter was known to take a quart of laudanum in twenty-four hours ; 80,000 drops would be 800 teaspoonfuls.

153 5. **Have untwisted . . . the accursed chain.** But see Appendix, pp. 255 *et seq.*, and note 252 28.

153 24. **The eloquent and benevolent [William Wilberforce].** These blanks were filled in by De Quincey, as in our text, in his (altered) reprint of this *Original Preface* in the enlarged *Confessions* of 1856. Wilberforce, born 1759, died 1833, was a famous orator, philanthropist, and abolitionist. In 1787 he and Thomas Clarkson (see note 133 9) began to agitate the slavery question, and they gained a final victory in 1807. See note 153 26, on *Mr. ——, the philosopher*.

153 25. **The late dean of [Carlisle, Dr. Isaac Milner].** Born 1750, died 1820 ; an intimate friend of Wilberforce. De Quincey adds in a long note in the edition of 1856 : " He was *nominally* known to the public as Dean of Carlisle, being colloquially always called *Dean* Milner ; but virtually he was best known in his own circle as the head of Queen's College, Cambridge, where he usually resided. . . . Wordsworth, who met him often at the late Lord Lonsdale's table, spoke of him uniformly as the chief potentate colloquially of his own generation, and as the man beyond all others (Burke being departed) who did not live upon his recollections, but met the demands of every question that engaged his sympathy by spontaneous and elastic movements of novel and original thought. As an opium-eater, Dean Milner was understood to be a strenuous wrestler with the physical necessity that coerced him into this habit. From several quarters I have heard that his daily *ration* was 34 grains (or about 850 drops of laudanum), divided into four portions, and administered to him at regular intervals of six hours by a confidential valet."

153 26. **Lord [Erskine].** Thomas Erskine, first Baron Erskine (1750–1823), was a famous jurist and pleader. His defence of Stockdale (1789) is especially celebrated. See Bradley's *Orations and Arguments*, Boston, 1897.

153 26. **Mr. ——, the philosopher.** De Quincey added in 1856 the following note on *Philosopher Dash, and the other blanks in the list of distinguished opium-eaters:* "Who is Mr. Dash, the philosopher? Really I have forgot. Not through any fault of my own, but on the motion of some absurd coward having a voice potential at the press, all the names were struck out behind my back in the first edition of the book, thirty-five years ago. I was not consulted, and did not discover the absurd blanks until months afterwards, when I was taunted with them very reasonably by a caustic reviewer. Nothing could have a more ludicrous effect than this appeal to shadows — to my Lord Dash, to Dean Dash, and to Mr. Secretary Dash. Very naturally it thus happened to Mr. Philosopher Dash that his burning light, alas! was extinguished irrecoverably in the general *mêlée.* Meantime, there was no excuse whatever for this absurd interference, such as might have been alleged in any personality capable of causing pain to any one person concerned. All the cases, except, perhaps, that of Wilberforce (about which I have at this moment some slight lingering doubts), were matters of notoriety to large circles of friends. It is due to Mr. John Taylor, the accomplished publisher of the work, that I should acquit *him* of any share in this absurdity."

154 21. **Their work-people were rapidly getting into the practice of opium-eating.** The following remarkable passage in Charles Kingsley's *Alton Locke: Tailor and Poet* (published in 1850), Chap. XII, to which attention is called by Garnett in his edition of the *Confessions*, bears striking testimony to the prevalence of the habit in the malarious Cambridgeshire fens. *Bor* (below) in the Cambridgeshire dialect is a common form of address for man or woman; *cf. neigh-bor.*

"'They as dinnot tak' spirits down thor, tak' their pennord o' elevation, then — women-folk especial.'

'What's elevation?'

'Oh! ho! ho! — yow goo into druggist's shop o' market-day, into Cambridge, and you'll see the little boxes, doozens and doozens, a' ready on the counter; and never a ven-man's wife goo by, but what calls in for her pennord o' elevation, to last her out the week. Oh! ho! ho! Well, it keeps women-folk quiet, it do; and it's mortal good agin ago pains.'

'But what is it?'

'Opium, bor' alive, opium!'

'But doesn't it ruin their health? I should think it the very worst sort of drunkenness.'

'Ow, well, yow moi soy that — mak'th 'em cruel thin then, it do; but what can bodies do i' th' ago?'"

154 33. **"That those eat now," etc.** *Cf.* the refrain in Parnell's *Vigil of Venus:*

> " Let those love now who never lov'd before;
> Let those who always lov'd, now love the more."

Parnell's poem is a translation of the *Pervigilium Veneris*, "written in the time of Julius Cæsar, and by some ascribed to Catullus," where the corresponding line reads :

> " Cras amet qui nunquam amavit; quique amavit, cras amet."

It should be noted in regard to the statement quoted above, which Parnell makes part of the title of his translation, that this poem is surely not by Catullus and that it is later than the time of Julius Cæsar.

155 8. **Φωναντα συνετοισι.** From Pindar, *Olympian Odes*, II, 153. Gray used this phrase as the motto for his Odes (1757). In a letter to Rev. J. Brown, Feb. 17, 1763, he renders it : " Vocal to the intelligent alone." *Cf.* Phelps, *Selections from Gray*, p. 150.

155 19. **I shall present the reader with the moral of my narrative.** See p. 252 and note 252 28.

156 11. **"Whose talk is of oxen."** *Cf.* Chaucer, *Parliament of Pirds*, lines 99 *et seq.*

> " The wery hunter, sleping in his bed,
> To wode ayein his mynde goth anoon ;
> The juge dremeth how his plees been sped ;
> The carter dremeth how his cartes goon "; etc.

156 19. **" Humani nihil a se alienum putat."** " Thinks nothing human foreign to him." *Cf.* Terence, *Heauton timoroumenos*, Act i, sc. 1, line 25 :

> " Homo sum : humani nil a me alienum puto."

156 29. **David Ricardo.** *Cf.* pp. 235–236. Ricardo, who lived from 1772 to 1823, published his chief work, *Principles of Political Economy and Taxation*, in 1817. He was in Parliament for some time.

156, footnote. **A third exception, etc.** William Hazlitt (1778–1830) is probably meant; a brilliant, but not too well-read, critic and essayist.

157 16. **For nearly ten years.** 1804–14, apparently.

157, footnote. **I know only one.** Professor Wilson is meant. *Cf.* note 106 19.

158 1. **In the twenty-eighth year, etc.** This would be the year August, 1812, to August, 1813. The " painful affection of the stomach"

has been declared by Dr. Eatwell, in his medical examination of De Quincey's case, Appendix to Page's *Life*, to be gastrodynia, or neuralgia of the stomach. This, he says, is brought on frequently in India by the insufficient and crude diet of the natives, and it yields in the end to the habitual use of opium. See De Quincey's account of his privations in Wales and London, pp. 168 *et seq.*, and the testimony of Berlioz, note 218 5.

158 16. **My father died, etc.** See notes 24 30 and 85 24.

158 17. **I was sent to various schools.** To Bath Grammar School, Winkfield, and Manchester Grammar School ; the second was a small "private" school. *Cf.* note 25 13.

158 33. **One of my masters.** Mr. Morgan, of Bath School.

159 3. **"And a ripe and good one."** *Cf.* Shakspere, *Henry VIII*, Act. iv, sc. 2, lines 51–52.

159 7. **A blockhead, who was in a perpetual panic.** Mr. Spencer, the master of Winkfield School.

159 9. **A respectable scholar.** Mr. Lawson, the head of Manchester School.

159 14. **Etonian brilliancy.** De Quincey refers to the special and almost exclusive care bestowed upon the classical training at Eton. Up to 1851 the regular curriculum was wholly classical, other than classical masters being attended during extra hours.

160 9. **This fourth . . . was a worthy man, etc.** The Rev. Samuel Hall, De Quincey's tutor in the "World of Strife" period, is meant. See p. 85, and note 85 24.

160 21. **A woman of high rank.** Lady Carbery. "A young woman some ten years older than myself, and who was as remarkable for her intellectual pretensions as she was for her beauty and her benevolence."— *Confessions*, Masson's Ed., Vol. III, p. 280. *Cf.* Vol. I, Chap. XV. Mrs. de Quincey's young friend, Miss Watson, had been married to Lord Carbery in 1792.

161 3. **Just remark of Dr. Johnson's, etc.** The passage in De Quincey's mind, as Professor Winchester has pointed out to me, is undoubtedly the following, from the impressive paper (No. 103) with which Johnson closed *The Idler :* "There are few things not purely evil, of which we can say, without some emotion of uneasiness, 'this is the last.' Those who never could agree together, shed tears when mutual discontent has determined them to final separation; of a place which has been frequently visited, though without pleasure, the last look is taken with heaviness of heart."

161 27. **My whole succeeding life, etc.** *Cf.* Introduction, p. xxii.

162 8. **The silence of a summer morning, etc.** *Cf.* De Quincey's reflections, p. 247.

162 18. **"Pensive citadel."** From Wordsworth's sonnet, beginning :

> " Nuns fret not at their convent's narrow room ;
> And hermits are contented with their cells ;
> And students with their pensive citadels."

162 30. **Eighteen years ago.** Nineteen. *Cf.* " Notice to the Reader," p. 433.

162 33. **A picture of the lovely ——.** " The housekeeper was in the habit of telling me that the lady had *lived* (meaning, perhaps, had been *born*) two centuries ago ; that date would better agree with the tradition that the portrait was a copy from Vandyke. All that she knew further about the lady was that either to the grammar school, or to that particular college at Oxford with which the school was connected, or else to that particular college at Oxford with which Mr. Lawson personally was connected, or else, fourthly, to Mr. Lawson himself as a private individual, the unknown lady had been a special benefactress. She was also a special benefactress to me, through eighteen months, by means of her sweet Madonna countenance. And in some degree it serves to spiritualise and to hallow this service that of her who unconsciously rendered it I know neither the name, nor the exact rank or age, nor the place where she lived and died. She was parted from me by perhaps two centuries ; I from her by the gulf of eternity."— DE QUINCEY'S note to revised *Confessions*, Masson's Ed., Vol. III, p. 297.

163 27. **"Of Atlantean shoulders,"** etc. *Cf.* Milton, *Paradise Lost*, Book II, lines 305–307, concerning Beelzebub in the council :

> " Sage he stood
> With Atlantean shoulders fit to bear
> The weight of mightiest monarchies."

163 29. **As spacious as Salisbury plain.** A great flat or slightly undulating district in Wiltshire, between Salisbury and Devizes.

164 15. **That might have wakened the Seven Sleepers.** The Seven Sleepers of Ephesus, so often referred to in this way, were, according to the legend, seven young· Christians who, having hidden themselves in a cave near Ephesus during the persecution under Decius (A.D. 249–251), fell asleep, and did not awake for two or three hundred years ; in the meantime Christianity had become established.

164 21. **Dr. [Lawson].** " In former editions of this work I created him a doctor ; my object being to evade too close an approach to the

realities of the case, and consequently to personalities," etc. — *Confessions*, Masson's Ed., Vol. III, p. 249.

164 32. **"With Providence my guide."** *Cf.* Milton, *Paradise Lost*, last four lines:

> " The world was all before them, where to choose
> Their place of rest, and Providence their guide :
> They hand in hand with wand'ring steps and slow,
> Through Eden took their solitary way."

165 5. **On other personal accounts.** For the sake of seeing Wordsworth. *Cf.* p. 95, and note 95 16; also p. 106.

165 6. **I bent my steps towards North Wales.** Not at once. *Cf.* Introduction, p. xxi.

165 28. **"Not to know them, argues one's self unknown."** *Cf.* Milton, *Paradise Lost*, Book IV, lines 830–831 :

> " Not to know me argues yourselves unknown,
> The lowest of your throng."

167 7. **High road to the Head.** To Holyhead, probably, whence travellers would take ship for Ireland, or the Isle of Man.

167 22. **A harsh and contemptuous expression, etc.** " I was wrong if I said anything in my anger," adds De Quincey in his enlarged *Confessions*, " that was disparaging or sceptical as to the bishop's intellectual pretensions; which were not only very sound, but very appropriate to the particular stations which he filled. For the Bishop of Bangor (at that time Dr. Cleaver) was also the head of Brasenose, Oxford — which college was indebted to him for its leadership at that era in scholarship and discipline. In this academic character I learned afterwards that he might be called almost a reformer, — a wise, temperate, and successful reformer; and, as a scholar, I saw many years later that he had received the laudatory notice of Porson [the famous Greek scholar]." — *Works*, Masson's Ed., Vol. III, pp. 323–324.

168 11. **In a fortnight I was reduced to short allowance.** There seems to be no doubt that De Quincey deliberately cut loose from his guardians at this time (so that he could receive no more money), even before he determined to go to London (*cf.* Masson's Ed., Vol. III, p. 338). He was afraid, says Japp in the latest life of De Quincey, of being caught and sent back to his guardians. *Cf.* Hogg, *De Quincey and his Friends*, p. 34, and *Confessions*, p. 180.

170 13. **" Dym Sassenach."** De Quincey gives us here, apparently, a very inaccurate version of the Welsh phrase, *Dim Seisnaeg*

(*Seisonaeg*, *Seisoneg*, or *Seisneg*), "No English," which the man no doubt used. *Sassenach*, I am told, is somewhat nearer the Gaelic or Irish form than it is the Welsh; but the spelling *dym* is not proper to either language. *Seisnaeg* is the Welsh corruption of the Teutonic *Seaxe*, *Seaxna*, "Saxons," the name applied by the conquered Britons to all the invading Germanic tribes.

170 25. **Mr. Shelley is right in his notions about old age, etc.** This passage was omitted when, at an advanced age, De Quincey made his enlarged edition of the *Confessions*. He refers, no doubt, to Shelley's *Revolt of Islam*, Canto II, stanza 33:

> " New lore was this — old age, with its gray hair,
>   And wrinkled legends of unworthy things,
> And icy sneers, is nought : it cannot dare
>   To burst the chains which life forever flings
>   On the entangled soul's aspiring wings,
> So is it cold and cruel, and is made
>   The careless slave of that dark power which brings
> Evil, like blight, on man, who, still betrayed,
> Laughs o'er the grave in which his living hopes are laid."

170 29. **Means which I must omit, etc.** De Quincey borrowed twelve guineas from two Oswestry lawyers, whom he had met in the Snowdon district. A fine passage in the enlarged *Confessions* gives an account of De Quincey's journey: "a favourable example," as Dr. Garnett remarks, "of that power of magnifying and dignifying ordinary things, and recounting trivial incidents with majestic circumlocution, which have made two hundred and seventy-five pages of small type out of two short magazine papers." *Cf. Works*, Masson's Ed., Vol. III, p. 339, and pp. 343-348.

171 20. **The same person to whose breakfast-table I had access allowed me to sleep in a large unoccupied house.** On his arrival in London, De Quincey betook himself at once to a money-lender, Dell. Dell referred him to Mr. Brunell or Brown, whose office was in this house, which, as De Quincey tells us (Japp, *De Quincey Memorials*, Vol. II, p. 270), "stands in Greek Street, on the west, and is the house on that side nearest to Soho Square, but without looking into the square." In the enlarged *Confessions* De Quincey describes both this house and its master thus: "The house was not in itself, supposing that its face had been washed now and then, at all disrespectable. But it wore an unhappy countenance of gloom and unsocial fretfulness, due in reality to the long neglect of painting, cleansing, and in some instances of repairing."

As to the chief tenant : " From the expression of his face, but much more from the contradictory and self-counteracting play of his features, you gathered in a moment that he was a man who had much to conceal, and much, perhaps, that he would gladly forget. His eye expressed wariness against surprise, and passed in a moment into irrepressible glances of suspicion and alarm. No smile that ever his face naturally assumed but was pulled short up by some freezing counteraction, or was chased by some close-following expression of sadness. One feature there was of relenting goodness and nobleness in Mr. Brunell's char-acter, to which it was that subsequently I myself was most profoundly indebted for an asylum that saved my life. He had the deepest, the most liberal, and unaffected love of knowledge, but, above all, of that specific knowledge which we call literature. His own stormy (and no doubt oftentimes disgraceful) career in life, that had entangled him in perpetual feuds with his fellow-men, he ascribed, with bitter impre-cations, to the sudden interruption of his studies consequent upon his father's violent death, and to the necessity which threw him, at a boyish age, upon a professional life in the lower branches of the law — threw him, therefore, upon daily temptations, by surrounding him with opportunities for taking advantages not strictly honourable, before he had formed any fixed principles at all. From the very first, Mr. Brunell had entered zealously into such conversations with myself as either gave openings for reviving his own delightful remembrances of classic authors, or brought up sometimes doubts for solution, sometimes perplexities and cases of intricate construction for illustration and disentanglement." — *Works*, Masson's Ed., Vol. III, pp. 350–351 ; Riverside Ed., Vol. I, pp. 430–432.

173 3. **Improving on the plan of Cromwell, every night he slept in a different quarter of London.** " Clarendon relates that after the dissolution of his last Parliament, Cromwell ' became more appre-hensive of danger to his own person' than formerly; that he wore armour under his clothes, preserved the utmost secrecy with regard to his movements, was difficult of access, and ' rarely lodged two nights together in one chamber, but had many furnished and prepared ; to which his own key conveyed him and those he would have with him, when he had a mind to go to bed' (*History of the Rebellion, etc.*, Book XV). Of later historians of credit, Lingard, naturally no advocate for Oliver, repeats these stories, and even Lingard remarks in a foot-note that Clarendon's ' testimony can prove nothing more than that such reports were current, and obtained credit among the Royalists.' From Carlyle's *Letters and Speeches of Oliver Cromwell*, Vol. V, we

gather, from trustworthy sources cited, that Cromwell took necessary precautions against the Royalist assassins and levelling fanatics who threatened his life, but that his bearing during the time Clarendon refers to was very different from that described on mere hearsay by the Royalist historian. In fact, Cromwell throughout treated the various plots — and they were many — against himself with considerable indifference; 'little fiddling things,' he termed them." — HUNTER.

173 31. **Whether this child,** etc. Dr. Garnett suggests that Dickens must have had this whole situation in mind when he drew the Marchioness and Sally Brass in *Old Curiosity Shop*.

174 3. **The dismal Tartarus.** In Homer and earlier Greek mythology, Tartarus was a deep, dark abyss, as far below Hades as earth is below Heaven. In later poets it came to be the place of punishment for the wicked, and often merely the lower world; in which sense apparently De Quincey uses it here.

174 29. **"Cycle and epicycle, orb in orb."** *Cf. Paradise Lost,* Book VIII, lines 82–84:

> " How gird the sphere
> With centric and eccentric scribbl'd o'er,
> Cycle and epicycle, orb in orb."

175 4. **As Dr. Johnson has recorded,** etc. See Mrs. Piozzi's *Anecdotes of the late Samuel Johnson, LL.D., during the last twenty years of his life,* London, 1786, pp. 102–103: "To make himself some amends indeed, he took his chocolate liberally, pouring in large quantities of cream, or even melted butter; and was so fond of fruit, that though he usually eat seven or eight large peaches of a morning before breakfast began, and treated them with proportionate attention after dinner again, yet I have heard him protest that he never had quite as much as he wished of wall-fruit, except once in his life, and that was when we were all together at Ombersley, the seat of my Lord Sandys."

175 11. **"The world was all before us."** *Cf. Paradise Lost,* Book XII, lines 646–647:

> " The world was all before them, where to choose
> Their place of rest, and Providence their guide."

176 13. **"Sine Cerere,"** etc. *Sine Cerere et Baccho friget Venus, i.e.,* " without food and wine love grows cold." See Terence, *Eunuchus,* Act iv, sc. 5, line 6.

176 20. **More Socratico.** After the manner of Socrates. Socrates, the great Greek philosopher (470–399 B.C.) was accustomed to pass

most of his time in public, wherever men were gathered in greatest number. In philosophical investigation he was wont by proposing a series of questions to lead a pupil from some evident truth to the conclusion he desired to attain. In this way the most valuable moral instruction (which Socrates set before all other) was imparted in the guise of agreeable conversation. This is the "Socratic method."

179 16. **To haunt — to way-lay.** *Cf.* Wordsworth, *She was a Phantom of Delight*, line 10:

> "To haunt, to startle, and way-lay."

179 23. **"Too deep for tears."** *Cf.* Wordsworth, *Intimations of Immortality*, last line.

180 13. **His late majesty.** George III, who had lately died (1820) when De Quincey wrote.

180 29. **Soliciting.** That is, "acting as solicitor or advocate for." *Cf.* De Quincey's *Revolt of the Tartars* (1837): "By way of soliciting his cause more effectually" (Riverside Ed., Vol. XII, p. 7; Masson's Ed., Vol. VII, p. 373).

182 8. **A Jew named D[ell].** "At this period (autumn of 1856), when thirty-five years have elapsed since the first publication of these memoirs, reasons of delicacy can no longer claim respect for concealing the Jew's name, or at least the name which he adopted in his dealings with the Gentiles. I say, therefore, without scruple, that the name was Dell : and some years later it was one of the names that came before the House of Commons in connexion with something or other (I have long since forgotten *what*) growing out of the parliamentary movement against the Duke of York, in reference to Mrs. Clark, &c. Like all the other Jews with whom I have had negotiations, he was frank and honourable in his mode of conducting business. What he promised he performed ; and, if his terms were high, as naturally they could not *but* be, to cover his risks, he avowed them from the first."—DE QUINCEY'S additional note, enlarged *Confessions*, Masson's Ed., Vol. III, pp. 364–365.

183 24. **I had also some from the Marquess of [Sligo].** Some of these letters may be read in Japp, *De Quincey Memorials*, Chap. IV. The third Earl of Altamont was created Marquis of Sligo, Dec. 29, 1800. His son, Lord Westport, De Quincey's young friend, then became by courtesy Earl of Altamont. The latter's mother was Lady Louisa Howe, daughter of the famous admiral, Earl Howe.

188 9. **A thought . . . prettily expressed by a Roman poet.** In his account of his experiences in Wales in the enlarged *Confessions*,

De Quincey writes (Masson's Ed., Vol. III, p. 330): "Against Thugs I had Juvenal's license to be careless in the emptiness of my pockets (*cantabit vacuus coram latrone viator*)," but adds this footnote: "I am afraid, though many a year has passed since last I read Juvenal, that the true classical sense of *vacuus* is *careless, clear from all burden of anxiety*, so that *vacuitas* will be the *result* of immunity from robbery. But suffer me to understand it in the sense of *free from the burden of property*; in which sense *vacuitas* would be the *cause* of such immunity." In the sense desired by De Quincey, and to which there seems to be no objection, the line (*Satires*, X, line 22) means: "An empty-pocketed tramp will sing in the face of a robber."

188 13. **A murder committed on or near Hounslow Heath.** A note in the enlarged *Confessions* testifies to De Quincey's remarkable interest in murders (*cf.* note 340 2 on *Murder Considered as one of the Fine Arts:* "Two men, Holloway and Haggerty, were long afterwards convicted, upon very questionable evidence, as the perpetrators of this murder. The main testimony against them was that of a Newgate turnkey, who had imperfectly overheard a conversation between the two men. The current impression was that of great dissatisfaction with the evidence; and this impression was strengthened by the pamphlet of an acute lawyer, exposing the unsoundness and incoherency of the statements relied upon by the court. They were executed, however, in the teeth of all opposition. And, as it happened that an enormous wreck of life occurred at the execution (not fewer, I believe, than sixty persons having been trampled under foot by the unusual pressure of some brewers' draymen forcing their way with linked arms to the space below the drop), this tragedy was regarded for many years by a section of the London mob as a providential judgment upon the passive metropolis." — *Works*, Masson's Ed., Vol. III, p. 370. Dr. Garnett adds the following: "The execution took place on February 23, 1807. The 'acute lawyer' was James Harmer, afterwards Alderman, and well known as proprietor of the 'Weekly Dispatch.' Nothing is said in Mr. Harmer's pamphlet of any conversation between Holloway and Haggerty having been overheard by a turnkey. The chief evidence against them was that of a man named Hanfield, who professed to have been an accomplice, but who was suspected of having falsely accused them to get himself liberated from the hulks."

188 24. **"Lord of my learning and no land beside."** *Cf.* Shakspere, *King John*, Act i, sc. 1, line 137 (said of Faulconbridge):

"Lord of thy presence and no land beside."

189 9.   **"To slacken virtue,"** etc.   From *Paradise Regained*, Book II, lines 455–456; but *tempt* should be *prompt*.

190 9.   **"Ibi omnis effusus labor!"**   From Virgil, *Georgics*, IV, 491–492 (of Orpheus): "There was all his labor lost!"

190 13.   **The Earl of D[esart].**   "I had known Lord Desart, the eldest son of a very large family, some years earlier, when bearing the title of Lord Castlecuffe.   Cuffe was the family name; and I believe that they traced their descent to a person of some historic interest — viz. that Cuffe who was secretary to the unhappy Earl of Essex during his treasonable *émeute* against the government of Queen Elizabeth." — DE QUINCEY'S note to enlarged *Confessions*, Masson's Ed., Vol. III, p. 372.   Henry Cuffe, for some time lecturer at Merton College, Oxford, was tried and executed in 1601.

190 26.   **Anonymously, an author.**   *Cf.* Introduction, p. xvi.

190 34.   **Her letters.**   Several of Mrs. de Quincey's letters are to be found in Page's (Japp's) *Life of De Quincey*, and more in Japp's *De Quincey Memorials;* they exhibit a great deal of administrative ability joined with an uncommon tenacity of opinion.

191 4.   **Lady M. W. Montague.**   Lady Mary Wortley Montagu (1689–1762) was the eldest daughter of the Earl of Kingston.   She spent several years in Constantinople with her husband; after her return she was the object of much admiration, especially from Pope; a quarrel with him made her the object of bitter attacks (as "Sappho," in the *Dunciad*, etc.).   She wrote some poems, but her literary fame rests upon her *Letters*, published in 1763.   *Cf.* note 67 3.

191 19.   **I remembered the story about Otway.**   Thomas Otway (1652–85) wrote a number of tragedies in the classical style; the best is *Venice. Preserved* (1682), to which De Quincey refers in the beginning of the *Revolt of the Tartars*.   The story here in his mind first appeared in the *Lives of the Poets* (ascribed to Theophilus Cibber, 1753), Vol. II, p. 335.   To avoid the importunity of creditors, we are told, Otway had retired in his last days to a public house on Tower Hill.   But, adds the chronicler, it is reported that, after suffering the torments of starvation, the dramatist begged a shilling of a gentleman in a neighboring coffee-house on April 14, 1685.   The gentleman gave him a guinea, whereupon Otway bought a roll, and was choked by the first mouthful.   The authenticity of this tale is extremely doubtful.

193 3.   **And unpropitious as those of a Saracen's head.**   The Saracen's head, horribly carved, was a frequent tavern sign.   *Cf.* De Quincey's *Works*, Masson's Ed., Vol. II, p. 350; Riverside Ed., Vol. III, pp. 469–470: "Being a very large woman, and, moreover, a masculine woman,

with a bronzed complexion, and always choosing to wear, at night, a turban, round hair that was as black as the 'Moors of Malabar,' she presented an exact likeness of a Saracen's Head, as painted over inn-doors."

193 19. A remote part of England. De Quincey went to Liverpool, to his friend Mrs. Best, where he remained while his guardians debated his future. See Japp, *De Quincey Memorials*, Vol. I, p. 92.

194 13. An address to —— in ——shire. To the Priory in Chester.

194 14. I have never heard a syllable. It was the work of the famous French poet, Alfred de Musset, to depict, in his recently recovered translation of the *Confessions*, a second meeting between the Opium-Eater and Anne. See Garnett, pp. 169–188, where the French of De Musset is given.

195 4. The ruin they had begun. At this point closed the instalment of the *Confessions* in the *London Magazine* for September, 1821, and the following note was appended :

"[The remainder of this very interesting article will be given in the next number. — ED.] "

195 8. Thy never-ending terraces. A range of houses is often named as a "Terrace," in England and Scotland especially, while retaining the street name. This is the case in the western (residence) portion of Oxford Street.

196 9. "That way I would fly for comfort" (*for rest*, more accurately, in 1856 edition). *Cf.* Psalm lv, 6 :

"Oh that I had wings like a dove, for then would I fly away and be at rest."

196 13. Second birth of my sufferings. *Cf.* Introduction, p. xxvi, and note 252 28.

196 17. Orestes was the son, according to Greek legend, of Agamemnon and Clytemnestra. He slew his mother and her paramour Ægisthus in vengeance for their murder of his father, and was then pursued by the Furies (called euphemistically "Eumenides, the well-wishers"). *Cf.* De Quincey's footnote.

196, footnote. φίλον ὕπνη κ.τ.λ. (ὕπνη should be ὕπνου). From Euripides, *Orestes*, 211 :

"O sweet balm of sleep, cure of disease."

197 10. "Sleep no more!" *Cf.* Shakspere, *Macbeth*, Act ii, sc. 2, line 35.

197 19. **I am again in London, etc.**   In August, 1821, when De Quincey was writing this for the *London Magazine*, he had already been three months away from his wife and children, whom he had left, as he says below, in that very cottage to which his desire had turned in the time of his vagrancy (*cf.* p. 196), from November, 1802, to March, 1803, when Wordsworth, the object of his youthful veneration, occupied it.

197, footnote 1. **ἡδὺ δούλευμα.** Euripides, *Orestes*, 221 : τὸ δούλευμ' ἡδύ, "sweet service." Electra wipes off the "clotted foam" from her brother's mouth.

197, footnote 2. **ἄναξ ἀνδρῶν.** A common Homeric appellative for Agamemnon. *Cf. Iliad*, I, 172.

197, footnote 3. **ὄμμα θεῖσ' εἴσω πέπλων.** *Cf.* Euripides, *Orestes*, 280. But Paley says Porson's ὄμμα, "face," should be κρᾶτα, "head."

199 16. **"The stately Pantheon."**   In the time to which De Quincey refers, the Pantheon, in Oxford Street near Poland Street, was a great concert room or theatre ; before 1854 we find it used as a great bazaar ; and now it is a wine warehouse. In the enlarged *Confessions* De Quincey adds this note : "'*Stately*': — It is but fair to say that Wordsworth meant to speak of the *interior*, which could very little be inferred from the mean, undistinguished outside, as seen presenting itself endways in Oxford Street."—*Works*, Masson's Ed., Vol. III, p. 380.   The reference is to the following lines in the opening stanza of Wordsworth's *Power of Music*, describing a street fiddler in London :

"Near the stately Pantheon you 'll meet with the same
In the street that from Oxford hath borrowed its name."

200 17. **φάρμακον νηπενθές.** "Drug banishing sorrow." *Cf.* Homer, *Odyssey*, IV, 220–221, where the reference is thought by many to be to opium. But *cf.* p. 243, and note 243 24.

200, footnote. **Mr. Flat-man, etc.** Thomas Flatman (1637–88) was a much better miniature painter than poet. He brought out, however, four editions of his *Poems and Songs*, and in the last, dated 1686, he printed for the first time *On the much lamented Death of our late Sovereign Lord King Charles II. of Blessed Memory. A Pindarique Ode*. De Quincey's quotation is a vague reminiscence of line 14, where the poet deplores the lack of a word (implying decease)

"Appropriate to *Crowned Heads*, who never ought to Die";

and line 25, where he adds that princes should

"Never submit to Fate, but only Disappear."

201 4. **"L'Allegro" and "Il Penseroso"** are the titles of Milton's well-known descriptive poems. *L'Allegro* means "the cheerful man," and *Il Penseroso* "the thoughtful man."

201 24. **Tuesday and Saturday,** *viz.*, the two days on which the *Gazette* is (or used to be) published (De Quincey's footnote, enlarged *Confessions*).

203 34. **"Ponderibus librata suis."** "Held in a state of equilibrium." *Cf.* Ovid, *Metamorphoses*, I, 13, and Cicero, *Tusculanae Disputationes*, V, 24.

204 3. **As some old gentleman says in Athenæus, etc.** De Quincey throws some doubt on this reference by omitting it in his enlarged edition. Athenæus, a Greek rhetorician and grammarian, produced about A.D. 200 his *Deipnosophistæ*, in which he gives a friend an account of a supposed banquet of scholars and wits. It is a storehouse of quotations, many of them from lost works.

204, footnote. **The brilliant author of "Anastasius."** Thomas Hope (1770–1831), "merchant prince, Oriental traveller," etc., published *Anastasius, or Memoirs of a Greek*, in 1819. The passage from this novel — which deserved a more enduring popularity — is given in full by Garnett, pp. 255–258.

205 7. **I happened to say to him.** De Quincey adds here in the enlarged edition the following footnote : "This surgeon it was who first made me aware of the dangerous variability in opium as to strength under the shifting proportions of its combination with alien impurities. Naturally, as a man professionally alive to the danger of creating any artificial need of opium beyond what the anguish of his malady at any rate demanded, trembling every hour on behalf of his poor children, lest, by any indiscretion of his own, he should precipitate the crisis of his disorder, he saw the necessity of reducing the daily dose to a *minimum*. But to do this he must first obtain the means of measuring the quantities of opium ; not the apparent quantities as determined by weighing, but the *virtual* quantities after allowing for the alloy or varying amounts of impurity. This, however, was a visionary problem. To allow for it was simply impossible. The problem, therefore, changed its character. Not to measure the impurities was the object ; for, whilst entangled with the operative and efficient parts of opium, they could not be measured. To separate and eliminate the impure (or inert) parts, this was now the object. And this was effected finally by a particular mode of boiling the opium. That done, the residuum became equable in strength ; and the daily doses could be nicely adjusted. About 18 grains formed his daily ration for many years. This, upon

the common hospital equation, expresses 18 times 25 drops of laudanum. But, since 25 is $= \frac{100}{4}$, therefore 18 times one quarter of a
hundred is = one quarter of 1800, and that, I suppose, is 450. So
much this surgeon averaged upon each day for about twenty years.
Then suddenly began a fiercer stage of the anguish from his disease.
But then, also, the fight was finished, and the victory was won. All
duties were fulfilled: his children prosperously launched in life; and
death, which to himself was becoming daily more necessary as a relief
from torment, now fell injuriously upon nobody." — *Works*, Masson's
Ed., Vol. III, pp. 385–386.

207 33. **"Next Friday, by the blessing of Heaven, I purpose,"**
etc., is changed, in the enlarged edition, to " Next Monday, wind and
weather permitting, I purpose," etc., and De Quincey adds this footnote : " My authority was the late Sir George Beaumont [Wordsworth's
friend], an old familiar acquaintance of the duke's. But such expressions are always liable to grievous misapplication. By 'the late' duke
Sir George meant that duke once so well known to the nation as the
partisan friend of Fox, Burke, Sheridan, &c., at the era of the great
French Revolution in 1789–93. Since *his* time, I believe there have been
three generations of ducal Howards : who are always interesting to the
English nation : first, from the bloody historic traditions surrounding
their great house; secondly, from the fact of their being at the head of
the British peerage." — *Works*, Masson's Ed., Vol. III, p. 388.

208 9. **Grassini sang at the Opera.** Josephina Grassini (1773–
1850), an Italian contralto, made her first appearance in 1794, and
was the reigning London favorite at the opening of the century. Her
Majesty's Theatre, or Opera House, where she sang, is on the corner
of Haymarket and Pall Mall, and dates from 1705. It was burned
down and rebuilt in 1789–90, enlarged in 1816–18, and the interior
again burned in 1867.

208 14. **The most pleasant place . . . for passing an evening.** " I
trust that my reader has not been so inattentive to the windings of my
narrative as to fancy me speaking here of the Brown-Brunell and
Pyment [Brunell's clerk] period. Naturally I had no money disposable
at that period for the opera. I am speaking here of years stretching
far beyond those boyish scenes — interludes in my Oxford life, or long
after Oxford." — DE QUINCEY's note, Masson's Ed., Vol. III, p. 389.

208 22. **In some interlude.** Apparently a vocal solo introduced
between the acts of an opera or the parts of an orchestral program.

208 24. **As Andromache.** The reference seems to be to a selection
from Grétry's *Andromaque*, which was produced at Paris in 1780.

208 31. **The fine extravaganza . . . in "Twelfth Night."** The opening speech of the play is meant: "If music be the food of love, play on," etc. *Cf.* also *Merchant of Venice*, Act v, sc. 1.

208 34. **A passage in the "Religio Medici."** This is worthy of a longer quotation: "For even that vulgar and Tavern-Musick, which makes one man merry, another mad, strikes in me a deep fit of devotion, and a profound contemplation of the First Composer. There is something in it of Divinity more than the ear discovers: it is an Hieroglyphical and shadowed lesson of the whole World, and creatures of GOD; such a melody to the ear, as the whole World, well understood, would afford the understanding. In brief, it is a sensible fit of that harmony which intellectually sounds in the ears of GOD."— Part II, sec. 9.

210 1. **A pleasure such as that with which Weld the traveller, etc.** "The women, on the contrary, speak with the utmost ease, and the language as pronounced by them appears as soft as the Italian. They have, without exception, the most delicate harmonious voices I ever heard, and the most pleasing, gentle laugh that it is possible to conceive. I have oftentimes sat among a group of them for an hour or two together, merely for the pleasure of listening to their conversation, on account of its wonderful softness and delicacy.".— I. WELD, JR., *Travels through the States of North Carolina, and the Provinces of Upper and Lower Canada during the years 1795, 1796, and 1797* (published 1799), pp. 411–412; 3d ed. (1800), Vol. II, p. 288. Garnett remarks that it is probably for the reason indicated by De Quincey that he has thought Finnish the most musical language he ever heard spoken.

210 16. **Marinus in his life of Proclus.** Proclus (A.D. 412–485) was a celebrated Neoplatonist philosopher, and author of a large number of philosophical works, as well as of works on grammar and a set of arguments against Christianity. Marinus of Flavia Neapolis in Palestine was a philosopher and rhetorician, and a disciple of Proclus. The obscurity of his *Vita Procli* is probably not greater than that produced by De Quincey in thus referring to an utterly unread work.

213 9. **The Cave of Trophonius.** De Quincey evidently refers to the well-known legend that a visitor to the oracle in the cave of Trophonius never smiled again. Hence the Greek saying of a dejected man, " He has visited the cave of Trophonius."

213 24. **Behmenism.** Jacob Böhme, or Behmen (1575–1624), a shoemaker of Görlitz in German Silesia, acquired celebrity by some rather recondite speculations in the region of mysticism and theosophy

213 25.   **Sir H. Vane, the younger** (1612–62) was one of the wisest and most disinterested of the Independent leaders in the controversy between the Parliament and Charles I.   After the Restoration he had the personal engagement of Charles II for his safety, but, the Convention Parliament being no longer in session, he was without shadow of equity tried, condemned, and executed.   At twenty-four Vane had been governor of Massachusetts, where he remained several years.   *Cf.* Milton's Sonnet *To Sir Henry Vane the Younger* (1652) and Wordsworth's Sonnet, *Great Men have been among us.*   Vane's tracts on politics and religion are of great interest, but he holds no place in the history of philosophy, strictly so called.

214 12.   **Oh! just, subtle, and mighty opium!**   This whole passage is doubtless suggested, as Professor Winchester points out, by the sublime apostrophe to Death with which Walter Raleigh closes his *History of the World:* " O, eloquent, just, and mighty Death ! whom none could advise, thou hast perswaded ; what none have dared, thou hast done ; and whom all the world flattered, thou only hast cast out of the world and despised : thou hast drawn together all the far stretched greatness, all the pride, cruelty, and ambition of man, and covered it all over with these two narrow words, *Hic jacet.*"

214 14.   **"The pangs that tempt the spirit to rebel."**   From Wordsworth's *White Doe of Rylstone*, Dedication:

> " And griefs whose aery motion comes not near
> The pangs that tempt the Spirit to rebel."

214 20.   **"Wrongs unredress'd and insults unavenged."**   From Wordsworth's *Excursion*, Book III, first part :

> " Not alone
> Dread of the persecuting sword, remorse,
> Wrongs unredressed, or insults unavenged,
> And unavengeable, defeated pride, . . ."

Quoted also in De Quincey's *Modern Greece*, Riverside Ed., Vol. XII, p. 352, Masson's Ed., Vol. VII, p. 340.

214 27.   **Beyond the splendour of Babylon and Hekatompylos.** Under King Nebuchadnezzar (604–561) the capital of Babylonia became a huge and splendid metropolis.   The palace, called by Nebuchadnezzar "the Admiration of Mankind," was of magnificent extent, and the Hanging Gardens, within the palace precincts, were reckoned one of the seven wonders of the world.   Hekatompylos, "*i.e.* the *hundred-gated* (from ἑκατόν, *hekaton*, a hundred, and πυλη, *pyle*, a gate)," adds De Quincey

in a footnote to enlarged *Confessions*. "This epithet of hundred-gated was applied to the Egyptian Thebes in contradistinction to the ἑπτάπυλος (*heptápylos*, or *seven-gated*) which designated the Grecian Thebes, within one day's journey of Athens." Thebes, part of which is now covered by Luxor, was the capital of Egypt, and its remains of temples and tombs are the most imposing and interesting relics of ancient Egyptian civilization.

214 28. **"From the anarchy of dreaming sleep."** From Wordsworth's *Excursion*, Book IV, near the beginning:

> "Who from the anarchy of dreaming sleep,
>   Or from its death-like void, with punctual care,
>   And touch as gentle as the morning light,
>   Restor'st us, daily, to the powers of sense
>   And reason's stedfast rule—..."

215 13. **The Bodleian.** The great library of Oxford University (the various colleges have also their own libraries), and in Great Britain second only to the library of the British Museum. It was formally named after Sir Thomas Bodley in 1604, having been reëstablished by him in 1597–1602. De Quincey was a more or less regular student at Oxford from 1800 to 1808.

216 10. **In the depth of mountains.** *Cf.* description of Dove Cottage, Grasmere, p. 226.

216 14. **Kant, Fichte, Schelling, etc.** De Quincey was one of the chief followers of Coleridge in the latter's effort to make the German transcendental philosophy, which dates from Immanuel Kant's *Critique of Pure Reason* (1781), at home in England. Some of De Quincey's best biographical writings concern Kant, and, in his own mind, his greatest distinction should have been as a philosopher. *Cf.* p. 229.

216 18. **A single female servant.** For an account of the misdoings attributed by De Quincey to this woman, "a foolish, selfish, and ignorant old maid," see Riverside Ed., Vol. III, pp. 610 *et seq.*; Masson's Ed., Vol. III, pp. 200 *et seq.*

216 18. **Honi soit qui mal y pense.** "Shame to him who thinks evil of it." The motto of the Order of the Garter, concerning which see pp. 58–59 and note 58 23.

216 31. **I am X. Y. Z., etc.** These initials were De Quincey's usual signature to his articles in the *London Magazine*. An article on John Paul Richter, in December, 1821, was signed *Grasmeriensis Teutonizans*.

216 32. **Custos Rotulorum.** "In England, the keeper of the rolls

or records (of the session of court) ; the chief civil officer of a county."
— *Century Dictionary.*

216 34. **"The rainy Sunday,"** etc.   *Cf.* p. 199.

217 15. **Medical advice from "Anastasius."**   *Cf.* p. 204 and note.

217 18. **Dr. Buchan.**   *Cf.* p. 202, footnote.

217 28. **Between every indulgence.**   It is interesting to see this
troublesome locution cropping out in so careful a writer as De Quincey.

217 34. **A very melancholy event.**   The death of little Catherine
Wordsworth, a great favorite of De Quincey, is thus referred to ; it
took place June 4, 1812, while De Quincey was on a visit to London.
Cf. his account in Riverside Ed., Vol. III, pp. 578 *et seq.* ; Masson's
Ed., Vol. II, pp. 440–445 : " Never, perhaps, from the foundations of
those mighty hills, was there so fierce a convulsion of grief as mastered
my faculties on receiving that heart-shattering news," etc.   *Cf.* also
note 248 29.

218 5. **A most appalling irritation of the stomach.**   *Cf.* references
to this trouble, pp. 158, 172.   As to the nature of this malady and its treatment by opium, see note 158 1.   " De Quincey's apology," adds Garnett,
" is further supported by the testimony of Berlioz," which runs in English
thus : " My father for a long time suffered from an incurable disease of
the stomach, which a hundred times brought him to the gates of the
tomb.   He almost ceased to eat.   The steady use of opium in considerable doses, from day to day, alone revived for a day his exhausted
powers.   Several years ago, worn out by his horrible suffering, he took
in one dose thirty-two grains of opium.   ' But, I confess,' he said to me
later in telling of his act, ' it was not to cure me.'   This frightful dose of
poison, instead of killing him, as he expected, dissipated almost at once
his sufferings, and restored him for the time to health."   " The ' frightful
dose,' according to De Quincey's calculation," remarks Dr. Garnett,
" would be equivalent to 800 drops, or 200 under the amount which he
[p. 222] speaks of as a trifle."

219 1. **In the next edition,** etc.   The actual revised *Confessions*
fairly fulfils this threat, by converting the two magazine articles into
nearly 250 closely printed pages.

219 28. **"Sweet men,"** etc.   The intention is evidently to quote
from the Prologue to the *Canterbury Tales*, lines 221 *et seq.*, of the
Friar :

> " Ful swetely herde he confessioun,
> And plesaunt was his absolucioun ;
> He was an esy man to yeve penaunce," etc.

219, footnote. **Followers of Zeno.** Zeno, who died about 264 B.C., founded about 308 the Stoic sect, which took its name from the " Painted Porch " (Στοὰ Ποικίλη) in the Agora at Athens, where the master taught. The Stoics held that men should be free from passion, and undisturbed by joy or grief, submitting themselves uncomplainingly to their fate. Such austere views are, of course, as far as possible removed from those of the Eudæmonist, who sought happiness as the end of life.

220 21. **No old gentleman, etc.** *Cf.* p. 204, footnote.

220 28. **Ramadan** is the ninth month of the Mohammedan year; each day of that month is observed as a fast from dawn to sunset.

221 27. **Νυχθημερον.** "A night and a day."

222 3. **"That moveth altogether, if it move at all."** From Words-worth's *Resolution and Independence:*

> " Motionless as a cloud the old Man stood,
> That heareth not the loud winds when they call
> And moveth all together, if it move at all."

222 8. **I understood him, or fancied that I did.** The abstruseness and involution of Kant's chief writings are proverbial.

222 21. **A Malay knocked at my door.** This Malay has been thought by some to be fictitious, — a notion which De Quincey's daughters reject with indignation. See Saintsbury, *Essays in English Literature, 1780–1860,* p. 440, and Japp, *De Quincey Memorials,* Vol. I, pp. 41, 51; Vol. II, p. 269. It is worth noting that De Quincey specifically rejects a similar notion in an article in the *London Magazine* for March, 1824. Discussing a review of his *Confessions* in the *New Edinburgh Review,* which lived from July, 1821, to April, 1823, he says : " As another point which, if left unnoticed, might affect something more important to myself than the credit of my taste or judgment, — let me inform my reviewer that, when he traces an incident which I have recorded most faithfully about a Malay to a tale of Mr. Hogg's [the Ettrick Shepherd is meant], he makes me indebted to a book which I never saw. In saying this I mean no disrespect to Mr. Hogg ; on the contrary, I am sorry that I have never seen it : for I have a great admiration for Mr. Hogg's genius, and have had the honour of his personal acquaintance for the last ten years." — *Works,* Masson's Ed., Vol. IX, p. 39, note 2.

222 23. **To a seaport.** " Viz., Whitehaven, Workington, &c.," inserts De Quincey in the text of the 1856 edition; he appends there this explanation : " Between the seafaring populations on the coast of Lancashire and the corresponding populations on the coast of Cumberland (such as Ravenglass, Whitehaven, Workington, Maryport, &c.)

there was a slender current of interchange constantly going on, and especially in the days of press gangs — in part by sea, but in part also by land." — *Works*, Masson's Ed., Vol. III, p. 402.

223 20. **The beautiful English face of the girl.** "This girl, Barbara Lewthwaite, was already at that time a person of some poetic distinction, being (unconsciously to herself) the chief speaker in a little pastoral poem of Wordsworth's. That she was really beautiful, and not merely so described by me for the sake of improving the picturesque effect, the reader will judge from this line in the poem, written perhaps ten years earlier, when Barbara might be six years old : —

'T was little Barbara Lewthwaite, a child of beauty rare ! '

This coming from William Wordsworth, both a fastidious judge and a truth-speaker of the severest literality, argues some real pretensions to beauty, or real at that time. But it is notorious that, in the anthologies of earth through all her zones, one flower beyond every other is liable to change, which flower is the countenance of woman. Whether in his fine stanzas upon ' Mutability,' where the most pathetic instances of this earthly doom are solemnly arrayed, Spenser has dwelt sufficiently upon this, the saddest of all, I do not remember." — DE QUINCEY'S note, enlarged *Confessions*. *Cf. Works*, Riverside Ed., Vol. I, pp. 437 *et seq.*; Masson's Ed., Vol. III, pp. 403, 460 *et seq.* But note the following from Wordsworth's preface to the poem in question, *The Pet Lamb* (1800) : "Barbara Lewthwaite, now living at Ambleside (1843), though much changed as to beauty, was one of two most lovely sisters. Almost the first words my poor brother John said, when he visited us for the first time at Grasmere, were, ' Were those two Angels that I have just seen ? ' and from his description I have no doubt they were those two sisters. . . . Barbara Lewthwaite was not in fact the child whom I had seen and overheard as described in the poem. I chose the name for reasons implied in the above; and will here add a caution against the use of names of living persons. Within a few months after the publication of this poem, I was much surprised, and more hurt, to find it in a child's school-book which, having been compiled by Lindley Murray, had come into use at Grasmere School where Barbara was a pupil; and, alas ! I had the mortification of hearing that she was very vain of being thus distinguished : and, in after-life, she used to say that she remembered the incident and what I said to her upon the occasion."

Spenser's *Cantos of Mutabilitie*, at the end of the *Faerie Queene*, do not touch upon the subject indicated by De Quincey.

223 31. **My knowledge of the Oriental tongues, etc.** *Cf.* note 12 4.

224 2. **Adelung's "Mithridates."** A work on Oriental languages by J. C. Adelung (1732–1806), a German philologist. It should, perhaps, be remarked that De Quincey here names together languages belonging to entirely distinct families.

226 1. **A third, etc.** He was also English, a surgeon at Brighton, De Quincey tells us in the enlarged edition.

226 12. **Let there be a cottage, standing in a valley.** "The cottage and the valley concerned in this description were not imaginary: the valley was the lovely one, *in those days*, of Grasmere ; and the cottage was occupied for more than twenty years by myself, as immediate successor, in the year 1809, to Wordsworth. Looking to the limitation here laid down — viz., *in those days* — the reader will inquire in what way *Time* can have affected the beauty of Grasmere. Do the Westmoreland valleys turn grey-headed ? O reader ! this is a painful memento for some of us ! Thirty years ago, a gang of Vandals (nameless, I thank heaven, to me), for the sake of building a mail-coach road that never would be wanted, carried, at a cost of £3000 to the defrauded parish, a horrid causeway of sheer granite masonry, for three-quarters-of-a-mile, right through the loveliest succession of secret forest dells and sly recesses of the lake, margined by unrivalled ferns, amongst which was the *Osmunda regalis*. This sequestered angle of Grasmere is described by Wordsworth, as it unveiled itself on a September morning, in the exquisite poems on the "Naming of Places." From this also — viz. this spot of ground, and this magnificent crest (the Osmunda) — was suggested that unique line, the finest independent line through all the records of verse,

' Or lady of the lake,
Sole-sitting by the shores of old romance.'

Rightly therefore did I introduce this limitation. The Grasmere before and after this outrage were two different vales."— DE QUINCEY'S footnote, enlarged *Confessions*, Masson's Ed., Vol. III, p. 406. *Cf.* note 127 3. The poem here referred to is IV in the *Poems on the Naming of Places;* "lake" in the extract was afterwards changed to "mere." De Quincey repeats his praise of this line, and regrets the change in it, in a footnote to the *Essay on Shelley*, Riverside Ed., Vol. VI, p. 604; Masson's Ed., Vol. XI, p. 370.

227 6. **"And at the doors and windows,"** etc. *Cf.* the actual lines in Thomson's poem, Canto I, stanza 43:

" And oft began
(So work'd the wizard) wintry storms to swell,
As heaven and earth they would together mell:
At doors and windows, threatening, seem'd to call
The demons of the tempest, growling fell,
Yet the least entrance found they none at all;
Whence sweeter grew our sleep, secure in massy hall."

227 17. **Mr. [Anti-Slavery Clarkson].** *Cf.* p. 133 and note 133 9.

227 29. **St. Thomas's day** is the twenty-first of December.

228 8. **I would have joined Dr. Johnson.** Professor Masson gives the following footnote: "Jonas Hanway, tourist, philanthropist, and author (1712–1786), and said to have been 'the first man who ventured to walk the streets of London with an umbrella over his head,' was a vehement opponent of tea, and got into conflict with Dr. Johnson on that subject, as appears from the following passage in Boswell's *Life of Johnson* (Temple Ed., Vol. I, p. 304):—'His defence of tea against Mr. Jonas Hanway's violent attack upon that elegant and popular beverage shows how very well a man of genius can write upon the slightest subject, when he writes, as the Italians say, *con amore.* I suppose no person ever enjoyed with more relish the influence of that fragrant leaf than Johnson. The quantities which he drank of it at all hours were so great that his nerves must have been uncommonly strong not to have been extremely relaxed by such an intemperate use of it. He assured me that he never felt the least inconvenience from it; which is a proof that the fault of his constitution was rather a too great tension of fibres than the contrary. Mr. Hanway wrote an angry answer to Johnson's review of his *Essay on Tea* (1756); and Johnson, after a full and deliberate pause, made a reply to it: the only instance, I believe, in the whole course of his life, when he condescended to oppose anything that was written against him.'" Concerning Hanway, see Dobson's *Eighteenth Century Vignettes*, 1892.

228 20. **Contrived "a double debt to pay."** From Goldsmith's *Deserted Village*, lines 229–230:

" The chest contrived a double debt to pay,
A bed by night, a chest of drawers by day."

228 33. **A parte ante, etc.** "From the part before and from the part after," *i.e.*, the teapot has always existed and is always to exist.

229 4. **But no, dear M[argaret].** As to De Quincey's wife, *cf.* Introduction, p. xxv.

229 11. **" Little golden receptacle."** *Cf.* p. 204, footnote.

229 17. **"Stately Pantheon."** *Cf.* p. 199 and note 199 16.

229 21. **German metaphysics.** *Cf.* p. 216 and note 216 14.

230 3. **I cannot fail . . . to be a gainer.** *Cf.* Woodhouse's description of De Quincey, quoted in Introduction, p. xxviii.

230 16. **An Iliad of woes.** *Cf.* the opening lines of Homer's *Iliad :*

> " Achilles' wrath, to Greece the direful spring
> Of woes unnumbered, heavenly Goddess sing."

230 18. **"As when," etc.** The lines in Shelley's poem, Canto V, stanza 23, read :

> " With hue like that when some," etc.

232 31. **Reading is an accomplishment of mine.** *Cf.* Woodhouse's *Conversations*, Garnett, pp. 198–199 ; Hogg's *De Quincey, etc.*, pp. 76–77 : " It seems to me, from the manner in which the Opium-Eater recited a few lines occasionally which he had occasion to quote, that the reading upon which in his Confessions he piques himself would scarcely appear good to most people. He reads with too inward a voice ; he dwells much upon the long vowels (this he does in his conversation, which makes it resemble more a speech delivered in a debating society than the varitonous discourse usually held among friends) ; he ekes out particular syllables, has generally much appearance of intensity, and, in short, removes his tone and manner too much from the mode of common language. Hence I could not always catch the words in his quotations, and though one acquainted with the quotation beforehand would relish it the more from having an opportunity afforded of dwelling upon it, and from hearing the most made of those particular parts for the sake of which it is brought forward, yet general hearers would be left far behind, and in a state of wonder at the quoter." Mr. H. G. Bohn, who used to see De Quincey in his father's bookshop, "remembers that he always seemed to speak in a kind of whisper." Others have admired the low silvery tone of his voice in conversation.

233 4. **John Kemble . . . Mrs. Siddons.** J. Kemble (1757–1823) was a famous English actor ; Mrs. Siddons (1755–1831) was easily the most celebrated of English actresses. De Quincey tells us (Riverside Ed., Vol. III, pp. 584–594 ; Masson's Ed., Vol. II, pp. 446–454) of his meeting Mrs. Siddons at the house of Hannah More (see note 128 9) in 1813 or 1814, and of her brilliant readings from Shakspere.

233 8. **Overstep the modesty of nature.** From *Hamlet*, Act iii, sc. 2.

233 13. **A young lady sometimes comes and drinks tea with us.** Probably Dorothy Wordsworth is meant.

233 17. **Often indeed he reads admirably.** In an early MS. of the *Confessions* this read "Blank verse he reads admirably," and it was followed by this interesting paragraph (*Posthumous Works*, Vol. I, pp. 318–319): "This, then, has been the extent of my reading for upwards of sixteen months. It frets me to enter those rooms of my cottage in which the books stand. In one of them, to which my little boy has access, he has found out a use for some of them. Somebody has given him a bow and arrows — God knows who, certainly not I, for I have not energy or ingenuity to invent a walking-stick — thus equipped for action, he rears up the largest of the folios that he can lift, places them on a tottering base, and then shoots until he brings down the enemy. He often presses me to join him; and sometimes I consent, and we are both engaged together in these intellectual labours. We build up a pile, having for its base some slender modern metaphysician, ill able (poor man!) to sustain such a weight of philosophy. Upon this we place the Dutch quartos of Descartes and Spinoza; then a third story of Schoolmen in folio — the Master of Sentences, Suarez, Picus Mirandula, and the Telemonian bulk of Thomas Aquinas; and when the whole architecture seems firm and compact, we finish our system of metaphysics by roofing the whole with Duval's enormous Aristotle. So far there is some pleasure — building up is something, but what is that to destroying? Thus thinks, at least, my little companion, who now, with the wrath of the Pythian Apollo, assumes his bow and arrows; plants himself in the remotest corner of the room, and prepares his fatal shafts. The bow-string twangs, flights of arrows are in the air, but the Dutch impregnability of the Bergen-op-Zooms at the base receives the few which reach the mark, and they recoil without mischief done. Again the baffled archer collects his arrows, and again he takes his station. An arrow issues forth and takes effect on a weak side of Thomas. Symptoms of dissolution appear — the cohesion of the system is loosened — the Schoolmen begin to totter; the Stagyrite trembles; Philosophy rocks to its centre; and, before it can be seen whether time will do anything to heal their wounds, another arrow is planted in the schism of their ontology; the mighty structure heaves — reels — seems in suspense for one moment, and then, with one choral crash — to the frantic joy of the young Sagittary — lies subverted on the floor! Kant and Aristotle, Nominalists and Realists, Doctors Seraphic or Irrefragable, what cares he? All are at his feet — the Irrefragable has been confuted by his arrows, the Seraphic has been found mortal, and the greatest philosopher and the least differ but according to the brief noise they have made."

233 18. **I read no book but one.** That is, Ricardo's *Political Economy*.

234 1. **De emendatione, etc.** "Of the amendment of the human mind." The fragment (1656) of similar title by the great pantheist sets forth the knowledge of truth as the highest good.

234 26. **The utter feebleness, etc.** "These vehement expressions of disdain are almost wholly omitted from subsequent editions. In an article in the *London Magazine* for March, 1824, De Quincey thus apologizes for the introduction of Ricardo into the Opium-Eater : —
' For this, as for some other passages, I was justly attacked by an able and liberal critic in the *New Edinburgh Review* [which lived only from July, 1821, to April, 1823], as for so many absurd irrelevancies : in that situation no doubt they were so ; and of this, in spite of the haste in which I had written the greater part of the book, I was fully aware. However, as they said no more than what was true, I was glad to take that, or any occasion which I could invent, for offering my public testimony of gratitude to Mr. Ricardo. The truth is, I thought that something might occur to intercept any more appropriate mode of conveying my homage to Mr. Ricardo's ear, which should else more naturally have been expressed in a direct work on political economy. This fear was at length realized — not in the way I had apprehended, viz., by my own death, but by Mr. Ricardo's. And, now, therefore, I felt happy that, at whatever price of good taste, I had in some imperfect way made known my sense of his high pretensions — although, unfortunately, I had given him no means of judging whether my applause were of any value. For during the interval between September, 1821, and Mr. Ricardo's death in September, 1823, I had found no leisure for completing my work on political economy.' [*Works*, Masson's Ed., Vol. IX, pp. 39-40.] The disinterested enthusiasm for intellectual beauty which led De Quincey, at some sacrifice of symmetry and propriety, to introduce Ricardo into the Opium-Eater, manifests one of the most prepossessing features of his own character." — GARNETT. *Cf.* 156 29 and note.

236 11. **"Prolegomena," etc.** This work, even in a fragmentary form, has not been preserved ; the same material may of course have been used in De Quincey's various writings on the subject.

236 17. **At a provincial press.** Kendal is meant, no doubt, where De Quincey had edited the *Westmoreland Gazette* in 1818-19.

236 28. **I have thus described and illustrated.** By this last word De Quincey endeavors adroitly to justify his digression on Ricardo, while at the same time he returns to his subject.

238 17. **Before Œdipus, etc.** These names call up some of the great civilizations of the past, — of Greece, of Palestine, and of Egypt.

239 32. **I was once told by a near relative, etc.** "The heroine of this remarkable case was a girl about nine years old ; and there can be little doubt that she looked down as far within the *crater* of death — that awful volcano — as any human being ever *can* have done that has lived to draw back and report her experience. Not less than ninety years did she survive this memorable escape ; and I may describe her as in all respects a woman of remarkable and interesting qualities. She enjoyed throughout her long life, as the reader will readily infer, serene and cloudless health ; had a masculine understanding ; reverenced truth not less than did the Evangelists ; and led a life of saintly devotion, such as might have glorified ' *Hilarion or Paul.*' — (The words in italics are Ariosto's.) — I mention these traits as characterising her in a memorable extent, that the reader may not suppose himself relying upon a dealer in exaggerations, upon a credulous enthusiast, or upon a careless wielder of language. Forty-five years had intervened between the first time and the last time of her telling me this anecdote, and not one iota had shifted its ground amongst the incidents, nor had any the most trivial of the circumstantiations suffered change. The scene of the accident was the least of valleys, — what the Greeks of old would have called an ἄγκος, and we English should properly call a dell. Human tenant it had none : even at noonday it was a solitude, and would oftentimes have been a silent solitude, but for the brawling of a brook — not broad, but occasionally deep — which ran along the base of the little hills. Into this brook, probably into one of its dangerous pools, the child fell : and, according to the ordinary chances, she could have had but a slender prospect indeed of any deliverance ; for, although a dwelling-house was close by, it was shut out from view by the undulations of the ground. How long the child lay in the water was probably never inquired earnestly until the answer had become irrecoverable : for a servant, to whose care the child was then confided, had a natural interest in suppressing the whole case. From the child's own account, it should seem that *asphyxia* must have announced its commencement. A process of struggle and deadly suffocation was passed through half consciously. This process terminated by a sudden blow apparently *on* or *in* the brain, after which there was no pain or conflict ; but in an instant succeeded a dazzling rush of light ; immediately after which came the solemn apocalypse of the entire past life. Meantime, the child's disappearance in the water had happily been witnessed by a farmer who

rented some fields in this little solitude, and by a rare accident was riding through them at the moment. Not being very well mounted, he was retarded by the hedges and other fences in making his way down to the water; some time was thus lost; but, once at the spot, he leaped in, booted and spurred, and succeeded in delivering one that must have been as nearly counted amongst the populations of the grave as perhaps the laws of the shadowy world can suffer to return!" — DE QUINCEY'S note to enlarged *Confessions*, Masson's Ed., Vol. III, p. 435. Dr. Garnett informs us, on the authority of Mrs. Baird Smith, that De Quincey's mother was the relative meant. De Quincey's quotation above is from Ariosto's *Orlando Furioso*, VIII, 45:

> " Such a call
> As e'er Hilarion had or holy Paul."

240 9. **Book of account, etc.** *Cf.* Revelations, xx, 12.

241 19. **A certain day in August, 1642.** "I think (but at the moment have no means of verifying my conjecture) that this day was the 24th of August. On or about that day Charles raised the royal standard at Nottingham; which, ominously enough (considering the strength of such superstitions in the seventeenth century, and, amongst the generations of that century, more especially in this particular generation of the Parliamentary War), was blown down during the succeeding night. Let me remark, in passing, that no falsehood can virtually be greater or more malicious than that which imputes to Archbishop Laud a special or exceptional faith in such mute warnings." — DE QUINCEY'S note to enlarged *Confessions*, Masson's Ed., Vol. III, p. 438. "The King's standard, giving the signal for the English Civil War, was raised on the Castle Hill at Nottingham on the evening of Monday the 22d of August 1642, and is said to have been blown down by a violent wind that night, — though Rushworth's account discredits that legend. I do not understand the grounds of De Quincey's defence of Laud at this point against the imputation of superstitious belief in omens. Whether his faith in such 'mute warnings' was 'special or exceptional,' in the sense of being stronger than was usual in his age, may admit of question; but that he was tremulously sensitive to dreams, omens, &c., is as certain as records can make anything." — MASSON.

241 30. **Paulus, or Marius.** Lucius Æmilius Paulus, surnamed Macedonicus (died 160 B.C.), and the still more famous Caius Marius (died 86 B.C.), are of course meant.

241 31. **The crimson tunic.** "The signal which announced a day of battle." — DE QUINCEY'S note to enlarged *Confessions*.

241 32. **Alalagmos.** "A word expressing collectively the gathering of the Roman war-cries — *Alála, Alála*." — DE QUINCEY'S note to enlarged *Confessions*. The word is Greek and from Greek ἀλαλή, "war cry." As Professor Kittredge points out to me, Pindar personifies ἀλαλά as the daughter of war.

242 1. **A set of plates by that artist** [Piranesi], **called his "Dreams."** "Piranesi never published any plates under this title, but many of his architectural drawings, though professedly representing actual edifices, are as visionary as Martin's views of Pandemonium. Charles Brockden Brown, after Hawthorne and Poe the most imaginative of American writers of fiction, was also fond of designing wholly ideal architecture in drawings of most elaborate execution." — GARNETT. Giovanni Battista Piranesi (died 1778) was an Italian engraver, whose fancy was especially seized by the idea of restoring in engravings the ruined architecture of Rome.

242 28. **From a great modern poet.** "What poet? It was Wordsworth; and why did I not formally name him? This throws a light backwards upon the strange history of Wordsworth's reputation. The year in which I wrote and published these Confessions was 1821; and at that time the name of Wordsworth, though beginning to emerge from the dark cloud of scorn and contumely which had hitherto overshadowed it, was yet most imperfectly established. Not until ten years later was his greatness cheerfully and generally acknowledged. I, therefore, as the very earliest (without one exception) of all who came forward, in the beginning of his career, to honour and welcome him, shrank with disgust from making any sentence of mine the occasion for an explosion of vulgar malice against him. But the grandeur of the passage here cited inevitably spoke for itself; and he that would have been most scornful on hearing the name of the poet coupled with this epithet of 'great' could not but find his malice intercepted, and himself cheated into cordial admiration, by the splendour of the verses." — DE QUINCEY'S note to *Confessions*, Masson's Ed., Vol. III, p. 439. *Cf.* p. 95 and note 95 16; also p. 106. The passage quoted is from the *Excursion*, Book II, near the end.

243 19. **Fuseli.** John Henry Fuseli (1741–1825) was a Swiss painter and art critic, most of whose active life was passed in England.

243 23. **The dramatist Shadwell.** Thomas Shadwell (1640–92) is most famous as Dryden's MacFlecknoe and Og (*cf. Absalom and Achitophel*, II); he had gained Dryden's enmity by satirizing him in the *Medal of John Bayes*. He succeeded Dryden as poet-laureate in

1688. Most modern critics agree that he was not quite so black as Dryden painted him :

> "The rest to some faint meaning make pretense,
> But Shadwell never deviates into sense." — *MacFlecknoe.*

243 24. **Homer is . . . rightly reputed to have known the virtues of opium.** "This idea is grounded on the passage in the *Odyssey* (Book IV) where Helen is represented as administering to Telemachus, in the house of Menelaus, a potion prepared from *nepenthes*, which made him forget his sorrows. It was evidently some narcotic, but is generally thought to have been an extract of hemp, which Galen says was given in his time to guests at banquets as a promoter of hilarity and enjoyment. Hippocrates was acquainted with the use of opium in medicine, and frequently prescribed it." — COOKE, *The Seven Sisters of Sleep*, Chap. II. "The Homeric *nepenthes* is the subject of a learned disquisition in Gronovius, tom. ii, by Petrus La Seine, who arrives at the extraordinary conclusion that it was *aurum potabile* [drinkable gold]." — GARNETT. *Cf.* p. 200 and note 200 17.

243 30. **To use a metaphysical word, "objective."** "This word, so nearly unintelligible in 1821, so intensely scholastic, and, consequently, when surrounded by familiar and vernacular words, so apparently pedantic, yet, on the other hand, so indispensable to accurate thinking, and to *wide* thinking, has since 1821 become too common to need any apology." — DE QUINCEY'S note to enlarged *Confessions*, Masson's Ed., Vol. III, p. 440.

243 35. **The last Lord Orford.** Horace Walpole (1717–97), third son of Sir Robert Walpole, Prime Minister, was a famous wit and letter writer, as well as author of the celebrated novel of the romantic and supernatural type, *The Castle of Otranto.*

246 8. **I fled from the wrath of Brama, etc.** The first three named compose the so-called Triad of the Hindu religion of Brahmanism. Brahma is the evolver of the universe, Vishnu its maintainer, and Siva its destroyer. Isis is the chief female deity of Egyptian mythology; Osiris, whose sister and female counterpart is Isis, is the creator and principle of good in that mythology. The ibis and the crocodile were sacred animals in Egyptian worship.

247 20. **The contemplation of death, etc.** See p. 7, where De Quincey refers to this passage, translates *cæteris paribus* into "other conditions remaining the same," and repeats the last of the three reasons given here with some additional discussion. *Cf.* also the opening of the first section of the *Dream-Fugue*, p. 330.

248 29. **The grave of a child, etc.** Catherine Wordsworth is meant. *Cf.* note 217 34.

249 15. **Shaded by Judean palms.** The picture is suggested by Judea on the Roman coins. *Cf. Works*, Riverside Ed., Vol. II, p. 56; Masson's Ed., Vol. I, p. 54.

249 34. **When we were both children.** "In the original MS. this was succeeded by the following passage, which was immediately cancelled by the writer, and has never appeared in any edition of the *Opium-Eater*. I am enabled to insert it here by the exceeding kindness of Mr. H. A. Page [pseudonym of Dr. A. H. Japp] : —

'This dream at first brought tears to one who had been long familiar only with groans: but afterwards it fluctuated and grew unsteady: the passions and the scenery changed countenance, and the whole was transposed into another key. Its variations, though interesting, I must omit.

'At length I grew afraid to sleep, and I shrunk from it as from the most savage torture. Often I fought with my drowsiness, and kept it aloof by sitting up the whole night and following day. Sometimes I lay down only in the day-time: and sought to charm away the phantoms by requesting my family to sit around me and to talk: hoping thus to derive an influence from what affected me externally into my internal world of shadows : but, far from this, I infected and stained as it were the whole of my waking experience with feelings derived from sleep. I seemed indeed to live and to converse even when awake with my visionary companions much more than with the realities of life. "Oh, X, what do you see? dear X, what is it that you see ?" was the constant exclamation of M[argaret], by which I was awakened as soon as I had fallen asleep, though to me it seemed as if I had slept for years. My groans had, it seems, wakened her, and, from her account, they had commenced immediately on my falling asleep.

'The following dream, as an impressive one to me, I shall close with: it grew up under the influence of that misery which I have described above as resulting from the almost paralytic incapacity to do anything towards completing my intellectual labours, combined with a belief which at the time I reasonably entertained that I should soon be called on to quit forever this world and those for whom I still clung to it.'

'As a final specimen,' etc., as printed, except that the words 'from 1820' do not appear in the original MS." — GARNETT, p. 263.

250 3. **The dream commenced, etc.** This paragraph is worthy of especial attention : De Quincey did nothing better in what he calls impassioned prose ; indeed, there is, perhaps, nothing better.

250 17. **I, as is usual, etc.** Hunter suggests a comparison of this with the passage in the *Mail-Coach*, beginning, " The situation here contemplated," p. 313.

250 22. **"Deeper than ever plummet sounded."** *Cf.* Shakspere, *Tempest*, Act v, sc. 1, line 56.

250 34. **With a sigh, such as the caves of hell, etc.** *Cf. Paradise Lost*, Book II, lines 746 *et seq.*, especially 787–789:

> " I fled, and cri'd out, DEATH ;
> Hell trembl'd at the hideous name, and sigh'd
> From all her caves, and back resounded DEATH."

The "incestuous mother" is Sin, mother of Death, and by him the mother of a pack of "yelling monsters."

252 28. **I triumphed.** "I am indebted for the following valuable note to De Quincey's biographer, Mr. H. A. Page [pseudonym of Dr. A. H. Japp], who is probably better acquainted with his circumstances than any but his very nearest relatives : —

'Accusations have been repeatedly made of late years against De Quincey for having asserted that he had made a final escape from the thraldom of opium, when such was not the case. This charge has been raised by writers otherwise favourable to him, and who should have been better informed. The chief cause of the misunderstanding is easily discovered. It arose from the very inadequate manner in which De Quincey, then only a few years before his death, was able to fulfil the task of expanding the Confessions as they stood at first into a volume the size of the series which Mr. James Hogg had happily been successful in getting him to put together as the "Collected Works." The original version is consistent with itself in all essential points: the later and enlarged version hardly is. Unless in the case of a very attentive reader, who has clearly in his mind the circumstances under which it was done, and is able to distinguish as he reads between the original and the added matter, difficulties and questionings are sure to arise about several matters of fact. De Quincey dove-tailed matter here and there into the book without carefully revising and rewriting the original portions as he should have done. The result is that in the earlier portion of the book we find him speaking of himself as a person who has had upwards of fifty years' experience of opium, and still indulging in it to a moderate extent, whereas at the end he speaks of himself as having attained a complete escape. He repeats, with merely the change of "seventeen" into "eighteen," the passage in the first edition where he had said, "the moral of the narrative is addressed to the opium-eater, and therefore of necessity limited in its application. If he is taught to fear and tremble, enough has been effected. But he may say that the issue of my case is at least a proof that opium, after an eighteen years' use and an eight years' abuse of its powers, may still be renounced." If the moral of the "Confessions of an Opium-Eater" is dependent on the fact of his having attained a complete escape from the power of the drug, then the final Confessions can really boast no moral even of the most limited application, since De Quincey, though he greatly reduced his doses, took opium up to the end of his days, — a fact which he very ingenuously confesses over and over again. The truth is, that the moral which he allowed to remain tacked to the Confessions as enlarged in 1856 is, like too many other morals tacked to less real narratives of pain and sorrow, utterly out of place and misleading, and should have been cancelled altogether. What he wrote at the close of the Confessions of 1821 was quite true of his condition at the time, but his after career presents a series of almost incredible fluctuations. We find him in 1855 giving express dates to four separate and signal prostrations under the influence of opium: the first in 1813–14; the second in 1817–18; the third in 1823–24; and the fourth in the period between 1841 and 1844 in Edinburgh or Glasgow. The record of the first two we have in the original Confessions; for the others we must refer to other documents. The struggle of 1843–44 was severe. He had again risen almost to his old excess in 1813–14; but by dint of daily exercise and resolution he somewhat suddenly reduced his dose to one hundred drops. "Effects so dreadful and utterly unconjectured by medical men succeeded, that I was glad to get back under shelter. Not the less I persisted, silently, surely descended the ladder, and suddenly found my mind as if whirled round on its true centre. It was as if a man had been in a whirlpool, carried violently by a headlong current, and before he could speak or think he was riding at anchor once more dull and untroubled as in days of infancy." In June, 1844, he succeeded in attaining a final *comparative* escape from opium, having brought his daily quantum down to six grains. "I would not say by any means," observes his daughter, "that he never exceeded this afterwards, but I am very sure he never much exceeded it." There are no more records of such struggles as those of 1817–18, and of 1844, though in 1848 he made a bold attempt to abstain totally: the general result of which is to be found in Page's memoir, vol. i, p. 354. He persevered for sixty-one days, but was compelled to return to his moderate dose, from which he never afterwards departed, as life otherwise was found to be insupportable. He resumed it on his own deliberate judgment, as of two evils very much the least. And not only did he justify the moderate indulgence in his own case, but he formulated a kind of general doctrine on the subject, which he thus summed up at p. 242 of the Confessions of 1856: — "Nervous irritation is the secret desolation of human life, and for this there is probably no adequate controlling power but that of opium, taken daily under steady regulation." If moral the final Confessions must have, then the pressure of facts would seem to point to this as the true one, rather than to any "triumph" or total abstinence. "Once in the toils of opium, reduce your dose to the very minimum, and keep it so by careful regulation and outdoor exercise," seems really to be the terms in which the moral of De Quincey's life as opium-eater would express itself.'

"It should be added, that the appendix to the original edition of the *Confessions*, in which De Quincey rather apologises for having conveyed to the reader 'the impression that I had wholly renounced the use of opium,' is omitted in the enlarged edition. He may have thought that he was supplying its absence by describing his 'escape' as 'a provisional stage, that paved the way subsequently for many milder stages, to which gradually my constitutional system accommodated itself.'" — GARNETT, *Confessions*, pp. 264–268.

253 1. **Innocent sufferer.** William Lithgow (1582–1645 ?), a Scotchman who travelled afoot through many parts of Europe, Asia, and Africa, was racked at Malaga in December, 1620. *The Totall Discourse of the Rare Aduentures and painfull Peregrinations of long nineteene Yeares*, etc., appeared in 1632.

253 24. **Jeremy Taylor conjectures, etc.** In the enlarged *Confessions* De Quincey alters the name to "Lord Bacon," and adds this note: "In all former editions I had ascribed this sentiment to Jeremy Taylor. On a close search, however, wishing to verify the quotation, it appeared that I had been mistaken. Something very like it occurs more than once in the bishop's voluminous writings: but the exact passage moving in my mind had evidently been this which follows, from Lord Bacon's 'Essay on Death': — 'It is as natural to die as to be born; and to a little infant perhaps the one is as painful as the other.'"

254 8. **"With dreadful faces,"** etc. *Paradise Lost*, Book XII, line 644.

254. **Appendix.** This appeared for the first time when the *Confessions* was published in book form in 1822. It was also published in the *London Magazine* for December, 1822, with the following introductory paragraph: "The interest excited by the two papers bearing this title, in our numbers for September and October, 1821, will have kept our promise of a Third Part fresh in the remembrance of our readers. That we are still unable to fulfill our engagement in its original meaning will, we are sure, be matter of regret to them as to ourselves, especially when they have perused the following affecting narrative. It was composed for the purpose of being appended to an edition of the Confessions in a separate volume, which is already before the public, and we have reprinted it entire, that our subscribers may be in possession of the whole of this extraordinary history."

255 15. **Fiat experimentum, etc.** "Let experiment be made on a common (worthless) body."

258 14. **Thierry and Theodoret.** Cf. *Thierry and Theodoret*, Act v, sc. 2.

258 25. **"I nunc,"** etc. "Go now, and ponder with thyself melodious lines." Horace, *Epistles*, II, 2, 76.

259 26. **"Infandum renovare dolorem."** "To renew (relate) the unspeakable grief." Virgil, *Æneid*, II, 3.

262 20. **Heautontimoroumenos.** Ἑαυτον-τιμορούμενος, "self-torturer," the title of one of Terence's plays.

262, footnote. **"Reculer pour mieux sauter."** "Go back to make a better leap."

263 7. **Is it for a Transcendental Philosopher, etc.** *Cf.* p. 216 and note 216 14.

264 16. **Si vivere perseverarent.** *Cf.* Suetonius, *Life of Caligula*, 38 : "Derisores vocabat, quod post nuncupationem vivere persevera-rent," etc. "He called [them] mockers, that after the announcement [that Caligula had been made joint heir with their children] persisted in living," etc.

FROM THE "SUSPIRIA DE PROFUNDIS"

The history of these remarkable pieces is unfortunately by no means clear; as we are not likely, however, to receive any further testimony on the subject, what information is now before us may be here summarized. In a note to Professor Lushington of Glasgow, evidently written in February, 1845, De Quincey says : "Perhaps I told you, when you were last over at Lasswade, of the intention I had (and was then carrying into effect) to write another *Opium Confessions;* or, if I did not tell you, it must have been only because I forbore to pester you too much with my plans — especially whilst unfinished, and liable to de-rangements more than one. Now, however, this particular plan, after occupying me for seven months of severe labour, is accomplished. Last Friday I received from the printer a sheet and something more (of 'Blackwood's Magazine'), containing the first part out of four. It bears for its title, 'Suspiria de Profundis; being a Sequel to the Con-fessions of an English Opium-Eater.' And the separate title of this first part is — 'The Affliction of Childhood.'. . . The four parts, when published in Blackwood through March, April, May, June, and July, will be gathered into a volume without any delay, and introduced by a letter of some length to my three daughters." The paper to which De Quincey here refers was preceded in *Blackwood* for March, 1845, by an *Introductory Notice* on the subject of Dreaming, and was followed by several detached paragraphs of lyrical prose; in the number for April there were a few more pages, without sub-titles, purporting to be a continuation of Part I; in May nothing was added; in June the conclusion of Part I appeared in the shape of four pieces, entitled, respectively, *The Palimpsest, Levana and Our Ladies of Sorrow, The Apparition of the Brocken*, and *Savannah-la-Mar*. To the second of these papers, *Levana*, De Quincey added this interesting, if somewhat baffling note : " The reader who wishes at all to understand the course of these Confessions ought not to pass over this dream-legend. There is no great wonder that a vision which occupied my waking thoughts in those years should reappear in my dreams. It was, in fact, a legend recurring in sleep, most of which I had myself silently written or sculptured in my daylight reveries. But its importance to the present Confessions is this, — that it rehearses or prefigures their course. This FIRST Part belongs to Madonna. The THIRD belongs to the 'Mater Suspiriorum,' and will be entitled *The Pariah Worlds*. The FOURTH, which terminates the work, belongs to the 'Mater Tenebrarum,' and will be entitled *The Kingdom of Darkness*. As to the SECOND, it is an interpolation requisite to the effect of the others, and will be explained in its proper place." In *Blackwood* for July appeared the beginning of Part II, printed without subdivision and with no sub-titles. And there, without warning, the series ended. In itself the note to *Levana* is not inconsistent with the statements made to Professor Lushington a few months before; yet its vagueness seems to indicate that the plan which then was announced as accomplished gave way before long to a different scheme — larger, and perhaps not so well worked out. Such a development is not only quite to be expected of De Quincey; but it is particularly evidenced by the fact that he spread Part I through three numbers of the Magazine. But apparently there was to be yet a third stage in the history of the *Suspiria*. Dr. Japp has recently published a list, recovered from De Quincey's papers, of titles for 32 *Suspiria* [Japp, *Posthumous Works of De Quincey*, Vol. I, p. 4. A dagger is here placed after pieces formerly published, and an asterisk after those recovered by Dr. Japp, and printed by him in the above work, Vol. I, pp. 7–23. Several detached paragraphs for *Suspiria* are also given by Japp, pp. 24–28] as follows :

(1) Dreaming.† (2) The Affliction of Childhood † and Dream Echoes.† (3) The English Mail-Coach.† (4) The Palimpsest of the Human Brain.† (5) Vision of Life.† (6) Memorial Suspiria.† (7) Levana and our Ladies of Sorrow.† (8) Solitude of Childhood.* (9) The Dark Interpreter.* (10) The Apparition of the Brocken.† (11) Savannah-la-Mar.† (12) The Dreadful Infant. (There was the glory of innocence made perfect; there was the dreadful beauty of infancy that had seen God.) (13) Foundering Ships. (14) The Archbishop and the Controller of Fire. (15) God that didst promise. (16) Count the Leaves in Vallombrosa. (17) But if I submitted with Resignation, not the less I searched for the Unsearchable — sometimes

in Arab Deserts, sometimes in the Sea.   (18) That ran before us in
Malice.   (19) Morning of Execution.   (20) Daughter of Lebanon.†
(21) Kyrie Eleison.   (22) The Princess that lost a Single Seed of
Pomegranate.*   (23) The Nursery in Arabian Deserts.   (24) The
Halcyon Calm and the Coffin.   (25) Faces! Angels' Faces!   (26) At
that Word.   (27) Oh, Apothanate! that hatest Death, and cleansest
from the Pollution of Sorrow.   (28) Who is this Woman that for
some Months has followed me up and down?   Her face I cannot see,
for she keeps for ever behind me.   (29) Who is this Woman that
beckoneth me and warneth me from the Place where she is, and in whose
Eyes is Woeful Remembrance?   I guess who she is.*   (30) Cagot and
Cressida.   (31) Lethe and Anapaula.   (32) Oh, sweep away, Angel,
with Angelic Scorn, the Dogs that come with Curious Eyes to gaze.

Of most intrinsic interest in this scheme is the testimony borne by it
to the fact that the *Suspiria* had indeed their origin in dreams, and
were, in fact, what De Quincey calls them, the "last Confessions" of an
Opium-Eater.   So far as the history of these pieces is concerned, this
list apparently dates from the years 1845–49.   It could hardly antedate
the note to *Levana*, in which the division into parts, entirely unrecog-
nized here, is made all-important.   On the other hand, *The English
Mail-Coach* came out in 1849 as a separate piece, and in a form too
extensive to allow it a place among the *Suspiria*, which in this list it
holds.   It seems clear that after the sudden close of the *Blackwood*
series, De Quincey continued to work upon these *Confessions;* the
Mail-Coach was one of them, which, outgrowing the proper size for
Suspiria, was thrown to the voracious magazines in 1849, in which year,
it will be noted, De Quincey published nothing else.   Now, however, in
1853, began the publication of the Hogg collective edition, and *The
Affliction of Childhood, Dream Echoes,* and *The Apparition of the
Brocken* were found useful to lend color and power to the *Autobiographic Sketches.*   But the unprinted *Suspiria* were to suffer far more
serious losses.   In the preface to the 1856 *Confessions* De Quincey
writes: "All along I had relied upon a crowning grace, which I had
reserved for the final pages of this volume, in a succession of some
twenty or twenty-five dreams and noon-day visions, which had arisen
under the latter stages of opium influence.   These have disappeared:
some under circumstances which allow me a reasonable prospect of
recovering them; some unaccountably; and some dishonourably.   Five
or six, I believe, were burned."   The *Daughter of Lebanon,* saved from
this "sudden conflagration," De Quincey appended to the *Confessions.*
It is clear, therefore, that the project of the *Suspiria* was in no way

abandoned by De Quincey (though it may have been by Blackwood), and that he actually wrote — roughly at least — three-quarters of the pieces called for by Dr. Japp's list. Finally it may be remarked that, although De Quincey did not live to add any collection of *Suspiria* to the Hogg Edition, Messrs. Black in the sixteenth (supplementary) volume of their reissue were able to publish the remains of the *Suspiria* formerly printed in *Blackwood*, with important corrections from the author's hand. From this revised text these selections are taken. They are found in *Works*, Masson's Ed., Vol. XIII, pp. 359–369; Riverside Ed., Vol. I, pp. 237–246, 253–256.

267 6. **On the foundation.** That is, on the endowment, holding free scholarships (in American phrase), which were probably provided for in the original grant to the college.

269 5. **She stood in Rama.** *Cf.* Jeremiah, xxxi, 15; Matthew, ii, 18.

269 33. **All this winter of 1844-5 within the bedchamber of the Czar, etc.** This reference is to the death, in August, 1844, of the Princess Alexandra, third daughter of the Czar Nicholas. She was nineteen years old.

270 30. **Norfolk Island,** in the South Pacific, east of Australia, was for some time used by Great Britain as a penal settlement. The galleys are likewise employed by France for the punishment of criminals.

271 19. **Amongst the tents of Shem.** *Cf.* Genesis, ix, 27.

273. **Savannah-la-mar.** This name occurs on the map as that of a small coast town in Jamaica; in that island De Quincey's brother Richard (Pink) was lost during a hunting trip in the Blue Mountains. Etymologically Savannah, a "plain," is English for the Spanish *Sabana*, a "sheet," or "plain"; *la mar* is of course Spanish for "the sea"; *cf. Sabana de la Mar*, the name of a coast town of Santo Domingo. The name is, however, not only very melodious in itself, but also suggestive of the dream De Quincey wishes to relate, that of a city sunk, with all its towers standing, beneath the ocean, yet still visible in calm weather. The meaning attached to the vision by De Quincey is that the future is God's present, — that in that truth lies the explanation of his mysterious workings by shocks, as of earthquake, and by grief.

274 11. **Fata-Morgana revelation.** Fata Morgana (Italian for "Morgana the fairy") is really the name of a sister of King Arthur in mediæval legend, but the name is given commonly to a mirage seen in the Straits of Messina, superstitiously supposed to be caused by Morgana.

274 32. **Clepsydra.** The clepsydra, as the context indicates, was a device for measuring time by water, which was discharged from a vessel through a small aperture.

THE ENGLISH MAIL–COACH

"In October 1849 there appeared in *Blackwood's Magazine* an article entitled *The English Mail-Coach, or the Glory of Motion*. There was no intimation that it was to be continued; but in December 1849 there followed in the same magazine an article in two sections, headed by a paragraph explaining that it was by the author of the previous article in the October number, and was to be taken in connexion with that article. One of the sections of this second article was entitled *The Vision of Sudden Death*, and the other *Dream-Fugue on the above theme of Sudden Death*. When De Quincey revised the papers in 1854 for republication in volume iv of the Collective Edition of his writings, he brought the whole under the one general title of *The English Mail-Coach*, dividing the text, as at present, into three sections or chapters, the first with the sub-title *The Glory of Motion*, the second with the sub-title *The Vision of Sudden Death*, and the third with the sub-title *Dream-Fugue, founded on the preceding theme of Sudden Death*. Great care was bestowed on the revision. Passages that had appeared in the magazine articles were omitted; new sentences were inserted; and the language was retouched throughout." — MASSON. *Cf.* above, pp. 470–473, and as to the revision, Professor Dowden's article, "How De Quincey worked," *Saturday Review*, Feb. 23, 1895. This selection is found in *Works*, Masson's Ed., Vol. XIII, pp. 270–327; Riverside Ed., Vol. I, pp. 517–582.

277 6. **He had married the daughter of a duke.** "Mr. John Palmer, a native of Bath, and from about 1768 the energetic proprietor of the Theatre Royal in that city, had been led, by the wretched state in those days of the means of intercommunication between Bath and London, and his own consequent difficulties in arranging for a punctual succession of good actors at his theatre, to turn his attention to the improvement of the whole system of Post-Office conveyance, and of locomotive machinery generally, in the British Islands. The result was a scheme for superseding, on the great roads at least, the then existing system of sluggish and irregular stage-coaches, the property of private persons and companies, by a new system of government coaches, in connexion with the Post-Office, carrying the mails and also a regulated number of passengers, with clockwork precision, at a rate of comparative speed, which he hoped should ultimately be not less than ten miles an hour. The opposition to the scheme was, of course, enormous; coach proprietors, innkeepers, the Post-Office officials themselves, were all against

Mr. Palmer; he was voted a crazy enthusiast and a public bore. Pitt, however, when the scheme was submitted to him, recognised its feasibility; on the 8th of August 1784 the first mail-coach on Mr. Palmer's plan started from London at 8 o'clock in the morning and reached Bristol at 11 o'clock at night; and from that day the success of the new system was assured. — Mr. Palmer himself, having been appointed Surveyor and Comptroller-General of the Post-Office, took rank as an eminent and wealthy public man, M. P. for Bath and what not, and lived till 1818. De Quincey makes it one of his distinctions that he 'had married the daughter of a duke,' and in a footnote to that paragraph he gives the lady's name as 'Lady Madeline Gordon.' From an old Debrett, however, I learn that Lady Madelina Gordon, second daughter of Alexander, fourth Duke of Gordon, was first married, on the 3d of April 1789, to Sir Robert Sinclair, Bart., and next, on the 25th of November 1805, to *Charles Palmer, of Lockley Park, Berks, Esq.* If Debrett is right, her second husband was not John Palmer of Mail-Coach celebrity, and De Quincey is wrong." — MASSON.

277, footnote. **Invention of the cross.** Concerning the *Inventio sanctae crucis*, see Smith, *Dictionary of Christian Antiquities*, Vol. I, p. 503.

278 4. **National result.** *Cf.* De Quincey's paper on *Travelling*, *Works*, Riverside Ed., Vol. II, especially pp. 313–314; Masson's Ed., Vol. I, especially pp. 270–271.

279 13. **The four terms of Michaelmas, Lent, Easter, and Act.** These might be called respectively the autumn, winter, spring, and summer terms. Michaelmas, the feast of St. Michael and All Angels, is on September 29. Hilary and Trinity are other names for Lent term and Act term respectively. Act term is the last term of the academic year; its name is that originally given to a disputation for a Master's degree; such disputations took place at the end of the year generally, and hence gave a name to the summer term. Although the rules concerning residence at Oxford are more stringent than in De Quincey's time, only eighteen weeks' residence is required during the year, six in Michaelmas, six in Lent, and six in Easter and Act.

279 17. **Going down.** *Cf.* "Going down with victory," *i.e.*, from London into the country.

279 30. **Posting-houses.** Inns where relays of horses were furnished for coaches and carriages. *Cf.* De Quincey on *Travelling*, *loc. cit.*

280 3. **An old tradition . . . from the reign of Charles II.** Then no one sat outside; later, outside places were taken by servants, and were quite cheap.

280 9. **Attaint the foot.** The word is used in its legal sense. The blood of one convicted of high treason is "attaint," and his deprivations extend to his descendants, unless Parliament remove the attainder.

280 14. **Pariahs.** *Cf.* note 74 27.

281 6. **Objects not appearing, etc.** *De non apparentibus et non existentibus eadem est lex*, a Roman legal phrase.

281 16. **"Snobs."** Apparently *snob* originally meant "shoemaker"; then, in university cant, a "townsman" as opposed to a "gownsman." *Cf. Gradus ad Cantabrigiam* (1824), quoted in *Century Dictionary:* "*Snobs.*— A term applied indiscriminately to all who have not the honour of being members of the university; but in a more particular manner to the 'profanum vulgus,' the tag-rag and bob-tail, who vegetate on the sedgy banks of Camus." This use is in De Quincey's mind. Later, in the strikes of that time, the workmen who accepted lower wages were called *snobs;* those who held out for higher, *nobs.*

283 33. **Fo Fo . . . Fi Fi.** "This paragraph is a caricature of a story told in Staunton's Account of the Earl of Macartney's Embassy to China in 1792." — MASSON.

284 4. **Ça ira** ("This will do," "This is the go"), "a proverb of the French Revolutionists when they were hanging the aristocrats in the streets, &c., and the burden of one of the most popular revolutionary songs, '*Ça ira, ça ira, ça ira.*'"— MASSON.

284 18. **All morality, — Aristotle's, Zeno's, Cicero's.** Each of these three has a high place in the history of ethical teaching: Aristotle for his so-called *Nicomachean Ethics* (*cf.* note 341 31); Zeno, who was the founder of the Stoic school of philosophy, as the teacher of an exalted system of morals (*cf.* note 219, footnote); Cicero for his *De Officiis*, " Of Duties."

285 9. **Astrological shadows.** Misfortunes due to being born under an unlucky star; *house of life* is also an astrological term.

285 24. **Von Troil's Iceland.** See note 48 24.

285 25. **A parliamentary rat.** One who deserts his own party when it is losing.

286 16. **"Jam proximus,"** etc. *Æneid*, II, lines 311–312: " Now next (to Deiphobus' house) Ucalegon (*i.e.*, his house) blazes! "

287 27. **Quarterings.** See p. 323, footnote, and note 323 2.

287 32. **Within benefit of clergy.** Benefit of clergy was, under old English law, the right of clerics, afterward extended to all who could read, to plead exemption from trial before a secular judge. This privilege was first legally recognized in 1274, and was not wholly abolished until 1827.

288 9. **Quarter Sessions.** This court is held in England in the counties by justices of the peace for the trial of minor criminal offences and to administer the poor-laws, etc.

288 26. **False echoes of Marengo.** General Desaix was shot through the heart, at the battle of Marengo (June 14, 1800); he died without a word, and his body was found by Rovigo (*cf. Memoirs of the Duke of Rovigo*, London, 1835, Vol. I, p. 181), "stripped of his clothes, and surrounded by other naked bodies." Napoleon, however, published three different versions of an heroic and devoted message from Desaix to himself, the original version being: "Go, tell the First Consul that I die with this regret, — that I have not done enough for posterity." (*Cf.* Lanfrey, *History of Napoleon the First*, 2d ed., London, 1886, Vol. II, p. 39.) Napoleon himself was credited likewise with the words De Quincey adopts. "Why is it not permitted me to weep," is one version (Bussey, *History of Napoleon*, London, 1840, Vol. I, p. 302). *Cf.* Hazlitt, *Life of Napoleon*, 2d ed., London, 1852, Vol. II, p. 317, footnote.

288, footnote. **The cry of the foundering line-of-battle ship Vengeur.** On the 1st of June, 1794, the English fleet under Lord Howe defeated the French under Villaret-Joyeuse, taking six ships, and sinking a seventh, the *Vengeur*. This ship sank, as a matter of fact, with part of her crew on board, imploring aid which there was not time to give them. Some 250 men had been taken off by the English; the rest were lost. On the 9th of July Barrère published a report setting forth "how the Vengeur, ... being entirely disabled, ... refused to strike, though sinking; how the enemies fired on her, but she returned their fire, shot aloft all her tricolor streamers, shouted *Vive la République*, ... and so, in this mad whirlwind of fire and shouting and invincible despair, went down into the ocean depths ; *Vive la République* and a universal volley from the upper deck being the last sounds she made." *Cf.* Carlyle, *Sinking of the Vengeur*, and *French Revolution*, Book XVIII, Chap. VI.

288, footnote. **La Garde meurt, etc.** "This phrase, attributed to Cambronne, who was made prisoner at Waterloo, was vehemently denied by him. It was invented by Rougemont, a prolific author of *mots*, two days after the battle, in the *Indépendant*." — FOURNIER'S *L'Esprit dans l'Histoire*, trans. Bartlett, *Familiar Quotations*, p. 661.

289 25. **Brummagem.** A vulgar form of Birmingham. *Cf.* note 69 5. *Cf.* also Shakspere, *Richard III*, Act i, sc. 4, line 55 :

"False, fleeting, perjured Clarence."

289 27.   **Luxor** occupies part of the site of ancient Thebes, capital of Egypt ; its antiquities are famous.   *Cf.* note 214 27.

290 9.   **But on our side . . . was a tower of moral strength, etc.** *Cf.* Shakspere, *Richard III*, Act v, sc. 3, lines 12–13 :

> " Besides, the king's name is a tower of strength,
> Which they upon the adverse party want."

291 1.   **Omrahs . . . from Agra and Lahore.**   Doubtless there is a reminiscence here of Wordsworth's *Prelude*, Book X, lines 18–20 :

> " The Great Mogul, when he
> Erewhile went forth from Agra or Lahore,
> Rajahs and Omrahs in his train."

Omrah, which is not found in *Century Dictionary*, is itself really plural of Arabic *amir* (ameer), a commander, nobleman.

291 23.   **The 6th of Edward Longshanks.**   A De Quinceyan jest, of course.   This would refer to a law of the sixth year of Edward I, or 1278, but there are but fifteen chapters in the laws of that year.

292 8.   **Not magna loquimur, . . . but vivimus.**   Not "we speak great things," but " we live " them.

293 21.   **Marlborough forest** is twenty-seven miles east of Bath, where De Quincey attended school.

294 18.   **Ulysses, etc.**   The allusion is, of course, to the slaughter of the suitors of Penelope, his wife, by Ulysses, after his return.   *Cf. Odyssey*, Books XXI–XXII.

295 3.   **About Waterloo,** *i.e.*, about 1815.   This phrase is one of many that indicate the deep impression made by this event upon the English mind.   *Cf.* p. 334.

295 17.   **" Say, all our praises,"** etc.   *Cf.* Pope, *Moral Essays: Epistle III, Of the Use of Riches*, lines 249–250 :

> " But all our praises why should lords engross,
> Rise, honest Muse ! and sing the Man of Ross."

296 3.   **Turrets.**   "Tourettes fyled rounde" appears in Chaucer's *Knight's Tale*, line 1294, where it means the ring on a dog's collar through which the leash was passed.   Skeat explains *torets* as " probably eyes in which rings will turn round, because each eye is a little larger than the thickness of the ring."   *Cf.* Chaucer's *Treatise on the Astrolabe*, Part I, sec. 2, " This ring renneth in a maner turet," " this ring runs in a kind of eye."   But Chaucer does not refer to harness.

297 2. **Mr. Waterton tells me.** Charles Waterton, the naturalist, was born 1782 and died 1865. His *Wanderings in South America* was published in 1825.

299 11. **Earth and her children.** This paragraph is about one-fifth of the length of the corresponding paragraph as it appeared in *Blackwood*. For the longer version see Masson's Ed., Vol. XIII, p. 289, note 2.

300 14. **The General Post-Office.** The present office was opened Sept. 23, 1829. St. Martin's-le-Grand is a church within the "city" of London, so named to distinguish it from St. Martin's-in-the-Fields, which faces what is now Trafalgar Square, and is, as the name indicates, outside the "city." The street takes its name from the church.

304 10. **Barnet** is a Hertfordshire village, eleven miles north of London.

305 33. **A "Courier" evening paper, containing the gazette.** A gazette was originally one of the three official papers of the kingdom; afterwards any official announcement, as this of a great victory.

306 17. **Fey.** This is not a Celtic word; it is the Anglo-Saxon *fæge* retained in Lowland Scotch, which is the most northerly English dialect. The word appears frequently in descriptions of battles; the Anglo-Saxon fatalistic philosophy teaching that certain warriors entered the conflict *fæge*, "doomed." Now the meaning is altered slightly : " You are surely fey," would be said in Scotland, as Professor Masson remarks, to a person observed to be in extravagantly high spirits, or in any mood surprisingly beyond the bounds of his ordinary temperament, — the notion being that the excitement is supernatural, and a presage of his approaching death, or of some other calamity about to befall him.

307 27. **The inspiration of God, etc.** This is an indication — more interesting than agreeeble, perhaps — of the heights to which the martial ardor of De Quincey's toryism rises.

309 13. **Cæsar the Dictator, at his last dinner-party, etc.** Related by Suetonius in his life of Julius Cæsar, Chap. LXXXVII: "The day before he died, some discourse occurring at dinner in M. Lepidus' house upon that subject, which was the most agreeable way of dying, he expressed his preference for what is sudden and unexpected" (repentinum inopinatumque praetulerat). The story is told by Plutarch and Appian also.

311 13. **Βιαθανατος.** "De Quincey has evidently taken this from John Donne's treatise : ΒΙΑΘΑΝΑΤΟΣ, *A Declaration of that Paradoxe or Thesis, That Self-homicide is not so naturally Sin, that it may never be otherwise*, 1644. See his paper on *Suicide, etc.*, Masson's ed.

VIII, 398 [Riverside, IX, 209]. But not even Donne's precedent justifies the word-formation. The only acknowledged compounds are βιαιο-θανασία, 'violent death,' and βιαιο-θάνατος, 'dying a violent death.' Even βιᾳ θανατος, 'death by violence,' is not classical."— HART. But the form βιαθάνατος is older than Donne and is said to be common in MSS. It should be further remarked that neither of the two compounds cited is classical. As to De Quincey's interpretation of Cæsar's meaning here, *cf.* Merivale's *History of the Romans under the Empire*, Chap. XXI, where he translates Cæsar's famous reply : " That which is least expected." *Cf.* also Shakspere, *Julius Cæsar*, Act ii, sc. 2, line 33.

313 25. **"Nature, from her seat,"** etc. *Cf.* Milton's *Paradise Lost*, Book IX, lines 780–784:

> " So saying, her rash hand in evil hour
> Forth reaching to the fruit, she pluck'd, she eat :
> Earth f lt the wound, and Nature from her seat
> Sighing through all her works gave signs of woe,
> That all was lost."

314 2. **So scenical, etc.** De Quincey's love for effects of this sort appears everywhere. *Cf.* the opening paragraphs of the *Revolt of the Tartars*, Masson's Ed., Vol. VII ; Riverside Ed., Vol. XII.

315 4. **Jus dominii.** " The law of ownership," a legal term.

315 14. **Jus gentium.** " The law of nations," a legal term.

315 30. **"Monstrum horrendum,"** etc. *Æneid*, III, 658. Polyphemus, one of the Cyclopes, whose eye was put out by Ulysses, is meant. *Cf. Odyssey*, IX, 371 *et seq.; Æneid*, III, 630 *et seq.*

316 1. **One of the Calenders, etc.** The histories of the three Calenders, sons of kings, will be found in most selections from the *Arabian Nights*. A Calender is one of an order of Dervishes founded in the fourteenth century by an Andalusian Arab ; they are wanderers who preach in market-places and live by alms.

316 10. **Al Sirat.** According to Mahometan teaching this bridge over Hades was in width as a sword's edge. Over it souls must pass to Paradise.

316 12. **Under this eminent man, etc.** For these two sentences the original in *Blackwood* had this, with its addition of good De Quinceyan doctrine : " I used to call him *Cyclops Mastigophorus*, Cyclops the Whip-bearer, until I observed that his skill made whips useless, except to fetch off an impertinent fly from a leader's head, upon which I changed his Grecian name to *Cyclops Diphrelates*

(Cyclops the Charioteer). I, and others known to me, studied under him the diphrelatic art. Excuse, reader, a word too elegant to be pedantic. And also take this remark from me as a *gage d'amitié*— that no word ever was or *can* be pedantic which, by supporting a distinction, supports the accuracy of logic, or which fills up a chasm for the understanding."

317 1. **Some people have called me procrastinating.** *Cf.* Page's *Life*, Chap. XIX, and Japp's *De Quincey Memorials*, Vol. II, pp. 45, 47, 49; also Introduction, p. xxxi.

318 11. **The whole Pagan Pantheon,** *i.e.*, all the gods put together; from the Greek Πάνθειον, a temple dedicated to all the gods.

319 2. **Seven atmospheres of sleep, etc.** Professor Hart suggests that De Quincey is here "indulging in jocular arithmetic. The three nights plus the three days, plus the present night equal seven."

319 17. **Lilliputian Lancaster.** The county town of Lancashire, in which Liverpool and Manchester, towns of recent and far greater growth, are situated.

320, footnote. "**Giraldus Cambrensis,**" or Gerald de Barry (1146–1220), was a Welsh historian; one of his chief works is the *Itinerarium Cambriæ*, or Voyage in Wales.

323 2. **Quartering.** De Quincey's derivation of this word in his footnote is correct, but its use in this French sense is not common. De Quincey, however, has it above, 287 27.

325 8. **The shout of Achilles.** *Cf.* Homer, *Iliad*, XVIII, 217 *et seq.*

326 10. **Buying it, etc.** De Quincey refers, no doubt, to the pay of common soldiers and to the practice of employing mercenaries.

328 1. **Faster than ever mill-race, etc.** The change in the wording of this sentence in De Quincey's revision is, as Masson remarks, particularly characteristic of his sense of melody; it read in *Blackwood:* "We ran past them faster than ever mill-race in our inexorable flight."

328 15. **Here was the map, etc.** This sentence is an addition in the reprint. Masson remarks "how artistically it causes the due pause between the horror as still in rush of transaction and the backward look at the wreck when the crash was past."

329 18. "**Whence the sound,**" etc. *Paradise Lost*, Book XI, lines 558–563.

330 3. **Woman's Ionic form.** In thus using the word Ionic De Quincey doubtless has in mind the character of Ionic architecture, with its tall and graceful column, differing from the severity of the Doric on the one hand and from the floridity of the Corinthian on the other. Probably he is thinking of a caryatid. *Cf.* the following version

of the old story of the origin of the styles of Greek architecture in Vitruvius, IV, Chap. I (Gwilt's translation), quoted by Hart: "They measured a man's foot, and finding its length the sixth part of his height, they gave the column a similar proportion, that is, they made its height six times the thickness of the shaft measured at the base. Thus the Doric order obtained its proportion, its strength, and its beauty, from the human figure. With a similar feeling they afterward built the Temple of Diana. But in that, seeking a new proportion, they used the female figure as a standard; and for the purpose of producing a more lofty effect, they first made it eight times its thickness in height. Under it they placed a base, after the manner of a shoe to the foot; they also added volutes to its capital, like graceful curling hair hanging on each side, and the front they ornamented with *cymatia* and festoons in the place of hair. On the shafts they sunk channels, which bear a resemblance to the folds of a matronal garment. Thus two orders were invented, one of a masculine character, without ornament, the other bearing a character which resembled the delicacy, ornament, and proportion of a female. The successors of these people, improving in taste, and preferring a more slender proportion, assigned seven diameters to the height of the Doric column, and eight and a half to the Ionic."

331 3.   **Corymbi.** Clusters of fruit or flowers.

331 28.   **Quarrel.** The bolt of a cross-bow, an arrow having a square, or four-edged head (from Middle Latin *quadrellus*, diminutive of *quadrum*, a square).

334 20.   **Waterloo and Recovered Christendom!** *Cf.* note 295 3.

339 29.   **The endless resurrections of His love.** The following, which Masson prints as a postscript, was a part of De Quincey's introduction to the volume of the Collective Edition containing this piece:

"'THE ENGLISH MAIL-COACH.' — This little paper, according to my original intention, formed part of the 'Suspiria de Profundis'; from which, for a momentary purpose, I did not scruple to detach it, and to publish it apart, as sufficiently intelligible even when dislocated from its place in a larger whole. To my surprise, however, one or two critics, not carelessly in conversation, but deliberately in print, professed their inability to apprehend the meaning of the whole, or to follow the links of the connexion between its several parts. I am myself as little able to understand where the difficulty lies, or to detect any lurking obscurity, as these critics found themselves to unravel my logic. Possibly I may not be an indifferent and neutral judge in such a case. I will therefore sketch a brief abstract of the little paper according to my original design, and then leave the reader to judge how far this design is kept in sight through the actual execution.

"Thirty-seven years ago, or rather more, accident made me, in the dead of night, and of a night memorably solemn, the solitary witness of an appalling scene, which threatened instant death in a shape the most terrific to two young people whom I had no means of assisting, except in so far as I was able to give them a most hurried warning of their danger; but even *that* not until they stood within the very shadow of the catastrophe, being divided from the most frightful of deaths by scarcely more, if more at all, then seventy seconds.

"Such was the scene, such in its outline, from which the whole of this paper radiates as a natural expansion. This scene is circumstantially narrated in Section the Second, entitled 'The Vision of Sudden Death.'

"But a movement of horror, and of spontaneous recoil from this dreadful scene, naturally carried the whole of that scene, raised and idealised, into my dreams, and very soon into a rolling succession of dreams. The actual scene, as looked down upon from the box of the mail, was transformed into a dream, as tumultuous and changing as a musical fugue. This troubled dream is circumstantially reported in Section the Third, entitled 'Dream-Fugue on the theme of Sudden Death.' What I had beheld from my seat upon the mail, — the scenical strife of action and passion, of anguish and fear, as I had there witnessed them moving in ghostly silence, — this duel between life and death narrowing itself to a point of such exquisite evanescence as the collision neared: all these elements of the scene blended, under the law of association, with the previous and permanent features of distinction investing the mail itself; which features at that time lay — 1st, in velocity unprecedented, 2dly, in the power and beauty of the horses, 3dly, in the official connexion with the government of a great nation, and, 4thly, in the function, almost a consecrated function, of publishing and diffusing through the land the great political events, and especially the great battles, during a conflict of unparalleled grandeur. These honorary distinctions are all described circumstantially in the First or introductory Section ('The Glory of Motion'). The three first were distinctions maintained at all times; but the fourth and grandest belonged exclusively to the war with Napoleon; and this it was which most naturally introduced Waterloo into the dream. Waterloo, I understand, was the particular feature of the 'Dream-Fugue' which my censors were least able to account for. Yet surely Waterloo, which, in common with every other great battle, it had been our special privilege to publish over all the land, most naturally entered the dream under the licence of our privilege. If not — if there be anything amiss — let the Dream be responsible. The Dream is a law to itself; and as well quarrel with a rainbow for showing, or for *not* showing, a secondary arch. So far as I know, every element in the shifting movements of the Dream derived itself either primarily from the incidents of the actual scene, or from secondary features associated with the mail. For example, the cathedral aisle derived itself from the mimic combination of features which grouped themselves together at the point of approaching collision — viz. an arrow-like section of the road, six hundred yards long, under the solemn lights described, with lofty trees meeting overhead in arches. The guard's horn, again — a humble instrument in itself — was yet glorified as the

organ of publication for so many great national events. And the incident of
the Dying Trumpeter, who rises from a marble bas-relief, and carries a marble
trumpet to his marble lips for the purpose of warning the female infant, was
doubtless secretly suggested by my own imperfect effort to seize the guard's
horn, and to blow the warning blast. But the Dream knows best; and the
Dream, I say again, is the responsible party."

ON MURDER CONSIDERED AS ONE OF THE FINE ARTS

SECOND PAPER. 1839.

This paper appeared originally in *Blackwood's Magazine* for November,
1839, nearly thirteen years after the publication of the First Paper. The
Postscript, called in America the "Three Memorable Murders," did not
come out till the Collective Edition in 1854. It is needless to say that
each one of these parts, if such they can be called at all, separated so
widely in time, can without serious loss be used by itself. This selection
is found in *Works*, Masson's Ed., Vol. XIII, pp. 52–69; Riverside Ed.,
Vol. XI, pp. 570–587.

340 1. **A good many years ago, etc.** In the original article in
Blackwood there was this opening paragraph: "DOCTOR NORTH — You
are a liberal man: liberal in the true classical sense, not in the slang
sense of modern politicians and education-mongers. Being so, I am
sure that you will sympathise with my case. I am an ill-used man, Dr.
North — particularly ill-used; and, with your permission, I will briefly
explain how. A black scene of calumny will be laid open; but you,
Doctor, will make all things square again. One frown from you,
directed to the proper quarter, or a warning shake of the crutch, will
set me right in public opinion; which at present, I am sorry to say,
is rather hostile to me and mine — all owing to the wicked acts of slan-
derers. But you shall hear." Dr. North was, of course, Professor Wilson,
— whose pseudonym was Christopher North, — De Quincey's friend,
and the chief adviser for many years of the publishers of the *Magazine*.

340 2. **A dilettante in murder.** De Quincey's interest in the great
murder mysteries of his time was intense. *Cf.* pp. 76, 396–397, and
note 396 28; see De Quincey's long letters on the Palmer and Madeline
Smith cases, Page's *Life*, Vol. II, pp. 115–117, 133–134; also the following footnote by Masson (Vol. XIII, p. 95): "An interesting pamphlet
just published [1890] by Mr. Charles Pollitt of Kendal, under the title
De Quincey's Editorship of the Westmorland Gazette, informs us that,
during the whole period of his editorship of that provincial Tory

journal (which extended, it now appears, exactly from 11th July 1818 to 5th November 1819), he was notably fond of filling his columns with assize reports and murder trials. 'During the whole of his connexion with the paper,' says Mr. Pollitt, 'assize news formed not only a prominent, but frequently an all-absorbing portion of the available space.' In illustration, Mr. Pollitt quotes the following editorial notice from the paper for 8th August 1818: — 'This week it will be observed that our columns are occupied almost exclusively with assize reports. We have thought it right to allow them precedency of all other news, whether domestic or foreign, for the three following reasons: — (1) Because to all ranks alike they possess a powerful and command-ing interest. (2) Because to the more uneducated classes they yield a singular benefit, by teaching them their social duties in the most im-pressive shape: that is to say, not in a state of abstraction from all that may explain, illustrate, and enforce them (as in the naked terms of the Statute), but exemplified (and, as the logicians say, *concreted*) in the actual circumstances of an interesting case, and in connexion with the penalties that accompany their neglect or their violation. (3) Because they present the best indications of the moral condition of society.' What the Westmorland people thought of this perpetual provision of horrors for them by the editor of the *Gazette* does not quite appear; but it seems to have been one of the causes of that dissatisfaction on the part of the proprietors of the paper which led, according to Mr. Pollitt, to the termination of De Quincey's editorship."

341 17. **Civilation.** In his second paper on *Sir William Hamilton*, which appeared in *Hogg's Instructor* in 1852 (*cf. Works*, Masson's Ed., Vol. V, pp. 318–332; Riverside Ed., Vol. IX, pp. 282–300), De Quincey again uses this word and explains it in the following footnote: "And what state may that be? As the word is a valuable word, and in some danger of being lost, I beg to rehearse its history. The late Dr. Maginn, with whom some of us may otherwise have had reason to quarrel, was, however, a man of varied accomplishments, — a wit, with singular readi-ness for improvising, and with very extensive scholarship. Amongst the peculiar opinions that he professed was this — that no man, however much he might *tend* toward civilisation, was to be regarded as having absolutely reached its apex until he was drunk. Previously to which consummation, a man might be a promising subject for civilisation, but otherwise than in *posse* it must be premature; so he must be considered as more or less of a savage. This doctrine he naturally published more loudly than ever as he was himself more and more removed from all suspicion of barbaric sobriety. He then became anxious, with tears in

his eyes, to proclaim the deep sincerity of his conversion to civilisation. But, as such an odiously long word must ever be distressing to a gentleman taking his ease of an evening, unconsciously, perhaps, he abridged it always after 10 P.M. into *civilation*. Such was the genesis of the word. And I therefore, upon entering it in my neological dictionary of English, matriculated it thus: — *Civilation*, by ellipsis, or more properly by syncope, or, rigorously speaking, by hiccup, from *civilisation*." Maginn brought the word into literature by using it in the *Noctes Ambrosianæ*, No. 4, July, 1822. In a note Mackenzie, the editor of the *Noctes*, speaks of the word as "one which he (Maginn) had invented and solely used for a long time."

341 31. **The Stagirite . . . placed virtue in the το μεσον.** Aristotle was called the Stagirite from his birthplace, Stagira, in Macedonia. According to his teaching, "ethical virtue is that permanent direction of the will which guards the mean [τὸ μέσον] proper for us. . . . Bravery is the mean between cowardice and temerity; temperance, the mean between inordinate desire and stupid indifference ; etc." — UEBERWEG, *History of Philosophy*, Vol. I, p. 169.

342 9. **In fact, I'm for peace, and quietness, etc.** In the original *Blackwood* version this sentence ran: " I'm for virtue, and goodness, and all that sort of thing." Immediately after it came this passage, the omission of which would seem to be a loss : "And two instances I'll give you to what an extremity I carry my virtue. The first may seem a trifle ; but not if you knew my nephew, who was certainly born to be hanged, and would have been so long ago, but for my restraining voice. He is horribly ambitious, and thinks himself a man of cultivated taste in most branches of murder, whereas, in fact, he has not one idea on the subject but such as he has stolen from me. This is so well known that the Club has twice blackballed him, though every indulgence was shown to him as my relative. People came to me and said — 'Now really, President, we would do much to serve a relative of yours. But still, what can be said ? You know yourself that he'll disgrace us. If we were to elect him, why, the next thing we should hear of would be some vile butcherly murder, by way of justifying our choice. And what sort of a concern would it be ? You know, as well as we do, that it would be a disgraceful affair, more worthy of the shambles than of an artist's *atelier*. He would fall upon some great big man, some huge farmer returning drunk from a fair. There would be plenty of blood, and *that* he would expect us to take in lieu of taste, finish, scenical grouping. Then, again, how would he tool ? Why, most probably with a cleaver and a couple of paving-stones: so that the whole *coup d'œil*

would remind you rather of some hideous Ogre or Cyclops than of the delicate operator of the 19th century.' The picture was drawn with the hand of truth; *that* I could not but allow, and, as to personal feelings in the matter, I dismissed them from the first. The next morning I spoke to my nephew: I was delicately situated, as you see, but I determined that no consideration should induce me to flinch from my duty. 'John,' said I, 'you seem to me to have taken an erroneous view of life and its duties. Pushed on by ambition, you are dreaming rather of what it might be glorious to attempt than what it would be possible for you to accomplish. Believe me, it is not necessary to a man's respectability that he should commit a murder. Many a man has passed through life most respectably without attempting any species of homicide — good, bad, or indifferent. It is your first duty to ask yourself, *quid valeant humeri, quid ferre recusent?* [Horace, *Ars Poetica*, 39–40 : "What your shoulders are equal to, what they refuse to bear?"] We cannot all be brilliant men in this life. And it is for your interest to be contented rather with a humble station well filled than to shock everybody with failures, the more conspicuous by contrast with the ostentation of their promises.' John made no answer; he looked very sulky at the moment, and I am in high hopes that I have saved a near relative from making a fool of himself by attempting what is as much beyond his capacity as an epic poem. Others, however, tell me that he is meditating a revenge upon me and the whole Club. But, let this be as it may, *liberavi animam meam* [" I have freed my mind"; *cf.* Ezekiel, iii, 19, 21]; and, as you see, have run some risk with a wish to diminish the amount of homicide." As to the Club here referred to, the First Part gives the following explanation in its "Advertisement": "Most of us who read books have probably heard of a Society for the Promotion of Vice, of the Hell-Fire Club founded in the last century by Sir Francis Dashwood, &c. At Brighton I think it was that a Society was formed for the Suppression of Virtue. That society was itself suppressed; but I am sorry to say that another exists in London, of a character still more atrocious. In tendency, it may be denominated a Society for the Encouragement of Murder; but, according to their own delicate εὐφημισμος [euphemism], it is styled the Society of Connoisseurs in Murder. They profess to be curious in homicide, amateurs and dilettanti in the various modes of carnage, and, in short, Murder Fanciers. Every fresh atrocity of that class which the police annals of Europe bring up, they meet and criticise as they would a picture, statue, or other work of art." The writer goes on to say that "one of the Monthly Lectures read before the society last year" has fallen into his hands, etc. ; the writer of our Second Paper is of course the author of the Lecture, not the writer of the Advertisement.

342 32. **For, if once a man, etc.** This is a rather famous sentence; and it must not be forgotten in connection with it that De Quincey was a double-dyed procrastinator. See note 317 1.

343 5 **Principiis obsta.** Ovid, *Remedia Amoris*, line 91 : " Make a stand against the first approaches."

343 21. **Laudator temporis acti [se puero].** Horace, *Ars Poetica*, line 173: " A praiser of past times, when he was himself a boy."

343 30. **" God's Revenge upon Murder."** *The Triumphs of God's Revenge against the Crying and Execrable Sin of Murder*, London, 1621. There were five later parts; all six were published together in 1635 ; and there was an enlarged edition in 1679 (Masson).

343 31. **A more ancient book, etc.** This book, which Nigel was reading just before he heard of the murder of the miser Trapbois (Chap. XXIV), is described by Scott thus : " The book was entitled *God's Revenge against Murther ;* not, as the bibliomaniacal reader may easily conjecture, the work which Reynolds published under that imposing name, but one of a much earlier date, printed and sold by old Wolfe."

343 33. **The " Newgate Calendar "** was a record of the lives of the most notorious criminals confined in Newgate prison in London.

344 2. **The great cause of degeneration in murder.** To the murder fancier the wholesale destruction by guillotine in the French Revolution must have seemed criminal !

344 8. **" Nor up the lawn,"** etc. This line having been taken from one of the closing stanzas of Gray's *Elegy*, De Quincey continues with a metrical parody of this stanza, describing the solitary poet :

> " There at the foot of yonder nodding beech
>   That wreathes its old fantastic roots so high
> His listless length at noontide he would stretch,
>   And pore upon the brook that babbles by."

344 31. **Brushing with hasty steps the dews away, etc.** This parodies Gray's stanza in the *Elegy :*

> " Haply some hoary-headed Swain may say,
>   Oft have we seen him at the peep of dawn
> Brushing with hasty steps the dews away,
>   To meet the sun upon the upland lawn."

As Masson points out, De Quincey produces four lines of verse, ending respectively with " away," " side," " hear," " aside."

345 8. **The great exterminating chef-d'œuvre, etc.** The two Williams murders are tellingly described by De Quincey in his *Postscript*, Masson's Ed., Vol. XIII, p. 70; *Three Memorable Murders*, Riverside Ed., Vol. XI, p. 588.

345 16. **La Bruyère.** Jean de La Bruyère (1645–96) was a French novelist. His great work was *Les Caractères*, "Characters," *i.e.*, Character Sketches. *Cf.* Sir Thomas Overbury's *Characters*.

346 15. **A second age of Leo the Tenth.** Leo X (Giovanni de'. Medici, 1475–1523), Pope from 1513, was "the only Pope who has bestowed his own name upon his age." The love of art and letters was his ruling passion. He recognized and fostered the genius of Raphael; and as to his patronage of literature, "every Italian man of letters, in an age of singular intellectual brilliancy, tasted or might have hoped to taste, of his bounty."

346 27. **The turning up of Thugs and Thuggism.** "It was about the year 1831 that the British authorities in India began really energetic measures for the suppression of the Thugs, — the sect or fraternity in Northern India whose practice it was, under the sanction of hereditary custom and religion, to waylay and murder travellers, carefully burying the bodies, and dividing the spoil. One of the first books on Thugs and Thuggism was Thornton's *Illustrations of the History and Practices of the Thugs*, published in 1837." — MASSON. See J. Hutton, *Thugs and Dacoits of India*, London, 1881, and Meadows Taylor, *Confessions of a Thug*, London, 1840.

347 2. **It passes my persimmon to tell you.** This is an effort on De Quincey's part to make use of American slang. *Cf.* the American proverb, "The longest pole knocks down the persimmons," and the expression, "Not a huckleberry to my persimmons." Other examples of American slang in De Quincey are "almighty fix," "gone coon," etc.

347 17. **"Et interrogatum,"** etc. "And it was asked of Toad-in-the-Hole — Where is that reporter? And it was answered with laughter — He has not been found." *Chorus.* "Then it was repeated by all, with laughter undulating, confused — He has not been found." *Non est inventus* is a Late Latin legal formula by which the issuer of a writ is informed that the person sought is not forthcoming. *Cf.* Nash's *Unfortunate Traveller* (1594), 1892, p. 194: "*Juliana* informed the pope of *Zacheries* and his practise, *Zachary* was sought for, but *non est inuentus*, he was packing long before."

347 23. **The Burke-and-Hare revolution in the art.** "In 1828 Edinburgh was horrified by the discovery that two Irishmen, William Burke and William Hare, with one or more accomplices, had been

carrying on a traffic in murder for the hideous purpose of selling the dead bodies as subjects for anatomical use.   Their method was to lure wayfaring strangers, beggar-women, idiots and such other poor creatures as were not likely to be missed, into the dens where they lived, especially into Burke's house in a court off the West Port, and there .o make them drunk, and then smother or strangle them.   It is computed that as many as sixteen victims had been thus disposed of before the horror was found out.   Condemned for one of the murders, Burke was hanged on the 28th of January 1829, his colleague Hare having, greatly to the disgust of the public, escaped the same doom by acting as king's evidence on the trial. — There is no more striking instance of the coining of a metonymy than in the immediate conversion of the name of the Edinburgh murderer of 1828 into a new word in the English language [*cf. boycott*].   People at once began to use the word *burk* (the final *e* dropped) as a verb for *suffocate*, whether in the literal sense of killing by suffocation (in which sense an anatomical lecture-room in a northern Scottish town was for a while popularly known as ' The Burking-House,' from the notion that subjects were obtained for it, or actually manufactured within its walls, by Burke's method), or in a more figurative sense in such phrases as ' His speech was *burked*,' *i.e.*, choked off or suppressed by the impatient audience. — Hare, whom the Edinburgh mob would have torn to pieces if they could have clutched him, disappeared from public view, and lived on, no one knows where, or in how many different places, under another name.   There is a legend that, as he was working somewhere as a plasterer's labourer, his fellow-workmen, finding out who he was, rolled him in lime or pelted him with lime, with the result of the total destruction of his eyesight. An old gray-haired man who used to sit begging by the railings of the National Gallery in Trafalgar Square, London, was pointed out to myself, more than twenty years ago [about 1870], as no other than the murderer Hare.   I was sceptical at the time, and rather because the look of the old man was not unvenerable; and I have heard since of the supposed identification of Hare with this or that similarly conspicuous blind mendicant in other localities." — MASSON.

348 5. **The Old Man of the Mountains.**   In the First Paper De Quincey says : " He was a shining light indeed, and I need not tell you that the very word 'assassin' is deduced from him.   So keen an amateur [*i.e.* lover of the art] was he that on one occasion, when his own life was attempted by a favourite assassin, he was so much pleased with the talent shown that, notwithstanding the failure of the artist, he created him a duke upon the spot, with remainder to the female line,

NOTES   491

and settled a pension on him for three lives." And the following is
added in a footnote : " The name 'Old Man of the Mountains' does
not designate any individual person, but was the title, — in Arabic
Sheikh-al-jebal, 'Prince of the Mountain,' — of a series of chiefs who
presided from 1090 to 1258 over a community or military order of
fanatical Mohammedan sectaries, called *The Assassins*, distributed
through Persia and Syria, but with certain mountain-ranges for their
headquarters. But, though there is no doubt that the words *assassin*
and *assassination*, as terms for secret murder, and especially for secret
murder by stabbing, are a recollection of the reputed habits of this old
Persian and Syrian community, the original etymology of the word
Assassins itself, as the name of the community, is not so certain. Skeat
sets it down as simply the Arabic *hashishin*, 'hashish-drinkers,' from
the fact or on the supposition that the agents of the Old Man of the
Mountains, when they were detached on their murderous errands,
went forth nerved for the task by the intoxication of *hashish*, or Indian
hemp." This etymology is universally accepted. *Cf.* Hewlett's *Richard
Yea-and-Nay*, 1900.

348 11. **Mr. von Hammer, etc.** "Von Hammer's *Geschichte der
Assassinen* was published in 1818. In a note to Gibbon's account of
the Assassins and the Old Man of the Mountains, he had acknowledged
his authority thus : — 'All that can be known of the Assassins of Persia
and Syria is procured from the copious, and even profuse, erudition of
M. Falconet in two *Mémoires* read before the Academy of Inscriptions';
to which this note by Milman is added in the 1839 edition of Gibbon: —
'Von Hammer's History of the Assassins has now thrown Falconet's
dissertation into the shade.' " — MASSON.

348 24. **Malleus hæreticorum.** "Hammer of the heretics," the title
of Charles Martel ; *cf.* below.

348 26. **The ship-carpenter's mallet.** The tool used by Williams
to strike down all his victims. See *Postscript*, or *Three Memorable
Murders* : Masson's Ed., Vol. XIII, p. 70 ; Riverside Ed., Vol. XI,
p. 588.

348 27. **Charles Martel** (Modern French *Marteau*, " hammer ") gained
his name by defeating the Saracens between Poitiers and Tours in 732.

349 12. **The Jewish Sicarii.** De Quincey shows an interest in
them elsewhere (*cf. The Essenes*, Riverside Ed., Vol. VIII, p. 113 ;
Masson's Ed., Vol. VII, p. 150). These Sicarii are referred to in Acts,
xxi, 38 : " Art not thou [Paul] that Egyptian which before these days
madest an uproar and leddest out into the wilderness four thousand
men that were murderers ? "

349 26. **Josephus.** Flavius Josephus (Jewish name Joseph ben Matthias, A.D. 38–100), the great Jewish historian, was of distinguished priestly ancestry, but from early years a sympathizer with Rome. In the Judæo-Roman war he was a leader, but he managed to save himself, and secured the favor of Vespasian and Titus, and a competency. He wrote *The Jewish War* in seven books, and *Antiquities of the Jews* in twenty books; his style has gained him the epithet of "the Hebrew Livy." *Cf.* De Quincey's treatment of him in *The Essenes* (see above).

349 28. **Jonathan himself, the Pontifex Maximus.** For this account of the murder of Jonathan the high priest, see Whiston's Josephus, *Antiquities*, Book XX, Chap. VIII, sec. 5.

350 7. **Three different parts.** The second important place is in the *Jewish War*, Book VII, Chap. X, sec. 1. The reference to Book I of the *War* concerns apparently Chap. XVI, sec. 4.

350 19. **Festus.** Porcius Festus, a Roman procurator in Palestine about 60–62 A.D.; the same with whom Paul was concerned, Acts, xxv.–xxvi.

351 1. **Father Mersenne, etc.** "Marin Mersenne, a monk of a convent near Paris, was born 1588 and died 1648. Among his works is a Commentary on Genesis, published at Paris in 1623 under the title *P. Marini Mersenni, ordinio minonem S. Francisci de Paula Quaestiones celeberrimae in Genesim, cum accurata Textus explicatione*. It is a large folio, each page divided into two columns, and with the columns numbered, and not the pages. De Quincey, with all his exactness, had not observed this, and is consequently wrong in his twice emphasized joke that the passage he cites is on 'page one thousand four hundred and thirty-one.' It is in *column* 1431, which would be *page* 716 only."—MASSON.

351 7. **Abelem, etc.** "That Abel had been torn to pieces by Cain with his teeth."

351 16. **"Frater," etc.** From Prudentius, *Hamartigenia*, Preface, lines 15–16.

352 8. **Finds it to be Cape.** That is, Cape Colony wine.

352 24. **Pancirollus . . . de rebus deperditis.** Guido Panciroli (1523–99), an Italian lawyer, was the author of a work on lost arts and inventions.

352 27. **The art of painting upon glass, of making the myrrhine cups.** *Cf.* as to the former art the following by C. H. Wilson in the *Encyclopædia Britannica:* "The manufacture of colored glass, which is the basis of the beautiful and interesting art of glass painting, originated at a period of remote antiquity, and the use of enamels, to vary

or ornament the surface, was known to the ancient Egyptians; but the formation of windows of mosaics of colored glass upon which the shapes of figures and ornaments are painted with an enamel fixed by fire is mediæval, and emphatically a Christian art. . . . Colored windows existed in St. Sophia at Constantinople in the 6th century." As to the myrrhine cups, see the *Century Dictionary*: "Murra (murrha, myrrha), in *Roman antiquities*, an ornamental stone of which vases, cups, and other ornamental articles were made. . . . Pliny is the only author who has attempted any detailed description of it. Unfortunately his accounts are so vague that the material cannot be positively identified, nor has anything been found in the excavations at Rome which is certainly known to be the ancient murra. In the opinion of the best authorities, however, it was fluor-spar, for of the known materials this is the only one found in abundance which has the peculiar coloration indicated by Pliny. The principal objections to this theory is that no fragments of fluor-spar vases have been found in Rome or its vicinity. Vessels of murra were at one time considered by the Romans as of inestimable value." *Cf.* Milton's *Paradise Regained*, Book IV, lines 118–120:

> " And how they quaff in gold,
> Crystal and myrrhine cups emboss'd with gems
> And studs of pearl."

Here the poet may have in mind the modern murrine or myrrhine glass, in making which gold and precious stones are embedded in the glass itself.

352 30. **Planudes.** Planudes Maximus, a Byzantine monk of the fourteenth century.

352 34. **Salmasius, etc.** Claude de Saumaise (1588–1653), of French birth, was the greatest scholar of his age in Western Europe. He became professor in Leyden in 1631; in 1649 he published his *Defensio Regia*, a defence of the government of Charles I, which brought out Milton's *Defensio pro Populo Anglicano* in reply. Flavius Vopiscus, of the fourth century, was the author of some of the lives of Roman emperors now collected in the *Historia Augusta*.

352 34. **'Est et elegans,' etc.** "That is also a choice epigram of Lucilius, where a doctor and an undertaker by compact so arrange that the doctor should kill all the sick committed to his care. And that he should turn them all over to his friend the undertaker to be laid out."

354 22. **In their lives, etc.** *Cf.* II Samuel, i, 23.

354 29. **Their names unfortunately are lost.** "In the Greek form of the epigram the Doctor figures as *Krateas* and the Pollinctor

as *Damon*. So the readers of the original article in *Blackwood* were informed in an editorial note which Wilson took the trouble to subjoin to De Quincey's text. The note was in these words : — 'Here is the Greek epigram — with a version. C. N. [*i.e.*, Christopher North]. We need not give the Greek here. Wilson's version (or was it his?) is as follows : —

> "Damon, who plied the undertaker's trade,
> With Doctor Krateas an agreement made
> What grave clothes Damon from the dead could seize
> He to the Doctor sent for bandages ;
> While the good Doctor — here no bargain-breaker —
> Sent all his patients to the Undertaker." ' " — MASSON.

JOAN OF ARC

This article appeared originally in *Tait's Magazine* for March and August, 1847 ; it was reprinted by De Quincey in 1854 in the third volume of his *Collected Writings*. It is found in *Works*, Masson's Ed., Vol. V, pp. 384–416 ; Riverside Ed., Vol. VI, pp. 178–215.

356 10. **Lorraine**, now in great part in the possession of Germany, is the district in which Domrémy, Joan's birthplace, is situated.

357 14. **Vaucouleurs.** A town near Domrémy ; *cf.* p. 362.

357 28. **En contumace.** "In contumacy," a legal term applied to one who, when summoned to court, fails to appear.

358 13. **Rouen.** The city in Normandy where Joan was burned at the stake.

358 25. **The lilies of France.** The royal emblem of France from very early times until the Revolution of 1789, when "the wrath of God and man combined to wither them."

359 5. **M. Michelet.** Jules Michelet (1798–1874) is said to have spent forty years in the preparation of his great work, the *History of France*. *Cf.* the same, translated by G. H. Smith, 2 vols., Appleton, Vol. II, pp. 119–169 ; or *Joan of Arc*, from Michelet's *History of France*, translated by O. W. Wight, New York, 1858.

359 8. **Recovered liberty.** The Revolution of 1830 had expelled the restored Bourbon kings.

359 20. **The book against priests.** Michelet's lectures as professor of history in the Collège de France, in which he attacked the Jesuits, were published as follows : *Des Jésuites*, 1843 ; *Du Prêtre, de la Femme et de la Famille*, 1844 ; *Du Peuple*, 1845. To the second De Quincey apparently refers.

359 26. **Back to the falconer's lure.** The lure was a decoy used to recall the hawk to its perch, — sometimes a dead pigeon, sometimes an artificial bird, with some meat attached.

360 6. **On the model of Lord Percy.** These lines, in Percy's Folio, ed. Hales and Furnivall, Vol. II, p. 7, run:

> " The stout Erle of Northumberland
> a vow to God did make,
> his pleasure in the Scottish woods
> 3 sommers days to take."

360 27. **Pucelle d'Orléans.** Maid of Orleans (the city on the Loire which Joan saved).

361 1. **The collection, etc.** The work meant is Quicherat, *Procès de Condamnation et Réhabilitation de Jeanne d'Arc*, 5 vols., Paris, 1841–49. *Cf.* De Quincey's note.

361 21. **Delenda est Anglia Victrix!** " Victorious England must be destroyed!" *Cf. Delenda est Carthago!* note 54 33.

361 27. **Hyder Ali** (1702–82), a Mahometan adventurer, made himself maharajah of Mysore and gave the English in India serious trouble; he was defeated in 1782 by Sir Eyre Coote. **Tippoo** Sahib, his son and successor, proved less dangerous and was finally killed at Seringapatam in 1799.

362 4. **Nationality it was not,** *i.e.*, nationalism — patriotism — it was not. *Cf. Revolt of the Tartars*, Riverside Ed., Vol. XII, p. 4 ; Masson's Ed., Vol. VII, p. 370, where De Quincey speaks of the Torgod as "tribes whose native ferocity was exasperated by debasing forms of superstition, and by a nationality as well as an inflated conceit of their own merit absolutely unparalleled." *Cf.* also footnote, p. 386.

362 4. **Suffren.** The great French admiral who in 1780–81 inflicted so much loss upon the British.

362 10. **Magnanimous justice of Englishmen.** As Professor Hart observes, the treatment of Joan in *Henry VI* is hardly magnanimous.

363 29. **That odious man.** *Cf.* pp. 371–372.

364 12. **Three great successive battles.** Rudolf of Lorraine fell at Crécy (1346); Frederick of Lorraine at Agincourt (1415); the battle of Nicopolis, which sacrificed the third Lorrainer, took place in 1396.

365 24. **Charles VI** (1368–1422) had killed several men during his first fit of insanity. He was for the rest of his life wholly unfit to govern. He declared Henry V of England, the conqueror of Agincourt, his successor, thus disinheriting the Dauphin, his son.

366 2. **The famines, etc.** Horrible famines occurred in France

and England in 1315, 1336, and 1353. Such insurrections as Wat Tyler's, in 1381, are probably in De Quincey's mind.

366 6. The termination of the Crusades. The Crusades came to an end about 1271. "The ulterior results of the crusades," concludes Cox in *Encyclopædia Britannica*, "were the breaking up of the feudal system, the abolition of serfdom, the supremacy of a common law over the independent jurisdiction of chiefs who claimed the right of private wars."

366 7. The destruction of the Templars. This most famous of the military orders, founded in the twelfth century for the defence of the Latin kingdom of Jerusalem, having grown so powerful as to be greatly feared, was suppressed at the beginning of the fourteenth century.

366 7. The Papal interdicts. "De Quincey has probably in mind such an interdict as that pronounced in 1200, by Innocent III, against France. All ecclesiastical functions were suspended and the land was in desolation." — HART. England was put under interdict several times, as in 1170 (for the murder of Becket) and 1208.

366 8. The tragedies caused or suffered by the house of Anjou, and by the Emperor. "The Emperor is Konradin, the last of the Hohenstaufen, beheaded by Charles of Anjou at Naples, 1268. The subsequent cruelties of Charles in Sicily caused the popular uprising known as the Sicilian Vespers, 1282, in which many thousands of Frenchmen were assassinated." — HART.

366 10. The colossal figure of feudalism, etc. The English yeomen at Crécy, overpowering the mounted knights of France, took from feudalism its chief support, — the superiority of the mounted knight to the unmounted yeoman. *Cf.* Green, *History of the English People*, Book IV, Chap. II.

366 15. The abominable spectacle of a double Pope. For thirty-eight years this paradoxical state of things endured.

367 15. The Roman martyrology. A list of the martyrs of the Church, arranged according to the order of their festivals, and with accounts of their lives and sufferings.

368 4. "Abbeys there were," etc. *Cf.* Wordsworth, *Peter Bell*, Part Second:

> "Temples like those among the Hindoos,
> And mosques, and spires, and abbey windows,
> And castles all with ivy green."

368 17. The Vosges . . . have never attracted much notice, etc. They came into like prominence after De Quincey's day in the Franco-Prussian War of 1870.

368 31. **Those mysterious fawns, etc.** In some of the romances of the Middle Ages, especially those containing Celtic material, a knight, while hunting, is led by his pursuit of a white fawn (or a white stag or boar) to a *fée* (*i.e.*, an inhabitant of the " Happy Other-world ") or into the confines of the "Happy Other-world " itself. Sometimes, as in the *Guigemar* of Marie de France, the knight passes on to a series of adventures in consequence of his meeting with the white fawn. I owe this note to the kindness of Mr. S. W. Kinney, A.M., of Baltimore.

369 4. **Or, being upon the marches of France, a marquis.** *Marquis* is derived from *march*, and was originally the title of the guardian of the frontier, or march.

369 13. **Agreed with Sir Roger de Coverley that a good deal might be said on both sides.** This expression is from the end of *Spectator* No. 122, where the Spectator, being asked by Sir Roger whether the redecorated tavern-sign is not still more like the Knight than the Saracen, replied, " that much might be said on both sides." It is likely, however, that De Quincey, who has evidently put the speech into the mouth of the wrong man, may have connected it in his mind with the discussion of witchcraft at the beginning of *Spectator* No. 117, where Addison balances the grounds for belief and unbelief somewhat as De Quincey does here.

370 7. **Bergereta.** A very late Latin form of French *bergerette*, " a shepherdess."

370 15. **M. Simond, in his " Travels."** The reference is to *Journal of a Tour and Residence in Great Britain during the years 1810 and 1811*, by Louis Simond, 2d ed., to which is added an appendix on France, written in December 1815 and October 1816. Edinburgh, 1817. De Quincey refers to this story with horror several times, but such scenes are not yet wholly unknown.

371 21. **A Chevalier of St. Louis.** The French order of St. Louis was founded by Louis XIV in 1693 for military service. After its discontinuance at the Revolution, this order was reinstated in 1814; but no knights have been created since 1830. " Chevalier " is the lowest rank in such an order; it is here erroneously used by De Quincey as a title of address.

371 22. **" Chevalier, as-tu donné,"** etc. " Chevalier, have you fed the hog?" **" Ma fille,"** etc., " My daughter, have you," etc. **" Pucelle,"** etc., " Maid of Orleans, have you saved the lilies (*i.e.*, France)?"

372 4. **The Oriflamme of France.** The red banner of St. Denis, preserved in the abbey of that name, near Paris, and borne before the French king as a consecrated flag.

372 22. **Twenty years after, talking with Southey.** In 1816 De Quincey was a resident of Grasmere; Southey lived for many years at Keswick, a few miles away; they met first in 1807. For De Quincey's estimate of Southey's *Joan of Arc*, see *Works*, Riverside Ed., Vol. VI, pp. 262–266; Masson's Ed., Vol. V, pp. 238–242.

372 28. **Chinon** is a little town near Tours.

373 3. **She " pricks " for sheriffs.** The old custom was to prick with a pin the names of those chosen by the sovereign for sheriffs.

374 9. **Ampulla.** The flask containing the sacred oil used at coronations.

374 10. **The English boy.** Henry VI was nine months old when he was proclaimed King of England and France in 1422, Charles VI of France and Henry V, his legal heir, having both died in that year. Henry's mother was the eldest daughter of Charles VI.

374 13. **Drawn from the ovens of Rheims.** Rheims, where the kings of France were crowned, was famous for its biscuits and gingerbread.

374 26. **Tindal's " Christianity as old as the Creation."** Matthew Tindal (1657–1732) published this work in 1732; its greatest interest lies in the fact that to this book more than to any other Butler's *Analogy* was a reply. Tindal's argument was that natural religion, as taught by the deists, was complete; that no revelation was necessary. A life according to nature is all that the best religion can teach. Such doctrine as this Joan preached in the speech ascribed to her.

374 27. **A parte ante.** "From the part gone before"; Joan's speech being three centuries earlier than the book from which it was taken.

375 9. **That divine passage in "Paradise Regained."** From Book I, lines 196–205.

376 34. **Patay** is near Orleans; Troyes was the capital of the old province of Champagne.

378 25. **"Nolebat," etc.** "She would not use her sword or kill any one."

379 24. **Made prisoner by the Burgundians.** The English have accused the French officers of conniving at Joan's capture through jealousy of her successes. Compiègne is 50 miles northeast of Paris.

379 27. **Bishop of Beauvais.** Beauvais is 43 miles northwest of Paris, in Normandy. This bishop, Pierre Cauchon, rector of the University at Paris, was devoted to the English party.

379 30. **"Bishop that art," etc.** *Cf.* Shakspere's *Macbeth*, Act i, sc. 5, line 13.

379 33. **A triple crown.** The papacy is meant, of course. The pope's tiara is a tall cap of golden cloth, encircled by three coronets.

380 17. **Judges examining the prisoner.** The judge in France questions a prisoner minutely when he is first taken, before he is remanded for trial. De Quincey displays here his inveterate prejudice against the French; but this practice is widely regarded as the vital error of French criminal procedure.

381 5. **A wretched Dominican.** A member of the order of mendicant friars established in France by Domingo de Guzman in 1216. Their official name was *Fratres Predicatores*, " Preaching Friars," and their chief objects were preaching and instruction. Their influence was very great, until the rise of the Jesuit order in the sixteenth century. The Dominicans Le Maitre and Graverent (the Grand Inquisitor) both took part in the prosecution.

381 31. **For a less cause than martyrdom.** *Cf.* Genesis, ii, 24.

383 14. **From the four winds.** There may be a reminiscence here of Ezekiel, xxxvii, 1–10, especially verse 9 : " Come from the four winds, O breath, and breathe upon these slain, that they may live."

383 30. **Luxor.** See note 214 27.

384 15. **Daughter of Cæsars.** She was the daughter of the German emperor, Francis I, whose sovereignty, as the name " Holy Roman Empire " shows, was supposed to continue that of the ancient Roman emperors.

384 17. **Charlotte Corday** (1768–93) murdered the revolutionist Marat in the belief that the good of France required it; two days later she paid the penalty, as she had expected, with her life.

385 18. **Grafton, a chronicler.** Richard Grafton died about 1572. He was printer to Edward VI. His chronicle was published in 1569.

385 20. **" Foule face."** *Foule* formerly meant " ugly."

385 21. **Holinshead.** Raphael Holinshed died about 1580. His great work, *Chronicles of England, Scotland, and Ireland*, was used by Shakspere as the source of several plays. He writes of Joan: " Of favor [appearance] was she counted likesome ; of person stronglie made, and manlie ; of courage, great, hardie, and stout withall."

386, footnote. **Satanic.** This epithet was applied to the work of some of his contemporaries by Southey in the preface to his *Vision of Judgement*, 1821. It has been generally assumed that Byron and Shelley are meant. See Introduction to Byron's *Vision of Judgment* in the new Murray Edition of Byron, Vol. IV.

388, footnote. **Burgoo.** A thick oatmeal gruel or porridge used by seamen. According to the Murray *Dictionary* the derivation is unknown; but in the *Athenæum*, Oct 6, 1888, quoted by Hart, the word is explained as a corruption of Arabic *burghul*.

393 30. English Prince, Regent of France. John, Duke of Bedford, uncle of Henry VI. "In genius for war as in political capacity," says J. R. Green, "John was hardly inferior to Henry [the Fifth, his brother] himself." — *A History of the English People*, Book IV, Chap. VI.

393 31. My Lord of Winchester. Henry Beaufort, Bishop of Winchester, half-brother of Henry IV. He was the most prominent English prelate of his time and was the only Englishman in the Court that condemned Joan. As to the story of his death, to which De Quincey alludes, see Shakspere, *2 Henry VI*, Act iii, sc. 3. Beaufort became cardinal in 1426.

394 17. Who is this that cometh from Domrémy? This is an evident imitation of the famous passage from Isaiah, lxiii, 1 : "Who is this that cometh from Edom, with dyed garments from Bozrah?" "Bloody coronation robes" is rather obscure, but probably refers to the fact that Joan had shed her own blood to bring about the coronation of her sovereign; she is supposed to have appeared in armor at the actual coronation ceremony, and this armor might with reason be imagined as "bloody."

394 22. She . . . shall take my lord's brief. That is, she shall act as the bishop's counsel. In the case of Beauvais, as in that of Winchester, it must be remembered that in all monarchical countries the bishops are "lords spiritual," on an equality with the greater secular nobles, the "lords temporal."

ON THE KNOCKING AT THE GATE IN "MACBETH"

This piece appeared originally in the *London Magazine* for October, 1823, as a part of the series called *Notes from the Pocket-Book of a Late Opium-Eater*. In the Collective Edition it was reserved for the last volume, which appeared after De Quincey's death. Consequently it remains unaltered, though De Quincey had expressed an intention of enlarging it. It is found in *Works*, Masson's Ed., Vol. X, pp. 389-394; Riverside Ed., Vol. IV, pp. 533-539.

395 3. The knocking at the gate, etc. See *Macbeth*, Act ii, scs. 2, 3. Coleridge in his Shakespeare Notes (*Works*, Vol. IV, p. 172) marked scene 3, with the exception of one sentence, as an interpolation ; and De Quincey's explanation of the meaning of the *Knocking* is an important part of the defence of the scene by Hales (*cf. The Porter in Macbeth, New Shakspere Society*, 1874; or *Essays and Notes on Shakespeare*) and others. For a convenient summary of the argument, see *Macbeth*, Arden Ed., Appendix F.

396 28. **In 1812, Mr. Williams made his début.** It was in December, 1811. (*Cf.* note, 345 8.) The comments following can best be understood as a foreshadowing of the *Murder as one of the Fine Arts* papers. They furnish a striking testimony to the early origin of De Quincey's interest in murder mysteries. *Cf.* note 340 2.

397 27. " **The poor beetle that we tread on.**" From Shakspere, *Measure for Measure*, Act iii, sc. 1, line 78 :

> " The sense of death is most in apprehension ;
> And the poor beetle, that we tread upon,
> In corporal sufferance finds a pang as great
> As when a giant dies."

398 4. "**With its petrific mace.**" *Cf.* Milton, *Paradise Lost*, Book X, lines 293-296 :

> " The aggregated soil
> Death with his mace petrific, cold and dry,
> As with a trident smote, and fix't as firm
> As Delos floating once."

398 14. **His feelings caught chiefly by contagion from her.** This view is by no means universal. *Cf.* Corson's *Introduction to Shakespeare*, pp. 244-251.

398 19. "**The gracious Duncan.**" *Macbeth*, Act iii, sc. 1, line 65.

398 20. "**The deep damnation,**" etc. *Macbeth*, Act i, sc. 7, line 20.

399 30. **Lady Macbeth is "unsexed."** *Cf. Macbeth*, Act i, sc. 5, lines 38-41.

ADDITIONAL NOTE

The following readings in this volume are not found in either of the standard editions :

46 4. **Seldom or never ;** both editions, *seldom or ever.*

63 12. **But otherwise ;** both editions, *or otherwise.*

266 11. **But that mighty system ;** both editions, *but by that mighty system.*

267 2. **This word ;** both editions, *this world.*

360 27. **Pucelle d'Orleans herself ;** both editions, *Pucelle d'Orleans for herself.*